SOCIAL WELFARE POLICY

Perspectives, Patterns, and Insights

SOCIAL WELFARE POLICY
Perspectives, Patterns, and Insights

Ira C. Colby
University of Texas, Arlington

The Dorsey Press   *WADSWORTH*
Chicago, Illinois 60604

Acquisition editor: Leo A. W. Wiegman
Project editor: Margaret Haywood
Production manager: Ann Cassady
Cover Design: Leon Bolognese & Associates
Compositor: Weimer Typesetting Co., Inc.
Typeface: 10/12 Palatino
Printer: R. R. Donnelley & Sons Company

LIBRARY OF CONGRESS
Library of Congress Cataloging-in-Publication Data

Social welfare policy : perspectives, patterns, and insights / [edited by] Ira C. Colby.

    p.   cm.

    ISBN 0-256-06226-9 (pbk.) 0-534-11037-1

    1. Public welfare—United States. 2. United States—Social policy. I. Colby, Ira C.
(Ira Christopher)

HV95.S619 1989   88–17612

361.6'1'0973—dc19   CIP

Preface

The case narrative was simple and direct: An anonymous caller reported that a fourteen-year-old female had been home alone for the past two days; the caller feared the child had not eaten during this time and wanted the Texas Department of Human Services to "do something."

Gloria Corder, the supervisor of the child protection services' unit, read the case and was torn about what action to take. On the one hand, Gloria wanted to send a worker out to verify the referral and provide any and all available services; yet, the department's policy clearly classified this case as a priority three—a letter would be sent to the caretakers outlining parental responsibilities.[1]

Gloria's experience illustrates the ongoing, and often frustrating, relationship between policy and practice. Policy, whether agency-based or the more general form of public policy, guides the extent and patterns of social work practice at all levels of intervention. In essence, practice is policy in action as intervention strategies are based on the inherent sanctions of a given policy. In the above case illustration, a social worker can violate agency policy because of a personal or professional conviction to verify the child's level of protection and safety, though such actions might result in disciplinary action. Yet, according to the National Association of Social Workers' Code of Ethics, social workers are obligated to work toward the development of effective, humane social policy. (Code of Ethics)

Thus, the professional dilemma occurs as the social worker implements a certain policy even though he or she disagrees with its prem-

---

[1]In Texas, each child protective services' referral is classified as a priority one, two, or three. A priority one requires that a worker begin work within twenty-four hours after the agency receives a referral; a priority two mandates that contact be made within ten days; a priority three requires no more action than a letter or phone call. Cases are prioritized based on a number of variables, including the alleged victim's age and the type and extent of the alleged abuse.

ise and resulting services because the practitioner often does not possess the tools, time, or possibly the desire to develop and manipulate a more equitable policy.

This anthology is built on the assumption that practice and policy are highly integrated with each other. As such, the social worker, whether new or experienced in the profession, must be knowledgeable of the integral relationship between practice and policy. Just as social workers are required to embody a variety of practice roles, practitioners must also be skillful with the tools associated with the field of policy—research, community organization, planning, administration, research, and direct service. (Gilbert and Specht, 1974, p. 16)

There are many excellent policy texts detailing a number of aspects related to the arena of social policy; some focus on policy formulation while others examine current public policies. Even with the breadth, depth, and variety of these texts, there remains a valuable and generally untapped body of literature that can add to our understanding of the nuances of the policymaking process. Such materials are found in professional journals, government publications, agency monographs, and unpublished theses.

The following pages bring together a sampling of high-quality reading to broaden our awareness and understanding of the policy arena. This anthology augments the fine policy texts available by providing, in a single companion volume, important original sources for which faculty must otherwise send the student to the library shelves. The number of articles included is selective when compared with other anthologies; the primary objective of this text is to acquaint students with provocative articles to further enrich their social policy knowledge base. In general, the articles are grouped around four broad topical areas typically explored in the beginning policy course: conceptual understanding, social welfare history, current policy issues, and future trends.

College- and university-based education provides us a unique opportunity to mature both socially and intellectually. The role of each course is different but the same—different in terms of content, the same in the goal of stretching our cognitive, affective, and psychomotor domains. We can, if we wish, glide through our classes and adopt a reaffirmation posture; that is, look for content that supports our previously held notions. On the other hand, we can accept the challenge of higher education to look beyond our current understandings and question why certain situations exist, even if the final answer challenges the core of our personal beliefs.

In the pages that follow, you will find that many of the articles will excite a range of emotions, from outright anger to positive inspiration. Look beyond your feelings as you read the articles and dissect what the authors are saying and, just as important, why they adopt such a position. Reflect on what you see in the classroom and how positions and class discussions relate to the readings. Remember, the key for professional growth is to stretch your intellect, develop creativity, be exposed to diversity, and be willing to risk and disclose your convictions.

This work is guided by the idea that the collected articles will stimulate thinking by describing differing perspectives in a specific area of policy analysis and force us to examine our own approach to practice. Many of this book's papers are controversial in their own regard, and even more so when coupled with other selections. Hopefully, readers will come away with an appreciation of the treasure trove of materials waiting to be ingested to stretch our policy-related knowledge for effective social work practice.

This anthology stems from two separate groups: faculty who instructed me in social work and my social policy students. From the former group, Charlotte Schriberg, Dojelo Russell, Tom Carlton, and Jean Jones helped me view issues and ideas from a social work frame of reference while I worked on my masters degree at Virginia Commonwealth University. During my doctoral studies at the University of Pennsylvania School of Social Work, June Axinn, Hal Levin, and Mark Stern supported, encouraged, guided, and refined my policy interests.

I am also indebted to those students over the years who struggled with the many readings I assigned and who provided feedback regarding their utility in the social policy course. This collection has emerged through their advice. Their hundreds of names are too many to mention, but through them I have been pushed to explore for more meaningful material. This work is dedicated to these folk and the students who follow in their footsteps.

Ira C. Colby

BIBLIOGRAPHY

Gilbert, N. and Specht, H. (1974). *Dimensions of Social Welfare Policy.* Englewood Cliffs, NJ: Prentice-Hall.

National Association of Social Workers, *Code of Ethics,* Silver Spring, MD: National Association of Social Workers.

CONTENTS

Part I Conceptual Foundation—Broadening the Knowledge Base 1

Article 1 Conceptions of Social Welfare 7
Harold Wilensky and Charles Lebeaux

Article 2 The Art of Savage Discovery: How to Blame the Victim 16
William Ryan

Article 3 Everyone Is on Welfare: "The Role of Redistribution in Social Policy" Revisited 34
Mimi Abramovitz

Article 4 The Nature of Poverty 47
George Gilder

Part II Social Welfare History—A Map to the Future 59

Article 5 Benjamin Franklin and the Poor Laws 68
Howell V. Williams

Article 6 Free Blacks in Antebellum Philadelphia: A Study of Ex-Slaves, Freeborn, and Socioeconomic Decline 89
Theodore Hershberg

Article 7 Building Character among the Urban Poor: The Charity Organization Movement 113
Paul Boyer

Article 8 The House of Refuge for Colored Children 135
Cecile P. Frey

Article 9   First Days at Hull-House   *155*
             Jane Addams

Article 10   Fifty Years of Social Security   *166*
             Martha A. McSteen

Part III   Issues Relating to Current Social Programs   *181*

Article 11   Budget Outlook—Summary, 1989-1993   *193*
             Congressional Budget Office

Article 12   Measuring Poverty   *202*
             Congressional Budget Office

Article 13   Issues in Addressing Poverty among Children   *226*
             Congressional Budget Office

Article 14   Federal Policy Changes and the Feminization of
             Poverty   *248*
             Rosemary C. Sarri

Article 15   The "Graying" of the Federal Budget and Its
             Consequences for Old-Age Policy   *261*
             Robert B. Hudson, Ph.D.

Article 16   The Long-Run Financing Problem: Basic
             Approaches   *284*
             Congressional Budget Office

Article 17   Family Medical Expenses in a Single Year   *295*
             Congressional Budget Office

Article 18   Workfare—Introduction   *302*
             Congressional Budget Office

Article 19   Community Mental Health Centers: A Look
             Ahead   *315*
             Allan Beigel, M.D.

Article 20   Pulling Together or Tearing Apart: Birds of a Feather
             Must Choose   *324*
             Robert J. Wineburg

Part IV   Practice, Politics, and the Social Welfare Agenda   *335*

Article 21   Factors Influencing Senate Voting Patterns on Social
             Work Related Legislation   *342*
             Joyce Littell Smith, MSW, and Gail Marie Sullivan, MSW

Article 22   Lobbying and Social Work   *356*
             Maryann Mahaffey

Article 23   Income Security   *370*
             James R. Storey

Article 24   A Social Agenda for the Eighties   *404*
*President's Commission for a National Agenda for the
Eighties*

Article 25   Nonwhites and the Demographic Imperative in Social
Welfare Spending   *437*
Martha N. Ozawa

Article 26   A Welfare Agenda for the End of the Century:
Recasting the Future on Foundations
of the Past   *455*
Robert Morris

Part I

Conceptual Foundation—
Broadening the Knowledge
Base

Why is it necessary to study social welfare policy? Couldn't time be better spent learning practice principles or human behavior? As noted in this anthology's introduction, policy may be characterized as one form of social work practice—social agencies or programs are guided by a set of policies which determine the type, form, and extent of services available to the community. Thus, one of the roles of policy is to outline the boundaries of social work services.

The Council on Social Work Education, the national accrediting body for social work education, identifies social policy as one of the five professional foundation learning areas required in all education programs; the others are human behavior, social work practice, social work research, and field practice. (Council, 1988) The Council notes that social policy courses

> (are) to prepare professionals to function as informed and competent practitioners in providing services and as knowledgeable and committed participants in efforts to achieve change in social policies and programs. Students are expected to develop skills in the use of and the application of scientific knowledge to the analysis and development of social welfare policy and services. They should know the structure of service programs and the history of the organized profession and other social welfare institutions. They should understand the legislative, judicial, and administrative policies, particularly as they affect current and emerging service programs. They should also acquire frameworks for analyzing social and economic policies in the light of the principles of social justice. Social work students should also gain an understanding of political processes and further the achievement of social work goals and purposes (Council, 1988, Appendix 1, 1–8, p. 126).

1

This mandate, while seemingly herculean in its dimensions, sets clear goals for social workers in the policy arena—skill in policy analysis, a sense of welfare history, knowledge of current social policy and programs, and the use of the art of political persuasion.

This first section of articles provides and clarifies the foundation upon which policy analysis and program development take place.

Policy analysis seems complicated at first glance. Yet, if we think of the process as applying a model with specific steps and questions, the task then becomes less confusing and more manageable. We must remember, though, that each step in the model must be addressed or the process will be incomplete. Think of a young child putting together a model airplane. Excitedly, the child tears the wrapper from the box, scatters pieces over the floor, quickly scans the directions, and then, with youthful enthusiasm and abandon, glues whatever pieces seem to fit, while the directions are ignored. The finished product may bear some resemblance to the picture on the box, but a number of pieces remain unattached to the model. Yes, the model is finished, but is it complete?

There are a number of analytic models to choose from practice. Neil Gilbert and Harry Specht (1974, pp. 24–53), for example, identify four basic questions to ask when examining social policy. Thomas Dye (1981, p. 20) details eight specific models, "each offering a separate way of thinking about policy. . . . " June Axinn and Herman Levin (1982) outline a historical approach, while others such as Charles Lindblom (1980), Charles Prigmore and Charles Atherton (1979), Thomas Meenaghan and Robert Washington (1980), Ralph Dolgoff and Donald Feldstein (1984), David Gil (1973), and Robert Morris (1985), among the many social welfare analysts, identify additional analytic processes. While many methods advanced by social workers are at our disposal, we must remember that other analytic processes have been refined and are utilized by many related disciplines, such as political science, public administration, urban affairs, and business administration, and they too may be adopted for social work purposes.

Even with an array of analytic models at our disposal, we are not yet ready to begin formal policy analysis—remember, a little knowledge is dangerous. In social work practice, human behavior, and social work research, there is a specific body of concepts and language applicable to each domain. Social policy also possesses its own unique set of concepts and resulting language.

The effective use of social policy requires us to communicate related concepts successfully. Communication involves the transmission, reception, and understanding of commonly shared concepts; in response to our messages, concepts are sent to us and involve our reception and understanding of the other system's conceptual clarity and application. As such, we must be able to access and apply concepts familiar to any system with which we wish to communicate. This can be accomplished in one of three ways—adopt the other system's concepts in total, force the other system to adopt our concepts, or develop some shared concepts.

Have you ever tried to speak with a non-English-speaking person? This is a difficult but exciting task as you both establish a common ground of understanding. Little by little you each learn some of the other person's language. Yet, you both rely on developing a commonly understood, shared series of concepts whose application to other persons would mean little, if anything; for example, nonsense words combining the two languages, gestures, grunts, or groans.

Each profession incorporates its own set of unique concepts so that its practitioners may communicate with one another and understand and be understood by other systems. In the first introductory level course in social work, new concepts seemed to blur as we struggled to figure out what was what, who was who, and how various social work pieces related to each other—casework, groupwork, CSWE, NASW, licensing, generalist practice, intervention, assessment, planning, and so on. We now take these concepts for granted as they are integral components of our professional thoughts, values, and behaviors. As we advance through the social work curriculum, additional concepts are added to our evolving and expanding professional base.

To understand the nature of social policy, we must be able to apply specific concepts—residual, institutional, equality, universal, optimum, selective, entitlement, means-tested, and so on—to our analytic model. Mere memorization of definitions is helpful, but concepts, through a series of learning stages, including knowledge development, comprehension, application, synthesis, organization, and evaluation, must be integrated within our professional knowledge base.

The goal of the articles in this section is to help the student develop, clarify, and broaden his or her professional conceptual social policy base. Many of the ideas discussed or positions taken in the following readings are generally alluded to in policy discussions or outlined in policy texts. Each of the authors exposes us to a detailed presentation of basic points, which in turn helps sort out the minute and sometimes ambiguous pieces of the policy puzzle.

ARTICLE 1: "CONCEPTIONS OF SOCIAL WELFARE"

We begin this section with the classic contribution by Harold Wilensky and Charles Lebeaux, "Conceptions of Social Welfare." Textbook after textbook refers to their classification scheme of *residual* and *institutional* programs. How a program is viewed or classified by society directly impacts levels of funding, types of services available, eligibility requirements, and how program participants are viewed and treated by the community at large. For example, food stamps is a residual program—there is minimal funding, eligibility is selective and means-tested, services are tightly controlled, and clients are negatively stigmatized. As a result, if the social work community wants to lobby for modifications in the Food Stamp Program, the impact of residual must be kept in the forefront of all political strategies; that is, how do we modify a program, which society would rather not offer, and convince lawmakers to adopt an "institutional" stance?

ARTICLE 2: "THE ART OF SAVAGE DISCOVERY"

William Ryan brings to our attention the way in which we often blame others for their plight while not considering the role that forces external to the individual play in the problem. For example, a person with an inadequate diet may be labeled as "ignorant" or "dumb" when it comes to taking care of himself or herself. Yet, what if this person has a full-time job, makes minimum wage, and cannot afford a complete dietary program? Does the nutritional problem stem from a lack of knowledge or from a low-paying job? Is the amount and quality of food a direct result of the money available to purchase food products?

Ryan asks us to consider the role of victim blaming in human services and how we blame clients for their situations, though often subconsciously.

Have you ever gone to a Child Protective Service office? What were your feelings about being there? Did you feel, "I'm not one of those 'abusers'; I don't molest children!"? Did you try to leave the waiting room quickly, avoiding eye contact with those sitting in the lounge area?

Or, have you ever walked into a county mental health office and felt ill at ease, saying to yourself, "I wonder what's wrong with them, I'm not crazy"? Upon leaving the office, a friend sees you from across the street. Did you tell your acquaintance that you were at the mental health office because of business for fear your friend may think you have some emotional problems you can't handle?

These are examples of *victim blaming*, a subtle process by which the belief that "they are at fault" influences our behavior. William Ryan outlines the destructive consequences of victim blaming. Part of his 1971 work is included to help us understand how the welfare system and resulting policy can blame the client for his or her particular crisis: The rape victim was asking for it, the sexual abuser is a pervert, the food stamp client is lazy.

If we blame clients for their life situations, the logical conclusion is that society has no, or at best a minimal, obligation to provide assistance. Further, if a client is at fault, we can then require him or her to meet certain obligations, such as workfare, to receive a particular service.

What if the client is not to blame but is a victim of constant changes in the technological society or an unforeseen crisis? Does the policy, either overtly or covertly, perpetuate the individual's social and economic status? Does the policy help the client out of or maintain his or her situation? What are the resulting client consequences? Are the social worker's behaviors any different? Ryan's piece helps us consider how and to what extent policy contributes to victim blaming.

ARTICLE 3: "EVERYONE IS ON WELFARE: 'THE ROLE OF REDISTRIBUTION IN SOCIAL POLICY' REVISITED"

Welfare is one of the most complex and misunderstood concepts in the human service system. For some, welfare is limited to programs for the poor (residual perspective), while others argue that welfare encompasses a broad range of services that allow individuals to maximize their fullest potential (institutional perspective).

Mimi Abramowitz's article on welfare applies the work of the famed British social scientist, Richard Titmuss, by exploring the nature of the American social welfare system. In this article, Abramowitz illustrates how welfare involves more than services to the poor; in fact, welfare strongly favors the worker. It is interesting to note the relationship between salary and welfare as Abramowitz documents that the more salary or prestige in one's employment position, the greater the amount and diversity of welfare benefits.

In looking at Abramowitz's work, consider three related points: First, what is your definition of welfare; second, should an individual receive special benefits due to his or her employment that are unavailable to the unemployed; and last, are worker benefits a form of welfare?

ARTICLE 4: "THE NATURE OF POVERTY"

Through the first three readings of this section, we have begun to sharpen our understanding of social policy concepts. As we consider why policy adopts a given shape or form, there is a need to consider differing points of view—challenges to our beliefs help sharpen our position while we become more aware of and sensitive to various issues associated with the given policy.

"The Nature of Poverty" was written by George Gilder, a staunch supporter of supply-side economics, the economic theory underlying the so-called Reagan Revolution of the 1980s. In this particular reading,

Gilder examines the status of poverty in the 1970s and challenges the need for a welfare system. To some people, Gilder presents a somewhat persuasive argument when he argues that many groups of people have "taken care of themselves" and risen out of poverty due to rugged individualism. To others, Gilder's views are sexist in nature, a total misunderstanding of social issues, which ultimately lead to residual social welfare programs, and directly oppose basic social work values which accent the worth and dignity of the individual. In particular, Gilder writes that faith, a male-headed household, and work will pull a family out of poverty's grasp.

What kind of perspective on people does Gilder propose? How are such views carried out in social welfare policy? Is Gilder correct? If not, how then do you argue with him based not on emotion but on the analytic process? Remember, policy analysis involves critiquing and eventually reasoning with others with whom, in many circumstances, you philosophically disagree. What would you say to Gilder if he were a visitor to your policy class? What do you think Abramowitz or Ryan would say and how would they formulate their positions?

BIBLIOGRAPHY

Axinn, J. & Levin, H. (1982). *Social Welfare, A History of the American Response to Need* (2nd ed.). New York: Harper and Row.

Council on Social Work Education. Commission on Accreditation. (1988). *Handbook of Accreditation Standards and Procedures.* Washington, DC: Council on Social Work Education.

Dolgoff, R. & Feldstein, D. (1984). *Understanding Social Welfare* (2nd ed.). New York: Longman.

Dye, T. (1981). *Understanding Public Policy* (4th ed.). Englewood Cliffs, NJ: Prentice-Hall.

Gil, D. (1973). *Unraveling Social Policy, Theory, Analysis, and Political Action Towards Social Equality.* Cambridge, MA: Schenkman Publishing Company.

Gilbert, N. & Specht, H. (1974). *Dimensions of Social Welfare Policy.* Englewood Cliffs, NJ: Prentice-Hall.

Lindblom, C. E. (1980). *The Policy-Making Process* (2nd ed.). Englewood-Cliffs, NJ: Prentice-Hall.

Meenaghan, T. M. and Washington, R. (1980). *Social Policy and Social Welfare, Structural Analysis.* New York: The Free Press.

Morris, R. (1985). *Social Policy of the American Welfare State, An Introduction to Policy Analysis* (2nd ed.). New York: Longman.

Prigmore, C. and Atherton, C. (1979). *Social Welfare Policy, Analysis and Formulation.* Lexington, Mass.: D.C. Heath and Company.

Article 1

CONCEPTIONS OF SOCIAL WELFARE

Harold Wilensky and Charles Lebeaux

What is meant by social welfare? Is it relief, and just for the poor? Is social insurance included? What of public recreation and parks? And if these are social welfare, why not public highways and the Tennessee Valley Authority? How about private industry's pension plans? And what of fee-charging social agencies and the "private practice" of social work?

We are not concerned here with formulating a view of what social welfare ought ideally to involve, but rather with its existing outlines and trends in the United States. Specifically, we will: (1) point out what seem to be the currently dominant concepts of welfare, and (2) state some criteria for delineating social welfare. Later chapters will discuss the implications of the dominant American conceptions of social welfare for the services and for the professional practice of social work.

Current Conceptions

Two conceptions of social welfare seem to be dominant in the United States today: The *residual* and the *institutional*. The first holds that social welfare institutions should come into play only when the normal structures of supply, the family and the market, break down. The second, in contrast, sees the welfare services as normal, "first line" functions of modern industrial society. These are the concepts around which drives for more or for less welfare service tend to focus. Not surprisingly, they derive from the ethos of the society in which they are found. They represent a compromise between the values of economic individualism and free enterprise on the one hand, and security, equality, and humanitarianism on the other. They are rather explicit among both social welfare professionals and the lay public.

The residual formulation is based on the premise that there are two "natural" channels through which an individual's needs are properly met: the family and the market economy. These are the preferred

SOURCE: From *Industrial Society and Social Welfare*, by Harold L. Wilensky and Charles N. Lebeaux. Copyright © 1958. Reprinted by permission of the Russell-Sage Foundation. Reprinted by permission of Russell-Sage Foundation, Inc.

structures of supply. However, sometimes these institutions do not function adequately: family life is disrupted, depressions occur. Or sometimes the individual cannot make use of normal channels because of old age or illness. In such cases, according to this idea, a third mechanism of need fulfillment is brought into play—the social welfare structure. This is conceived as a residual agency, attending primarily to emergency functions, and is expected to withdraw when the regular social structure—the family and the economic system—is again working properly. Because of its residual, temporary, substitute characteristic, social welfare thus conceived often carries the stigma of "dole" or "charity."

The residual concept was more popular in the United States before the Great Depression of 1929 than it is now. That it is consistent with the traditional American ideology of individual responsibility and by-your-own-bootstrap progress is readily apparent. But it does not reflect the radical social changes accompanying advanced industrialization, or fully account for various aspects of contemporary social welfare activity.

The second major formulation of social welfare is given in a widely used social work textbook as "the organized system of social services and institutions, designed to aid individuals and groups to attain satisfying standards of life and health. It aims at personal and social relationships which permit individuals the fullest development of their capacities and the promotion of their well-being in harmony with the needs of the community."[1] (2: p. 4; cf. 3.) This definition of the "institutional" view implies no stigma, no emergency, no "abnormalcy." Social welfare becomes accepted as a proper, legitimate function of modern industrial society in helping individuals achieve self-fulfillment. The complexity of modern life is recognized. The inability of the individual to provide fully for himself, or to meet all his needs in family and work settings, is considered a "normal" condition; and the helping agencies achieve "regular" institutional status.

While these two views seem antithetical, in practice American social work has tried to combine them, and current trends in social wel-

---

[1]This is a typically vague definition of the "institutional" view. Contemporary definitions of welfare are fuzzy because cultural values regarding the social responsibilities of government, business, and the individual are now in flux. The older doctrines of individualism, private property and free market, and of minimum government provided a clear-cut definition of welfare as "charity for unfortunates." The newer values of social democracy—security, equality, humanitarianism—undermine the notion of "unfortunate classes" in society. All people are regarded as having "needs" which *ipso facto* become a legitimate claim on the whole society. Business and government as channels to supply these needs have vastly broadened their responsibilities. Both the older and newer doctrines coexist today, creating conflicts and ambiguities in values which are reflected in loose definitions of social welfare.

fare represent a middle course. Those who lament the passing of the old order insist that the second ideology is undermining individual character and the national social structure. Those who bewail our failure to achieve utopia today, argue that the residual conception is an obstacle which must be removed before we can produce the good life for all. In our view, neither ideology exists in a vacuum; each is a reflection of the broader cultural and societal conditions described in . . . and with further industrialization the second is likely to prevail.

Criteria for Delineating Social Welfare

Keeping in mind this ideological dualism, we can now look at the substance of social welfare. What are the main distinguishing characteristics of activities which fall within the range of welfare practice in America today?[2]

1. Formal Organization. Social welfare activities are formally organized. Handouts and individual charity, though they may increase or decrease welfare, are not organized. Likewise, services and help extended within such mutual-aid relationships as family, friends and neighbors, kinship groups, and the like are not included in the definition of social welfare structure. It is recognized that there is a continuum running from the most informal to the most formal, and that in-between cases—the mutual-aid welfare services of a small labor union, church, or fraternal society—cannot be precisely classified. The distinction is clear in principle, however, and important.

Modern social welfare has really to be thought of as help given to the stranger, not to the person who by reason of personal bond commands it without asking. It assumes a degree of social distance between helped and helper. In this respect it is a social response to the shift from rural to urban-industrial society. Help given within the family or friendship group is but an aspect of the underlying relationship. Welfare services are a different kind of "help." We must think here of the regular, full-time, recognized agencies that carry on the welfare business.

---

[2]All institutions, of course, undergo change over time, both in form and function. However, some continuing identify is usually clear. Thus, the historical continuity and interconnection of social welfare institutions can be traced—from hospitals first designed as a place for the poor to die, to modern community hospitals serving the health needs of all; from sandpiles for the children of working mothers, to the tennis courts and baseball tournaments of a modern recreation program; from poorhouses to Social Security.

2. Social Sponsorship and Accountability. Social auspice—the existence of socially sanctioned purposes and methods, and formal accountability—is the crucial element in social welfare service versus comparable service under profit-making auspices. If mobilization of resources to meet needs is not accomplished by the family or through the market economy, some third type of organization must be provided, and this is typically the society as a whole acting through government (city, state, federal), or a smaller collectivity operating through a private social agency. (Cf. 5; p. 13.)

Some mechanism for expressing the public interest and rendering the service accountable to the larger community is an essential part of social sponsorship. For public welfare services in a democratic society, the mechanism is simply the representative structure of government. For voluntary agencies accountability is typically, though less certainly, achieved through a governing board. That some of these boards are self-perpetuating, unresponsive to changing needs and isolated from constituencies, does not deny the principle of accountability, any more than oligarchy denies it in the public welfare arena. The principle is acknowledged in privately as well as publicly sponsored organizations.

3. Absence of Profit Motive as Dominant Program Purpose. Just as the needs-service cycle within the family is excluded from the concept of social welfare, so generally are those needs which arise and are fulfilled within the bounds of the three enterprise system. The services and goods produced by the market economy and purchased by individuals with money derived from competitive participation in that economy are not social welfare. Profitable and most fee-for-service activities are excluded. But there are cases difficult to classify.

Social welfare objectives can be intimately associated with what is basically profit-making enterprise, as when a private business provides recreation facilities, pension plans, or nurseries for its employees. The view may be taken, on the one hand, that since such services attend human wants quite peripheral to the purpose of the organization, they neither share in nor alter the nature of the underlying profit-making activity. The latter remains nonwelfare, while the former are essentially social welfare programs under business auspices. This view gains support from the observation that separate structures for the administration of welfare services often develop within the business enterprise, and constitute a kind of "social auspice." An industrial pension plan, for instance, usually has a trust fund separate from the financial operations of the company; a separate office with its own physical facilities will be

set up to administer it; the policy-making group—board or committee—will often have employee or union representation, especially if the plan is collectively bargained; and its operation will
likely come under some degree of government regulation.

On the other hand, the view may be taken that industry-spon-
sored welfare programs are simply part of the conditions of employment, a substitute for wages. Industries provide restrooms and
run recreational programs to compete for a labor supply and maintain employee morale and efficiency. Pensions, in this view, are a
kind of deferred wage. Programs are often administered not through
separate administrative offices, but by the business accounting or
personnel office. Even when separate administrative structures are
created, this does not alter the underlying program purpose of facilitating production.[3]

Thus, the degree to which an industrial welfare program may
be considered social welfare varies inversely with extent of emphasis on a contractual relationship between two parties seeking a
mutually rewarding arrangement, and directly with extent of social sponsorship and control. It is clear, nevertheless, that industrial welfare programs affect the development of social welfare
institutions. The Supplemental Unemployment Benefits scheme, for
instance, creates pressure for expanded unemployment insurance,
and private pension plans are integrated with OASI in planning
for retirement. Our discussion of social welfare expenditures . . .
will therefore include data on industrial welfare programs.

Some aspects of professional fee-for-service practice are also
difficult to classify. Most Americans probably would think—and
without derogatory implication—that professions as well as trades
are primarily ways of making a living (often a kind of small business), and thus nonwelfare in nature. Yet it is a fact that many
individual professional practitioners—physicians, lawyers, and
dentists particularly—observe what appears to be a semi-social
welfare practice of scaling fees according to ability to pay. Fee-
scaling in private practice, however, is often a professional norm,
part of a formal code of ethics. As such, its meaning and nature

---

[3]It is true that men's motives vary; and businessmen are not an exception. What
we are talking about here is not individual motives but organizational purposes. Many
business leaders may acquire a sense of trusteeship going beyond their obligations to
the shareholders. Thus, multi-plant companies have been known to avoid shutdown
of an unprofitable unit because of major disruption to the local community. But one
cannot say that the enterprise purpose is to save declining communities, any more
than one can call dropping 50 cents in a blind man's hat Aid to the Blind.

derive from a different context—professionalism—and it can be seen as a device by which a group with a monopoly of an indispensable service protects its fee-taking privilege. Where the professional "charges what the traffic will bear," there is no ambiguity, and his activity is clearly nonwelfare in nature.

To the extent that the private practice of social casework resembles other fee-for-service professions, it, too, is rather clearly outside the field of social welfare. Solo practice of social work is as yet so little developed, however, that it cannot be seen how close it will hew to the model of the other professions.

4. Functional Generalization: An Integrative View of Human Needs. Since almost any of the gamut of culturally conditioned human needs may be unmet and since human capacities which can be developed are many, welfare services to meet needs and enhance capacities will be varied. Placing babies in foster homes, operating a recreation program, administering social insurance, developing medical service in a rural community—the substantive activities here have little in common; a great variety of activities may take on a social welfare aspect. From the standpoint of the welfare structure as a whole, these activities are properly described as "functionally generalized"; that is, welfare services are found attached to, or performing in place of, medical institutions, the family, education, industry—wherever there is "unmet need." It will be noticed that this concept is closely related to that of residuality discussed above; what other institutions do not do, it is the job of welfare to do. To the extent that it is the function of social welfare to come in and "pick up the pieces" in any area of need, it must lack attachment to any given area.

From this characteristic derives, in part at least, the comprehensive view of human needs and personality that distinguishes social work from other professions. An international study by the United Nations of training for social work concludes that social work seeks to assist

. . . individuals, families and groups in relation to the many social and economic forces by which they are affected, and differs in this respect from certain allied activities, such as health, education, religion, etc. The latter . . . tend to exclude all save certain specific aspects of the socio-economic environment from their purview. . . . The social worker, on the other hand, cannot exclude from his consideration any aspect of the life of the person who seeks help in solving problems of social adjustment . . . [or any] of the community's social institutions that might be of use to the individual. . . (5: p. 13)

Individual agencies are, of course, specialized and limited in function; but the welfare field is inclusive. It is because social welfare is "functionally generalized" that we exclude the school system, which tends to be segmental in its approach to its clientele.

5. Direct Concern with Human Consumption Needs. Finally, how are government welfare services to be distinguished from other government services, since all are socially sponsored? It is possible to place governmental activities on a continuum which ranges from services primarily concerned with the functional requisites of the society . . . and only indirectly with the fate of the individual, to those which provide direct services to meet immediate consumption needs of individuals and families. At the "indirect" end of this continuum, following the analysis of Hazel Kyrk, are government activities "inherent in the nature of the state . . . such as the national defense, the preservation of law and order, the administration of justice, the exercise of regulatory functions. . . ." Intermediate are road building, flood control, forest conservation, and other such services, "the benefits of which are so remote in time or diffused among the population that they will not be privately provided." At the direct services end are those where "specific beneficiaries can be identified, although there are also general benefits. . . . Schools and universities, recreational facilities, libraries, museums, concerts, school books and lunches, subsidized housing, medical and hospital services. In this last group of services described are those which are distinctly for consumer use and enjoyment." (4: pp. 148–149)[4]

In the last group fall the welfare services. Of course, social welfare programs serve the needs of both the larger social structure and the individual consumer. The unemployment compensation program in the United States, for example, has been designed as an anti-depression weapon as well as a means of alleviating the

---

[4]An interesting parallel to the distinction Kyrk makes here has been noted with respect to Soviet state institutions where, since "everything is government," it might also be expected that everything would be social welfare. Sociologist Vucinich observes, however, that in the U.S.S.R.: "Soviet experts in jurisprudence make a sharp distinction between social institutions . . . and Soviet enterprises. Institutions (post offices, telegraphic services, scientific laboratories, schools, and the like) are, in the economic sense, nonproductive units which draw their funds from the state budgets and are not considered independent juridical persons. Enterprises, on the other hand, have their 'own' budgets . . . , their 'own' basic capital (machines, tools, etc.) and working capital." (6: pp. 9–10)

individual distress accompanying unemployment. But it is the latter, rather than the former, aspect of the program which from the present point of view qualifies it as a social welfare activity.

A nineteenth century view of government in the United States saw its functions restricted to "activities inherent in the nature of the state." The veto of Dorothea Dix's mental hospital bill in 1854, it will be remembered, was based on President Pierce's belief that the life conditions of individuals were no proper concern of government. Today many government services are directed specifically to individuals, and it is these which tend to be identified as social welfare.

It is thus an additional distinguishing attribute of social welfare programs that they tend to be aimed directly at the individual and his consumer interests, rather than at the general society and producer interests; that they are concerned with human resources as opposed to other kinds of resources. Soil conservation, subsidy of the merchant marine, development of water power resources, much as these redound ultimately to human welfare, are not typically defined as social welfare; but feeding the hungry, finding homes for dependent children, even provision of recreational facilities are so defined. This is the point of the stipulation in the definition of welfare given by Kraus,[5] that welfare services have "direct effects on welfare and health of individuals and families," and of Cassidy's definition of the social services as "those organized activities that are primarily and directly concerned with the conservation, the protection, and the improvement of human resources." (1: p. 13)

In sum, the major traits which, taken together, distinguish social welfare structure in American (made explicit here as criteria to define the field of analysis) are:

1. Formal organization
2. Social sponsorship and accountability
3. Absence of profit motive as dominant program purpose
4. Functional generalization: integrative, rather than segmental, view of human needs
5. Direct focus on human consumption needs

The major weakness in definition occurs in the area of socially sponsored, nonprofit services which affect nearly everyone in the so-

---

[5]At a meeting of the United States Committee of the International Conference of Social Work, New York City, June 17, 1955.

ciety. It would seem, for instance, that public education might be classed among the social services, as it is in England (and by a few American welfare experts, for example, Ida C. Merriam). In the U.S. there is apparently a tendency to exclude from the welfare category any service, no matter how identified with welfare it may have been in origin, which becomes highly developed, widespread in its incidence among the population, and professionally staffed by persons other than social workers. Helen Witmer notes social insurance as an example of a welfare service which has tended to move out of the welfare area after it became a "usual institutional arrangement." (7: pp. 484–486) This seems to be consistent with the residual conception and its view of the welfare services as emergency, secondary, peripheral to the main show. As the residual conception becomes weaker, as we believe it will, and the institutional conception increasingly dominant, it seems likely that distinctions between welfare and other types of social institutions will become more and more blurred. Under continuing industrialization all institutions will be oriented toward and evaluated in terms of social welfare aims. The "welfare state" will become the "welfare society," and both will be more reality than epithet.

REFERENCES

1. Cassidy, Harry M., *Social Security and Reconstruction in Canada*. Bruce Humphries, Inc., Boston, 1943.
2. Friedlander, Walter A., *Introduction to Social Welfare*. Prentice-Hall, New York, 1955, p. 4.
3. Kraus, Hertha, *Common Service Resources in a Free Society*. Association for the Study of Community Organization, New York, 1954. Mimeographed.
4. Kyrk, Hazel, *The Family in American Economy*. University of Chicago Press, Chicago, 1953.
5. United Nations, Department of Social Affairs, *Training for Social Work: An International Survey*. Columbia University Press, New York, 1950, p. 13.
6. Vucinich, Alexander S., *Soviet Economic Institutions: The Social Production Units*. Stanford University Press, Stanford, Calif., 1952.
7. Witmer, Helen L., *Social Work: An Analysis of a Social Institution*. Farrar and Rienhart, New York, 1942.

Article 2

THE ART OF SAVAGE DISCOVERY
How to Blame the Victim

William Ryan

I

Twenty years ago, Zero Mostel used to do a sketch in which he impersonated a Dixiecrat Senator conducting an investigation of the origins of World War II. At the climax of the sketch, the Senator boomed out, in an excruciating mixture of triumph and suspicion, "What was Pearl Harbor *doing* in the Pacific?" This is an extreme example of Blaming the Victim.

Twenty years ago, we could laugh at Zero Mostel's caricature. In recent years, however, the same process has been going on every day in the arena of social problems, public health, anti-poverty programs, and social welfare. A philosopher might analyze this process and prove that, technically, it is comic. But is is hardly ever funny.

Consider some victims. One is the miseducated child in the slum school. He is blamed for his own miseducation. He is said to contain within himself the causes of his inability to read and write well. The shorthand phrase is "cultural deprivation," which, to those in the know, conveys what they allege to be inside information: that the poor child carries a scanty pack of cultural baggage as he enters school. He doesn't know about books and magazines and newspapers, they say. (No books in the home: the mother fails to subscribe to *Reader's Digest.*) They say that if he talks at all—an unlikely event since slum parents don't talk to their children—he certainly doesn't talk correctly. (Lowerclass dialect spoken here, or even—God forbid!—Southern Negro. (*Ici on parle nigra.*) If you can manage to get him to sit in a chair, they say, he squirms and looks out the window. (Impulsive-ridden, these kids, motoric rather than verbal.) In a word he is "disadvantaged" and "socially deprived," they say, and this, of course, accounts for his failure (*his* failure, they say) to learn much in school.

Note the similarity to the logic of Zero Mostel's Dixiecrat Senator. What is the culturally deprived child *doing* in the school? What is wrong

SOURCE: From *Blaming the Victim* by William Ryan. Copyright © 1971 by William Ryan. Reprinted by permission of Pantheon Books, a division of Random House, Inc.

with the victim? In pursuing this logic, no one remembers to ask questions about the collapsing buildings and torn textbooks, the frightened, insensitive teachers, the six additional desks in the room, the blustering, frightened principals, the relentless segregation, the callous administrator, the irrelevant curriculum, the bigoted or cowardly members of the school board, the insulting history book, the stingy taxpayers, the fairy-tale readers, or the self-serving faculty of the local teachers' college. We are encouraged to confine our attention to the child and to dwell on all his alleged defects. Cultural deprivation becomes an omnibus explanation for the educational disaster area known as the inner-city school. This is Blaming the Victim.

Pointing to the supposedly deviant Negro family as the "fundamental weakness of the Negro community" is another way to blame the victim. Like "cultural deprivation," "Negro family" has become a shorthand phrase with stereotyped connotations of matriarchy, fatherlessness, and pervasive illegitimacy. Growing up in the "crumbling" Negro family is supposed to account for most of the racial evils in America. Insiders have the word, of course, and know that this phrase is supposed to evoke images of growing up with a long-absent or never-present father (replaced from time to time perhaps by a series of transient lovers) and with bossy women ruling the roost, so that the children are irreparably damaged. This refers particularly to the poor, bewildered male children, whose psyches are fatally wounded and who are never, alas, to learn the trick of becoming upright, downright, forthright all-American boys. Is it any wonder the Negroes cannot achieve equality? From such families! And, again, by focusing our attention on the Negro family as the apparent *cause* of racial inequality, our eye is diverted. Racism, discrimination, segregation, and the powerlessness of the ghetto are subtly, but thoroughly, downgraded in importance.

The generic process of Blaming the Victim is applied to almost every American problem. The miserable health care of the poor is explained away on the grounds that the victim has poor motivation and lacks health information. The problems of slum housing are traced to the characteristics of tenants who are labeled as "Southern rural migrants" not yet "acculturated" to life in the big city. The "multi-problem" poor, it is claimed, suffer the psychological effects of impoverishment, the "culture of poverty," and the deviant value system of the lower classes; consequently, though unwittingly, they cause their own troubles. From such a viewpoint, the obvious fact that poverty is primarily an absence of money is easily overlooked or set aside.

The growing number of families receiving welfare are fallaciously linked together with the increased number of illegitimate children as twin results of promiscuity and sexual abandon among members of the lower orders. Every important social problem—crime, mental illness, civil disorder, unemployment—has been analyzed within the framework of the victim-blaming ideology. In the following pages, I shall present in detail nine examples that relate to social problems and human services in urban areas.

It would be possible for me to venture into other areas—one finds a perfect example in literature about the underdeveloped countries and the Third World, in which the lack of prosperity and technological progress is attributed to some aspect of the national character of the people, such as lack of "achievement motivation"—but I plan to stay within the confines of my own personal and professional experience, which is, generally, with racial injustice, social welfare, and human services in the city.

I have been listening to the victim-blamers and pondering their thought processes for a number of years. That process is often very subtle. Victim-blaming is cloaked in kindness and concern, and bears all the trappings and statistical furbelows of scientism; it is obscured by a perfumed haze of humanitarianism. In observing the process of Blaming the Victim, one tends to be confused and disoriented because those who practice this art display a deep concern for the victims that is quite genuine. In this way, the new ideology is very different from the open prejudice and reactionary tactics of the old days. Its adherents include sympathetic social scientists with social consciences in good working order, and liberal politicians with a genuine commitment to reform. They are very careful to dissociate themselves from vulgar Calvinism or crude racism; they indignantly condemn any notions of innate wickedness or genetic defect. "The Negro is *not born* inferior," they shout apoplectically. "Force of circumstance," they explain in reasonable tones, "has *made* him inferior." And they dismiss with self-righteous contempt any claims that the poor man in American is plainly unworthy or shiftless or enamored of idleness. No, they say, he is "caught in the cycle of poverty." He is trained to be poor by his culture and his family life, endowed by his environment (perhaps by his ignorant mother's outdated style of toilet training) with those unfortunately unpleasant characteristics that make him ineligible for a passport into the affluent society.

Blaming the Victim is, of course, quite different from old-fashioned conservative ideologies. The latter simply dismissed victims as inferior, genetically defective, or morally unfit; the emphasis is on the intrinsic, even hereditary, defect. The former shifts its emphasis to the environmental causation. The old-fashioned conservative could hold firmly to the belief that the oppressed and the victimized were born that way— "that way" being defective or inadequate in character or ability. The new ideology attributes defect and inadequacy to the malignant nature of poverty, injustice, slum life, and racial difficulties. The stigma that marks the victim and accounts for his victimization is an acquired stigma, a stigma of social, rather than genetic, origin. But the stigma, the defect, the fatal difference—though derived in the past from environmental forces—is still located *within* the victim, inside his skin. With such an elegant formulation, the humanitarian can have it both ways. He can, all at the same time, concentrate his charitable interest on the defects of the victim, condemn the vague social and environmental stresses that produced the defect (some time ago), and ignore the continuing effect of victimizing social forces (right now). It is a brilliant ideology for justifying a perverse form of social action designed to change, not society, as one might expect, but rather society's victim.

As a result, there is a terrifying sameness in the programs that arise from this kind of analysis. In education, we have programs of "compensatory education" to build up the skills and attitudes of the ghetto child, rather than structural changes in the schools. In race relations, we have social engineers who think up ways of "strengthening" the Negro family, rather than methods of eradicating racism. In health care, we develop new programs to provide health information (to correct the supposed ignorance of the poor) and to reach out and discover cases of untreated illness and disability (to compensate for their supposed unwillingness to seek treatment). Meanwhile, the gross inequities of our medical care delivery systems are left completely unchanged. As we might expect, the logical outcome of analyzing social problems in terms of the deficiencies of the victim is the development of programs aimed at correcting those deficiencies. The formula for action becomes extraordinarily simple: change the victim.

All of this happens so smoothly that it seems downright rational. First, identify a social problem. Second, study those affected by the problem and discover in what ways they are different from the rest of us as a consequence of deprivation and injustice. Third, define the differences as the cause of the social problem itself. Finally, of course, assign a government bureaucrat to invent a humanitarian action program to correct the differences.

Now no one in his right mind would quarrel with the assertion that social problems are present in abundance and are readily identifiable. God knows it is true that when hundreds of thousands of poor children drop out of school—or even graduate from school—they are barely literate. After spending some ten thousand hours in the company of professional educators, these children appear to have learned very little. The fact of failure in their education is undisputed. And the racial situation in America is usually acknowledged to be a number one item on the nation's agenda. Despite years of marches, commissions, judicial decisions, and endless legislative remedies, we are confronted with unchanging or even widening racial differences in achievement. In addition, despite our assertions that Americans get the best health care in the world, the poor stubbornly remain unhealthy. They lose more work because of illness, have more carious teeth, lose more babies as a result of both miscarriage and infant death, and die considerably younger than the well-to-do.

The problems are there, and there in great quantities. They make us uneasy. Added together, these disturbing signs reflect inequality and a puzzlingly high level of unalleviated distress in America totally inconsistent with our proclaimed ideals and our enormous wealth. This thread—this rope—of inconsistency stands out so visibly in the fabric of American life, that it is jarring to the eye. And this must be explained, to the satisfaction of our conscience as well as our patriotism. Blaming the Victim is an ideal, almost painless, evasion.

The second step in applying this explanation is to look sympathetically at those who "have" the problem in question, to separate them out and define them in some way as a special group, a group that is *different* from the population in general. This is a crucial and essential step in the process, for that difference is in itself hampering and maladaptive. The Different Ones are seen as less competent, less skilled, less knowing—in short, less human. The ancient Greeks deduced from a single characteristic, a difference in language, that the barbarians— that is, the "babblers" who spoke a strange tongue—were wild, uncivilized, dangerous, rapacious, uneducated, lawless, and, indeed, scarcely more than animals. Automatically labeling strangers as savages, weird and inhuman creatures (thus explaining difference by exaggerating difference) not infrequently justifies mistreatment, enslavement, or even extermination of the Different Ones.

Blaming the Victim depends on a very similar process of identification (carried out, to be sure, in the most kindly, philanthropic, and intellectual manner) whereby the victim of social problems is identified as strange, different—in other words, as a barbarian, a savage. Discovering savages, then, is an essential component of, and prerequisite to, Blaming the Victim, and the art of Savage Discovery is a core skill that must be acquired by all aspiring Victim Blamers. They must learn how to demonstrate that the poor, the black, the ill, the jobless, the slum tenants, are different and strange. They must learn to conduct or interpret the research that shows how "these people" think in different forms, act in different patterns, cling to different values, seek different goals, and learn different truths. Which is to say that they are strangers, barbarians, savages. This is how the distressed and disinherited are redefined in order to make it possible for us to look at society's problems and to attribute their causation to the individuals affected.

II

Blaming the Victim is an ideological process, which is to say that it is a set of ideas and concepts deriving from systematically motivated, but *unintended*, distortions of reality. In the sense that Karl Mannheim[1] used the term, an ideology develops from the "collective unconscious" of a group or class and is rooted in a class-based interest in maintaining the *status quo* (as contrasted with what he calls a *utopia*, a set of ideas rooted in a class-based interest in *changing* the *status quo*). An ideology, then, has several components: First, there is the belief system itself, the way of looking at the world, the set of ideas and concepts. Second, there is the systematic distortion of reality reflected in those ideas. Third is the condition that the distortion must not be a conscious, intentional process. Finally, though they are not intentional, the ideas must serve a specific function: maintaining the *status quo* in the interest of a specific group. Blaming the Victim fits this definition of all counts, as I will attempt to show in detail in the following chapters. Most particularly, it is important to realize that Blaming the Victim is not a process of *intentional* distortion although it does serve the class interests of those who practice it. And it has a rich ancestry in American thought about social problems and how to deal with them.

Thinking about social problems is especially susceptible to ideological influences since, as John Seeley has pointed out,[2] defining a social problem is not so simple. "What is a social problem?" may seem an ingenuous question until one turns to confront its opposite: "What human problem is *not* a social problem?" Since any problem in which people are involved is social, why do we reserve the label for some problems in which people are involved and withhold it from others? To use Seeley's example, why is crime called a social problem when university administration is not? The phenomena we look at are bounded by the act of definition. They become social problems only by being so considered. In Seeley's words, *"naming* it as a problem, after naming it as a *problem."*

It is only recently, for example, that we have begun to *name* the rather large quantity of people on earth as the *problem* of overpopulation, or the population explosion. Such phenomena often become proper predicaments for certain solutions, certain treatments. Before the 1930's, the most anti-Semitic German was unaware that Germany had a "Jewish problem." It took the Nazis to *name* the simple existence of Jews in the Third Reich as a "social problem," and that act of definition helped to shape the final solution.

We have removed "immigration" from our list of social problems (after executing a solution—choking off the flow of immigrants) and have added "urbanization." Nowadays, we define the situation of men out of work as the social problem of "unemployment" rather than, as in Elizabethan times, that of "idleness." (The McCone Commission, investigating the Watts Riot of 1966, showed how hard old ideologies die; it specified both unemployment *and* idleness as causes of the disorder.) In the near future, if we are to credit the prophets of automation, the label "unemployment" will fade away and "idleness," now renamed the "leisure-time problem," will begin again to raise its lazy head. We have been comfortable for years with the "Negro problem," a term that clearly implies that the existence of Negroes is somehow a problematic fact. *Ebony* magazine turned the tables recently and renamed the phenomenon as "The White Problem in America," which may be a good deal more accurate.

We must particularly ask, "To whom are social problems a problem?" And usually, if truth were to be told, we would have to admit that we mean they are a problem to those of us who are outside the boundaries of what we have defined as the problem. Negroes are a problem to racist whites, welfare is a problem to stingy taxpayers, delinquency is a problem to nervous property owners.

Now, if this is the quality of our assumptions about social problems, we are led unerringly to certain beliefs about the causes of these problems. We cannot comfortably believe that *we* are the cause of that which is problematic to us; therefore, we are almost compelled to believe that *they*—the problematic ones—are the cause and this immediately prompts us to search for deviance. Identification of the deviance as the cause of the problem is a simple step that ordinarily does not even require evidence.

C. Wright Mills analyzed the ideology of those who write about social problems and demonstrated the relationship of their texts to class interest and to the preservation of the existent social order.[3] In sifting the material in thirty-one widely used textbooks in "social problems," "social pathology," and "social disorganization," Mills found a pervasive, coherent ideology with a number of common characteristics.

First, the textbooks present material about these problems, he says, in simple, descriptive terms, with each problem unrelated to the others and none related in any meaningful way to other aspects of the social environment. Second, the problems are selected and described largely according to predetermined norms. Poverty is a problem in that it deviates from the standard of economic self-sufficiency; divorce is a problem because the family is supposed to remain intact; crime and delinquency are problematic insofar as they depart from the accepted moral and legal standards of the community. The norms themselves are taken as givens, and no effort is made to examine them. Nor is there any thought given to the manner in which norms might themselves contribute to the development of the problems. (In a society in which everyone is assumed and expected to be economically self-sufficient, as an example, doesn't economic dependency almost automatically mean poverty? No attention is given to such issues.)

Within such a framework, then, deviation from norms and standards comes to be defined as failed or incomplete socialization—failure to learn the rules or the inability to learn how to keep them. Those with social problems are then viewed as unable or unwilling to adjust to society's standards, which are narrowly conceived by what Mills calls "independent middle class persons verbally living out Protestant ideas in small town America." This obviously, is a precise description of the social origins and status of almost every one of the authors.

In defining social problems in this way, the social pathologists are, of course, ignoring a whole set of factors that ordinarily might be considered relevant—for instance, unequal distribution of income, social stratification, political struggle, ethnic and racial group conflict, and inequality of power. Their ideology concentrates almost exclusively on the failure of the deviant. To the extent that society plays any part in social problems, it is said to have somehow failed to socialize the individual, to teach him how to adjust to circumstances, which, though far from perfect, are gradually changing for the better. Mills' essay provides a solid foundation for understanding the concept of Blaming the Victim.

This way of thinking on the part of "social pathologists," which Mills identified as the predominant tool used in *analyzing* social problems, also saturates the majority of programs that have been developed to *solve* social problems in America. These programs are based on the assumption that *individuals* "have" social problems as a result of some kind of unusual circumstances—accident, illness, personal defect or handicap, character flaw or maladjustment—that exclude them from using the ordinary mechanisms for maintaining and advancing themselves. For example, the prevalent belief in America is that, under normal circumstances, everyone can obtain sufficient income for the necessities of life. Those who are unable to do so are special deviant cases, persons who for one reason or another are not able to adapt themselves to the generally satisfactory income-producing system. In times gone by these persons were further classified into the worthy poor—the lame, the blind, the young mother whose husband died in an accident, the aged man no longer able to work—and the unworthy poor—the lazy, the unwed mother and her illegitimate children, the malingerer. All were seen, however, as individuals who, for good reasons or bad, were personal failures, unable to adapt themselves to the system.

In America health care, too, has been predominantly a matter of particular remedial attention provided individually to the more or less random group of persons who have become ill, whose bodily functioning has become deviant and abnormal. In the field of mental health, the same approach has been, and continues to be, dominant. The social problem of mental disease has been viewed as a collection of individual cases of deviance, persons who—through unusual hereditary taint, or exceptional distortion of character—have become unfit for normal activities. The solution to these problems was to segregate the deviants, to protect them, to give them *asylum* from the life of the community for which they were no longer competent.

This has been the dominant style in American social welfare and health activities, then: to treat what we call social problems, such as poverty, disease, and mental illness, in terms of the individual deviance of the special, unusual groups of persons who had those problems. There has also been a competing style, however—much less common, not at all congruent with the prevalent ideology, but continually developing parallel to the dominant style.

Adherents of this approach tended to search for defects in the community and the environment rather than in the individual; to emphasize predictability and usualness rather than random deviance; they tried to think about preventing rather than merely repairing or treating—to see social problems, in a word, as social. In the field of disease, this approach was termed public health, and its practitioners sought the cause of disease in such things as the water supply, the sewage system, the density and quality of housing conditions. They set out to prevent disease, not in individuals, but in the total population, through improved sanitation, inoculation against communicable disease, and the policing of housing conditions. In the field of income maintenance, this secondary style of solving social problems, focused on poverty as a predictable event, on the regularities of income deficiency. And it concentrated on the development of standard, generalized programs affecting total groups. Rather than trying to fit the aged worker ending his career into some kind of category of special cases, it assumed all sixty-five-year-old men should expect to retire from the world of work and have the security of an old age pension, to be arranged through public social activity. Unemployment insurance was developed as a method whereby all workers could be protected against the effects of the normal ups and downs of the business cycle. A man out of work could then count on an unemployment check rather than endure the agony of pauperizing himself, selling his tools or his car, and finding himself in the special category of those deserving of charity.

These two approaches to the solution of social problems have existed side by side, the former always dominant, but the latter gradually expanding, slowly becoming more and more prevalent.

Elsewhere[4] I have proposed the dimension of *exceptionalism-universalism* as the ideological underpinning for these two contrasting approaches to the analysis and solution of social problems. The *exceptionalist* viewpoint is reflected in arrangements that are private, voluntary, remedial, special, local, and exclusive. Such arrangements imply that problems occur to specially defined categories of persons in an unpredictable manner. The problems are unusual, even unique, they are exceptions to the rule, they occur as a result of individual defect, accident, or unfortunate circumstance and must be remedied by means that are particular and, as it were, tailored to the individual case.

The universalistic viewpoint, on the other hand, is reflected in arrangements that are public, legislated, promotive or preventive, general, national, and inclusive. Inherent in such a viewpoint is the idea that social problems are a function of the social arrangements of the community or the society and that, since these social arrangements are quite imperfect and inequitable, such problems are both predictable and, more important, preventable through public action. They are not unique to the individual, and the fact that they encompass individual persons does not imply that those persons are themselves defective or abnormal.

Consider these two contrasting approaches as they are applied to the problem of smallpox. The medical care approach is exceptionalistic; it is designed to provide remedial treatment to the special category of persons who are afflicted with the disease through a private, voluntary arrangement with a local doctor. The universalistic public health approach is designed to provide preventive inoculation to the total population, ordered by legislation and available through public means if no private arrangements can be made.

A similar contrast can be made between an exceptionalistic assistance program such as Aid to Families with Dependent Children and the proposed universalistic program of family allowances based simply on the number of children in a family. The latter assumes that the size of a family should automatically be a consideration in income supplementation, since it is in no way taken into account in the wage structure, and that it should be dealt with in a routine and universal fashion. The AFDC program, on the other hand, assumes that families need income assistance only as a result of special, impoverishing circumstances.

Fluoridation is universalistic; it is aimed at preventing caries in the total population; oral surgery is exceptionalistic, designed to remedy the special cases of infection or neglect that damage the teeth of an individual. Birth control is universalistic; abortion exceptionalistic. It has been said that navigational aids have saved far more lives than have rescue devices, no matter how refined they might be. The compass, then, is universalistic, while the lifeboat is exceptionalistic.

The similarity between exceptionalism and what Mills called the "ideology of social pathologists" is readily apparent. Indeed, the ideological potential of the exceptionalist viewpoint is unusually great. If one is inclined to explain all instances of deviance, all social problems, all occasions on which help is provided to others as the result of unusual circumstances, defect, or accident, one is unlikely to inquire about social inequalities.

This is not to devalue valid exceptionalistic services. Despite fluoridation, some instances of caries and gum disease will require attention; despite excellent prenatal care, handicapped children will occasionally be born; husbands will doubtless continue to die unexpectedly at early ages, leaving widows and orphans in need. And at any given moment, the end products of society's malfunctioning—the miseducated teenager, the unskilled adult laborer, the child brain-damaged as a result of prenatal neglect—will require service that is predominantly exceptionalistic in nature.

The danger in the exceptionalistic viewpoint is in its impact on social policy when it becomes the dominant component in social analysis. Blaming the Victim occurs exclusively within an exceptionalistic framework, and it consists of applying exceptionalistic explanations to universalistic problems. This represents an illogical departure from fact, a method, in Mannheim's words, of systematically distorting reality, of developing an ideology.

Blaming the Victim can take its place in a long series of American ideologies that have rationalized cruelty and injustice.

Slavery, for example, was justified—even praised—on the basis of a complex ideology that showed quite conclusively how useful slavery was to society and how uplifting it was for the slaves.[5] Eminent physicians could be relied upon to provide the biological justification for slavery since after all, they said, the slaves were a separate species—as, for example, cattle are a separate species. No one in his right mind would dream of freeing the cows and fighting to abolish the ownership of cattle. In view of the average American of 1825, it was important to preserve slavery, not simply because it was in accord with his own group interests (he was not fully aware of that), but because reason and logic showed clearly to the reasonable and intelligent man that slavery was good. In order to persuade a good and moral man to *do* evil, then, it is not necessary first to persuade him to *become* evil. It is only necessary to teach him that he is doing good. No one, in the words of a legendary newspaperman, thinks of himself as a son of a bitch.

In late-nineteenth-century America there flowered another ideology of injustice that seemed rational and just to the decent, progressive person. But Richard Hoffstadter's analysis of the phenomenon of Social Darwinism[6] shows clearly its functional role in the preservation of the *status quo*. One can scarcely imagine a better fit than the one between this ideology and the purposes and actions of the robber barons, who descended like piranha fish on the America of this era and picked its bones clean. Their extraordinarily unethical operations netted them not only hundreds of millions of dollars but also, perversely, the adoration of the nation. Behavior that would be, in any more rational land (including today's America), more than enough to have landed them all in jail, was praised as the very model of a captain of modern industry. And the philosophy that justified their thievery was such that John D. Rockefeller could actually stand up and preach it in church. Listen as he speaks in, of all places, Sunday school:

> The growth of a large business is merely a survival of the fittest. . . . The American Beauty rose can be produced in the splendor and fragrance which bring cheer to its beholder only by sacrificing the early buds which grow up around it. This is not an evil tendency in business. It is merely the working-out of a law of nature and a law of God.[7]

This was the core of the gospel, adapted analogically from Darwin's writings on evolution. Herbert Spencer and, later, William Graham Sumner and other beginners in the social sciences considered Darwin's work to be directly applicable to social processes: ultimately as a guarantee that life was progressing toward perfection but, in the short run, as a justification for an absolutely uncontrolled, laissez-faire economic system. The central concepts of "survival of the fittest," "natural selection," and "gradualism" were exalted in Rockefeller's preaching to the status of laws of God and Nature. Not only did this ideology justify the criminal rapacity of those who rose to the top of the industrial heap, defining them automatically as naturally superior (this was bad enough), but at the same time it also required that those at the bottom of the heap be labeled as patently *unfit*—a label based solely on their position in society. According to the law of natural selection, they should be, in Spencer's judgment, eliminated. "The whole effort of nature is to get rid of such, to clear the world of them and make room for better."

For a generation, Social Darwinism was the orthodox doctrine in the social sciences, such as they were at that time. Opponents of this ideology were shut out of respectable intellectual life. The philosophy that enabled John D. Rockefeller to justify himself self-righteously in front of a class of Sunday school children was not the product of an academic quack or a marginal crackpot philosopher. It came directly from the lectures and books of leading intellectual figures of the time, occupants of professorial chairs at Harvard and Yale. Such is the power of an ideology that so neatly fits the needs of the dominant interests of society.

If one is to think about ideologies in America in 1970, one must be prepared to consider the possibility that a body of ideas that might seem almost self-evident is, in fact, highly distorted and highly selective; one must allow that the inclusion of a specific formulation in every freshman sociology text does not guarantee that the particular formulation represents abstract Truth rather than group interest. It is important not to delude ourselves into thinking that ideological monstrosities were constructed by monsters. They were not; they are not. They are developed through a process that shows every sign of being valid scholarship, complete with tables of numbers, copious footnotes, and scientific terminology. Ideologies are quite often academically and socially respectable and in many instances hold positions of exclusive validity, so that disagreement is considered unrespectable or radical and risks being labeled as irresponsible, unenlightened, or trashy.

Blaming the Victim holds such a position. It is central in the mainstream of contemporary American social thought, and its ideas pervade our most crucial assumptions so thoroughly that they are hardly noticed. Moreover, the fruits of this ideology appear to be fraught with altruism and humanitarianism, so it is hard to believe that it has principally functioned to block social change.

III

A major pharmaceutical manufacturer, as an act of humanitarian concern, has distributed copies of a large poster warning "Lead Paint Can Kill!" The poster, featuring a photograph of the face of a charming little girl, goes on to explain that if children *eat* lead paint, it can poison them, they can develop serious symptoms, suffer permanent brain damage, even die. The health department of a major American city has put out a coloring book that provides the same information. While the poster urges parents to prevent their children from eating paint, the coloring book is more vivid. It labels as neglectful and thoughtless the mother who does not keep her infant under constant surveillance to keep it from eating paint chips.

Now, no one would argue against the idea that it is important to spread knowledge about the danger of eating paint in order that parents might act to forestall their children from doing so. But to campaign against lead paint *only* in these terms is destructive and misleading and, in a sense, an effective way to support and agree with slum landlords—who define the problem of lead poisoning in precisely these terms.

This is an example of applying an exceptionalistic solution to a universalistic problem. It is not accurate to say that lead poisoning results from the actions of individual neglectful mothers. Rather, lead poisoning is a social phenomenon supported by a number of social mechanisms, one of the most tragic by-products of the systematic toleration of slum housing. In New Haven, which has the highest reported rate of lead poisoning in the country, several small children have died and many others have incurred irreparable brain damage as a result of eating peeling paint. In several cases, when the landlord failed to make repairs, poisonings have occurred time and again through a succession of tenancies. And the major reason for the landlord's neglect of this problem was that the city agency responsible for enforcing the housing code did nothing to make him correct this dangerous condition.

The cause of the poisoning is the lead in the paint on the walls of the apartment in which the children live. The presence of the lead is illegal. To use lead paint in a residence is illegal; to permit lead paint to be exposed in a residence is illegal. It is not only illegal, it is potentially criminal since the housing code does provide for criminal penalties. The general problem of lead poisoning, then is more accurately analyzed as the result of a systematic program of lawbreaking by one interest group in the community, with the toleration and encouragement of the public authority charged with enforcing that law. To ignore these continued and repeated law violations, to ignore the fact that the supposed law enforcer actually cooperates in lawbreaking, and then to load a burden of guilt on the mother of a dead or dangerously-ill child is an egregious distortion of reality. And to do so under the guise of public-spirited and humanitarian service to the community is intolerable.

But this is how Blaming the Victim works. The righteous humanitarian concern displayed by the drug company, with its poster, and the health department, with its coloring book, is a genuine concern, and this is a typical feature of Blaming the Victim. Also typical is the swerving away from the central target that requires systematic change and, instead, focusing in on the individual affected. The ultimate effect is always to distract attention from the basic causes and to leave the primary social injustice untouched. And, most telling, the proposed remedy for the problem is, of course, to work on the victim himself. Prescriptions for cure, as written by the Savage Discovery set, are invariably conceived to revamp and revise the victim, never to change the surrounding circumstances. They want to change his attitudes, alter his values, fill up his cultural deficits, energize his apathetic soul, cure his character defects, train him and polish him and woo him from his savage ways.

Isn't all of this more subtle and sophisticated than such old-fashioned ideologies as Social Darwinism? Doesn't the change from brutal ideas about survival of the fit (and the expiration of the unfit) to kindly concern about characterological defects (brought about by stigmas of social origin) seem like a substantial step forward? Hardly. It is only a substitution of terms. The old, reactionary exceptionalistic formulations are replaced by new progressive, humanitarian exceptionalistic formulations. In education, the outmoded and unacceptable concept of racial or class differences in basic inherited intellectual ability simply gives way to the new notion of cultural deprivation: there is very little functional difference between these two ideas. In taking a look at the phenomenon of poverty, the old concept of unfitness or idleness or laziness is replaced by the newfangled theory of the culture of poverty. In race relations, plain Negro inferiority—which was good enough for old-fashioned conservatives—is pushed aside by fancy conceits about the crumbling Negro family. With regard to illegitimacy, we are not so crass as to concern ourselves with immorality and vice, as in the old days; we settle benignly on the explanation of the "lower-class pattern of sexual behavior," which no one condemns as evil, but which is, in fact, simply a variation of the old explanatory idea. Mental illness is no longer defined as the result of hereditary taint or congenital character flaw; now we have new causal hypotheses regarding the ego-damaging emotional experiences that are supposed to be the inevitable consequence of the deplorable child-rearing practices of the poor.

In each case, of course, we are persuaded to ignore the obvious: the continued blatant discrimination against the Negro, the gross deprivation of contraceptive and adoption services to the poor, the heavy stresses endemic in the life of the poor. And almost all our make-believe liberal programs aimed at correcting our urban problems are off target; they are designed either to change the poor man or to cool him out.

IV

We come finally to the question, Why? It is much easier to understand the process of Blaming the Victim as a way of thinking than it is to understand the motivation for it. Why do Victim Blamers, who are usually good people, blame the victim? The development and application of this ideology, and of all the mythologies associated with Savage Discovery, are readily exposed by careful analysis as hostile acts—one is almost tempted to say acts of war—directed against the disadvantaged, the distressed, the disinherited. It is class warfare in reverse. Yet those who are most fascinated and enchanted by this ideology tend to be progressive, humanitarian, and, in the best sense of the word, charitable persons. They would usually define themselves as moderates or liberals. Why do they pursue this dreadful war against the poor and the oppressed?

Put briefly, the answer can be formulated best in psychological terms—or, at least, I, as a psychologist, am more comfortable with such a formulation. The highly-charged psychological problem confronting this hypothetical progressive, charitable person I am talking about is that of reconciling his own self-interest with the promptings of his humanitarian impulses. This psychological process of reconciliation is not worked out in a logical, rational, conscious way; it is a process that takes place far below the level of sharp consciousness, and the solution—Blaming the Victim—is arrived at subconsciously as a compromise that apparently satisfies both his self-interest and his charitable concerns. Let me elaborate.

First, the question of self-interest or, more accurately, class interest. The typical Victim Blamer is a middle class person who is doing reasonably well in a material way; he has a good job, a good income, a good house, a good car. Basically, he likes the social system pretty much the way it is, at least in broad outline. He likes the two-party political system, though he may be highly skilled in finding a thousand minor flaws in its functioning. He heartily approves of the profit motive as the propelling engine of the economic system despite his awareness that there are abuses of that system, negative side effects, and substantial residual inequalities.

On the other hand, he is acutely aware of poverty, racial discrimination, exploitation, and deprivation, and, moreover, he wants to do something concrete to ameliorate the condition of the poor, the black, and the disadvantaged. This is not an extraneous concern; it is central to his value system to insist on the worth of the individual, the equality of men, and the importance of justice.

What is to be done, then? What intellectual position can he take, and what line of action can he follow that will satisfy both of these important motivations? He quickly and self-consciously rejects two obvious alternatives, which he defines as "extremes." He cannot side with an openly reactionary, repressive position that accepts continued oppression and exploitation as the price of a privileged position for his own class. This is incompatible with his own morality and his basic political principles. He finds the extreme conservative position repugnant.

He is, if anything, more allergic to radicals, however, than he is to reactionaries. He rejects the "extreme" solution of radical social change, and this makes sense since such radical social change threatens his own well-being. A more equitable distribution of income might mean that he would have less—a smaller or older house, with fewer yews or no rhododendrons in the yard, a less enjoyable job, or, at the least, a somewhat smaller salary. If black children and poor children were, in fact, reasonably educated and began to get high S.A.T. scores, they would be competing with *his* children for the scarce places in the entering classes of Harvard, Columbia, Bennington, and Antioch.

So our potential Victim Blamers are in a dilemma. In the words of an old Yiddish proverb, they are trying to dance at two weddings. They are old friends of both brides and fond of both kinds of dancing, and they want to accept both invitations. They cannot bring themselves to attack the system that has been so good to them, but they want so badly to be helpful to the victims of racism and economic injustice.

Their solution is a brilliant compromise. They turn their attention to the victim in his post-victimized state. They want to bind up wounds, inject penicillin, administer morphine, and evacuate the wounded for rehabilitation. They explain what's wrong with the victim in terms of social experiences *in the past*, experiences that have left wounds, defects, paralysis, and disability. And they take the cure of these wounds and the reduction of these disabilities as the first order of business. They want to make the victims less vulnerable, send them back into battle with better weapons, thicker armor, a higher level of morale.

In order to do so effectively, of course, they must analyze the victims carefully, dispassionately, objectively, scientifically, empathetically, mathematically, and hardheadedly, to see what made them so vulnerable in the first place.

What weapons, now, might they have lacked when they went into battle? Job skills? Education?

What armor was lacking that might have warded off their wounds? Better values? Habits of thrift and foresight?

And what might have ravaged their morale? Apathy? Ignorance? Deviant low class cultural patterns?

This is the solution of the dilemma, the solution of Blaming the Victim. And those who buy this solution with a sigh of relief are inevitably blinding themselves to the basic causes of the problems being addressed. They are, most crucially, rejecting the possibility of blaming, not the victims, but themselves. They are all unconsciously passing judgments on themselves and bringing in a unanimous verdict of Not Guilty.

If one comes to believe that the culture of poverty produces persons *fated* to be poor, who can find any fault with our corporation-dominated economy? And if the Negro family produces young men *incapable* of achieving equality, let's deal with that first before we go on to the task of changing the pervasive racism that informs and shapes and distorts our every social institution. And if unsatisfactory resolution of one's Oedipus complex accounts for all emotional distress and mental disorder, then by all means let us attend to that and postpone worrying about the pounding day-to-day stresses of life on the bottom rungs that drive so many to drink, dope, and madness.

This is the ideology of Blaming the Victim, the cunning Art of Savage Discovery. The tragic, frightening truth is that it is a mythology that is winning over the best people of our time, the very people who must resist this ideological temptation if we are to achieve nonviolent change in America.

NOTES

1. Karl Mannheim, *Ideology and Utopia*, trans. Louis Wirth and Edward Shils (New York: Harcourt, Brace & World, Inc., A Harvest Book, 1936). First published in German in 1929.
2. John Seeley, "The Problems of Social Problems," *Indian Sociological Bulletin*, II, No. 3 (April, 1965). Reprinted as Chapter Ten in *The Americanization of the Unconscious* (New York: International Science Press, 1967), pp. 142–48.
3. C. Wright Mills, "The Professional Ideology of Social Pathologists," *American Journal of Sociology*, XLIX, No. 2 (September, 1943), pp. 165–80.
4. William Ryan, "Community Care in Historical Perspective: Implications for Mental Health Services and Professionals," *Canada's Mental Health*, supplement No. 60, March-April, 1969. This formulation draws on, and is developed from, the *residential-institutional* dimension outlined in H. L. Wilensky and C. N. Lebeaux, *Industrial Society and Social Welfare* (paperback ed.; New York: The Free Press, 1965). Originally published by Russell Sage Foundation, 1958.
5. For a good review of this general ideology, see I. A. Newby, *Jim Crow's Defense* (Baton Rouge: Louisiana State University Press, 1965).
6. Richard Hofstadter, *Social Darwinism in American Thought* (revised ed.; Boston: Beacon Press, 1955).
7. William J. Ghent, *Our Benevolent Feudalism* (New York: The Macmillan Co. 1902), p. 29.

Article 3

EVERYONE IS ON WELFARE: "THE ROLE OF REDIS-TRIBUTION IN SOCIAL POLICY" REVISITED

Mimi Abramovitz

> Hitherto, our techniques of social diagnosis and our conceptual frame-works have been too narrow. We have compartmentalized social welfare as we have have compartmentalized the poor. The analytic model of social policy that has been fashioned on only the phenomena that are clearly visible, direct and immediately measurable is an inadequate one. It fails to tell us about the realities of redistribution which are being generated by the processes of technological and social change and by the combined effects of social welfare, fiscal welfare and occupational welfare.[1]

In a now classic article, "The Role of Redistribution in Social Policy," the British sociologist Titmuss argued that the view of social policy as redistributive or as politically assigning claims from

> one set of people who are said to produce and earn the national prod-ucts to another set of people who may merit compassion and charity but not economic rewards for productive service . . . [is] a very limited and inadequate model of the working of social policy in the second half of the twentieth century.[2]

By limited, Titmuss meant (1) that the social welfare system as we know it is only the visible part of a larger three-part system of welfare that also includes tax and fringe benefits and (2) that taken together, the social, fiscal, and occupational welfare systems favor the privileged over the poor.

Titmuss's views are especially relevant today, now that Reagan-omics has placed issues of redistribution back on the social policy agenda. As poverty rates rise and social programs on which the poor rely are cut, today's tax and spending policies seek to revive the sagging econ-omy by shifting capital from the public to the private sector—from those in need to those who can save and invest. The result, according to the Congressional Budget Office (CBO) is a net loss in income for those

SOURCE: Copyright 1983, National Association of Social Workers, Inc. Reprinted with permission, from *Social Work*, Vol. 28, No. 6 (1983, November-December), pp. 440–445.

who earn less than $10,000 a year, but a net increase for those earning more.[3]

Social workers know that Reaganomics is unfair to their clients and themselves, but being afraid of economics, they often cannot explain why. With the intent of demystifying economics, this article uses Titmuss's model of three welfare systems to examine the government's tax and spending policies.[4] Special attention is paid to the largely invisible but expanding system of tax expenditures. When these benefits are combined with more traditional social welfare benefits, nearly everyone is "on welfare." The author argues that by lowering the tax liability of upper-income individuals and large corporations, the tax code redistributes income from the "have-nots" to the "haves" and increasingly operates as a "shadow" welfare state.

Three Welfare Systems

Nearly twenty years ago, Titmuss observed that programs of the welfare state, tax code provisions, and fringe benefits—despite different names and administrative auspices—all recognized the similar dependencies of old age, childhood, widowhood, sickness, and the need for income support, health care, education, employment, and housing. The welfare state, he pointed out, is only the tip of the "social welfare iceberg." What are submerged are a "fiscal welfare" system that offers income support to individuals and families through the tax code and an "occupational welfare" system that offers similar aid through fringe benefits.

A brief review shows that social welfare programs such as social security, Supplemental Security Income (SSI), Aid to Families with Dependent Children (AFDC), Medicare and Medicaid, public housing, and public education have a counterpart in both the tax code and the fringe benefit systems. For example, social security, private pensions, and lowered income taxes for the aged all provide retirement income for those over 65. Just as Medicaid and Medicare help finance the cost of health care, so do private health insurance available to workers as a fringe benefit and tax deductions for medical expenses above 5 percent of a taxpayer's gross income. As in the case of recipients of public housing, the government aids private homeowners through deductions for property taxes, mortgage interest, and special tax rates on capital gains for sales of homes. Some corporations also provide housing assistance to higher-paid executives. AFDC provides income support to families with children, but so do income tax deductions for dependents. Government-supported day care centers for the working poor parallel both employer-sponsored day care for children of employees and the tax deduction for child care available to working parents. Education and training subsidies received by the poor do not differ significantly from either education benefits provided by employers or untaxed scholarship income and tax exemptions for parents of college students aged 19 and over.

All three systems of welfare represent considerable dollar amounts. In 1979, the government's social welfare expenditures were about $400 billion, as were employers' outlays for occupational benefits.[5] In 1982, the U.S. Treasury allowed over $250 billion in uncollected taxes, although not all lost tax dollars reflected social welfare functions.[6] In brief, the fiscal and occupational welfare systems operate as a shadow welfare state.[7]

As Titmuss concluded, in addition to recognizing the same common human needs, all three welfare systems are redistributive—each is

> concerned with changing the individual and family pattern of current and future claims on resources set by the market, set by the possession of accumulated past rights and set by the allocation made by Government to provide for national defense and other non-market sectors.[8]

Titmuss adds that all three systems favor the middle and upper classes. Applied to the U.S. government's tax and spending programs, Titmuss's framework reveals how both direct social spending and indirect tax expenditures redistribute income upwards by providing extensive benefits to the nonpoor.

Social Welfare: Serving the Middle Class

Social welfare programs—the direct public provision of cash and in-kind benefits to individuals and families, free or at below market cost—are popularly regarded as serving only the poor. In fact, programs of the welfare state not only assist the nonpoor, but, with respect to dollars spent, benefit levels, and survival of programs, upper-income groups fare best with social welfare programs.

In their review of the antipoverty decade, Plotnik and Skidmore found that although the absolute amount of social welfare expenditures nearly doubled between 1965 and 1972, the portion spent on the poor changed little, hovering around 40 percent.[9] The CBO also reported that social welfare benefits often go to those least in need. In 1980, although 49 percent of federal expenditures were paid directly to individuals and families, only 13 percent of these dollars went for programs that used poverty or need as a criterion for receiving aid.[10] Moreover, the average benefit levels in programs such as social security and unemployment insurance (programs available to people regardless

TABLE 1   Average Monthly Benefits per Person in Social Welfare Programs

	Benefit Amount
Social Security (1980)[a]	
Disabled worker	$352.07
Retired worker	321.09
Widow/widower	271.45
Unemployment insurance (1980)[b]	448.74
Supplemental Security Income (1981)[c]	
Total	118.46
Blind	152.83
Disabled	143.18
Aged	102.02
Aid to Families with Dependent Children (1980)[d]	
Per recipient	90.61
Per family	288.71

SOURCE: U.S. Department of Health and Human Resources, Social Security Administration, Social Security Bulletin 45 (June 1982), (a) Table M-13, p. 33; (b) Table M-37, p. 51; (c) Table M-27, p. 41; (d) Table M-32, p. 46.

of income) tend to be higher than those of AFDC and SSI and other means-tested programs serving only the poor (see Table 1).

Finally, recent studies have shown that Reagan's social program cuts fall heaviest on the poor, who feel the cuts most acutely.[11] Nordhaus wrote that Reaganomics "decimated" programs for the poor but attacked middle-class entitlements much less severely.[12] Income-support programs for the poor, Nordhaus calculated, would decline by 9.3 percent a year between 1981 and 1983, after having grown at an annual rate of 9.3 percent between 1973 and 1981. In contrast, it was predicted that between 1981 and 1983 programs serving the middle class would continue to expand, albeit at a slower rate—their annual growth rate would fall from 6.0 percent to 2.3 percent. In its evaluation of the Administration's 1982 budget, the CBO concluded that

> reduction in federal benefit payments for individuals will be greatest for households with incomes below $10,000. In 1983, households with incomes below $10,000 will lose on an average of about $360 in federal benefits, while those with incomes over $80,000 will lose on an average of about $120. Total federal savings will be about $17 billion in 1983,

about two-thirds of which will come from reductions affecting households with incomes below $20,000.[13]

The effect is compounded by the income tax cut, which offsets loss of benefits among the rich but not for the poor, who earn too little to pay any taxes.

The welfare state has always benefited the middle class, but, since the economic crisis surfaced in the mid-1070s, the trend has intensified. From 1950 (and probably earlier) until the mid-1970s, federal payments actually reduced the income gap, if only slightly. The *National Journal* reported that the poorest fifth of families had 3.1 percent of all personal income in 1950 and 3.9 percent in 1975. But by 1979 their share dropped to 3.8 percent, and the *National Journal* predicted it would fall to 3.7 percent in 1981. Federal transfer programs did grow during these years, but they concentrated less frequently on the poor, who received 26.4 percent of federal transfers in 1974 but only 21.5 percent in 1981. Meanwhile, the share of the most affluent families rose from 13.9 to 16.1 percent.[14]

Reaganomics has accelerated these trends even further, arguing that cash transfers to the poor interfere with market dynamics and weaken the overall economy and that economic recovery requires putting more dollars into the hands of wealthy individuals and of the management of large corporations who, it is believed, are more likely to work, save, and invest. It is not surprising that Reagan's policies cut social programs while strengthening the fiscal welfare system.

Fiscal Welfare: Benefits for the Affluent

Fiscal welfare, administered by the Internal Revenue Service, provides income support to individuals and families indirectly through tax exemptions, deductions, and credits known in today's budget parlance as "tax expenditures." Tax expenditures are

> those revenue losses attributable to provisions of Federal tax laws which allow a special exclusion, exemption or deduction from gross income or which provide a special credit, a preferential rate of tax, or a deferral of tax liability.[15]

Popularly known as tax "loopholes," tax expenditures are revenues deliberately not collected. First counted in 1967, tax expenditures have grown in number from 50 to 104. The cost to the government in lost revenues has mounted accordingly from $36.6 billion in 1967 to $253.5 billion in fiscal year 1982, or from 4.4 percent to 8.4 percent of the gross national product (GNP).[16]

The Economic Recovery Act of 1981 extended this system, adding eight new tax benefits and expanding twenty-one others, while reducing only two. The 1982 Tax Equity and Fiscal Responsibility Act, passed in part as a backlash to the revenue losses produced in 1981, reduced thirteen tax expenditures and increased only two. Nonetheless, tax dollars not collected because of tax expenditures will rise by $20 billion between 1982 and 1983 and are projected to equal $439 billion, about one-third of the government's spending, in fiscal 1987.[17]

Even more than social welfare benefits, tax expenditures favor the middle and upper classes. Only those who earn enough to pay taxes and to itemize can use them, and the benefits become more valuable as one's earnings, and, therefore, one's income tax rate, rise. It is not surprising that, in 1980, tax expenditures equaled less than 10 percent of the adjusted gross income of those earning $50,000 or less a year but 22.3 percent for those earning more.[18] Moreover, they were worth more to the average upper-income family for whom interest on mortgages and property tax benefits amounted to $1,100 a year compared to $10 estimated for the average low-income family. Similarly, health care deductions for the bottom income families were estimated at $40 compared to $450 for those at the top.[19]

Tax benefits favoring upper-income groups often claim more federal dollars than comparable social programs serving the poor. In 1981, the government did not collect some $30 billion in taxes to homeowners, but spent less than $7 billion for low-income housing.[20] Similarly, between 1975 and 1979, tax subsidies for health care rose at an annual rate of 19 percent compared to 17 percent for Medicare and 13 percent for Medicaid, which serve the aged and the poor respectively.[21]

Finally, the middle class benefits from the Administration's cutting direct spending while allowing tax expenditures to grow. Although Congress reduced direct spending by $130 billion for fiscal years 1982–1984, it also spent another $82 billion in tax benefits.[22] As one critic of Reaganomics pointed out, whittling down the $266 billion in 1982 tax expenditures by one-seventh could have yielded the Treasury more than the $35 billion cut from the domestic budget that year.[23]

Corporate Welfare: Business Subsidies

Like individuals and families, corporations ask for and receive "welfare" through both direct government outlays and tax expenditures. Although Titmuss did not include it in his discussion, when corporate welfare is counted, the upward bias of the welfare system is even greater.

Among the most important sources of government aid to business are direct outlays for military spending, which both subsidize corporate production costs and guarantee sales. In a recent study of Defense Department contracts, the Council on Economic Priorities found eight of the ten largest contractors to be "defense dependent": each of the eight contractors earned 25 percent or more of its revenues from defense-related work between 1970 and 1979; each received one hundred billion dollars in defense contracts, and 50 percent of the sales of each were secured by purchases from the Defense Department and the National Aeronautics and Space Administration.[24] The Reagan Administration plans to spend more than $1.5 trillion on defense between 1981 and 1986, raising the military budget from $162 billion in fiscal 1981 to $343 billion by fiscal 1986.[25]

Agriculture is a long-time recipient of government aid in the form of price supports for such products as tobacco, sugar, and dairy products. In 1981, sugar subsidies guaranteed U.S. farmers at least eighteen cents a pound for their sugar, several cents above world market prices.[26] The government's sugar support program will cost taxpayers at least $200 million between fiscal years 1982 and 1985, will force consumers to pay $2 billion more for sugar products, and will require the government to borrow more than $1 billion. In 1981, Congress also mandated that the Secretary of Agriculture support the dairy industry by buying milk, cheese, and butter. This $2.2 billion-a-year "welfare" grant includes $110 million a year to store 500 million pounds of butter.[27]

The auto industry is a more recent applicant for corporate welfare. The chairperson of General Motors (GM), who in 1979 condemned federal aid to the financially troubled Chrysler Corporation as a basic challenge to the philosophy of the United States, defended his own request for some $440 million in government aid as necessary to remain competitive.[28] In 1981, GM requested financial assistance for purchasing land, site preparation, and tax abatements from federal, state, and local governments to construct an assembly plant in the Detroit area.

Even thriving companies seek and receive government aid to lower their production costs and increase their profits. In 1977 and 1978, the American Broadcasting Corporation (ABC) successfully requested some $32 million in tax exemptions, abatements, and low-interest loans from various New York City agencies. These benefits, granted in years of record profits for the company, covered most of ABC's expansion costs. Likewise, the Bank of New York and the Smith Barney Investment House won $22 million and $2 million respectively in property tax reductions as incentives to build in New York City. If denied the reductions, they threatened to abandon their projects or take them elsewhere.[29]

The Reagan Administration plans to increase federal tax benefits to business from $48.7 billion in 1981 to $122 billion in 1987 by expanding key industrial tax write-offs, such as investment tax credits, accel erated depreciation, and safe harbor leasing.[30] All told, such tax benefits will lower the effective tax rate on corporations, which is already at 28 percent.[31] In 1982, for the first time since 1941, corporate income taxes were less than 2 percent of the GNP.[32]

Discussion

Tax expenditures—clearly a shadow welfare state for the well-to-do—in many ways parallel the social welfare system for the poor: Both address similar needs, raise an individual's disposable income, and lower government revenues. For these reasons, the CBO observed that any feature included in a government spending or loan program can be duplicated as a tax subsidy.[33]

Yet tax expenditures receive less government scrutiny and review than direct spending programs, even though the costs of both in many cases are "uncontrollable" (that is, benefits are automatically available to whomever meets statutory requirements). Tax expenditures require neither annual appropriations nor periodic authorizations. Because they create little, if any, new bureaucracy, tax expenditures win Congressional approval more easily and remain on the books longer than direct spending programs, while going relatively unnoticed by the public at large. Less subject to the perils of the budget process, this "welfare" for the affluent not only pays more, but is more permanent and secure. In fiscal 1982, for example, although Congress cut $2 billion in direct spending for health care (mostly for the aged and the poor), there was no review of the $16.6 billion in federal revenues lost from not taxing employers' contributions for employees' medical benefits.[34] Funds for school lunches were reduced while tax breaks for business lunches continued.[35]

The low visibility of tax expenditures obscures the reality that, when considered in addition to social welfare benefits, tax expenditures allow nearly everyone to be "on welfare." One key difference is that tax benefits do not carry the stigma of "public assistance." Beneficiaries think of themselves as receiving an incentive, not a handout—as working hard, not violating the work ethic. Underpaying income taxes is a challenge, not welfare fraud—although the dollar amounts lost to the government must be considerably higher.[36]

The low visibility and nonwelfare identity of tax expenditures also obscure the extent to which the shadow welfare state quietly favors the privileged over the poor. Indeed, tax expenditures help make the overall tax code more regressive by lowering the tax bill of the affluent while increasing that of the middle class and the working poor. Rea-

gan's tax program also reduces the proportion of federal revenues raised through progressive income taxes while raising the highly regressive payroll taxes that fall heaviest on the middle class (see Table 2).
steady proportion of all federal revenues, ranging from a low of 40 percent to a high of 47 percent, but during the same period the corporate share dropped precipitously from 25.6 percent to 12.4 percent.[37] The Economic Recovery Act of 1981 and the Tax Equity and Fiscal Responsibility Act of 1982 intensified these trends: The portion of federal revenues raised by personal income taxes grew from 47.2 percent in 1981 to 48.3 percent in 1982, while the corporate share fell to a new low of 8.3 percent. Meanwhile, since 1950, social security payroll taxes, which take proportionately more income from lower- than higher-paid workers, grew significantly from 11.1 percent in 1950 to 32.6 percent in 1982. This regressive social insurance tax is projected to climb to 37.1 percent of all federal revenues by 1988.[38]

The 1981 cut in tax rates also helped upper-income groups the most. Their tax burden dropped significantly because of a reduction in the maximum tax rate on "unearned income" (for example, unincorporated business profits, dividends, interest, capital gains, and other sources of personal income concentrated in upper-income brackets). Meanwhile, the 1981 income tax cuts for low-income taxpayers were offset by inflation, higher social security taxes, and new local and state taxes.

Many believe current proposals to replace the graduated income tax with a simplified flat or single tax rate will only intensify these regressive trends. Two senior tax officials of the Treasury Department pointed out that a flat tax would conflict with the ability-to-pay principle on which the current income tax is based.[39] According to a *New York Times* editorial, "The price of simplicity in such a flat tax is an enormous redistribution of income."[40]

Tax expenditures have always redistributed income upwards. As an alternative to direct public aid, the relative generosity and lack of stigma of tax expenditures recommend them as a more humane way to provide economic assistance. However, as a supplemental and concealed system of welfare for wealthy individuals and corporations, tax expenditures remain unequal and unfair.

The exclusion of tax expenditures from traditional conceptualizations of welfare also perpetuates a narrow and compartmentalized view of the welfare state. In this view, only the poor receive aid, making them especially vulnerable to cuts when the government's economic policies go awry. By exposing the welfare features of the tax code (and fringe benefit system), Titmuss's three-part welfare state broadens the meaning of social welfare and points to a restructuring of the tax code as a strategy for the active pursuit of distributive justice.

TABLE 2 Federal Revenues by Source

Revenue Source by Type of Tax	Actual			Estimated		Baseline Projection			
	1980	1981	1982	1983	1984	1985	1986	1987	1988
Individual income	244.1	285.9	298.1	285.8	294.9	320.8	345.8	371.6	400.0
Corporate income	64.6	61.1	49.2	40.3	55.8	65.2	74.0	83.1	87.7
Social insurance	157.8	182.7	201.1	212.1	232.1	258.2	283.2	303.4	326.2
Excise	24.3	40.8	36.3	37.7	41.6	41.5	36.4	35.5	35.9
Estate and gift	6.4	6.8	8.0	6.1	5.9	5.6	5.0	4.6	4.3
Other	19.9	21.9	25.0	24.1	23.0	23.6	23.8	23.8	24.1
Total	517.1	599.3	617.8	606.2	653.4	714.9	768.3	821.9	878.2
As a Percentage of Total Revenues									
Individual income	47.2	47.7	48.3	47.2	45.1	44.9	45.0	45.2	45.6
Corporate income	12.5	10.2	8.0	6.6	8.5	9.1	9.6	10.1	10.0
Social insurance	30.5	30.5	32.6	35.0	35.5	36.1	36.9	36.9	37.1
Excise	4.7	6.8	5.9	6.2	6.4	5.8	4.7	4.3	4.1
Estate and gift	1.2	1.1	1.3	1.0	0.9	0.8	0.7	0.6	0.5
Other	3.9	3.7	4.0	4.0	3.5	3.3	3.1	2.9	2.7
Total	100.0	100.0	100.0	100.0	100.0	100.0	100.0	100.0	100.0
As a Percentage of the Gross National Product									
Individual income	9.5	10.0	9.8	8.9	8.4	8.4	8.3	8.3	8.3
Corporate income	2.5	2.1	1.6	1.3	1.6	1.7	1.8	1.9	1.8
Social insurance	6.1	6.4	6.6	6.6	6.6	6.8	6.8	6.8	6.8
Excise	0.9	1.4	1.2	1.2	1.2	1.1	0.9	0.8	0.7
Estate and gift	0.2	0.2	0.3	0.2	0.2	0.1	0.1	0.1	0.1
Other	0.8	0.8	0.8	0.8	0.7	0.6	0.6	0.5	0.5
Total	20.1	20.9	20.4	19.0	18.7	18.7	18.5	18.4	18.3

SOURCE: Congressional Budget Office, *Reducing the Deficit: Spending and Revenue Options* (Washington, D.C.: U.S. Governmental Printing Office, February 1983), p. 228.

NOTES AND REFERENCES

1. Richard M. Titmuss, "The Role of Redistribution in Social Policy," *Social Security Bulletin*, 39 (June 1965), p. 20.
2. Ibid., p. 15.
3. *Effects of Tax and Benefit Reductions Enacted in 1981 for Households in Different Income Categories*, special study prepared pursuant to separate requests of Senator Ernest Hollings and Chairman James R. Jones (Washington, D.C.: Congressional Budget Office, February 1982), p. 24. (Mimeographed.)
4. For more on Reaganomics, see Mimi Abramovitz and Thomas Hopkins, "Reaganomics and the Welfare State," *Journal of Sociology and Social Welfare*, 10 (December 1983).
5. Ann Kallman Bixby, "Social Welfare Expenditures, Fiscal Year 1979," *Social Security Bulletin*, 44 (November 1981), p. 3; and Barry Friedman and Leonard Hausman, "The Welfare Safety Net? Private vs. Public," *Brandeis Quarterly*, 2 (January 1982), p. 7.
6. Congressional Budget Office, *Tax Expenditures: Budget Control Options and Five Year Budget Projections for Fiscal Years 1983–1987* (Washington, D.C.: U.S. Government Printing Office, November 1982), p. xiv.
7. The occupational welfare system is not discussed in this article. It may be noted, however, that the tax structure supports the fringe benefit system by not taxing employers' contributions for various fringe benefits nor counting these benefits as part of the income earned by employees.
8. Titmuss, "The Role of Redistribution in Social Policy," p. 16.
9. Robert D. Plotnik and Felicity Skidmore, *Progress Against Poverty: A Review of the 1964–1974 Decade* (New York: Academic Press, 1975), pp. 73–74.
10. Congressional Budget Office, *Reducing the Federal Budget: Strategies and Examples for Fiscal Years 1982–1986* (Washington, D.C.: U.S. Government Printing Office, February 1981), p. 9.
11. Joel Havenmann, "Sharing the Wealth: The Gap Between Rich and Poor Grows Wider," *National Journal*, 14 (October 23, 1982), p. 1795.
12. William B. Nordhaus, "The Budget: Let Them Eat Jelly Beans," *New York Times*, October 21, 1981.
13. Congressional Budget Office, *Effects of Tax and Benefit Reductions*, p. 111.
14. Havenmann, "Sharing the Wealth," p. 1792.
15. Congressional Budget Office, *Tax Expenditures: Current Issues and Five Year Budget Projections for Fiscal Years 1982–1986* (Washington, D.C.: U.S. Government Printing Office, 1981), p. 1.
16. Congressional Budget Office, *Tax Expenditures: Budget Control Options and Five Year Budget Projections for Fiscal Years 1983–1987*, p. xiv.
17. Ibid., p. 15, Appendix A, Table A.
18. Pamela Fessler, "Congress Urged to Scrutinize Tax Breaks That Cost U.S. Billions in Lost Revenues," *Congressional Quarterly Weekly Report*, 40 (January 30, 1982), p. 157.
19. Havenmann, "Sharing the Wealth," p. 1794.

20. Congressional Budget Office, *Tax Expenditures: Current Issues and Five Year Budget Projections for Fiscal Years 1982–1986*, p. 19; and U.S. Office of Management and Budget, *The Budget of the U.S. Government, Fiscal Year 1981* (Washington, D.C.: U.S. Government Printing Office, 1981), p. 272.
21. Gail Wilensky, "Government and the Financing of Health Care." Paper presented at the American Economic Association Meeting, Washington, D.C., December 30, 1981.
22. Fessler, "Congress Urged to Scrutinize Tax Breaks That Cost U.S. Billions in Lost Revenues," p. 155.
23. William Coyne, "Wealthfare? No." *New York Times*, September 8, 1981, p. 23.
24. Council on Economic Priorities, "Newsletter," Pub. No. N81–4, June 1981. See also Philip Taubman, "Arms Makers Seen Gaining Politically," *New York Times*, June 18, 1981: and Merril Sheils, "Politics of Arms Spending," *Newsweek*, June 22, 1981, p. 68.
25. Lester Thurow, "Beware of Reagan's Military Spending," *New York Times*, May 31, 1981, Sec. 3, p. 3.
26. Seth King, "Senate Defeats Move to End Sugar Subsidy," *New York Times*, September 18, 1981, p. 21; "Too Sweet a Deal for Sugar Growers," Editorial, *New York Times*, May 19, 1981, p. 14; "A Shameful Sugar Policy," Editorial, *New York Times*, May 10, 1982, p. 20.
27. Peter Peyser, "Sugar Daddy," *New York Times*, September 10, 1981, p. 31.
28. William Serrin, "Huge New GM Plant, Like Many, to Get Subsidies," *New York Times*, February 25, 1982, p. 12.
29. Sidney Schanberg, "Blue Chip Underdogs," *New York Times*, January 26, 1982, p. 15.
30. Congressional Budget Office, *Tax Expenditures: Budget Control Options and Five Year Budget Projections for Fiscal Years 1983–1987*, Table A, p. 51.
31. Karen Arenson, "The Quiet Repeal of the Corporate Income Tax," *New York Times*, August 2, 1981.
32. Congressional Budget Office, *Reducing the Federal Deficit: Strategies and Options*, a report to the Senate and House Committees on the Budget, Part III (Washington, D.C.: U.S. Government Printing Office, February 1982), p. 187.
33. Congressional Budget Office, *Tax Expenditures: Current Issues and Five Year Budget Projections For Fiscal Years 1982–1986*, p. 46.
34. Since this article was written, such a tax was proposed by President Reagan in his 1983 State of the Union Message and introduced by Rep. Barber B. Conable, Jr. (R-N.Y.). As of April 18, 1983, the Health Cost Containment Tax Act of 1983 (H 2574) was in the House Ways and Means Committee. See Elizabeth Wehr, "$90.6 Billion Health Outlays Seen Despite Major Changes in System Sought by Reagan." *Congressional Quarterly Weekly Report*, 41 (February 5, 1983), pp. 275–277; and Andy Plattner, "Economic Troubles Top List of Problems Facing Congress," *Congressional Quarterly Weekly Report*, 41 (January 29, 1983), p. 207.
35. Fessler, "Congress Urged to Scrutinize Tax Breaks That Cost U.S. Billions in Lost Revenues," p. 156.

36. Jerome Kurtz and Joseph Pechman, "Tax Fraud Hyperbole," *New York Times,* July 12, 1982, p. 15.
37. Congressional Budget Office, *Baseline Budget Projections: Fiscal Years, 1982–1986* (Washington, D.C.: U.S. Government Printing Office, 1981), p. 26.
38. Congressional Budget Office, *Baseline Budget Projections for Fiscal Years 1984–1988,* a report to the Senate and House Committees on the Budget, Part II (Washington, D.C.: U.S. Government Printing Office, 1983), p. 26.
39. Edward Cowan, "Flat Income Tax Gaining Advocates," *New York Times,* May 25, 1982, Sec. 4, p. 6.
40. "Yes, There Is a Better Income Tax," Editorial, *New York Times,* June 6, 1982, Sec. 4, p. 20.

Article 4

THE NATURE OF POVERTY

George Gilder

Living in a world of wealth, the upper classes of Americans have long listened straight-faced and unboggled to the most fantastic tales from the world of the poor. Although inclined to accept Ernest Hemingway's assurances that the rich differ from us chiefly in having more money, we have been willing to suppose that the poor were some alien tribe, exotic in culture and motivation, who can be understood only through the channels of credentialed expertise.

It helped that many of the poor were black. They looked different; perhaps they were different. There came forth a series of authoritative fables: blacks are allegedly matriarchal by nature; like the Irish, the Jews, and other urban immigrants before them, their IQ's were shown to be genetically lower[1] (possibly, in the case of blacks, because of cramped cranial spaces); and they were found to be markedly prone to violent crime and slovenly living. Nonetheless, we could not judge them, it was said by those of liberal spirit, without being guilty of ethnocentrism or cultural imperialism. A propensity for violence, low intelligence, and fatherless homes, it was implied, constitutes a reasonable adaptation to poverty from which we may all learn much.

This attitude, however, required a spirit of cultural relativism so heroic that it could not serve for long, particularly in political formulations. So new approaches emerged, allegedly more enlightened, but with implications equally farfetched. Slavery, discrimination, and deprivation, it was said, have so abused the black psyche that all sorts of new ministrations and therapies are needed to redeem it; racism and unemployment still inflict such liabilities that vast new programs of public employment and affirmative action are required to overcome them. The reasonable inference arises that even though blacks are not genetically inferior, science proves them to be so damaged by racism and poverty that they are inferior now.

Not only do these notions cause serious strain to the spirit of liberalism when confronting specific specimens of this maimed but deserving race, but such attitudes also perpetuate the idea that the poor,

SOURCE: From *Wealth and Poverty* by George Gilder. Copyright © 1981 by George Gilder. Reprinted by permission of Basic Books, Inc., Publishers.

for whatever reason, are still very different from us. This belief permits a series of new fables to arise, some explicit, most implicit in government programs.

For example, most of us work for money and enjoy leisure. The poor, it is implied, despite their generally more onerous jobs, do not. They so lust for labor, so they tell all inquiring scholars, that their willingness to work is unaffected by levels of welfare and in-kind support substantially higher than the available wage; they even clamor to enter the work force in the face of effective tax rates on work (through reductions in welfare payments) of nearly 100 percent.

All American ethnic groups in the past rose out of poverty partly by learning English and downplaying their own languages. The current foreign poor, mostly Hispanic, are thought to require instruction chiefly in their native tongue, for reasons of ethnic pride.

Middle-class Americans are demonstrably devastated by divorce and separation: they leave their jobs, income plummets, health deteriorates; they drink and philander; their children behave badly in school. But the poor and their children are assumed to be relatively unshaken by a plague of family breakdowns; at least any resulting lower income and employment levels are said to be due to discrimination, and the behavior of the children is regarded to be little influenced by the absence of fathers.

Most American men earn more money than their wives; men that don't tend to leave, or be left, in large numbers. Yet poor men are assumed to be unaffected by the higher relative incomes available to their wives from welfare and affirmative action, which are alleged to have no relationship to high rates of unemployment and illegitimacy.

Perhaps most important of all, every successful ethnic group in our history rose up by working harder than other classes, in low-paid jobs, with a vanguard of men in entrepreneurial roles. But the current poor, so it is supposed, can leapfrog drudgery by education and credentials, or be led as a group from poverty, perhaps by welfare mothers trained for government jobs. These views depict the current poor as a race so alien to the entire American experience, so radically different in motive and character from whites, that one can speak in terms of a new form of bigotry.

The notion of liberal racism is perhaps needlessly provocative. Liberals are not racists any more than all but a small, dwindling, and utterly uninfluential minority of other Americans are. But the response of the dominantly liberal media to the racial situation is so quixotic and peculiar as to be reprehensible in its own special way. For example, anyone who has spent any time at all among the American political and economic elite knows that it is desperately eager to appoint blacks to high positions whenever they are reasonably able to perform the duties. The more prestigious American universities avidly pursue black Ph.D.'s and pay them on average some two thousand dollars more than white professors with similar credentials and experience.[2] Yet every American newspaper and magazine treated the appointment of Franklin Thomas as head of the Ford Foundation as if it were some amazing triumph, a startling breakthrough, although Thomas had previously turned down a post in the U.S. cabinet, had already served as temporary chief of the the Whitney Foundation, professed the same impeccably fashionable views as his predecessor, McGeorge Bundy, and was chosen with the highest possible enthusiasm by the board.

Similarly, it has been demonstrated many times in American politics that blacks can get elected to virtually any office, particularly in big cities, if they are sufficiently resourceful politicians. Yet the editorial pages of *The New York Times* and *The New York Post* explained both Percy Sutton's defeat in the 1976 Democratic mayoral primary and their own refusal to endorse him by labored implications that the city was "unready" for a black mayor "at this time." Actually, the newspapers refrained from endorsing Sutton and the people refrained from voting for him because, although a pleasant and intelligent man, he was an unimpressive campaigner who conducted a lackluster drive for the office. He did as well as he did chiefly by getting unanimous black support. His defeat had nothing to do with racism, despite his own hapless claims to the contrary, encouraged by *The New York Times.*

The refusal of American leaders to tell the truth about blacks is more important when it comes to black poverty. The prevailing expressed opinion is that racism and discrimination still explain the low incomes of blacks. This proposition is at once false and invidious. Not only does it slander white Americans, it deceives and demoralizes blacks. Not only does it obstruct the truth, it encourages, by its essential incredibility, the alternate falsehood, held in private by many blacks and whites, that blacks cannot now make it in America without vast federal assistance, without, indeed, the very government programs that in fact account for the worst aspects of black poverty and promise to perpetuate it. Finally, the liberal belief in bigotry as an explanation for the condition of blacks leads to still more preposterous theories about the alleged poverty of other groups, from women to Hispanics, and to a generally manic-depressive vision of the economy, in which poverty is seen both as more extreme and more remediable than it is.

The first thing to understand is that regardless of the affluence of the American economy, we live in a world full of poor people. Modern transport and communications ensure that increasing numbers will be both eager and able to reach our shores. Unless we wish to adopt an immoral and economically self-destructive policy of prohibiting immigration, there will be poverty in America for centuries to come. The policies and approaches we have adopted in our neurotic concern about blacks will likely be applied to many millions of others. The potential injury that could be inflicted on our economy and on the poor people in it is quite incalculable. But, on the basis of the long and thoroughly unambiguous experience of our government in blighting the lives of blacks and Indians, one can only predict that the damage will be tragically great.

To get a grip on the problems of poverty, one should also forget the idea of overcoming inequality by redistribution. Inequality may even grow at first as poverty declines. To lift the incomes of the poor, it will be necessary to increase the rates of investment, which in turn will tend to enlarge the wealth, if not the consumption, of the rich. The poor, as they move into the work force and acquire promotions, will raise their incomes by a greater percentage than the rich; but the upper classes will gain by greater absolute amounts, and the gap between the rich and the poor may grow. All such analyses are deceptive in the long run, however, because they imply a static economy in which the *numbers* of the rich and the middle class are not growing.

In addition, inequality may be favored by the structure of a modern economy as it interacts with demographic change. When the division of labor becomes more complex and refined, jobs grow more specialized; and the increasingly specialized workers may win greater rents for their rare expertise, causing their incomes to rise relative to common labor. This tendency could be heightened by a decline in new educated entrants to the work force, predictable through the 1990s, and by an enlarged flow of immigration, legal and illegal. Whatever the outcome of these developments, an effort to take income from the rich, thus diminishing their investment, and to give it to the poor, thus reducing their work incentives, is sure to cut American productivity, limit job opportunities, and perpetuate poverty.

Among the beneficiaries of inequality will be the formerly poor. Most students of the problems of poverty consider the statistics of success of previous immigrant groups and see a steady incremental rise over the years, accompanied by the progressive acquisition of educational credentials and skills. Therefore, programs are proposed that foster a similar slow and incremental ascent by the currently poor. But the incremental vision of the escape from poverty is mostly false, based on a simple illusion of statistical aggregates that conceals everything important about upward mobility. Previous immigrants earned money first by working hard; their children got the education.[3]

The rising average incomes of previous groups signify not the smooth progress of hundreds of thousands of civil-service or bureaucratic careers, but the rapid business and professional successes of a relative few, who brought their families along and inspired others to follow. Poor people tend to rise up rapidly and will be damaged by a policy of redistribution that will always hit new and unsheltered income and wealth much harder than the elaborately concealed and fortified winnings of the established rich. The poor benefit from a dynamic economy full of unpredictable capital gains (they have few capital losses!) more than from a stratified system governed by educational and other credentials that the rich can buy.

THE ONLY dependable route from poverty is always work, family, and faith. The first principle is that in order to move up, the poor must not only work, they must work harder than the classes above them. Every previous generation of the lower class has made such efforts. But the current poor, white even more than black, are refusing to work hard. Irwin Garfinkel and Robert Haveman, authors of an ingenious and sophisticated study of what they call *Earnings Capacity Utilization Rates*, have calculated the degree to which various income groups use their opportunities—how hard they work outside the home. This study shows that, for several understandable reasons, the current poor work substantially less, for fewer hours and weeks a year, and earn less in proportion to their age, education, and other credentials (even *after* correcting the figures for unemployment, disability, and presumed discrimination) than either their predecessors in American cities or those now above them on the income scale.[4] (The study was made at the federally funded Institute for Research on Poverty at the University of Wisconsin and used data from the census and the Michigan longitudinal survey.) The findings lend important confirmation to the growing body of evidence that work effort is the crucial unmeasured variable in American productivity and income distribution, and that current welfare and other subsidy programs substantially reduce work. The poor choose leisure not because of moral weakness, but because they are paid to do so.

A program to lift by transfers and preferences the incomes of less diligent groups is politically divisive—and very unlikely—because it incurs the bitter resistance of the real working class. In addition, such an effort breaks the psychological link between effort and reward, which is crucial to long-run upward mobility. Because effective work consists not in merely fulfilling the requirements of labor contracts, but in "putting out" with alertness and emotional commitment, workers have to understand and feel deeply that what they are given depends on what they give—that they must supply work in order to demand goods. Parents and schools must inculcate this idea in their children both by instruction and example. Nothing is more deadly to achievement than the belief that effort will not be rewarded, that the world is a bleak and discriminatory place in which only the predatory and the specially preferred can get ahead. Such a view in the home discourages the work effort in school that shapes earnings capacity afterward. As with so many aspects of human performance, work effort begins in family experiences, and its sources can be best explored through an examination of family structure.

Indeed, after work the second principle of upward mobility is the maintenance of monogamous marriage and family. Adjusting for discrimination against women and for child-care responsibilities, the Wisconsin study indicates that married men work between two and one-third and four times harder than married women, and more than twice as hard as female family heads. The work effort of married men increases with their age, credentials, education, job experience, and birth of children, while the work effort of married women steadily declines. Most important in judging the impact of marriage, husbands work 50 percent harder than bachelors of comparable age, education, and skills.[5]

The effect of marriage, thus, is to increase the work effort of men by about half. Since men have higher earnings capacity to begin with, and since the female capacity utilization figures would be even lower without an adjustment for discrimination, it is manifest that the maintenance of families is the key factor in reducing poverty.

Once a family is headed by a woman, it is almost impossible for it to greatly raise its income even if the woman is highly educated and trained and she hires day-care or domestic help. Her family responsibilities and distractions tend to prevent her from the kind of all-out commitment that is necessary for the full use of earning power. Few women with children make earning money the top priority in their lives.

A married man, on the other hand, is spurred by the claims of family to channel his otherwise disruptive male aggressions into his performance as a provider for a wife and children. These sexual differences alone, which manifest themselves in all societies known to anthropology, dictate that the first priority of any serious program against poverty is to strengthen the male role in poor families.

These narrow measures of work effort touch on just part of the manifold interplay between family and poverty. Edward Banfield's *The Unheavenly City* defines the lower class largely by its lack of an orientation to the future. Living from day to day and from hand to mouth, lower class individuals are unable to plan or save or keep a job. Banfield gives the impression that short-time horizons are a deep-seated psychological defect afflicting hundreds of thousands of the poor.

There is no question that Banfield puts his finger on a crucial problem of the poor and that he develops and documents his theme in an unrivaled classic of disciplined social science. But he fails to show how millions of men, equally present oriented, equally buffeted by impulse and blind to the future, have managed to become far-seeing members of the middle classes. He also fails to explain how millions of apparently future-oriented men can become dissolute followers of the sensuous moment, neglecting their jobs, dissipating their income and wealth, pursuing a horizon no longer than the most time-bound of the poor.

What Banfield is in fact describing in his lower-class category is largely the temperament of single, divorced, and separated men. The key to lower-class life in contemporary America is that unrelated individuals, as the census calls them, are so numerous and conspicuous that they set the tone for the entire community. Their congregation in ghettos, moreover, magnifies greatly their impact on the black poor, male and female (though, as Banfield rightly observes, this style of instant gratification is chiefly a male trait).

The short-sighted outlook of poverty stems largely from the breakdown of family responsibilities among fathers. The lives of the poor, all too often, are governed by the rhythms of tension and release that characterize the sexual experience of young single men. Because female sexuality, as it evolved over the millennia, is psychologically rooted in the bearing and nurturing of children, women have long horizons within their very bodies, glimpses of eternity within their wombs. Civilized society is dependent upon the submission of the short-term sexuality of young men to the extended maternal horizons of women. This is what happens in monogamous marriage; the man disciplines his sexuality and extends it into the future through the womb of a woman. The woman gives him access to his children, otherwise forever denied him; and he gives her the product of his labor, otherwise dissipated on temporary pleasures. The woman gives him a unique link to the future and a vision of it; he gives her faithfulness and a commitment to a lifetime of hard work. If work effort is the first principle of overcoming poverty, marriage is the prime source of upwardly mobile work.

It is love that changes the short horizons of youth and poverty into the long horizons of marriage and career. When marriages fail, the man often returns to the more primitive rhythms of singleness. On the average, his income drops by one-third and he shows a far higher propensity for drink, drugs, and crime. But when marriages in general hold firm and men in general love and support their children, Banfield's lower-class style changes into middle-class futurity.

The key to the intractable poverty of the hardcore American poor is the dominance of single and separated men in poor communities. Black "unrelated individuals" are not much more likely to be in poverty than white ones. The problem is neither race nor matriarchy in any meaningful sense. It is familial anarchy among the concentrated poor of the inner city, in which flamboyant and impulsive youths rather than responsible men provide the themes of aspiration. The result is that male sexual rhythms tend to prevail, and boys are brought up without authoritative fathers in the home to instill in them the values of responsible paternity: the discipline and love of children and the dependable performance of the provider role. "If she wants me, *she*'ll pay," one young stud assured me in prison,[6] and perhaps, in the welfare culture, she can and will. Thus the pattern is extended into future generations.

In his concern with present and future orientation, Banfield was right about the role of time in upward mobility. "Capital," as the Austrian school of economists tells us, "*is* time"—the delay in consumption entailed by extended modes of production. In poor communities, it might be said, all time is present time, and capital—in its human form of work effort combined with education and savings—does not adequately accumulate to provide income and wealth. But a more fundamental way of defining the stagnant lower class is by its lack of family structure. The men's links to children and future are too often insufficient to induce work and thrift.

British demographer E. A. Wrigley has even argued that the emergence of these direct and exclusive links to children in the nuclear family was a prerequisite of the industrial revolution. In slow-developing areas of Eastern Europe and Asia, he maintains, marriage took place within the compass of extended families, and fathers were not expected to support their children alone. But as early as the Elizabethan period in England and in other industrially precocious parts of Western Europe, a couple normally could not marry until the man had demonstrated his ability to provide for an independent household. As I wrote in *Sexual Suicide*, "Sexual energies were directly tied to economic growth, and since strong sanctions were imposed on premarital sex, population growth was directly tied to economic productivity."[7]

As Wrigley wrote, "Preindustrial men lived their lives in a moving present," devoted to "short term prospects."[8] Such men could not find the time to make capital, could not bring themselves to work, save, and forgo rewards in the name of an unseen and unknowable future. It was firm links between work, wealth, sex, and children that eventually created a future-oriented psychology in the mass of Western European men. Wrigley concludes: "So often said to be the result of industrialization and urban living," the nuclear family, in fact, "preceded it by centuries" and facilitated the long-term development of the highly motivated industrial bourgeoisie and work force.[9]

Although this is an oversimplified account of both Wrigley and the industrial revolution, it expresses his crucial point: that "the act of marriage is necessarily one which stands centrally in the whole complex of social behavior."[10] In particular, it stands centrally to a man's attitude toward time, and thus toward saving and capital. Conversely, a condition of widespread illegitimacy and family breakdown can be a sufficient cause of persistent poverty, separating men from the extended horizons embodied in their children.

An analysis of poverty that begins and ends with family structure and marital status would explain far more about the problem than most of the distributions of income, inequality, unemployment, education, IQ, race, sex, home ownership, location, discrimination, and all the other items usually multiply regressed and correlated on academic computers. But even an analysis of work and family would miss what is perhaps the most important of the principles of upward mobility under capitalism—namely, faith.

Banfield understood this moral dimension better than he comprehended the role of families. One of the reasons why *The Unheavenly City* missed the importance of family structure, perhaps, was an earlier study Banfield had made of a completely stagnant Italian village riddled with nuclear families but devoid of faith.[11] Here the devotion to the interests of the family was so short-sighted and fanatical, fears of the future so paralyzing, and mutual suspicions so rife that all group endeavor failed, making impossible the kinds of large-scale organization necessary to a modern economy.

From his Italian experience Banfield developed a theory, anthropologically very dubious, that extended families represent an advance over nuclear ones. As nice as they are, extended families without a core of nuclear responsibility tend to thwart economic development. But Banfield amply proves his central theme: that family alone will not suffice.

Banfield has arrived at that point, eventually reached by every profound explorer of social and economic life, at which an appeal is made to a higher morality. He identifies it with secular concepts such as cooperation, public spirit, and long time horizons. Adolph A. Berle, contemplating the contrast between prosperous and dominantly Mormon Utah and indigent, chiefly secular Nevada next door, concluded his study of the American economy with the rather uneconomic notion of a "transcendental margin,"[12] possibly kin to Leibenstein's less glamorous X-efficiency and Christopher Jencks's timid "luck."[13] Lionel Tiger identifies this source of unexplained motion as "evolutionary optimism—the biology of hope,"[14] and finds it in the human genes. Ivan Light, in his fascinating exploration of the sources of difference between entrepreneurial Orientals and less venturesome blacks, resolved on "the spirit of moral community."[15] Irving Kristol, ruminating on the problems of capitalism, sees the need for a "transcendental justification."[16] They are all addressing, in one way or another, the third principle of upward mobility, and that is faith.

Faith in man, faith in the future, faith in the rising returns of giving, faith in the mutual benefits of trade, faith in the providence of God are all essential to successful capitalism. All are necessary to sustain the spirit of work and enterprise against the setbacks and frustrations it inevitably meets in a fallen world; to inspire trust and cooperation in an economy where they will often be betrayed; to encourage the forgoing of present pleasures in the name of a future that may well go up in smoke; to promote risk and initiative in a world where the rewards all vanish unless others join the game. In order to give without the assurance of return, in order to save without the certainty of future value, in order to work beyond the requirements of the job, one has to have confidence in a higher morality: a law of compensations beyond the immediate and distracting struggles of existence.

The nuclear families of Tuscany lacked this faith, and the polygynous company of Mormons possessed it. This faith sustained the overseas Chinese, working for years far from their wives. This faith roused and inspired thousands of American blacks in the pits of the Great Depression, when under the auspices of "Father Divine" they launched hundreds of successful businesses in America's inner cities. Between 1933 and 1937 God, Inc., as its eponymous leader called his effort, became Harlem's leading landlord, operated innumerable groceries, ran ten dry cleaners, sponsored twenty or thirty hucksters selling vegetables, fruit, and fish "at evangelical prices" from small wagons, and managed a coal business shuttling trucks between New York and Pennsylvania.

Meanwhile the group also sustained similar enterprises in Newark, Jersey City, Bridgeport, and Baltimore, and fed thousands of wholesome ten-cent meals—and even more free ones—to near starving blacks. Divine's Lieutenant Faithful Mary headed a kitchen in Newark that prepared food for some 96,000 people in one depression year. By 1953, when, unhappily, Divine absconded in ungodly circumstances, his empire embraced "peace garages," construction and painting firms, tailors, furriers, hotels and photographic studios, and an employment service for domestic servants.[17]

The employment service brought thousands of Father Divine's "angels" to serve in the kitchens and nurseries of white families in downtown Manhattan. Two of these domestics, Gratifying Love and Ezekiel, once took me, as a boy of eight, to Harlem, to visit the divine sanctum, appointed in ivory and velvet, and I fell to my tremulous knees before His then empty throne.

Father Divine is known as a fraud. But if God works in mysterious ways, and if the Black Panthers are to be praised for giving breakfasts to little school children, after extorting them from terrified small grocers, Father Divine deserves the gratitude of many, for giving meals and meaning to the lives of some million blacks. He demonstrated conclusively that blacks, like every other group in America's cities, can create and sustain enterprise even when their families fail. Faith, in all its multifarious forms and luminosities, can by itself move the mountains of sloth and depression that afflict the world's stagnant economies; it brought immigrants thousands of miles with pennies in their pockets to launch the American empire of commerce; and it performs miracles daily in our present impasse.

In general, however, upward mobility depends on all three principles—work, family, and faith—interdependently reaching toward children and future. These are the pillars of a free economy and a prosperous society. They are being eroded now in America by the intellectual and political leaders of perhaps the freest and most prosperous of all the world's societies.

NOTES

1. Thomas Sowell, "Race and I. Q. Reconsidered," in Thomas Sowell, ed., *American Ethnic Groups* (Washington, D.C.: The Urban Institute, 1977), p. 208.
2. Richard B. Freeman, "Discrimination in the Academic Marketplace," in Sowell, ed., *American Ethnic Groups*, pp. 167–200.
3. Andrew Greeley, "The Ethnic Miracle," *The Public Interest*, No. 45 (Fall 1976), pp. 20–36.
4. Irwin Garfinkel and Robert Haveman, with the assistance of David Betson, U.S. Department of Health, Education and Welfare, *Earnings Capacity, Poverty, and Inequality*, Institute for Research on Poverty Monograph Series (New York: Academic Press, 1977), pp. 32 and passim.
5. Ibid.
6. George Gilder, *Visible Man: A True Story of Post-Racist America* (New York: Basic Books, 1978), p. 188.
7. George Gilder, *Sexual Suicide* (New York: Quadrangle/The New York Times Book Co., 1973); rev. ed. (New York: Bantam Books, 1974), p. 90.
8. E. A. Wrigley, *Population and History* (New York: McGraw-Hill, 1969), pp. 76–77.
9. Ibid., p. 13.
10. Ibid., p. 116.
11. Edward Banfield, *The Moral Basis of a Backward Society* (New York: The Free Press, 1958; paperback ed., 1967).
12. Adolph Berle, *American Economic Republic* (New York: Harcourt, Brace & World, 1963), chapter 7.
13. Christopher Jencks et al., *Inequality: A Reassessment of the Effect of Family and Schooling in America* (New York: Basic Books, 1972).
14. Lionel Tiger, *Optimism, the Biology of Hope* (New York: Simon & Schuster, 1979).
15. Ivan H. Light: *Ethnic Enterprise in America* (Berkeley: University of California Press, 1972), pp. 170–172.
16. Irving Kristol, *Two Cheers for Capitalism* (New York: Basic Books, 1978), p. 262.
17. Light, *Ethnic Enterprise*, pp. 141–142 and 149.

Part II

Social Welfare History— A Map to the Future

"History . . . do we have to?" "Can't we look at current programs?" "What's the purpose of memorizing dates?" Typical and understandable responses to the study of history by individuals whose primary concern is to provide services to those in some form of social, emotional, or economic discomfort.

The study of social welfare history is probably one of the least understood areas of the social work curriculum. History is often approached with a certain amount of apprehension, framed with stoic student responses, and guided with lingering doubts regarding the relatedness of previous, sometimes centuries old, transactions to the technological society of the twentieth century. History is a map to the future that details prior experiences, outlines previously traveled routes, and points out the resulting hazards.

Social workers are not immune to the use of history in practice. For example, the social history of a client system provides vital information in determining a course of intervention. The selection of one particular strategy or theory is based on the worker's analysis of his or her practice in a historical context; that is, a particular approach that has been most appropriate in the past will again be implemented under similar conditions.

The ability to use the client's (social history) or worker's (practice history) past has a valuable place in the social worker's repertoire of knowledge and skills. Similarly, knowledge of welfare history also plays a significant role in current practice. Is it a recent phenomenon that identifies women, children, and elders as the "worthy poor," individuals society has some obligation to help during periods of economic or social crisis? Over three centuries ago, the 1601 English Poor Laws identified these groups as being eligible for public aid—thus the nation's commitment of assistance, no matter how grudgingly, to these groups is solidified in time and reinforced through the development of numerous forms of public policies.

We can look at the current public debate regarding lowering or eliminating minimum wage laws as an example of history's relatedness to the present. In the eighteenth century, the English implemented the Speenhamland Act which tied the financial level of public assistance to a community's wage scale. Basically, the law called for public aid to be set below the financial level of the "lowest paid" worker in a community. The law's rationale rested on the belief that an individual would not work if he or she could receive similar amounts in public assistance (remember, there has been and still remains the notion that people are inherently lazy and will take the easiest way out). Not wanting to make public assistance a comfortable life-style and desiring to "get the poor back to work," public assistance payments remain lower than minimum wage. Now the policy question—What will happen to public aid *if* the minimum wage is lowered or eliminated? If history is right, we can postulate that welfare payments will be lowered. Given the existing minimal levels of public assistance, such as a national per capita average of forty-seven cents per meal in food stamps allowances, to what level might such payments be lowered?

Other examples of the importance of social welfare history to present-day social work issues can be cited, but the point is clear that social work is not confined to a vacuum of the present; rather, there exists a rich and exciting history to assist and impact our decision-making process. The questions then are, How do we approach the study of history? What should we be looking for? and What happens to our newfound knowledge?

There are a number of approaches to the study of history. One of the more common though disliked methods is the memorization of dates: In 1601 the English Poor Laws were organized, in 1865 the Freedmen's Bureau was established, in 1912 the Girl Scouts were founded, and so on. While knowledge of when events took place is important (as well as impressive to friends and colleagues when you are able to drop a date during a conversation), this helps us minimally in the overall scheme of welfare analysis.

A second avenue, and, in general, one of the more utilized approaches to the study of social welfare history, is the *chronological* method of study. Under this format, we examine history beginning at one point in time, generally starting with the 1601 Poor Laws, and move in a year-by-year, decade-by-decade, or century-by-century style until our study brings us to the present. This methodology has greater utility than memorizing dates as we at least become acquainted with time relationships between events. For example, the progressive years of the early twentieth century proved to be a fertile period for enactment of laws delineating rights—a variety of child protective policies were passed in many states in an adult-based society, and women's issues crystallized with the ratification of the Nineteenth Amendment in 1920 (see Chambers, 1967, chaps. 2 and 3).

Closely tied to this method is the identification of significant actors in social history, such as Benjamin Franklin, General O. O. Howard, William Booth, Dorothea Dix, Jane Addams, Mary Richmond, Paul Kellog, Edward Devine, Florence Kelly, Grace Abbott, Edith Abbott, Clifford Beers, Charles Loring Brace, and Harry Hopkins (Stroup, 1986; *Encyclopedia*, 1987). The knowledge of *who* was involved with *what* helps us gain a fuller picture of our past, and, in a manner of speaking, rounds out the study of chronological history.

The intent of examining social welfare history, however, goes far beyond the memorization of facts and developing a somewhat rote approach to its chronology. From a policy perspective, we identify trends or themes that have been threaded throughout the fabric of our past. Richard Spano clearly set forth this approach when writing

> we are not so much concerned with history as history but with the HISTORICAL CONTEXT of social policies and programs; historical context is the soil in which social policy grows and takes root. If social policy is viewed as a plant, historical context consists of the air, water, and ground in the immediate area that will shape the growth of the plant (Spano, 1986, p. 39).

In this style of inquiry, we also locate, if possible, the beginnings of policy trends and examine *how* they evolved throughout time. For example, the 1601 English Poor Laws identified *who* the worthy poor were, *what* level of government was accountable for services, and *how* services should be provided. Throughout American history the *who* of the Poor Laws have remained the same (women, elders, children, and the infirm), while the *what* and *how* remain central to the arguments of social welfare responsibility—should the state and local community identify standards and programs or should the federal government set nationwide standards; should services be cash or in kind?

The study of history reveals how some themes over time have been modified. For example, June Axinn and Herman Levin (1982) document the evolution of armed forces veterans as "worthy" recipients of federal aid; the Depression years of the 1930s radically changed the roles and relationships between the federal, state, and local governments in the provision and responsibility of social services (Axinn and Levin, 1982; Chambers, 1967; and Trattner, 1974).

This form of study is analytic in style and places us in the role of investigator rather than consumer—we become partners with history, looking for clues to better understand and explain current issues.

This investigative style mandates that we ask questions, seek answers, and piece together parts of our mosaic of social history. In this approach, we look at an event and its actors in terms of the context of the period; that is, we don't apply late twentieth-century beliefs and values to positions taken or policies formulated in previous decades or centuries. Rather, we look to the past within its unique time frame and the context of the values and beliefs of that era. The Freedmen's Bureau, for example, superficially seems to have been a post–Civil War strategy that assisted the former Southern slaves' movement into a free society. Tentative analysis of Bureau programs lend support to such a stance. Yet, closer examination of the Bureau's policies and resulting programs support the conclusion that the Bureau institutionalized segregation by establishing a dual social and economic structure well in advance of the Black Codes and Jim Crow Laws (Rabinowitz, 1980; Colby, 1985).

The articles chosen for this section move the reader to a more detailed analytic plain. When viewed together, the articles shed light on some current welfare themes and propels us through the surface of social history.

ARTICLE 5: "BENJAMIN FRANKLIN AND THE POOR LAWS"

Benjamin Franklin is generally depicted as a balding, portly, grandfather type who helped the eighteenth-century American colonies join together in nationhood. His energies and contributions were legendary in his time: His resumé includes authorship of numerous works, including *Poor Richard's Almanac*, and ownership of the *Pennsylvania Gazette*, which became the nation's largest circulating paper under his leadership. He organized the first fire company in Pennsylvania; founded the first circulating library in the country; organized the American Philosophical Society; helped establish the Pennsylvania Hospital; conceived the theory of electricity; outlined positive and negative poles; and invented a variety of items including the Franklin stove, bifocals, and the lightning rod. He was one of the more creative characters during the nation's formative years.

Franklin had an economic side—one to which our basic high school and college American history texts seldom allude—that challenged the purpose and function of public assistance and, in particular, the 1601 English Poor Laws.

Howell Williams's manuscript provides an opportunity to examine Franklin's welfare-related philosophy. According to Williams, Franklin felt that people would rather not work; that each person was responsible for his or her own welfare; that public and private welfare encouraged "idleness, dependence, and vice"; and that the poor were in no position to ask for aid since they provided no work-related services to society. Such ideas are not uncommon in twentieth-century America, and in fact dominate so-called conservative political thinking.

Franklin represented the mainstream of the seventeenth- and eighteenth-centuries' thinking which was integrated into various forms of social policy. Williams opens the door to social welfare history by examining the basic antipublic assistance positions in colonial America. Franklin was not the sole believer in nor the originator of such thinking, but his stature in early America requires us to consider both what he said and why he took such positions. As you read about Franklin, reflect back to Gilder's ideas in article 4. Are the ideas similar, separated only by 200 years? In fact, could Franklin have authored Gilder's comments?

ARTICLE 6: "FREE BLACKS IN ANTEBELLUM PHILADELPHIA"

When considering eighteenth- and nineteenth-century race relations, people simplistically categorize the South as racist while the North embraced social and economic equality. People, events, and geographical regions in the period preceding the Civil War are often dichotomized as "good" versus "evil," North versus South, Lincoln versus plantation owners.

Are these positions accurate assessments? For example, did Lincoln believe in racial equality? During the famed 1858 Lincoln-Douglas debates, Lincoln's position was clear when he stated: "I am not, nor ever have been in favor of bringing about in any way the social and political equality of the white and black races . . . and I as much as any other man am in favor of having the superior position assigned to the white race" (Stampp, 1965, pp. 32–33). This statement typifies Lincoln's belief that racial equality was unacceptable, while segregating the races was the sole way to prevent "racial amalgamation" (Stampp, 1965, p. 35).

Was the North the sole caretaker of racial equality and harmony? Were Northern blacks granted equal access to schools, jobs, housing, and social care? Theodore Hershberg's article examines the state of black life in early nineteenth-century Philadelphia and provides direct evidence that segregation was a significant component of the social and economic order.

If Hershberg's analysis that segregation was a mainstay in Northern life is correct, what sort of social policies could we expect to be implemented by the victorious North following the Civil War? Is it accurate to assume that Northerners would change their beliefs or is it more logical that the Northern philosophy of racial segregation would dominate the South?

While Hershberg provides significant information into the status of nineteenth-century race relations, his work also serves as an excellent model for conducting historical research. Note his research techniques and the sources he accesses to develop a data base. Hershberg easily demonstrates how to quantify history in order to make significant findings based on "hard numbers."

ARTICLE 7: "BUILDING CHARACTER AMONG THE URBAN POOR, THE CHARITY ORGANIZATION MOVEMENT"

The YMCA, settlement houses, recreation programs, and asylums were among the many different types of institutions that emerged during the nineteenth century. Each serviced a particular population group with unique programs and services. The 1800s was an era of social experimentation as an array of program strategies were designed with the overt goal of making the urban-based nation morally stronger.

The Charity Organization Society, commonly referred to as the COS, originated in England and first came to America in 1877. The program, while sharpening the concept of *scientific charity*, a specific process for determining client eligibility for programs, provided a fertile ground for the evolution of the future profession we now call social work.[1]

Paul Boyer outlines the dimensions of the COS and its operations. In Boyer's piece, however, some interesting features begin to emerge. Certain ideas discussed in previous readings take shape in programs as services take on a certain moral flavor—individual character flaws are highlighted, with clients to blame for their difficulties.

Boyer allows us to question the nature of the emerging welfare system. Are clients morally corrupt? Do workers have a responsibility to modify a client's morals? Whose morals are correct—the social agency's, the workers', or the clients'? These are interesting questions as they direct our attention not only to services but also to the social worker's role in the social welfare system.

---

[1]Social work is historically tied to a number of nineteenth- and twentieth-century programs. Casework, for example, can be traced to the COS; group practice stems from the settlement movement, and community practice is closely tied to the United Way experiences.

ARTICLE 8: "THE HOUSE OF REFUGE FOR COLORED CHILDREN"

Cecile Frey critiques another nineteenth-century institution, albeit minor in comparison to the COS, directed toward black children. As with the Boyer article, we again must reflect on the nature of institutions and in particular how programs and services impacted minorities.

What was the purpose of the House of Refuge? Why the emphasis on work, guided by the notion of "Christian morality"? Were such programs geared toward social change or social control? Were the COS and the House of Refuge similar in terms of intent and function, if so how, and, just as important, why?

As we read Frey's work, consider Hershberg's work in article 6 on the role of free blacks in the North. How does the House of Refuge reflect or relate to Boyer's thesis? Are race relations patterns beginning to solidify in the social and helping order?

ARTICLE 9: "FIRST DAYS AT HULL-HOUSE"

Jane Addams—social worker, Nobel Peace Prize winner, advocate—was a person who lived what she believed. As a social worker, Addams helped shape the destiny of the then fledgling human service profession; as a person, Jane Addams remained a dominant force in society and, in a sense, kept in the forefront of America's consciousness the nation's responsibilities and obligations to the disadvantaged.

With close friend Ellen Starr, Jane Addams established Hull-House in Chicago, a settlement home which provided a variety of programs, from education to entertainment, to neighborhood people. Hull-House extended beyond the geographic boundaries of a Chicago neighborhood as the organization became a social and political force within Chicago with its reverberations felt in other urban centers of the country.

The Addams manuscript provides insight into urban life of early twentieth-century metro America. Look at Addams's words and keep in mind the ideas of the preceding two centuries—How have such philosophies and beliefs impacted the poor of the 1900s? What was the intent of Addams and Starr? Was their work victim blaming? How did Hull-House deal with the previous century's belief in moral manipulation?

ARTICLE 10: "FIFTY YEARS OF SOCIAL SECURITY"

In August 1935, President Franklin Roosevelt signed into law the Social Security Act. The law was to provide for the general welfare by establishing a system of Federal old-age benefits, and by enabling the several States to make more adequate provision for aged persons, blind persons, dependent and crippled children, maternal and child welfare, public health, and the administration of their unemployment compensation laws; to establish a Social Security Board; to raise revenue; and for other purposes (see Axinn and Levin, 1982, pp. 218–30).

The Social Security Act radically rearranged governmental relationships for the social welfare system. The federal government became responsible for most social programs which, since the 1601 English Poor Laws, had been within the scope of state and local governments. Additionally, the 1935 act set the framework for the emergence of the now often referred to *welfare state.*

Martha McSteen outlines the genesis of the U.S. Social Security Program and highlights changes during the program's first fifty years of transactions. This article is important on two points: First, we have a clear and understandable presentation outlining the purpose and evolution of social security (on its own merits, this alone is reason enough to become familiar with this piece) and, second, we are able to assess the extent to which public assistance and social insurance programs embody the philosophical beliefs of the previous years regarding social welfare. Do we see Franklin's or Addams's ideas played out in social security? Or, is there a mix of their positions? If there is a mix, that is, some programs adopt a Franklin-type philosophy while others subscribe to the Addams stance, what is it about that program or service which leads to the particular philosophical identification?

BIBLIOGRAPHY

Axinn, J. and Levin, H. (1982). *Social Welfare, A History of the American Response to Need* (2nd ed.). New York: Harper and Row.

Chambers, C. A. (1967). *Seedtime of Reform, American Social Service and Social Action, 1918–1933.* The University of Michigan Press, Ann Arbor Paperbacks.

Colby, I. (1985). The Freedmen's Bureau: From Social Welfare to Segregation. *Phylon, XLVI* (3), 219–230.

Encyclopedia of Social Work (Vol. 17, Nos. 1 and 2). (1987). Silver Spring, MD: National Association of Social Workers.

Rabinowitz, H. (1980). *Race Relations in the Urban South, 1865–1890.* Chicago, IL: University of Illinois Press.

Spano, R. (1986). Creating the Context for the Analysis of Social Policies: Understanding the Historical Context. In Donald E. Chambers (Ed.). *Social Policy and Social Programs, A Method for the Practical Public Policy Analyst* (pp. 38–53). New York: Macmillan.

Stampp, K. (1965). *The Era of Reconstruction, 1865–1877.* New York: Vintage Books.

Stroup, H. (1986). *Social Welfare Pioneers.* Chicago, IL: Nelson-Hall.

Trattner, W. (1974). *From Poor Law to Welfare State, A History of Social Welfare in America.* New York: The Free Press.

Article 5

BENJAMIN FRANKLIN AND THE POOR LAWS

Howell V. Williams

Benjamin Franklin, statesman, diplomat, scientist, was also our first American economist. It is interesting that his writings severely criticized the statutory provision for aid to the poor and needy. He advocated repeal of the poor laws long before the writings of Malthus roused fervid support in England and America for that extreme change in public policy; and he challenged the Elizabethan provision of public aid for the poor which had been made part of the system of poor relief in every colony in America.

Franklin's most extensive discussions of the poor laws were written in England during his almost continuous residence there from 1757 to 1775. This period of his residence in England was one of intensive discussion and general condemnation of the poor laws. Squires, clergymen, justices, legislators, and landowners wrote pamphlets and contributed articles to the press on the subject. Public discussion was caused by exaggerated ideas of the rise in the costs of poor relief.[1] Franklin's interest in economic and political questions soon impelled him to join in the discussion.

The Franklin writings on the poor law covered the period from 1753, when he was aged forty-seven, to 1789, a year before his death at the age of eighty-four. The most important of these writings include the "Letter to Peter Collinson, Philadelphia, May 9, 1753"; "Essay on the Price of Corn, and Management of the Poor" (London, 1766); "Essay on the Laboring Poor," (London, April, 1768); and "Letter to Baron Francis Maseres, London, June 17, 1772."

The "Letter to Peter Collinson"[2] in 1753 introduced Franklin's principal argument against poor laws. He began by asserting that English

SOURCE: Reprinted with permission from *Social Service Review*, Vol. 18 (1944), pp. 77–91.

[1]Cf. Sidney and Beatrice Webb, *English Poor Law History*, Part I: *The Old Poor Law* (London: Longmans, Green, 1927), p. 265.

[2]*Works of Benjamin Franklin* (Sparks ed.), VII, 66–68. The letter was first printed in the *Gentleman's Magazine* (London), January, 1834. In addition to discussing poor laws in the letter, Franklin dwelt upon the economic aspects of Indian life, the progress of education in America, and the problem of assimilating German immigrants. Peter Collinson (1694–1768), English naturalist and antiquarian, was an intimate friend and

laborers lacked industry and thrift, while German workers showed both qualities; and he observed:

> When I consider that the English are the offspring of Germans, that the climate they live in is much of the same temperature, and when I see nothing in nature that should create this difference, I am tempted to suspect it may arise from the constitution; and I have sometimes doubted whether the laws peculiar to England, which *compel the rich to maintain the poor,* have not given the latter a dependence, that very much lessens the care of providing against the wants of old age.

Franklin went on to include private and sectarian charities in his criticism. He stated that the poor in Protestant countries on the Continent of Europe were generally more industrious than those in Catholic countries, and he concluded: "May not the more numerous foundations in the latter for the relief of the poor have some effect towards rendering them less provident?"

The thesis that provision for the needy tends to destroy the personal qualities of industry and thrift was based on Franklin's belief that the sharp spur of necessity and a longing for freedom from toil are the motivations for labor and that any security against the economic hazards of life will only cause increased pauperism. Franklin continued:

> It seems certain that the hope of becoming at some time of life free from the necessity of care and labor, together with the fear of penury, are the mainsprings of most people's industry. To those, indeed, who have been educated in elegant plenty, even the provision made for the poor may appear misery; but to those who have scarce ever been better provided for, such provision may seem quite good and sufficient. These latter, then, have nothing to fear worse than their present condition, and scarce hope for anything better than a parish maintenance. So that there is only the difficulty of getting that maintenance allowed while they are able to work, or a little shame they suppose attending it, that can induce them to work at all; and what they do, will only be hand to mouth.

Franklin proceeded to apotheosize the principle that industry and thrift are destroyed by aid to the poor by identifying it with the laws of nature and God:

> To relieve the misfortunes of our fellow creatures is concurring with the Deity; it is godlike, but, if we provide arrangement for laziness, and support for folly, may we not be found fighting against the order of God and nature, which perhaps has appointed want and misery as the proper

---

a regular correspondent. He became acquainted with Franklin through his interest in electrical experiments. He corresponded with other Colonial men of science and was a contributor to the Public Library of Philadelphia.

punishments for, and cautions against, as well as necessary consequences of, idleness and extravagance? Wherever we attempt to amend the scheme of Providence, and to interfere with the government of the world, we had need be very circumspect, but we do more harm than good.

The letter was concluded by an interesting comment on workhouses,[3] which at that time Franklin believed might serve not only to employ the poor but also, by an unpleasant atmosphere, to act as a deterrent to applications for public aid. He stated:

> They [the poor] should therefore have every encouragement we can invent, and not one motive to diligence be subtracted; and the support of the poor should not be by maintaining them in idleness, but by employing them in some kind of labor suited to their abilities of body, as I am informed begins of late the practice in many parts of England, where workhouses are erected for that purpose. If these were general, I should think the poor would be more careful, and work voluntarily to lay up something for themselves against a rainy day, rather than run the risk of being obliged to work at the pleasure of others for a bare subsistence, and that too under confinement.

Franklin did not again mention workhouse care as a satisfactory mode of relief; and it must be concluded, in view of his subsequent strenuous attacks on all forms of poor relief, that he did not continue to regard workhouses as an exception.

But by 1766, when he was residing in England, Franklin was more forthright in questioning the poor laws, and for the first time advocated outright repeal. He made the following statement in the essay "On the Price of Corn, and Management of the Poor":

> I am for doing good to the poor, but I differ in opinion about the means. I think the best way of doing good to the poor, is, not making them easy *in* poverty, but leading or driving them *out* of it. In my youth, I travelled much, and I observed in different countries, that the more public provisions were made for the poor, the less they provided for themselves, and of course became poorer. And, on the contrary, the less was done for them, the more they did for themselves, and became richer.[4]

England's statutory provision for the economically needy, as well as private charitable aid, acted, he thought, to increase poverty by destroying industry, thrift, and independence. He said:

---

[3]In England the term "workhouse" was used as synonymous with "poorhouse" or "poor farm" or "almshouse" in America.

[4]*Works*, II, 355–60. The essay was originally published in the London *Chronicle* in 1766 under the pseudonym of "Arator." It appeared in *Political, Miscellaneous, and Philosophical Pieces*, ed. Benjamin Vaughan (London, 1779), pp. 57–63.

There is no country in the world where so many provisions are established for them [the poor]; so many hospitals to receive them when they are sick and lame, founded and maintained by voluntary charities; so many almshouses for the aged of both sexes, together with a solemn law made by the rich to subject their estates to a heavy tax for the support of the poor. Under all these obligations, are our poor modest, humble, and thankful? And do they use their best endeavours to maintain themselves and lighten our shoulders of this burthen? On the contrary, I affirm, that there is no country in the world in which the poor are more idle, dissolute, drunken, and insolent. The day you passed that act, you took away from before their eyes the greatest of all inducements to industry, frugality, and sobriety, by giving them a dependence on somewhat else than a careful accumulation during youth and health, for support in age or sickness. . . . In short, you offered a premium for the encouragement of idleness, and you should not now wonder that it has had its effect in the increase of poverty.

Franklin advised the repeal of the English poor laws and painted a glowing picture of the benefits that would ensue:

Repeal that law, and you will see a change in their manners. *Saint Monday* and *Saint Tuesday* will soon cease to be holidays. *Six days shalt thou labour,* though one of the old commandments long treated as out of date, will again be looked upon as a respectable precept; industry will increase, and with it plenty among the lower people; their circumstances will mend, and more will be done for their happiness by inuring them to provide for themselves, than could be done by dividing your estates among them.[5]

---

[5]The American economist, Willard Phillips, who edited Franklin's economic writings in the Sparks edition of his works, stated in an editorial comment on this essay: "This paper was published nine years before the 'Wealth of Nations,' and takes the same view of the English poor-laws that is taken in that work" (see *Works,* II, 360 n.). But, on the contrary, there is no similarity between Franklin's comments and those of Adam Smith. When the latter discussed the English poor laws, he took a stand only on the settlement and removal provisions, which he condemned as hindering the mobility of labor and violating "natural liberty and justice"; he did not criticize the other sections of the laws (cf. Adam Smith, *Wealth of Nations,* Cannan ed., I, 137, 435, 141 f.). Conversely, Franklin did not mention settlement or removal but condemned the basic provision of the laws. Phillips also cited the position later taken by Malthus that public and private assistance to the destitute are rendered futile by the tendency of population increase to outstrip food supply. Of this thesis he said: "This is a result from which the characteristic philanthropy of Franklin would have revolted. He certainly would not have maintained that the resourceless sick, maimed, poor, and those destitute of the discretion requisite to support themselves should . . . be abandoned to perish of want." Again, his interpretation must be challenged. Franklin advocated the repeal of the poor laws and the limitation of private charities, as emphatically as Malthus did.

Franklin suggested changes in poor law administration in 1766, in addition to his advocacy of repeal. He recommended that each English parish should be required to print and distribute a list of the names of all recipients of poor relief and the names and amounts of those paying poor rates.[6] He asserted that this system would act as a check on applications for aid, and would restrain the approval by poor relief officials, and inform voters of the affairs of the parish. Apparently he believed the last-named factor might result in action either to lower the poor rates or actually to repeal the poor laws.

Another essay, "On the Laboring Poor,"[7] was written in London in 1768. Franklin stated that he had heard much invective in England during the preceding two years about the hardheartedness of the rich and much complaint of the great oppressions suffered by the laboring poor and wished to present the other side of the question. He asserted that the condition of the poor in England was by far the best in Europe. Men of fortune, he said, who had passed the poor laws had voluntarily subjected their own estates, and the estates of others, to the payment of a "tax for the maintenance of the poor, encumbering those estates with a kind of rent-charge for that purpose, whereby the poor are vested, as it were, in all the estates of the rich."

Franklin reiterated his stand that the poor laws induced dependency and poverty by destroying self-reliance when he said:

> But I fear that the giving mankind a dependence on any thing for support, in age or sickness, besides industry and frugality during youth and health, tends to flatter our natural indolence, to encourage idleness and prodigality, and thereby to promote and increase poverty, the very evil it was intended to cure; thus multiplying beggars instead of diminishing them.

Import duties on foreign-manufactured goods and the prohibition of manufacturing in the colonies were held to be examples of the generosity of the rich toward the poor. Franklin wrote as follows:

> There are so many laws for the support of our laboring poor, made by the rich, and continued at their expense; all the difference of price, between our own and foreign commodities, being so much given by our rich to the poor; who would indeed be enabled by it to get by degrees above poverty, if they did not, as too generally they do, consider every increase of wages, only as something that enables them to drink more and work less; so that their distress in sickness, age, or times of scar-

---

[6]"Remarks to Owen Ruffhead" (London, 1766) in *Posthumous Writings*, ed. William Temple Franklin, II, 31 n. These comments also appear in *Miscellaneous Pieces*, p. 63 n.

[7]*Works*, II, 367–71.

city, continues to be the same as if such laws had never been made in their favor.

It seems unlikely that Franklin actually believed that the returns from protected manufacturers went to the workers in the form of higher wages; and, furthermore, the statement contradicted Franklin's strong stand that protectionism lowers the standard of living of the great body of consumers. Apparently, the statement did reflect his estimate of the habits and character of laborers.

Two novel economic principles were advanced in the 1768 essay: first, that the poor benefit by luxurious and superfluous expenditures by the rich; and, second, that the poor receive annually in the form of wages the whole of the clear revenues of a society. The following statement is important:

> Much malignant censure have some writers bestowed upon the rich for their luxury and expensive living, while the poor are starving, etc.; not considering that what the rich expend, the laboring poor receive in payment for their labor. It may seem a paradox if I should assert, that our laboring poor do in every year receive *the whole revenue of the nation;* I mean not only the public revenue, but also the revenue or clear income of all private estates, or a sum equivalent to the whole. . . . *Our laboring poor receive annually the whole of the clear revenues of the nation,* and from us they can have no more.

Franklin admitted that it might be said that wages were too low but that in most cases this was due to the underbidding of the seekers of employment. A law might be passed to raise wages, he said, but the price of manufacturing would then increase, foreign sales would fall accordingly, and unemployment would be the end result. Having disposed of minimum-wage legislation, anticipating one ground of the stand later taken by the laissez faire English economists, Franklin inquired into other remedies for low wages. His conclusion embodied the recurrent thesis that the idleness and dissipation of the poor were the causes of their poverty, and the remedy for low wages therefore lay in their own hands. His observations on this point are interesting:

> I have said, a law might be made to raise their wages; but I doubt much whether it could be executed to any purpose, unless another law,, now indeed almost obsolete, could at the same time be revived and enforced; a law, I mean, that many have often heard and repeated, but few have ever duly considered. *Six days shalt thou labor.* This is as positive a part of the commandment, as that which says, *The seventh day thou shalt rest.* But we remember well to observe the indulgent part, and never think of the other. *Saint Monday* is generally as duly kept by our working people as *Sunday;* the only difference is, that, instead of employing their time cheaply at church, they are wasting it expensively at the alehouse.

Another viewpoint on the care of the poor is found in Franklin's "Letter to Baron Francis Maseres,"[8] written in London, June 17, 1772. Maseres was one of the early proponents of care of the poor by providing annuities for them to purchase; and his proposal was that parliament authorize the parishes to act as corporations and sell old age annuities to the poor. The annuities would be payable quarterly, at a maximum rate of £20, to men at the age of fifty and women at the age of thirty-five. Coverage would be achieved through voluntary purchases, each payment to be not less than £5. The funds would be invested in national securities at 3 per cent interest. A bill making provision for annuities passed the House of Commons in 1773, but failed in the upper house, principally because the landowners became alarmed at a provision making the parish rates security for the payment of annuities in case of a deficiency of funds.

Maseres sent Franklin a copy of the plan in 1772 and asked for his comments. The reply stated that the provision for annuities was an "excellent plan," but Franklin's succeeding remarks indicate that this was no more than a polite phrase. Franklin went on to make a counterproposal to Maseres, based on his observation of private homes for old people in Holland. These homes, he said, were handsome and well-furnished homes for the aged, requiring the payment of a fixed sum for entrance. Administration was carried on by volunteer committees of private citizens, a feature that appealed to Franklin's laissez faire ideas. Franklin commented:

> These institutions seem calculated to *prevent* poverty, which is rather a better thing than *relieving* it; for it keeps always *in the public eye* a state of comfort and repose, with freedom from care in old age, held forth as an encouragement to so much industry and frugality in youth as may at least serve to raise the required sum (suppose 50 pounds) that is to intitle a man or woman at 50 to a retreat in these houses. And in acquiring the sum, habits may be acquired that produce such affluence before this age arrives, as to make the retreat unnecessary, and so never claimed.

Franklin believed that such homes would be more advantageous in other ways than the annuity plan. Every unclaimed right would revert to the house, whereas all annuities would be claimed. He also asserted that "the prospect of a distant annuity will not be so influencing on the minds of young people as the constant view of the comfort enjoyed in those homes, in comparison of which, even the payment and *receipt* of annuities are private transactions."

---

[8]The letter was first published in 1819 in *Posthumous Writings*, II, 54–57. It was also included in J. R. McCulloch (ed.), *A Select Collection of Scarce and Valuable Economical Tracts* (London, 1859), pp. 201–3.

Franklin then posed a question, as he frequently did to express a conviction and gain a point, i.e., whether or not one or more of the homes in each county would result in "promoting industry and frugality among the lower people" and "of course lessening the enormous weight of the poor tax."

The counterproposal for the establishment of private homes for the aged, entered through private purchase, was consistent with Franklin's idea that individual thrift and industry could provide for the economic needs of old age and that any public or private project in the field should be of a nature to stimulate the maximum development of those qualities.

Franklin left no doubt that he intended his remarks on statutory poor relief for universal application. He extended them specifically to the poor laws of America in the "Letter to Alexander Small,"[9] written in Philadelphia, November 5, 1789. In this letter he said:

> I have long been of your opinion, that your [English] legal provision for the poor is a very great evil, operating as it does to the encouragement of idleness. We have followed your example, and begin now to see our error, and, I hope, shall reform it.

Private Charitable Programs

Although Franklin believed that private charitable assistance in the form of material aid was as inimical to industry and character as the poor laws, he extended support to welfare organizations offering educational or what might today be called "case-work" services. His comments on the administration and programs of service of certain early private charities are suggestive of later developments in the private social work field, eventually affecting public assistance practices.

Franklin's essay "Hints for Consideration Respecting the Orphan School-House in Philadelphia"[10] gives some of his views on private charities. He observed: "Charitable institutions, however originally well intended and well executed at first for many years, are subject to be in a course of time corrupted; mismanaged, their funds misapplied or perverted to private purposes." He recommended as a corrective measure that authority to govern the agency be vested in a permanent body of directors, who would establish regulations, carry on inspections, and supervise the manager—a form of organization that has proved efficient and practicable.

Other plans for the orphan school bore the stamp of Franklin's individualistic philosophy. He would have the orphans given credit for

---

[9]*Works*, X, 407.
[10]*Ibid.*, I, 59 f.

any funds brought in, and he would also credit them with the results of their labor, after subtracting their indebtedness for their maintenance and education. At discharge any credits would be paid the orphan, or, if there was a debit, the orphan would be "exhorted to pay, if ever able, but not to be compelled." Those with credits would be "exhorted" to give part back to the institution, or at least to remember it favorably later. The managers would continue to counsel and advise the orphans after they had left the institution.

Franklin's activities as president of the Pennsylvania Society for Promoting the Abolition of Slavery[11] show that he realized the utility of what may be termed early forms of case-work assistance. He stated that the purpose of the society was

> to instruct, to advise, to qualify those, who have been restored to freedom, for the exercise and enjoyment of civil liberty, to promote in them habits of industry, to furnish them with employment suited to their age, sex, talents, and other circumstances, and to procure for their children an education calculated for their future situation in life. . . .

The working plan of the society was drafted by Franklin. A committee of inspection superintended the general conduct of free Negroes, offered them advice, instruction, protection from wrongs, and other friendly offices. A committee of guardians placed Negro children in suitable homes and as far as possible exercised the right of guardianship over them. A committee on education supervised the schooling of free Negro children and youths, influencing them to attend established schools or providing instruction. The committee also kept records of the births, marriages, and manumissions of Negroes. A committee on employment sought jobs for able-bodied free Negroes, on the basis that unemployment would induce "poverty, idleness, and many vicious habits." The committee attempted the institution of simple and useful manufactures and assisted those who were qualified in starting a business.

Franklin's will has been an object of study by persons interested in the form of bequests for private charitable and educational activities. Franklin left funds for the establishment of free schools in Boston, where he received his education, and for loans for the training of apprentices in Boston and Philadelphia.[12] The loan funds included £1,000 for citizens of Boston and the same amount for citizens of Philadelphia. Loans were to be made in amounts of £15–60 to young married artificers who were under twenty-five years of age, who had served a successful ap-

---

[11]*Ibid.*, II, 513–16.
[12]The will is printed in *Works*, I, 599–612.

prenticeship, who were of good moral character, and who could produce bonds for repayment in ten equal annual instalments of 5 per cent interest a year. Franklin made elaborate calculations as to the growth of the funds, estimating that each fund would grow to £131,000 in one hundred years and £4,061,000 at the end of two hundred years.

Great difficulty attended the execution of the will, because of the narrow qualifications and the changes in the nature of vocational training. The funds did not grow as Franklin had anticipated.[13] The will is an example of the limitations of the "dead hand," when long-time or self-perpetuating bequests are made in a rigid and narrow pattern and without provision for liquidation or modifications in accordance with social and economic changes.

Bases of Franklin's Poor Law Criticism

Franklin's criticism of statutory poor relief rested on multiple grounds, some no more than practical observations, others attempts to advance economic principles or establish the nature of "economic man." They were sometimes inconsistent with his views on other economic topics. Unlike his English contemporary, Adam Smith, Franklin showed little sympathy for the dignity and worth of the laboring classes.

That the spur of economic want, or the fear of want, was necessary to stir the laborer to work, Franklin held to be a law of nature and God.[14] He believed the "natural" state of working persons was one of sloth, wastefulness, and dissipation.[15] "The common people do not work for pleasure generally, but from necessity," he stated; and, if wages become higher or provisions cheaper, they respond by idleness.[16] And, since "industry in all shapes, in all instances, and by all means, should be encouraged and protected; indolence, by every possible method rooted out,"[17] the poor laws, which provided a security against economic want and fear of want, should be eliminated. His harsh estimate of the nature of "economic man" made him conceive of public assistance as an injurious device.

Franklin's narrow philosophical and social horizon and the class preconceptions of his day did not permit him to view human motivations in their full complexity and promise. He did not perceive that human laws giving economic aid to the destitute are an essential part of a society whose goals include at least a minimum standard of living

---

[13]See William Cabell Bruce, *Benjamin Franklin Self-revealed* (1917), I, 151–53.
[14]See *Works,* VII, 67.
[15]See *ibid.,* II, 368 f.
[16]*Ibid.,* pp. 393 f.
[17]*Ibid.,* p. 390.

for all its members. He showed no evidence of the vision and the optimism which might have led him to hold that human laws may so modify the social and economic environment as to modify human character and bring about increasingly more adequate human personalities.

Franklin's second basic stand is closely related to his first principle. He held that individual industry, thrift, and initiative are sufficient to meet the economic needs of life, and a statutory provision for the needy acts only to destroy those qualities and bring on increasing poverty. He believed that each individual was responsible for his economic welfare, as even the aged and disabled should have prepared for adversity while they had youth and health, and that any lessening of this responsibility would encourage individuals toward indolence and vice. The working of the economic system, in Franklin's opinion, required that individuals should be left undisturbed to gain their livelihood and their future security by selling their labor.

Franklin's conception of the individual economic man operating without governmental intervention was partly derived from his observations of the youthful and unexploited economic environment of the American colonies. It must have been colored by the remarkable personal success he himself had met with as a gifted enterpriser. This environmental and personal background did not incline him to delve into the economic causes of destitution or to test his assumptions by intensive investigation or historical study.[18]

The Franklin ideal of life was the exercise of thrift, caution, and diligence. He preached the virtues of industry and "settled low content," and his motto "industry and frugality" constantly appeared in his works. He believed that industry and frugality tend to increase the wealth, power, and grandeur of a nation more than any other virtues. He said:

> It has been computed by some political arithmetician that, if every man and woman would work for four hours each day on something useful, that labor would produce sufficient to procure all the necessaries and

---

[18]One passage in Franklin's writings contradicts his otherwise consistently strong thesis that individuals may control their economic destinies. He made the following statement in *The Internal State of America*, written after the Revolutionary War: "There can be no country or nation existing, in which there will not be some people so circumstanced, as to find it hard to gain a livelihood; people who are not in the way of a profitable trade, and with whom money is scarce, because they have nothing to give in exchange for it; and it is always in the power of a small number to make a great clamor" (*Works*, II, 462). On the other hand, as has been shown, Franklin believed that persons could save enough while working to provide for any later periods of adversity.

comforts of life, want and misery would be banished out of the world, and the rest of the twenty-four hours might be leisure and pleasure.[19]

In Franklin's opinion even the taxes and duties imposed on the American colonies by England might not be wholly injurious if they would incline the colonists toward the practice of thrift and industry. He made the following statement during his residence in England prior to the Revolutionary War:

> I hope my country folks will remain as fix'd in their Resolutions of Industry and Frugality till these acts are repealed. And, if I could be sure of that, I should almost wish them never to be repealed; being persuaded, that we shall reap more solid and extensive Advantages from the steady Practice of those two great Virtues, than we can possibly suffer Damage from all the Duties of Parliament of this kingdom can levy on us.[20]

Franklin's stand that individuals can and should be completely responsible for their economic welfare is demonstrated in the maxims he published in *Poor Richard's Almanack*. The sayings epitomized the self-reliant man, who needed no help from the body politic and should not be hindered by the existence of poor laws from relying on his own industry, thrift, and virtue. The sayings were household words in Europe and America.

He thought that his *Almanack* was generally read, and he "considered it as a proper vehicle for conveying instruction among the common people, who bought scarcely any other books." He therefore filled "all the little spaces that occurred between the remarkable days in the Calendar, with proverbial sentences," to inculcate "industry and frugality" as the means of "procuring wealth, and thereby securing virtue"; for he thought it was more difficult "for a man in want to act always honestly," as (to use one of those proverbs) it is "hard for an empty sack to stand upright."[21]

The following maxims of Poor Richard illustrate Franklin's teaching that thrift and industry will provide personal security:

> If we are industrious, we shall never starve; for at the working man's house hunger looks in, but dares not enter.
> For age and want save while you may, no morning sun lasts a whole day.
> Sloth makes all things difficult, and industry all things easy.
> A penny saved is two pence clear. A pin a-day is a groat a-year. Save and have.

---

[19]*Works*, II, 451.

[20]*Ibid.*, V, 203.

[21]*Life and Writings of Benjamin Franklin*, ed. William Duane (New York, 1859), I, 38.

Laziness travels so slowly, that Poverty soon overtakes him.

At a great Pennyworth pause awhile.

Then plough deep while sluggards sleep, and you shall have corn to sell and to keep. Work while it is called, for you know not how much you may be hindered to-morrow.

A man may, if he knows not how to save as he gets, keep his nose all his life to the grindstone, and die not worth a groat at last.

It would be thought a hard government, that should tax its people one-tenth part of their time, to be employed in its service; but idleness taxes many of us much more; sloth, by bringing on diseases, absolutely shortens life. Sloth, like rust, consumes faster than labor wears; while the used key is always bright, as Poor Richard says. But dost thou love life, then do not squander time, for that is the stuff life is made of, as Poor Richard says.

He that riseth late must trot all day, and shall scarce overtake his business at night; while Laziness travels so slowly, that Poverty soon overtakes him. Drive thy business, let not that drive thee; and Early to bed, and early to rise, makes a man healthy, wealthy, and wise, as Poor Richard says.[22]

It was Franklin's belief that thrift and industry could operate to give individuals the economic necessities of life even more freely in America than in Europe, because of the ease of securing ownership of land, the fertility of the soil, and the unused natural resources. Thus there was even less reason for a statutory provision for the needy. Franklin disregarded the decisions of all the Colonial assemblies to enact laws to provide for the destitute; he ignored the economic problems in his own state, Pennsylvania, and the experience with the needy disabled, aged, and unemployed persons who had found it necessary from the time of the earliest settlements to apply for aid to the public authorities.

Any person in America, Franklin believed, could go into the boundless woods, which "afford freedom and subsistence to any man who can bait a hook or pull a trigger."[23] "The vast quantity of forest land we have yet to clear, and put in order for cultivation, will for a long time keep the body of our nation laborious and frugal."[24] He painted this picture of the economic situation in America:

The only Encouragement we hold out to Strangers are, a good Climate, fertile Soil, wholesome Air and Water, plenty of Provision and Fuel, good pay for Labour, kind Neighbors, Good Laws, Liberty; and a hearty

---

[22]See Thomas Herbert Russell (ed.), *The Sayings of Poor Richard* (n.d.), pp. 10, 34 f., 35, 37, 39; *Works* (Smyth ed.), III, 407 ff.; (Sparks ed.), II, 95 f., 98.

[23]*Works* (Sparks ed.), IV, 209 f.

[24]*Ibid.*, II, 450.

welcome; the rest depends upon a Man's own Industry and Virtue. Lands are cheap, but they must be bought. All settlements are undertaken at private Expence; the Publick contributes nothing but Defence and Justice.[25]

The third argument that Franklin advanced in opposition to the poor laws was based on a comparative examination of the degrees of thrift and industry in countries with different methods of care for the needy. As has been shown, he attributed idleness, dependence, and vice among the working classes in England and France to the existence of public and private provision for the poor.[26]

This argument rests on little more than practical observations and arbitrary deductions. They may or may not have been sagacious, but they certainly did not have any scientific basis. Approached systematically and objectively, in order to establish his position, it would have been necessary to assay and isolate the many complex factors that went into the degree of industry and thrift of the people of a particular country. Franklin did not consider such factors as wage levels, working conditions, distribution of income, and degree of industrialism.

Franklin's fourth position was that the luxurious and superfluous expenditures of the rich benefit the poor by resulting in a demand for their labor.[27] Since he believed that the whole revenue of a society went to laborers, the poor could ask for no more, least of all for aid for which they rendered no service.

"If the rich curtail their desires, or wishes," Franklin asserted in 1774, "their riches serve, in proportion to their not using them, no more than ore in an unworked mine."[28] He amplified the position in a letter to Benjamin Vaughan in 1784, in which he said:

> I am not sure, that in a great state its luxury is capable of a remedy, nor that the evil is in itself always so great as it is represented. . . . Is not the hope of being one day able to purchase and enjoy luxuries a great spur to labor and industry? May not luxury, therefore, produce more than it consumes, if without such a spur people would be, as they are naturally enough inclined to be, lazy and indolent? . . . a shilling spent idly by a fool, may be picked up by a wiser person, who knows better what to do with it. It is therefore not lost. A vain, silly fellow builds a

---

[25]*Ibid.*, IX, 497 f.

[26]See *ibid.*, II, 359; VII, 66f.

[27]See *ibid.*, II, 369 f. Franklin's assertions that luxurious expenditures may be of general benefit do not harmonize with his earlier teachings on frugality, parsimony, and avoidance of ostentatious spending. It may be significant that Franklin began to temporize on luxurious expenditures after he himself had achieved wealth, fame, and social position.

[28]*Ibid.*, p. 393.

fine house, furnishes it richly, lives in it expensively, and in a few years ruins himself; but the masons, carpenters, and smiths, and other honest tradesmen have been by his employ assisted in maintaining and raising their families; the former has been paid for his labor and encouraged, and the estate is now in better hands.[29]

The position that the luxurious expenditures of the rich are a benefit to wage-earners is not economically defensible. It is a species of the "made-work fallacy." The wealth of a society rests on the nature and the amount of production of the necessary and convenient goods and services. To the extent that production is diverted into superfluities for a small section of the people, the wealth of the society is diminished and the standard of living for the whole is lowered.[30]

---

[29]*Ibid.*, pp. 448–50.

[30]The similarity between Franklin's stand and the tenets of the cynical English philosopher, Bernard de Mandeville (1670–1733) is marked. Franklin had known Mandeville during the stay in London (1724–26) and was familiar with his works. Franklin's economic ideas were sometimes borrowed, and the occasion and the possibility existed in this instance. If the borrowing occurred, Franklin had distinguished company, as research has disclosed that Mandeville influenced Adam Smith, Hume, Berkeley, Hutchinson, Malthus, and Montesquieu.

Mandeville originated the idea that luxurious expenditures benefit the poor, as asserted in Franklin's work. It was part of the former's notorious maxim that "private vices are public benefits." He also anticipated Franklin in arguing that the laboring poor work only from dire necessity. Mandeville stated: "Every Body knows that there is a vast number of Journeymen Weavers, Tailors, Clothworkers, and twenty other Handicrafts; who, if by four Days Labour in a Week they can maintain themselves, will hardly be persuaded to work the fifth; and that there are Thousands of labouring Men of all sorts, who will, tho' they can hardly subsist, put themselves to fifty inconveniences, disoblige their Masters, pinch their Bellies, and run in Debt, to make Holidays. When Men shew such an extraordinary proclivity to Idleness and Pleasure, what reason have we to think that they would ever work, unless they were oblig'd to it by immediate Necessity?"

Mandeville held that the superfluous purchases of the rich are the basis of trade and industry in a nation and give employment to its laborers. "He that gives the most Trouble to thousands of his Neighbors," said Mandeville, "and invents the most operose Manufactures is, right or wrong, the greatest Friend to the Society." He illustrated his contention by the famed parable of the bees.

Franklin was also writing in the tradition of Mandeville in his criticism of statutory assistance and private charities. Mandeville had written such passages as the following: "Charity, where it is too extensive, seldom fails of promoting Sloth and Idleness, and is good for little in the Commonwealth but to breed Drones and destroy Industry. The more Colleges and Alms-houses you build the more you may." He also opposed charity schools, a position that brought a storm of denunciation about his head. He held that national wealth and the enjoyment of life by the favored classes requires a multitude of laborious poor and "to make the Society happy and People easy under the meanest Circumstances, it is requisite that great Numbers of them should be Ignorant as well as Poor."

Franklin's position that luxurious expenditures benefit the poor was related to the novel thesis that the laboring poor receive in the form of wages all of the clear revenue of a society. Since the laborers receive all of the revenues, he asserted, they cannot expect to receive more.[31] Cannan, the English economist, showed that Franklin's theory was an erroneous conception of the nature of the circulation of wealth.[32] Carey later pointed out that the stand would mean that no income was going into capital savings, which certainly was not true, and, furthermore, that a demand for commodities does not necessarily mean a demand for labor.[33] It may be added that Franklin's position shows the mistaken idea that national wealth rests on monetary circulation, instead of consisting of the nature, volume, and distribution of the production of goods and services.

Stand against Governmental Intervention

Franklin's opposition to statutory poor relief was a part of his laissez faire convictions. He was a strong believer in a minimum of public functions and was opposed to governmental intervention to meet the economic needs of the poor, just as he was opposed to intervention for the rich in the form of bounties and protective tariffs. He believed that a government should be characterized not only by passivity but also by frugality. However, he supported a moderate amount of public works, such as bridges, roads, canals, and other projects "tending to the common felicity."[34]

Franklin's stand against governmental intervention is shown in his remarks on "restraint of trade." He commended Colbert's slogans of *laissez-nous faire* and *pas trop gouverner* and stated:

> Most of the statutes, or acts, edicts, arrêts, and placarts of parliaments, princes, and states, for regulating, directing, or restraining of trade, have, we think, been either political blunders, or jobs obtained by artful men for private advantage, under pretence of public good.[35]

And the following statement gives a general application to governmental nonintervention.

---

[31]See *Works* (Sparks ed.), II, 369 f.

[32]Edwin Cannan, *A History of the Theories of Production and Distribution in English Political Economy* (3d ed., 1924), p. 36 n.

[33]Lewis J. Carey, *Franklin's Economic Views* (1928), pp. 218 f. Carey dealt briefly with some of Franklin's poor law views. They were not treated in W. A. Wetzel's monograph on *Benjamin Franklin as an Economist*, or by Mott and Jorgenson in *Benjamin Franklin*.

[34]*Works* (Sparks ed.), X, 26 f.

[35]*Ibid.*, II, 401.

Naturally one would imagine, that the interest of a few individuals should give way to general interest; but individuals manage their affairs with so much more application, industry, and address, than the public do theirs, that general interest most commonly gives way to particular. We assemble parliaments and councils, to have the benefit of their collected wisdom; but we necessarily have, at the same time the inconvenience of their collected passions, prejudices and private interests. By the help of these, artful men overpower their wisdom, and dupe its possessors; and if we may judge the acts, *arrêts,* and edicts, all the world over, for regulating commerce, an assembly of great men is the greatest fool on earth.[36]

Poor relief was second only to regulation of trade as a field which Franklin would leave untouched by legislation. His earnest injunction, since statutory poor relief existed in America and England, was for repeal of the laws.[37]

Franklin was an important figure in legislative affairs, and the assembly was a small, unicameral group in which personal influence could play an effective role. From 1785 to 1788 he was the chief executive officer, then called the "president," of the new state of Pennsylvania.

Franklin's writings on the poor laws demonstrate strong convictions on the subject, and obviously he must have considered their application in the Pennsylvania statutes while he was burgess, and later as president. It may be indicative of his known interest that, while he was in London, he was notified of the passage of the poor law of 1766, providing incorporated managers of the poor for Philadelphia and surrounding districts.[38] The letter containing a description of the new law was sent by the assembly committee on correspondence.

It is probable that Franklin, who was politically skilful and knew when not to press an issue, withheld efforts to repeal or limit the poor laws in Pennsylvania because of his sense of political expediency and not because he had changed his stand on the question. He wrote at one time in a letter to a friend that "to get the bad Customs of a Country changed, and new ones, though better, introduced, it is necessary first to remove the Prejudices of the People, enlighten their ignorance,

---

[36]*Ibid.,* p. 448.

[37]See *ibid.,* p. 359; X, 407. On his general condemnation of governmental intervention in economic affairs, a younger contemporary, Dugald Stewart (1753–1828), the Scotch philosopher and political economist, observed that "the expressions *laissez-faire* and *pas trop gouverner* are indebted chiefly for their extensive circulation to the short and luminous comments of Franklin, which has so extraordinary an influence on public opinion in the old and new world" (Carey, *op. cit.,* pp. 160 f.).

[38]See Worthington C. Ford (ed.), *Benjamin Franklin Papers in the Library of Congress* (Washington, 1905), p. 14.

and convince them that their Interest will be promoted by the proposed Changes; and this is not the Work of a Day."[39] Repeal of the
Pennsylvania poor laws would not have been the "work of a day," and
Franklin's efforts on the subject were principally centered on "enlight-
enment of the people." He kept his opposition to the poor laws intact—
less than a year before his death at the age of eighty-four he deplored
America's adoption of the English poor law system.[40]

The contemporary influence of Franklin's writings on the poor laws,
as distinct from his direct personal influence, could not have been great,
as his writings on the subject were not immediately and widely
circulated[41] in America.

Nor did his eminent position in Philadelphia result in the consideration of his analyses of the poor laws by early poor law committees.
In 1827, when a committee was appointed to report remedies for the
defects of the poor law system in Philadelphia and surrounding districts, no mention was made of Franklin's poor law views.[42] The same
year a poor law report to the Board of Guardians of the Poor of Philadelphia made no reference to the poor law views of Philadelphia's most
distinguished son.[43]

However, Franklin's activities in founding the Pennsylvania Hospital in Philadelphia in 1751 provided a model for a later experiment in
poor law administration and finance in that city, undertaken while he
was in London as agent for the province. Franklin had been approached in 1751 by a friend who was soliciting contributions for a

---

[39]*Works* (Smyth ed.), IX, 614 f.

[40]See *Works* (Sparks ed.), X, 407.

[41]The views contained in his letters, for example, were not available for many years.
The "Letter to Peter Collinson," written in 1753, was not published until 1834, and
then appeared in the *Gentleman's Magazine* in London. The "Letter to Francis Maseres," 1772, was first published in 1819, again in London. The two letters first appeared in America in 1840 in the Sparks edition of Franklin's works. The essays "On
the Price of Corn, and Management of the Poor" and "On the Laboring Poor," which
were first published in journals in London in 1766 and 1768, respectively, and must
have had at least a limited circulation in the American colonies, were written under
pseudonyms. The former essay was first published under Franklin's name in London
in 1779 and in America in 1809. The latter essay first appeared under his name in
America in 1840 in the Sparks edition of his works.

[42]See William Boyd, Mathew Carey, *et al.*, *Report of the Committee Appointed at a town
meeting of the citizens of the City and County of Philadelphia on the 23d of July, 1827, To
consider the Subject of the Pauper System of the City and districts, and to Report Remedies for
its defects* (Philadelphia, 1827).

[43]Thomas Earp *et al.*, *Report of the Committee appointed by the Board of Guardians of the
Poor of the City and Districts of Philadelphia to visit the cities of Baltimore, New York, Providence, Boston, and Salem* (Philadelphia, 1827).

hospital for the sick poor but who was meeting with little success. Franklin strongly approved the project[44] and worked out a strategy for securing public and private support.[45]

Franklin petitioned the provincial assembly for an appropriation of £2,000 for a hospital for the needy sick and mentally ill of the province—the appropriation to become effective only if private contributions of an equal amount were raised. The plan included incorporation of the private contributors into a managing body for the hospital, with the necessary corporate powers. A bill embodying the plan was introduced through Franklin's influence, passed without difficulty,[46] a drive for private matching donations was promptly successful, and the hospital was established.

The year 1766 was a year of trade stagnation, unemployment, and suffering in Philadelphia. Increasing complaints came from that city about the burden of the poor tax. The overseers of the poor informed the assembly that the poor tax was so great that it could not be raised or repeated, because of the stagnation of business. The almshouse was reported too small, and "provision for work" was deemed essential.[47]

The Franklin plan of financing and administering the Pennsylvania Hospital seemed so successful that the provincial assembly attempted to solve the vexatious problems of financing and operating poor relief in Philadelphia by application of the same method. A bill was prepared and passed the assembly.[48] The Preamble stated that the poor taxes in Philadelphia were burdensome, while, on the other hand, there were many individuals who would be willing to make voluntary contributions.

The act provided that persons in Philadelphia and the surrounding districts who contributed £10 annually to the almshouse and workhouse would be made a body politic for the operation of the institution. They were given power to elect a board of twelve managers and a treasurer each year. They had the authority to erect a new almshouse and workhouse, issue rules, borrow funds, receive gifts, issue reports, etc. The new almshouse was to care for the impotent needy and the workhouse was for the able-bodied. The overseers of the poor were retained to collect taxes and receive applications for outdoor aid. Upon

---

[44]See this *Review*, II (1928), 469–86.

[45]See *Works* (Sparks ed.), I, 164–66.

[46]*Pa. Laws, 1751*, chap. 390. Looking back over the project, Franklin declared: "I do not remember any of my political manoeuvres, the success of which at the time gave me more pleasure; or wherein, after thinking of it I more easily excused myself for having made calculated use of cunning" (*Works* [Sparks ed.], I, 166).

[47]See *Archives of Pennsylvania* (ser. 8), VIII, 5823 f.

[48]*Pa. Laws, 1766*, chap. 534.

complaint of two managers that a person was of disorderly conduct and likely to become chargeable, two magistrates might commit him to the workhouse for three months, unless he provided security.[49]

The assembly soon learned that the financial plan they had borrowed did not work perfectly in the different setting. Private contributions were made, and managers assumed their duties. But they did not have sufficient funds for the buildings planned, and during the year 1767 it was necessary to authorize debts of £3,000 for completion of the project.[50] Difficulties between the managers and the overseers of the poor arose soon after the passage of the act. The managers stopped outdoor relief to save expenses, and overseers vehemently protested the need for discretionary grants of that mode of assistance.[51] The overseers refused to levy taxes for the managers, and the assembly found it necessary in 1768 to authorize justices of the peace or city aldermen to order the overseers to levy poor taxes, upon complaint of the managers that funds were needed.[52] A forfeit of £50 was set as the penalty for refusal by the overseers.

Further difficulties arose during the Revolutionary War because of the impoverishment of many of the contributors and the deaths of others. Few successors replaced the early contributors. In 1779 the assembly passed an act[53] declaring the tax rate insufficient and noting that the occupation of Philadelphia by the British had resulted in depletion of the ranks of contributors and managers. Managers and a treasurer for the almshouse and workhouse were appointed by name in the act, and the tax was raised to 1s. 6 d. for each pound of property and 36s. per poll for each freeman not otherwise rated, to be repeated as often as necessary.

The assembly of 1782 provided[54] that the overseers were to take over the management of the almshouse and workhouse if managers were not elected or if they failed to carry out their duties. The act stated that the care of the poor was expensive and likely to increase and that it was difficult to secure more than a small number of private contributors.

In 1784, the managers accused the overseers of hampering superintendence of the almshouse and workhouse. The overseers petitioned

---

[49]There is no evidence that Franklin was consulted about the application of his plan to statutory poor relief. However, he was notified of the passage of the act.

[50]*Pa. Laws, 1767*, chaps. 552, 567.

[51]Charles Lawrence, *History of the Philadelphia Almshouses and Hospitals* (Philadelphia, 1905), p. 24.

[52]*Pa. Laws, 1768*, chap. 573.

[53]*Pa. Laws, 1779*, chap. 839.

[54]*Pa. Laws, 1782*, chap. 562.

the assembly in 1787, asking for consolidation of the managers and the overseers. The managers retorted that the overseers were remiss in the collection of taxes and furthermore were engaging in unlawful collusions. In 1789 the "Contributors to the relief and employment of the Poor in the City of Philadelphia" failed to elect managers and the overseers were given their duties. The poor law system borrowed from Franklin's hospital plan was defeated by administrative conflict between the semipublic managers and the overseers of the poor and by the failure of the private contributors to provide continuous funds and the requisite attention to administration.[55] The plan which had worked successfully for the privately administered Pennsylvania Hospital was not adaptable to the public poor relief system.

Franklin's popular writing on economic individualism probably influenced the course of statutory poor relief in America and abroad more than his direct analyses of the subject. This influence was indirect and cannot be precisely measured, but there is ample evidence of its importance. It was expressed through the medium of *Poor Richard's Almanack*[56] and its reprints. Franklin published the almanac from 1732 to 1757, selling about ten thousand copies annually. The maxims of thrift, industry, and virtue rested on the assumption that each individual was responsible for his economic situation and could make his material life secure by the exercise of the proper qualities.

The effect of Franklin's maxims was to popularize economic individualism both in Europe and in America and to help create public attitudes inimical to governmental intervention for the destitute. The keystone of opposition to statutory poor relief in the nineteenth century was the allegation that it destroyed individual industry, thrift, and foresight, which were held sufficient to provide the material necessities of existence without public aid.

---

[55]For details of the administration of the Philadelphia Almshouse and Workhouse during 1766–89 see William C. Heffner, *History of Poor Relief Legislation in Pennsylvania 1682–1913* (Cleona, Pa., 1913), pp. 101–6 and Lawrence, *op. cit.*, pp. 30–35.

[56]The *Almanack* of 1757 assembled the proverbs in a connected discourse, "The Way to Wealth," in order to make a greater impression. Its influence is shown by the fact that the discourse was "copied in all the newspapers of the American continent, reprinted in Britain on a large sheet of paper to be stuck up in houses; two translations were made of it in France, and great numbers bought by the clergy and gentry to distribute among their poor parishioners and tenants" (*Works* [Duane ed.], p. 39).

Article 6

FREE BLACKS IN ANTEBELLUM PHILADELPHIA:
A Study of Ex-Slaves, Freeborn, and Socioeconomic Decline

Theodore Hershberg

Afro-American history in general has received a great deal of attention from historians in the past decade. The same cannot be said about the history of black Americans who were free before the Civil War. Studies published since Leon Litwack's *North of Slavery* have considered racial discrimination in the legal tradition, the relationship between race and politics, the establishment of black utopian communities, and the role of blacks in the abolitionist movement.[1] With a few exceptions notable in the earlier studies of the free Negro by Luther P. Jackson and John Hope Franklin, the literature lacks a solid empirical base, a sophisticated methodological and theoretical approach, and a focus on the black community itself.[2] There exists an important need for new studies of the family and social structure, of the development of community institutions such as the church, school and beneficial society, of migration and social mobility.[3]

Antebellum Philadelphia offers the historian an important opportunity to study each of these topics. The free-black population of the city had its roots in the eighteenth century. Its free-black population in 1860, more than 22,000, was the largest outside of the Slave South and second only to Baltimore. All-black churches, schools, and voluntary societies were numerous. The National Negro Convention Movement met for the first time in Philadelphia in 1830, and the city hosted such meetings frequently thereafter. Many of the leading black abolitionists such as James Forten, Robert Purvis, and William Still were Philadelphians. Most significantly for the historian, the data describing all facets of this history are extant. The black history collections and the papers of the Pennsylvania Abolition Society at the Historical Society of Pennsylvania and the Library Company of Philadelphia are even richer for the antebellum period than the Schomburg Collection of the New York Public Library.

In many ways this essay resembles a preliminary progress report.[4] Despite the research and analysis that remain to be done, it is appropriate to discuss several important themes which emerge early in the study of nineteenth-century black Philadelphians: the socioeconomic deterioration of the antebellum black community, the condition of the ex-slaves in the population, and the value of understanding the urban experience for the study of black history.

A Context of Decline

The decision of the Pennsylvania Abolition Society in 1837 to take a census of Philadelphia's free-Negro population was made for both a specific and a general purpose. The specific purpose was to defeat the move, already underway in Harrisburg, to write into the new state constitution the complete disfranchisement of Pennsylvania blacks. The general purpose was "to repel" those who denounced "the whole of the free colored people as unworthy of any favor, asserting that they were nuisances in the community fit only to fill alms houses and jails."[5]

The strategy employed to accomplish these ends reveals a good deal about the faith which the abolitionists had in hard fact and reasoned argument. The data from the census were presented to the delegates at Harrisburg and to the public at large in the form of a forty-page pamphlet summarizing the findings.[6]

The pamphlet argued that disfranchisement should be defeated because the free-Negro population made a worthy contribution to the well-being of the entire community. Blacks paid considerable taxes and rents, owned property, were not disproportionately paupers and criminals, cared for their own underprivileged and, finally, put money as consumers into the income stream of the general economy. The facts contained in the published pamphlet, therefore, "gave great satisfaction affording the friends of the colored people strong and convincing arguments against those who were opposed to their enjoying the rights and privileges of freemen."[7]

Although unsuccessful in the specific purpose—blacks were disfranchised in Pennsylvania until 1870 when the Fifteenth Amendment was adopted—the Abolitionists and Quakers undertook further censuses in 1847 and 1856.[8] As in 1838, these later censuses were followed with printed pamphlets which duly noted the discrimination and problems facing free Negroes and counseled patience to the "magnanimous sufferers," as they referred to their Negro brethren. The general tone of the pamphlets, however, was *optimistic* and pointed to important *gains* made in past decades. The overall optimism, however, proved unfounded when the actual manuscript censuses were submitted to computer analysis.

The "friends of the colored people," unfortunately, had been carried away by their admirable purpose. It was one thing to document that free Negroes were not worthless, that they could indeed survive

TABLE 1

Census: Pa. Abol. Soc. 1838

Variables	Total Households					Male-Headed Households				
	All Freeborn	Ex-slave HH's	Ex-slave HH HD's	Ex-slave HH HD's Bought Selves	All Freeborn	All	Free HD's	Ex-slave HH's Ex-slave Heads All	Manumitted	Bought Selves
Non church goers	17.8%	9.3%	5.4%	3.2%	18.5%	10.5%	13.5%	4.8%	7.1%	3.7%
White churches	5.5%	5.1%	5.7%	7.5%	5.2%	4.3%	4.1%	4.6%	3.8%	5.1%
Baptist	8.7%	10.3%	11.4%	12.9%	8.1%	11.0%	10.0%	12.7%	13.9%	12.8%
Methodist	70.7%	76.5%	74.1%	76.3%	71.1%	75.1%	77.7%	70.6%	70.9%	75.6%
Episc.	7.0%	4.8%	4.7%	2.2%	8.1%	4.6%	0.4%	5.1%	3.8%	2.6%
Presbyt.	7.6%	5.3%	6.7%	5.4%	7.8%	5.8%	4.7%	7.6%	7.6%	5.1%
Cath.	4.1%	1.1%	1.3%	1.1%	2.6%	1.3%	0.9%	2.0%	2.5%	1.3%
Misc.	1.9%	2.0%	1.7%	2.2%	2.3%	2.2%	2.4%	2.0%	1.3%	2.6%
HH chld attnd	27.6%	29.2%	29.0%	35.4%	29.7%	35.9%	35.3%	37.2%	36.5%	38.3%
HH chld not attnd	22.5%	25.4%	15.9%	22.9%	25.2%	28.3%	32.2%	20.1%	17.6%	24.7%
Chld attnd	55.0%	67.1%	71.7%	71.2%	54.9%	61.4%	55.7%	72.7%	75.0%	70.8%
HH w/ members	56.4%	56.1%	60.8%	64.6%	52.0%	57.7%	53.8%	65.2%	62.3%	69.1%
Members	27.1%	27.0%	35.1%	32.4%	25.5%	26.2%	22.6%	34.5%	34.6%	33.0%
White collar	4.0%	5.4%	8.2%	4.9%	4.2%	5.4%	4.4%	7.0%	7.3%	5.1%
Skilled	17.6%	16.6%	18.8%	20.7%	17.5%	15.6%	14.2%	18.4%	17.1%	20.3%
Unskilled	78.4%	78.1%	73.1%	74.4%	78.3%	79.0%	81.4%	74.6%	75.6%	74.7%

outside of the structured environment of slavery and even that they could create a community with their own churches, schools, and beneficial societies; but it was quite another thing to argue that the people and the institutions they created actually *prospered* in the face of overwhelming obstacles. It is not so much that the Abolitionists and Quakers were wrong, as that they went too far. And in so doing, they obscured a remarkable deterioration in the socioeconomic condition of blacks from 1830 to the Civil War.

Beginning in 1829 and continuing through the ensuing two decades, Philadelphia Negroes were the victims of half a dozen major anti-black riots and many more minor mob actions. Negro churches, schools, homes, and even an orphanage were set on fire. Some blacks were killed, many beaten, and others run out of town.[9] Contemporaries attributed the small net loss in the Negro population between 1840 and 1850 in large part to riots.[10] In the same decade, white population grew 63 percent. While it is important to maintain the perspective that the anti-black violence occurred within a larger context of anti-Catholic violence, this knowledge must have been small comfort to Philadelphia Negroes.

A victimized minority, one reasons, should organize and bring *political* pressure on local government officials. But black Philadelphians after 1838, as we have seen, were denied even this remedy. Disfranchisement of all Negroes, even those citizens who owned sufficient property to vote in all elections during the previous 23 years, was all the more tragic and ironic because, at the same time, all white males in Pennsylvania over the age of 21 were specifically given the right to vote.

In addition to the larger, less measurable forces such as race riots, population decline,[11] and disfranchisement, after 1838 black Philadelphians suffered a turn for the worse in wealth, residential segregation, family structure, and employment.

The antebellum black community was extremely poor. The total wealth—that is, the combined value of real and personal property holdings—for three out of every five households in both 1838 and 1847 amounted to sixty dollars or less. This fact, it can be noted in passing, precludes the use of simple economic class analysis in determining social stratification in the black community.[12] The distribution of wealth itself, moreover, was strikingly unequal within the black population. In both 1838 and 1847 the poorest half of the population owned only one-twentieth of the total wealth, while the wealthiest 10 percent of the population held 70 percent of the total wealth; at the very apex of the community, the wealthiest 1 percent accounted for fully 30 percent of the total wealth.[13]

Between 1838 and 1847, there was a 10 percent decrease in per capita value of personal property and a slight decrease in per capita

TABLE 2

| Census: Pa. Abol. Soc. 1838 | Total Households (3,295) (12,084 Persons) | | | | | Male-Headed Households (2,361) (9,609 Persons) | | | | |
| | | | Ex-slave HH HD's | Ex-slave HH HD's | | | | Ex-slave HH's | Ex-slave HH's | Ex-slave HH's |
Variables	All Freeborn	Ex-slave HH's	Ex-slave HH HD's	Bought Selves	All Freeborn	All	Free HD's	All	Heads Manumitted	Bought Selves
Total HH's	2489	806	314	96	1760	601	394	207	85	81
Total persons	8867	3217	1013	358	6966	2643	1852	791	312	327
Fam. size (w/o singles)	3.88	4.27	3.84	4.12	4.06	4.40	4.70	3.99	3.80	4.72
Two-par HH (%)	77.0	79.8	79.3	90.5	99% of all male-headed households with 2 or more persons were two-parent households.					
$0–20 (%)	23.9	19.6	17.5	10.4	21.8	16.3	19.0	11.1	16.5	6.2
$21–40 (%)	21.1	19.6	19.7	11.5	18.6	18.1	19.5	15.5	16.5	8.6
$41–90 (%)	17.8	15.1	14.6	11.5	16.7	14.0	14.7	12.6	12.9	11.1
$91–240 (%)	18.6	21.1	18.8	25.0	20.9	23.0	22.6	23.7	24.7	28.4
$241 + (%)	18.6	24.6	29.3	41.7	22.1	28.6	24.1	37.2	29.4	45.7
Ave. TW	$252	$268	$295	$388	$257	$317	$284	$380	$388	$409
Ave. PP*	$176	$175	$191	$223	$181	$204	$180	$249	$269	$252
All HH's Ave. RP	$76	$93	$105	$164	$69	$113	$103	$131	$119	$157
Owners only Ave. RP	$987	$730	$567	$527	$768	$770	$1017	$564	$776	$472
% RP owners	7.7	12.8	18.5	31.2	9.0	14.6	10.1	23.2	15.3	33.3
Ave. rent	$48	$50	$47	$53	$53	$55	$55	$54	$49	$56

TW = Total Wealth   PP = Personal Property   RP = Real Property   HH = Household

*There is little observable difference between the ave. PP for all HH's and the ave. PP for owners only: 95%–100% of all HH's owned PP.

total wealth among Philadelphia blacks. Although the number of households included in the 1847 census was 30 percent greater than in 1838, the number of real property holders fell from 294 to 280, and their respective percentages fell from 9 to 6 percent. There was, in other words, despite a considerable increase in the number of households, both absolute and percentage decrease in the number of real property holders.

Another way of highlighting the decline is to create roughly equal population groups, rank them by wealth and determine at what point in the rank order blacks ceased to include owners of real property. In 1838 owners of real property extended through the wealthiest 30 percent of the ranked population; in 1847 they extended less than half as far. In 1838, moreover, it required a total wealth holding of between two hundred and three hundred dollars in order to own real property; by 1847 an individual required a total wealth holding twice as high before he could purchase land or own a home.

This statistic is complemented by a measurable rise in residential segregation over the decade. Disfranchisement (perhaps as valuable to us as a symptom of contemporary feelings about Negroes as it was a cause), a decade of race riots, and a general backlash against abolitionist activities, all contributed to the creation of a social atmosphere in which it was considerably more difficult for even the wealthiest of Negroes to acquire real property. It is tempting to conclude quite simply that rising racism meant that a far higher price had to be paid in order to induce a white man to sell land to a black man. Stating such a conclusion with complete confidence, however, requires further *comparative* research in order to determine if instead this phenomenon applied equally to all ethnic groups, i.e., a period of generally appreciating land values.

The actual measurement of residential segregation depends upon the use of a "grid unit"—an area roughly one by one and one-quarter blocks—and is a vast improvement over far larger geographical entities such as districts or wards. Each Negro household was located on detailed maps and its precise grid unit recorded. All variables about each household, then, are observable and measurable in small, uniquely defined units.

Residential segregation is measured in two dimensions: 1. the *distribution* of the household population—that is, the number of grid units in which Negro households were located; and 2. the *density* of the population—that is, the number of Negro households per grid. Residential segregation was rising in the decade before 1838, and it increased steadily to 1860. Between 1838 and 1847 average density increased 13 percent in all grid units inhabited by blacks; more importantly, however, the percentage of households occupying the most dense grid units (those with more than one hundred black households) increased by almost 10

percent. Between 1850 and 1860 the average density changed very little, but the trend toward settlement in the more dense grids continued. By 1860 the number of households occupying the most dense grid
units reached more than one in four, an increase of 11 percent over the
previous decade and the high point between 1838 and 1880. During the
Civil War decade, residential segregation fell off but rose again from
1870 to 1880 as migration from the South swelled the Negro population
of Philadelphia to 31,700, an increase of 43 percent over both the 1860
and 1870 totals.

Data from the Abolitionist and Quaker censuses, the U.S. Census
of 1880, and W. E. B. Du Bois's study of the seventh ward in 1896–97
indicate, in each instance, that two-parent households were characteristic of 78 percent of black families. That statistical average, however,
belies a grimmer reality for the poorest blacks. There was a decline in
the percentage of two-parent households for the poorest fifth of the
population from 70 percent in 1838 to 63 percent ten years later; and
for the poorest half of the black population the decline was from 73
percent to 68 percent. In other words, among the poorest half of the
community at mid-century, roughly one family in three was headed by
a female.[14]

An unequal female-male sex ratio no doubt indirectly affected family
building and stability. Between 1838 and 1860 the number of black
females per 1,000 black males increased from 1,326 to 1,417. For whites
in 1860 the corresponding figure was 1,088. Between 1860 and 1890 the
sex ratio for blacks moved in the direction of parity: 1,360 in 1870,
1,263 in 1880, and 1,127 in 1890. The age and sex distribution throughout the period 1838 to 1890 indicates that the movement away from,
and after 1860 back toward, equal distribution of the sexes was due to
a change in the number of young black males in the 20 to 40 age bracket.
Changes in this age bracket usually result from two related factors:
occupational opportunities and in- and out-migration rates. The re-
markably high excess of females over males throughout the period
probably reflects poor employment opportunities for black men (while
the demand for black female domestics remained high) accompanied
by net out-migration of young black males. The gradual improvement
of industrial opportunities for young black males after 1860, accompanied by net in-migration of increasing numbers of young black men
reduced the excess of black females. The sociological consequences
of such an imbalance in the sex ratios are familiar: illegitimacy, delinquency, broken homes, and such. In light of these statistics, it is
surprising that the percentage of two-parent households was as high
as it was.

More important for our purposes, however, is another measure of
the condition of the entire black population often obscured by the debate over the matrifocality of the black family, focusing as it does on

narrow statistical analysis of traditional household units. How many blacks were living outside of black households? How many were inmates of public institutions? How many were forced not only to delay beginning families, but to make lives for themselves *outside* the black family unit, residing in boarding houses as transients or living in white homes as domestic servants?[15]

The data indicate that there was a slow but steady rise in the percentage of black men and women who found themselves outside the black family. Between 1850 and 1880 their numbers nearly doubled. By 1880, six thousand persons—slightly less than one-third of the adult population (inmates, transients, and servants combined) were living outside the normal family structures. One out of every five adults lived and worked in a white household as a domestic servant. That so many Negroes took positions outside their traditional family units is testimony to the strength and pervasiveness of the job discrimination that existed at large in the economy; that this occurred within a context of widening occupational opportunities for whites, a benefit of increasing industrialization and the factory system, makes it even more significant. In 1847 less than one-half of 1 percent of the black male workforce was employed in factories. And this came at a time, it should be remembered, when thousands of Irish immigrants were engaged in factory work.

Blacks were not only denied access to new jobs in the expanding factory system, but because of increasing job competition with the Irish they also lost their traditional predominance in many semiskilled and unskilled jobs. The 1847 census identified 5 percent of the black male workforce in the relatively well-paying occupations of hod carrier and stevedore. The following letter to a city newspaper written in 1849 by one "P. O." attests to the job displacement.

> That there may be, and undoubtedly is, a direct competition between them (the blacks and Irish) as to labor we all know. The wharves and new buildings attest this fact, in the person of our stevedores and hod-carriers as does all places of labor; and when a few years ago we saw none but blacks, we now see nothing but Irish.[16]

"P. O." proved perceptive indeed. According to the 1850 U. S. Census the percentage of black hod carriers and stevedores in the black male workforce fell in just three years from 5 percent to 1 percent. The 1850 Census, moreover, reported occupations for the entire country and included 30 percent more black male occupations than the 1847 Census; nevertheless the absolute number of black hod carriers fell sharply from 98 to 28 and stevedores from 58 to 27.

A similar pattern of increasing discrimination affected the ranks of the skilled. Blacks complained not only that it was "difficult for them to find places for their sons as apprentices to learn mechanical trades,"[17] but also that those who had skills found it more difficult to practice them. The "Register of Trades of the Colored People," published in 1838 by the Pennsylvania Abolition Society to encourage white patronage of black artisans, noted that 23 percent of 656 skilled artisans did not practice their skills because of "prejudice against them."[18] The 1856 Census recorded considerable deterioration among the ranks of the skilled. The percentage of skilled artisans not practicing their trades rose from 23 percent in 1838 to approximately 38 percent in 1856. Skilled black craftsmen were "compelled to abandon their trades on account of the unrelenting prejudice against their color."[19]

Job discrimination, then, was complete and growing: blacks were excluded from new areas of the economy, uprooted from many of their traditional unskilled jobs, denied apprenticeships for their sons and prevented from practicing the skills they already possessed. All social indicators—race riots, population decrease, disfranchisement, residential segregation, per capita wealth, ownership of real property, family structure, and occupational opportunities—pointed toward socioeconomic deterioration within Philadelphia's antebellum black community.

Ex-slave and Freeborn

Among the 3,300 households and 12,000 persons included in the 1838 census, about one household in four contained at least one person who although free in 1838 had been born a slave. Living in these 806 households were some 1,141 ex-slaves or 9 percent of the entire population.

What was the condition of the ex-slave relative to his freeborn brother? Were ex-slaves in any way responsible for the socioeconomic deterioration just described? Contemporaries perceived two very different effects of direct contact with slavery. "Upon feeble and common minds," according to one view, the slave experience was "withering" and induced "a listlessness and an indifference to the future." Even if the slave somehow managed to gain his freedom, "the vicious habits of slavery" remained, "worked into the very grain of his character." But for others "who resisted . . . and bought their own freedom with the hard-earned fruits of their own industry," the struggle for "liberty" resulted in "a desire for improvement" which "invigorated all their powers and gave energy and dignity to their character as freemen."[20] An analysis of the data permits us to determine whether both groups were found equally in antebellum Philadelphia or whether one was more representative of all ex-slaves than the other.

The richness of detail in the census schedules allows us to make several important distinctions in the data describing the ex-slave households. We know which of the 806 households were headed by ex-slaves themselves—314—and how these 40 percent of all ex-slave households were freed—if, for instance, they were "manumitted" or if, as they put it, they had "bought themselves."

We are dealing, then, with several ex-slave categories: 1. 493 households in which at least one ex-slave lived, but which had a free-born household head; I shall refer to this group as free-headed, ex-slave households; 2. 314 households in which at least one ex-slave lived, but which had an ex-slave household head; I shall refer to this group as ex-slave-headed households. In this second group of ex-slave-headed households, I have selected two subgroups for analysis: a. 146 ex-slave household heads who were manumitted, and b. 96 ex-slave household heads who bought their own freedom.[21]

Cutting across all of these groups is the dimension of sex. The census identified household heads as males, females, and widows. There was a strong and direct relationship between family size, wealth, and male sex, so that the largest families had the most wealth and the greatest likelihood of being headed by a male. Because there was also a strong and direct relationship between sex and almost all other variables, with males enjoying by far the more fortunate circumstances, it is important to differentiate by sex in comparing the general condition of the ex-slave groups to that of the freeborn population. Ex-slaves differed from their freeborn neighbors in a variety of significant social indicators:

Family Size.   The family size of all ex-slave households was 10 percent larger than households all of whose members were freeborn: 4.27 persons as compared to 3.88. Families of ex-slave households headed by freeborn males and those families headed by males who bought their own freedom were 20 percent larger; 4.70. The instances in which freeborn families were larger occurred only where female and, to a lesser extent, widow ex-slave households were involved. (This, by the way, is the general pattern in most variables; in other words, ex-slave females and widows more closely resembled their freeborn counterparts than ex-slave males resembled freeborn males.)

Two-Parent Household.   Two-parent households were generally more common among the ex-slaves. Taken together, two-parent households were found 80 percent of the time among ex-slaves, while the figure for the freeborn was 77 percent. A significant difference, however, was found in the case of ex-slave household heads who bought their own freedom. In this group 90 percent were two-parent households.

Church.   For two basic reasons the all-black church has long been recognized as the key institution of the Negro community: first, an

oppressed and downtrodden people used religion for spiritual sustenance and for its promise of a better life in the next world; second,
with the ability to participate in the political, social, and economic
spheres of the larger white society in which they lived sharply curtailed, Negroes turned to the church for fulfillment of their secular
needs.

Important in the twentieth century, the church was vital to blacks
in the nineteenth. Philadelphia Negroes were so closed off from the
benefits of white society that church affiliation became a fundamental
prerequisite to a decent and, indeed, bearable existence.[22] For this reason, nonchurch affiliation, rather than poverty, was the distinguishing
characteristic of the most disadvantaged group in the community. Nonchurchgoers must have enjoyed few of the benefits and services that
accrued to those who were affiliated with a church in some manner.
The socioeconomic profile of nonchurchgoers is depressing. They fared
considerably less well than their churchgoing neighbors in all significant social indicators: they had smaller families, fewer two-parent
households, high residential density levels, and they were disproportionately poor. Their ratios for membership in beneficial societies and
for the number of school-age children in school was one-fourth and
one-half, respectively, that of the larger community. Occupationally they
were decidedly overrepresented among the unskilled sectors of the
workforce.

In this sense, then, the percentage of households with no members attending church is a more valuable index of general social condition than any other. Eighteen percent of the freeborn households had
no members attending church; for all ex-slave households the figure
was *half* as great. Although ex-slave households were one in four in the
community-at-large, they were less than one in ten among households
with no members attending church. The ratios were even lower (one
in 20) for ex-slave-headed households and lowest (one in 30) for
ex-slaves who bought themselves.

About 150 households or 5 percent of the churchgoing population
of the entire community attended 23 predominately white churches.
These churches had only "token" integration, allowing a few Negroes
to worship in pews set apart from the rest of the congregation. Ex-
slaves of all groups attended white churches in approximately the same
ratio as did the freeborn—one household in 20.

The churchgoing population of the entire community consisted of
2,776 households distributed among five religious denominations:
Methodists (73 percent), Baptists (9 percent), Presbyterians (7 percent),
Episcopalians (7 percent), and Catholics (3 percent). Methodists wor-
shipped in eight and Baptists in four all-black congregations scattered

throughout the city and districts. Together they accounted for more than eight of every ten churchgoers. The various ex-slave groups were found more frequently among Methodists and more frequently among Baptists.

In any case, Methodists and Baptists differed little from each other and to describe them is to characterize the entire community: poor and unskilled. Within each denomination, however, a single church—Union Methodist and Union Baptist—served as the social base for their respective elites. And while ex-slaves attended all of the community's all-black churches, it was in these two churches where the ex-slaves were most frequently found. The ex-slave members of these two churches shared the socioeconomic and cultural characteristics of the community's elite denominations, the Episcopalians and the Presbyterians; and it should not be surprising, therefore, to find ex-slaves of all groups underrepresented in each of these last two denominations.

Beneficial Society.   Next to the church in value to the community were the all-black beneficial societies. These important institutions functioned as rudimentary insurance groups which provided their members with relief in sickness, aid during extreme poverty and burial expenses at death.

There were over 100 distinct societies in antebellum Philadelphia. They grew out of obvious need and were early manifestations of the philosophy of "self-help" which became so popular later in the nineteenth century. Almost always they were affiliated directly with one of the all-black churches. The first beneficial society, known as the "Free African Society," was founded in 1787. A dozen societies existed by 1815, fifty by 1830, and 106 by 1847.

Slightly more than 50 percent of freeborn households were members of the various societies. Making good the philosophy of "self-help," half a century before Booker T. Washington, the societies found ex-slaves more eager to join their ranks than freeborn blacks. Each group of ex-slaves had a higher percentage of members, especially ex-slave-headed households (61 percent), ex-slaves who purchased their own freedom (65 percent), and the males among the latter group (70 percent).

Membership in beneficial societies varied significantly by wealth and status. Ranking the entire household population in 30 distinct wealth categories revealed that, beginning with the poorest, the percentage of membership rose with increasing wealth until the wealthiest six categories. For this top 11 percent of the population, however, membership in beneficial societies declined from 92 to 81 percent. Among the wealthiest, and this applied equally to ex-slaves, there was less need for membership in beneficial societies.

Education.   One household in four among the freeborn population sent children to school. For ex-slave households the corresponding figure was more than one in three. Ex-slave households had slightly fewer children, but sent a considerably greater percentage of their children to school. For freeborn households the percentage was 55 percent; for all ex-slave households 67 percent; and for ex-slave-headed households the figure rose to 72 percent. To the extent that education was valuable to blacks, the ex-slaves were better off.

Location and Density.   Small groups of ex-slaves clustered disproportionately in the outlying districts of Kensington, Northern Liberties, and Spring Garden. Twenty-five percent of the entire black population of Philadelphia, they comprised about 35 percent of the black population in these areas. Most ex-slaves, however, lived in the same proportions and in the same blocks as did the freeborn population.

More interesting than the pattern of their distribution throughout the city, however, was the level of population density in which they lived, i.e., the number of black neighbors who lived close by. To calculate the number of black households in a grid unit of approximately one and one-fourth blocks, three density levels were used: 1–20, 21–100, and in excess of 100 households per grid unit.[23]

The less dense areas were characterized by larger families, greater presence of two-parent households, less imbalance between the sexes, and fewer families whose members were entirely nonnatives of Pennsylvania. In these areas lived a disproportionately greater number of wealthy families, and among them, a correspondingly overrepresented number of real property owners. Here white-collar and skilled workers lived in greater percentages than elsewhere in the city, and unskilled workers were decidedly few in both percentage and absolute number. The major exceptions to the distribution of wealth and skill came as a result of the necessity for shopkeepers and craftsmen to locate their homes and their businesses in the city's more densely populated sections.

Ex-slave households were more likely than freeborn households to be found in the least dense areas (one in four as compared with one in five). Conversely, ex-slave households were less likely to be found in those areas with the greatest density of black population.

Wealth.   The parameters of wealth for Negroes in antebellum Philadelphia have already been described. The community was impoverished. Poverty, nevertheless, did not touch all groups equally. In terms of average total wealth, including both real and personal property, free-headed ex-slave households differed little from the freeborn population. In considering the ex-slave-headed household, however, differences emerge. Average total wealth for this group was 20 percent greater; for males in this group 53 percent greater; and for males who freed themselves, 63 percent greater.

The most significant differences in wealth by far occurred in real property holding. One household in 13 or slightly less than 8 percent among the freeborn owned real property. For all ex-slave households the corresponding ratio was one in eight; for ex-slave-headed households, one in five; for males who were in this group one in four; and most dramatically, for males who purchased their own freedom, one in three owned real property. To these ex-slaves, owning their own home or a piece of land must have provided something (perhaps a stake in society) of peculiarly personal significance. Distribution of wealth, to view the matter from a different perspective, was less unequal for ex-slave households, particularly ex-slave household heads. The poorest half of the freeborn and ex-slave-headed households owned 5 and 7 percent respectively of the total wealth; for the wealthiest quarter of each group the corresponding figure was 86 and 73 percent; for the wealthiest tenth, 67 and 56 percent; and for the wealthiest one-hundredth, 30 and 21 percent. Overall wealth distribution, in other words, while still skewed toward pronounced inequality, was more equally distributed for ex-slave household heads in the middle and upper wealth categories.

Occupation.   The final area of comparison between the ex-slaves and the freeborn is occupation.[24] Analysis of the data using the same classification schema for Negroes as for white ethnic groups confirms an earlier suspicion that, although such schemata are necessary in order to compare the Negro to white ethnic groups, they are entirely unsatisfactory tools of analysis when social stratification in the Negro community is the concern. Despite the fact that the Negroes who comprised the labor force of antebellum Philadelphia described themselves as engaged in four hundred different occupations, a stark fact emerges from the analysis: there was almost no occupational differentiation!

Five occupations accounted for 70 percent of the entire male workforce: Laborers (38 percent), porters (11.5 percent), waiters (11.5 percent), seamen (5 percent), and carters (4 percent); another 10 percent were employed in miscellaneous laboring capacities. Taken together, eight out of every ten working men were unskilled laborers. Another 16 percent worked as skilled artisans, but fully one-half of this fortunate group were barbers and shoemakers; the other skilled craftsmen were scattered among the building-construction (3.2 percent), home-furnishing (1.3 percent), leather goods (1.2 percent), and metal work (1.2 percent) trades. Less than one-half of one percent of Negroes, as pointed out in another context, found employment in the developing factory system. The remaining 4 percent of the labor force were engaged in white-collar professions. They were largely proprietors who sold food or second-hand clothing from vending carts, and should not be considered as "storeowners."

The occupational structure for females was even less differentiated than for males. More than eight out of every ten women were employed in day-work capacities (as opposed to those who lived and worked in white households) as domestic servants: "washers" (52 percent), "day workers" (22 percent), and miscellaneous domestics (6 percent). Fourteen percent worked as seamstresses, and they accounted for all the skilled workers among the female labor force. Finally, about 5 percent were engaged in white-collar work, which, like the males, meant vending capacities in clothing- and food-selling categories.

It should come, then, as no surprise that there were few distinctions of significance in the occupational structure of the ex-slaves and freeborn workforces. The differences in vertical occupational categories find male ex-slave household heads more likely to be in white-collar positions (7 percent as opposed to 4 percent for the freeborn), equally distributed in the skilled trades, and slightly less represented in the unskilled occupations (75 percent as opposed to 78 percent). Within the horizontal categories there were few important differences. Male ex-slave household heads were more likely than the freeborn to be employed as porters, carpenters, blacksmiths, preachers, and clothes dealers.

In summary, then, we find the ex-slaves with larger families, greater likelihood of two-parent households, higher affiliation rates in church and beneficial societies, sending more of their children to school, living more frequently in the least dense areas of the county, generally wealthier, owning considerably more real property, and being slightly more fortunate in occupational differentiation. By almost every socioeconomic measure the ex-slave fared better than his freeborn brother. While ex-slaves were distributed throughout the socioeconomic scale, they were more likely to be part of the community's small middle class which reached into both the lower and upper strata, characterized more by their hard-working, conscientious and God-fearing life style than by a concentration of wealth and power.

An Urban Perspective

On the basis of the data presented it is possible to state two conclusions, offer a working hypothesis, and argue for the necessity of an urban perspective. First, the relatively better condition of the ex-slave, especially the ex-slave who was both a male and who bought his own freedom, confirms the speculations of a few historians that the slave-born Negro freed before the Civil War was exceptional: a uniquely gifted individual who succeeded in internalizing the ethic of deferred gratification in the face of enormous difficulties.[25] More striking was the fact that the socioeconomic condition of the great majority of ex-slaves was not markedly inferior to that of the freeborn. That ex-slaves were generally better off than freeborn blacks, however, should not suggest anything more than relative superiority; it does not imply prosperity and should not obscure the generally impoverished and deteriorating condition of the black community. Second, because the remaining 91 percent of Philadelphia's antebellum black population was freeborn, the dismal and declining socioeconomic circumstances of that population cannot be attributed to direct contact with the "slave experience." Direct contact with slavery was undoubtedly a *sufficient* cause of low status and decay; it most certainly was not a *necessary* cause.[26]

In a very important sense the first conclusion has little to do with the second. The latter is not arrived at because those who had direct contact with slavery fared better in the city than those who were born free. The second conclusion is not based upon a recognition that slavery was less destructive or benign (although in some aspects it certainly could have been so), but rather that the antebellum Northern city was destructive as well. It is significant to understand that slavery and the discrimination faced by free Negroes in the urban environment were both forms of racism which pervaded the institutions and informed the values of the larger white society.

The comparison of the freeborn and the ex-slave was undertaken in an effort to learn more about the question that students of the black experience want answered: What was the effect of slavery on the slaves? In the case of antebellum Philadelphia the ex-slaves may not be representative of the slave experience. If they were, however, our insight would necessarily be limited to the effect of the mildest slavery system as it was practiced in Maryland, Delaware, and Virginia.[27]

Deemphasizing direct contact with slavery does not imply that the institution of slavery, and the debasement and prejudice it generated, did not condition the larger context. The indirect effect of slavery cannot be underestimated. The pro-slavery propaganda provided the justification not only for the institution, but for the widespread discriminatory treatment of the free Negro both before and long after emancipation.

Yet, on the other hand, one must not allow this understanding, or an often overwhelming sense of moral outrage, to lead to a monolithic interpretation of the effects of the slave experience. Stanley Elkin's treatment of slavery may be in error, but few historians doubt that his urging of scholars to end the morality debate and to employ new methods and different disciplines in the study of slavery was correct and long overdue.

There is no historically valid reason to treat the slave experience as entirely destructive or entirely benign; nor, for that matter, does historical reality necessarily fall midway between the two. It may be more useful to study the problems that blacks faced at different times and in different places in their history and make the attempt to trace their historical origins rather than to begin with slavery and assume that it represented in all instances the historical root. Some of the problems faced by blacks may more accurately be traced to the processes of urbanization, industrialization, and immigration, occurring in a setting of racial inequality, rather than to slavery.

One of the most significant contributions to black history and sociology in recent years presents data that suggest the post-slavery, possibly urban, origins of the matrifocal black family. In groundbreaking essays on the Negro family after the Civil War, Herbert Gutman has demonstrated convincingly that traditional interpretations of slavery and its effect on the black family are seriously misleading. Examining "the family patterns of those Negroes closest in time to actual chattel slavery," Gutman did not find "instability," "chaos," or "disorder." Instead, in fourteen varied Southern cities and counties between 1865 and 1880, he found viable two-parent households ranging from 70 to 90 percent.[28]

It is significant to note that of the areas studied by Gutman the four lowest percentages of two-parent households were found in cities: Natchez and Beaufort, 70 percent; Richmond, 73 percent; and Mobile, 74 percent. The urban experience was in some way responsible for the weaker family structure, and for a whole set of other negative socioeconomic consequences, all of which are found in the Philadelphia data.

Yet the city is more than a locale. Slavery itself underwent major transformations in the urban setting.[29] Sustained advances in technology, transportation, and communication made the city the context for innovation; and the innovation, in turn, generated countless opportunities for upward mobility for those who could take advantage of them. And here was the rub. Blacks, alone among city dwellers, were excluded not only from their fair share, but from almost any chance for improvement generated by the dynamics of the urban milieu. That the exclusion was not systematic, but, by and large, incidental, did not make it any less effective. The city provided an existence at once superior to and inferior to that of the countryside: for those who were free to pursue their fortunes, the city provided infinitely more opportunities and far greater rewards; for those who were denied access altogether (or for those who failed) the city provided scant advantages and comforts. There were few interstices.

The data presented in this essay point to the destructiveness of the urban experience for blacks in nineteenth-century Philadelphia.[30] To proceed, data comparing the black experience to that of other ethnic groups are necessary and they are forthcoming. Although much research remains, it is possible to offer a hypothesis. The forces that shaped modern America—urbanization, industrialization, and immigration—operated for blacks within a framework of institutional racism and structural inequality. In the antebellum context, blacks were unable to compete on equal terms with either the native-white-American worker or the thousands of newly arrived Irish and German immigrants. Philadelphia Negroes suffered in the competition with the Irish and Germans and recovered somewhat during the Civil War and Reconstruction decades, only to suffer again, in much the same circumstances, in competition with the "new" immigrant groups, this time the Italians, Jews, Poles, and Slavs who began arriving in the 1880s. Best characterized as a low-status economic group early in the century, Philadelphia's blacks found themselves a deprived and degraded caste at its close.

Students of black history have not adequately appreciated the impact of the urban experience. In part this is due to several general problems: to the larger neglect of urban history; to unequal educational opportunities which prevented many potential black scholars from study and other students from publication; to difficulties inherent in writing history "from-the-bottom-up"; and to present reward mechanisms which place a high premium on quickly publishable materials involving either no new research or shoddy and careless efforts.

There are, however, other and more important considerations, with no little sense of irony. The moral revulsion to slavery prevented development of alternative explanations of low status and decay. In the immediate post-slavery decades and throughout the twentieth century blacks and their white allies took refuge in an explanation used by many abolitionists before them, namely, that slavery and not racial inferiority was responsible for the black condition. They were, of course, not wrong: It was rather that they did not go far enough. It was, and still is, much easier to lament the sins of one's forefathers than it is to confront the injustices in more contemporary socioeconomic systems.

Although August Meier and Elliot Rudwick titled their well-known and widely used text, *From Plantation to Ghetto,* and, with the little data available to them, subtly but suggestively wove the theme of the impact of urban environment through their pages, scholars have been slow to develop it in monographic studies.

The Philadelphia data from 1838 to 1880 enable one to examine this theme in minute detail. Although 90 percent of the nation's black population in 1880 was Southern and overwhelmingly rural, the key to the twentieth century lies in understanding the consequences of the migration from the farm to the city. The experience of Philadelphia Negroes in the nineteenth century foreshadowed the fate of millions of black migrants who, seeking a better life, found different miseries in what E. Franklin Frazier called the "cities of destruction."

If we are to succeed in understanding the urban experience, we must dismiss simplistic explanations which attribute all present-day failings to "the legacy of slavery" or to "the problems of unacculturated rural migrants lacking the skills necessary to compete in an advanced technology." We must understand, instead, the social dynamics and consequences of competition and accommodation among different racial, ethnic, and religious groups, taking place in an urban context of racial discrimination and structural inequality.

NOTES

1. Leon Litwack, *North of Slavery* (Chicago, 1961); Arthur Zilversmit, *The First Emancipation* (Chicago, 1967); Eugene H. Berwanger, *The Frontier Against Slavery: Western Anti-Negro Prejudice and the Slavery Extension Controversy* (Urbana, 1967); V. Jacques Voegeli, *Free but Not Equal: The Midwest and the Negro During the Civil War* (Chicago, 1969); James A. Rawley, *Race and Politics* (Philadelphia, 1969); Eric Foner, *Free Soil, Free Labor, Free Men* (New York, 1970); William and Jane Pease, *Black Utopia* (Madison, 1963); Benjamin Quarles, *Black Abolitionists* (New York, 1969); Carleton Mabee, *Black Freedom: The Non-Violent Abolitionists, 1830 to the Civil War* (New York, 1970).
2. Luther P. Jackson, *Free Negro and Property Holding in Virginia 1830–1860* (New York, 1942), and John Hope Franklin, *The Free Negro in North Carolina, 1790–1860* (Chapel Hill, 1943); there are, of course, many other state and local studies: W. E. B. Du Bois, *The Philadelphia Negro* (Philadelphia, 1899); Edward R. Turner, *The Negro in Pennsylvania* (Washington, 1911); John Russell, *The Free Negro in Virginia, 1830–1860* (Baltimore, 1913); John Daniels, *In Freedom's Birthplace: A Study of Boston's Negroes* (Boston, 1914); James M. Wright, *The Free Negro in Maryland* (New York, 1921); Robert A. Warner, *New Haven Negroes* (New Haven, 1940); Emma Lou Thornbrough, *The Negro in Indiana* (Indianapolis, 1957). Especially valuable articles include Carter Woodson, "The Negroes of Cincinnati Prior to the Civil War," *Journal of Negro History* 1 (January 1916); Charles S. Sydnor, "The Free Negro in Mississippi before the Civil War," *American Historical Review* 32 (July 1927); E. Horace Fitchett, "The Origin and Growth of the Free Negro Population of Charleston, South Carolina," *Journal of Negro History* 26 (October 1941); J. Merton England, "The Free-Negro in Ante Bellum Tennessee," *Journal of Southern History* 9 (February 1943).
3. There are, of course, important beginnings. Among are E. Franklin Frazier's *The Free Negro Family* (Nashville, 1932) and Carter G. Woodson's *The Education of the Negro Prior to 1861* (Washington, 1915), *History of the Negro Church* (Washington, 1921), and *Free Negro Heads of Families in the United States* (Washington, 1925). Fortunately there are studies of the free Negro currently underway and others awaiting publication which will make important contributions to the literature. I am aware of the following studies: Ira Berlin, University of Illinois, Chicago Circle, on the free Negro in the Upper South; Rhoda Freeman, Upsala College, on the free

Negro in New York; Carol Ann George, Oswego State College, on the free Negro church; Laurence Glasco, University of Pittsburgh, on the free Negro in Buffalo and Pittsburgh; Floyd Miller, Hiram College, on Martin Delany and the colonization movement; Carl Oblinger, Johns Hopkins University, on free Negro communities in Southeastern Pennsylvania towns; Armisted Robinson, University of Rochester, on free Negroes in Memphis; Harry Silcox, Temple University, on free Negro education in Philadelphia and Boston; Arthur O. White, College of Education, University of Florida, on the free Negro in Boston; Marina Wikramanayake, University of Texas, El Paso, on the free Negro in Charleston.

4. For a description of the data compiled by the Philadelphia Social History Project, see Appendix II.

5. Edward Needles, *Ten Years' Progress: A Comparison of the State and Condition of the Colored People in the City and County of Philadelphia from 1838 to 1847* (Philadelphia, 1849), pp. 7–8.

6. Pennsylvania Abolition Society, *The Present State and Condition of the Free People of Color of the City of Philadelphia and Adjoining Districts* (Philadelphia, 1838).

7. Needles, *op. cit.*, pp. 7–8.

8. Society of Friends. *Statistical Inquiry into the Condition of the People of Color of the City and Districts of Philadelphia* (Philadelphia, 1849); Benjamin Bacon. *Statistics of the Colored People of Philadelphia* (Philadelphia, 1859), second ed., revised.

9. Sam Bass Warner, Jr., *The Private City* (Philadelphia, 1968), see ch. 7, "Riots and the Restoration of Order," pp. 125–57.

10. Society of Friends, *op. cit.*, p. 7.

11. There was also a net population loss for blacks of 0.17 percent between 1860 and 1870; the white population in the same decade, however, increased some 20 percent.

12. Social distinctions indispensable to the study of social stratification do exist among this 60 percent of the household population; however, they do not emerge along economic lines. Households averaging thirty dollars of total wealth are not distinctively different from households worth twenty dollars or fifty dollars. Important social distinctions can be determined by using specific noneconomic measures such as church affiliation or a more general noneconomic measure such as "life style" which, in turn, is described by a number of other variables: residence, family structure, education, occupation, etc.

13. The unequal distribution of wealth was not unique to the black population. Stuart Blumin, "Mobility and Change in Ante-Bellum Philadelphia," in Stephan Thernstrom and Richard Sennett, eds., *Nineteenth-Century Cities* (New Haven, 1969) found greater inequality among a sample of the entire Philadelphia population in the U.S. Census for 1860 than I did among all blacks in the Abolitionist and Quaker censuses in 1838 and 1847: the wealthiest 10 percent of 1860 owned 89 percent of the wealth and the wealthiest 1 percent owned 50 percent of the wealth. Data describing the universe of black, Irish, and German property-holders in the U.S. Census for Philadelphia in 1860, however, indi-

cate that inequality was pronounced in all three groups: in each case the wealthiest 10 percent of the population owned about 88 percent of the wealth. The Lorenz measures for the blacks, Irish, and Germans were .95, .94, and .92 respectively.

14. Ninety-nine percent of all male-headed households were two-parent households as well. Female-headed households in the Abolitionist and Quaker censuses were invariably one-parent households.

15. The data necessary to answer a series of important questions concerning the black men and women who lived and worked in white households as domestic servants will soon be available. Their age structure, marital status, mobility, social status, and the possibility of their families living close by will be examined. It will be valuable to know whether "live-in" service was a short-term or long-term experience and to determine its effects on family-building, family structure, and child-rearing techniques. Perhaps the most important question, and one which relates this form of employment to the experience of other ethnic groups, is whether such employment was seen by blacks as severely limiting, demeaning, and poor-paying—engaged in only because there were no other occupational alternatives available to them—or if they embraced such work as their own domain, desirable and pleased by the standards of living it afforded them.

16. The *Daily Sun*, November 10, 1849. I am indebted to Bruce Laurie who originally came across this letter in his rigorous research on ethnic divisions within the working class of antebellum Philadelphia.

17. *Register of the Trades of the Colored People in the City of Philadelphia and Districts* (Philadelphia, 1838), pp. 1–8.

18. Appendix to the *Memorial from the People of Color to the Legislature of Pennsylvania*, reprinted in *Hazard's Register*, 1832, Vol. IX, p. 361.

19. Benjamin C. Bacon, *Statistics of the Colored People of Philadelphia* (Philadelphia, 1859), second ed., pp. 13–15.

20. Needles, *op. cit.*, p. 2.

21. The data describing the ex-slaves and the freeborn, although comprehensive, are not complete; specific age, specific place of birth, and length of residence information are not included in the census. Such data will become available for a significant number of individuals only after linkage between censuses (especially between the Quaker census of 1847 and the U.S. Census of 1850) is accomplished because the latter began in 1850 to list age and place of birth data for every individual. While no explicit data exist in any of the censuses describing the length of residence, linkage will provide approximations of this information, especially where in-migrants (those not listed in 1838 but found in ensuing censuses) are concerned.

David Gerber of Princeton University pointed out to me that the absence of such data in this essay may represent serious limitations, for "there may well be intervening variables which offer a better and very different interpretation of the data than the simple fact of free-birth and ex-slave status." No doubt other variables such as age and length of residence will affect some of my conclusions; however, I am of the opinion that when such information is analyzed the essential findings will remain intact. The most significant differences between the ex-slave and the freeborn are found among a specific group of ex-slaves: those who purchased their own freedom. This information makes it clear that we are dealing not with children who left slavery before its mark was firmly implanted on them, but with adults who must have worked long and hard in order to save up the money necessary to secure their freedom. I do not believe that knowing their exact age or length of residence in the city would affect to a greater degree their peculiarly high level of achievement in Philadelphia.

22. The data describing church affiliation are derived from the Abolitionist and Quaker census categories "name of religious meeting you attend" and "number attend religious meeting." These terms and the very high percentage of positive respondents make it clear that we are not dealing here with formal, dues-paying, church membership, but rather with a loose affiliation with a church.

23. Admittedly crude at this stage of research, the population density technique of analysis nevertheless yields interesting and important information; and with refinement promises to be an invaluable tool for the study of neighborhood, and its relation to social mobility, class ecology, and community structure.

24. The construction of meaningful occupational categories has thus far proven to be the most difficult part of the research. While constructing such categories for the Irish, German, and native white American workforce (currently underway) is certainly complex, one at least has the benefit of considerable occupational differentiation which provides vertical distance, a prerequisite for the study of social mobility and social stratification. Some 13 vertical categories including white collar/skilled/unskilled, nonmanual/manual, proprietary/nonproprietary, and combinations of these schemata, and 102 horizontal categories including building-construction, food, clothing, and domestic service were constructed for the study of the black occupational structure.

25. See the discussion of the "hiring-out system," pp. 38–54, in Richard C. Wade, *Slavery in the Cities* (New York, 1964). It is highly likely that many of the ex-slave household heads who bought their freedom had, in fact, experienced the hiring-out system first-hand and migrated to Philadelphia.

26. There is some reason to believe that the total number of ex-slaves (1,141 or one out of every five persons who migrated to Pennsylvania) is understated. 1838 was not too early for free blacks to fear being sent South illegally or legally as runaway slaves. It is understandable, therefore, that despite the fact that Philadelphia blacks were asked by their clergymen to cooperate with the two census-takers (a white Abolitionist, Benjamin Bacon, and the black minister of the First African Presbyterian Church, Charles Gardner), many blacks who had in fact been born slaves reported instead that they had been born free. Although it is impossible to determine whether those who were nonnatives of Pennsylvania had been in fact slave-born or freeborn, the likelihood that ex-slaves are

underestimated is further supported by the fact that 50 percent of the black population had been born outside of Pennsylvania.

Of course, the important consideration concerns the consequences of understating the actual number of ex-slaves among the black population. If the socioeconomic condition of the ex-slaves who identified themselves as freeborn was significantly worse than the actual freeborn, and if their numbers were sufficiently large enough, the conclusions offered in this essay would to a certain extent be compromised. The problem, however, can be resolved.

Consider the following: for the same reasons that one suspects that the ex-slaves are underenumerated, it is unlikely that many blacks born free or slave in the free states migrated to Philadelphia. It is also unlikely that more than a few elderly Pennsylvania-born blacks who had once been slaves were included in the 1838 census: Pennsylvania's gradual emancipation law had been passed in 1780. When we speak of the ex-slaves, whether or not correctly identified in the census, therefore, we can be fairly certain that they were not natives of Pennsylvania, but had migrated from the Upper South. When all freeborn migrants (read as including a significant number of unidentified ex-slaves) were compared to all freeborn natives their socioeconomic profile was strikingly similar to that of the identified ex-slaves. In other words, the one population cohort in which unidentified ex-slaves might be found was at least as well off as the freeborn native population and in some important respects was better off.

27. To determine the effect of slavery on the slaves as compared to blacks who were born free or who won their freedom before the Civil War, we would have to look someplace after 1865. No one has yet found any data for the post-Emancipation period that distinguishes the freed men from the freeborn (or from those freed before the Civil War). We can make the assumption that because 94 percent of the blacks in the South were slaves in 1860, a significant percentage of the migrants from the South after the Civil War were ex-slaves. But even if we discount the fact that if the the migrants came from Maryland, Delaware, or the District of Columbia they were more likely to have been free before the Civil War (55 percent of all blacks in these areas were free in 1860), we are still left with the problem of representativeness. To put it another way, even if we had data that distinguished the freed men from the freeborn we would still be left with only the typical migrant, not the typical ex-slave. There is every reason to believe that Carter Woodson was correct in his observation that the migrants who came to the cities of the North before the Great Migration were not typical at all, but rather, representatives of the "Talented Tenth." The migrants who came after 1910, and especially after 1915, although not "typical" of the millions of Southern blacks who did not migrate, were nevertheless far more representative of Southern blacks than those who migrated before them. They came to the North for different reasons than did those who left the South a generation earlier, say between 1875 and 1900. The "push and pull" factors

(floods, drought and the boll weevil, and the demand for industrial labor heightened by the end of immigration from Europe) which led to the Great Migration simply were not operative in the earlier period. Those who came before 1900 were probably motivated for different reasons; the problems they faced in the South and the opportunities they saw in the North, if not different in kind, were certainly different in degree.

The logic of the situation suggests that we examine a Northern city during the period of the Great Migration, which had a significantly large antebellum black community and which experienced migration from the South between 1865 and 1900, hoping to identify and study three distinct groups of blacks: natives-of-the-city, migrants arriving before 1900 (the "Talented Tenth") and migrants arriving after 1900 (the "typical" migrant). The problem with this approach is twofold: first, we would no longer be dealing with the "typical" ex-slave, but with his children; second, the data necessary to distinguish the three groups among the population are not available.

28. Herbert Gutman, "The Invisible Fact: Negro Family Structure Before and After the Civil War," paper read at the *Association for the Study of Negro Life and History* (Birmingham: October 1969) and in a revised form at the *Organization of American Historians* (Los Angeles: April 1970). Also see Gutman, *The Black Family in Slavery and Freedom, 1750–1925* (New York, 1976).

29. Richard Wade, *op. cit.*, "The Transformation of Slavery in the Cities," pp. 243–82.

30. A major interest of my research is to develop and make explicit for the city the characteristics of an "urban component" which distinguishes the urban from the rural experience. There is certainly general agreement that urban conditions differ from rural ones in significant dimensions: family structure, sex ratios, mortality, fertility, housing conditions, diet, educational and occupational opportunities plus the intangibles of values and expectations. In future work, however, I hope to demonstrate that it is seriously misleading to treat these urban/rural differences monolithically. The racial discrimination and structural inequality of the city affected each ethnic group differently. The advantages of the city were never equally available for all.

Article 7

BUILDING CHARACTER AMONG THE URBAN POOR
The Charity Organization Movement

Paul Boyer

Josephine Shaw was a pretty and vivacious young woman of Boston, the daughter of a prominent old family, when the Civil War began. But when her beloved brother Robert Gould Shaw and her husband of a year, Charles Russell Lowell, were killed in battle, a great gash was torn across the familiar contours of her life, leaving it permanently altered. Donning the black mourning garb she would wear for the rest of her life, the twenty-year-old widow and new mother plunged into a round of charitable activity that led eventually to the directorship of the New York Charity Organization Society.[1]

What was "charity organization"? Why did it so appeal to Mrs. Lowell and others of her generation? And why does it merit a chapter in a study of social control in the American city?

While some urban moral reformers of the Gilded Age tried to work through the church, many others operated outside ecclesiastical channels. These ostensibly secular efforts took many forms and were aimed at many targets. "Social purity" organizations in a number of cities directed their fire against those who advocated municipal toleration of prostitution. (When the Saint Louis City Council began an experiment with regulated prostitution in the city in 1870, alarm bells rang in moral-reform circles all over the country.) Anthony Comstock's vice society and its counterparts focused on the urban purveyors of obscene literature, gambling schemes, and contraceptives. Elbridge Gerry's Society for the Prevention of Cruelty to Children (founded in 1875 in New York, and later extended to other cities) combated not only the physical abuse of the young but their moral degradation as well.[2]

And, like the antebellum mill owners of Lowell, a few Gilded Age industrialists tried to supervise the moral lives of their employees. The best known of these was George Pullman, builder of railroad sleeping cars, who in 1880 founded the town of Pullman on the outskirts of Chicago to house his workers and their families. As both employer and landlord (houses were rented, never sold), Pullman made his company

SOURCE: Reprinted by permission of the publishers from *Urban Masses and Moral Order In America, 1820–1920*, by Paul Boyer, Cambridge, Massachusetts: Harvard University Press, Copyright © 1978 by the President and Fellows of Harvard College.

town a controlled environment reflecting his own moral standards. Brothels, dance halls, and gambling establishments were banished, and liquor was available only in a hotel patronized by visitors rather than the resident workers. To fill the vacuum created by the absence of alcohol, he developed a variety of positive alternatives, as he explained in an 1882 interview: "We have provided a theatre [limited to plays of the "utmost propriety"], a reading room, billiard room, and all sorts of outdoor sports, and by this means our people soon forget all about drink, . . . and we have an assurance of our work being done with greater accuracy and skill."[3]

But single issue societies and paternalistic efforts like Pullman's did not represent the major innovative thrust of Gilded Age urban moral reformism. In these years, increasing numbers of middle-class Americans became persuaded that only a comprehensive, systematic, and orchestrated effort could stave off moral decay and social disintegration among the urban masses. Out of this conviction grew the charity organization movement, which for a few heady decades seemed to hold out the promise that the chronic moral and social concerns associated with the slums were at last on the road to solution.

Reduced to essentials, the charity organization movement rested on three simple but sweeping assumptions: first, the roots of urban poverty lay in the moral deficiencies and character flaws of the poor; second, the eradication of the slum evil depended upon bringing the poor to recognize and correct these deficiencies; and third, the realization of this goal would require a greater degree of cooperation among the diverse, often overlapping charitable societies of the typical large city. These were the ideas that struck the generation of the 1870s and 1880s with such revelatory force and drew thousands of middle-class volunteers into charity organization work.

Developments in England provided the immediate inspiration. In 1864 a well-to-do London woman named Octavia Hill had begun to buy and renovate tenements and rent them to poor families whom she then visited regularly, not only as landlady but as moral guardian. Soon Hill was managing over 400 rooms, and sympathetic observers were marveling at the "social and moral reformation" as she "gradually fashioned each tenement into a 'home.' "[4]

What Octavia Hill attempted individually, the London Society for Organizing Charitable Relief and Repressing Mendicity (1869) tried to achieve institutionally. Influenced by the earlier work of the Reverend Thomas Chalmers in Edinburgh and guided by the able Charles Stewart Loch, general secretary from 1875 to 1913, this organization worked to expose professional beggars, eliminate indiscriminate almsgiving, and bring about the moral rehabilitation of the poor.[5]

It was a onetime volunteer in London charitable work, the Anglican clergyman S. Humphreys Gurteen, who founded the first American charity organization society, in Buffalo, in 1877. Having witnessed the New York draft riots of 1863, Gurteen could never forget the "revolting spectacle."

> 5,000 men, women and children sweeping down the leading avenue of the city in the darkness of night, the lurid flames of a hundred torches disclosing a scene of wild license scarcely surpassed by any single incident of the French Revolution; women, and mothers at that, with their bare breasts exposed to the winds of heaven, brandishing deadly weapons and uttering foul and loathsome language; . . . while the very air as they passed was polluted by their drunken breath.[6]

The rail and shipping center of Buffalo, where Gurteen was associate rector of Saint Paul's Episcopal Cathedral, had suffered severely in the Depression of the mid-1870s, and in the turbulent year 1877 it seemed that the scenes of 1863 might soon be reenacted. Such grim forebodings form the backdrop of Gurteen's appeals on behalf of the charity organization idea. *"We shall have ourselves alone to blame,"* he wrote, *"if the poor, craving for human sympathy, yet feeling their moral deformity, should some find day wreak their vengeance upon society at large."*[7]

For all the urgency of his rhetoric, Gurteen's proposed remedy was hardly new in 1877. In addition to the English precedents, a number of Americans—Boston's Joseph Tuckerman, Cincinnati's Thomas H. Perkins, New York's Robert Hartley, and others—had earlier urged comprehensive moral-control strategies almost identical to those of the charity organization enthusiasts: the division of the city into districts; the compilation of dossiers on everyone requesting relief; and the use of middle-class visitors to approach the uplift task on a family-by-family basis.[8]

What happened in 1877 was not that a new approach to urban moral control was discovered but that the moment was ripe for one that had been around for years. Labor violence had raged in many cities that summer; the urban moral challenge seemed beyond the capacity of existing organizations; and the non-Protestant character of the new immigrants sharply limited the effectiveness of traditional church-based approaches. So it was that from its beginnings in Buffalo, "charity organization" spread like wildfire in the later 1870s and the 1880s, quickly becoming, as one historian has noted, almost a fad. By the 1890s over 100 cities had charity organization societies; the movement had attracted an impressive array of able leaders; journals like *Lend-a-Hand* (Boston), *Charities Review* (New York), and *Charities Record* (Baltimore) were providing publicity and a forum for ideas; and the annual

National Conference of Charities and Corrections (NCCC) had emerged to give the leadership an opportunity to formulate policy and discuss issues of common concern.[9]

Like the supporters of the AICP in an earlier day, the men and women who rallied to the charity organization movement believed implicitly that urban poverty was mainly the result not of economic or structural maladjustments in society, but of the individual failings of the poor themselves. Indeed, the judgmental moralism that had from the beginning shaped American responses to the slum found its fullest expression in the charity organization movement.

The conviction that the able-bodied poor were *personally responsible* for their condition saturates the handbooks, journals, speeches, and even private correspondence of the early charity organization leaders. These were not callous people. They could write feelingly of the physical circumstances of slum life—the overcrowding, the epidemics, the infant mortality, the poor nutrition, the family disruption—but like William Ellery Channing a generation before, they always probed for the moral flaws that underlay such conditions. "Misery and suffering," declared one handbook, "are the inevitable results of idleness, filth, and vice." In most instances, agreed a Boston leader, poverty's roots lay in "the characters of the poor themselves." S. Humphreys Gurteen left no doubts on this score in his influential *Handbook of Charity Organization* (1882). It was "self-indulgence" and other personal failings, he asserted, that produced urban poverty, turned the tenement household into a "sickening and ghastly caricature of a 'home,' " and made the "moral atmosphere" of the slum "as pestilential as the physical."[10] (Influenced by advances in germ theory and epidemiology, the early charity organization spokesmen often employed public-health analogies, speaking freely of moral "infections," "contagions," and "plague spots.")

The task, then, was what Gurteen called "the moral elevation of the poor," or, in Mrs. Lowell's more poetic phrase, "moral oversight for the soul." Others spoke of the need to "diffuse character" among the poor and to "lead these cramped and fettered lives into the knowledge and practice of something better than they have yet known."[11] It is impossible to understand the charity organization movement without grasping the intensity of this underlying concern. Eradication of that "immoral taint" festering at the core of every slum was the central, compelling goal.

The career of Josephine Shaw Lowell offers a revealing insight into the kinds of experiences that could engender such a powerful reform commitment. Although of old Boston stock, Josephine grew up on Staten Island, where her family had established residence to be near the New York eye specialist treating her mother. The coming of the Civil War initially produced in her a mood of spiritual exaltation. "These are extraordinary times and splendid," she wrote in her diary in August 1861. "This war will purify the country of some of its extravagance and selfishness . . . It can't help doing us good; it has begun to do us good already. It will make us young ones much more thoughtful and earnest, and so improve the country. I suppose we need something every few years to teach us that riches, luxury and comfort are not the great end of life." She soon realized, though, that in nearby Manhattan, especially in the slums, lived many who did not share her mood. Attending the theater in October 1862, she was shocked when an antiwar scene was enthusiastically applauded, and noted particularly that the cowardly display had been confined to the cheaper upper-gallery seats.[12] Then in July 1863 came the terrible antidraft riots and, a few days later, word that her brother Robert had been cut down in South Carolina under heroic circumstances. The war touched her even more deeply, as we have seen, when in October 1864 her husband was killed in action. Six weeks later she bore their child, a daughter.

Her role as a passive if passionate social onlooker was at an end. She plunged into work for the Freedmen's Bureau, investigated conditions in Staten Island's jail and almshouse, and in 1876 was appointed to the New York State Board of Charities. When the charity organization movement began soon after, she was at once drawn to it. A founder of the New York City Charity Organization Society in 1882, she was for twenty-five years its guiding spirit. Through speeches, articles, and the book *Public Relief and Private Charity* (1884) she became one of the movement's best known national leaders.

Though Mrs. Lowell's career was involved with urban immigrants, she viewed them with an unsentimental and sometimes even hostile eye. "Often it is brains more than anything else that is lacking to the poor," she once observed. And while her outlook eventually shifted somewhat, in the 1870s and 1880s she staunchly insisted that the charity organization movement's central aim was not the amelioration of physical hardship ("We exaggerate the importance of physical suffering," she believed), but rather the moral oversight of the poor, even if the process proved "as painful as plucking out an eye or cutting off a limb." As for relief of the needy, her position was equally tough-minded: society should "refuse to support any except those whom it can control."[13]

In committing herself to the charity organization movement, Josephine Shaw Lowell found a career that enabled her not only to sublimate her bitterness and perhaps even hatred toward the urban poor who had behaved so ignobly during her own and the nation's great ordeal but to instill into them something of the moral strength and sense of purpose that her martyred brother and husband had displayed on the battlefield.

The visionary and sometimes vague rhetoric with which Mrs. Lowell and her cohorts espoused their moral goals did not prevent them from developing a detailed and clear-eyed strategy for achieving those goals. Indeed, they dismissed most urban charitable effort as naive and misdirected. Random and sentimental almsgiving, they contended, was not only inefficient but downright injurious in failing to discriminate between the few whose destitution was the result of external circumstance (such as the death or injury of a breadwinner) and the vast majority for whom it was simply the outward badge of inner moral deficiency. Providing alms to persons of the latter type could do "fatal moral injury," argued Mrs. Lowell, for their "salvation" became nearly impossible if they grew to believe that society would cushion them from the consequences of their failings. This was particularly true of individuals in whom higher and lower impulses were at war: the normally hardworking laborer, for example, who periodically went on a spree. The aim, obviously, was not to coddle such waverers with handouts, but to stiffen their powers of resistance; not just to apply external balm to their moral illness, but to "cure it internally."[14]

They rejected, too, the church-related approaches dominant a generation before and still prevalent in the Gilded Age. The moral regeneration of the slums, declared Gurteen (himself a clergyman!), would never be achieved by "pulpit or platform oratory . . ., the distribution of tracts and pledges . . ., street preaching or the occasional visit of clergy or city missionary." Charity organization "should never be in the hands of the clergy," he warned, and no one connected with it should "use his or her position for the purposes of proselytism or spiritual instruction." Church-sponsored relief work, charged Mary Richmond of the Baltimore COS, was usually a covert form of bribery for church attendance. The basic support for charity organization, asserted Gurteen bluntly, must come from "business and professional men" and "noble-hearted women of the wealthier class," not from "missionaries . . ., prayer meetings and Bible classes."[15] The church had had its chance at urban moral control; now it was time for others! With the urban masses overwhelmingly non-Protestant, the architects of the new movement were determined to avoid sectarian taint.

Underlying the charity organization strategy was the assumption that the urban poor had degenerated morally because the circumstances of city life had cut them off from the elevating influence of their moral betters. This notion crops up repeatedly in the literature of the movement. In small-town society, observed a charity organization speaker at the NCCC in 1884, one individual of "lofty character and high purpose" could influence hundreds of his neighbors and fellow townsmen; in the city, such influence was "practically impossible."[16] In the village, agreed charity organization leader Charles D. Kellogg in 1887, neighbors of many years' standing could easily exchange "counsel [and] admonition," and "speak of each other's affairs with fuller knowledge and discernment." In cities, by contrast, "the classes which wealth and poverty and occupation make have drifted apart, and are more monotonously uniform . . . [S]urface and rapid transit . . . distributes population according to wealth; and the poorer stratum is in one district, the middle classes in another, and the rich upon some Beacon or Murray Hill. There is no solvent of social ties like urban life."[17] The urgent task, then, was to restore the social ties that urbanization had severed—to re-create between the classes the "natural relations . . . of which life in a city has robbed them," and establish "neighborliness . . . as a feature of civic life." Such a "reunion between the classes," insisted S. Humphreys Gurteen, could not fail to have a "civilizing and healing influence."[18]

But how: The somewhat paradoxical answer, in the words of one COS leader, was to devise some "machine," some "artifice," for re-creating in the city those "natural" social relations essential to the development of character among the poor.[19] Not surprisingly, that "artifice" was the charity organization movement itself.

The first step in reopening the moral conduits between the classes was simply to learn more about the lives of the poor. In simpler days, such knowledge came naturally through numerous informal channels; now a mechanism was needed to penetrate the slums. The "fundamental law" of charity organization, wrote Gurteen, "is expressed in one word, INVESTIGATE." The nerve center of every charity organization society was the central file where information on the city's poor was systematically accumulated, arranged, and stored. By the mid-1890s, the New York City COS held data on 170,000 families or individuals, and could supply information by return mail to anyone "charitably interested" in a particular family. Thanks to its records system, boasted an early historian of the movement, charity organization was the first moral-welfare movement "to apply scientific methods to human relationships."[20]

The procedures may have been "scientific," but the data itself reflected the movement's moralistic preoccupations, focusing on character and behavior as well as on the family's history and economic situation. Is the applicant "well conducted and industrious"? ask the model questionnaires included in Gurteen's *Handbook of Charity Organization*. Is he "temperate and steady"? What is the family's general moral condition?[21] Endlessly the probing went on, seeking to pinpoint the character flaws that were surely somewhere present.

The investigative feature of the undertaking was profoundly appealing to the middle-class COS volunteers, perhaps because the sheer mass of dossiers offered deceptively tangible assurance that the complex and disturbing human reality they documented had somehow been subdued and rendered manageable. A charity organization society, declared a Boston leader, was a "clearinghouse" that could help rees-tablish "orderly and effective relations" among the city's varied ele-ments. When each of the "individual units" of the urban mass had been "located, guided, helped, and controlled," declared another speaker rather grandly in 1891, "we shall have a model state of society."[22]

The Friendly Visitor

But the accumulation of information was only a first step. Once the needy family had been investigated, its moral flaws diagnosed, and a COS file established, the harder task remained: actually to effect the needed transformation. The crucial factor at this stage—and indeed the keystone in the entire charity organization structure—was the "friendly visitor." This was a middle-class or upper-class volunteer—usually female—who each week visited a limited number of slum families to which she had been assigned by the COS district supervisor. By the early 1890s some 4,000 friendly visitors were regularly knocking on tenement doors in Boston, New York, Brooklyn, Baltimore, and other major cities from coast to coast.[23]

It is difficult today to recapture the excitement that this aspect of charity organization generated. Here at last was the key to urban America's redemption. "Charity Organization perfectly carried out would produce a state of society nearer the Christian ideal than has ever yet been known," exclaimed one leader in 1884. Three years later Charles D. Kellogg described friendly visiting somewhat more mili-tantly (Haymarket had intervened) as the movement's "right arm of aggressive work." He envisioned an army of 100,000 friendly visitors sweeping "like a tidal wave" over urban America, "flooding every part" with "sweetness and order and light."[24]

How would the friendly visitor achieve such wonders where so many others had failed? The first step—as the Reverend Ward Stafford had urged as long ago as 1817—was simply to establish a human tie across the barriers of class, religion, and nationality. The central object of the entire scheme, wrote Gurteen, was to promote "the *personal* in-tercourse of the wealthier citizens with the poor at their homes" and thereby bring together "the extremes of society in a spirit of honest friendship." Once class divisions had been overcome, and the friendly visitors had begun to "think of the poor as husbands, wives, sons and daughters, members of households as we are ourselves instead of con-templating them as a class different from ourselves," they could start to "impart to the cheerless tenement or the wretched hovel, a little of their own happiness."[25]

However, if mere camaraderie or a temporary lift in spirits were the only result, the encounter could be worse than useless. "It is a mistake to believe that any letting of ourselves down will ever lift them up," friendly visitors were advised. "The 'hail fellow, well met' air which we sometimes see in those who would avoid condescension, often leads to rash relations with those we would benefit, and consequent disappointment."[26]

The friendly visitor's profoundly serious purpose was to use "*the moral support of true friendship*" to bring about transformations of character: to embed in the poor a "new desire to live rightly" and to marshal more effectively their own resources of "energy and self-control."[27] In Boston, friendly visitors were given explicit instructions on this point: "Your duty to the family requires you to consider their moral good, and not the gratification of your own emotions . . . You who are strong, give some of your strength to those who are weak . . . You who love industry, teach it to the idle. You in your strength of character, steady the stumbling."[28]

For all their pride in being nonsectarian and scientific, charity organization leaders easily lapsed into the rhetoric of earlier evangelical urban-reform crusaders in urging the friendly visitors to persevere in their vital mission: "We must keep at work continually, season after season, pulling up the seeds of degradation and destitution, cultivating the thrift, self-dependence, industry, virtue, [and] health, as well as the intellectual and social natures of our poor friends."[29] In trying to define the changes they envisioned, they typically fell back on the familiar litany of middle-class virtues: honesty, thrift, sobriety, self-dependence, and respect for "the dignity of honest work."[30] In fact, however, specificity was unnecessary, for the friendly visitor understood her task implicitly: to bring the poor to share her own values and moral standards—to make them more like herself.

But—and here matters became delicate indeed—the visitor must never *appear* to be seeking such a transformation. The pose of simple friendship and "neighborliness" had to be sustained. "Avoid anything like dictation," Gurteen cautioned. "Treat even the poorest with the same delicacy of feeling and kind consideration that you would wish to have shown to yourself." The handbook for friendly visitors in Boston made the same point: "Do not announce yourself as a visitor of any charitable organization, but as a *friend* or neighbor anxious to know those among whom you live."[31] And it was reiterated by the keynote NCCC speaker in 1890: "human hearts are not like cattle—they cannot be driven . . . [E]ach one of the vast multitude of the wayward or ignorant . . . must be handled like an individual . . . if the germs of the higher life within him are to burst the matted soil and seek the light."[32] *Handled like an individual!* The phrase not only captures the quintessential COS outlook but reveals how precarious was this effort to create, through the magic of friendly visiting, an urban social order where currents of personal moral influence might flow once again between the upper social ranks and the poor.

The "friendship" offered by the friendly visitor was thus of a rather special kind. Seemingly artless and spontaneous (when the visitor was skilled in her role), it was in fact simply the necessary first step in a larger moral-uplift process. Only by "holding on with firm grip, until at last you reach the heart-strings of someone in the family," wrote one COS leader in 1891, could the friendly visitor achieve that larger goal.[33]

With so much at stake, the friendly visitor was urged to plan her strategy with all the care of a military commander besieging an entrenched stronghold. If "her" family frittered away its meager resources on short-term pleasures and petty vices, for example, she was advised not to expound the virtue of thrift but to *demonstrate* it by planning some "pleasant occasion" to which the family members might "look forward from one week or month to another" and thereby gradually acquire the habit of delayed gratification. Even the "gift of a plant or picture or some other tasteful suggestive object of beauty" could play a part in this delicate process of character building.[34] Delegates to the 1895 NCCC were told of the amazing results when a friendly visitor set out to stimulate the "artistic imagination" of an "unruly" boy by taking him to the art museum: "When he went home, he could not begin again slashing up the furniture with his pocket knife, or beating his younger brother; for on every pine chair and table, as well as on his brother's jacket, arose visions of a soldiers' camp-fire at sunset, of a cardinal in his crimson robe of state, of three boats sailing out into the moonlight. He soon became a good boy."[35]

More important than any such stratagem, however, was the friendly visitor's own personality, as it gradually unfolded during her repeated visits. Almost by osmosis, the charity organization literature sometimes seems to suggest, the faithful friendly visitors would slowly "impart their own virtues" to the poor. The "life of the visitor," declared the leader of the Minneapolis COS, would be "the light that guides them to self-help, respectability, and multiplying opportunities."[36]

For all the talk of "neighborliness" and even of "guidance," what was involved here was social control of a quite explicit variety. The aim, wrote Gurteen, was to subject the poor to "the firm though loving government of heroic women." Once the friendly visitor had become a slum family's "acknowledged friend," he added, she would be "a power in that home."[37] *Power* was the issue, and in the shadowy struggle to gain moral leverage over the poor, the friendly visitor had certain important strategic advantages. Although she did not herself distribute relief, she helped compile the dossiers that were then made available not only to relief agencies but also to prospective employers, landlords, banks, "charitably interested individuals," and even the police. However glossed over, this fact could not long be concealed, and it surely added further tension to the already strained and ambiguous encounters between the needy family and its self-invited "friend." In *Democracy and Social Ethics* (1902), settlement-house leader Jane Addams offered a telling analysis of the "moral deterioration" which, she believed, frequently resulted from the relationship between slum family and charity visitor.

> When the agent or visitor appears among the poor, and they discover that under certain conditions food and rent and medical aid are dispensed from some unknown source, every man, woman, and child is quick to learn what the conditions may be, and to follow them . . . [T]o the visitor they gravely laud temperance and cleanliness and thrift and religious observance. The deception in the first instances arises from a wondering inability to understand the ethical ideals which can require such impossible virtues, and from an innocent desire to please.[38]

By 1902, when this insightful criticism was published, the once-confident charity organization movement was beset by doubt and division. As early as 1891 an NCCC committee reported that the future of friendly visiting seemed "not altogether encouraging."[39] A year later, the Boston Associated Charities, while singling out one ethnic group, summed up a more general frustration friendly visitors were experiencing in dealing with some of their slum "neighbors."

> Until the Italians became numerous, we had at least intelligent means of communication with most of the families we knew. We not only spoke the same language, but they knew what we were talking about when we urged the advantages of temperance, industry, or economical living. Though their acquiescence in our standards might be feigned and though they might never live up to them, we seldom failed to agree in theory. [But the Italians] are truly foreigners to us. We do not speak a common language; our standards have no meaning to them, and we may well doubt whether they have any applicability.[40]

Even more dispiriting was the mounting criticism from those who should have been the movement's strongest supporters. In an 1890 symposium on poverty published in a Boston reform magazine, Benjamin O. Flower's *Arena*, one participant bitterly attacked the city's Associated Charities as a monopolistic "syndicate," and urged readers to consider the "torture" endured by needy families upon discovering that their relief application had caused "their names, history, and troubles to be spread in a written record to be coddled and gossiped over; [and] the privacy of their home to be invaded by inquisitive visitors whose unasked advice is the substitute for practical relief."[41]

The criticism increased in the mid-1890's as a devastating Depression called into question the two ideological pillars of the charity organization movement; that poverty was rooted in individual flaws, and that those flaws could be remedied through personal uplift effort. If, as the economic crisis of 1893–1897 seemed to make clear, the physical and moral dislocations of slum life were often the result of causes beyond individual control, where was the justification for the hand-crafted, family-by-family CC3 approach? As the Depression worsened, even so conservative an organization as the American Academy of Political and Social Science could publish an essay by a sociologist-reformer that scornfully dismissed the entire charity organization ethos: "It is said that the interests of the laborers are subserved best if the well-to-do classes do their charities for them . . . The time has passed when one class . . . will longer accept this sort of advice . . . The traditional charity . . . is a gift from success to failure, from superiority to apparent inferiority, from one who pities to one who is an object of pity."[42]

Their guiding principles confounded by events, the charity organization movement and its foot soldiers, the friendly visitors, lost their aggressive confidence and went on the defensive. "The work is developed under great discouragements in most of our large cities," acknowledged Amos G. Warner in 1894. The once path-breaking movement was subsiding into "mere officialism," agreed a Baltimore leader.[43] The familiar urban moral-control cycle, from initial enthusiasm to baffled discouragement, was playing itself out yet again.

Charity Organization and the Settlement-House Movement: Conflicts and Continuities in Urban Moral Uplift

Of all the late-nineteenth-century challenges to the assumptions of the charity organization movement, none was more pointed than that which came from the settlement houses. The history of the settlement movement—thanks in large part to Jane Addams's role in it—is comparatively well known.[44] Originating in London, the idea took root in America in 1886 with the opening of Stanton Coit's Neighborhood Guild in New York City. Three years later came the College settlement in New York and Jane Addams's Hull House in Chicago. By the end of the century over 100 settlement houses had sprung up in the immigrant sections of most big cities, and for young college-bred volunteers, the movement had acquired much of the cachet that "charity organization" had possessed two decades earlier.[45]

From the first, relations between the upstart settlement movement and the older charity organization societies were strained, reflecting in part their differing perceptions of the urban moral situation and the duty of the middle classes toward the poor. A typical encounter occurred at the NCCC in 1896 when a charity organization speaker made the usual allusions to the failings of the urban poor and the need for "moral force" to lift them up. The next speaker, Mary McDowell of the University of Chicago Settlement, adopting the self-deprecatory yet slightly mocking tone at which settlement workers excelled, commented that she could not bring herself to criticize a filthy tenement apartment when she knew that smoke and soot were pouring into it from unregulated factories nearby. "When I try to apply some of that 'moral force' Mr. Ayres has spoken of," she concluded, "somehow I don't know how."[46]

The sarcasm flowed in both directions. At the NCCC the year before, COS leader Mary Richmond criticized the naiveté of youthful settlement-house residents who too readily abandoned their own convictions to accept uncritically the outlook of those among whom they lived. "They are bowled over," mocked Richmond, "by the first labor leader, or anarchist, or socialist" they meet.[47]

In retrospect, this quarrel appears as something of a family spat. The two movements had more in common than either liked to admit. Indeed, the early settlement houses were often viewed as extensions of the COS approach; settlement volunteers were simply "friendly visitors" who actually took up residence in the poor neighborhood, creating a model middle-class household: orderly, cultivated, temperate, and industrious. Josephine Shaw Lowell, bestowing her blessing on the settlement movement in 1895, described it as simply another means by which the privileged could "awaken nobler ambitions and create higher ideals" in the slums.[48]

For all their criticism of the COS's self-righteousness, the settlement leaders, too, fundamentally judged urban working-class life by their own solidly middle-class standards. Robert A. Woods of Boston's South End House, a staunch prohibitionist who advocated the isolation and segregation of tramps, alcoholics, paupers, and other unfit types, viewed the settlement house as the nucleus of purified slum neighborhoods that would ultimately banish rowdiness, drunkenness, and vice from their midst.[49] Even the determinedly tolerant Jane Addams eyed her Hull House neighbors from behind a barricade of moral and social preconceptions. She found much of value in immigrant life, but, as Allen Davis has noted, she also never really questioned that "the lower-class environment of saloons, dance halls, and street life needed to be . . . made more like a middle- or upper-class neighborhood." A wholly conventional morality underlay her 1913 work on prostitution, *A New Conscience and an Ancient Evil*, and in *The Spirit of Youth and the City*

Streets (1909) she harshly criticized almost every aspect of urban mass culture. "Let us know the modern city in its weakness and wickedness," she wrote, "and then seek to rectify and purify it."[50]

If the moral outlook of the hundreds of now-obscure settlement volunteers who didn't write books or achieve fame could be recovered, we might find—despite Mary Richmond's charge that they were all being radicalized—a far higher degree of continuity with the conservative assumptions and strategies of the charity organization societies than the sniping between the two movements might suggest.

But this is not to say that the differences were all illusory. While the social-control impulse was present in the settlement movement, it was usually expressed in more nuanced terms, and subjected to more soul-searching scrutiny, than in the aggressively moralistic early COS pronouncements. More sensitive to the ambiguities involved in their encounters with the urban poor, chastened by the Depression of the 1890s, and determined to recognize the "admirable" qualities as well as the "failings" of their working-class neighbors, the settlement leaders generally muted their negative moral judgments or placed them within a larger framework of positive comment.

Furthermore, the young settlement workers were more responsive than the older COS leaders to the newer social thought, with its emphasis on the role of environment in shaping behavior and morals. Accordingly, their activism tended toward environmentalist rather than individualistic remedies. At times this environmentalism was rather baldly moralistic, as in their advocacy of movie censorship, dance hall regulation, and sometimes prohibition, but the settlements also supplied recruits for a wide range of reforms aimed at bettering not only the *moral* environment of the urban poor, but their *industrial* environment as well: campaigns for wage-and-hour legislation, child-labor laws, factory-safety regulations, etc.[51] While the charity organizations accumulated masses of data on individuals and families, the settlement workers—equally fascinated by statistics—chose the neighborhood, the political ward, or the industry as their unit of investigation. *Hull-House Maps and Papers* (1895), with its bristling pages of maps, graphs, charts, and statistical tables profiling Chicago's entire South Side, is a notable example of this broadened perspective.

When the settlement workers' moral-uplift efforts *were* directed at individuals, they typically involved not the inculcation of specific values or patterns of behavior, but what would later be called "consciousness raising": awakening the urban immigrants to the larger world beyond the tenement or factory, the richness of their cultural heritage, and the possibilities of community organization and cooperative effort. The most "difficult task" of any settlement house, said Mary

K. Simkhovitch of New York's Greenwich House, was to assist the poor to become "a consciously effective group."[52]

If the two reforms had much in common, then, there were also important differences of emphasis. A crucial summation of those differences—and a major salvo in the running feud between the charity organizers and the settlement workers—was Jane Addams's 1902 work *Democracy and Social Ethics.* The book begins with a fifty-seven page critique, characteristically gentle but devastating, of the charity organization movement and its substitution of "a theory of social conduct for the natural promptings of the heart." Confronted by the "daintily clad charitable visitor" with her air of moral superiority, wrote Addams, the poor usually responded with a superficial complaisance masking their true feelings: "good-natured and kindly contempt." The "scientific" social investigation in which the charity organization societies took such pride she compared to eighteenth-century botany, "when flowers were tabulated in alphabetical order." In a key passage, she simply inverted a classic charity organization formulation: the moral defects of the poor were not the *cause* of their poverty, she suggested, but a *consequence* of "the struggle for existence, which is so much harsher among people near the edge of pauperism."[53] When the National Conference of Charities and Correction, long a forum for COS pronouncements on the moral shortcomings of slum dwellers, elected Jane Addams president in 1904—two years after *Democracy and Social Ethics*—the symbolic import of the moment was not lost on the partisans of either movement.

Beset by criticism, their ideology under challenge, charity organization spokesmen tried to adapt to the altered climate of the 1890s by soft-pedaling their preoccupation with the failings of the poor and paying more attention to environmental factors.[54] A COS spokesman in 1896 portrayed friendly visitors not only as agents of individual moral uplift but also as instruments for marshaling public sentiment against child labor, sweatshops, and other exploitative aspects of the industrial system.[55] At the NCCC gathering of 1897, Edward T. Devine, the new general secretary of the New York COS, implicitly dismissed two decades of charity organization rhetoric as he poked fun at the heavily moralistic aura of the typical COS office: "Sometimes a caller . . . will bring in the word 'worthy' or 'deserving,' doubtfully, as if not exactly accustomed to use it when talking of their neighbors, but as if thinking that no other classification would be quite in place in a charity organization office, just as we half unconsciously drop into the use of such semi-technical words as 'acute' and 'chronic,' when speaking to a physician, or 'believer' and 'unbeliever,' in a clergyman's presence."[56] At the same conference, a Chicago leader, discussing "Friendly Visiting as a Social Force," rejected the old preoccupation with the individuals and single families. Displaying a sociological map of a Chicago immigrant ward, he described how a group of COS visitors, working as a team, had helped establish a neighborhood employment committee, a savings bank, a women's workroom, and a forty-acre cooperative vegetable garden.[57]

The turn toward environmentalism is evident, too, in several important books produced by charity organization leaders in the 1890s. In *The Development of Thrift* (1899), Mary Willcox Brown blamed the fact that the poor were often "stunted" in spirit as well as in body on their "wretched material environment." Amos Warner in *American Charities* (1894), explicitly rejecting the view that eradication of the slums depended exclusively or even primarily on individual "moral reformation," offered a list of "objective" causes of poverty that included "Bad Industrial Conditions," "Defective Legislation," and "The Undue Power of Class Over Class."[58]

Similarly, Mary Richmond's widely used COS manual of 1899, *Friendly Visiting among the Poor,* was marked by a positive attitude toward the poor far different from the earlier handbooks of Gurteen and others. (Her own background, as well as the shifting intellectual climate, helped determine her outlook. Orphaned at two, she passed a poverty-stricken girlhood with working-class relatives and worked for two years at starvation wages in New York City before joining the Baltimore COS in 1889.) Like the contemporary settlement-house leaders, she warned COS volunteers against rigid moralism and urged receptivity to every hint of goodness and nobility in the poor. Rather than isolating specific character traits or behavioral details, she advised, the charity visitor should try to grasp "the family life as a whole," including the "joys, sorrows, opinions, feelings, and entire outlook upon life." ("One never feels acquainted with the poor family until [one] has had a good laugh with them," she added in a later work.) Only a "benighted social reformer," she wrote acerbically, "thinks of all who drink as drunkards, and of all the places where liquor is sold as dens of vice."[59] (A charity worker with such an attitude would not long have survived in Baltimore!)

At the same time, however, these works also reveal that even in the wake of a catastrophic Depression, the charity organization leadership continued to be preoccupied with the moral sources of poverty. Along with his "objective" causes of destitution, Amos Warner drew up a lengthy list of "subjective" causes, including "Indolence," "Lubricity," "Lack of Judgment," "Unhealthy Appetites," "Shiftlessness," "Abuse of Stimulants and Narcotics," and "Disregard of Family Ties." (Indeed, one of his "objective" causes was "Evil Associations and Surroundings," revealing how easily the new "environmentalist" outlook could be accommodated to the old moralism.) Discussing the

"Personal Causes of Individual Degeneration," Warner deplored the grossness of "the rougher class of day laborers" among whom "the whole undercurrent of thought . . . is thoroughly base and degrading." The "inherent uncleanness of their minds," he concluded, ruins them for positions requiring "alertness and sustained attention" and thus "prevents them from rising."[60]

Even for Mary Richmond, a heightened concern with the human realities of slum life did not override a continued belief that deficiencies of character figured prominently among the causes of poverty, and that a part of the charity worker's duty was to lead the poor to a higher moral plane. "Character is at the very center of this complicated problem" of poverty, she wrote in *Friendly Visiting among the Poor.* Neglect of "the discipline that makes character," she added in another work of this period, was a "common fault of modern philanthropy." It was on a foundation of individual industry and thrift, she argued, that "all the social virtues are built." Richmond also believed that any household that violated the strict Victorian division of sexual roles (the husband the breadwinner, the wife devoting herself exclusively to domestic duties) would quickly become "a breeding place of sin and social disorder." This, in part, was what she had in mind when she urged COS visitors to work to strengthen "true" home life among the poor and to transform "the sham home into a real one." In addition to warning children about "bad reading" and "low theatrical performances," she wrote, the friendly visitor must help the husband who had "lost his sense of responsibility toward wife and children to regain it," dissuade restless wives from seeking outside employment, and introduce messy housekeepers to "the pleasures of a cleanly, well-ordered home."[61]

In important ways, then, *Friendly Visiting among the Poor* reaffirmed the long-standing charity organization hope that the poor would "unconsciously imitate" the middle-class visitor and gradually adopt her values. Like the antebellum Sunday school ideologists, Richmond suggested that this influence could be especially effective with the young. "We should not despair of the children, if we can attach them to us and give them a new and better outlook upon life."[62]

But this was, after all, a book of 1899 and not 1879, and Richmond, acknowledging that some of her ideas might seem "old fashioned," adopted a decidedly defensive tone as she refurbished the old verities: "Some . . . question our right to go among [the poor] with the object of doing them good, regarding it as an impertinent interference with the rights of the individual. But . . . [w]e must interfere when confronted by human suffering and need. Why not interfere effectively?"[63]

The efforts to bring charity organization abreast of the shifting social and intellectual climate of the 1890s could not conceal the fact that the movement as its founders had conceived it was fading with the old century itself. The early leaders were passing from the scene, taking their bold moral certitudes with them.

But despite its eventual decline, the charity organization movement for a crucial twenty-year period in the Gilded Age provided a powerful rationale and institutional outlet for the urban social-control impulses of the American middle class. In these decades when the middle class was in fact abandoning the immigrant cities and their complex problems—fleeing to the suburbs, retreating into tight neighborhood enclaves, dismissing municipal politics with ridicule, and allowing the industrial capitalism that was shaping the city to proceed unchecked and uncontrolled—charity organization had provided the illusion that in the moral realm, at least, it was still firmly at the helm.

NOTES

1. William R. Stewart, *The Philanthropic Work of Josephine Shaw Lowell* (New York, Macmillan, 1911), pp. 3–133.
2. David J. Pivar, *Purity Crusade; Sexual Morality and Social Control, 1868–1900* (Westport, Conn., Greenwood Press, 1973); Paul S. Boyer, *Purity in Print; Book Censorship in America* (New York, Charles Scribner's Sons, 1968), pp. 1–22; Joseph M. Hawes, *Children in Urban Society: Juvenile Delinquency in Nineteenth-Century America* (New York, Oxford University Press, 1971), pp. 138–142. Through the efforts of the Gerry society, juveniles in Manhattan were barred from saloons, theaters, and brothels, and action was taken to clear the streets of the "flower girls" who were often simply under-age prostitutes.
3. Stanley Buder, *Pullman: An Experiment in Industrial Order and Community Planning, 1880–1930* (New York, Oxford University Press, 1967), pp. 64, 69. For a discussion of another, less well known experiment along these lines—Vandergrift, Pa., "The Pullman of Western Pennsylvania" founded in the 1890s by the Apollo Iron and Steel Company—see Roy Lubove, *Twentieth Century Pittsburgh: Government, Business, and Environmental Change* (New York, John Wiley and Sons, 1969), pp. 17–18.
4. S. Humphreys Gurteen, *A Handbook of Charity Organization* (Buffalo, N.Y., 1882), pp. 41, 42, 72; Verl S. Lewis, "The Development of the Charity Organization Movement in the United States, 1875–1900. Its Principles and Methods" (D.S.W. diss., Western Reserve University, School of Applied Social Sciences, 1954), pp. 24–28.
5. Kathleen Woodroofe, *From Charity to Social Work in England and the United States* (London, Routledge and Paul, 1962), p. 28.
6. Gurteen, *Handbook*, p. 45.
7. Ibid., p. 48; Lewis, "Development of the Charity Organization Movement," p. 61.
8. More recently, in 1866, the Detroit City Mission Board had proposed a scheme for systematic visitation and moral uplift among the poor that, in the view of one admiring contemporary, was "almost utopian in its

completeness." Silas Farmer, *History of Detroit and Wayne County and Early Michigan,* 3rd ed. (New York, 1890; reissued, Detroit, Gale Research, 1969), p. 650.

9. Gurteen, *Handbook,* p. 18; Lewis, "Development of the Charity Organization Movement," p. 2; Nathan Irvin Huggins, *Protestants against Poverty: Boston's Charities, 1870–1900* (Westport, Conn., Greenwood Pub., 1971), p. 9.

10. Gurteen, *Handbook,* pp. 21, 38; Constance M. Green, *Washington: Capital City, 1879–1950* (Princeton, N.J., Princeton University Press, 1963), p. 70; Mrs. Glendower Evans, "Scientific Charity," *Proceedings of the National Conference of Charities and Correction, Sixteenth Annual Session, San Francisco, 1889* (Boston, 1889), p. 27 (hereafter, NCCC, *Proc.*). See also Huggins, *Protestants against Poverty,* p. 73, quoting Anna L. Meeker in *Lend-a-Hand* (1886) and S. Humphreys Gurteen, *Provident Schemes* (Buffalo, 1879), p. 76.

11. Lewis, "Development of the Charity Organization Movement," p. 120, quoting Lenora Hamlin, a Saint Paul, Minnesota, COS leader; Gurteen, *Handbook,* p. 49; Stewart, *Philanthropic Work of Josephine Shaw Lowell,* p. 179. See also Mary Willcox Brown, *The Development of Thrift* (New York, 1899), p. 6; NCCC, *Proc.* (1889), p. 27 (Mrs. Glendower Evans); Charles S. Fairchild, "Objects of Charity Organization," ibid. (1884), p. 68.

12. Stewart, *Philanthropic Work of Josephine Shaw Lowell,* pp. 16 (quote from diary), 35 (the theater incident).

13. Josephine Shaw Lowell, *Public Relief and Private Charity* (New York, 1884), pp. 68, 94; Stewart, *Philanthropic Work of Josephine Shaw Lowell,* pp. 146, 212–213.

14. Gurteen, *Handbook,* p. 32 (see also pp. 12, 109); Stewart, *Philanthropic Work of Josephine Shaw Lowell,* pp. 172, 212.

15. Gurteen, *Handbook,* p. 67; Lewis, "Development of the Charity Organization Movement," p. 131; Mary E. Richmond, *Friendly Visiting among the Poor; A Handbook for Charity Workers* (New York, [1899]; reissued, Montclair, N.J., Patterson Smith, 1969), p. 173. See also Gurteen, *Provident Schemes,* p. 17. This hostility to church-sponsored philanthropy also reflected the COS's desire to rationalize urban charity by eliminating the competition and overlapping efforts of numerous special-interest benevolent organizations.

16. Fairchild, "Objects of Charity Organization," p. 66.

17. NCCC, *Proc.* (1887), p. 134.

18. Gurteen, *Handbook,* pp. 109, 39; Fairchild, "Objects of Charity Organization," p. 66.

19. Ibid., p. 65.

20. Frank D. Watson, *The Charity Organization Movement in the United States* (New York, Macmillan, 1922), p. 218; Gurteen, *Handbook,* p. 30. In 1894 one COS spokesman urged the development of a standardized COS telegraph code to facilitate intercity COS communications. Amos G. Warner, *American Charities: A Study in Philanthropy and Economics* (New York, 1894), p. 382.

21. Gurteen, *Handbook,* pp. 160–161.

22. George D. Holt, "The Relation of Charity Problems to Social Problems," NCCC, *Proc.* (1891), pp. 120–121; Mrs. Glendower Evans, "Scientific Charity," p. 26. See also comments by Charles D. Kellogg quoted in NCCC, *Proc.* (1877), p. 125.
23. Lewis, "Development of the Charity Organization Movement," p. 190; Robert H. Bremner, *From the Depths; The Discovery of Poverty in the United States* (New York, New York University Press, 1956), p. 52.
24. NCCC, *Proc.* (1887), pp. 132–133 (Kellogg); Fairchild, "Objects of Charity Organization," p. 68.
25. Gurteen, *Handbook*, pp. 116, 113; Gurteen, *Provident Schemes*, pp. 72, 74.
26. "Rules and Suggestions for Visitors of the Associated Charities" (Boston, 1879), p. 8. (This pamphlet is reprinted as app. C in Lewis, "Development of the Charity Organization Movement.")
27. Marian C. Putnam, "Friendly Visiting," NCCC, *Proc.* (1877), p. 151; ibid. (1889), p. 27 (Mrs. Glendower Evans); Gurteen, *Handbook*, p. 176. See also Lenora Hamlin, "Friendly Visiting," *Charities Review*, 6 (June 1897), 322.
28. Robert Treat Paine, 1879 address quoted in Lewis "Development of the Charity Organization Movement," p. 120.
29. Frances A. Smith, "Continued Care of Families," NCCC, *Proc.* (1895), p. 87.
30. See, e.g., Gurteen, *Handbook*, pp. 39, 182 (quoted phrase); Lewis, "Development of the Charity Organization Movement," pp. 114 (quoting the constitution of the Boston Associated Charities) and app. C ("Rules and Suggestions for Visitors of the Associated Charities.")
31. Ibid.; Gurteen, *Handbook*, pp. 224, 225.
32. Alexander Mackay-Smith, "The Power of Personality in Redemptive Work," NCCC, *Proc.* (1890), p. 20.
33. Holt, "Relation of Charity Problems to Social Problems," p. 121.
34. Green, *Washington: Capital City*, p. 70; "Rules and Suggestions for Visitors of the Associated Charities," p. 4.
35. Smith, "Continued Care of Families," p. 89.
36. Holt, "Relation of Charity Problems to Social Problems," p. 121; Smith, "Continued Care of Families," p. 90.
37. Gurteen, *Handbook*, p. 117; Gurteen, *Provident Schemes*, p. 32.
38. Jane Addams, *Democracy and Social Ethics* (New York, Macmillan, 1902; reissued, Cambridge, Mass., Harvard University Press, 1964, edited with introduction by Anne Firor Scott), pp. 27–28.
39. "Report of the Committee on the Organization of Charity," NCCC, *Proc.* (1891), p. 113. See also, for similar pessimism, Charles D. Kellogg, "Charity Organization in the United States," ibid. (1893), p. 84.
40. Quoted in Roy Lubove, *The Professional Altruist: The Emergence of Social Work as a Career* (Cambridge, Mass., Harvard University Press, 1965; reissued, New York, Atheneum, 1971), p. 17.
41. "Destitution in Boston: A Symposium," *Arena*, 2 (Nov. 1890), 734. The author of this comment was Edward Hamilton.
42. John Graham Brooks, "The Future Problem of Charity and the Unemployed," *Annals of the American Academy of Political and Social Science*, 5 (July 1894), 14–15.

43. Jeffrey R. Brackett, "The Charity Organization Movement: Its Tendency and Its Duties," NCCC, *Proc.* (1895); Warner, *American Charities*, p. 390.

44. For a good recent study see Allen F. Davis, *Spearheads for Reform: The Social Settlements and the Progressive Movement, 1890–1914* (New York, Oxford University Press, 1967).

45. Bremner, *From the Depths*, pp. 60–61; Davis, *Spearheads for Reform*, pp. 8–12.

46. Mary E. McDowell, "Friendly Visiting," NCCC, *Proc.* (1896), p. 254.

47. Quoted in Lewis, "Development of the Charity Organization Movement," p. 122.

48. Stewart, *Philanthropic Work of Josephine Shaw Lowell*, pp. 185–186.

49. Eleanor H. Woods, *Robert A. Woods: Champion of Democracy* (Boston, Houghton Mifflin, 1929), pp. 198–202, 238–248, 250–256; Davis, *Spearheads for Reform*, pp. 75–76, 92.

50. Jane Addams, *The Spirit of Youth and the City Streets* (New York, Macmillan, 1909; reprinted, Urbana, University of Illinois Press, 1972, introduction by Allen F. Davis), pp. 14, xxvi–xxvii (Davis quote). When the sexual behavior of urban youth did not follow "the traditional line of domesticity," she wrote, it was "a cancer in the very tissues of society and . . . a disrupter of the securest social bonds" (ibid., p. 15).

51. Davis, *Spearheads for Reform*, chap. 6: "The Settlements and the Labor Movement."

52. Quoted in ibid., p. 75.

53. Addams, *Democracy and Social Ethics*, pp. 16, 25, 26, 44, 64.

54. This did not represent a total about-face, for the question of the physical circumstances of slum life had had a distinct if subordinate place in COS writings from the beginning. As early as 1879, for example, S. Humphreys Gurteen had written of "people who live huddled together in vile tenements and overcrowded dwellings and who have been allowed through the guilty negligence of their fellow-townsmen to float down the stream and through the floodgates of sanitary neglect and to land at last in physical, moral, aye, and spiritual degradation." Gurteen, *Provident Schemes*, p. 35. See also Gurteen, *Handbook*, p. 181.

55. P. W. Ayres, "Report of the Committee on Charity Organization," NCCC, *Proc.* (1896), p. 238.

56. Edward T. Devine, "The Value and the Dangers of Investigation," ibid. (1897), p. 194.

57. Charles F. Weller, "Friendly Visiting as a Social Force," ibid. (1897), pp. 201–202.

58. Warner, *American Charities*, pp. 26, 28; Brown, *The Development of Thrift*, p. 6.

59. Richmond, *Friendly Visiting among the Poor*, pp. 45, 180, 57; and introduction by Max Siporin, esp. pp. xix–xx ("good laugh" quote from Mary Richmond's *The Good Neighbor in the Modern City* [1907]).

60. It was on these grounds that Warner opposed supplying birth-control information to the poor: it would simply "promote sensuality." Warner, *American Charities*, pp. 28, 67–68.

61. Richmond, *Friendly Visiting among the Poor*, pp. 9, 45, 47, 73, 86, 109. Richard Sennett has suggested that concern by middle-class reformers

about family stability in the slums was in part a projection of their interest in preserving and strengthening the *middle-class* family as a "bulwark against confusion" in new suburbs where traditional community structures were much weakened or absent altogether. Richard Sennett, *Families against the City: Middle-Class Homes of Industrial Chicago, 1872–1890* (Cambridge, Mass., Harvard University Press, 1970; reissued, New York, Vintage Books, 1974), pp. 42–43, 237 (quoted passage).

62. Ibid., p. 92.
63. Ibid., pp. 12, 45.

Article 8

THE HOUSE OF REFUGE FOR COLORED CHILDREN

Cecile P. Frey

The House of Refuge of Philadelphia, which opened its doors late in 1828, was established by a group of benevolent citizens who wanted to remove child offenders from adult prisons. Historically, until the 19th century, children accused of crimes were, if found guilty, placed into the adult jails then in existence. When the House was first opened, its founders did not require that the inmates be of any particular race. However, after the first year, no black child was admitted to the House.[1] Until 1850, when the House of Refuge for Colored Children was opened in Philadelphia, youthful offenders of that race were placed in adult prisons rather than in any separate facility. The 1850 facility marked the only time in the 19th century that a northern state opened such an institution designed specifically for blacks, and it is therefore unique and interesting to the historian. The reasons for the establishment of the House of Refuge for Colored Children paralleled in many ways the establishment of the earlier House, and it therefore seems advisable to review the reasons such institutions arose early in the 19th century.

Implicit in the founding of the original House and the later one for Colored Children is the concept of social control. This idea argues that the motivation of the reformers of the 19th century, whatever they overtly stated or implied, was one of social control of deviant elements of the increasingly heterogeneous society. As Trattner says, " . . . .In an attempt to cope with the disturbing social and economic conditions and to restore a sense of community to urban America, moralism succeeded benevolence, public aid and private charity were transformed into mechanisms for social control."[2] According to Trattner, a "growing concern over child welfare . . . resulted above all else from the fact that many citizens viewed the child as the key to social control."[3]

Steven Schlossman, too, sees the importance of social control in the attitudes of 19th-century reformers. In discussing the New York House of Refuge, but then generalizing from there, he states: "Sponsors were very frank about potential social control uses of the Refuge.

SOURCE: Reprinted with permission from The Association for the Study of Afro-American Life and History. *Journal of Negro History,* copyright © 1981, Vol. 66, No. 1, (September), pp. 10–25.

Recognizing the timeless appeal of a 'law and order' issue, they stressed a variety of control functions in the yearly requests for additional legislative funds."[4]

The program for the inmates in Philadelphia, established by 1829 and maintained in both Houses throughout the century, presented the keys to social control over the inmates by the managers.[5] Schooling, for example, was designed to give the students a basic instruction in reading, writing, and numbers.[6] The founders believed that literacy was an excellent cure for poverty and indolence, and the Rules and Regulations stated that "the school shall be provided with all the necessary apparatus to instruct the children in spelling, reading, writing, arithmetic, geography, and bookkeeping."[7]

The teaching of the ethics of Protestantism was an integral and pervasive part of all the activities of both Houses. Each employee was instructed to "endeavor to unfold . . . the advantages of a moral and religious life, and impress upon them a conviction of the evils and miseries that attend the wicked and profligate."[8] The teachers too were expected to teach morality, and each child who left either House as an apprentice was given a Bible.

The third aspect of the program that was to serve as a socializing experience was work. As the Rules and Regulations stated, "The introduction of labour into the Refuge will be regarded principally with reference to the moral benefits rather than the profits to be derived from it. If the employment should not be productive of much pecuniary advantage, still the gain to the City and State will eventually prove very considerable, from the reformation, and consequently reduced number of offenders."[9]

The Managers of the Houses (they were the same until the end of the century) reiterated the belief prevalent in the 19th century that children could be remolded into socially accepted behaviors because of their plasticity.[10] Therefore, they stressed the importance of moral retraining. They felt that delinquents had one characteristic which marked them as a "class, separated from the rest of society. . . . It is the habit of doing wrong, more or less confirmed . . . [and] required to be eradicated before any hope can be entertained of their improvement."[11] The program of the original House of Refuge, and of the House of Refuge for Colored Children as well, was to serve to retrain, to educate, to impart morality, and to incarcerate potentially harmful deviants. Because of the increasing numbers and visibility of poor, vagrant, and delinquent children in the city as the 19th century progressed, Philadelphia citizens found it necessary to establish institutions to try to combat this growing problem.[12]

Before discussing the House of Refuge for Colored Children, one must review briefly the history of blacks in Pennsylvania. They had been in the colony even before William Penn had landed in 1681, and the institution of slavery was practiced until 1780. In that year, the Act for the Gradual Abolition of Slavery was passed by the Pennsylvania legislature. This provided that no child thereafter born in Pennsylvania should be a slave. The children of slaves born before 1780 were to be bond-servants until they reached the age of 28, so that beginning in 1808 there were a series of emancipations. Slaves were encouraged to learn trades; hence, competition for jobs increased between black and white laborers.[13] The constitution of 1790 gave black males the franchise; however, because of a series of events that occurred between 1820 and 1850, the status of blacks in Philadelphia diminished greatly.[14]

Blacks in Pennsylvania were affected greatly by events beyond their control, and as the issue of race became more heated, the city of Philadelphia became, in effect, more racist. Prejudice, especially overt prejudice, increased greatly.[15] By 1837, blacks had lost even the right to vote.[16] As Turner has said: "It was repeatedly said by representative men in the most public places that negroes were and must remain an inferior and degraded race. It was felt that they had made no progress, that they could make none, and that they should not be allowed to make any."[17]

Statistics of the antebellum period noted the disproportionate number of blacks in prisons and the alms house. The first census of blacks, conducted by the Pennsylvania Society for Promoting the Abolition of Slavery, commented: "When we consider that, owing to the feelings and prejudices of the community . . . it is not a matter of surprise that a considerable number of them should be dependent on public support."[18] The same report argued that a disproportionate number of blacks were in prison because there was no other place to incarcerate youth of that race. Its authors recommended the establishment of an institution similar to the House of Refuge, "in which colored minors may be separated from old and practiced offenders. . . . There is no doubt similar good effects would flow from it, as have attended the institution for whites."[19]

As racial prejudice increased, the socioeconomic position of the black community declined. Especially after 1837, blacks were essentially powerless to argue against the dictates of the white community. Poverty increased; as Theodore Hershberg has pointed out: "The total wealth—that is, the combined value of real and personal property holdings—for three out of every five households, in both 1838 and 1847, amounted to $60 or less . . . the distribution of wealth itself, moreover, was strikingly unequal within the black population."[20]

The period of the late 1830's and 1840's was marked by an increased atmosphere of violence and crime in Philadelphia. Riots, gangs, and increased numbers of crimes against property all marked this era

The ineffectiveness of local government in dealing with these problems[21] merely exacerbated the tendency to violence of the various ethnic groups of the community.[22] Often the victims, and sometimes the attackers, were black.[23]

The Managers of the House of Refuge were aware of the problem of black delinquents. As early as 1831, they passed a resolution "to construct the necessary buildings for the suitable accommodation of coloured juvenile delinquents of both sexes. . . ."[24] Nothing, however, was done immediately, and the black children of Philadelphia waited almost 20 years more before they could enter a House constructed specifically for them.

What happened to poor and delinquent black children before 1850? There were some alternative institutions into which they could be placed. One institution, founded by private benevolence, was the Association for the Care of Colored Orphans, established by the Society of Friends in 1822, and opened as a home for "qualified" children. Originally occupying a building on 13th and Callowhill Streets, the establishment was attacked by a mob in 1837. After that, the Association moved the home to 44th Street and Haverford Avenue. At this location, its managers admitted children from 18 months to 8 years of age. At 8, most were indentured out to masters in the country.[25]

Many more black youngsters found their way into the Philadelphia almshouse. Both the census of 1838 and the census of 1849 reported disproportionate numbers of blacks in the Almshouse, and this included black youth. The earlier census reported that one-seventh of the total almshouse population of 1837 was black, including 106 men and boys. These included eighteen under the age of 21. There were also 33 females under the age of 18 listed in the same report. Of the boys, 12 were there because they were "destitute"; women were not classified in the same way, so it is impossible to understand from the data why they were residents.[26] The 1849 report again commented on the disproportionate number of blacks in the almshouse.[27]

A third dumping ground for black juvenile offenders was the adult prison. Again, the bare statistics seemed to indicate a higher proportion of the inmate population of both jails and prisons was black. However, since no breakdown by age was given, it is impossible to ascertain how many of the inmates would have been in the House of Refuge if they had been white.[28] Hence, black delinquents were handled by society in the most convenient way possible—by callously placing them in existing institutions rather than constructing institutions specifically designed to rehabilitate them.

Since reformers believed that early habit formation of a child could make him into either a good citizen or a criminal, and since they believed that the earlier a child was admitted to the House of Refuge, the better were his chances for reformation, it follows that they also believed that the early admissions of black children to such an institution could transform these children from potential criminals into law-abiding citizens who would accept the white, middle class values of the Managers. This concept is stated repeatedly in appeals to the public for the establishment of a House of Refuge for Colored Children that various committees proposed throughout the 1840's.[29]

In 1841, a committee of the Managers of the House of. Refuge reported on the advisability of establishing a separate House for Colored Children. The publication advised that, in fact, the "law establishing the House of Refuge contemplates no differences of colour as distinguishing the classes which shall be admitted."[30] Black children who might have been sent to the House by magistrates and judges, however, were provided for "elsewhere," because no "suitable accommodations for them" were available; "and the knowledge of the community, that they were not prepared to receive them, has doubtless prevented applications."[31] Frank Packard, the chairman, was careful to note that the New York House of Refuge did in fact accept black children.

The prevailing attitudes towards blacks were clearly reflected in the following excerpt from the same pamphlet: "Their [blacks'] opportunities for the improvement in morals or useful learning of any kind, we know to be extremely limited . . . in the habits and associations of the lowest grades there is an assimilation to the irrational animals— which, if seen among whites, would excite universal commiseration."[32]

The committee estimated that in Philadelphia there were 3,337 black children living there between the ages of 5 and 15, "and of this number a large portion are neither at schools nor trades." Therefore, it was "presumed that among so great a number of poor idle, ignorant children there are many who need the care and discipline, and the reforming influence of such an Institution as the House of Refuge."[33] The purpose of the new Refuge was the "cutting down and rooting out the young shoots of licentiousness and crime. . . ."[34] The state was to "remove the colored delinquent from the haunts of iniquity and from the influence of temptation and evil example, and put him under restraint and discipline. . . ."[35] As with the earlier House of Refuge, the institution was to be preventive as well as a place to rehabilitate after the fact.

The original idea of the 1841 committee was to erect a new building adjacent to the buildings of the White Department then in operation; in capital letters, it was noted that "our report is founded on the assumption, that this total and invariable separation is practicable and will be full secured."[36] This was no doubt included to assure the public that no deviation from the norm of segregation was contemplated. The necessity for separation was, in fact, never fully explained; it seemed rather that this was an accepted mode of practice in the city; the schools were completely segregated, as were religious facilities and benevolent institutions.[37]

The Annual Report for 1842 made no mention of the report issued by the 1841 committee. In fact, it was not until 1844 that another mention of the possibility of the establishment of a separate house for black children arose. In that year, the Managers merely mentioned that they had "long regretted the want of an Asylum, where the vicious or neglected children of the coloured population might be properly trained."[38] The 1846 report, which recapitulated the events of 1845, again stated that nothing concrete had been done, and an appeal was made to a "community . . . ever distinguished for its philanthropy."[39]

When one considers the general unrest in Philadelphia that occurred in the 1840's,[40] it is perhaps easier to understand why the Managers felt that they had to "train" the children of the black population before they became like their parents. In addition, the census figures for the early 1840's, and the reports of such institutions as the Philadelphia almshouse and Eastern penitentiary, showed a disproportionate number of black inmates.

In 1845, a series of four letters published in a Philadelphia newspaper advocated the establishment of a House of Refuge for Colored Juvenile Delinquents. Again, the arguments used were much the same as those used by the committee to investigate the possibility of its establishment some years earlier. In essence, the first letter argued that the more youthful an offender was at the time of rehabilitation, the better would the "community . . . be the essential gainer."[41] Since blacks were most prone to violate the law, those with the least advantages would profit most.[42]

The second letter argued that, since the blacks constituted a larger number of the poor and downtrodden, from a benevolent point of view they were most worthy of benefitting from such an institution.[43]

The third letter argued that, because of the prejudices held by the white community, a Refuge should be established "on the principle of simple justice alone. . . ."[44] It was the whites who had brought blacks to America as slaves, yet prevented them (after the abolition of slavery in Pennsylvania) from "rising in their condition. . . ."[45]

The last letter, designed to combat the argument that black youth would not benefit from admission to a House of Refuge, because "the African race" is "more prone to vice, and less capable of moral elevation than the European," argued that "even if blacks could not reach as high on the moral scale as the European, it is also true that it [sic] may be raised far higher by judicious training than without it. . . ."

The author concluded by stating that he believed the theory of an essential and permanent moral difference in races is false; and "this view is sustained by historical facts."[46]

The above statements deserve some comment, for they reflect clearly certain concepts about nature and nurture, and attitudes about children, that were held by members of the articulate classes during the 1840's. First, it must be noted that nowhere does the anonymous author argue for integration. He has accepted without question that any change in the status of black delinquents would, of necessity, involve segregation. Second, the concept of early training as a means of effecting desirable behavior is evident, especially in the last three letters. Third, the idea of benevolence is still prominent in the argument. Last, the concept of social control of deviant behavior is obvious. The issue of law and order is by no means a 20th century phenomenon; those who wish to create changes in society felt free to use it for persuasive purposes much earlier.

On March 10, 1846, a meeting was called by the Society for Alleviating the Miseries of the Public Prisons "for the purpose of adopting measures to secure the establishment of a Refuge for Coloured Juvenile Delinquents, in connection with the Institution already established. . . ."[47] As a result of this meeting (conducted, it should be noted, by a committee consisting solely of middle class white males), an appeal was issued to the citizens of Philadelphia for money. Again, statistics of admissions, deemed "authentic" by the Committee, were presented to reinforce the case for its establishment.[48] These illustrated the disproportionate numbers of black criminals in the community, and the logical conclusion was that "if a House of Refuge be necessary for the White, it is doubly requisite for the Coloured portion of our community."[49] In essence, the committee members believed that "it is cheaper to pay, at the present time, for the correction of vicious and idle habits in the young, than at a future period be compelled to defray the expenses of Police, Criminal Courts, Penitentiaries, and Alms-Houses. . . ."[50]

The Board of Managers of the original House offered to spend $25,000 for the erection of such a building, and hoped that public donations would contribute a like amount. It was clearly noted that "there shall be a total separation of the inmates of the two departments of the Institution."[51] There is no evidence that any black person was considered either as a member of the Board or as an employee of the proposed House.

Once the "good" citizens of Philadelphia decided to pursue the idea of a House of Refuge for blacks, they solicited the opinions of other influential members of the community to bolster their case. Again no blacks were included. *The Annual Report* for 1847 excerpted some of the letters, including those by such local luminaries as Richard Vaux (later mayor of Philadelphia); Francis Wharton, a leading juror of the day; and Anson V. Parsons, an Associate Judge of the Court of Common Pleas. The stress in the letters was the need for a House of Refuge for blacks as a means of social control and a method of teaching them good habits before they became the "desparate and savage offenders" referred to by Francis Wharton in his letter.[52] In fact, the only mention of the feelings of members of the black community was included in the Minutes book of the Board of Managers of the House of Refuge for Jan. 4, 1848: "It affords the Board much pleasure to be able to state that the proposed erection of a Refuge exclusively for colored children, meets the unqualified approval of a number of our most intelligent respectable citizens of color, to whom the plan has been explained; and that there is no doubt that it will be approved by our colored population generally."[53] Who these people were, however, was never mentioned, nor in later Minutes was there any follow-up of the plan to present the idea to "our colored population generally."

By 1848, the status of the new institution had already been decided. According to the *Annual Report* of that year, the Managers stated that they had gathered over $14,000 from private subscriptions. In addition, they had managed to save some money from the existing institution, and had purchased a lot "in the District of Spring Garden, in the vicinity of Girard College. . . . "[54] The original plan was to build, during the following year, a refuge for Colored Children, with accommodations for 100 inmates, and "a capacity within the walls for the erection of buildings for the reception of 150 additional inmates. . . . "[55] Land was saved on another portion of the lot to build a new House of Refuge for white children; this latter building was completed in 1854.

The plans for the buildings were consistent with the beliefs of the Managers as to classification and separation. There was to be total separation of the boys and girls; the first (or best) and second classes were each to have a playground and work-room, and the members of one class were not to be permitted to talk to those of the other. The third class, which was to consist of the most "depraved" inmates, was to be kept "in separate confinement, with a suitable allowance of out of door exercise for the preservation of health . . . [and] where no conversation between the inmates shall be permitted."[56] Since no money was available to erect the separate cells for members of this class, the Managers planned to add it when the money became available. It must be noted that no building for absolute separation was ever erected; hence, children of the third class were probably mixed in with those of the first two.

The opening of the House of Refuge for Colored Children took place at the end of December, 1849. The occasion was marked by a speech by the Hon. William D. Kelley, in which many of the beliefs and ideas of the Managers were expressed. Kelley said that Philadelphia was suffering from "riot and tumult," caused by the "wayward and restless youths who congregate at the street corners. . . ."[57] The new House was to aid those whose parents, for whatever the reasons, allowed them to remain undisciplined and ignorant. In essence, it was to serve the same function for the black community that the 1828 House did for the white children of the poorer classes.[58] In both instances, the idea of noblesse oblige pervaded.

In 1850, an act was passed by the Pennsylvania legislature that enabled the Inspectors of the Prisons of the County of Philadelphia, under the direction of the Court of Quarter Sessions, to transfer and deliver "with their assent, any colored convicts, under the age of 21, committed to said prison, and when so transferred they shall be dealt with as other minors committed and delivered to said Managers."[59]

The *Twenty-Second Annual Report* illustrates how fully the program for the black children had been implemented. By that year, staff included a superintendent, two teachers (for the boys' and girls' schools), and a matron.[60] It was not until 1881 that the Board of Managers began using the same superintendent for both institutions, and this was due to certain failures on the part of the administration as well as an effort to cut costs.

The number of black children who entered the House increased steadily after 1850, but there were always fewer than the parallel number in the White Department. The ages of the former generally were one and one-half to two years lower than those of the same sex admitted to the White Department. In 1850, 93 black children were admitted to the newly opened institution[61]; by 1892, when the House of Refuge for boys (both black and white) was moved to Glen Mills, there was an average of 141 boys and 31 girls.[62] By 1855, the state legislature had codified entrance into both institutions by two means: through the courts, or on recommendation of parents or friends. From 1856 to 1860, black children were admitted for the following reasons: want of friends; on complaint; and vagrancy; as well as by the more normal procedure of admission through court.[63] These three designations were never given for the white children admitted during these years, and by 1861 were dropped entirely by the authors of the annual reports.

As soon as the new House was opened, the demand for its services proved greater than what the Managers had anticipated. *The Annual Report* for 1851 noted:

> It was estimated that the average number of inmates for the past year would be 60; but the number actually received has been much greater, and the applications so numerous that the Managers have been constrained to decline receiving, from the City and County of Philadelphia, except under peculiar circumstances, inmates over the age of 16 years, until additional accommodations can be erected.[64]

By 1853, the Managers notified the magistrates of Philadelphia that they could receive children up to the age of 14 only, "except under peculiar circumstances." They appealed to the citizens for additional money ($10,000) to build the facilities they needed to accommodate 125 additional inmates.[65] By 1854, much of the money was collected, and the new building was begun. The estimate of $10,000 was raised in that year to $22,500, and again an appeal was issued to the citizens.[66] Even a casual look at the statistics of admission show that overcrowding was to remain a continuous problem in both the black and white departments until the end of the century.

Ostensibly because of overcrowding and a disproportionately high death rate among the black children, the Managers decided that the House of Refuge for Colored Children should be moved to the country. During 1858, for example, eight children died, and this was blamed on the "law of climate" and the "results of intermixture of race," plus a "tendency to scrofulous and pulmonary diseases in so many of them. . . ."[67] The Managers failed to take into account such reasons as poor earlier environment and poor nutrition as causes for increased mortality. The other argument used for the move, aside from benevolence, was that the whites could be better classified if there were more room for them, and the Managers intended to replace the black inmates within the city with white ones.[68]

Elisha Swinney, who was superintendent of the Colored Department in 1860, was most sensitive to the problems of these children. As he stated: "In this department, we have difficulties to meet that are not found among the white children. To a white boy, inducements may be held out to make efforts to elevate himself to some important position in life. Not so with these colored children. We cannot say, you may attain to such a high calling or position in life; to that of a physician, lawyer, legislator, governor. . . . There are few opportunities given them whereby they might prove themselves capable of filling higher positions."[69]

Swinney was refreshingly honest in his report. In truth, opportunities for blacks in Philadelphia became increasingly rare as the country moved towards the Civil War and the influx of immigrants to fill menial positions increased. Hence, Swinney understood that it was necessary for social control that blacks be made to limit their expectations, and to strive rather for realistic, if humble, goals.[70]

In 1861, the Managers again expressed a desire to send the black children to the country, because "experience has proved that a climate, so far north as Pennsylvania, is unfavorable to the African constitution."[71] The Managers desired to find a small farm a "convenient distance from the city" to instruct "in agriculture and horticulture, and be better able to find comfortable homes in the country (as apprentices), and be prepared for immigration to Liberia."[72]

The last mention of moving the Colored Department to the country appeared in the Annual Report of 1864. The Board asked the community for $50,000, $25,000 to be paid a year for two years. Liberia was not mentioned, and the plan was never implemented.[73]

In 1881, the management of both the Colored and White Departments was placed under the direction of a single superintendent, J. Hood Laverty. The Annual Report for that year noted that this was "to reduce expenditures and for greater efficiency."[74] This did not imply that there was any attempt at integration, however. In 1883, statistics for the White and Colored Departments were reported together, although distinctions as to sex and color were still made. In 1892, the black girls were moved into the White Department, and all the boys, both black and white, were moved to the country. By 1893, statistics from Glen Mills (the new facility) no longer distinguished between black and white inmates. However, cottages remained segregated, housing either black or white inmates.[75] In 1908, all of the girls were moved to a sister institution of Glen Mills, Sleighton Farms.

The programs established at the House of Refuge for Colored Children paralleled those of the original House of Refuge. There was a strong emphasis on the importance of work in the House; children were indentured out at the completion of their "rehabilitation"; and pervasive in all aspects of life in the institution was the desire to retrain the children according to the precepts of Christian morality in order to convert them from potential criminals into sober, self-sufficient, law-abiding citizens. Hence, the desire for social control of inmates served as the major goal of the Managers.

The program of education was considered to be a terminal one. The Managers saw it as a means of imparting what they considered to be a minimum amount of literacy, as well as a means of introducing their ideas about values and morality to a group who otherwise might not have been exposed to them. Especially before 1870, literacy was believed by the reformers to be a means of preventing poverty and crime. Hence, the stress was continuously on discipline and moral instruction. After the House of Refuge for Colored Children was opened in 1850, the Managers maintained four separate schools: one for white boys, a second for white girls, a third for black boys, and a fourth for black girls. All the teachers were white, and this condition remained at least until the House was moved to Glen Mills. Teachers in all four schools commented on the degree of illiteracy among the children, both black and white. Since education was not yet compulsory in Pennsylvania, and inmates in both Houses were drawn from the lowest socioeconomic classes of society, this is hardly surprising. As Mary Howard, teacher of the black girls, noted: "The school was opened on the 13th of March, 1850, with twelve girls; out of that number, but one could read in words of two syllables; but one could perform a sum in addition. . . ."[76] That same year, the teacher of the white girls noted that only two of the 42 girls could read: "Twenty-one could read a little; seven could spell words of two, three, and four letters; one knew the alphabet, and eleven were ignorant of it."[77]

The Managers recognized that the ignorance of the children was not confined to criminals and potential criminals. Rather, the lack of educational opportunities was much more general. The Annual Report for 1856 noted their concern, and estimated that 20,000 children in Philadelphia were receiving no education.[78] By implication, these were the children of the poorest, least powerful people. By 1860, the Managers included in their report a plea for compulsory common school education. Although public schools had already been established, especially in urban areas, the Managers recognized that parents and guardians were not compelled to send their children to school by law, and often did not.[79]

Despite the pleas for a better public education, the problem of illiteracy continued to be a major one with the inmates of the House. Little difference in literacy was found between the white and black children, with large portions of both being either totally illiterate or able to read only the simplest words.

By 1889, the problems of illiteracy continued unabated. In that year, only 13 of the black boys admitted could read well, 16 could read "fairly," 21 could read "easy lessons," 17 knew the alphabet only, and 16 were ignorant even of the alphabet. When one considers that the average age of the boys admitted was over 13, it is easy to understand the concern.[80] Girls, too, had a wide variety of abilities. Of the 44 admitted that year, six could read well, eight could read "fairly," 15 could read easy lessons, 10 knew the alphabet only, and eight were ignorant of the alphabet.[81]

The problem of illiteracy merely reflected the lack of educational opportunities of blacks in the larger society, and to those lower class white children who entered the White Department as well. Essentially, the Managers saw the rudiments of a basic education as necessary to reform the inmates, and the program of instruction stressed such fundamentals as reading, writing, and basic arithmetic. Included for those with some literacy was American history, but the stress was always primarily on the basics.[82]

The education received by the children was heavily laced with the Managers' values as a method of "moral retraining." This underlying philosophy was summed up in the Annual Report of 1873: "Necessary as their physical and literary education is, their moral training is considered far more important. To it unceasing attention is given. Every morning and evening they have social worship, and on Sundays they receive religious instruction in the Chapels and Sunday Schools."[83]

Moral retraining was not limited to the classroom. Rather, it was pervasive in all programs of the House, which offered its inmates a form of Protestantism in both the formal sense and morality as a method of re-formation of evil habits. Implicit in this was the concept of social control.[84] In a contest held by the Managers in 1855, designed to elicit essays on the causes and cures of juvenile delinquency, two of the three winning articles said that a prime cause of delinquency was the failure on the part of parents to instill religious and moral principles in their children.[85] In its responsibilities, it was the duty of the state to remove children from their families if the parents failed to instill moral values, in order to avoid the perpetuation of such evils.[86]

One additional point must be made. Although the Managers claimed that the religion preached by the visiting ministers was nonpartisan, this was not true. The nondenominationalism was limited to members of various Protestant sects, and all the visiting ministers were, of course, white. It was not until 1887 that priests were permitted to enter the House to counsel Catholic inmates.[87] Even then, Catholics and Jews were not permitted to hold services; and it was not until May 28, 1891, because of the advice of the Manager's attorney, that non-Protestant groups were permitted to conduct services. This occurred because of a ruling by the state legislature allowing such services to be conducted in adult jails and prisons.[88] Black children, therefore (as were Catholic and Jewish children), were exposed only to Protestant ministers (always white) in an effort to retrain them in the "paths of righteousness" according to the latter's beliefs and values.

Like religious training and education, work under the contract system was an integral and important aspect of the total program in the House of Refuge. It too can be viewed as a method of social control. Until 1884, the system of contract labor was the one employed, and this enabled the Managers to reap some financial gain as well as to provide the children with the understanding of the importance of work in 19th-century America. This system was certainly not unique in the

House. According to Harry Elmer Barnes, in his classic work on penology in Pennsylvania, ". . . Labor was introduced in the newly organized penitentiaries in the quarter of the century following 1790, primarily for its deterrent and reformative virtues and secondarily as a means of partially defraying the cost of maintaining the penal institutions. . . ."[89]

The kind of work the children were exposed to, regardless of the goals of the Managers in assigning it, was dull and repetitive because of the sameness of the operation and the length of time per day (up to four hours) spent at the tasks. In 1853, for example, the black boys were employed in the following ways:

Making umbrella furniture . . 40
Shoemaking 3
Making cane seats 17
Miscellaneous . . . . .24[90]

The Annual Report for that year complained about the difficulties of securing positions for the black boys (as apprentices) once they were ready to leave the House. Girls did all the housework, cooking, and sewing for the institution. After 1870, some of them were assigned to the Hosiery shop, but they were always a minority of the total female population.

The emphasis on work for both its own sake and as a preparation for later life was a common theme in the writings of the Managers. Again, as in other aspects of the program, the element of social control is present. Children were to learn the importance of regular work, so that they would be the kind of citizens later who would turn neither to crime nor the public dole as a means of survival. Rather they would, by means of practical experience while in the House, learn not only the use of tools but also "habits of industry and regularity."[91]

Despite the protests of superintendents of prisons and the House of Refuge, by 1884 the system of contract labor was eliminated by law. As the Annual Report for that year noted: "The late legislation in regard to the conduct of Reformatories greatly embarrassed the Board. They are forbidden to make contracts for the employment of the pupils, and are required to enter into contracts for the supplies of the establishment. . . ."[92]

The reality of the situation was that the workshops did continue. In the Annual Report for 1885, the Managers noted that the legislature had passed a law forbidding contract labor, but failed to make an "appropriation to meet the expense of compensating instructors, and for the purchase of machinery, tools, and raw materials. . . ."[93] The shops continued to operate under the new conditions presented by the law. These included tailoring, shoemaking, cane-seating, and iron-working.

Some boys were taught baking, others the management of boilers and steam-fitting. Even after the move to Glen Mills, the position of work (and the erection of shops for the boys) played a prominent part in the rehabilitation of the inmates. As in all other aspects of the institution, absolute segregation within the workshops was maintained.

Once the children left the House, after a stay of one to two years, the Managers continued in many instances to retain some control over them. In order to do so, the apprenticeship system was continued throughout the 19th century, despite the fact that the tradition had begun to die out rapidly as the century progressed.[94] The Managers saw the collapse of apprenticeship as a viable means of rehabilitation as one of the great evils of the 19th century. In the *Prize Essays on Juvenile Delinquency*, originally published in 1855, one winner disparaged the wage system, by which a boy learned a specific function of a machine rather than a craft.[95]

Boys and girls were both indentured through the auspices of the Indenturing Committee, which consisted of eight members "whose duty it shall be to decide upon all applications for apprentices, and to indenture them with their consent."[96] Girls of both races were most frequently apprenticed to learn "housewifery," boys to a variety of occupations, most frequently farming. Black boys were also indentured to barbers and as waiters.[97]

After 1850, the Managers felt the children, both black and white, should be placed "a distance from the city, and the evil associations connected therewith," so that "still more favorable results might be realized."[98] By 1857, the Managers had secured permission to indenture white inmates outside the state of Pennsylvania.[99] On April 22, 1858, Pennsylvania Law 452 was passed, extending to the Managers the right to send black inmates out of the State, "providing that the said Board of Managers are not permitted to bind such colored inmates to persons residing within slave states."[100] This practice, including sending boys to the West, was to be the practice for the remainder of the century. Nowhere is there any evidence that their parents or guardians were ever consulted.

As the numbers of children apprenticed out became greater, because of the increase in numbers admitted to the House, the Managers found it increasingly necessary to establish organized communication between the masters and the institution. Therefore, in 1857, a person was hired as a Visiting Agent. It was his function to place boys, especially in the West, and to visit those already placed in order to check their behavior. The Managers therefore extended their effective influence over the children until they reached the age of majority in many instances. Children were given both a Bible and letter of advice when they left the House. They were to serve to reinforce the beliefs of the

Managers, that children should be moral, obedient, and patient. Along with such admonitions as "If your life be hereafter exemplary the errors of your infancy will be forgiven and forgotten," and "In our happy country every honest person may claim the reward he merits," children were instructed to avoid those who might lead them into vice.[101] As with other aspects of the program, advice was given equally to white and black children.

The House of Refuge for Colored Children, then, paralleled in many ways the House of Refuge opened in 1828 which was de facto for whites only. Both institutions were designed to establish a system of social control over potentially dangerous deviants and to retrain children into the values of the reformers who founded them. These included the necessity for a basic education, an appreciation of work, and the desire for the children under their care to be sober, conscientious, and self-supporting once they re-entered society. The Managers believed the best way to do this was through a total program that consumed every waking hour of the children, with subdivisions of work and education, both literally interspersed with teachings of Protestant morality. Even after the children had left the House and entered a program of apprenticeship, the Managers maintained control over them, in an effort to insure their development into adults. Until the 20th century, the blacks who found their way into the House created for them were totally segregated; even after the boys moved to Glen Mills and the black and white girls were combined, this condition persisted.

As a means of social control, the House of Refuge served to remove black delinquents and potential delinquents from the streets, and as a method of retraining them into an acceptance of the morality and standards of the reformers (all white) who founded the institution. That no member of either the black or white community of the 19th century protested the segregation by race merely is testimony to the racism that existed in the larger Philadelphia society at the time, and in no way should the separation in the House be considered as anything but a reflection of larger society. It was the practice in both public and private institutions until well into the 20th century, and in fact, much still remains, even the City of Brotherly Love.

NOTES

1. History of the Boys, 1828–1829. This is a handwritten account, unpaginated, which listed one child admitted during the period as "Negro."
2. Walter Trattner, *From Poor Law to Welfare State* (New York: Free Press, a Division of Macmillan Co., 1974), p. 67.
3. *Ibid.*, p. 97.

4. Steven Schlossman, "Juvenile Justice in the Age of Jackson," *Teachers College Record*, V. 76, No. 1 (Sept., 1974), p. 125.
5. For a detailed schedule, see *Rules and Regulations for the Government of the House of Refuge* (Philadelphia, 1829), pp. 77–78.
6. *The Forty-Third Annual Report of the Board of Managers of the House of Refuge* (Philadelphia: H. B. Ashmead, 1871), pp. 25–26. This report announced the introduction of a three hour afternoon session in the school, because "a school session in the morning, and then again in the evening, after a long day had been spent in work, play, etc., did not seem to be the most propitious plan for mental improvement."
7. *Rules and Regulations . . . .*, pp. 20–21.
8. *Ibid.*, p. 47.
9. *Ibid.* When the Pennsylvania legislature decided that prison labor should not be for profit of the institution, however, the Managers were upset; by that year, they were realizing profits of over $5,000 from their shops.
10. David Rothman, *The Discovery of the Asylum* (New York: Little Brown and Co., 1971), p. 70.
11. *Fifth Annual Report of the House of Refuge of Philadelphia* (Philadelphia: William Brown, 1833), p. 6.
12. William Tilghman, "An Account of the Measures Taken to Establish the House of Refuge." Handwritten account, unpaginated, found at Glen Mills.
13. W. E. B. DuBois, *The Philadelphia Negro* (New York: Noble Offset Printers, 1967), p. 17. First issued in 1899.
14. *Ibid.*, p. 25.
15. See for example Rev. H. Easton, *A Treatise on the Intellectual Character and Civil and Political Condition of the Colored People of the United States, and the Prejudice Exercised Towards Them* (Boston: Isaac Knapp), 1837.
16. Edward R. Turner, *The Negro in Pennsylvania* (New York: Arno Press, 1969), p. 145. Originally printed 1911.
17. *Ibid.*, p. 147.
18. *Present State and Condition of the Free People of Color, of the City of Philadelphia and Adjoining Districts as Exhibited by a Report of a Committee of the Pennsylvania Society for Promoting the Abolition of Slavery* (Philadelphia: Merrihew and Gunn, 1838), p. 12.
19. *Ibid.*, p. 17.
20. Theodore Hershberg, "Free Blacks in Antebellum Philadelphia: A Study of Ex-Slaves, Freeborn, and Socioeconomic Decline," *Journal of Social History*, Vo. 5, No. 2 (Winter, 1971–72), p. 183.
21. Sam Bass Warner, *The Private City* (Philadelphia: Univ. of Pennsylvania Press, 1971), pp. 138–140.
22. Rowland Berthoff, *An Unsettled People: Social Order and Disorder in American History* (New York: Harper and Row, 1971), p. 231. Also see Elizabeth Geffen, "Violence in Philadelphia in the 1840's and 1850's," *Pennsylvania History*, Vol. XXVI, No. 4 (Oct., 1969), pp. 381–410.
23. For accounts of individual riots in which blacks were involved, see *Hazard's Register of Pennsylvania, Devoted to the Preservation of Facts and Every*

Kind of Useful Information Respecting the State of Pennsylvania, Vol. XIV: or John Scharf and Thompson Westcott, *History of Philadelphia*, Vol. 2 (Philadelphia: L. Everts and Co., 1854), p. 1455.

24. *Third Annual Report of the House of Refuge of Philadelphia* (Philadelphia: J. Harding, 1831), p. 6.

25. Scharf and Westcott, Vol. 2, p. 1455.

26. *The Present State and Condition . . . .*, pp. 12–13.

27. *A Statistical Inquiry into the Condition of the People of Colour of the City and Districts of Philadelphia* (Philadelphia: Kite and Walton, 1849), p. 25.

28. *The Present State and Condition . . . .*, p. 17. For an explanation of why more blacks than whites were admitted (based on the argument of unequal justice under the law) see *A Statistical Inquiry . . . .*, p. 27.

29. See, for example, *Report on the Practicability and Necessity of a House of Refuge for Coloured Juvenile Delinquents in Philadelphia* (Philadelphia: Brown, Bicking and Guilbert), 1841.

30. *Ibid.*, p. 3.

31. *Ibid.*, p. 4.

32. *Ibid.*, p. 5.

33. *Ibid.*, p. 6.

34. *Ibid.*, p. 7.

35. *Ibid.*, p. 10.

36. *Ibid.*, p. 11.

37. See, for example, Harry Silcox, "Delay and Neglect: Negro Public Education in Antebellum Philadelphia, 1800–1864," *Pennsylvania Magazine of History and Biography*, Vol. XCVII, No. 4 (Oct., 1973), pp. 444–464.

38. *Sixteenth Annual Report of the House of Refuge* (Philadelphia: E. G. Dorsey, 1844), p. 5.

39. *Eighteenth Annual Report of the House of Refuge* (Philadelphia, 1846), p. 10.

40. See Elizabeth Gefien.

41. "House of Refuge No. 1," *Pennsylvanian*, Vol. XXVI, No. 3860 (Jan. 10, 1845), p. 2.

42. *Ibid.*

43. "House of Refuge No. 2," *Pennsylvanian*, Vol. XXVI, No. 3861 (Jan. 11, 1845), p. 2.

44. "House of Refuge No. 3," *Pennsylvanian*, Vol. XXVI, No. 3863 (Jan. 14, 1845), p. 2.

45. *Ibid.*

46. "House of Refuge No. 4," *Pennsylvanian*, Vol. XXVI, No. 3864 (Jan. 15, 1845), p. 2. "Raised" in this sense implies elevation of blacks to a higher moral state (at least in the eyes of reformers of the day).

47. *Committee Report* of the Philadelphia Society for Alleviating the Miseries of the Public Prisons (March 10, 1846), p. 2.

48. *An Appeal to the Public on Behalf of a House of Refuge for Coloured Juvenile Delinquents* (Philadelphia: T. K. and P. G. Collins, 1846), p. 3.

49. *Ibid.*, pp. 4–6.

50. *Ibid.* The same arguments were used from 1826 to 1828, when the Managers were fighting for public acceptance of the original House. See, for example, Robert Vaux, *An Address from the Managers of the House of Refuge, to their Fellow Citizens* (Philadelphia: Solomon Conrad, 1828) or *Notices of the Origin and Successive Efforts to Improve the Discipline of the Prison at Philadelphia* (Philadelphia: Harding), 1826.

51. *Ibid.*, p. 9.

52. *Nineteenth Annual Report of the House of Refuge* (Philadelphia: T. K. and P. G. Collins, 1847), pp. 10–11.

53. Minutes of the Board of Managers of the House of Refuge, Jan. 4, 1848.

54. *Twentieth Annual Report of the House of Refuge* (Philadelphia: T. K. and P. G. Collins, 1848), p. 10.

55. *Ibid.*

56. *Twenty-First Annual Report of the House of Refuge* (Philadelphia: T. K. and P. G. Collins, 1850), p. 13. This is consistent with the Pennsylvania Plan of solitary confinement, in which inmates, by reading the Bible and contemplating their sins alone, were expected to repent. Their only visitor was to be a minister. The most famous prison of this type to be erected in nineteenth century America was the Prison at Cherry Hill (Phila.).

57. William D. Kelley, *Address Delivered at the Colored Department of the House of Refuge, De. 31, 1849* (Philadelphia: T. K. and P. G. Collins, 1850), p. 13.

58. *Ibid.*, pp. 20–21.

59. Pennsylvania Law 570, April 25, 1850; Section C.

60. *Twenty-Second Annual Report of the House of Refuge* (Philadelphia: T. K. and P. G. Collins, 1850), p. 19.

61. *Sixty-Fourth Annual Report of the Board of Managers of the House of Refuge* (Philadelphia: Franklin Printing), 1892.

62. *Ibid.*

63. *Twenty-Eight Annual Report of the Board of Managers of the House of Refuge* (Philadelphia: Ashmead, 1856) to *Thirty-Second Annual Report of the Board of Managers of the House of Refuge* (Philadelphia: Ashmead), 1860.

64. *Twenty-Third Annual Report of the House of Refuge* (Philadelphia: T. K. and P. G. Collins, 1851), p. 60.

65. *Twenty-Fifth Annual Report of the Board of Managers of the House of Refuge* (Philadelphia: T. K. and P. G. Collins, 1853), p. 10.

66. *Twenty-Sixth Annual Report*, p. 9.

67. *Thirty-First Annual Report of the Board of Managers of the House of Refuge* (Philadelphia: Ashmead, 1859), pp. 10–11.

68. *Ibid.*, p. 11.

69. *Thirty-Second Annual Report*, p. 44.

70. *Ibid.*

71. *Thirty-Third Annual Report of the Board of Managers of the House of Refuge* (Philadelphia: Ashmead, 1861), p. 12

72. *Ibid.*, p. 11.

73. *Thirty-Sixth Annual Report*, p. 18.
74. *Fifty-Third Annual Report of the Board of Managers of the House of Refuge* (Philadelphia: Franklin Printing), 1881.
75. *Sixty-Fourth Annual Report* and *Sixty-Fifth Annual Report of the Board of Managers of the House of Refuge* (Philadelphia: Fell), 1893.
76. *Twenty-Third Annual Report*, pp. 36–37.
77. *Ibid.*, p. 34.
78. *Twenty-Eighth Annual Report*, p. 4.
79. *Thirty-Second Annual Report*, p. 6.
80. *Sixty-First Annual Report of the Board of Managers of the House of Refuge* (Philadelphia: Franklin Printing, 1889), p. 33.
81. *Ibid.*, p. 34.
82. See, for example, any of the annual reports. Detailed lists of studies, including texts used, were given.
83. *Forty-Fifth Annual Report of the Board of Managers of the House of Refuge* (Philadelphia: Ashmead, 1874), p. 9.
84. See, for example, Clifford Griffin, "Religious Benevolence as Social Control," *Mississippi Valley Historical Review,* Vol. XLIV, No. 3 (Dec., 1957), pp. 423–444.
85. *Prize Essays on Juvenile Delinquency,* introd. by Cecile P. Remick (Norwood, Pa.: Norwood Editions), 1976. Originally published in 1855.
86. *Ibid.*, pp. 13–44.
87. Minutes of the Board of Managers, March 31, 1887.
88. Minutes of the Board of Managers, May 28, 1891.
89. Harry Elmer Barnes, *Evolution of Penology in Pennsylvania* (Indianapolis: Bobbs-Merrill, 1927), p. 237.
90. *Twenty-Fifth Annual Report*, p. 23.
91. See, for example, *Thirty-Third Annual Report*, p. 9.
92. *Fifty-Sixth Annual Report of the Board of Managers of the House of Refuge* (Philadelphia: Friends' Book Assoc., 1884), pp. 1–2.
93. *Fifty-Seventh Annual Report of the Board of Managers of the House of Refuge* (Philadelphia: Franklin Printing, 1885), p. 30.
94. Trattner, p. 100.
95. *Prize Essays on Juvenile Delinquency,* pp. 13–14.
96. Quoted in Robert H. Bremner, *Children and Youth in America: A Documentary History* (Cambridge: Harvard Univ. Press, 1970), p. 41.
97. *Sixty-First Annual Report*, p. 18.
98. *Twenty-Second Annual Report*, pp. 9–10.
99. *Articles of Association, Acts of Incorporation, Acts of Assembly, of the State of Pennsylvania, and Decrees of the Court, together with the Statistics of Other States Relating to the House of Refuge* (Philadelphia: Franklin Printing, 1885), p. 17.
100. *Ibid.*
101. *Thirty-Second Annual Report*, p. 61.

Article 9

FIRST DAYS AT HULL-HOUSE

Jane Addams

The next January found Miss Starr and myself in Chicago, searching for a neighborhood in which we might put our plans into execution. In our eagerness to win friends for the new undertaking, we utilized every opportunity to set forth the meaning of the Settlement as it had been embodied in Toynbee Hall, although in those days we made no appeal for money, meaning to start with our own slender resources. From the very first the plan received courteous attention, and the discussion, while often skeptical, was always friendly. Professor Swing wrote a commendatory column in the *Evening Journal,* and our early speeches were reported quite out of proportion to their worth. I recall a spirited evening at the home of Mrs. Wilmarth, which was attended by that renowned scholar, Thomas Davidson, and by a young Englishman who was a member of the then new Fabian society and to whom a peculiar glamour was attached because he had scoured knives all summer in a camp of high-minded philosophers in the Adirondacks. Our new little plan met with criticism, not to say disapproval, from Mr. Davidson, who, as nearly as I can remember, called it "one of those unnatural attempts to understand life through coöperative living."

It was in vain we asserted that the collective living was not an essential part of the plan, that we would always scrupulously pay our own expenses, and that at any moment we might decide to scatter through the neighborhood and to live in separate tenements; he still contended that the fascination for most of those volunteering residence would lie in the collective living aspect of the Settlement. His contention was, of course, essentially sound; there is a constant tendency for the residents to "lose themselves in the cave of their own companionship," as the Toynbee Hall phrase goes, but on the other hand, it is doubtless true that the very companionship, the give and take of colleagues, is what tends to keep the Settlement normal and in touch with "the world of things as they are." I am happy to say that we never resented this nor any other difference of opinion, and that fifteen years later Professor Davidson handsomely acknowledged that the

SOURCE: From *Twenty Years At Hull House* by Jane Addams (New York: Macmillan, 1910).

advantages of a group far outweighed the weaknesses he had early pointed out. He was at that later moment sharing with a group of young men, on the East Side of New York, his ripest conclusions in philosophy and was much touched by their intelligent interest and absorbed devotion. I think that time has also justified our early contention that the mere foothold of a house, easily accessible, ample in space, hospitable and tolerant in spirit, situated in the midst of the large foreign colonies which so easily isolate themselves in American cities, would be in itself a serviceable thing for Chicago. I am not so sure that we succeeded in our endeavors "to make social intercourse express the growing sense of the economic unity of society and to add the social function to democracy." But Hull-House was soberly opened on the theory that the dependence of classes on each other is reciprocal; and that as the social relation is essentially a reciprocal relation, it gives a form of expression that has peculiar value.

In our search for a vicinity in which to settle we went about with the officers of the compulsory education department, with city missionaries, and with the newspaper reporters whom I recall as a much older set of men than one ordinarily associates with that profession, or perhaps I was only sent out with the older ones on what they must all have considered a quixotic mission. One Sunday afternoon in the late winter a reporter took me to visit a so-called anarchist Sunday School, several of which were to be found on the northwest side of the city. The young man in charge was of the German student type, and his face flushed with enthusiasm as he led the children singing one of Koerner's poems. The newspaperman, who did not understand German, asked me what abominable stuff they were singing, but he seemed dissatisfied with my translation of the simple words and darkly intimated that they were "deep ones," and had probably "fooled" me. When I replied that Koerner was an ardent German poet whose songs inspired his countrymen to resist the aggressions of Napoleon, and that his bound poems were found in the most respectable libraries, he looked at me rather askance and I then and there had my first intimation that to treat a Chicago man, who is called an anarchist, as you would treat any other citizen, is to lay yourself open to deep suspicion.

Another Sunday afternoon in the early spring, on the way to a Bohemian mission in the carriage of one of its founders, we passed a fine old house standing well back from the street, surrounded on three sides by a broad piazza which was supported by wooden pillars of exceptionally pure Corinthian design and proportion. I was so attracted by the house that I set forth to visit it the very next day, but though I searched for it then and for several days after, I could not find it, and at length I most reluctantly gave up the search.

Three weeks later, with the advice of several of the oldest residents of Chicago, including the ex-mayor of the city, Colonel Mason, who had from the first been a warm friend to our plans, we decided upon a location somewhere near the junction of Blue Island Avenue, Halsted Street, and Harrison Street. I was surprised and overjoyed on the very first day of our search for quarters to come upon the hospitable old house, the quest for which I had so recently abandoned. The house was of course rented, the lower part of it used for offices and store-rooms in connection with a factory that stood back of it. However, after some difficulties were overcome, it proved to be possible to sublet the second floor and what had been the large drawing-room on the first floor.

The house had passed through many changes since it had been built in 1856 for the homestead of one of Chicago's pioneer citizens, Mr. Charles J. Hull, and although battered by its vicissitudes, was essentially sound. Before it had been occupied by the factory, it had sheltered a second-hand furniture store, and at one time the Little Sisters of the Poor had used it for a home for the aged. It had a half-skeptical reputation for a haunted attic, so far respected by the tenants living on the second floor that they always kept a large pitcher full of water on the attic stairs. Their explanation of this custom was so incoherent that I was sure it was a survival of the belief that a ghost could not cross running water, but perhaps that interpretation was only my eagerness for finding folklore.

The fine old house responded kindly to repairs, its wide hall and open fireplaces always insuring it a gracious aspect. Its generous owner, Miss Helen Culver, in the following spring gave us a free leasehold of the entire house. Her kindness has continued through the years until the group of thirteen buildings, which at present comprises our equipment, is built largely upon land which Miss Culver has put at the service of the Settlement which bears Mr. Hull's name. In those days the house stood between an undertaking establishment and a saloon. "Knight, Death, and the Devil," the three were called by a Chicago wit, and yet any mock heroics which might be implied by comparing the Settlement to a knight quickly dropped away under the genuine kindness and hearty welcome extended to us by the families living up and down the street.

We furnished the house as we would have furnished it were it in another part of the city, with the photographs and other impedimenta we had collected in Europe, and with a few bits of family mahogany. While all the new furniture which was bought was enduring in quality, we were careful to keep it in character with the fine old residence. Probably no young matron ever placed her own things in her own house with more pleasure than that with which we first furnished Hull-House. We believed that the Settlement may logically bring to its aid all those adjuncts which the cultivated man regards as good and suggestive of the best life of the past.

On the 18th of September, 1889, Miss Starr and I moved into it, with Miss Mary Keyser, who began by performing the housework, but who quickly developed into a very important factor in the life of the vicinity as well as in that of the household, and whose death five years later was most sincerely mourned by hundreds of our neighbors. In our enthusiasm over "settling," the first night we forgot not only to lock but to close a side door opening on Polk Street, and were much pleased in the morning to find that we possessed a fine illustration of the honesty and kindliness of our new neighbors.

Our first guest was an interesting young woman who lived in a neighboring tenement, whose widowed mother aided her in the support of the family by scrubbing a downtown theater every night. The mother, of English birth, was well bred and carefully educated, but was in the midst of that bitter struggle which awaits so many strangers in American cities who find that their social position tends to be measured solely by the standards of living they are able to maintain. Our guest has long since married the struggling young lawyer to whom she was then engaged, and he is now leading his profession in an eastern city. She recalls that month's experience always with a sense of amusement over the fact that the succession of visitors who came to see the new Settlement invariably questioned her most minutely concerning "these people" without once suspecting that they were talking to one who had been identified with the neighborhood from childhood. I at least was able to draw a lesson from this incident, and I never addressed a Chicago audience on the subject of the Settlement and its vicinity without inviting a neighbor to go with me, that I might curb any hasty generalization by the consciousness that I had an auditor who knew the conditions more intimately than I could hope to do.

Halsted Street has grown so familiar during twenty years of residence that it is difficult to recall its gradual changes—the withdrawal of the more prosperous Irish and Germans, and the slow substitution of Russian Jews, Italians, and Greeks. A description of the street such as I gave in those early addresses still stands in my mind as sympathetic and correct.

> Halsted Street is thirty-two miles long, and one of the great thoroughfares of Chicago; Polk Street crosses it midway between the stockyards to the south and the shipbuilding yards on the north branch of the Chicago River. For the six miles between these two industries the street is lined with shops of butchers and grocers, with dingy and gorgeous saloons, and pretentious establishments for the sale of ready-made

clothing. Polk Street, running west from Halsted Street, grows rapidly more prosperous; running a mile east to State Street, it grows steadily worse, and crosses a network of vice on the corners of Clark Street and Fifth Avenue. Hull-House once stood in the suburbs, but the city has steadily grown up around it and its site now has corners on three or four foreign colonies. Between Halsted Street and the river live about ten thousand Italians—Neapolitans, Sicilians, and Calabrians, with an occasional Lombard or Venetian. To the south on Twelfth Street are many Germans, and the side streets are given over almost entirely to Polish and Russian Jews. Still farther south, these Jewish colonies merge into a huge Bohemian colony, so vast that Chicago ranks as the third Bohemian city in the world. To the northwest are many Canadian-French, clannish in spite of their long residence in America, and to the north are Irish and first-generation Americans. On the streets directly west and farther north are well-to-do English-speaking families, many of whom own their houses and have lived in the neighborhood for years; one man is still living in his old farmhouse.

The policy of the public authorities of never taking an initiative, and always waiting to be urged to do their duty, is obviously fatal in a neighborhood where there is little initiative among the citizens. The idea underlying our self-government breaks down in such a ward. The streets are inexpressibly dirty, the number of schools inadequate, sanitary legislation unenforced, the street lighting bad, the paving miserable and altogether lacking in the alleys and smaller streets, and the stables foul beyond description. Hundreds of houses are unconnected with the street sewer. The older and richer inhabitants seem anxious to move away as rapidly as they can afford it. They make room for newly arrived immigrants who are densely ignorant of civic duties. This substitution of the older inhabitants is accomplished industrially also, in the south and east quarters of the ward. The Jews and Italians for the finishing for the great clothing manufacturers, formerly done by Americans, Irish, and Germans, who refused to submit to the extremely low prices to which the sweating system has reduced their successors. As the design of the sweating system is the elimination of rent from the manufacture of clothing, the "outside work" is begun after the clothing leaves the cutter. An unscrupulous contractor regards no basement as too dark, no stable loft too foul, no rear shanty too provisional, no tenement room too small for his workroom, as these conditions imply low rental. Hence these shops abound in the worst of the foreign districts where the sweater easily finds his cheap basement and his home finishers.

The houses of the ward, for the most part wooden, were originally built for the one family and are now occupied by several. They are after the type of the inconvenient frame cottages found in the poorer suburbs twenty years ago. Many of them were built where they now stand; others were brought thither on rollers, because their previous sites had been taken for factories. The fewer brick tenement buildings which are three or four stories high are comparatively new, and there are few large tenements. The little wooden houses have a temporary aspect, and for this reason, perhaps, the tenement-house legislation in Chicago is totally inadequate. Rear tenements flourish; many houses have no water supply save the faucet in the back yard, there are no fire escapes, the garbage and ashes are placed in wooden boxes which are fastened to the street pavements. One of the most discouraging features about the present system of tenement houses is that many are owned by sordid and ignorant immigrants. The theory that wealth brings responsibility, that possession entails at length education and refinement, in these cases fails utterly. The children of an Italian immigrant owner may "shine" shoes in the streets, and his wife may pick rags from the street gutter, laboriously sorting them in a dingy court. Wealth may do something for her self-complacency and feeling of consequence; it certainly does nothing for her comfort or her children's improvement nor for the cleanliness of anyone concerned. Another thing that prevents better houses in Chicago is the tentative attitude of the real estate men. Many unsavory conditions are allowed to continue which would be regarded with horror if they were considered permanent. Meanwhile, the wretched conditions persist until at least two generations of children have been born and reared in them.

In every neighborhood where poorer people live, because rents are supposed to be cheaper there, is an element which, although uncertain in the individual, in the aggregate can be counted upon. It is composed of people of former education and opportunity who have cherished ambitions and prospects, but who are caricatures of what they meant to be—"hollow ghosts which blame the living men." There are times in many lives when there is a cessation of energy and loss of power. Men and women of education and refinement come to live in a cheaper neighborhood because they lack the ability to make money, because of ill health, because of an unfortunate marriage, or for other reasons which do not imply criminality or stupidity. Among them are those who, in spite of untoward circumstances, keep up some sort of an intellectual life; those who are "great for books," as their neighbors say. To such the Settlement may be a genuine refuge.

In the very first weeks of our residence Miss Starr started a reading party in George Eliot's *Romola*, which was attended by a group of young women who followed the wonderful tale with unflagging interest. The weekly reading was held in our little upstairs dining room, and two members of the club came to dinner each week, not only that they might be received as guests, but that they might help us wash the dishes afterward and so make the table ready for the stacks of Florentine photographs.

Our "first resident," as she gaily designated herself, was a charming old lady who gave five consecutive readings from Hawthorne to a most appreciative audience, interspersing the magic tales most delightfully with recollections of the elusive and fascinating author. Years before she had lived at Brook Farm as a pupil of the Ripleys, and she came to us for ten days because she wished to live once more in an atmosphere where "idealism ran high." We thus early found the type of class which through all the years has remained most popular—a combination of a social atmosphere with serious study.

Volunteers to the new undertaking came quickly; a charming young girl conducted a kindergarten in the drawing room, coming regularly every morning from her home in a distant part of the North Side of the city. Although a tablet to her memory has stood upon a mantel shelf in Hull-House for five years, we still associate her most vividly with the play of little children, first in her kindergarten and then in her own nursery, which furnished a veritable illustration of Victor Hugo's definition of heaven—"a place where parents are always young and children always little." Her daily presence for the first two years made it quite impossible for us to become too solemn and self-conscious in our strenuous routine, for her mirth and buoyancy were irresistible and her eager desire to share the life of the neighborhood never failed, although it was often put to a severe test. One day at luncheon she gaily recited her futile attempt to impress temperance principles upon the mind of an Italian mother, to whom she had returned a small daughter of five sent to the kindergarten "in quite a horrid state of intoxication" from the wine-soaked bread upon which she had breakfasted. The mother, with the gentle courtesy of a South Italian, listened politely to her graphic portrayal of the untimely end awaiting so immature a wine bibber; but long before the lecture was finished quite unconscious of the incongruity, she hospitably set forth her best wines, and when her baffled guest refused one after the other, she disappeared, only to quickly return with a small dark glass of whisky, saying reassuringly, "See, I have brought you the true American drink." The recital ended in seriocomic despair, with the rueful statement that "the impression I probably made upon her darkened mind was that it is the American custom to breakfast children on bread soaked in whisky instead of light Italian wine."

That first kindergarten was a constant source of education to us. We were much surprised to find social distinctions even among its lambs, although greatly amused with the neat formulation made by the superior little Italian boy who refused to sit beside uncouth little Angelina because "we eat our macaroni this way"—imitating the movement of a fork from a plate to his mouth—"and she eat her macaroni this way," holding his hand high in the air and throwing back his head, that his wide-open mouth might receive an imaginary cascade. Angelina gravely nodded her little head in approval of this distinction between gentry and peasant. "But isn't it astonishing that merely table manners are made such a test all the way along?" was the comment of their democratic teacher. Another memory which refuses to be associated with death, which came to her all too soon, is that of the young girl who organized our first really successful club of boys, holding their fascinated interest by the old chivalric tales, set forth so dramatically and vividly that checkers and jackstraws were abandoned by all the other clubs on Boys' Day, that their members might form a listening fringe to *The Young Heroes*.

I met a member of the latter club one day as he flung himself out of the House in the rage by which an emotional boy hopes to keep from shedding tears. "There is no use coming here any more, Prince Roland is dead," he gruffly explained as we passed. We encouraged the younger boys in tournaments and dramatics of all sorts, and we somewhat fatuously believed that boys who were early interested in adventures or explorers might later want to know the lives of living statesmen and inventors. It is needless to add that the boys quickly responded to such a program, and that the only difficulty lay in finding leaders who were able to carry it out. This difficulty has been with us through all the years of growth and development in the Boys' Club until now, with its five-story building, its splendid equipment of shops, of recreation and study rooms, that group alone is successful which commands the services of a resourceful and devoted leader.

The dozens of younger children who from the first came to Hull-House were organized into groups which were not quite classes and not quite clubs. The value of these groups consisted almost entirely in arousing a higher imagination and in giving the children the opportunity which they could not have in the crowded schools, for initiative and for independent social relationships. The public schools then contained little hand work of any sort, so that naturally any instruction which we provided for the children took the direction of this supplementary work. But it required a constant effort that the pressure of poverty itself should not defeat the educational aim. The Italian girls in the sewing classes would count that day lost when they could not carry home a garment, and the insistence that it should be neatly made seemed a super-refinement to those in dire need of clothing.

As these clubs have been continued during the twenty years they have developed classes in the many forms of handicraft which the newer education is so rapidly adapting for the delight of children; but they still keep their essentially social character and still minister to that large number of children who leave school the very week they are fourteen years old, only too eager to close the schoolroom door forever on a tiresome task that is at last well over. It seems to us important that these children shall find themselves permanently attached to a House that offers them evening clubs and classes with their old companions, that merges as easily as possible the school life into the working life and does what it can to find places for the bewildered young things looking for work. A large proportion of the delinquent boys brought into the juvenile court in Chicago are the oldest sons in large families whose wages are needed at home. The grades from which many of them leave school, as the records show, are piteously far from the seventh and eighth where the very first instruction in manual training is given, nor have they been caught by any other abiding interest.

In spite of these flourishing clubs for children early established at Hull-House, and the fact that our first organized undertaking was a kindergarten, we were very insistent that the Settlement should not be primarily for the children, and that it was absurd to suppose that grown people would not respond to opportunities for education and social life. Our enthusiastic kindergartner herself demonstrated this with an old woman of ninety, who, because she was left alone all day while her daughter cooked in a restaurant, had formed such a persistent habit of picking the plaster off the walls that one landlord after another refused to have her for a tenant. It required but a few weeks' time to teach her to make large paper chains, and gradually she was content to do it all day long, and in the end took quite as much pleasure in adorning the walls as she had formerly taken in demolishing them. Fortunately the landlord had never heard the æsthetic principle that the exposure of basic construction is more desirable than gaudy decoration. In course of time it was discovered that the old woman could speak Gælic, and when one or two grave professors came to see her, the neighborhood was filled with pride that such a wonder lived in their midst. To mitigate life for a woman of ninety was an unfailing refutation of the statement that the Settlement was designed for the young.

On our first New Year's Day at Hull-House we invited the older people in the vicinity, sending a carriage for the most feeble and announcing to all of them that we were going to organize an Old Settlers' Party.

Every New Year's Day since, older people in varying numbers have come together at Hull-House to relate early hardships and to take for the moment the place in the community to which their pioneer life entitles them. Many people who were formerly residents of the vicinity, but whom prosperity has carried into more desirable neighborhoods, come back to these meetings and often confess to each other that they have never since found such kindness as in early Chicago when all its citizens came together in mutual enterprises. Many of these pioneers, so like the men and women of my earliest childhood that I always felt comforted by their presence in the house, were very much opposed to "foreigners," whom they held responsible for a depreciation of property and a general lowering of the tone of the neighborhood. Sometimes we had a chance for championship; I recall one old man, fiercely American, who had reproached me because we had so many "foreign views" on our walls, to whom I endeavored to set forth our hope that the pictures might afford a familiar island to the immigrants in a sea of new and strange impressions. The old settler guest, taken off his guard, replied, "I see; they feel as we did when we saw a

Yankee notion from down East"—thereby formulating the dim kinship between the pioneer and the immigrant, both "buffeting the waves of a new development." The older settlers as well as their children throughout the years have given genuine help to our various enterprises for neighborhood improvement, and from their own memories of earlier hardships have made many shrewd suggestions for alleviating the difficulties of that first sharp struggle with untoward conditions.

In those early days we were often asked why we had come to live on Halsted Street when we could afford to live somewhere else. I remember one man who used to shake his head and say it was "the strangest thing he had met in his experience," but who was finally convinced that it was "not strange but natural." In time it came to seem natural to all of us that the Settlement should be there. If it is natural to feed the hungry and care for the sick, it is certainly natural to give pleasure to the young, comfort to the aged, and to minister to the deep-seated craving for social intercourse that all men feel. Whoever does it is rewarded by something which, if not gratitude, is at least spontaneous and vital and lacks that irksome sense of obligation with which a substantial benefit is too often acknowledged.

In addition to the neighbors who responded to the receptions and classes, we found those who were too battered and oppressed to care for them. To these, however, was left that susceptibility to the bare offices of humanity which raises such offices into a bond of fellowship.

From the first it seemed understood that we were ready to perform the humblest neighborhood services. We were asked to wash the newborn babies, and to prepare the dead for burial, to nurse the sick, and to "mind the children."

Occasionally these neighborly offices unexpectedly uncovered ugly human traits. For six weeks after an operation we kept in one of our three bedrooms a forlorn little baby who, because he was born with a cleft palate, was most unwelcome even to his mother, and we were horrified when he died of neglect a week after he was returned to his home; a little Italian bride of fifteen sought shelter with us one November evening, to escape her husband who had beaten her every night for a week when he returned home from work, because she had lost her wedding ring; two of us officiated quite alone at the birth of an illegitimate child because the doctor was late in arriving, and none of the honest Irish matrons would "touch the likes of her"; we ministered at the deathbed of a young man, who during a long illness of tuberculosis had received so many bottles of whisky through the mistaken kindness of his friends, that the cumulative effect produced wild periods of exultation, in one of which he died.

We were also early impressed with the curious isolation of many of the immigrants; an Italian woman once expressed her pleasure in the red roses that she saw at one of our receptions in surprise that they had been "brought so fresh all the way from Italy." She would not believe for an instant that they had been grown in America. She said that she had lived in Chicago for six years and had never seen any roses, whereas in Italy she had seen them every summer in great profusion. During all that time, of course, the woman had lived within ten blocks of a florist's window; she had not been more than a five-cent car ride away from the public parks; but she had never dreamed of faring forth for herself, and no one had taken her. Her conception of America had been the untidy street in which she lived and had made her long struggle to adapt herself to American ways.

But in spite of some untoward experiences, we were constantly impressed with the uniform kindness and courtesy we received. Perhaps these first days laid the simple human foundations which are certainly essential for continuous living among the poor: first, genuine preference for residence in an industrial quarter to any other part of the city, because it is interesting and makes the human appeal; and second, the conviction, in the words of Canon Barnett, that the things which make men alike are finer and better than the things that keep them apart, and that these basic likenesses, if they are properly accentuated, easily transcend the less essential differences of race, language, creed, and tradition.

Perhaps even in those first days we made a beginning toward that object which was afterward stated in our charter: "To provide a center for a higher civic and social life; to institute and maintain educational and philanthropic enterprises, and to investigate and improve the conditions in the industrial districts of Chicago."

Article 10

FIFTY YEARS OF SOCIAL SECURITY

Martha A. McSteen*

Today, we celebrate the 50th anniversary of the Federal social insurance program, now known simply as "Social Security," that emerged in 1935 as part of the Nation's response to the plight of its elderly. The Social Security program of the 1980's is the direct descendant of the limited program of the contributory old-age benefits enacted in 1935. The program, which today covers virtually all jobs, continues to have certain basic characteristics found in the original program; that is, eligibility is earned through work in covered jobs, participation is generally compulsory, the amount of the benefits is related to covered earnings, the program is intended to provide a base of protection, and benefits are financed primarily through dedicated payroll taxes paid by workers and their employers.

Yet, while the program fundamentals have remained the same over 5 decades, much has changed. As American work and life patterns have changed, so too Social Security has been adapted to meet current expectations. The legislative history of the program, described briefly below, shows clearly how Social Security has retained its essential characteristics as it has evolved to keep pace with the times.

Foundations of Change

By the end of the First World War, a primarily agrarian American society had become a primarily urban, industrialized one. Thus, on the eve of the Great Depression of the 1930's, a larger proportion of the American people were dependent on cash wages for their support than ever before. By 1932, however, unemployment reached 34 percent of the nonagricultural workforce. Between 1929 and 1932, national income dropped by 43 percent, per capita income by 19 percent. By the mid-1930's, the lifetime savings of millions of people had been wiped out.

*The author wishes to acknowledge the assistance provided by the following members of the Social Security Administration's Office of Legislative and Regulatory Policy: Peggy S. Fisher, Director, and Timothy K. Evans and Richard L. Griffiths, staff, of the Division of Retirement and Survivors Benefits.

SOURCE: *Social Security Bulletin*, Vol. 48, No. 8 (1985, August), pp. 36–44.

For vast numbers of aged people, and people nearing old age, the loss of their savings brought with it the prospect of living their remaining years in destitution. At the height of the Depression, many old people were literally penniless. One-third to one-half of the aged were dependent on family or friends for support. The poor houses and other relief agencies that existed at the time to assist people who had fallen on hard times were financed mainly from charity and local funds. They could not begin—either financially or conceptually—to respond adequately to the special needs of the aged brought about by the cataclysmic events of the Depression.

Although by 1934, 30 States had responded by providing pensions for the needy aged, total expenditures for State programs for the aged that year were $31 million—an average of $19.74 a month per aged person. As the Depression worsened, benefits to individuals were cut further to enable States to spread available funds among as many people as possible.

Various national schemes to provide income to the aged received substantial attention. These included the Townsend Old-Age Revolving Pension Plan and a plan called "Share the Wealth," advanced by Louisiana Senator Huey P. Long. Under the Townsend plan, every American over age 60 was to get a monthly pension, provided he or she did not work and promised to spend the entire payment during the month. Under Long's plan, large personal fortunes would be liquidated to finance (1) pensions for the aged and (2) cash payments to every family sufficient to buy a home, a car, and radio.

Due in large part to the public and congressional pressures for some Federal response to the chaotic conditions of the time, in June 1934, a Committee on Economic Security was established by Executive Order of President Franklin Roosevelt. This Cabinet-level Committee, chaired by Frances Perkins, the Secretary of Labor, was given the task of developing constructive, long-term proposals for the prevention of all the major causes of economic insecurity. Given the desperate conditions of the time, the Committee's major attention was focused on programs to protect the unemployed. Yet, amid some controversy about the feasibility and constitutionality of such a plan, there developed from the work of the Committee a proposal for compulsory, contributory old-age insurance, which was ultimately enacted as part of the Social Security Act.

The Social Security Act, enacted on August 14, 1935, provided a new federally administered system of social insurance for the aged financed through payroll taxes paid by employees and their employers. Under the system, which applied only to workers in commerce and industry, people would earn retirement benefit eligibility as they worked. With some exceptions, benefits would be related to workers' average covered earnings, and workers could not have earnings and still be eligible for benefits. No benefits were provided for spouses or children, and lump-sum refunds were provided to the estates of workers who died before age 65 or before receiving at least the equivalent in benefits of their taxes plus interest. Collection of payroll taxes began in 1937, and benefit payments were scheduled to begin in 1942.

The Early Years

Even as the Social Security legislation moved through the Congress in the late winter and spring of 1935, it was acknowledged by many supporters that the old-age program then under consideration was but a first step in providing comprehensive protection for American workers against loss of earnings. President Roosevelt, in signing the Social Security Bill into law noted that "This law, too, represents a cornerstone in a structure which is being built but is by no means complete." In May 1937, the month in which the old-age program survived a crucial constitutional test in the landmark **Helvering v. Davis** case (in which the employer Social Security payroll tax was found constitutional), the Senate Committee on Finance and the Social Security Board jointly appointed an Advisory Council on Social Security. This outside advisory group, which would be the first of many to study and make recommendations concerning Social Security over the years,[1] was instructed to study possible ways of making the program more fully effective sooner than contemplated under the 1935 law.

The Council's fundamental finding was an endorsement of contributory old-age insurance as a way of preventing dependency in old age and thereby reducing reliance on needs-tested assistance. Further, the Council recommended a benefit structure that, in addition to basic benefits for workers, would provide protection for aged wives, widows, and surviving children starting in 1940.

Based on the Advisory Council's recommendations and recognizing the heavy dependence of most families on the male wage earner at that time, the Congress, in 1939, enacted legislation that eliminated lump-sum payroll tax refunds and provided benefits for aged wives and widows, young children of retired and deceased workers, young widows caring for a child beneficiary, and dependent parents of retired and deceased workers.

---

[1]Appointment of outside advisory bodies has long been institutionalized as a tradition in Social Security policymaking. Numerous advisory bodies have met over the years, and most of the changes made in Social Security have been based in large part on their studies and recommendations. The law has since 1956 required periodic appointment of Advisory Councils.

The Committee on Ways and Means of the House of Representatives and the Senate Committee on Finance, in their reports on the 1939 amendments, reasoned that "Under a social-insurance plan the primary purpose is to pay benefits in accordance with the probable needs of the beneficiaries rather than to make payments to the estate of a deceased person regardless of whether or not he leaves dependents."

The 1939 legislation also provided a new method of computing benefits, based on average monthly earnings instead of on cumulative wages. The net effect of the 1939 amendments was to increase the annual cost of benefits payable during the early years and to decrease the annual cost of benefits payable during later years. Over the long range, the average annual cost of benefits remained about the same as under prior law.

In addition to these changes in benefits, the 1939 amendments made basic changes in the financing of the Social Security program by establishing the Old-Age and Survivors Insurance Trust Fund and by changing the size of the financial reserves held by the program. The provisions of prior law would have resulted in the accumulation of a huge reserve fund over the years, similar to the reserves built up by private pension plans. The new legislation was designed to constrain the accumulation of reserves and, in effect, to move the financing of the program toward "pay-as-you-go" financing. This change in the reserve concept allowed the immediate payment of benefits to retired workers and to their dependents and survivors without increasing Social Security tax rates. This change in financing also permitted a 3-year postponement of the increases in the Social Security tax rate that had been scheduled for 1940.

Other recommendations of the 1938 Council that were enacted in 1939 included:

- Provision for benefits to start in 1940 instead of 1942;
- Revision of the earnings test, allowing earnings of $14.99 a month before benefits were withheld; and
- A method of measuring whether an individual had worked long enough in covered employment to get a benefit—based on "quarters of coverage"—the measure on which today's methods are based.

Following implementation of the 1939 amendments, the basic Social Security program was in place. It would remain essentially unchanged over the 1940's as the Nation concentrated its efforts on fighting World War II and toward building a healthy post-war economy. Social Security legislation enacted during these years included further postponement of tax rate increases, minor changes in coverage, and provision for coordinating the survivor benefits payable under the Social Security and Railroad Retirement Acts. Nevertheless, Social Security grew in importance both to the aged and to the economy. The number of beneficiaries grew from about 222,000 at the end of 1940 to over 3 million in 1949. Average monthly benefits grew only slightly, however—from $22.60 for a retired worker in 1940 to $26 at the end of the decade—less than the rate of inflation.

The Post-War Era

By the end of the immediate post-war period, Social Security had arrived at a major crossroads.

- The purchasing power of benefits had been sharply reduced by inflation. (By 1950, the cost of living had risen by three-quarters since 1939.)
- There was growing recognition that, as the Committee on Economic Security had pointed out, the hazards of economic insecurity due to disability were at least as great as the hazards faced by retirees.
- The program had not reduced the need for public assistance among older persons. On the contrary, the percentage of the aged receiving old-age assistance was somewhat larger (22.5) in 1950 than it had been in 1940 (21.7).

To help it determine the appropriate ongoing role of social insurance in the Nation's income support system, in 1947, the Senate Committee on Finance named an Advisory Council on Social Security. The findings of this Council formed a major milestone in the history of Social Security by reaffirming in the post-Depression era the social insurance principles established in the 1930's. In the Introduction to its report, the Council said:

> Opportunity for the individual to secure protection for himself and his family against the economic hazards of old age and death is essential to the sustained welfare, freedom, and dignity of the American citizen. For some, such protection can be gained through individual savings and other private arrangements. For others, such arrangements are inadequate or too uncertain. Since the interest of the whole Nation is involved, the people, using the Government as the agency for their cooperation, should make sure that all members of the community have at least a basic measure of protection against the major hazards of old age and death.

With respect to the existing old-age and survivors insurance (OASI) program, the Council was unanimous in finding three major deficiencies: inadequate coverage; unduly restrictive eligibility requirements for older workers; and inadequate benefits. To remedy these problems, the Council recommended a general benefit increase; a doubling of the minimum benefit; provision of benefits for additional dependents and survivors; and extension of coverage beyond the original boundaries of commerce and industry to self-employed workers, farm and domestic workers, Federal civilian employees not under a retirement system, State and local governmental employees, and employees of nonprofit organizations. In order to provide more adequate benefits to workers in these groups who were already middle-aged or older when their jobs were first covered, the Council recommended a "new-start" benefit computation.

The 1948 Advisory Council also strongly recommended extension of the social insurance approach to provide a program of cash benefits to the permanently and totally disabled. The program recommended by the Council would pay benefits after a 6-month waiting period only to those with severe and long-lasting disabilities, would provide for expenditures of Social Security funds for rehabilitation of disabled workers, and would terminate benefits to workers who refused to accept physical examinations or rehabilitation.

As its first order of business, in 1950, the Congress addressed the erosion in the value of Social Security benefits due to the inflation that had occurred since the inception of the program. The 1950 amendments provided for general benefit increases and increases in the minimum benefit that amounted to an across-the-board increase of about 77 percent. Echoing the view of the 1948 Advisory Council with respect to the ongoing role for the Social Security system, the Senate Committee on Finance said in its report of the 1950 amendments:

> Your committee's impelling concern in recommending passage of [this bill] has been to take immediate, effective steps to cut down the need for further expansion of public assistance, particularly old-age assistance. . . . We believe that improvement of the American social-security system should be in the direction of preventing dependency before it occurs, and of providing more effective income protection, free from the humiliation of a test of need . . .

To finance this substantial benefit increase and other program improvements, the 1950 amendments increased the contribution and benefit base (the amount of annual wages subject to Social Security taxes and creditable for benefits) from $3,000 to $3,600 and provided a revised schedule of gradually increasing tax rates for employers, employees, and the newly covered self-employed. The new law also repealed a never-used provision which authorized appropriations to the program from general revenues if they were needed. These changes made clear the Congress' rejection of Federal general revenues as a major source of Social Security financing and underscored its view that Social Security should be self-supporting in both the short range and the long range.

The Congress also began in 1950 to focus on the coverage deficiencies identified by the 1948 Council. These deficiencies, of course, had previously been recognized by the framers of the original law. At the inception of Social Security, there had been virtually unanimous agreement among supporters of the social insurance concept that, in order to assure adequate protection to the greatest number of workers, coverage should be both compulsory and as nearly universal as possible. Universal, compulsory coverage was also looked upon as the best means of spreading the cost of the program over the largest possible group, and thus avoiding problems of adverse selection and windfall benefits.

As noted earlier, the 1935 Act provided compulsory coverage for workers in commerce and industry; initially, about 6 in 10 jobs were covered. Coverage was not extended to other jobs for a number of reasons. Administrative considerations prevented quick development of methods of collecting taxes and providing coverage for the self-employed and for farm workers. Some groups, primarily railroad workers and Federal employees, already had retirement systems. In addition, legal and constitutional concerns involving taxation of States and localities prevented immediate extension of coverage to employees of State and local governments.

By 1950, with a decade of experience under the Social Security program behind them, the Congress concluded that many of the obstacles to universal coverage were not as formidable as they had appeared at the beginning. Thus, legislation enacted in 1950 extended coverage to several major categories of workers, including regularly employed farm and domestic workers; nonfarm self-employed persons (except professionals); Federal civilian workers; and, at the election of employees and employers, State and local government employees not covered under another retirement program and employees of nonprofit organizations other than ministers.

Because many of the workers newly covered under the 1950 amendments were already middle-aged or older, the principle of enabling newly covered older workers to become insured more easily and making their benefits more comparable to those of other covered workers with similar earnings was established. The 1950 amendments included a so-called "new-start" benefit computation that based benefit amounts on earnings after 1950 and companion provisions for measuring insured status in terms of work after 1950.

Four years later (1954), another 10 million workers' jobs were covered; in 1956, another million were added. Social Security legislation enacted in 1954 and 1956 extended coverage to (among others) the farm self-employed, certain groups of professional self-employed (generally with the exception of physicians), members of the uniformed services, and State and local government employees under a retirement system, under various conditions. Thus, by the mid-1950's, some 20 years after enactment of Social Security, the protection offered under the program was available to 90 percent of workers.

During the 1950's, the Congress also undertook lengthy consideration of another of the 1948 Advisory Council's recommendations—extension of Social Security protection to disabled workers.

The House-passed version of the 1950 Social Security Amendments would have provided for a program of disability insurance along the lines recommended by the Council, but the final bill made no such provision. Instead, the 1950 amendments provided for extension of the State-Federal public assistance program to the permanently and totally disabled, as had been urged by a minority of the Advisory Council's members.

Later, in 1954, the Congress enacted a disability "freeze" provision. No cash disability benefits were payable under this provision, but workers who were permanently and totally disabled and who also met insured status tests could have their Social Security earnings records frozen as of the date of their disability. Through the "freeze" provision, disabled workers could prevent their retirement benefits from being diluted by many years of no earnings. Other provisions of the 1954 amendments provided for expansion of State vocational rehabilitation programs to address the difficult problem of rehabilitating the severely disabled.

Eight years after the 1948 Advisory Council had recommended it, Congress in 1956 established a cash disability insurance program—with benefits first payable in 1957—with essentially the same eligibility requirements passed by the House in 1950. Because of concern about the high costs of a disability program and potential abuse, however, benefits were payable only to workers who were at least 50 years old. These amendments established basic principles under which the disability program continues to operate today:

- "Disability" is defined as the inability to engage in substantial gainful activity (prior to legislation in 1965, permanent disability was required; the 1965 legislation provided the present-law requirement that the disability be expected to last at least 12 months or be expected to result in death);
- Disability must be established on the basis of objective medical evidence;
- Eligibility is based on both duration and recency of work in covered employment;
- Benefits are paid only after a waiting period;

- A proportion of Social Security funds may be spent for rehabilitation of disabled workers; and
- Workers who refuse to accept physical examinations or rehabilitation may lose their benefits.

In 1958, the insured status requirements for disability benefits were relaxed through elimination of the currently insured status requirement and benefits were extended to spouses and children of disabled workers. Two years later, the minimum age requirement for disabled workers was eliminated and a trial work period provision added to encourage disabled workers to return to work.

The 1960's

By 1960, then, the old-age, survivors, and disability insurance (OASDI) programs were essentially in place as we know them today. Coverage under the program had been made nearly universal, so that virtually all people reaching retirement age in the decades to come would be able to establish benefit eligibility. Over the 1960's, the OASDI programs were refined through legislation to create new categories of beneficiaries, to increase benefits so as to maintain their purchasing power, and to adjust tax rates to assure adequate program financing. Moreover, legislation enacted in 1961 lowered the age of benefit eligibility for men. When the Social Security program was established, benefits were made available to men and women at age 65. The Social Security Amendments of 1956 had provided benefits for women as early as age 62. Benefits received prior to age 65 were reduced to take account of the longer period over which they would be received. The 1961 amendments extended eligibility for reduced benefits to include men.

In its examination of the adequacy of Social Security protection for the aged and the disabled, the 1965 Advisory Council came to the conclusion "that cash benefits alone are not enough." In its report, the Council said that:

> Monthly cash benefits, if adequate, can meet regularly recurring expenses such as those for food, clothing and shelter, but [they] are not a practical way to meet the problem that the aged and disabled face in the high and unpredictable costs of health care, costs that may run into the thousands of dollars for some and amount to very little for others. Security in old age and during disability requires the combination of a cash benefit and insurance against a substantial part of the costs of expensive illness.

The Council found in part that, while health care expenditures for the aged were twice as high as those of younger people, the great majority of the aged were neither well-off nor had adequate health insurance. Further, they found that, by the 1960's, the inability of the aged to meet health care costs had become the single most important reason that older people applied for public assistance. Based on these findings, the Council recommended establishment of a program to provide, through a contributory, social insurance mechanism, protection against the costs of hospital and related inpatient services for the aged and disabled. In order to protect people who were already old, the Council recommended that hospital insurance protection be provided initially without regard to insured status; that is, that people at or near retirement age be grandfathered into the new program.

Even as the Council was meeting, the Congress was actively considering proposals to provide health insurance benefits. In 1965, the Congress passed "Medicare" legislation, which, while it essentially embodied the Advisory Council's recommendations, differed in two major respects. First, in addition to providing protection against hospital costs through a payroll tax financed hospital insurance (HI) program, the plan enacted also included a voluntary program to be financed through monthly premiums and Federal general revenues. This supplementary medical insurance (SMI) program was designed to meet the costs of physicians' services and other outpatient care. Second, only people aged 65 and over, rather than both the aged and disabled, would for Medicare. (A few years later, in 1972, Medicare protection was extended to people who had been receiving cash disability benefits for 24 months or more.)

The Last 15 Years

With the advent of Medicare, the body of programs which we refer to today as "Social Security" was complete. Yet, while there have been no major additions to the system over the last 15 years or so, there has been continuing public and congressional reassessment of the ongoing role of Social Security in the Nation's income support structure. For example, the 1975 Advisory Council on Social Security firmly endorsed the basic purposes and principles of the program, noting that:

> The earnings-related OASDI program should remain the Nation's primary means of providing economic security in the event of retirement, death, or disability. It should be supplemented by effective private pensions, individual insurance, savings, and other investments; and it should be undergirded by effective means-tested programs. Future changes in OASDI should conform to the fundamental principles of the program: universal compulsory coverage, earnings-related benefits paid without a test of need, and contributions toward the cost of the program from covered workers and employers.

With respect to the OASDI programs, legislative considerations over these years have focused on three fundamental issues:

- Maintaining the value of benefits over time;
- Assuring the financial soundness of the system; and
- Structuring the disability program so as to maintain its responsiveness to the needs of the disabled while curbing the potential for abuse.

As noted earlier, the Congress acted to increase benefits from time to time during the 1950's and 1960's. Nevertheless, there was concern that during the intervals between these ad hoc benefit increases, inflation eroded the purchasing power of benefits. The 1971 Advisory Council examined this issue and recommended that Social Security benefits be adjusted automatically to keep pace with increases in prices. The Council said:

> An automatic adjustments system would, the Council believes, give to both present and future beneficiaries a greater sense of security than would exist if a benefit increase can take place only after an action by the Congress. Beneficiaries would be assured, by virtue of an explicit provision in the law, that the purchasing power of their benefits would not deteriorate because of inflation.

In order to assure that Social Security would provide a consistent level of protection to workers over time as earnings levels rose and to restrain payroll tax rates as benefit levels increased, the Council further recommended that the contribution and benefit base be increased automatically to reflect earnings growth. In conjunction with these recommendations, the Council also recommended that actuarial cost estimates for the program be based on assumptions that earnings levels would rise over time.[2] The Council also reaffirmed the view of prior Councils that the program should be financed on a current-cost basis in the near term and advocated frank recognition of this policy in longer-range financial planning.

In 1972, the Congress approved legislation that established automatic cost-of-living adjustments (COLA's) in benefits based on price increases as measured by the Consumer Price Index and provided for automatically increasing the maximum amount of earnings covered under the system. Moreover, the payroll tax schedule adopted in 1972

---

[2]Before 1972, actuarial estimates of program costs over the long range were based on level cost assumptions—that is, it was assumed that wage and price levels, as well as benefit levels, would remain unchanged over the 75-year valuation period. As wages did in fact increase, surpluses accumulated that could be and were used to finance benefit increases.

reflected the 1971 Council's recommendations with respect to both the basis for 75-year cost estimates and current-cost financing. Soon after the automatic COLA provision took effect, it became evident that combining the automatic-indexing procedures with the existing benefit table resulted in a computation procedure that, because it took into account both wage and price increases, unduly increased benefits for workers who would retire in the future. This overcompensation resulted in cost projections which showed that the tax rates scheduled in the law would be inadequate to meet the long-range costs of the program.

Based on the recommendations of the 1975 Advisory Council, the Congress in 1977 addressed the problems by establishing a new "decoupled" benefit-computation formula for workers becoming newly eligible or dying after 1978. Under the new formula, which replaced the benefit table in the law, initial benefits are increased to reflect increases in average wages before workers reach retirement age, and the purchasing power of benefits in guaranteed after retirement through cost-of-living increases.

At the time that the 1977 amendments were enacted, it was thought that, due to the lower long-range costs resulting from the new benefit formula, changes the Congress made in the tax rate schedule would be adequate to finance benefit payments well into the next century. However, over the next few years, the Nation experienced a period of spiraling inflation and high unemployment along with low or negative real wage growth. These worse-than-expected economic conditions created a two-pronged drain on Social Security in the short term.

- Benefit expenditures were pushed up rapidly by high inflation, while payroll taxes went up more slowly because of the relatively slower growth in wages; and

- High unemployment reduced payroll taxes.

In addition, new long-range projections showed that the decline in the birth rate and the likelihood of increased life expectancy would both have negative effects on Social Security; in the 21st century, fewer workers would be paying taxes and retirees would be receiving benefits longer.

Due to these problems, it soon became clear that without significant further congressional action, the OASI Trust Fund would be unable to pay benefits on time by some point in the 1980's. Thus, in December 1981, President Reagan announced the formation of the National Commission on Social Security Reform (NCSSR) "to work with the President and the Congress to reach two specific goals: propose realistic, long-term reform to put social security back on a sound financial footing and forge a working bipartisan concensus so that the necessary reforms will be passed into law."

The NCSSR reported on January 20, 1983. Based on the recommendations of the NCSSR, the Congress enacted the so-called "bipartisan compromise" 1983 amendments. This package of provisions was designed to resolve the financing crisis by sharing the burden among affected groups, present and futures. Among the major provisions of the 1983 legislation that became effective in the near term were:

- Advances in tax rate increases already scheduled in the law for employees and employers;
- Permanent increases in self-employment tax rates;
- Delays in the effective date of automatic COLA's in benefits from June to December of each year; and
- Inclusion of up to half of benefits in taxable income for certain high-income beneficiaries (and appropriation of the resulting revenues to the trust funds).

In the long range, in recognition of improvements in longevity, the 1983 amendments provided for gradually increasing the age of eligibility for unreduced retirement benefits. Workers born after 1937 will be the first to be affected by this change; the provision will be fully effective for workers born after 1959, for whom unreduced benefits will be available at age 67. Benefits will continue to be available at age 62, but the reduction in benefits at age 62 will increase as the age of eligibility for unreduced benefits increases.

As a result of enactment of the 1983 legislation, OASDI benefits can be paid on time in the short run and well into the next century on the basis of even the most pessimistic economic and demographic assumptions used by the Social Security Trustees in making projections. During the 1990's, current projections show, substantial excesses of income over outgo will replenish program reserves and build up substantial trust funds. After the turn of the century, program costs will rise substantially as the baby boom generation reaches retirement age, and use of trust fund assets will be necessary.

With the enactment of the 1983 amendments, which assured the soundness of the Social Security system both through the 1980's and well into the 21st century, the Congress once again reaffirmed its commitment to the use of the social insurance mechanism as the Nation's first line of defense against dependency in old age, disability, or upon the death of a worker.

During the past decade and a half, the disability insurance program has also undergone substantial change. During the early 1970's, the disability insurance (DI) program began to experience tremendous growth. As the decade unfolded, it became clear that continuing rapid growth in the DI program was beginning to pose a serious threat to the DI Trust Fund. Studies aimed at discovering the causes of the unexpected growth in the disability program suggested that (1) the beneficiary rolls included many ineligibles, and (2) the program structure tended to discourage people who might be able to return to work from doing so.

The Social Security Disability Amendments of 1980 included a limit on monthly family disability benefits, additional work incentive provisions, and administrative improvements, including mandatory reviews, at least once every 3 years, of the continuing eligibility of disabled beneficiaries whose disabilities are not necessarily permanent. On the basis of these amendments, the financial solvency of the DI Trust Fund was restored, and, in fact, the trust fund was projected to increase rapidly after 1981.

Shortly after implementation of the 1980 amendments, however, the periodic review provision began to be criticized by the public and Congress. Although, beginning in 1982, the Social Security Administration and the Department of Health and Human Services made many administrative changes to deal with these criticisms, public and congressional attention remained fixed on the DI program, as advocacy groups for the disabled petitioned Congress for legislative relief. Throughout 1982 and 1983, amidst great controversy, the Congress considered a variety of reforms to mitigate the effects of the periodic review process.

These efforts culminated in the enactment of the Social Security Disability Benefits Reform Act of 1984. The major provisions are mandatory application of a medical improvement standard in continuing disability reviews, continuation of disability benefit payments during appeal of termination decisions, and a moratorium on reviews of cases involving mental impairments pending development of revised review criteria.

Conclusion

Today, 37 million people get Social Security benefits of more than $15 billion a month; OASDI benefits this year will total $188 billion. In 1985, about 122 million people will work in employment covered under Social Security, which applies today to 95 percent of all jobs in our economy.

As a Nation, we can take particular pride in having made the Social Security program the most successful domestic program in our history. Over the years, Social Security has been a vital contributor to the security of virtually all Americans. Today, 50 years after its inception, it remains the foundation of well-being for us in our later years or if we are disabled and for our families if we die before retirement.

Part III

Issues Relating to Current Social Programs

A social welfare program is the direct result of policy action from one of two routes: by federal, state, and/or local government initiative or through the efforts of the private sector via an agency's board of trustees or directors. Social workers are employed in both the public and private arenas, and, as a result, knowledge of the intricacies of both policymaking systems is indispensable. All social workers have direct contact with public policy—policy enacted by the federal government—and must be cognizant of issues related to the variety of such policies.

As a result of the common interaction social workers have with it, this section centers on public policy. Bear in mind that many of the problems identified and discussed in the following articles are often the same or similar to the dilemmas experienced by practitioners employed in private-sector programs.

What do we mean by social welfare? Does it include food stamps, general assistance, medicaid, subsidized school meals? Yes, these are part of social welfare and probably are most often thought of by the community at large when they think about welfare. If we follow this definition, social welfare takes on a residual, narrow, and Franklin-type perspective and becomes "programs to aid the poor."

The federal government, on the other hand, defines social welfare in broad terms by including seven program areas: (*Social Security Bulletin*, 1982)

- Social insurance
- Education
- Veterans' programs
- Public aid

181

- Housing
- Health
- Other social welfare

Veterans are welfare recipients? Senior citizens receiving social security retirement are on welfare? Children going to public school are welfare clients? Aren't we going a bit overboard at this point by identifying seventh graders as public welfare recipients?

Not really. If we look back to Mimi Abramowitz's article in Part 1, we are reminded that social welfare involves the redistribution of resources. Redistribution takes many forms—free textbooks in public schools, reduced meal cost for all public school children, lower family food costs through food stamps, or agricultural price subsidies.

Awareness and knowledge of the federal government's social welfare scheme is critical in order not to be caught by the emotional rhetoric, a by-product of many welfare debates. For example, a diatribe often leveled against social workers is that welfare is wasteful and cutting unneeded expenditures will save the government money. In the 1984 federal social welfare budget, 50.94 percent of welfare expenditures were in social insurance; 22.62 percent were for education; while 13.37 percent were for public aid programs, such as AFDC, food stamps, SSI, social services, work relief, low-income energy programs, surplus foods, and temporary and emergency employment services. (*Social Security Bulletin*, 1982) These three program areas, social insurance, education, and public aid, were the three most costly federal welfare programs, accounting for nearly 87 percent of national welfare expenditures. As a result, these program areas are most susceptible to potential budget reductions.

One of the so-called untouchable program areas is social insurance. Can you imagine a politician's chances of being elected on a platform supporting reductions in social security benefits to seniors? What are the chances of being elected to public office for a candidate who supports reduced funding for public education, the second most expensive welfare program? Education too is a so-called sacred cow protected from budget cutters. When running for president in 1980, Ronald Reagan vowed to eliminate the federal Department of Education. Yet, with less than six months left in his administration, Reagan appointed a replacement Secretary of Education to carry on the work of his administration. *But* what if a candidate supports financial cuts in public aid programs, the third most expensive welfare program? Ah, now we're talking.

Yet, we're really talking ignorance. In 1984, public aid expenditures reached $89.8 billion compared to a total welfare budget exceeding $671.9 billion. What kind of dent is made in social expenditures by reducing public aid? Let's say public aid programs are cut by 25 percent ($22.5 billion). That's a good political stance, but what will it do to welfare expenditures? The answer is that while the cuts will reduce total social welfare expenditures by a little more than 3.3 percent, the reduction or elimination of services will negatively impact millions of Americans who depend on government support to meet basic human needs.

Social workers have been and continue to be considered the main providers, defenders, and advocates of the social welfare system. To carry out these roles successfully, the social worker must have two types of policy-related knowledge. First, from a practice perspective, the social worker possesses a general knowledge of program eligibility, forms of service, and levels of assistance; second, from a policy perspective, the social worker encompasses awareness and knowledge of the issues directly impacting the quality and extent of services while working toward needed improvements and additions in the current range of social welfare programs.

One of the difficulties in learning about a particular social welfare program in an academic course is that policy and resulting services change yearly, and in some instances, on a monthly basis. Thus, to tell you that eligibility for food stamps mandates that an individual have no more than $x in financial assets should not be taken as rock solid truth; there is a chance that this could change tomorrow or might have changed yesterday.

This section of readings directs our attention not to program design, but to present-day issues which impact the quality and extent of provided services. While reading the various selections in this portion of the text, keep in mind the previous articles on social history. Are particular themes from the seventeenth, eighteenth, and nineteenth centuries threaded through current programs? For example, does social welfare take on a moral control perspective? To what extent does the issue of public versus private responsibility shape current programs? Who are the current "worthy" recipients and why do they maintain this status while others do not? How does the past, in general, relate to present services and program philosophy?

ARTICLE 11: "BUDGET OUTLOOK— SUMMARY 1989–1993"

The Congressional Budget Office (CBO) serves the U.S. Congress as an investigatory agency. A member of Congress can request this nonpartisan federal agency to report on the specifics of a proposed policy or examination of social issues. Each year, the CBO produces a wealth of materials relating to federal programs; topics have ranged from analysis of the president's credit budget to physicians' reimbursements.

The CBO annually examines the federal budget in context with the nation's economy and, based on its findings, makes short-term projections for funding levels, deficits, and program impact. Generally issued in January of each year, this report analyzes how the nation's economic vitality will affect the federal budget. A second and related CBO report, published later each spring, identifies various options for reducing the national deficit. This latter report details potential reductions in national defense, entitlement programs, agricultural price supports, nondefense discretionary spending, and personal costs.[1]

This CBO article provides access to current funding levels in line with future economic projections and is a useful tool when we consider how programs will be funded, what level funding should take, and what other parts of the federal budget might be trimmed to increase funding in social welfare.

ARTICLE 12: "MEASURING POVERTY"

Periodically, the media note that poverty rates have increased or decreased for a given period. When such announcements are made, charges and countercharges are leveled against the success or failure of certain antipoverty public policies. One group will generally charge that the poverty figures are inaccurate; that is, the figures are too low or too high.

Given that social work is firmly rooted in working with and advocating on behalf of the poor and near-poor, we must have a clear and firm understanding of how poverty is measured. Further, we need to be aware of limitations and weaknesses of current measures and understand the implications of alternative measures.

This article focuses our attention on how poverty rates are determined while examining the inherent difficulties with the present measure. This work, generated by the Congressional Budget Office, brings to our attention alternative methods for computing poverty rates. To illustrate how these various measures impact the poverty rate, the article applies each proposed measure to children in poverty. These examples allow us to see how poverty rates are increased or decreased with the same population, depending on which criteria are applied.

As you read this article, consider the importance of having a clear and accurate poverty measure. For example, if we can show that pov-

---

[1]For example, see Congressional Budget Office. *Reducing the Deficit: Spending and Revenue Options, A Report to the Senate and House Committees on the Budget—Part II.* (March 1986). Washington, DC: U.S. Government Printing Office.

erty is low, how will funding for antipoverty programs be affected: Conversely, if poverty is determined to be high, should program funding be increased? Is it possible to play with statistics to support your view, that is, can we in fact define people out of poverty even though their reality remains in poverty?

ARTICLE 13: "ISSUES IN ADDRESSING POVERTY AMONG CHILDREN"

Women and children account for over 60 percent of the individuals in poverty and, as such, remain central figures in social welfare concerns. The extent of poverty among children is large; over 14 million children, one in every five youths, were living in conditions below the poverty threshold during the mid-1980s.

It may be trite to say that our future is our children, yet if so many of our young people are in the grasp of poverty, what does the future hold for them and, subsequently, for other members of society?

This article, taken from a 1985 CBO study which examined the nature of children's poverty, stimulates our thinking regarding child welfare programs while also directing our attention to a basic question—what is our responsibility to youth, especially those in need of services?

When reading this piece, consider the role of federal programs in terms of victim blaming, as outlined by Ryan in Article 2. Do current services and program alternatives cut to the heart of the problem; that is, do or will such programs ameliorate poverty among children? In a more philosophical sense, what should our federal commitment be to children—might the government intervene with a comprehensive child welfare program or with minimal services reflecting a Ben Franklin or George Gilder philosophy?

ARTICLE 14: "FEDERAL POLICY CHANGES AND THE FEMINIZATION OF POVERTY"

Rosemary Sarri's work goes hand-in-hand with the preceding CBO study on children and permits the reader to look at how policy changes of the 1980s impacted the Aid to Families with Dependent Children (AFDC) program, the primary federal program that assists poor families with children.

Based on interviews with 3,200 AFDC families, Sarri documents that crises due to inadequate income, loss of employment, and lack of health care often resulted in increased behavioral problems among AFDC children. Sarri concludes that fiscal cuts in AFDC have further entrenched these families in poverty.

The same questions asked of the preceding reading are again applicable to Sarri's work. Must we also acknowledge what is and should be the nation's commitment to families, especially those who are economically disadvantaged? Should the government provide assistance to push low-income families above the poverty threshold? Or, should families receive minimal aid with the primary responsibility for economic survival and growth remaining with the adult caretaker or his or her extended family? An equally important issue deals with the status of women in society—how does AFDC help women economically and socially? Does AFDC provide women access to the opportunity structure or does the program create another barrier to social and economic equality?

ARTICLE 15: "THE 'GRAYING' OF THE FEDERAL BUDGET AND ITS CONSEQUENCES FOR OLD-AGE POLICY"

We are all growing old; the aging process began at the moment of birth. In cultures throughout the world, elders hold a place of honor and respect, as seniors are often sought out for their advice and wisdom.

Americans face a serious dilemma with regard to aging. As health fields have become more sophisticated, life expectancy has increased, providing additional productive and active years for our elders. Yet, social policies have been slow to reflect such changes and effectively confront the resulting problems faced by older persons. Use of free time, health and illness, housing, transportation, and economic issues are among the many difficulties confronting seniors.

Historically, American seniors have been treated favorably in social welfare, with specific or categorical policies having been implemented to provide a greater degree of life satisfaction. Robert Hudson, however, raises the specter that elder policy faces political attacks threatening the most vulnerable seniors—the "old-old," minority aged, and widows.

The questions asked regarding women and children are also relevant to seniors' issues. Who is responsible for our seniors? The individual? Their families? Can we legislate that a senior's family be economically responsible for him or her? Should society care for seniors who are unable to provide for themselves? If society is to care for seniors, what type and level of services should be provided? Should federal benefits be cash, in kind, voucher, or some other form of benefit?

ARTICLE 16: "THE LONG-RUN FINANCING PROBLEM: BASIC APPROACHES"

In Article 10, McSteen detailed the first fifty years of the social security program. In the mid-1970s, however, the program exposed its Achilles' heel to a fragile economy. During this period of national economic uncertainty, declining levels of workers' contributions, coupled with the increased program participation, forced the Social Security Administration to draw from its savings to offset increasing expenses. Critics of social security charged that the system was fast becoming bankrupt and its future survival required immediate overhauling of the present program.

In 1981, the National Commission on Social Security Reform convened as a result of Presidential Executive Order No. 12335. Chaired by Allan Greenspan, this bipartisan group was directed to (a) review the financial condition of the social security program, (b) identify funding problems, (c) analyze potential solutions, and (d) provide recommendations. (Report of the National Commission, 1983) The Commission's work was completed in January 1983, with a number of their recommendations implemented shortly thereafter.

This article, part of a CBO study conducted during the National Commission's transactions, identifies a number of critical issues surrounding social security and reviews several program options. But why, if a Presidential Commission met and seemingly resolved relevant issues, should we be concerned with social security, especially since many of the Commission's recommendations were implemented? Very simply put, the social security program continues to be in a financially tenuous position. A number of the commissioners reported that their work would hold the social security program in place through the first quarter of the twenty-first century, at which time it would be necessary to once again modify the program. Others, however, have charged that the social security program will be insolvent by the beginning of the twenty-first century.

The twenty-first century seems far in the future, but it really isn't. Many readers of this anthology will conduct the majority of their professional work then. They will be a vital part of the new century. For many of today's employees, the beginning of the twenty-first century will be one of retirement with, in some instances, primary dependence on social security retirement programs.

In this reading, consider the history of social security, why the program came about, and its overall place in society. What are realistic goals for a social security program in a technological society? Remember, social security in 1935 was structured in an industrial society—we are now in a technological society with different needs, a different social and economic context. Consider the obligations made to those participating or who will soon be eligible to take part in the various social security programs—seniors, women, children, widows, survivors, disabled. Do these obligations remain intact? Should they be rearranged or modified due to the ever-changing context of society?

ARTICLE 17: "FAMILY MEDICAL EXPENSES IN A SINGLE YEAR"

According to the U.S. Census Bureau, in 1985 over 31.3 million individuals were not covered by either public or private health insurance (Bureau of the Census, 1986, p. 9). Another way of considering this particular fact is that the total resident population of the following states is slightly less than the entire uninsured U.S. population: Maine, New Hampshire, Vermont, Massachusetts, Connecticut, Rhode Island, New Jersey, Maryland, Virginia, and West Virginia (Hoffman, 1986, pp. 220–221). As to medical insurance, 15.5 percent of youth under age 16 and 21.4 percent of those persons between the ages of 16 and 24 have none; 19.3 percent of the black population and 23.5 percent of the Spanish-origin population have no medical coverage (Bureau of the Census, 1986, p. 37).

Health care presents a critical dilemma to our society. Is health care a right, that is, can all people receive treatment no matter the costs, or is health care a privilege, so that only those who can afford to pay direct or indirect costs should receive medical attention? Should a hospital emergency room treat patients without knowing if the provided care can be paid directly by the client or by his or her insurance company? Should a hospital be able to refuse services to a patient due to the individual's inability to pay? If not, then who is ultimately responsible for defraying medical costs?

Such questions easily spur conflict as, in effect, we try to quantify the value of human life. Yet, there is a problem in our health care system as costs increase at unparalleled rates, coupled with the large number of individuals not covered by public, private, or employee health insurance programs. Our nation's federal health care system is built around medicare and medicaid, augmented by private insurance companies. Even with this structure, one illness, whether it is minor or major, can sap an individual's or family's savings. According to Allan Little, a health crisis can place a family into *crisis poverty*—an unexpected event which drains one's income and resources (Little, 1971).

This reading examines health care costs for the nonelderly, generally individuals not covered by either medicare or medicaid. This CBO article reviews medical expenses for one year and discusses three major findings: first, about 5 percent of all families exceed $5,000 in annual medical expenses; second, the expenses in so-called high-cost families tend to be for one person; and third, the proportion of inpatient hospital expenses is large among high-cost families.

The cost of health care is often thought of in relation to vulnerable population groups, in particular the poor and elders. This article reminds us that the middle class also faces unexpected financial crises which can propel a once-prosperous family into the web of fiscal poverty.

What then is society's role in health care? Should the nation provide catastrophic health insurance? Should the individual bear responsibility for his or her health needs? How do we define that point at which an individual no longer is responsible for his or her expenses? As we think about costs for catastrophic care, let's also try to identify why health care costs have risen in the past few years. Does the government's role include controlling escalating health care provider costs? Is it appropriate for the government to regulate the private sector as tightly as the public domain?

ARTICLE 18: "WORKFARE—INTRODUCTION"

Workfare requires that public assistance recipients participate in some work, training, or education program in order to receive a program's grant. Workfare is a controversial topic—some charge that workfare places clients in undesirable jobs which provide no chance for upward mobility; proponents note that workfare offers clients a chance to develop marketable skills and a sense of self-worth.

Workfare has been one of the consistent requirements for client program participation throughout American social welfare history. Leon Ginsberg and Kevin Meehan note that we

> need look back no further than the New Deal of President Franklin Deiano Roosevelt and to recall the Works Progress Administration, the Civil Conservation Corps, and the National Youth Administration. Similar efforts were part of the Economic Opportunity Act of 1964, popularly known as the War on Poverty, under President Lyndon B. Johnson. . . . Work programs have been persistent in American social welfare and are likely to remain so (Ginsberg and Meehan, 1987, p. 27).

This CBO article examines work-related programs for AFDC families and outlines the general goals and purposes of workfare programs. As we consider the role of work-related programs in social welfare, let's keep in mind some questions asked by Ginsberg and Meehan: "What responsibility does the government have to provide jobs or welfare benefits to its people? Are jobs and welfare benefits considered rights or privileges? What responsibility do welfare recipients have to repay society for the benefits they receive?" (Ginsberg and Meehan, 1987, p. 28). We might also consider the various views of people as previously discussed by Gilder, Ryan, Addams, Williams, and Abramowitz with particular reference to the poor—how do the poor contribute to society's growth? Should the level of aid be based on the rate of participation in the workforce? Should welfare recipients be required to participate in work or educational training programs as a requirement to receive public assistance? Are such programs victim blaming? Do workfare programs provide the poor access to the so-called opportunity structure?

ARTICLE 19: "COMMUNITY MENTAL HEALTH CENTERS: A LOOK AHEAD"

Mental health is a primary area of practice interest to the social work community—in the early 1980s, over 25 percent of NASW's members were employed in mental health settings; in 1986, the CSWE reported that 23.8 percent of social work graduate students were majoring in mental health (Morales and Sheafor, 1986, p. 30; *Statistics*, 1987, p. 40). As a result of the profession's involvement in mental health programs, we also maintain a significant interest in related policy issues.

In 1963, the Community Mental Health Act provided federal funding to develop local, community-based mental health centers. People, regardless of income, were provided access to a variety of services, including inpatient and outpatient care, partial hospitalization, emergency intervention, and education/consultation. The original act was amended in 1975 to extend services to children and seniors.

The community mental health centers, or CMHCs, have been a key program development in the mental health field since its inception. The success of the CMHCs, as noted by DiNitto and Dye, (1983, p. 128), rests with the active support and involvement of the communities served. Without referrals from the police, schools, hospitals, and other local services and agencies, a CMHC will not be able to meet its program function of providing comprehensive care to an entire community.

Allen Beigel's brief article examines the status of the CMHC in relation to reduced federal funding. Based on funding patterns of the 1980s, Beigel outlines his predictions for community-based mental health programs, which he argues will negatively impact local services. Beigel takes us one step further, however, by offering alternative policies which he feels will minimize the negative impact of reduced federal support.

This piece provides an opportunity to examine the impact of reduced federal funds with increased fiscal responsibility placed in the local community for services. What if a community is unable or unwilling to fund mental health programs: How will reduced funding impact the quality of services? Will it increase workloads and limit available services (for example, eliminate existing programs or offer only centralized programs, or increase user fees?) Should the federal government provide needed funding to financially poor communities in order to offer mental health services? Will public mental health programs become available only to those communities which are able to afford them?

ARTICLE 20: "PULLING TOGETHER OR TEARING APART"

Part 3 of this anthology has brought to our attention a number of critical issues in social welfare, issues we must consider in policy analysis and program development. The dilemmas facing the social welfare community are numerous and multifaceted. Yet, what if program personnel consider only their particular problems and argue "My problem is more important than yours"? The obvious consequence is division within the social welfare community.

In a period of scarce resources, we tend to first fight for what we need and only when these problems are resolved will we look to help others. This is a dangerous state of affairs in human services—programs will work against rather than with each other.

Robert Wineberg outlines the dangers associated with the problems of reduced resources and identifies specific steps that local program staff can take to avoid splitting local coalitions. Wineberg optimistically argues that communities can overcome the coordination problems inherent in periods of reduced funding.

From a policy perspective, what steps should we take to avoid this problem? Why are agencies placed in this competitive posture? Is a divided social service community less powerful than a coordinated system? Is it realistic for agency personnel to move beyond personal needs during periods of limited resources, especially if the survival of the individual's agency is threatened?

BIBLIOGRAPHY

Bureau of the Census, Current Population Reports, Series P-70, No. 8. (1986). *Disability, Functional Limitation, and Health Insurance Coverage: 1985/1986.* Washington, DC: U.S. Government Printing Office.

DiNitto, D. and Dye, T. (1983). *Social Welfare, Politics and Public Policy.* Englewood-Cliffs, NJ: Prentice-Hall.

Ginsberg, L. and Meehan, K. (1987, Spring/Summer). Workfare in Rural America: The West Virginia Experience. *Human Services in the Rural Environment,* 10 (4), 11 (1), (pp. 22–28).

Hoffman, M. (Ed.). (1986). *The World Almanac and Book of Facts, 1987.* New York: Pharos Books.

Little, A. (1971). Poverty: Types, *Encyclopedia of Social Work* (pp. 929–948). New York, NY: National Association of Social Workers.

Morales, A. and Sheafor, B. (1986). *Social Work, A Profession of Many Faces* (4th ed.). Boston, MA: Allyn and Bacon.

Social Security Administration. (1982). *Social Security Bulletin.* Washington, DC: Government Printing Office.

Statistics on Social Work Education in the United States: 1987. (1987). Washington, DC: Council on Social Work Education.

Report of the National Commission on Social Security Reform. (1983). Washington, DC: Government Printing Office.

Article 11

BUDGET OUTLOOK—SUMMARY, 1989–1993

Congressional Budget Office

In the closing days of 1987, the Congress and the Administration negotiated and largely put in place a plan to reduce the budget deficit for 1988 and 1989. At the same time, in the wake of the stock market collapse, signs of some temporary weakness in the economy began to emerge. The Congressional Budget Office (CBO) now anticipates that the economy will experience a pronounced slowdown in growth in early 1988, but will regain strength in the second half of 1988 and in 1989. On the basis of CBO's economic assumptions and a continuation of current budgetary policies, the federal deficit is projected to rise from $150 billion in 1987 to $157 billion in 1988 and $176 billion in 1989, before dropping to $167 billion in 1990.

These baseline budget projections assume that revenues, offsetting receipts, and entitlement spending are projected according to the laws now on the statute books. Defense and nondefense discretionary appropriations are assumed to be held constant in real terms. The baseline projections are, therefore, not forecasts of future budgets, which will doubtless include numerous policy changes. This year CBO has made minor changes in its baseline to make it identical to the budget base as specified in the Balanced Budget and Emergency Deficit Control Reaffirmation Act of 1987 (Public Law 100–119). Having a single baseline is intended to help focus attention on the fundamentals of the budget situation and reduce any confusion stemming from minor conceptual differences.

The Short-Run Budget Situation

On November 16, as required by the Balanced Budget Reaffirmation Act of 1987, CBO reported that the budget deficit for 1988 would be $180 billion under laws then in effect. It also projected a deficit of $186 billion in 1989 and $166 billion in 1990. These estimates were based on CBO's August economic and technical estimating assumptions. How have the budget estimates changed since November?

SOURCE: *The Economic and Budget Outlook: Fiscal Years 1989–1993*, Washington, DC: The Congress of the United States Congressional Budget Office, February, 1988.

On November 20, Congressional leaders and the President announced that they had reached a budget agreement covering the next two fiscal years. This agreement, or budget summit, was intended to reduce the deficit by $30 billion in 1988 and $46 billion in 1989 from the Balanced Budget Act baseline. The results of the budget summit were almost entirely incorporated in two bills—the continuing resolution of appropriations (Public Law 100–202) and the Omnibus Budget Reconciliation Act of 1987 (Public Law 100–203)—signed by the President on December 22. These laws reduced the 1988 deficit by an estimated $34 billion, comprising $23 billion in lower spending and $11 billion in additional revenues. The projected deficit reduction will then swell to $36 billion in 1989 and $40 billion in 1990, assuming that spending programs subject to annual appropriation action are allowed to grow by only the rate of inflation (see Summary Table 1).

While policymakers were working hard to reduce the deficit, however, a deterioration in the economic outlook was eroding some of their improvements. CBO's updated economic assumptions add $9 billion to the deficit in 1988, $21 billion in 1989, and $33 billion in 1990, compared with the November estimates. In 1988 and 1989, most of these changes result from lower tax revenues brought on by the forecast of a slowdown in economic growth. By 1990, however, the primary factor is a projected increase in interest rates, which adds to the costs of servicing the national debt.

Changes in technical estimating methods and assumptions have increased the projected deficit slightly—by $2 billion in 1988, $6 billion in 1989, and $8 billion in 1990—since CBO's November report. These reestimates result primarily from newly available data that permit a better estimate of the effects of the Tax Reform Act of 1986 (Public Law 99–514). Technical revisions in outlay estimates, while large for some individual programs, are negligible in total in most years.

The recent policy actions and economic and technical reestimates have not changed the pattern of the deficit: it fell sharply in 1987, will rise in 1988 and 1989, and will fall again in 1990. This jagged shape is largely the result of the phase-in of the Tax Reform Act of 1986 and of various one-time outlay savings. Tax reform added $22 billion to revenues in 1987 but reduces tax collections by $10 billion in 1988 and $16 billion in 1989. Asset sales and other one-time spending cuts hold down outlays by $15 billion in 1987 and $7 billion in 1988. The 1988 savings result from loan prepayments permitted by the recent appropriation and reconciliation bills. Were it not for these special factors, the pattern of the deficits would be much smoother, as shown in Summary Figure 1. The deficit would have fallen less sharply in 1987—to about $187 billion—and would then fall further to about $160 billion, where it would remain for several years.

SUMMARY TABLE 1   Baseline Deficit Projections for 1988–1990 (by fiscal year)

	Actual		Projections		
	1986	1987	1988	1989	1990
	In Billions of Dollars				
November 1987 Base deficit for Balanced Budget Act	221	150	180	186	166
Changes for:					
Enacted legislation	—	—	−34	−36	−40
Updated economic					
assumptions	—	—	9	21	33
Technical reestimates	—	—	2	6	8
Total changes	—	—	−23	−10	1
February 1988 Baseline deficit	221	150	157	176	167
Adjustments for:					
Tax reform	—	22	−10	−16	−4
One-time outlay savings	2	15	7	a/	a/
Total adjustments	2	37	−3	−17	−4
Adjusted deficit	223	187	154	159	163
	As a Percentage of GNP				
Baseline deficit	5.3	3.4	3.4	3.5	3.1
Adjusted deficit	5.4	4.2	3.3	3.2	3.1

a. Less than $500 million.

SOURCE: Congressional Budget Office

    The baseline deficits of $176 billion in 1989 and $167 billion in 1990 are well above the Balanced Budget Reaffirmation Act targets of $136 billion and $100 billion. The amount of deficit reduction required in 1989 is limited by law to $36 billion. Implementing the rest of the budget summit in 1989 would produce about $3 billion in additional outlay reductions in discretionary appropriations from the 1989 baseline and $0.4 billion in additional revenues resulting from further increases in Internal Revenue Service enforcement resources. But even with these further savings, another $32 billion in deficit reduction would still be required. (Asset sales of $3.5 billion, although required by the budget

SUMMARY FIGURE 1   Deficit Adjusted for Tax Reform Act and One-Time Savings

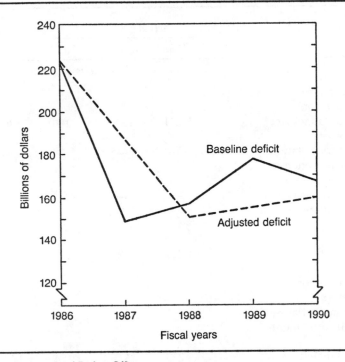

SOURCE: Congressional Budget Office

summit, may not be counted as savings under the terms of the Balanced Budget Reaffirmation Act.) If the Office of Management and Budget (OMB) comes up with similar estimates this summer, across-the-board cuts would be required of roughly 9 percent in defense programs and 13 percent in nondefense programs from their baseline levels.

These cuts could be avoided if OMB's estimate of the deficit were within $10 billion of the target—that is, less than $146 billion. While using more favorable economic assumptions could reduce the projected deficit to that level, relying on this approach to get through the 1989 budget year would make the 1990 deficit reduction task that much harder. Taking no action this year beyond that required by the budget summit would leave the 1990 deficit around $160 billion, according to CBO's current estimates. With a 1990 deficit target of $100 billion, the excess deficit would be $60 billion, almost double the amount of deficit reduction achieved in the first year of the summit.

The Short-Term Economic Outlook

Just as the budget summit agreement for 1988 and 1989 was prompted by the stock market collapse of October 19, so will budgetary developments for 1988 and 1989 be driven by the economic aftermath of the crash. The drop in share values wiped out hundreds of billions of dollars of consumer wealth and contributed to a drop in consumption. Excluding automobiles, real personal consumption fell at a 1 percent rate in the fourth quarter of 1987—the first decline since 1981.

As a result of the weakness in consumption, business piled up unsold inventories throughout 1987, but especially in the fourth quarter. CBO expects that the attempt to reduce inventory accumulation will act as a drag on the economy in early 1988. Real federal purchases of goods and services are also expected to fall, reflecting successive years of budgetary stringency.

Some brighter signs, however, suggest that the economy will avoid a recession. Real net exports have started to improve as a result of three years of dollar depreciation, and net exports are likely to be the major engine of growth in 1988 and 1989. Because the saving rate has already increased substantially, further declines in consumption are not anticipated.

The financial crisis was the impetus for a major shift in monetary policy. From the Louvre accord in February 1987 through October, the Federal Reserve's stated aims were to support the value of the dollar and to dampen inflationary expectations. In pursuing these aims, the Federal Reserve was forced to keep up interest rates. After the crash, however, it permitted interest rates to fall even at the cost of a depreciating dollar. This situation is likely to create inflationary pressures by the end of 1988 that will cause the central bank to shift back to a less accommodating stance.

CBO's short-run economic forecast for 1988 and 1989 is shown in Summary Table 2. In addition to the monetary policy just described, the forecast assumes that federal fiscal policies are consistent with CBO's baseline revenue and outlay projections. The immediate outlook for the economy is substantially weaker than CBO expected in August. With a sluggish first half, real gross national product (GNP) is expected to grow by only 1.8 percent in 1988 (measured from fourth quarter to fourth quarter). The unemployment rate will average 6.2 percent for 1988 as a whole, the same as the previous year. In 1989, growth is expected to return to a 2.6 percent rate, roughly the same as that assumed in CBO's summer projections and only slightly lower than in

SUMMARY TABLE 2   CBO Forecast for 1988 and 1989 (by calendar year)

	Actual 1987	Forecast 1988	1989
Fourth Quarter to Fourth Quarter (Percent change)			
Real Gross National Product	3.8	1.8	2.6
GNP Deflator	3.3	3.9	4.2
Consumer Price Index (CPI-W)	4.5	4.9	4.8
Calendar-Year Average (Percent)			
Three-Month Treasury Bill Rate	5.8	6.2	6.7
Ten-Year Government Note Rate	8.4	9.3	9.5
Civilian Unemployment Rate	6.2	6.2	6.1

SOURCE: Congressional Budget Office.

the last three years. Consumer price inflation, which totaled 4.5 percent in 1987, is expected to reach 4.9 percent in 1988 and 4.8 percent in 1989. The GNP deflator is expected to increase more slowly than the Consumer Price Index, since the step-up in inflation is driven mainly by import prices, which do not add to the GNP deflator.

As a result of the slow real growth and the Federal Reserve's accommodative stance in the first half of 1988, there will be little immediate pressure on interest rates. Later in the year, the three-month Treasury bill rate should begin to rise in response to the higher inflation rate. For the year as a whole, CBO projects that the bill rate will average 6.2 percent. Ten-year government note yields will rise even more sharply, averaging 9.3 percent for the year, as they incorporate expectations of still greater inflation in the future resulting from the accommodative monetary policy. In 1989, the resumption of growth and the Federal Reserve's anticipated tightening will cause short-term real interest rates to continue rising. Long-term rates in 1989, however, are projected to be relatively flat.

Like all economic forecasts, this one is very uncertain. For one thing, it depends on the success of the Federal Reserve in supplying the economy with enough credit to avoid a recession, without reigniting inflation or undermining the dollar. It also assumes that the long-awaited improvement in net exports has finally arrived and will accelerate in 1988. On the other hand, the economy could prove stronger than in this forecast if CBO has overestimated the extent of consumer retrenchment.

Another way of addressing the uncertainty of the forecast is to look at the historical record. For fiscal years 1978 through 1987, two-thirds of CBO's forecasts of nominal GNP for the budget year were within 2.8 percent of the actual outcome. Because 10 years is a very small sample on which to base a conclusion, however, CBO has also developed an uncertainty measure using a statistical approach. This measure produces a somewhat higher margin of uncertainly—4.2 percent of GNP. Based on this second measure of uncertainty, there is a two-thirds chance that the 1989 deficit will fall within $49 billion of the level projected by CBO.

SUMMARY TABLE 3 Baseline Budget Projections and Underlying Assumptions

	Actual 1987	1988	1989	1990	1991	1992	1993
	Budget Projections						
	(By fiscal year, in billions of dollars)[a]						
Revenues	854	897	953	1,036	1,112	1,181	1,262
Outlays	1,005	1,055	1,129	1,203	1,269	1,332	1,396
Deficit	150	157	176	167	158	151	134
	Economic Assumptions						
	(by calendar year)						
Nominal GNP Growth (percent change)	5.9	5.8	6.8	6.8	6.8	6.9	6.9
Real GNP Growth (percent change)	2.9	2.3	2.6	2.6	2.6	2.7	2.7
Implicit GNP Deflator (percent change)	3.0	3.4	4.1	4.1	4.1	4.1	4.1
CPI-W [b] (percent change)	3.6	4.5	4.9	4.6	4.4	4.4	4.4
Civilian Unemployment Rate (percent)	6.2	6.2	6.1	6.0	5.9	5.9	5.8
Three-Month Treasury Bill Rate (percent)	5.8	6.2	6.7	6.6	6.4	6.1	5.9
Ten-Year Government Note Rate (percent)	8.4	9.3	9.5	9.0	8.4	7.8	7.4

a. The baseline estimates include Social Security, which is off-budget.

b. Consumer Price Index for urban wage earners and clerical workers.

SOURCE: Congressional Budget Office.

Longer-Run Baseline Projections

Beyond 1989, CBO's economic assumptions are not a forecast of future conditions but are projections based on historical trends. The projections do not include business cycles. They assume that the economy's long-term growth depends largely on the growth of the labor force and that output per worker will grow at about the same rate it has in recent years. CBO's five-year economic projections and the corresponding baseline budget projections are presented in Summary Table 3.

SUMMARY FIGURE 2   Major Economic Assumptions

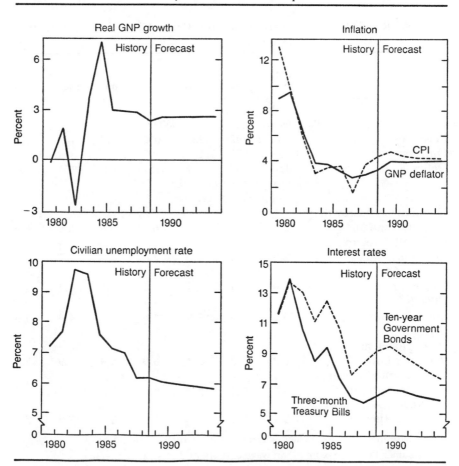

SOURCES: Congressional Budget Office; Department of Commerce, Bureau of Economic Analysis; Department of Labor, Bureau of Labor Statistics; Federal Reserve Board.

In the projections, real GNP grows at an average annual rate of about 2.7 percent from 1989 to 1993, while the civilian unemployment rate falls to about 5.8 percent (see Summary Figure 2). As measured by the GNP deflator, inflation stays at 4 percent, close to the postwar average. Consumer price inflation is slightly higher, however, because of further declines in the dollar and increases in import prices over the medium term. After 1989, real interest rates decline to levels consistent with their average since exchange rates began floating in 1971. Cyclical changes will presumably affect the level of activity during the projection years, but there is no way of predicting when they will occur or what will precipitate them. Thus, the projections should be considered as an average of a number of possible paths the economy might take.

Under these longer-run assumptions, the baseline deficit is projected to decline slowly from $176 billion in 1989 to $134 billion in 1993. The deficit shrinks because revenues are boosted by both inflation and real growth, while outlays rise only slightly faster than the rate of inflation. Compared with the size of the nation's economy, the baseline deficit falls from 3.1 percent of the gross national product in 1990 to 2.1 percent in 1993.

This report attempts to quantify for the first time the uncertainty inherent in these long-term economic and budget projections. The approach used is an extension of the analysis in CBO's report of last summer of the accuracy of budget-year estimates. The analysis suggests that there are about two chances in three that the level of real GNP in 1993 will turn out to be within 7 percent of its projected value, or that the average real growth rate between 1987 and 1993 will be between 1.6 percent and 3.6 percent. As a result, there is a two-in-three chance that the 1993 deficit will be within $125 billion of its projected value of $134 billion. This large degree of uncertainty illustrates the point made earlier that the longer-run projections should be viewed only as a general indicator of budgetary trends and not as a forecast of future budgets.

Article 12

MEASURING POVERTY

Congressional Budget Office

Since the early 1960s, the official definition of poverty has been one developed by Mollie Orshansky for the Social Security Administration.[1] That definition compares the total cash income of an individual's family with a poverty threshold based on a multiple of the cost of a nutritionally adequate diet for a family of that size and composition: if the family income is below the threshold, each member of the family is officially classified as poor.

The official poverty definition has been criticized on a variety of grounds, among them that income received in the form of goods and services—generally called in-kind income—is not counted, that the thresholds are set improperly, that taxes should be treated consistently in income measures and the thresholds, and that the basic concept of a poverty rate cannot measure the degree of poverty. These problems were clearly recognized by Orshansky and others when the poverty definition was established, but the need for a workable definition meant that compromises had to be made. Further, most of the issues that pose problems today were substantially less important 20 years ago.[2]

SOURCE: *Reducing Poverty Among Children*, Washington, DC: The Congress of the United States Congressional Budget Office, May 1985.

[1]There are actually two official poverty definitions. The Orshansky measure is used by the Bureau of the Census to assess which people were poor during an earlier year. The Office of Management and Budget (OMB) measure is used to determine eligibility for federal antipoverty programs. The OMB measure—which is actually calculated each year by the Department of Health and Human Services—is derived by inflating the most recent Census poverty thresholds based on the prior year's change in the Consumer Price Index for Urban Consumers (CPI-U). The focus here is on the Census definition.

[2]This discussion does not consider what may be the most significant problem in measuring poverty—the underreporting of income in the Current Population Survey (CPS). Comparisons of CPS data—the basis for poverty estimates—and income data from programs and the Internal Revenue Service indicate that a significant fraction of income does not show up in the CPS. To the extent that low-income families underreport their income, this would lead to overstated poverty rates. At the same time, underreporting has not changed by much over time, so changes in poverty statistics are likely to be more accurately measured than levels. In any case, no better data are available.

ISSUES ASSESSING POVERTY AND THE CURRENT MEASURE

What constitutes poverty is inherently a subjective judgment, depending in part on the views of the observer and in part on the use to which a poverty measure is to be put. Any assessment of poverty compares resources available to a family against a standard of need: if the resources are less than the standard, the family is labeled "poor." At issue are two basic questions: what resources should be considered to be available to meet need standards, and at what level should the standards be set?

It is generally agreed that available resources should include all cash income, but questions are raised about non-cash income and assets. Because in-kind income—that is, income received as goods or services—cannot be used to satisfy general needs, it is unclear how such income should be counted; in essence, the issue is one of valuation. Whether assets should be counted beyond the income they produce is also debated, especially in the case of assets that do not generate cash income, such as owner-occupied homes. These issues are discussed in greater detail below.

Need standards are necessarily arbitrary and are defined relative to societal norms. What one person views as inadequate can be seen by another as being fully satisfactory, and what would be considered poverty in a wealthy country like the United States could be an extremely high living standard in a developing country where average incomes are low. At the same time, the choice of poverty thresholds should be determined, at least in part, by the purpose behind the poverty measure. If the measure is to be used primarily as an indicator of what is happening to the number of poor people over time, assessed in terms of an absolute standard of what constitutes poverty, thresholds should be fixed in real terms even though the levels are arbitrary. If, instead, the measure is to be used as an eligibility criterion for assistance programs, thresholds should indicate levels of well-being below which it is agreed that the government should provide aid. Finally, if the measure is meant to assess the well-being of those who are worst off in relation to the rest of the population, thresholds should be set and varied over time to equal some fraction of average living standards.

Measuring poverty is complicated, partly because it is difficult to define need standards and thus required resources, and partly because required and available resources may not be measured in comparable units. If need standards could be defined as minimum amounts of each consumption good or service, available resources would be adequate if they made it possible to obtain the needed amount of each item—that is, if cash resources were sufficient to purchase necessary items not available in kind. Setting standards for how much of each good a family must have to escape poverty, however, is difficult—if not impossible. Resource requirements have therefore been defined in aggregate dollar terms—the poverty thresholds. (See the following section for further discussion of this issue.)

The problem would end here if available resources were also only in dollars: a family with cash income at or above the thresholds would be able to meet the need standards and thus not be poor. But resources are not all monetary; families can get food stamps, subsidized housing, subsidized health insurance, and other goods and services in kind rather than in cash. Because need standards are defined in monetary terms and not on the basis of how much of each consumption item is required to avoid poverty, it is difficult to determine what amounts of in-kind resources would satisfy those needs.

Measuring poverty thus requires two things:

- A definition of what constitutes the standard and the resources required to satisfy those needs, and

- Assessment of whether individual families have the necessary resources.

Defining Need Standards and Resource Requirements

There is no objective method of defining need standards and resource requirements. In principle, standards should represent the minimum amount of each category of goods and services that is necessary for a socially acceptable, minimum standard of living, while resource requirements should be what is necessary to attain those standards. Because there are official nutritional standards, a minimum food bundle that satisfies those standards can be used to define the basic need for food. Such standards do not exist, however, for housing, medical care, clothing, and other requirements, and there is wide disagreement about what standards should be. Moreover, standards set, even for food, are necessarily subjective, reflecting the prevailing living conditions for the nation as a whole and the perceptions of the people defining the standards.

Orshansky skirted the question of quantifying need standards for specific items by establishing poverty thresholds that represent resource requirements. These thresholds were defined as the cost of a bundle of food, multiplied by the ratio of income to food expenditures. Minimum food costs were taken from the economy food plan, the least expensive of four diets determined by the Department of Agriculture

(USDA) to meet basic nutritional needs.[3] The income needed to be non-poor was then set equal to three times the cost of the economy food plan, based on a 1955 survey indicating that families of three or more persons spent one-third of their after-tax income on food. Because food requirements vary with household composition, separate poverty thresholds were calculated for different family types based on size, number of children, and the age and sex of the family's head.[4] Over time, these thresholds have been adjusted for inflation, initially to reflect changes in food prices and more recently to account for changes in the general price level (see further discussion below).

While the Orshansky formulation conveniently sidesteps the issue of defining minimum requirements for every consumption item, its very simplicity means that it cannot accurately measure basic needs for all—or perhaps any—households. For example, because women require less food than men, the original thresholds for female-headed households were set below those for male-headed households, even though needing less food has no effect on requirements for housing, clothes, and other necessities.[5] Unless there is a fixed relationship between food requirements and other needs, defining poverty thresholds as a fixed multiple of poverty-level food costs for different groups can only approximate true resource requirements.

Similarly, objections can be raised against the simplifying assumption that, because in 1955 families with three or more members spent one-third of their income on food, need standards can be defined as three times the cost of food. Families spend a smaller share of their budget on food as their incomes rise. Consequently, poor families spend a larger than average fraction of their incomes on food, and the fraction of income spent on food by all families therefore understates that fraction. Thus, the poverty thresholds derived from the average budget

---

[3]Even here, however, there is disagreement. The Department of Agriculture has defined both economy and thrifty food plans, the first of which was designed as "emergency and temporary" and the second of which is used as the basis for food stamp allotments. Neither represents the minimum-cost food bundle for meeting nutritional standards, since both allow for a varied diet that includes those foods normally consumed by Americans. Even so, the USDA acknowledges that a person would have to be quite knowledgeable to maintain a nutritional diet with either food plan.

[4]To account for the higher fixed costs of smaller families, multipliers greater than three were used for couples and persons living alone; these multipliers were 3.88 and 5.92, respectively. All other differences in thresholds stem from differences in assumed food needs.

[5]The threshold distinction based on sex of household head was dropped in 1981; currently 48 thresholds are defined for nine sizes of families with nonelderly heads and two sizes of families with elderly heads, with further differentiation based on number of children

share going for food overstate needs based on normal expenditures of low-income households. In addition, changing relative prices between food and non-food items mean that a fixed relationship between food and non-food expenditures is unlikely to hold over time. If food prices rise less rapidly than other prices, the budget share needed for non-food items would increase and the income requirement would be more than three times the cost of a minimum food bundle.

Updating the thresholds to account for price changes also presents problems, because current methods may not accurately reflect variations in resources required to avoid poverty. Before 1969, the thresholds were adjusted annually for inflation based on changes in the Consumer Price Index for food. That procedure implicitly assumed that the income-to-food-expenditure ratio was unchanging and that resource requirements therefore would grow at the same rate as food prices.[6] Since 1969, the basis for inflation adjustment has been the Consumer Price Index (CPI) for all goods and services. This revised methodology does not assume a constant ratio of income to food expenditures, but it does assume that changes in relative prices do not affect the need standards for families.

The major failing of this inflation-adjustment procedure comes from the possibility that prices of goods purchased by poor families might change at a different rate from prices of goods represented in the CPI. Low-income families spend relatively more of their income on food and energy and relatively less on their own homes than does the average family. When prices of food and energy rose faster than the CPI during the early 1970s, the official poverty thresholds failed to reflect these adverse relative price movements. At the end of that decade, rapidly increasing homeownership costs meant that the CPI grew faster than prices generally; during that period, poverty thresholds probably increased in real terms. If poverty thresholds are intended to represent the cost of obtaining a minimum bundle of consumption needs, updating them based on the CPI probably misstates actual costs.

A further objection to the current methodology involves the question of what should be included in the measures of income and food expenditure used to calculate the multiplier. The original analysis counted only cash income after taxes on the income side and food purchases on the food side. Because farm families grow some of their own food, adjustments were made to poverty thresholds for the farm pop-

---

[6]Alternatively, the procedure could be viewed as assuming that all prices were changing at the same rate, so using the CPI for food to inflate the thresholds was equivalent to using the CPI for all items. This last assumption was clearly false, however.

ulation to reflect their reduced need for cash to buy food.[7] In the early 1960s, this approach made sense, since most income was in cash, and, other than for farm families, relatively little food was received as transfers or in-kind payments. This situation has changed, however, with the growth during the last two decades of government transfer programs (such as food stamps, Medicaid, and housing assistance) that provide non-cash aid and the rapid increase in the proportion of employee compensation paid in the form of fringe benefits (such as pensions, health and life insurance, and employer-provided meals). Ignoring the values of these in-kind benefits in either the numerator or the denominator of the multiplier calculation will yield a less accurate measure of the income-to-food-expenditure ratio.

At the same time, defenders of the current multiplier argue that the poverty measure should be absolute and unchanging over time, except to reflect general inflation. If the original multiplier calculations accurately measured the income-to-food-expenditure relationship at the time, there is no need to determine a new multiplier taking into account the growth in in-kind benefits, even if such benefits were counted as income. The need standards, according to this argument, should continue to be based on the original multiplier analysis to avoid raising (or lowering) poverty standards over time, and hence to maintain continuity in poverty statistics.

A final objection is that poverty thresholds make no allowance for geographic variation in the cost of living. What few data are available indicate that maintaining a given standard of living can be markedly more expensive in some locations than in others; yet a single set of poverty thresholds, invariant with respect to location, is used to determine whether people are poor. Families officially classified as poor but living in low-cost areas could well be better off than similar families with incomes above the poverty line who live where costs are high.

Despite these criticisms, the lack of an objective means of defining a family's basic needs for each individual consumption item leaves no better way of setting absolute poverty thresholds.[8] While recognizing

---

[7]This adjustment was somewhat arbitrary, however. Thresholds for farm families were set at 70 percent of non-farm thresholds, even though there was little evidence to support such a value. The percentage was raised to 85 percent in 1969 and to 100 percent in 1981 on the assumption that only a small fraction of farm families rely on home production for a significant portion of their food.

[8]The entire issue of defining poverty in terms of need standards could be avoided by setting thresholds relative to median family income. This approach argues that poverty is not absolute, but rather is a function of the standard of living of the average family. The Orshansky multiplier approach itself is not entirely absolute in that the

the shortcomings of the methodology, this study follows the basic Orshansky multiplier approach in most of the alternative definitions it examines. At the same time, changes are considered that could reduce the impact of some of those shortcomings.

Assessing the Adequacy of Resources

Currently, a family's poverty status is obtained by comparing its total pre-tax, cash income with the relevant poverty threshold. If its annual income falls short of the threshold, the family and all of its members are classified as poor. This section discusses four problems with this approach: no account is taken of the family's non-cash income; wealth and period-to-period fluctuations in income are ignored; the income considered is gross of taxes, while the thresholds are based on after-tax income; and no distinction is made between families that are barely poor and those whose income is far below the threshold.

In-Kind Income.   Perhaps the most frequently mentioned criticism of the official poverty measure is that it ignores non-cash income. A family receiving $200 worth of food stamps each month, living in public housing, and getting subsidized health insurance is considered to be no better off than an otherwise identical family getting none of those benefits. This almost certainly misstates the relative well-being of the two families. Since accepting such income is voluntary, the recipient family is almost certain to be helped and cannot be made worse off. At the same time, any amount of a given good in excess of the minimum requirement has no value in terms of meeting other needs. A family is still poor if it cannot afford all basic needs, regardless of how much food or housing or any other single good it has. Consequently, receipt of non-cash income reduces poverty with respect to other goods only to the extent that it frees cash income to buy those other goods.

By this argument, a particular form of non-cash income should be considered in assessing poverty status only up to a value representing that part of the poverty threshold that would be expected to be allocated to that good. For example, if the poverty threshold for a family were $800 per month and the family was expected to spend 30 percent on housing, the value of housing assistance provided to the family each

---

income-to-food-expenditure ratio is based on a national average, thus taking into account the normal standard of living. Similarly, the economy food plan is not a least-cost diet, but rather a low-cost diet that allows for a varied food menu containing the kinds of food consumed by average Americans.

month should not exceed $240 (30 percent of $800) less the family's own cash expenditures on housing when determining whether or not the family is poor. Any additional non-cash income given in the form of housing does not help the family meet its need for $560 per month (70 percent of $800) for non-housing expenditures.[9] (Since the excess over $240 may substantially improve the family's well-being, however, one might argue that it ought not to be completely excluded from measurement.)

Wealth and the Accounting Period. The official poverty definition ignores wealth except to the extent that a family's assets generate cash income; only income received during the calendar year is compared with the poverty threshold.[10] But a family's well-being depends less on income than on consumption and the ability to satisfy basic needs. A family with significant accumulated savings can continue to consume, even if its income disappears entirely for a year or two, and such a family would not normally be considered poor. At the same time, savings cannot replace income forever, and almost all families with no income at all will eventually become poor in consumption terms.

What is at issue here is the accounting period over which poverty is assessed; the length of that period can greatly affect the measured poverty rate. The official poverty measure uses a one-year accounting period, long enough to smooth out most short-term fluctuations in incomes such as those caused by periods of illness. Even so, some incomes are more volatile, perhaps because employment is less regular or because payment comes only at the completion of major tasks, and even an annual accounting period fails to capture the true nature of a family's financial situation. Savings may enable such families to maintain an even consumption pattern; in such cases, the official poverty measure is misleading. This argues for some means of reflecting wealth in assessing poverty.

Two issues mitigate this argument, however. First, good measures of wealth do not exist, and individuals in general do not have a good sense of what their wealth is. While surveys could gather data on wealth just as they do on income, the results would likely be inaccurate because people tend not to know either the extent of their assets or their

---

[9]As noted above, the current poverty thresholds do not indicate basic needs for individual consumption items. That the thresholds represent income needed to satisfy specific needs is implicit, however.

[10]One form of wealth not considered here is employer contributions to pension plans. Because such wealth cannot be used for current consumption, one might argue that it should be ignored in assessing poverty status. Others might argue that because pensions reduce the need for other savings, they should be counted.

value. Second, even if wealth could be measured accurately, it is unclear how it should be incorporated into a measure of poverty. Should a family be expected to spend all its savings in a given year? Over three years? If so, wealth (or one-third of wealth) should be counted as income. Or should wealth be expected to provide a particular percentage return? Then that percentage of a family's wealth should be considered to be the same as income. That might still be an inaccurate measure of the family's ability to satisfy its immediate consumption needs, however, because some forms of wealth are difficult to transform into cash quickly.

One particular form of wealth—housing—presents special problems. For most homeowners, their homes are probably their largest assets and form the bulk of their wealth. More important, their homes provide them with places to live, for what might be a lower annual cash cost than for similar, rented housing. The family's investment in their home yields a return, not in money income like most financial assets, but rather as housing which is neither valued in dollars nor counted as income in assessing poverty status. By ignoring this in-kind income (often called imputed rent by economists), the official poverty measure understates the resources available to homeowner families to meet their consumption needs.[11] However, omitting the value of services provided by a family's own home—and, to a lesser extent, the value of services provided by other durable goods such as automobiles—yields an inaccurate assessment of its poverty status.

Taxes.   There are two consistent methods of dealing with taxes in measuring poverty. On the one hand, pre-tax income could be compared with poverty thresholds defined to include tax payments as a resource need; on the other hand, income net of taxes could be compared with poverty thresholds defined as resources required to cover non-tax needs. Official poverty statistics follow neither course but rather compare pre-tax income with poverty thresholds based on after-tax income. Twenty years ago when the poverty measure was devised, this treatment of income made little difference since poor families paid little or nothing in taxes. Rising payroll taxes and bracket creep in the federal income tax have increased the tax liabilities of low-income households, however; in 1984, families with four members and with earnings at the poverty level owed more than 10 percent of their income in federal taxes—up from 4 percent in 1978. This is a significant

---

[11]In part, imputed rent is ignored because it is difficult to obtain accurate data through surveys (the source of other information used to calculate poverty statistics).

reduction in resources available to such families to meet their consumption needs.

In addition, the current treatment of taxes in measuring poverty fails to distinguish the different resource needs of families with and without tax liabilities. Two families with the same pre-tax incomes will not be equally well off if one has income from earnings that are subject to payroll and income taxes, while the other has income from untaxed transfer payments. Consistency requires either that pre-tax incomes be compared with resource needs for consumption and taxes or that after-tax incomes be assessed against consumption needs alone.

Pre-tax incomes are more easily determined than after-tax incomes, since there is wide variation in taxes paid by families with similar before-tax incomes. At the same time, this variation means that poverty thresholds incorporating average tax liabilities would not accurately represent the resource needs of different families. Because there is much less variation in incomes required for consumption goods and services, thresholds reflecting after-tax needs might provide greater accuracy.

Degree of Poverty.   Poverty statistics classify families and individuals as either poor or not poor; this simplification severely limits the usefulness of the poverty rate as an indicator of the condition of low-income families. The degree of poverty matters as well, and the inability of the poverty rate to measure degree has several implications. First, the measure separates similar families, and groups together quite different families. A family with income just below the poverty threshold is much more like a family with income just above the threshold than it is like a family with no income at all, yet it appears to be no different from the latter family in the poverty rate statistics. Second, poverty rates do not tell how poor families are. A situation in which every family in the poorest 15 percent of the population has an income $200 below the poverty threshold appears identical to one in which each of those families has an income of only $200, yet clearly the latter presents much greater cause for concern. Third, the poverty rate cannot give a complete picture of the effectiveness of antipoverty programs. In terms of its effect on the poverty *rate*, a program that provided a small amount of additional income to many families just below the poverty line, thus moving them out of poverty, would seem more effective than a program that gave significant resources to the very poor but did not pull any of its beneficiaries above the official poverty line.

The poverty gap—the aggregate amount of cash income by which all poor families fall below the poverty level—is a measure that serves to mitigate these problems somewhat but not completely. It distinguishes sharply between the polar cases cited above: if all poor families are just below the poverty threshold, the poverty gap is relatively small; if all of the poor have virtually no incomes, the gap is large. Further, the poverty gap provides a good measure of the effectiveness of antipoverty programs. The extent to which any program raises measured incomes of the poor will be directly reflected in the poverty gap; benefits going to those at or above the poverty line have no effect on it, however.

At the same time, the poverty gap fails to distinguish which of the poor are helped by improvements in the national economy or by assistance programs. Although providing $1,000 additional annual income to a family who is $1,000 below the poverty threshold has the same effect on the poverty gap as providing the same $1,000 to a family with no income, the latter approach is almost certain to be better in terms of reducing the effects of poverty. Differential impacts on the poor can be distinguished by examining the distribution of the poor and near-poor around the poverty thresholds, considering, for example, the number of families with incomes between 0 and 50 percent of the poverty thresholds, between 50 percent and 75 percent, between 75 percent and 100 percent, between 100 percent and 125 percent, and so on. Changes in this distribution could then show the effects on the poor of antipoverty programs, a drop in unemployment, or other events. It is difficult, however, to summarize the meaning of a given distribution or to compare two different distributions. In any event, there is probably no single measure that tells policymakers all they should know about poverty. Using several measures is probably the best approach.

ALTERNATIVE MEASURES OF POVERTY

This section examines alternative measures of poverty, focusing on various ways of changing the definition of income to include non-cash resources and to exclude taxes paid, and of adjusting the poverty thresholds with which income is compared.

Counting In-Kind Income and Excluding Taxes from Income

A significant part of income is received in a wide range of in-kind forms. Employers often pay part of the costs of health and life insurance for workers and their families, and sometimes provide meals and housing. The government offers aid to low-income families and individuals through food stamps, school nutrition programs, Medicaid, and housing subsidies for both renters and homeowners. These benefits now comprise nearly two-thirds of all means-tested assistance given to poor households.[12] Medicare provides medical care for the elderly and disabled without regard to recipients' incomes.

Taxes have also grown in importance for low-income families. For a family of four at the poverty level, combined federal payroll and personal income tax liability has grown from 4 percent of income in 1978 to over 10 percent in 1984. More than one-third of all families below the poverty level pay some taxes; for those families, the two taxes average more than 6 percent of income.

Because these in-kind benefits and taxes have a significant effect on the well-being of low-income families, they should be incorporated in assessments of poverty status. Ignoring these factors, which have a large and growing impact on the resources of poor families, yields inaccurate measures of the ability of the poor to satisfy basic needs.

Three questions arise with regard to counting non-cash income and excluding taxes:

- Which kinds of non-cash income can and should be included?
- How should non-cash income be valued?
- Which taxes should be omitted in calculating incomes?

Which Kinds of Non-Cash Income Can and Should Be Included? This question has both practical and theoretical parts. On the one hand, if a more inclusive income measure is to be applied, one must be able to determine how much of each kind of non-cash income a family receives. In principle, all benefits that improve a family's ability to obtain goods and services should be included. From a practical viewpoint, however, it is often difficult to determine exactly what in-kind income a family receives. On the other hand, even if one could observe receipt of every form of non-cash income, not all of those forms improve a family's ability to satisfy current needs; for example, employer-provided pension benefits may generate resources that the family can use in retirement but not money with which to buy food today.

What non-cash benefits could be counted as income in practice is determined by the data available. While new survey information is forthcoming, the best current source (the Current Population Survey, or CPS) includes data only on receipt of food stamps, school lunches, housing assistance, and medical care provided through Medicaid,

---

[12]Department of Commerce, Bureau of the Census, *Estimates of Poverty Including the Value of Noncash Benefits: 1983*, Technical Paper 52, Table A, p. viii.

Medicare, and private insurance.[13] The Bureau of the Census has estimated alternative ways of valuing each of these four in-kind transfers; the assessment offered below of in-kind income includes only these four items.[14]

How Should Non-Cash Income Be Valued?   To allow combining cash and non-cash incomes, each non-cash benefit must be assigned a cash value, but there is no consensus on how this should be done. The Bureau of the Census has devised three different valuation approaches, each with advantages and drawbacks.[15]

Market value is an estimate of what the good or service would cost if bought in the private market. This is generally easiest to estimate, since there is often a comparable item available for sale for which a price or cost can be found.[16] However, the market value may greatly exceed the value to recipients, if recipients would not have chosen to buy as much of the good or service had they been given its market value in cash, or if in-kind benefits do not free up resources equal to their market value for use in satisfying other needs. In fact, valuing in-kind benefits at their market value can lead to absurd conclusions: an example often cited is that by using the market-value approach and valuing Medicaid benefits at average cost (that is, the market value is defined to be the average cost of health care services provided), there would be no elderly poor living alone in New York State because the insurance value of Medicare and Medicaid provided to them exceeds the poverty threshold for single people.

The *recipient/cash equivalent value* (R/CE) addresses this problem by trying to estimate how much cash individuals would have to be given in place of the non-cash benefit to make them feel equally well off. This value cannot be greater than the market value of the benefit; cash equal

---

[13]The Survey of Income and Program Participation (SIPP) will provide a wealth of information on 40 different sources of income and 13 classes of assets, but data from SIPP are now available only for the last two quarters of 1983. When more SIPP data are released, it will be possible to determine the receipt of a much wider range of non-cash incomes than with current data bases.

[14]One additional issue involves the inclusion of medical care: should long-term institutional medical care be included at all? Because poverty rates are calculated only for the noninstitutionalized population, only the value of noninstitutional care is included.

[15]See Department of Commerce, Bureau of the Census, *Alternative Methods for Valuing Selected In-Kind Transfer Benefits and Measuring Their Effect on Poverty*, Technical Paper 50, March 1982 (see especially Chapters 4 and 5).

[16]For some items, this is not the case. Medicaid, for example, has no comparable counterpart in the private market. The market value for Medicaid is calculated as an insurance value, based on total program costs.

to the market value would enable recipients to purchase the in-kind transfer and be at least as well off as with the transfer. Usually, the R/CE value is less than the market value; in most cases, recipients would prefer to be given a combination of goods rather than a large amount of only one good; they would thus exchange the in-kind transfer for less than its market value in cash, which could then be used to buy a variety of goods.[17]

For some analysts, the R/CE value is quite appealing since it bases the valuation on the individual's own assessment of the benefit's worth. On the other hand, others would argue that society should judge what in-kind transfers to the poor should be and that self-perceptions of the poor should be ignored. Further, while the R/CE value is conceptually clear, its practical application requires strong assumptions about people's behavior or preferences.[18]

The *budget-share value* assumes that the value of an in-kind benefit cannot exceed the amount that families with cash incomes near the poverty level would spend on that specific item (the "poverty share"). The value of a non-cash benefit is then taken to be the lesser of the market value (as defined above) and this poverty share. This approach addresses the fact that in-kind transfers do not necessarily free up resources for use in satisfying other needs; only to the extent that the transfers replace previously purchased goods or services do recipients have more money to spend on consumption goods.

---

[17]If the recipient would have purchased at least as much of the item as was received, the transfer frees up cash equal to its market value, so the recipient/cash equivalent value must equal the market value. If the recipient would have purchased less, the recipient/cash equivalent value will generally be lower than market value because consumers usually do not choose to spend all additional income on any one good; they would be willing to give up some of the market value of the in-kind benefit in order to achieve more variety in their consumption.

[18]In particular, the Bureau of the Census approach assumes that the value that recipients place on in-kind benefits is equal either to the average expenditure on the item by similar families with similar incomes who do not receive in-kind transfers or to the market value of the benefit, whichever is less. For example, if a family is given housing with a market value of $5,000, and if similar families not receiving housing assistance spend an average of $4,000 on housing, the R/CE value would be $4,000. If the market value of the assistance were only $3,500, the R/CE value would also be $3,500.

An alternative approach uses utility functions to estimate the additional income a family would need to be as well off as with the in-kind benefits. This approach suffers because utility functions are unobservable, and strong assumptions therefore have to be made to obtain estimates. See Department of Commerce, Bureau of the Census, *Alternative Methods for Valuing Selected In-Kind Transfer Benefits and Measuring Their Effect on Poverty,* Technical Paper 50, March 1982, pp. 28–31, 38–44, 58–69, and 127–134.

The budget-share value method has potentially serious shortcomings, however. First, it assumes that recipients of in-kind income value that income as much as people with cash-only incomes near the poverty level. Second, it implicitly assumes that the poverty level is correctly defined. If in-kind income is counted in assessing poverty status, different thresholds may be appropriate. (This issue is discussed in greater detail below.)

The budget-share value method could be used to partition poverty thresholds into resource requirements for individual classes of goods. If poverty shares—that is, normal expenditures by families near the poverty level—were used to define resource requirements for specific goods and services, the budget-share value would constrain in-kind transfers to meet only the poverty-level requirement for the good or service in question.[19]

The dollar valuations of in-kind benefits developed by the Bureau of the Census vary significantly across the three approaches. In general, the market value is highest, while the recipient/cash equivalent value is lowest. Because measuring in-kind transfers at market value often overstates the availability of resources for purchasing goods and services—and thus the ability to meet basic needs—the analysis presented here uses only the budget share and the recipient/cash equivalent values. Specific estimates are those made by the Bureau of the Census.

Which Taxes Should Be Omitted in Calculating Incomes? Because poverty thresholds are based on the relationship between after-tax income and food expenditures, it would be consistent to exclude taxes from the income used to assess poverty status. In essence, the thresholds represent the minimum disposable income required to be nonpoor. Both payroll and income taxes must be subtracted from pretax income to determine disposable income that can then be compared with the thresholds.[20] On the other hand, because thresholds are based on consumption needs including sales taxes, the latter taxes should not

---

[19]The circularity of this approach may lead to significant under- or overstatement of needs. If the poverty thresholds in fact represent the cost of meeting basic needs, and if families at the thresholds in fact purchase those basic needs, their budget shares represent poverty thresholds for individual items. On the other hand, if poverty thresholds are not what is needed to be nonpoor, or families at the poverty line buy too little or too much of some goods, the budget shares would not accurately denote resources needed to meet basic needs for specific items.

[20]One can argue that payroll taxes finance retirement benefits and therefore may allow families to reduce savings and increase current consumption. For families in poverty, however, it is unlikely that saving for retirement would occur in the absence of payroll taxes.

be removed, as they represent part of the cost of goods and services. Similarly, because they are part of shelter costs and are thus part of normal expenditures, property taxes should not be subtracted from gross income. In the following analysis, income is evaluated net of payroll and state and federal income taxes, but inclusive of other taxes.[21]

Establishing Income Thresholds for Assessing Poverty Status

The thresholds currently used to assess poverty status have been set by multiplying the cost of a nutritionally adequate food bundle by the ratio of after-tax income to food expenditures for families with three or more members. These thresholds are updated over time in line with changes in the CPI for all items. Neither the income nor the food expenditure calculations include in-kind benefits, and it is therefore argued that the thresholds are inappropriate benchmarks to use if non-cash income is counted as a resource. This line of reasoning asserts that if income includes in-kind items, the income-to-food-expenditures ratio must be recalculated with in-kind benefits included in both halves of the ratio. This recalculation would require that the dollar value of in-kind food (such as food stamps, school lunches and other food programs, employer-provided meals, and food grown for personal consumption) be added to cash expenditures for food and that the dollar value of all non-cash income (including employer-provided health and life insurance, housing assistance, Medicare and Medicaid, and food items) be added to after-tax cash income. The revised ratio of these two values would then be multiplied by the cost of an inexpensive food plan to obtain a threshold against which total cash and non-cash income could be compared.

In response to this argument, others contend that there is no need to revise the poverty thresholds to account for non-cash income, because neither income nor consumption included much in kind at the time of the original multiplier calculation, which was based on a 1955 survey. If total food consumption required one-third of total income before in-kind benefits were significant—then increases in non-cash income and transfers should not affect the income-to-food-expenditure ratio, but rather should only require that the non-cash income be included in the poverty assessment. A hypothetical example clarifies this line of reasoning. Assume the multiplier based on cash income (which was then essentially the total) and food expenditures were exactly three,

---

[21]It would be equally correct to compare pre-tax needs and pre-tax income, but—as noted above—wide variations in tax liability make estimating pre-tax needs difficult.

and that the cost of a minimal food plan was $200 per month; the poverty threshold is thus $600 ($200 × 3). A family with $600 or more in cash income and no non-cash benefits would thus be nonpoor. Now suppose that the family was given $100 in food benefits and $100 in housing assistance, and that its housing costs were at least $100. The family would now need only $400 cash income to meet its needs as defined by the poverty level; the non-cash food benefits satisfy half of its food needs and the housing assistance provides some or all of its shelter, leaving only $400 of other needs (the balance of food and housing requirements and all others). On the other hand, if non-cash income was significant in the earlier period, adjustments in the multiplier would be required.

Comparing total incomes—cash plus in-kind—with current poverty thresholds would ignore changes in consumption patterns over time. In that sense, the poverty measure would be constant in absolute terms. However, relative prices have changed over time, and families—both poor and nonpoor—have reacted by adjusting their consumption patterns, buying more of relatively cheaper goods and less of relatively expensive ones. To the extent that this has occurred, current poverty thresholds do not have the same meaning as when they were originally defined. To reflect changing relative prices and changing income patterns, the thresholds would require revision.

If the multiplier is to be adjusted to account for the inclusion of in-kind income, an additional question is raised: what group should be used as the basis for estimating the income-to-food-expenditure relationship? Orshansky took data for all income groups in the population—partly because that was what was available. But critics complain that this approach biases the multiplier—and, thus, the poverty thresholds—upward because higher-income families spend a smaller fraction of their income on food. If the intent is to characterize the income needs of families at the poverty level, it may be more logical to use data for the low-income population. At the same time, using expenditure information only for the poorest families probably would result in bias in the other direction: those below the poverty level spend a very high proportion of their income on food by necessity, and a multiplier based on the spending patterns of these families would be too low. An intermediate choice would be a group containing neither the poorest nor the richest families.

Another issue regarding thresholds is the basis on which they should be adjusted for inflation. Currently, thresholds are indexed by the CPI for all items. This is appropriate to the extent that the way in which prices are combined in calculating the CPI represents expenditure patterns of families around the poverty level. If this is not the case and if prices for some commodities are changing faster than prices for others, indexation based on the CPI will yield less accurate threshold adjustments than a price index based on actual purchases by poor families. Such a CPI for the poor does not now exist. It could be established, however, based either on the actual consumption patterns of poor families or on a consumption bundle representing the poverty level. While the latter would be conceptually consistent with inflating poverty thresholds, the former would be calculated without defining specific components of poverty-level consumption.

A final issue is whether poverty should be measured in absolute or relative terms. The official poverty measure does not assess whether families have enough income simply to survive. Instead, it takes some account of accepted standards of what constitutes a reasonable quality of life in the United States. Poverty thresholds are thus not strictly absolute, but are at least somewhat relative. Some critics argue that this should be made explicit by setting the thresholds equal to a fixed percentage of median family income. If this were done, what is defined as poverty level would keep pace with average living standards in the country. In practice, the relationship between current poverty thresholds and median income has followed a downward trend, falling during periods of real growth and increasing during periods of stagflation. The poverty level for a family of four declined from 49 percent of the median income of four-person families in 1959 to 33 percent in 1973 and then rose to 35 percent in 1983. Thus, while the official poverty thresholds might (with the qualifications mentioned above) indicate the income required to obtain a minimum acceptable standard of living, they do not allow for changing perceptions of minimum needs brought about by increasing national income. For the latter, a relative measure would be needed.

Critics maintain that a relative poverty measure is an indicator not of poverty but rather of income inequality, since it measures the fraction of the population with incomes below a fixed percentage of median incomes. If being poor is defined as having income below thresholds defined in relative terms, then poverty can be eradicated only by reducing inequality among incomes of the poor and near-poor. General economic growth that causes all incomes to rise by 10 percent or 50 percent or 100 percent would have no impact on measured poverty at all, even though it would be hard to argue that those people at the bottom of the economic ladder would not be much better off as a result of the growth. In essence, the two measures answer different questions. An absolute measure tells how many people are unable to attain a specific living standard, while a relative measure assesses how well the poor are doing in relation to national norms.

One example of a relative poverty measure is included in the estimates presented below. The poverty level for a family of four was set at 50 percent of the median family income. Thresholds for other family sizes and compositions were set to maintain the same ratio with current official thresholds as for a family of four. This approach yields thresholds about 19 percent above the official thresholds in 1982.

STATISTICS ON POVERTY OF CHILDREN

This section presents 12 different measures of the poverty of children—the official measure used by the Bureau of the Census and 11 alternative measures obtained by varying the definition of income and the poverty thresholds with which incomes are compared. The alternatives are offered as illustrations of how the measurement of poverty might be changed, not as proposed revisions of the current measure. Statistics based on the alternative measures indicate how poverty rates and gaps would vary if definitions were changed; they are not meant to be viewed as "better" measures.

The 12 measures are based on three definitions of income and four sets of poverty thresholds. One definition of income is cash only, the same as is used in the official measure. The other definitions calculate income as cash plus the value of in-kind receipts of food stamps, school lunches, housing assistance, and medical care, minus federal and state income and payroll taxes. One alternative uses the recipient cash equivalent value of in-kind benefits, while the other uses the budget-share approach.

The lowest of the four sets of thresholds is a reindexation of the original 1965 thresholds, based on changes in the cost of a poverty consumption bundle.[22] The current thresholds are also used based on the argument given above that no changes in the thresholds are required and to provide a comparison with official poverty statistics. A third set of thresholds is based on a recalculation of the multiplier relating food expenditures to total cash and in-kind income for the entire population.[23] Finally, relative thresholds based on median family in-

---

[22]This CPI for the poor is based on expenditure patterns for poor people and families obtained from the 1972–1973 Consumer Expenditure Survey (CEX). Using published components of the CPI and reweighting with expenditure shares of the poor, it was found that costs for the poor rose about 203 percent between 1965 and 1982. Applying that increase to the 1965 poverty threshold for a family of four ($3,223) yields a reindexed 1982 poverty threshold of $9,757, about 1 percent less than the actual 1982 threshold of $9,862 for four-person families. For a complete discussion of the methodology, see Roberton Williams, "Inflation and the Poor" (Unpublished paper, April 1982).

[23]"New multiplier" thresholds were calculated using estimates of total cash plus in-kind income after taxes and food expenditures—with in-kind benefits measured using

come provide the highest poverty lines. Table 1 presents the estimated values for these alternative sets of poverty thresholds for 1982. (Because the most recent Census Bureau estimates of tax liabilities and the value of in-kind income needed to calculate incomes for some poverty measures are for 1982, all poverty statistics reported here are for that year.)

Poverty Rates

Under any particular set of thresholds, poverty rates for children in all families using the different income measures vary only slightly—never by more than about 10 percent—while differences in poverty rates across alternative thresholds are roughly proportional to variations in the thresholds themselves. The 1982 poverty rate for children under age 18 varied from 19.4 percent to 27.7 percent across all 12 measures—compared with 21.9 percent under the official definition (see Table 2). The bulk of the variation was the result of the 20 percent difference between the highest and lowest thresholds; the widest variation across income definitions is from 19.4 percent to 21.6 percent for reindexed thresholds, the lowest values. Whether income is measured in terms of cash only, or inclusive of in-kind benefits and exclusive of taxes, poverty rates for all children as a group are relatively constant.

For individual family types, however, poverty rates vary much more across the alternative definitions. For children living in families headed by single women, the broader income definitions yield lower poverty rates—as much as one-sixth lower—regardless of what threshold is used. On the other hand, poverty rates for children in two-parent families decline only slightly or increase by as much as 10 percent. Variation in the effects of alternative definitions results from differences in the relative importance of in-kind income and taxes for different family types. Families headed by single women are likely to receive more in-kind assistance and to pay less in taxes than are married-couple families. As a result, broadening the income definition is likely to have a greater positive effect for families headed by single women than for married couples.

---

the recipient cash equivalent value. In 1978, these values for all families of three or more people were estimated to be $14,067 and $3,532, respectively. The multiplier is the ratio of those two figures, or 3.98. The poverty threshold for a family of four was calculated by multiplying that ratio times the annual cost of the Thrifty Food Plan in 1982—$2,794.20. Poverty thresholds for other family sizes were obtained by multiplying the four-person threshold times the ratio of official thresholds for the given family size and for a four-person family.

TABLE 1   Alternative Poverty Thresholds, 1982 (in dollars)

Family Size and Structure [a]	Reindexed Threshold [b]	Official Threshold	Revised Multiplier [c]	Relative Threshold [d]
One Person	4,849	4,901	5,528	5,823
Age 15–64	4,966	5,019	5,661	5,963
Age 65 and over	4,577	4,626	5,218	5,496
Two People	6,214	6,281	7,085	7,463
Under age 65	6,418	6,487	7,317	7,708
Age 65 and over	5,774	5,836	6,583	6,934
Three People	7,611	7,693	8,678	9,140
Four People	9,757	9,862	11,124	11,717
Five People	11,560	11,684	13,180	13,881
Six People	13,066	13,207	14,897	15,691
Seven People	14,876	15,036	16,961	17,864
Eight People	16,541	16,719	18,859	19,863
Nine People or More	19,488	19,698	22,219	23,403
Ratio to Official Threshold	0.989	1.000	1.128	1.188

a. For all measures, thresholds for different family sizes are based on ratios between official thresholds for four-person families and the family size in question; for example, the reindexed threshold for five-person families equals $9,757 × ($11,684/9,862). This assumes that the ratio of thresholds for any two family sizes is the same across the four alternatives.

b. The reindexed threshold is obtained by inflating the official 1965 threshold for a family of four by the change in the CPI for poor families.

c. Revised multiplier thresholds are obtained by estimating both income and food expenditures, inclusive of in-kind benefits, recalculating the income-to-food-expenditure ratio, and multiplying that ratio times the 1982 Thrifty Food Plan amount for a family of four.

d. The relative threshold for a family of four is set at 50 percent of the median income for all families.

SOURCE: Department of Commerce, Bureau of the Census, *Characteristics of the Population Below the Poverty Level: 1982*, Current Population Reports, Consumer Income Series P-60, No. 144, and the Congressional Budget Office.

Variation across family types in the effects of changing the poverty definition means that the composition of the population of poor children changes as well, although the differences are not great. Of all poor children under the official definition in 1982, 51 percent lived with their single mothers, while only 42 percent lived with both parents. If poverty had instead been assessed by comparing the budget-share

TABLE 2 Poverty Rates of Children Using Alternative Illustrative Definitions of Income and Poverty Thresholds of Family Type, 1982

Threshold [a] and Income Measure [b]	Children in Family Type [c]						
	All Families	Two-Parent	Single Parent	Single Mother	Single Father	No Parent	Teenage Mother
Official Thresholds							
Cash Only	21.9	12.3	51.1	54.0	21.9	44.9	47.4
Cash Equivalent	20.7	12.3	46.3	48.8	21.1	41.1	43.4
Budget Share	19.8	12.0	43.5	45.8	20.8	39.7	40.6
Reindexed Thresholds							
Cash Only	21.6	12.1	50.8	53.6	21.9	44.4	47.4
Cash Equivalent	20.3	12.0	45.5	47.9	20.8	40.6	43.0
Budget Share	19.4	11.7	42.5	44.7	20.3	39.2	39.5
New Multiplier Thresholds							
Cash Only	24.9	14.9	55.3	58.3	24.6	48.3	53.4
Cash Equivalent	25.6	16.3	53.7	56.7	24.5	48.1	54.9
Budget Share	25.2	16.2	52.6	55.5	24.2	47.4	53.0
Relative Thresholds							
Cash Only	26.4	16.3	57.2	60.3	25.9	50.2	57.0
Cash Equivalent	27.7	18.2	56.8	59.7	27.1	50.3	56.7
Budget Share	27.3	18.0	55.7	58.6	27.3	49.8	56.6

a. See Table 1 for definitions of alternative thresholds and their 1982 values.

b. Cash only is pre-tax income from all sources. Cash equivalent is total cash income plus the recipient cash equivalent value of food stamps, school lunches, housing assistance, and medical care received in kind, less federal and state income and payroll taxes. Budget share is the same as cash equivalent except that in-kind benefits are measured at their budget-share value.

c. Children include all unmarried people under 18 years of age, except those under 15 years of age who live alone. This definition excludes about 110,000 married people under age 18 and about 200,000 people under age 15 who are living alone.

SOURCE: Congressional Budget Office tabulations of March 1983 Current Population Survey, including Bureau of the Census imputations of the value of the in-kind income and of taxes.

measure of income with the new multiplier thresholds, poor children in two-parent families would have outnumbered those in families headed by single women 48 percent to 45 percent. While these effects may be small—under either measure, each group comprises nearly half of all poor children—they may influence perceptions about which types of families most need assistance.

TABLE 3   Poverty Gaps for All Families with Children, under Alternative Illustrative Definitions of Income and Poverty Thresholds, 1982 (all values in billions of dollars)

Income Measure [a]	Poverty Thresholds [b]			
	Reindexed	Official	New Multiplier	Relative
Cash Only	25.3	26.0	34.0	38.2
Cash Equivalent	17.9	18.5	26.5	30.9
Budget Share	16.9	17.5	25.3	29.6

NOTE: Children include all unmarried people under 18 years of age, except those under 15 years of age who live alone. This definition excludes about 110,000 married people under age 18 and about 200,000 people under age 15 who are living alone.

a. Cash only is pre-tax income from all sources. Cash equivalent is total cash income plus the recipient cash equivalent value of food stamps, school lunches, housing assistance, and medical care received in kind, less federal and state income and payroll taxes. Budget share is the same as cash equivalent except that in-kind benefits are measured at their budget-share value.

b. See Table 1 for definitions of alternative thresholds and their 1982 values.

SOURCE: Congressional Budget Office tabulations of March 1983 Current Population Survey, including Bureau of the Census imputations of the value of the in-kind income and of taxes.

Poverty Gaps for Poor Families with Children

Using broader income measures would yield poverty gaps markedly lower than under the current poverty definition, regardless of which thresholds are used (see Table 3). Because large amounts of in-kind transfers go to poor families with children, their inclusion as income would close as much as one-third of the official poverty gap for those families. Using budget-share values would have somewhat larger effects than using cash-equivalent values, since the former are greater on average. As noted above, poverty gaps provide a more complete assessment of the status of the poor, since they reflect not only the number of poor people but also their degree of poverty.[24]

---

[24]By definition, higher thresholds result in much larger poverty gaps, but that adds little information about the degree of poverty. Most of the increase stems from the additional resources needed to reach the higher thresholds by families that are poor under both sets of thresholds· relatively little increase results from more families being labeled as poor.

Distribution of Poor Children
Around Poverty Thresholds

One can obtain a more complicated but also more complete picture of the well-being of children by examining the distribution of children around the poverty thresholds (see Table 2). By the official poverty measure, nearly three-fourths of poor children (or 16 percent of all children) are in families that have incomes below 75 percent of poverty. An additional 6 percent of all children are not poor, but have incomes within 25 percent of poverty. The broader income definitions change this picture somewhat. If either cash-equivalent or budget-share measures of income are used, only about half of poor children are in families with incomes below 75 percent of the thresholds. The families of nearly one-tenth of all children have incomes within 25 percent above poverty. These numbers are little different if alternative thresholds are used.

These distributions indicate two things. First, many of the poor are well below the poverty level, regardless of how income is measured, and a significant fraction of those that are not poor are only just above the poverty line. Second, in-kind transfers and taxes have a marked leveling effect on incomes: the combination pulls both those people below and those above poverty toward the thresholds.

Article 13

ISSUES IN ADDRESSING POVERTY AMONG CHILDREN

Congressional Budget Office

Government by its very nature affects the well-being of all citizens and influences how many of them are poor. Through monetary and fiscal policies and regulations, government affects the condition of the economy, and thus, among other things, how readily workers can find jobs and the stability of the value of the money they earn. Also, the taxes collected by government determine how much income is available to people to meet consumption needs. In addition, governments at all levels administer a wide variety of programs intended to aid people—both individuals and families with children—who remain in or near poverty even during periods of economic expansion and low inflation.

This chapter briefly describes the issues that arise in determining the scope of direct government efforts to aid low-income families with children, and in designing specific policies. It then examines the current federal role. This chapter concludes with an overview of options for altering current policies. . . .

THE OBJECTIVES OF GOVERNMENT POLICY AND ISSUES IN DESIGNING AID

Government policies that deal specifically with childhood poverty are intended to address several broad objectives: to ensure that some minimum level of resources is available to meet the basic needs of children for food, shelter, health care, and other necessities; to protect children from some of the adverse effects that poverty may have, including impairments to their physical and mental development; and to help poor families achieve economic independence. Underlying these policies are concerns to avoid creating incentives for families to break up; to maintain work incentives for those who are able to work; and to provide aid as efficiently as possible. Most people would also argue that government efforts should endeavor to treat similar people similarly, consistent with other policy goals.

SOURCE: *Reducing Poverty Among Children*, Washington, DC: The Congress of the United States Congressional Budget Office, May, 1985.

While considerable consensus exists concerning policy objectives, there is much less agreement regarding the scope or design of specific policies. Four broad issues arise in designing antipoverty efforts:

- What should be the scope of government's responsibility?
- Who should be helped?
- What form should assistance take?
- How should direct aid be delivered?

What Should Be Government's Responsibility?

Society's judgment concerning the appropriate division of responsibilities between the public and private sectors has shifted over time. In the United States until this century, private charity provided a large fraction of aid for poor people; the assistance that came from the public sector was financed almost exclusively by states and localities. During the Depression, however, the scope of poverty increased greatly, and the capacity of the private sector and of subnational governments to address basic needs of the poor diminished; as a result, the role of the federal government was broadened. In addition to the enactment of new programs, the federal government's role as a regulator of economic activity was considerably expanded. For example, the Fair Labor Standards Act of 1938 established a federal minimum wage for many jobs.

With the shift in the economy brought about by World War II, some of the direct federal aid—particularly that which was funneled through states and localities to finance public-sector employment—was phased out. Federal aid expanded again during the 1960s and 1970s, and its scope was broadened significantly. Over the past few years, growth in most assistance programs has been slowed and, in some cases, reversed, but the basic policies remain largely the same.

The effect of federal tax policy on the poor has also varied over time. Prior to World War II, approximately 90 percent of the population was below tax entry levels in the federal income tax. Even in the late 1940s and the early 1950s, tax entry levels were much higher, relative to median family income, than they are now. By 1964, the erosion of the value of the personal exemption led the Congress to enact a minimum standard deduction designed to exempt the very low-income population from the income tax. Enactment of the Earned Income Tax Credit (EITC) in 1975 to benefit families with children, and creation of the zero bracket amount in 1977, further raised tax entry levels for families with children. In fact, 1975–1979 was the only period during the last 25 years in which tax entry levels significantly exceeded the poverty thresholds. Since that time, a growing proportion of poor families have paid income taxes. Moreover, the Social Security payroll tax rate has risen from 3 percent in 1960 to just over 7 percent in 1985. In 1984, about one-third of all poor families paid some federal tax.

Debate continues as to the appropriate role of government. Some argue that only government can mobilize the resources necessary to help the poor, and that more assistance is needed in light of the recent rise in the number of poor children. Others contend that while some direct government involvement is necessary to ensure that people who cannot support themselves can achieve some minimum level of subsistence, in practice the government has gone well beyond what was needed and has created a welfare class that is dependent on public aid. They argue that only by sharply curtailing government's role can incentives be created for the poor to take the initiative to move themselves out of poverty. Some critics also contend that certain government efforts to raise the incomes of disadvantaged groups—such as establishing minimum wage rates—have actually made them worse off, and that relaxing or eliminating these laws and regulations will expand their job opportunities.

Disagreement also exists as to the level of government—federal, state, or local—that should provide whatever aid is made available. Some people argue that state and local agencies can better identify the families who are in need of help and the form that assistance should take. Others—citing differences in the willingness and fiscal capacity of different states and localities to aid low-income people—contend that the responsibility for helping meet the minimum needs of those who are least well-off should rest with the federal government. They note that only the federal government is in a position to assure that similar families in different locations are treated similarly.[1]

In the area of tax policy, there is less apparent controversy. Though disagreement about particular means may exist—for example, raising the zero bracket amount or increasing the personal exemption—it is widely held that people with incomes below the poverty lines should not have to pay any income tax.

Who Should Be Helped?

One of the central issues in designing specific policies intended to reduce childhood poverty or alleviate its effects is who should be helped.

---

[1]Further, if assistance is locally determined and funded, differences in aid—and in taxes to finance it—might draw some poor people to areas providing higher benefits, and some taxpayers to areas with lower taxes. Only the federal government can ensure that incentives for migration resulting from benefit and tax differentials are avoided.

Defining the Minimum.   From one perspective, deciding who should receive cash or in-kind assistance to help meet basic consumption needs involves defining the minimum amount of resources that the government should assure is available to support a child. Put another way, at what level of resources should government's responsibility cease? Setting the minimum at a relatively high level provides aid to a greater number of children at a higher cost. It may also extend aid to families in which parents or guardians could support their children without help and may create incentives for people to depend on public aid instead of their own efforts. Setting highly restrictive eligibility requirements—and less generous minimum benefits—decreases government costs and increases incentives for people to become self-reliant, but it also risks leaving some children living below an acceptable standard. It is much more difficult to quantify needs for many services, and, thus, to determine the minimum amount of aid and who should receive it.

Related to this choice is the question of whether eligibility criteria and minimum benefits should differ geographically. National standards treat all recipients alike, but they fail to take into account differences among areas such as in the cost of living, or in the preferences of their citizens for aiding the poor.

Defining the Household.   Another question is whether the type of household in which children live should affect eligibility for assistance. For example, aid can be provided to low-income families with children regardless of the composition of the household; or assistance can be denied to households in which there are two parents, one of whom is physically able to work and is free of child care responsibilities. The former approach assures that some assistance is available to all children living below the minimum established for the particular program, but it increases costs to the government and may reduce incentives that parents have to seek or accept employment. In contrast, denying aid to intact two-parent families reduces government costs and increases the parents' work incentives. It also creates incentives for families to break up, however, and creates hardships for some children—either because of decisions made by their parents or guardians not to work, because the employed adults are unable to earn enough to raise their families to the minimum standard, or because the adults cannot find jobs.

A related question is whether parents or guardians should be required to do some work in exchange for the aid they receive, or if they should be required to participate in training programs to enhance their long-term employment prospects. A work requirement may reduce the net cost of aid, depending on the value of the work done and the expense of administering the work requirement. Such a requirement may also increase the chances that those employed will become self-sufficient in the future. Job-training requirements can have an even greater long-term impact—depending on the effectiveness of the training—but they add to government costs, at least in the short run. Moreover, either approach may require the government to provide or finance child care, since the adults have to be away from their children for some part of the day. Also, if the parents refuse to participate, their children lose government help.

Defining Coverage.   Still another question is whether aid should be available on an entitlement basis for all individuals who qualify and seek assistance, or if benefits should be provided to only some of those who could qualify. Entitlement programs treat all eligible people alike, but their costs are harder to control, requiring amendments to authorizing statutes. Appropriated programs are easier to control on an annual basis, but they generally result in some potential beneficiaries receiving less help than others, or none at all.

Finally, there is the question of whether people not currently in need should be helped so that they will not become needy in the future. In essence, the choice is when to assist the poor—earlier with preventive efforts, or later with ameliorative ones. Preventive policies may avoid deprivation for children and may reduce federal costs in the long run, but only to the extent that those who are at risk can be identified and effectively served.

What Form Should Assistance Take?

Another issue in designing antipoverty policies concerns the form that assistance from the government should take.

The Type of Aid.   On one level, this concerns whether aid should be provided in the form of cash or in-kind transfers that meet current needs; services to help the poor deal with some of the consequences of poverty; or human capital development programs, designed to enhance skill and or other labor market policies that could increase self-sufficiency.[2]

Direct transfers help families meet immediate needs but do not deal with the underlying causes of poverty. Such aid may also reduce

---

[2]Human capital consists of the knowledge, skills, abilities, and experience that a person can use in employment or any other task. It includes basic skills such as reading and writing, as well as specialized skills applicable only to specific jobs. It also encompasses developed traits, such as punctuality and reliability, that contribute to success in labor markets.

people's incentives to support themselves. A secondary issue is whether the government should provide cash or in-kind assistance. The former approach allows recipients to determine what use they make of their additional resources and may be more efficient, since it does not involve the government in deciding how much and what form any good or service should take. On the other hand, providing cash grants to low-income parents and guardians on behalf of their children carries no assurance that the aid will be used to meet particular needs of the children.

Services such as child welfare aid and educational assistance are special forms of in-kind assistance designed to prevent or reduce some of the potential adverse effects of poverty on children. Human capital development programs aimed at parents are designed to attack the causes of poverty by helping families earn more adequate incomes. Neither of these forms of aid offers help in meeting ongoing consumption needs. They may, however, be of great benefit to families who need more than short-term income supplements to overcome the causes or effects of their poverty.

Meeting Needs of Different Types of Families. A related question is what forms of assistance are best suited to particular types of poor families with children. The answer depends, in part, on the circumstances facing those families. Table 1 classifies poor children by the duration of their spells of poverty and whether adult members of their families are generally employed.

Nearly 60 percent of poor children live in families that have members who normally work at jobs that keep them above the poverty line,

TABLE 1 Distribution of Poor Children by Duration of Poverty and Family Labor Force Attachment (In percent of all children ever poor)

| Labor Force Attachment | Duration of Poverty | |
	Short Term[a]	Long Term[b]
Working[c]	59	14
Nonworking[d]	14	14

a. Poor fewer than four years in a five-year period.
b. Poor for four or five years in a five-year period.
c. Head of family (and spouse, if any) worked at least 500 hours in at least three out of five years.
d. Head of family (and spouse, if any) worked fewer than 500 hours in at least three out of five years.

SOURCE: University of Michigan, Survey Research Center analysis of Panel Study of Income Dynamics Data for 1968 through 1982.

but who are not currently employed for enough hours or at high enough wages to escape poverty. In general, incomes of these families—the short-term, working poor—will rise above the poverty thresholds in a relatively short time without intervention. Short-term income supplements can help bridge their periods of poverty, while employment assistance programs and national economic policies that create job opportunities can shorten the length of time that they are poor.

About one in seven poor children lives in a family that is in economic transition—the nonworking, short-term poor. These families are likely either to be headed by single parents—especially single mothers—or to be young families just entering their working years. In some of these families, adult members may be able to obtain work fairly easily. In other instances, parents may lack necessary skills or experience. Altering labor market regulations to expand employment opportunities, or increasing training and employment assistance, can help such people find jobs more easily. Income supplements provide them with resources to meet their short-term needs.

Another one in seven poor children is in a family where there is a working adult, but where spells of poverty are lengthy, presumably because earners lack skills or are able to find only intermittent or part-time work. This group is also likely to include families whose size contributes to their poverty. These families may also benefit from training programs to develop labor market skills, in combination with employment assistance to help them find better jobs. At the same time, transfer programs can increase their current resources, while social services can help ameliorate the consequences of their long-term poverty.

The remaining one in seven poor children—and the most difficult group to deal with—lives in a family that has no attachment to the labor market and therefore no likelihood of becoming self-sufficient. These nonworking, long-term poor families include: single-parent families, especially those headed by women, in which child care responsibilities make regular employment difficult; families whose normal earners are disabled to the extent that they cannot work; and families whose adult members have such inadequate skills or labor force attachments that they cannot or will not find and hold jobs. Because they provide essentially no support for themselves through earnings, and because they are poor for extended periods, these families impose the greatest demands on social welfare programs and account for a disproportionate share of those programs' costs. Intensive employment and training programs, as well as child care services, can aid those who have the potential and willingness to work. Workfare programs can also be appropriate for this group and for welfare recipients who can work but choose not to do so. Finally, transfers and social services help those such as the disabled who cannot work.

How Should Direct Aid Be Delivered?

A final set of questions concerns how direct assistance should be delivered in order to have the greatest impact at the lowest cost. Cash assistance, for example, can be provided either directly or through the administrative apparatus of the income tax system. Providing aid through the federal tax system may, in certain instances, be administratively simpler than through a direct spending program, but it increases the complexity of the tax code and limits aid to those who file returns. Similarly, direct spending programs financed by the federal government can be administered either by the federal government or by states and localities. More important, however, is the degree of flexibility given to local administrators. Greater flexibility enables them to respond to specific circumstances, but reduces federal control and may lead to differential treatment of similar families.

Other administrative questions arise in particular types of programs. For example, in-kind aid can be provided as actual commodities or as vouchers that can be used to buy specified goods. Services can be provided either by government offices or by publicly funded private agencies. Human capital development can be provided through public schools, other government-operated agencies, or the private sector.

THE CURRENT FEDERAL ROLE

The federal government currently plays a wide and diverse role in aiding poor families with children. Direct assistance policies provide cash, in-kind benefits, services to relieve the problems faced by poor families with children, and employment and training aid intended to help them support themselves in the long run. In addition, federal statutes and regulations affect the availability of low-wage jobs and the minimum amounts that workers can be paid. Finally, the federal tax system in general, and certain provisions in particular, affect the well-being of low-income families.

A number of cash and in-kind assistance programs—plus a tax credit for some families with low earnings—help low-income families with children meet their basic needs.[3] Coverage is uneven, however,

---

[3]This section considers only programs funded in whole or part by the federal government that are specifically designed to aid the poor. Some serve only children or families with children, while others serve those groups as part of a larger clientele. Other programs not considered here also reduce poverty by providing cash income to various groups. For example, Social Security survivors' benefits paid to spouses and children of deceased workers keep many families out of poverty. Because they are not targeted primarily toward poor families, however, they are not discussed in this section.

Further, the focus of this section is on antipoverty programs that have the greatest

and average benefits vary geographically, sometimes greatly. Food Stamps—a federally financed program that helps families afford a minimally adequate diet—is the only assistance that is available to essentially all families in or near poverty. Aid to Families with Dependent Children (AFDC), which provides cash assistance, and Medicaid, which finances health care services, are shared federal/state responsibilities. Aid under these programs is available to most children living in single-parent families with incomes less than state-established minimums that are generally well below the poverty thresholds. States also determine whether assistance is provided to children living in two-parent families. This core of assistance is supplemented by subsidized housing programs, which reduce shelter costs for some low-income families with children; the Earned Income Tax Credit which reduces the tax liability, or provides cash payments, for low-income families with children and low earnings; and school-based meal programs that subsidize breakfasts and lunches for low-income children whose schools choose to participate.

The federal government also provides funding for a broad range of social services and education programs intended to alleviate some of the adverse consequences of poverty, and for employment and training intended to help the parents of poor children work their way out of poverty. Most of this aid is available through annually appropriated programs that serve only a small share of those who are eligible. Finally, direct spending programs are complemented by provisions of the tax system that subsidize wages for low-income workers and that help reduce families' child care costs.

As the following review indicates, current antipoverty efforts vary greatly in who is helped, what form assistance takes, and how aid is financed and administered.

Cash Transfer Programs

Cash assistance is provided to some poor families through the Aid to Families with Dependent Children (AFDC) program and through a provision of the federal income tax (see Table 2).

The AFDC program is the principal federal device to assure that some minimum amount of resources is available to help meet the daily needs of low-income children. States administer the program,

---

impact on families with children. Some programs, such as Supplemental Security Income (SSI), benefit a small number of children but are primarily targeted toward other groups—in this case, the elderly and the disabled.

TABLE 2 Current Cash Transfer Programs that Assist Poor Families with Children

Program	Aid Provided	Eligible Groups	Number of people Served in 1984 (in millions)[a]	Administered by:	Estimated Fiscal Year 1985 Budgetary Cost (in billions of dollars)
Aid to Families with Dependent Children	Cash grants	Low-income single-parent and some two-parent families with children	10.9	State	8.7 Federal 7.6 State ── 16.4 Total
Earned Income Tax Credit	Refundable tax credit	Taxpaying units with children and low earnings	5.6[b]	Federal	1.9 Federal [c]

a. Average monthly participation for AFDC; number of tax returns claiming the EITC.
b. Estimate for calendar year 1986.
c. Estimate for fiscal year 1986.

SOURCES: Congressional Budget Office and various federal sources.

operating within federal guidelines, and they are free to establish their own income eligibility requirements and benefit levels. Costs are shared between the federal and state governments. Outlays for AFDC are expected to total $16.4 billion in fiscal year 1985, with slightly more than half contributed by the federal government.[4]

AFDC eligibility criteria and benefit levels vary greatly among states. They reflect differing judgments concerning who should be served and the appropriate scope of aid, and result in widely differing treatment for similar families living in different places. In January 1985, gross income limits for a single parent with two children ranged from $346 per month in South Carolina to $1,576 in Vermont (the median was $779). As of the same date, the maximum benefit for a single-parent, two-child family with no income was as low as $96 per month in Mississippi and as high as $719 in Alaska (the median was $327).

States also differ in their treatment of children of married couples. While children of single parents—and of married couples when one spouse is incapacitated—are eligible in all states, only about half the states allow any children in married-couple families to receive benefits through the unemployed parents program, AFDC-UP.[5] These differences reflect in part differing judgments concerning the tradeoff between maintaining work incentives and encouraging families to remain together.[6] Finally, there are differences among states in whether adult recipients are required to perform some work in exchange for their benefits.

Assistance is also provided to working poor families through the Earned Income Tax Credit. The EITC may be viewed both as a wage supplement for the working poor with children, and as an offset for Social Security contributions. It reduces tax bills for those who would otherwise owe taxes; it is paid in cash to families with no tax liability who file the necessary forms. For families with very low earnings, this may provide an incentive to work.[7]

---

[4]The federal share of benefit costs can vary from 50 percent to a maximum of 83 percent, depending on per capita incomes in each state. On average, the federal government pays 55 percent of benefit costs.

[5]The 24 states that offer AFDC-UP generally pay higher benefits and have larger caseloads. About two-thirds of all AFDC families live in those states. States may also provide general assistance to poor families that are categorically ineligible for AFDC.

[6]There are some work incentives within AFDC-UP, since it requires at least one parent to be registered in an employment program. If the primary earner works more than 99 hours per month, however, the family is ineligible for benefits.

[7]For families with earnings between $6,500 and $11,000, the EITC is a work disincentive, however, since it raises their income and their marginal tax rate, both of which reduce the value of additional work hours.

In-Kind Transfer Programs

In addition to providing cash, the federal government provides aid to poor families with children through in-kind transfer for food, medical care, and housing (see Table 3).

In fiscal year 1985, an average of about 20 million people—over 80 percent of whom are in households with children— will be assisted each month through the Food Stamp program at a total cost of just over $12 billion. This program, benefit costs of which are funded entirely by the federal government, provides vouchers that can be used to buy food products.[8] Nearly all people in families with gross cash incomes below 130 percent of the poverty guidelines, "countable" incomes below 100 percent of the guidelines, and countable assets below $1,500 are eligible.[9] This is the only universally available entitlement among government transfer programs. School breakfast and lunch programs also provide free and reduced-price meals to poor children attending the over 80 percent of schools that offer at least one of the two programs. Federal outlays for these programs are expected to total about $3 billion in fiscal year 1985.

Funded by both states and the federal government, Medicaid finances medical care for all AFDC recipients, almost all families receiving Supplemental Security Income, and other people whom states may designate as "medically needy." Within federal guidelines, Medicaid programs are designed and run by state agencies, with eligibility rules and benefit levels varying widely across states. Over 20 million people currently receive Medicaid benefits, which will cost states and the federal government more than $40 billion in fiscal year 1985.

The bulk of housing aid is provided through rental assistance programs that currently pay a share of the rent for about 4 million low-income households living either in publicly or privately owned dwellings. This aid is primarily targeted toward elderly or handicapped individuals and families and to nonelderly families with children; as of 1983, about 41 percent of rental assistance went to the latter group, which made up nearly 45 percent of the eligible population. Eligibility and benefit levels are set by the federal government but vary across

---

[8]Administrative costs are paid essentially equally by states and the federal government. For some specific expenses, such as computerizing case management and combating fraud and abuse, the federal share is greater than half.

[9]Countable income is gross income less a standard deduction and deductions for work expenses, child care, excess housing costs, and medical care for the elderly. Households with an elderly member need not satisfy the gross income test and may have as much as $3,000 in assets.

TABLE 3 Current In-Kind Transfer Programs that Assist Poor Families with Children

Program	Aid Provided	Eligible Groups	Number of People Served in 1984 (in millions)	Administered by:	Estimted Fiscal 1985 Budgetary Cost (In billions of dollars)
Food Stamps	Food vouchers	Most low-income families and individuals	20.9[a]	Federal	11.5 Federal[a] 0.8 State ___ 12.3 Total[a]
School Lunch, Breakfast	Free and reduced-price meals	Students with family incomes below 185% of poverty level	11.6[b]	State	3.1 Federal
Medicaid	Free or low-cost medical care	All AFDC and most SSI recipients; all children under 5 in families meeting AFDC income and resource requirements (after phase-in); some medically needy	21.5	State	22.6 Federal 17.1 State ___ 39.7 Total

| Housing Assistance | Subsidized housing units | Families and elderly and handicapped individuals with low incomes | 9.3 | Local | 11.0 Federal[c] |
| Low-income Energy Assistance | Assistance in meeting home energy costs | Most low-income families and individuals | N.A. | State | 2.1 Federal |

NOTE: N.A. = Not available.

a. Excludes food aid to Puerto Rico.
b. Average daily participation in free and reduced-price lunch programs in October 1984. A total of 3.1 million children received free or reduced-price breakfasts, some of whom also receive free or reduced-price lunches.
c. Excludes outlays of $14 billion to redeem outstanding Public Housing Authority notes used to finance capital costs. Also excludes forgone local property taxes.

SOURCES: Congressional Budget Office and various federal sources.

housing markets, reflecting differences in family incomes and housing costs. Spending for housing assistance is expected to total close to $11 billion in 1985. Unlike the other transfers, housing assistance is not an entitlement; it currently serves just under one-third of all eligible households with children.

Eligibility requirements differ greatly among cash and in-kind transfer programs. Rather than serving a single well-defined group of poor families, each program sets its own eligibility criteria—targeting different types of families, while trying to constrain program costs and maintain appropriate incentives related to work effort and family stability. For example, state-specific income cutoffs for AFDC benefits vary from about one-half the federal poverty thresholds to more than twice the poverty levels.[10] By contrast, food stamps are available to families whose gross incomes are less than 130 percent of the poverty level. Housing assistance is provided almost exclusively to families with incomes at or below half of the local median adjusted for family size—in 1983, the income cutoff for a four-person family ranged from 77 percent to 176 percent of the national poverty threshold.[11]

Ameliorative and Preventive Programs

A wide range of programs offer services both to ameliorate the current adverse effects of poverty and to prevent future poverty among children (see Table 4). These programs differ from the previously discussed antipoverty programs in a number of ways. First, many of them address specific problems that face some families with children—problems that may or may not be the result of poverty. Therefore, poverty status alone is frequently insufficient to guarantee eligibility, as families must also demonstrate need for the specific services offered. Second, although federal funding is supplied for all of these programs, in some cases it is only a small part of the total expenditure for a particular service. In general, social services are delivered by local agencies under state direction; they are thus unevenly distributed both within

---

[10]For three-person families, income limits for AFDC are based on need standards that vary among states. Maximum payment levels are well below this, however, ranging from 13 percent to 79 percent of poverty thresholds.

[11]Asset limits also vary across the various programs. AFDC allows $1,000 of assets (excluding a house and up to $1,500 equity in one car), while families are eligible for food stamps as long as their assets are less than $1,500—$3,000 if there is an elderly member—from which the value of a home, some of the value of cars, and the values of specific other assets are excluded. Housing programs, on the other hand, have no explicit asset limit. If net family assets exceed $5,000, however, the greater of actual asset earnings or an imputed return from assets—using the current passbook interest rate—is included as income in determining eligibility.

TABLE 4 Current Programs that Ameliorate the Effects of Poverty on Children

Program	Aid Provided	Eligible Groups	Number of People Served in 1984 (in millions)	Administered by:	Estimted Fiscal 1985 Budgetary Cost (In billions of dollars)
Social Services Block Grant	Child care, child welfare, adoption, foster care, family planning, information and referral services	Determined by state	N.A.	State	2.8 Federal
Child Welfare Title IV-B	Foster care payments, child welfare services	Families in need of child welfare services	N.A.	State	0.2 Federal N.A. State
Title IV-E	Foster care payments	Foster families of children who are eligible for AFDC	0.1[a]	State	0.5 Federal 0.4 State
Child Support Enforcement	Location of absent parents, and assistance in establishing and collecting child support	All families with an absent parent, with priority given to AFDC recipients	8.0[b]	State	0.6 Federal
Title X of Public Health Service Act	Family planning services	All individuals, with priority given to low-income clients	3.7	Federal/local	0.1 Federal

TABLE 4 *(concluded)*

Program	Aid Provided	Eligible Groups	Number of People Served in 1984 (in millions)	Administered by:	Estimted Fiscal 1985 Budgetary Cost (In billions of dollars)
Supplemental Food Program for Women, Infants, and Children (WIC)	Nutritional supplements, health care screening	Nutritionally-at-risk women, infants, and children under age 5, with family incomes below 185% of poverty[c]	3.0[a]	State/local	1.5 Federal
Head Start	Educational, social, nutritional, and medical services	Low-income preschool children	0.4	Federal/local	1.0 Federal
Chapter I—Compensatory Education	Compensatory education	Educationally disadvantaged children	5.9[d]	State/local	3.5 Federal

NOTE: N.A. = Not available.

a. Average monthly participation.
b. Seventy-seven percent AFDC cases, 23 percent non-AFDC families.
c. States are allowed to set income eligibility guidelines between 100 percent and 185 percent of poverty. The majority use 185 percent of poverty as the upper eligibility limit.
d. Because of forward funding, this reflects funding provided in fiscal year 1983.

SOURCES: Congressional Budget Office and various federal sources.

and across states. Finally, most of these programs are not entitlements; limited funding can restrict service levels with the result that some areas lack services entirely.

The largest general social services program is the Social Services Block Grant, which is currently funded at $2.8 billion. Under this program, states are allowed to fund, at their discretion, a wide range of services—including child care, child welfare, foster care, and adoption services. Other child welfare programs include Title IV-B and IV-E of the Social Security Act, which contribute to state funding for child welfare services. Eligibility for these services is based primarily on need for service, although poverty status is also considered in some cases.

The Supplemental Food Program for Women, Infants, and Children (WIC) provides nutritional supplements to approximately 3 million low-income infants, children, and pregnant women who are at nutritional risk, at a 1985 cost of $1.5 billion. Education programs, such as the Head Start program and Chapter I—Compensatory Education— provide low-income children with educational experiences that they may not receive at home. While Head Start has several other aims as well, these programs share the goal of fostering children's mental development in order to improve their future ability to learn and become self-sufficient. Finally, programs related to teenage parenthood work to prevent teenage pregnancy and childbearing (which are closely linked to future poverty) through family planning and family life education. These programs also provide services to teenage parents to help them overcome the disadvantages of being an adolescent parent.

Programs to Promote Employability

The federal government sponsors several programs and provides tax credits that are intended to promote employability, either by expanding opportunities for employment and training or by subsidizing child care costs to enable parents to work or acquire additional education (see Table 5). The federal cost of these activities is expected to total about $6 billion in the current fiscal year—$3.5 billion in outlays for employment and training programs; $0.4 billion in forgone revenues for a tax subsidy to encourage employers to hire disadvantaged workers; and $2.2 billion in forgone revenues for tax subsidies for child care costs to enable parents to work or to attend school.

The largest of the employment and training activities is the state block grant program authorized by Title II-A of the Job Training Partnership Act of 1982 (JTPA). Through this program, the federal government provides funds for training and related services for disadvantaged youth and adults. Other programs authorized by JTPA include a summer jobs program and the Job Corps, each of which is exclusively targeted toward disadvantaged youth. These programs are administered

TABLE 5 Current Programs to Promote Employability for Poor Families with Children

Program	Aid Provided	Eligible Groups	Number of People Served in 1984[a] (in millions)	Administered by:	Estimated Fiscal 1985 Budgetary Cost (In billions of dollars)
Job Training Partnership Act (JTPA) Title II-A	Training and related services	Economically disadvantaged people	1.2[b]	State/local	1.9 Federal
JTPA Summer Youth Employment and Training	Summer jobs	Economically disadvantaged youth	0.8[b]	State/local	0.8 Federal
Job Corps	Training and related services in residential centers	Economically disadvantaged youth	0.1	Federal	0.6 Federal
Work Incentive Program (WIN)	Job search and other assistance to achieve self-support	AFDC recipients	0.2	State/local	0.3 Federal
Targeted Jobs Tax Credit (TJTC)	Tax subsidy for employers hiring eligible workers	Economically disadvantaged youth, welfare recipients, and other designated groups	0.6	Federal	0.4 Federal
Dependent Care Tax Credit	Nonrefundable tax subsidy for child care costs	Users of child care to enable parents to work or go to school	5.0	Federal	2.2 Federal

a. Number of people for JTPA, Jobs Corps, and WIN; number of certifications for TJTC; number of taxpayers claiming the child care tax credit for 1982.
b. 1984 program year (July 1984 to June 1985).

SOURCES: Congressional Budget Office and various federal sources.

by states and localities, which select participants and design training, within federal guidelines. The programs are controlled through annual appropriations and serve only a small proportion of all eligible people.

The Work Incentive (WIN) program—another appropriated program—is targeted exclusively toward AFDC recipients. The workfare components of AFDC and other transfer programs are also intended to increase employment of disadvantaged people. Finally, the Targeted Jobs Tax Credit (TJTC) subsidizes the wages of disadvantaged workers by reducing the tax liability of their employers, thereby improving the workers' employability. Unlike the direct-spending training programs, TJTC is an entitlement.

Employment for poor families with children—and participation in training programs—is facilitated by assistance with child care. Direct subsidies for child care costs are currently provided primarily through the Social Services Block Grant, although data on actual spending by states for this purpose are not available. The dependent care credit in the individual income tax essentially refunds up to 30 percent of a family's child care costs—up to a maximum of $1,440. The credit is limited, however, to the extent of the family's tax liability, since it is not refundable. Businesses are encouraged to provide child care facilities for their employees through the deductibility of the costs of such care and the exclusion of the value of child care from the taxable income of employees.

OVERVIEW OF OPTIONS FOR HELPING CHILDREN IN POVERTY

Options for altering current federal policies to help poor children are as varied as the views regarding the appropriate role of government and the dynamics of poverty. As noted earlier, collective judgments concerning what the direct role of the federal government should be in meeting both immediate and long-run needs of poor children have changed appreciably over time, as reflected in the history of federal involvement. Much disagreement remains concerning the effectiveness of current efforts and the direction that policy changes should take in the future.

The Scope of Possible Changes

Alternatives to current policies include some that would comprehensively restructure the current welfare system—either by altering it or by doing away with large parts of it—and others that would leave the major elements of it intact, but would change either who is helped, how much assistance is provided to those who are eligible, or how aid is delivered. The variety of both comprehensive and incremental options reflects the wide range of views concerning government's responsibility and how it should be pursued.

Some proposals to substantially restructure the current system are premised on concerns regarding its fragmented nature and its uneven treatment of children living in different types of families or in different places. People who share these concerns have periodically proposed making the federal government fully responsible for providing a minimum income floor for all families with children. Such changes could involve federalizing the AFDC program and, perhaps, Medicaid as well. Under some alternatives, other responsibilities that are now partially federal—such as support for elementary and secondary education—would be shifted entirely to states and localities. Comprehensive proposals of this sort would often involve increasing total federal resources devoted to aiding low-income families with children.

Other proposals for comprehensive change start from a very different premise—that the current public assistance system constitutes a substantial disincentive for low-income people to take responsibility for improving their own well-being. Those who hold this view contend that the federal government could best promote the long-term welfare of poor families by providing less direct aid, thereby compelling them to rely more fully on their own initiative. Some would combine this approach with removal of labor-market regulations that, they claim, substantially restrict the availability of low-paid jobs.

Comprehensive reform of the tax system—such as proposals currently being debated in the Congress—could also substantially affect the well-being of low-income families with children. For example, provisions that determine the tax entry level (the lowest income level at which taxes are owed)—including increasing the zero bracket amount or the personal exemption—could substantially change the tax liability of many such families.

While debate continues concerning these and other possible comprehensive changes, discussions in the Congress each year tend to be dominated by specific proposals to modify existing policies. These incremental approaches also vary greatly, however, reflecting the same disagreements regarding the causes and cures of poverty. Some proposals, for example, would either expand eligibility or increase benefits under existing programs in order to increase resources available to low-income families to meet immediate consumption needs. Others are designed to increase the opportunity for low-income people to become self-reliant, by, for example, increasing direct spending for job training, requiring that recipients of public assistance perform some work as a condition of their receiving aid, or altering government policies that may now limit private-sector job opportunities.

Options Examined in this Paper

This paper describes more than 40 specific options that would alter existing federal policies affecting poor children and their families. While most of the options examined here would be considered incremental changes, some would involve fairly substantial modifications. Also, wide-ranging change could be accomplished by combining some of the individual options discussed here. Comprehensive proposals for wholesale shifts are not considered, nor are proposals to alter substantially how the tax system is structured or how it operates.

Two fundamental issues must be faced in deciding what the federal government should do to aid poor children. First, how effective would a particular approach be? This question is often difficult to answer fully. Even when the amount of aid is easily quantified, as in the case of cash benefits for poor families, it is difficult to know how much assistance actually reaches the children and thus what the impact will be on their well-being. In other cases, such as the provision of many social services, it is inherently difficult to assess the effectiveness of alternative policies. This paper presents evidence about the impacts of existing federal efforts and quantifies, where possible, the likely impacts of program changes on beneficiaries.

Even if there is general agreement that a particular approach is effective, however, the large projected federal budget deficits facing this nation generally require difficult tradeoffs. Because most proposals to modify current policies would require additional outlays or would reduce revenues, other demands on the government and limited tax revenues conflict with the desire to aid these children. As the Congress struggles to reduce deficits, choices among these competing factors are particularly difficult. Estimates of the budgetary effects are presented, when feasible, for the options examined here.

Article 14

FEDERAL POLICY CHANGES AND THE FEMINIZATION OF POVERTY

Rosemary C. Sarri

The deteriorating economic conditions of women relative to men is now common knowledge, as the frequent use of the term, "the feminization of poverty," suggests [Pearce and McAdoo 1981]. Since 1980 there has been a dramatic increase, from 30 million to 34 million (13 % to 15%), in the number of persons below the poverty level in the United States, but the increase in the numbers of women and children below the poverty level has greatly exceeded that of men or aged individuals. In 1982 nearly 50% of all poor families were headed by women. One out of five children is now being reared in a family whose income is below the poverty level; for minority children, the statistic is one of two, and for female-headed black households, two out of three children are living in poverty [U.S. Dept. of Commerce, Bureau of the Census 1983]. Even more shocking is the fact that in no state in the United States does any family receiving Aid to Families with Dependent Children (AFDC) receive a cash grant or non-income transfers that bring their total income up to the poverty level. These families are poor regardless of alimony, child support, welfare benefits, or their own earnings, and they remain poor after receiving welfare benefits because of the level at which these are provided [Pearce 1982; Children's Defense Fund 1984].

Although both Nixon and Carter established welfare reform as a major social policy goal during their administrations, it was Reagan who successfully accomplished the most significant welfare reform in recent history. Within his first year in office the "Reagan reforms" were introduced to Congress, passed into law, and implemented in states and localities throughout the United States. In contrast to the highly controversial Nixon and Carter proposals, which extended benefits, guarantees, and resources, the Reagan changes, by reducing cost and caseloads through raising the tax rate on welfare to 100% and by establishing lower and more restrictive gross income limits, effected measurable reductions in expenditures in several major social welfare programs serving the poor—in particular, the working poor and women.

SOURCE: Rosemary Sarri, "Federal Policy Changes and the Feminization of Poverty," *Child Welfare* Vol. 64, No. 3, (1985), pp. 235–247.

The changes that took place under the Omnibus Budget Reconciliation Act (OBRA) have undoubtedly increased and hastened the feminization of poverty, but this movement has been under way for a much longer period of time. It is the acceleration since 1980 that has become a matter of public concern. Between 1960 and 1982 the number of female-headed households rose from 4.2 to 9.5 million (9.3% to 15.4% of all families). Among blacks the growth was even greater—from 21% to 42%; and particularly for blacks, being born and reared in a single-parent, female-headed household is associated with long-term poverty. Bane and Ellwood [1983] noted that the average black child born into a female-headed household will remain poor for 22 years. Moreover, 75% of all black children lived in a family that received some AFDC income between 1969 and 1978. Thus, it seems clear that the poverty of women and children is a profoundly serious problem in the United States and demands an immediate response because of its short- and long-term negative potential for society.

Examined here are the federal policy changes that resulted in the elimination of AFDC, food stamps, and Medicaid benefits for employed recipients whose earnings and work-related expenses were above the state level of need that provided the basis for determination of eligibility for income support. The policy changes effected under the provisions of the Omnibus Budget and Reconciliation Act of 1981 sharply restricted eligibility and benefits for the working poor. These provisions included: (1) establishment of a cap on eligibility for gross income at 150% of the state need standard; (2) elimination of the earned income disregard provision after 4 months; (3) establishment of a cap on child care and other work-related expenses; (4) advance counting of earned income tax credit and income of all minor children; and (5) the requirement that stepparent income be included in determining eligibility and benefits of all minor children.

AFDC Reforms and the Well-Being of Terminated Recipients

The United States has reluctantly extended income supports to its needy citizens—even when those in need are primarily children unable to care for themselves. It has been suggested that the term "Mean Society" is more appropriate than "Great Society." Many income support programs for families are gender-marked, in that they are far more punitive toward women than toward men. They have explicit and implicit requirements controlling the roles and behavior of women recipients. On the one hand, women are to have the primary socialization responsibilities for children; on the other hand, they are expected to fulfill those responsibilities without long-term public income support.

In recent years conservatives have expressed much concern about the likelihood that income support through AFDC would result in increased psychological deficiencies and deviant behavior. Gilder [1981] and Anderson [1978], for example, argue that attitudes will develop in the minds of recipients such that they will not attempt to become self-supporting and will be divorced from the current realities of the world of work; moreover, they will transmit these attitudes to their children, resulting in intergenerational perpetuation of AFDC support. These conservative advocates direct almost no attention to the work effort of these women, or to the consequences for them of being limited by a variety of factors to low-income, sex-segregated occupations [U.S. Commission on Civil Rights 1983].

Along with the larger numbers of all women who are entering the labor force, single mothers also are trying to work. Between 1950 and 1980 the number of women in the labor force grew from 18.4 to 44.6 million, or from 28.8% to 42.6% of the total labor force. In 1980 [U.S. Commission on Civil Rights 1982] single-parent female heads of households worked at least some part of the year, and the sharpest increase occurred among women with children. Mothers with children under age 6 were responsible for 60% of the gain. Most of these women were employed in low-paying and unskilled jobs with few or no benefits. The median weekly earnings for families maintained by women with only one worker was $198 versus $411 for families headed by a single male and $473 for married-couple families.

Despite the compelling data to the contrary and perhaps because of ideologies, policy makers in the Reagan administration accepted the conservative thesis about the dangers of welfare dependency and sought to implement changes whereby working-age, able-bodied, poor women, the "marginally" poor, would be weaned away from AFDC and other income supports. No consideration was given to environmental factors such as economic recessions, double-digit unemployment, sex discrimination in employment—all of which would make it impossible for these women to earn the income needed by their families. Also ignored was the fact that 40% of all AFDC recipients who leave AFDC have incomes below the poverty level in the years following AFDC support [Bane and Ellwood, 1983].

Conceptual Framework

We examined the impact of OBRA policies on working women and sought to determine how these women coped in their efforts to maintain individual and family well-being when confronted with an environmentally induced problem—termination of AFDC benefits: cash income, food stamps, and/or Medicaid insurance, as well as housing, energy, child care, or school lunch allowances in some special circumstances. Our guiding hypothesis was that both objective (e.g., economic need) and subjective factors (e.g., perceived stress) would influence the respondent's coping behavior, but that responses would be mediated by informal (e.g., kin, friends, and neighbors) and formal (e.g., social agencies) social networks and by the availability of resources such as health insurance associated with employment. It was expected that coping behavior might be adaptive or maladaptive in terms of the family's subsequent well-being.

Crisis and stress theories have long recognized that the same objective event may have different functional effects depending upon (1) how it is perceived; (2) the decision-making and problem-solving strategies subsequently undertaken; and (3) the environmental response to those strategies. The perception of an event such as a crisis is further conditioned by both individual sociopsychological factors and by the situational context within which it occurs. Thus, when confronted by changes in AFDC policy that reduced incentives to work, how did women conceive their options? What steps, if any, did they take to overcome the impact of their loss of income so as to restore their family's well-being? How important in a woman's decision making was her need for Medicaid protection? Understanding the factors that went into the decisions of these women will help us clarify those for whom remaining on AFDC is a positive act of coping and those for whom it reflects lack of reality testing and/or motivational problems.

Once initial decisions on work and other possibilities have been made, it is important to detail the various strategies that women employ to master their problems in balancing work, income, and family needs. As Belle, Dill, and their colleagues [1982] observed in their Boston study of AFDC families and stress, the environment of low-income women frequently opposes their efforts to master problematic situations [Dill, 1980; Belle, 1982]. Strategies that would be effective in more hospitable social contexts may fail to produce desired results for certain working AFDC recipients.

Methodology

In 1982, six counties in Michigan with unemployment rates from 9% to 20% were selected. Three had rates of unemployment at the low end and three had rates at the upper end of the range. Variation in unemployment rate was selected as a critical sampling variable because of the wide variation in unemployment in Michigan counties in 1982 (6%–34%). Counties were selected as a critical unit for analysis because the social services programs in Michigan are administered through county government, and some discretion remains at that level in decision making about services and service delivery.

With the cooperation and assistance of the Michigan Department of Social Services, all recipients terminated from AFDC because of the OBRA policies during the period September 1, 1981, and April 1, 1982, were identified. A total of 3,200 women were identified in the six counties and samples were selected randomly by county.

Respondents were contacted by mail to obtain their consent for participation in the study. All of the interviews were completed in their homes. Each interview obtained information on welfare experience and attitudes, health, household composition, income and expenses, employment, education, marital experience and family background, parenting and child care, formal and informal social supports, and coping behavior.

Personal and Social Characteristics

The median age of the respondents was 33 years: 37% were nonwhite and more than 9 in 10 were urban residents. Seventy-six percent had completed high school or its equivalent; 30% had some post-secondary education, and 12% were enrolled in school, including college, business school, and other technical programs at the time of the interview.

Seventy-seven percent identified themselves as single parents, but there were other adults or children not belonging to the respondent residing in more than half of the households. There were 2.1 children in the average household, but only 1.8 children had been included in the formal AFDC unit at the time of termination. Most of the children were stepchildren, nieces, or nephews. Among the other adults, 31% were female, and 80% of the respondents reported that most of these adults made some contribution to the household income. However, that contribution was often small, variable, and sporadic. Few reported that child support was ever received from the children's fathers.

Fifty percent of the respondents had been married once; 25% had been married two or more times; an equal number had never been married. Two-thirds grew up in traditional two-parent households with blood relatives. Although our data do not permit the conclusion that they were reared in low-income families, most of their fathers had working class occupations—90% were employed full-time. Forty-eight percent of their mothers were employed more than 50% of the time while they were growing up and also were employed in working class occupations.

TABLE 1   Personal and Social Characteristics of Working Former AFDC Recipients

(N = 279)	
Median Age	33 years
% Non-white	37%
Education:	
Less than grade 12	19%
High school grad or GED	76%
Some post-secondary	30%
Currently enrolled	12%
Average No. of Children:	
In household	2.1
In AFDC UNIT	1.8
Marital Status:	
Age at first marriage	19 years
% Currently married	15%
% Married 1+ times	18%
% Married once	50%
% Never married	31%
Respondent's Family Background:	
% reared in 2-parent family	76%
% father employed full-time	90%
% mother employed half-time or more	48%
Household Mobility in 1982:	
% moved 1 or more times	23%
% households with persons moving out	23%
% households with persons moving in	29%
% total percent of households with some recomposition	53%

Given the difficulties that were encountered in attempting to locate and contact these respondents, it was not surprising to learn that they reported high levels of mobility. Twenty-three percent had moved one or more times in 1982. Twenty-nine percent of the households had one or more persons move in with them and 23% had someone move out. Overall, 53% experienced at least one major household change during 1982. Many respondents moved in with parents, their own siblings, and friends as a way of stretching meager resources.

Intrafamilial conflict was overwhelmingly the major factor that led to marital disruption, separation, and/or divorce. No one stated that the availability of welfare was a factor in their decision. The conflict appeared to have been serious and long-standing, for 45% reported that their spouses had been repeatedly violent toward them or their children or both; 55% reported that there was serious general conflict in the family. Several respondents reported still being in fear of being battered, but few had access to or had ever received any services from a domestic violence program.

Bane and Ellwood [1983] reported that the single largest cause of movement into poverty was the decline in the household head's income—overall 37%, but 60% for male heads and 14% for female heads, indicating that for female-headed households it is not a strong predictor of poverty. Instead, the poverty "spells" begin when a woman becomes a female household head, especially if she has young children, and periods of poverty last far longer for her. In this Michigan survey, 74% reported that they applied for AFDC when their marriage or partnership broke up, and these results are clearly similar to those of Bane and Ellwood. The findings apply to children also, because 70% of the AFDC caseloads are composed of children.

Welfare Use and Experience

Some researchers and policy makers argued that AFDC earner families would not attempt to return to the rolls once they were terminated [Anderson 1978; Stockman 1983; and Nathan et al. 1982], although others argued just the opposite. The former asserted that women would obtain adequate income through full-time employment and seemed unaware that many of the women would encounter any problems in meeting the cost of child care or health insurance because they were employed in uncovered industries. The cited writers also failed to note that many AFDC recipients eligible for termination were already employed full-time, but could not earn sufficient income given the types of jobs and compensation typically available to low-income working women.

The overall return rate for women to AFDC, Medicaid, and/or food stamps in the Michigan sample was 55.9% over an 18-month interval, as the results in Table 2 indicate. County differences were pronounced, with higher rates in the counties with high unemployment. One anomaly occurred in one county that had a relatively low unemployment rate but a high rate of AFDC return (26%). In that county a number of "workfare" programs supported with federal grants were implemented, and eligibility restrictions were apparently less rigidly enforced.

Higher numbers of women received food stamps (43%) and Medicaid (31.9%) after having been terminated. The terminations were implemented beginning October 1, 1981, and by December 1981, 70% of

TABLE 2   Support after Termination[a]

	(N = 279)			
	AFDC %	Medicaid Only %	Food Stamps Only %	One or More Programs %
Received assistance for at least one month between termination and interview	24.0	31.9	43.0	55.9
% on Medicaid or food stamps at interview	0	21.9	12.0	27.7
% returned to AFDC after termination and following reapplication	24.0	10.0	33.0	39.8

[a]This sample includes only those cases fully meeting all OBRA criteria, but excluding those terminated because of the stepfather rule since their situations varied substantially from this sample.

this sample had been terminated—primarily because of having too-high income rather than other criteria applicable in OBRA. Among the 24% who reapplied and were successful in their reapplication, their average monthly benefit at the time of the interview was $111 higher than it had been when they were terminated. State benefits were not increased, but these women who returned were not working and therefore became eligible for the larger amount. Thus, the state experienced greater cost when the women had to return to AFDC.

Fewer than 10% of the respondents understood the details of the policy decision, knew how much income they would have, or how much property they could have before they would be terminated. Only 7% ever appealed a decision of the Department of Social Services, but among those who did, 61% were successful. Only one-third reported that they were informed that they might continue to be eligible for food stamps after termination.

Forty-four percent reapplied for welfare after being terminated, and an additional 37% said that they wanted or needed to reapply, for an overall total of 73%. More than half visited the local social services office an average of three times to inquire about or reapply for benefits. Among the 41% who did not reapply, 69% said they did not do so because they thought they were ineligible. Need for health insurance was the most frequently stated need (39%), and that was not surprising, because 37% did not have health insurance coverage for their children.

Ten percent of the sample were terminated because of the application of the "stepfather" rule. Among that group, many initially had far higher household incomes than those headed by females, but several returned to AFDC when their husbands deserted them as a result of the increased unwanted burden. Among the remainder, they were usually terminated more rapidly and received fewer benefits of all types, regardless of their income level. Many of these families then ended up receiving far higher AFDC benefits than they had received prior to termination when the stepfather lived with the family. Undoubtedly, the social costs of another family disruption were equally great or greater for these women and children.

Constraints on Well-Being

Crises.   Having to cope with crises such as having no money or food, a serious illness, death, family violence, and problems of their children were almost routine for these families, as Table 3 indicates. Nearly 9 out of 10 ran out of money at least once, and 62% reported that they were without money 7 or more times. Forty-eight percent were without food at least once, and a quarter ran out of food more than 7 times. Several interviewers visited households in which there

TABLE 3   Crisis Following Termination[a]

(N = 279)	
	%
1. Ran out of money	89
2. Ran out of food	48
3. Became seriously ill	38
4. Borrowed over $300	36
5. Had someone important die	33
6. Had problems with partner	34
7. Had furnace or major appliance break	31
8. Had something bad happen to a child	28
9. Been a victim of crime	11
10. Been to court or was arrested	12
11. Had gas turned off	9
12. Had electricity turned off	6
13. Had something repossessed	4
14. Had some other crises	24

[a]"Since January 1982 how many times, if at all, have you . . ." Data reported are for response of one or more times.

was no food available and where respondents were extremely anxious because of their children. Many reported that they always ran out of food at the end of the month when wages were gone and emergency food was unavailable.

Respondents said that the following problems were the *most* serious experienced in 1982: lack of money (28%); lack of food (10%); having something bad happen to their children (14%); having someone close die (9%); and own illness (7%). Women with lower incomes experienced somewhat more crises, particularly those involving crime and lack of money, but the relationship was not strong—probably because the income range was limited relative to overall need and because nearly all experienced several serious crises during the year. Several reported suicides within the family, serious fires, rape, and other crises.

Living below the poverty level as a single female head of household is likely to result in frequent experience with serious crises, but we do not have information about the frequency of crises being experienced by other families in Michigan at this time, other than the report of a Detroit survey that indicated considerable suffering among all families experiencing unemployment, but far below the extent of suffering among these women. In a recent survey in the Detroit metropolitan area, Kelly and Sheldon [1983] observed that 27% to 33% of all families surveyed reported problems in obtaining sufficient food and clothing; 26% to 35% had specific illnesses; and over half reported serious money management problems.

Because the respondents in the Michigan study were employed mothers, child care was a serious problem, particularly after they were terminated from AFDC, because they not only lost child care allowances, they found that public child care programs were terminated in 1981 and 1982 because of cutbacks in Title XX and Title IV-A [U.S. Dept. of Commerce 1983 a]. Half of the respondents had children under 12 and 87% of these women reported that they needed child care in order to work. The child care providers that they were able to obtain included relatives, 53%; private sitter, 28%; older sibling, 9%. Non-white mothers were more likely to use relatives, and white mothers often used private sitters and older children, sometimes keeping them out of school for that purpose.

Women with older children appear to have encountered problems at least as serious as those with young children. More than one-third were called to school for special conferences, and 22% reported that children were suspended at least once. A small number had been expelled, were referred to juvenile court, were sent to special schools, were committed to institutions, or had been victimized by a crime. The numbers, although small, were disproportionately greater than would be expected in a random sample of families with children of these ages [Danziger 1982].

Social Support Networks in Crises

Families who had relatives nearby to assist them reported that they relied heavily on parents, grandparents, and siblings for all types of support: housing, money, food, child care, and transportation, as well as counsel and sympathy. Women with older children and with larger families relied on their own family for all types of assistance.

The findings in Table 4 reveal essentially the same pattern of social support for the time at which the respondent was terminated and for the time at which she experienced the most serious crises during 1982. Only in the case of health care personnel was there a substantial increase; given the amount of illness that these families experienced during 1982, such a change could be expected. Overall, few received any help from formal help-giving organizations such as social agencies, except for emergency food and occasional emergency housing. These findings corroborate those of Van Houten et al. [1982]. They observed that 45% of the recipients of public social services are households headed by single women, of whom 62% are AFDC recipients. Problems observed were similar to those noted in this study (e.g., child care and protection, financial need, employment).

TABLE 4   Social Support Network in Crisis[a]

	When cut from AFDC %	Most serious problem in 1982[b] %
	(N = 279)	
Parents, sibs, or other relatives	73	70
Friends	61	52
Own children	46	48
Boyfriend or partner	36	42
Physician, nurse, or clinic	10	20
Social worker or counselor	12	13
Police	0	9
Lawyer	6	7
Minister	8	8

[a]"I'm going to read you a list of people and places. For each tell me whether or not you contacted them about ___ problem when you were terminated."
[b]Most serious problem in 1982.

Conclusion

The findings from this research provide ample evidence that federal policy changes have had a profound impact and that they are increasing poverty in the United States through alterations in the social structure that they have brought about [Smeeding 1983; Danziger 1983; Stallard et al. 1983; Pearce 1982]. Poverty is a painful reality for millions of American women and children—just as it is for millions throughout the world. Short-term "Band-Aid" solutions are not sufficient to reverse this condition. What is required is a thoroughgoing analysis of the basic elements of the social structure, policies, ideologies, and traditions that led to the development of the modern welfare state. That knowledge will enable us to design effective solutions, but it must be supported by strong advocacy on the part of the entire social welfare community and especially those interested in the status of women and the well-being of children.

REFERENCES

Anderson, M. Welfare. Stanford, CA: Hoover Institute Press, 1978.

Bane, M. J., and Ellwood, D. Slipping Into and Out of Poverty: The Dynamics of Spells. Cambridge, MA: Urban Systems Research and Engineering, 1983.

Belle, D., ed. Lives in Stress. Beverly Hills, CA: Sage, 1982.

Children's Defense Fund. A Children's Defense Budget: An Analysis of the 1984 Budget. Washington, DC: Children's Defense Fund, 1984.

Danziger, S. K. "Postprogram Changes in the Lives of AFDC Support Work Participants: A Quantitative Assessment." Journal of Human Resources, 16, 4 (1983): 637–48.

———. "Children in Poverty: The Truly Needy Who Fall Through the Safety Net." Children and Youth Services Review 4, 1/2 (1982).

Dill, Diane; Feld, E.; Martin, J.; Burkeman, S.; and Belle, D. "The Impact of the Environment on the Coping Efforts of Low-Income Mothers." Family Relations 29 (October 1980); 503–509.

Gilder, George. Wealth and Poverty. New York, NY: Basic Books, 1981.

Kelly, Robert, and Sheldon, Eleanor. The Effects of Unemployment on People's Lives in Detroit. Detroit, MI: Wayne State University, Dept. of Sociology, 1983.

Nathan, R.; Dearborn, P. M.; Goldman, C. A., et al. "Initial Effects of the Fiscal Year 1982 Reductions in Federal Domestic Spending," in Reductions in U.S. Domestic Spending, edited by J. Ellwood. New Brunswick, NJ: Transaction Books, 1982.

Pearce, D. The Poverty of Our Future: The Impact of Reagan Budget Cuts on Women, Minorities and Children. Washington, DC: Center for National Policy Review, 1982.

Pearce, D., and McAdoo, H. Women and Children: Alone and in Poverty. Washington, DC: National Advisory Council on Economic Opportunity, September 1981.

Smeeding, T. "Recent Increase in Poverty in the U.S.: What the Official Estimates Fail to Show." Testimony before the House Ways and Means Subcommittee on Oversight, Public Assistance and Unemployment Compensation. Washington, DC, October 18, 1983.

Stallard, K.; Ehrenreich, B; and Sklar, H. Poverty in the American Dream: Women and Children First. Boston, MA: South End Press, Institute for New Communications, 1983.

Stockman, D. A. "Poverty in America." Statement before the House Ways and Means Subcommittee on Oversight, Public Assistance and Unemployment, U.S. Congress, Washington, DC, Executive Office, OMB, November 3, 1983.

U.S. Commission on Civil Rights. Unemployment and Underemployment Among Blacks, Hispanics, and Women. Washington, DC: U.S. Commerce Clearinghouse Publication No. 73, November 1982.

———. A Growing Crisis: Disadvantaged Women and Their Children. Washington, DC: U.S. Commission on Civil Rights Clearinghouse Publication No. 78, May 1983.

U.S. Department of Commerce, Bureau of the Census. Child Care Arrangements of Working Mothers: June, 1982. Washington, DC: Bureau of Census Current Population Reports P-23, No. 129, 1983 a.

———. Bureau of the Census. Money Income and Poverty Status of Families and Persons in the United States. Current Population Reports P-60, No. 140. Washington, DC: U.S. Government Printing Office, July 1983 b.

Van Houten, T.; Schroeder, A.; and King, L. S. "Single Female-Headed Families and Public Social Services—Questions for the '80s." Children and Youth Services Review 4, 12 (1982): 209–221.

Article 15

THE "GRAYING" OF THE FEDERAL BUDGET AND ITS CONSEQUENCES FOR OLD-AGE POLICY[1]

Robert B. Hudson, PhD[2]

The aging, long a favored social-welfare constituency in the United States, are in the early stages of being confronted with a series of obstacles which may put their favored status—and its concomitant material and symbolic benefits—in jeopardy. Rapidly rising public policy costs for meeting the needs of an aging population, a nascent but growing reassessment of policy benefits directed toward the elderly, and competitive pressures from other social-welfare constituencies are now threatening two of the aging's longstanding political resources—their singular legitimacy as a policy constituency and their political utility to other actors in the policy process.

These developments hold the clear potential for fundamentally altering old-age politics and policy. The widespread public sympathy and narrower political calculations which have been featured in the passage of many old-age policy enactments will increasingly give way to competitive and cost-based pressures, the effect being to produce a more inclusive and zero-sum politics of aging.

Three likely outcomes can be expected to result from these shifts. Major new policy initiatives or appropriations beyond those provided for under existing legislation will meet with new and perhaps overwhelming resistance. Demographic trends and existing statutory provisions already require that public expenditures for the aged will increase dramatically, and it is these increases which may in large part preclude additional enactments. For those subgroups of the aging population having special needs and not having benefitted proportionally from existing policies—the "old-old," minorities, and women—these pressures may have particularly deleterious consequences.

More critical appraisal of aging policy may also place agencies serving the elderly under new and harder scrutiny. The existence and operations of these agencies have served a number of political agendas

SOURCE: Reprinted by permission of *The Gerontologist*, Vol. 18, No. 5, October, 1978.
[1]The author's work is supported by a Research Career Development Award (5-KO4-AG00005) from NIA, NIH.
[2]The author wishes to thank James Schulz and Alan Sager for their very helpful comments on an earlier draft of this article.

as well as serving the elderly, and these other agendas are changing. As the aging come to be viewed increasingly as a political *problem* and less as a source of political *opportunity*, the role and utility of these agencies will be assessed more in terms of problem resolution than problem recognition.

Finally, these changes in the political environment will pose new challenges to the aging and to groups organized on their behalf. The political influence of aging interest groups will be put to a new and sterner test. The outcome will be of central interest to potential beneficiaries of new policies and, to a lesser extent, to those who have engaged in the professional debate focused on the extent of the political power of the aging and their organizations.

The following pages examine the ways in which the political factors influencing aging policy are changing, some of the reasons behind these changes, and the consequences they may have for the aging and the policies, groups, and agencies which serve them. The consequences cannot be predicted with certainty, but to the extent that perceptions and realities in the larger environment evolve as anticipated, consequences on the order of those suggested here can be expected.

Past Policies and Traditional Resources

Past policy enactments for the aging have been of two kinds: "breakthrough" and "constituency-building." Breakthrough policies consist of those legislative initiatives that have first involved the federal government in providing or guaranteeing fundamental social-policy benefits. Constituency-building policies are those that recognize and provide sustenance to related interests organized around common client, problem, or geographical concerns. The aging have contributed to, and benefited from, breakthrough activities in income maintenance and health care and have been able to create "policy space" for themselves and their allies in a cluster of social-services policies.

Critical to these legislative successes have been the aging's political legitimacy and their political utility. Legitimacy is perhaps the most effective of political resources because it connotes the belief that something or someone should be supported. Legitimacy may also obviate the need for power because, where pervasive, its presence precludes the necessity of overcoming resistance or opposition. This is why legitimate governments do not need to post policemen on every corner and— at a more modest level—in large part why the aging have secured major public-policy benefits without overt demonstrations of political muscle.

Political utility is a more proximate and instrumental concept and one that frequently builds on legitimacy. Knowing that a given group or proposal is viewed positively, other actors will seize on it in order to pursue agendas of their own. Congressmen have furthered careers by intoning the virtues of states' rights, the family farm, the "American canal in Panama," and, one may add, the policy needs of older Americans. As the following discussion will suggest, Congressmen are not the only actors who engage in this practice. In the case of aging policy, actors with a variety of agendas have helped themselves and their interests while helping the aging as well.

The Aging and Policy Breakthroughs.   The legitimacy and utility of the aging have led to their being both the principal beneficiaries and most functional constituency in the legislative struggles leading to the federal government's involvement in economic security, health-care financing, and guaranteeing minimum income. The objective needs of the elderly—a major factor contributing to their legitimacy—was beyond question and widely perceived at the time of each of the relevant enactments. Old Age Assistance and Old Age Insurance were enacted at a time when only an estimated 10% of the older population had any form of pension protection whatsoever; Medicare coverage was directed toward an older population whose hospital costs were twice as high and whose hospital stays were twice as long as the rest of the population; and Supplemental Security Income (SSI) payments provided a modicum of adequacy and equity to impoverished older persons whose benefits (per recipient) were as low as $38 and $47 in some states as recently as 1973. While statistics such as these were important in documenting the income and health needs of older persons, they served primarily to confirm what most persons already knew or suspected.

A more fundamental influence was the widely held belief that most older persons were impoverished or ill for reasons which were no fault of their own. Few would have disagreed with Franklin Roosevelt's statement, made while Governor of New York, that:

> Poverty in old age should not be regarded either as a disgrace or necessarily as a result of lack of thrift or energy. Usually it is a mere by-product of modern industrial life. . . . No greater tragedy exists in modern civilization than the aged, worn-out worker who after a life of ceaseless effort and useful productivity must look forward for his declining years to a poorhouse (Roosevelt, 1938).

Public support for the aged in the Medicare case had similar origins; the aged "were one of the few population groupings about whom one could not say the members should take care of their financial-medical problems by earning and saving more money" (Marmor, 1970). The relative lack of controversy around the idea of providing a minimum income to the aged, blind, and disabled allowed for the enactment of SSI whereas the broader Family Assistance Plan went down to defeat. Writing about the Family Assistance Plan (FAP) controversy, Moynihan (1973) notes simply that "from the earliest discussions it had always been assumed that any welfare-reform proposal would increase benefit levels and establish national minimum standards in the 'adult' categories."

The unquestioned needs of the older population and widespread sympathy towards them found in each of these instances provided what can be termed a "permissive consensus." For that consensus to be acted upon, however, required the involvement of some set of more proximate actors, and in each case that involvement took place. But the agendas these other actors pursued were broader than just meeting the particular needs of older persons. While the proponents in each of these episodes had genuine interest in remedying the problems besetting older persons, different concerns which they addended to that of helping the aging may have been of equal or greater importance. Put simply, the needs of and sympathy for older persons were useful to others; older persons were of instrumental value as well as being valued in their own right.

The principal actors in each of these major legislative cases hoped that by concentrating on the elderly or by attaching their proposals to the elderly they could establish a broader principle or assure yet more extended coverage. Roosevelt postponed for a year submitting his old-age assistance legislation until proposals to insure unemployed workers and establish a contributory old-age insurance system could be readied. His reasoning was that the OAA legislation would pass easily and that the others might well go down to defeat if not attached to that popular proposal (Altmeyer, 1968). National health insurance proponents, having witnessed the defeat of Truman's comprehensive health package, focused their subsequent efforts exclusively, not only on the elderly in general but on Social Security beneficiaries in particular, successfully taking advantage of both the group and the policy (Marmor, 1970). The inclusion of the adult categories into the FAP proposal clearly served to legitimize the broader proposal, and as it turned out, the legislation eventually enacted covered only these categories. The aging have reaped great benefits from these policies not only because they are seen as legitimate and deserving recipients but because executive branch leadership and those favoring an expanded social policy role for the national government have seen it in their interests to have such policies in place.

In the process leading to enactment of these policies, organized old-age interests appear to have been of only conditional or minimal importance. Only with Medicare, where the testaments of older persons and the lobbying activities of the National Council of Senior Citizens were prominently featured, does a conventional "pressure politics" model seem at all applicable. In the case of Old Age Assistance, the Townsend Movement lent a sense of urgency but emerged relatively late in the process and well beyond the critical policymaking circle. SSI was designed in a setting almost totally apart from organized social-welfare concerns, a fact indirectly attested to by the legislation's being mentioned only twice in passing in Henry Pratt's recent booklength discussion of "the gray lobby" (1976). Other factors were clearly at work.

The Aging and Constituency-Building.   In addition to these three major enactments, a number of smaller programs have been enacted on behalf of the elderly and numerous other policy constituencies in recent years. While containing needed in-kind benefits for the target populations, these "distributive" policies (Lowi, 1964) are more notable for the political benefits which accrue to the more central figures involved in the enactment process. Policies of this kind and the political relationships which foster them have been widely discussed under a variety of colorful rubrics: "subgovernments" (Cater, 1964); "interest group liberalism" (Binstock, 1972; Lowi, 1969); "self-regulatory politics" (Salisbury, 1968); "the social pork barrel" (Stockman, 1975); "cozy triangles" (Davidson, 1977).

The popularity of these distributive policies and their political utility to different actors are not difficult to see. They *optimize political credit* by lending recognition to particular constituencies and by involving administrators who both consume and disburse appropriated funds. By legislating such programs, elected officials appear responsible in meeting perceived public needs while relieving pressures being generated by organized constituency interests. These programs also animate public bureaucracies by providing them with specific policy responsibilities and often provide a major role to organized interests in the program's implementation.

At the same time, distributive policies *minimize political costs* by entailing monetary expenditures which are only modest when weighed against the problem in question and by defining the role of program implementors as that of distributing funds rather than regulating behaviors. The hallmark of these programs is that the actual costs of each one (as contrasted with the sum of the costs of all of them) are too diffused to be perceived by the taxpayers who ultimately foot the bill. Implementation of these programs is characterized by disbursement of funds through vertical networks of corresponding agencies at different levels of government. This, in turn, means that the dangers of infringing on the prerogatives of related, but operationally separate, programs can be minimized if not avoided altogether.

The legitimacy, utility, and presumed electoral strength of the elderly have made them frequent beneficiaries of distributive policy. Recognition of the policy legitimacy of the aging and the political credit it brings is an important factor in social service, housing, home care, nutrition, senior center, and training programs which have been enacted for the elderly and is perhaps the principal purpose served by the conferences, committees, and councils on aging found at all levels of government. As has been forcefully argued elsewhere (Binstock, 1972), however, the programs have served as well to finance the work of large numbers of professionals, providers, and advocates. It is these groups, more than the elderly themselves, that have been the motivating force behind these programs. As with all in-kind programs, it is these groups which consume the actual appropriations while the formally targeted population receives what those appropriations happen to buy.

On the cost side, these distributive policies have raised relatively few problems because the elderly—unlike business, labor, or unwed mothers—have engendered no natural opposition and because the costs of these programs are minimal relative to what might be done. The most telling indictment of distributive/in-kind programs generally lies in their legislative language invariably enumerating a wide range of problems to be remedied while, at the same time, the relatively meager appropriations make for spotty geographical and functional coverage and render the notion of "entitlement" near myth. The monumental backlogs of older persons desiring services under Titles III and VII of the Older Americans Act and Title XX of the Social Security Act provide clear evidence of the inequities inherent in these in-kind programs.

The purpose of the foregoing discussion has been to suggest some of the political reasons responsible for the different policy benefits the aging as a population have come to enjoy. There are trends now emerging, however, that may lessen the political legitimacy and utility of the aging and that may place severe pressures on both new initiatives and existing policies.

Emerging Political Pressures

Three discernible sets of factors are going to make further major initiatives for the elderly much more difficult to bring about and are going to place under harder scrutiny the programmatic and political utility of the in-kind programs serving the elderly. Growing absolute and relative cost burdens for meeting the needs of the older population, increasing debate over the actual distribution and intensity of older persons' needs, and sharpening compensation for limited discretionary social-welfare dollars are likely to erode traditional sources of support for the aging while yielding new competitive and cost-based pressures.

These factors hold the potential of bringing basic changes to the old-age policy universe.

Most of the comments and arguments in the following sections are made with regard to the *aggregate* older population. The principal theme of this discussion is that benefits targeted on the aging are now beginning to generate major competitive and cost pressures. What this does not say or intend is (a) that these benefits, as expensive as they are becoming, are necessarily adequate or (b) that all older persons have shared in the policy gains which have been made by the older population in general. No one could live decently on the minimum income benefits currently guaranteed through SSI. Publicly-supported health benefits for older persons are limited in terms of the costs which are covered and/or the persons who are eligible. The lack of an entitlement feature in many of the in-kind programs denies services to eligible persons for no reason other than that they arrived after the money ran out. Clearly, by even a modest standard of absolute need, current old-age policies can be deemed inadequate.

As the following discussion will suggest, however, older persons have done *relatively* well in the arena of public policy as contrasted with other population groupings whose aggregate needs can be argued to be equally pressing. It is this growing sense of relative deprivation on the part of other groups coupled with the monetary costs of old-age policies which form the core of the present discussion.

The conclusions to be drawn concerning older persons and public policy are that those older persons whose needs are the greatest may suffer disproportionately from these new external pressures and that these new pressures may come to bear, as well, on agencies serving older persons.

A final introductory note centers on the question of inflation and how real are the monetary increases discussed below. In the area of cash transfers, benefit increases have, for the most part, more than kept pace with inflation. In the area of health care, however, much of the reported increases in expenditures are the result of medical inflation rather than expansion or liberalization of benefits. Thus, despite massive increases in Medicare and Medicaid costs, older persons today have higher out-of-pocket medical expenses than they did 10 years ago. It is essential that facts such as this be made known and be appreciated in order that emerging political pressures do not deny needed relief to that large number of older persons who continue to remain very much "at risk."

Cost Pressures.   Rapidly rising budgetary charges for existing policies targeted on older persons are the principal source of public and official pressures on old-age policies. Cash payments under the

Old Age and Survivors Insurance portion of Social Security doubled between 1970 ($26.3 billion) and 1975 ($54.8 billion), and costs for this program are budgeted at $87.2 billion for FY 1979, with an anticipated rise to over $120 billion by 1983 (U. S. Office of Management and Budget, 1978a; U. S. Social Security Administration, 1976). The rise in the number of older persons by eight million over the next 25 years, the increasing percentage of them who will have Social Security coverage, and the declining proportion of working-age to old-age populations will all further exacerbate these pressures.

While many consider these costs to be qualitatively different from other portions of the federal budget because of their separate funding base and their earmarked purpose, Social Security is a "pay-as-you-go" rather than a true annuity system. Current contributions are paid out to current beneficiaries rather than being invested and set aside for the individual contributor. This feature has been made especially visible by the recent $227 billion Social Security tax package and the yet more recent attempts by Congress to roll it back. Taxes are invariably unpopular, but the intensity of the public outcry about a program as politically sacred as OASI has been nothing short of remarkable:

> For 40 years, Social Security was the linchpin of all liberal politics. You literally couldn't do too much for the elderly, the disabled and the ill. But now the costs of that largess have come home with a vengeance, and the middle-class working families have let their congressmen hear from them. Never again will Social Security benefits be increased without Congress looking nervously over its shoulder (Broder, 1978).

This tax increase, combined with evidence that the populace has misgivings about the soundness, equity, and investment value of Social Security (Eldred, 1977), suggests that "the peculiar mix of rational self-interest, fiscal illusion, and symbolic manipulations" posited by Mitchell (1977) as the "paradoxical" sources of support for Social Security may be unravelling.

Health is the second major area where the magnitude of current expenditures for the aging is very large and rapidly escalating. Medicare expenditures have risen from $3.2 billion in the program's first year to $16.9 billion in 1976 (Gibson et al., 1977), are budgeted at $29.4 billion for FY 1979, and are projected to be $44.5 billion by 1983 (U. S. Office of Management and Budget, 1978a). Assuming an 11% annual medical inflation rate, Medicare will cost over $90 billion by 1990, and this estimate does not incorporate the increasing numbers of persons who will be eligible for Medicare coverage.[3]

---

[3]Principally because of disability coverage, approximately 15% of Medicare expenditures are targeted on persons defined in terms other than age (Social Security Administration, 1978).

TABLE 1   Estimated Nursing Home Care Costs

Year	Total Nursing Care Cost (in millions)	Nursing Care Cost Borne by Public Programs (excluding OASI)	% of Cost Borne by Public Programs (excluding OASI)
1976	$10,600	$5,856	55.2%
1975	9,100	5,014	55.1
1974	7,450	3,801	51.0
1973	6,650	3,264	49.1
1972	5,860	2,465	42.1

SOURCES: Worthington (1975); Gibson et al., (1977).

Cost increases in long-term care have been among the most pronounced in recent years and will grow ever larger as the number of persons over age 75 increases 60% by 2000 (Brotman, 1977). While aggregate national health expenditures (public and private) quadrupled between 1960 and 1974, and were up 50% between 1970 and 1974, nursing home costs rose 1500% and 200% during the same periods (Worthington, 1975). In the two-year period, 1974–76, the latter costs have increased another 42%. And, as indicated in Table 1, nursing home costs borne by public programs have also risen steadily.[4]

Congressional Budget Office (CBO) estimates show long-term care costs continuing their rapid increase. The CBO projects public long-term care costs under current authorizations increasing from the present CBO estimate of $5.7 billion to $15–$17 billion by 1985. Were Medicare home health benefits liberalized to include nonskilled services and were home-based services mandated under Medicaid, the estimated cost of publicly-financed long-term care services would rise to $18–$28 billion by 1985. Long-term care insurance would increase the latter estimate roughly 2½ times (Congressional Budget Office, 1977a). Wershow (1977) estimates that the costs of room, board, and nursing care of the most severely afflicted long-term care patients (organic brain syndrome) could alone rise to $20 billion by 2000.

The costs of publicly supported health policies for older persons are less apparent to the public than is the OASI program, and factors other than the numbers and needs of older people lie behind much of the health cost increases. Nonetheless, the aging currently receive nearly 90% of the services funded through Medicare, 38% of those funded through Medicaid, and 49% of the $48.4 billion of public money spent

---

[4]Roughly 75% of the nation's total nursing home expenditures are for the elderly (Gibson et al., 1977)

on health care in the U.S. (Gibson et al., 1977). The proportion of health dollars targeted on the elderly being so substantial, it seems inevitable that political pressures from cost-conscious government officials and benefit-seeking populations will find the aged relatively disadvantaged in new public initiatives in health. The concern older persons might well have is stated succinctly by Anderson (1976):

> In pure self-interest, if I were an elderly person, I would not approve universal health insurance, because resources will not increase in proportion to demand. The aged will then have to scramble for scarcer resources than if the only government program were Medicare. As the pressure on resources builds up in the system, side-effects may include a weakening of the taboo on the "right to die," and an increase in "store houses" for the aged, nursing homes, and old-age homes.

Firm estimates of cost increases in the smaller in-kind programs directed toward the elderly are difficult to make because these are neither entitlement nor, for the most part, means-tested programs. It seems certain, however, that the growth in these programs will be substantially less than in those just discussed. Because they are not entitlement programs, there is no "automatic" cost escalator. Moreover, costs generated by the entitlement programs benefitting the elderly will put added pressures on these discretionary in-kind programs, such as the Older Americans Act. And, to the extent that these programs have been enacted for their nonprogrammatic or political utility, they may continue to serve their political function without great increases in substantive benefits.

Policy Success and Improved Well-Being.   At the same time public expenditures for the aging have been increasing—and in part because of these expenditures—various indices of older persons' well-being have shown improvement. While these developments are welcome and to be expected, they are also serving to alter perceptions of older persons and their needs held by both the population at large and the older population itself. As older persons are shown or perceived to be better off while costs for public programs directed toward them escalate, political pressures on these programs seem certain to increase.

Poverty among the older population has declined sharply in recent years. U.S. Census Bureau (1977) data show the percentage of older persons in poverty declining from 35.2% in 1959, to 28.5% in 1966, to 21.6% in 1971, and to 15.3% in 1975. The University of Wisconsin Institute for Research on Poverty, employing different measures, estimates that only 5% of the older population was in poverty in 1976 (Watts & Skidmore, 1977). There has also been a modest decline in the proportion of older persons in the overall poverty population (Plotnick,

1975a). Principal among the factors in this decline has been public cash and in-kind transfers to the elderly. Foremost among these has been increased OASI benefits. Since the first major benefit increase awarded to retired workers and their dependents in 1950, benefit levels have risen dramatically: 1950: $64; 1955: $129; 1960: $152; 1965: $173; 1970: $227; 1975: $384. While these are current dollar figures, the cost of living has only slightly more than doubled over the same 1950–1975 period (U.S. Office of the President, 1976). Plotnick (1975b) has calculated the probabilities of different demographic groups of the "pretransfer poor" escaping from poverty when cash transfers were factored in. While there was considerable variation among different age groupings, the probabilities for aged individuals (regardless of race, marital status, region, or education) were consistently higher than for younger persons. Widows and elderly Black couples continued, however, to have less than a 50–50 "chance" of being brought out of poverty through these public programs. The Congressional Budget Office (1977b), using complicated modeling techniques, has also estimated the effect of public programs in reducing poverty among older persons. The differential impact of the major income and in-kind programs were calculated to be as shown in Table 2.

Some selected broader measures of well-being also show betterment in the overall status of the aged. Life expectancy at age 65 has increased from 12.8 years in 1940 to 14.4 years in 1960, to 15.6 years in 1974 (U.S. Bureau of the Census, 1975). Death rates for persons aged 75–84 have declined from 112 per 1,000 in 1940, to 87/1,000 in 1960, to 79/1,000 in 1973 (U.S. Nation Center for Health Statistics, 1976). Between 1958 and 1974, the number of "restricted-activity days" for persons aged 65+ has declined from 47.3 to 38.0 per year (Munnell, 1976). It is important to note, however, that Shanas (1976) found no change

TABLE 2   Families Aged 65-and-over below the Poverty Level under Alternative Definitions: FY 1976

	Families in Poverty (Age 65+)	
	No. (000)	%
Pretax/Pretransfer income	9,297	57.7
Pretax/Post-social insurance income	2,977	18.5
Pretax/Post-money transfer income	2,107	13.1
Pretax/Post-in-kind transfer income	646	4.0
Posttax/Post-total transfer income	654	4.1

SOURCE: Congressional Budget Office, Poverty Status of Families under Alternative Definitions of Income. Background Paper 17 (January, 1977b).

in the health status of older persons in her 1975 restudy of the research which she originally conducted in 1962. The higher salaries and wages, expanded private pension coverage, and higher levels of education (Neugarten, 1974; Skolnick, 1976) make it appear likely, nonetheless, that in many aspects of their lives—including, perhaps, health—coming generations of older persons will be better-off.

These improvements in the length and quality of life of the older population are changing how the aging view themselves and how others may view the aging and their needs. It is clear and understandable that the aging do not wish to be viewed as dependent or be segregated from the remainder of the population. The Gray Panthers have been perhaps most vocal in demanding social inclusion, but public and private efforts geared toward independent living, elimination of mandatory retirement, and a nonstereotypical media image are each directed toward older persons not being viewed as something apart. Their increased well-being will make these demands more insistent and—at least for the "young-old"—more realistic.

All this will not, however, be without its political consequences. Older persons have received their indisputably high proportion of public benefits in large part because they were, in fact, singularly disadvantaged and were so viewed by others. If—on an aggregate basis—they are now less disadvantaged and wish to be perceived as such, the question of why they should continue to receive special policy treatment immediately arises. Were costs and competitive claims not so pressing, it might be possible for older persons to have an improved existence, a positive image, and disproportionate public benefits. However, these other constraints are present and growing, and it seems likely that, in conjunction with improved well-being and image, they pose a threat to future public benefits. As bluntly put by Samuelson in an article widely circulated in the *Washington Post* (1978), "The more the elderly seem to be enjoying themselves, and the healthier they are, the more young workers may resent it."

Competitive Spending Pressures. The third factor portending negative consequences for old-age policy is the contrast between policy benefits which are made available to the elderly and those made available to other population groups. Some of these have been alluded to above and many of the others are widely known, but these disparities will take on increasing political importance as the costs of old-age programs continue to escalate and as the policy needs of the overall aging population come under more careful scrutiny.

Publicly-financed medical benefits are currently weighted heavily toward the elderly, and the bulk of those benefits aid older persons defined officially as nonpoor. While the elderly are confronted by health costs three times greater than the rest of the population, public funds pay 68% of these higher per capita costs while paying only 28% of the lower bills of the younger population (Mueller & Gibson, 1976). Just under 80% of the $23.7 billion in federal health outlays for older persons in 1977 was spent for persons defined as nonpoor as contrasted with 51% of the $18.7 billion spent on behalf of the nonpoor population under age 65 (U.S. Office Management and Budget, 1977a). Medicare is the major factor both in the high public coverage for older persons generally and for nonpoor older persons in the older population. Its enactment, however, preceded the major economic advances of the older population and the "rise of the young-old." No one advocates or envisages reductions in Medicare benefits, but the status of older persons has undergone some significant changes from what it was depicted to be during the lengthy debate leading up to Medicare's enactment in 1965.

Another unexpected and costly development has been the rising proportion of Medicaid payments targeted on the elderly. Devoted largely to long-term care costs, roughly 40% of Medicaid funds are now assisting the elderly. There can be no question that these benefits are aiding the very neediest of the aged—and often for inappropriate and substandard care—but pressures exist here as well. These rising costs are inevitably impinging on other social-welfare budgets. Testifying before the House Select Committee on Aging, Massachusetts Secretary of Human Services, Jerald Stevens (1977) spoke of these added consequences:

> Because of the escalating costs in Medicaid, we in Massachusetts are not able to provide a cost-of-living increase for AFDC recipients which is a particularly severe burden on the poor people. Additionally, we are not able to provide all the services we think are necessary for either the mentally ill, or for adolescents who need a number of types of care. So, the Medicaid pressure is felt not only in terms of making cuts, or trying to improve management inside Medicaid, but has a very strong ripple effect on all other human service programs—a negative impact on all other human services programs.

The aging have fared relatively well when compared to other social-welfare constituencies in additional areas. AFDC payments never equalled those under the Old Age Assistance Program (Steiner, 1966) and have fallen further behind given the guaranteed minimum and cost-of-living features in the present SSI program. In public housing, where shortages for all eligible populations are chronic, the percentage of units occupied by the elderly has increased markedly, rising from 27% in 1964 to 41% in 1972 (Department of Housing and Urban Development figures cited in Steiner, 1971; and in Gold et al., 1976). Fifty percent of recent public housing construction has been devoted to elderly housing (Steiner, 1971). Recent HUD initiatives to concentrate community development bloc grants in "core" areas are designed in part to assist younger welfare populations at the relative expense of suburban areas where, it has been argued, senior citizen projects tend to dominate.

A number of tax provisions at both the state and federal levels have singled out the elderly for special treatment. In the instances of prescription drug and property tax relief, the rationale lies in the disproportionate burden which falls on the elderly in both of these areas. The double personal-tax exemption and the capital gains exemption for low and moderately valued owner-occupied residences in the federal tax code recognizes the low incomes of older persons. The retirement-income-tax credit seeks to make amends to those elderly who do not benefit from another tax advantage enjoyed by most older persons (viz., the total tax exemption of Social Security and Railroad Retirement income [Schulz, 1976]).

As with publicly-financed health benefits, the issues increasingly coming to the fore concern costs, distribution of benefits within the older population, and inequities between older and younger persons who are similarly situated. The Office of Management and Budget has made the following estimates of the costs (Table 3—income lost to the Treasury) of different federal tax provisions benefitting the elderly. Despite the rationale that these tax provisions are designed to aid the low and moderate income elderly, Surrey (1973) estimates that nearly half of the dollar benefits accrue to older persons whose incomes exceed $10,000. And, as is true with exemptions generally, greater benefits accompany higher incomes. The equity issue between older and younger populations is clear, if controversial: younger persons with low in-

TABLE 3 Loss of Federal Tax Receipts Due to Special Provisions for the Aged

Special Provision	Loss ($$)
Extra personal exemptions for the elderly	$1.4 billion
Exclusion of Social Security benefits	3.8 billion
Exclusion of Railroad Retirement benefits	.2 billion
Tax credit to the elderly	.2 billion
	$6.0 billion[a]

[a]Total figure is higher than sum of the components because of higher tax brackets recipients would be in were these provisions eliminated.

SOURCE: U. S. Office of Management and Budget (1978b).

comes, high health-care costs, and nonliquid assets do not share many of the tax advantages enjoyed by older persons (Pechman, 1977).

Political and Policy Consequences

Rising costs of public policies targeted on older persons, improved well-being of the aggregate older population, and continued disparity between policy benefits bestowed on older persons and others in the population are undermining the political legitimacy and utility of the aging, and this decline will bring with it further consequences.

The political legitimacy of the aging has rested in the widespread belief that, as a class of persons, they are singularly disadvantaged by low incomes, poor health, and a particular vulnerability brought on by their place in the life-cycle. This generalized pattern is no longer valid and will become less so with time. The improved status of many older persons is already known in policy circles, but the cost and equity factors are generating questions among the populace at large as to the overall needs of older persons. Furthermore, as cost pressures yield greater opposition to policy initiatives for older persons and as competitive pressures yield separate spending demands, incumbents of elected office will find support of old-age policies more of a mixed political blessing than has been the case. As the policy legitimacy of the aged constituency erodes, so will its utility to other political actors. At least three more proximate consequences will stem from these changes and the pressures producing them.

New Appropriations for Old Policies.   Clearest and most notable in this regard are the new appropriations which will be required to meet existing statutory obligations directed primarily towards older persons. What the Office of Management and Budget classifies as "relatively uncontrollable" expenditures have quadrupled in the last decade, and the rate of increase is accelerating. Obligations for the elderly represent the major element of overall "uncontrollable" spending, which now constitutes nearly ¾ of all federal outlays. Spending under the OASI portion of Social Security, totaling $71 billion in 1977, is expected to rise to over $120 billion by 1983 (U.S. Office of Management and Budget, 1978a). Total outlays for the aging, survivors, and retirees under OASI, civilian and military retirement and insurance plans, Railroad Retirement, SSI, Medicare, and Medicaid were $122 billion in 1977 (author's estimate from OMB figures). The corresponding figure for the FY 1979 budget is $148 billion, or 29.6% of the total budget. HEW Secretary Califano estimates that if present trends continue, "real" spending on behalf of the elderly will triple by 2010 (Califano, 1978). Unfortunately, the factors which contribute to the cost escalation in these areas—number of beneficiaries, levels of benefits, inflation—appear as well to be largely uncontrollable. The first is fixed by demography; the second is constrained by politics; and the third—especially in the health area—has remained nearly impervious to attempts to rein it in.

The principal consequence of these fixed charges is that they severely limit the ability of the government to embark on new initiatives. These costs, coupled with more general budgetary concerns to which they contribute, are already impeding progress in major areas such as national health insurance and welfare reform. But because roughly ½ of the uncontrollable expenditures are attributable to aging-related policies, they can be expected to place a particularly heavy burden on new activities in this area. When an article addressing the escalation in costs of aging policies is entitled "The Withering Freedom to Govern" (Samuelson, 1978), one gets a sense—although perhaps an exaggerated one—of the obstacles which are likely to be encountered.

Locating "new" money to provide greater income, housing, health, and social service benefits for those older persons whose needs and numbers are growing will be very difficult. Tax increases are unlikely for any number of reasons: concern over existing budget deficits, economic problems associated with siphoning off "productive capital" from the private sector, increasing restiveness among taxpayers generally. The further notion that additional revenues should be targeted on the elderly—even those with dire needs—will encounter stiff resistance from taxpayers and competitive constituencies alike.

What largely remains then is reallocating funds earmarked by statute or expectations for other purposes. The question here is simply "whose" pot should be raided? The feeling is widespread in governmental circles and elsewhere that spending for health and welfare functions generally is already excessive; and, within the health and welfare community, it is widely—if not openly—held that "the elderly" get too much. Who will sit idly by and see more spending targeted on older persons if they perceive it to be at their expense?

A third and hardly pleasant alternative lies in reallocating public expenditures for the aging toward those subgroups of the aging population deemed most in need. Despite the valid issues concerning large numbers of relatively well-off older persons receiving significant public policy benefits, reallocation of aging monies raises difficult political and normative questions. The largest single expenditure and the one where the equity issues can be most forcefully argued is in the OASI portion of Social Security. Yet, the benefit structure here—as contrasted with the system's financing—is already progressive, and at least one analyst advocates making it less progressive now that SSI is in place to pick up the "social adequacy" function being served partially by OASI

(Munnell, 1976). Medicare currently covers hospital and medical costs which few persons—regardless of age—can reasonably be expected to shoulder themselves. Medicaid benefits are more extensive but are denied to those even with only very modest means. A case can be made for reducing or scaling some of the tax advantages enjoyed by older persons, but only the taxing of Social Security benefits would raise truly significant revenues, and action along those lines is not in the offing in any event. One might expect cuts in the in-kind service programs such as the Older Americans Act, but the revenues freed by such action are not sufficient to finance major new initiatives. It does seem likely, however, that the budgetary growth experienced by these programs in recent years will not continue, a conclusion supported by the President's FY 1979 budget.

A final potential answer to the allocation question involves more cost-effective and, hopefully, appropriate uses of funds contained within the cost-escalation projections presented earlier. Assuming that no downward revisions occur in the cash-benefit estimates for OASI or SSI, the principal item here would focus on health allocations. And, because acute-care coverage is dominated by the medical establishment and deemed fundamental by health-care consumers, the reallocations here are most likely to fall in the long-term care area.

Whether reallocation of long-term care resources—principally away from the current institutionally-based pattern—can lead to monetary savings is a major concern of the Health Care Financing Administration, the Administration on Aging, and other federal and state agencies. No consensus has emerged from the several existing studies related to this question. Relatively favorable cost findings concerning noninstitutional services are reported in Hurtado et al. (1972) study of an HMO population and in the Nielson et al. (1972) study of a posthospitalized population. However, Burton et al. (1974) and Greenberg (1974) report that deinstitutionalization of nursing home patients resulted in very limited cost savings, largely because of the small number of persons in their studies who could be appropriately discharged. Preliminary findings from a panel study by Sager (1977) indicate that for five of nine patients for whom there are discharge data, institutional care was less expensive. Further studies, involving different placement options and subject to widespread replication, will be necessary before it can be determined whether home care and other noninstitutional services can lead to more efficient expenditure of the major resources being devoted to long-term care.

New Demands on Old Agencies.   Budgetary constraints may be only one of a number of new pressures which will be brought to bear on agencies serving older persons. As the older population comes to be increasingly viewed as a public-policy problem rather than as a target of political opportunity, agencies serving the elderly will be placed under new and harder scrutiny. Not only will questions of accountability be raised more frequently, but the questions will be less on the order of "what are you doing for the elderly?" and more along the lines of "what has been the effect of your activities on alleviating pressing needs and controlling growing public-policy costs?"

These tougher accountability questions will be asked of many agencies dealing with the aging such as the Social Security Administration, the Health Care Financing Administration, and the Veterans Administration, but they may be put most directly to the Administration on Aging. Because of its origins, the characteristics of its authorizing legislation, and past perceptions of its role and responsibilities, AoA may find itself hard pressed to provide adequate responses. Historically, AoA has been formally charged with being a "focal point" for governmental concern for the elderly, but the absence of adequate funding, staffing, authority, and concerted outside interest has kept AoA from playing this role, even assuming it was a role AoA wished to play. Instead, AoA has found itself trying to administer a series of fairly large and increasingly decentralized grant-in-aid programs providing a wide array of social services throughout the country. To this point, its serving to recognize the aging as a policy constituency and provide discretionary service dollars has been sufficient to generate requisite levels of political support.

The question now arises as to whether AoA will become the scapegoat for ongoing problems which are not of AoA's making but the resolution of which a revisionist history will claim to have long been the rationale behind its existence. Critics will see a large service-delivery infrastructure and will see as well an increasing volume of unmet needs among an expanding population. Before, it was sufficient to demonstrate that agencies in business to serve the elderly blanketed the country; now, people will search for evidence that there has been some resolution of the problems which these agencies have been established to address. There are, of course, a number of reasons to exonerate AoA, but the questions must be directed somewhere, and AoA is the agency which has had the most proximate responsibility. The agency which serves to recognize a constituency in a benign environment is transformed into a lightning rod attracting problems in a hostile environment. The lofty language expressing concern becomes a legislative mandate demanding results.

Under these conditions, AoA will be under increasing pressure to demonstrate a capacity for problem-solving. While it may continue to lend recognition to the needs of older persons and oversee the disbursement of limited funds for those purposes, it runs the risk of being viewed as just another social-services program under the larger umbrella of the Office of Human Development Services if confined to these roles. The area where AoA might best make its mark appears to be in long-term care, and AoA has, in fact, been making concerted efforts in this direction in recent months. Many of the services currently funded through the Older Americans Act are related to long-term care, but these services have been fragmented, are not confined to persons who have pressing long-term care needs, and are yet to be effectively meshed with the larger array of institutionally-oriented long-term care programs.

There is some leeway for demonstration projects which might show how these current shortcomings can be alleviated, but AoA does not currently have the authority to move the state and area agencies collectively in this direction. These agencies have, in fact, become more autonomous actors within the hierarchy of aging agencies because of their growth relative to other agencies at their respective levels of government and because of the latitude provided them under the Older Americans Act. However, for AoA to maintain a place for itself at the national level, it will increasingly need the capacity to impose a more singular rationale on the program activities under its aegis. An agency's shifting from a constituency-based to a problem-oriented focus carries the danger of losing existing support while seeking it from new and different sources, but the new realities of aging policy in Washington may warrant the risk in AoA's case.

New Political Pressures on a New Policy System.   For the larger aging community, securing additional benefits will increasingly entail overcoming the presence of new resistence and the decline of the legitimacy and utility which have been the mainstays of its political support. Monetary and opportunity costs have caught up with material benefits and perhaps even symbolic ones. Elected officials can no longer lend unquestioned support to aging initiatives, competing interests can no longer remain uninvolved, and budgetary officials on both the legislative and executive side may be decidedly hostile.

The political power of the aging, its extent long the subject of debate, will be put to a sterner test than it has faced to this point. The political legitimacy and utility of older persons have always lent a spurious quality to claims which equate the aging's political power with the policy benefits which they have gained. In the coming period, where scrutiny will supplant sympathy, that question should at least be resolved. Success in securing new benefits and maintaining existing ones will depend as never before on the ability of the aging and their organizations to demonstrate that they have the capability of imposing negative sanctions on those who choose not to support them. Costs and competitive pressures combined with the thought that the aging are not to be slighted will put decision-makers in a new and uncomfortable position when it comes to aging issues. Should they choose to continue supporting aging initiatives, it will be valid testimony to the aging and their organizations having transformed their numbers into an effective political resource.

Even if political pressure generated by the aging turns out to be relatively effective, a question remains as to what ends this pressure will be directed. It will be used if necessary—and probably success-fully—to maintain policy gains already won. It is easier to defeat moves to rescind existing benefits than it is to gain enactment of new ones. Beyond defensive actions, the aging constituency will continue to press for liberalization and extension of benefits under existing authoriza-tions. These efforts will include income and in-kind policies alike. In-creases in OASI cash benefits beyond those called for under existing formulas will be difficult to bring about, but there will certainly be moves in this direction. Broadening of Medicare benefits will continue to be pressed, but it seems unlikely that significant changes will be made independent of the larger debate on national health insurance. The interests of the aging and those favoring a public presence in the health sector were both well served by Medicare's enactment, but now extension of benefits to new population groups may take precedence over expansion of benefits to the currently entitled older population. Pressures both for and against expansion of social-services benefits will, as indicated earlier, grow more intense.

Largely left out of these efforts and whatever successes they may bring—as has often been the case in the past—will be the most vulner-able of the older population. In proportion to numbers and needs, the income, health, and service benefits directed toward the old-old, the minority old, the isolated, and widowed are slight. That the working years of most of these persons preceded the era of broad private pen-sion and health-care coverage as well as the more recent expansion of public benefits renders them yet more disadvantaged. None of this is, of course, unknown, but ironically recognition of the intense needs of these groups is coming at just the time when the pressures discussed here may constrain initiatives for the entire aging population. If, in addition, the organized aging community—younger, better-off, and now concerned about its own prerogatives—fails to give high priority to the needs of the vulnerable elderly, the latter's well-being may continue to suffer. Responsible elected and bureaucratic leadership will work toward more liberal and appropriate public benefits, but these efforts may be thwarted in the presence of cost-based pressures and in the absence of counterbalancing supportive pressures. For the old-old to be the vic-tims of constraints generated by policies from which they were largely excluded would be reprehensible.

REFERENCES

Altmeyer, A. J. *The formative years of Social Security.* Univ. Wisconsin Press, Madison, 1968.

Anderson, O. W. Reflections on the sick aged and helping systems. In B. L. Neugarten & R. J. Havighurst (Eds.), *Social policy, social ethics, and the aging society.* National Science Found., USGPO, Washington, 1976.

Binstock, R. H. Interest group liberalism and the politics of aging. *Gerontologist,* 1972, 2, 265–280.

Broder, D. The end for an era of liberal legislation. *Boston Globe,* February 15, 1978.

Brotman, H. B. Population projections: Part 1. Tomorrow's older population (to 2000). *Gerontologist,* 1977, *17,* 203–209.

Burton, R. M., Damon, W. W., et al. Nursing home cost and care: An investigation of alternatives. Ctr. for Study of Aging & Human Development, Duke Univ., Durham, NC, 1974.

Califano, J. A., Jr. The aging of America: Questions for the four-generation society. Presentation before American Academy of Political and Social Science, Philadelphia, April, 1978.

Cater, D. *Power in Washington.* Random House, New York, 1964.

Davidson, R. H. Breaking up those "cozy triangles": An impossible dream? In S. Welch & J. G. Peters (Eds.), *Legislative reform and public policy.* Praeger, New York, 1977.

Eldred, G. W. Does the public support the Social Security program? *Journal of Risk and Insurance,* 1977, *44,* 2, 179–191.

Gibson, R. M., Mueller, M. S., & Fisher, C. R. Age differences in health-care spending, FY 1976. *Social Security Bulletin,* 1977, *40,* 3–14.

Gold, B., Kutza, E., & Marmor, T. R. United States social policy on old age: Present patterns and predictions. In B. L. Neugarten and R. J. Havighurst (Eds.), *Social policy, social ethics, and the aging society.* National Science Found., USGPO, Washington, 1976.

Greenberg, J. The costs of in-home services: A planning study of services to noninstitutionalized older persons in Minnesota. Governor's Council on Aging, Minneapolis, 1974.

Hurtado, A. V., Greenlick, M. R., McCabe, M., & Saward, E. W. The utilization and costs of home-care and extended-care facility in a comprehensive, prepaid group practice program. *Medical Care,* 1972, *10,* 8–16.

Lowi, T. J. American business, public policy, case-studies, and political theory. *World Politics,* 1964, 16–677–715.

Lowi, T. J. *The end of liberalism.* W. W. Norton, New York, 1969.

Marmor, T. R. *The politics of Medicare.* Routledge & Kegan Paul, London, 1970.

Mitchell, W. C. *The popularity of Social Security: A paradox in public choice.* American Enterprise Inst., Washington, 1977.

Moynihan, D. P. *The politics of a guaranteed income.* Vintage, New York, 1973.

Mueller, M. S., & Gibson, R. M. Age differences in health-care spending, FY 1975. *Social Security Bulletin,* 1976, *39,* 18–30.

Munnell, A. H. The future of Social Security. *New England Economic Review,* 1976, July/August, 3–28.

Neugarten, B. L. Age groups in American society and the rise of the young-old. *Annals,* 1974, 415, 187–198.

Nielson, M., Blenkner, M., Bloom, M., Downs, T., & Beggs, H. Older persons after hospitalization: A controlled study of home-aide service. *American Journal of Public Health,* 1972, *62,* 1094–1101.

Pechman, J. A. *Federal tax policy* (3rd Ed.). The Brookings Inst., Washington, 1977.

Plotnick, R. D. The changing character of poverty. In R. D. Plotnick & F. Skidmore, *Progress against poverty.* Academic Press, New York, 1975. (a)

Plotnick, R. D. Poverty and the public cash-transfer system, 1965–1972. In R. D. Plotnick & F. Skidmore, *Progress against poverty.* Academic Press, New York, 1975. (b)

Pratt, H. J. *The Gray Lobby.* Univ. Chicago Press, 1976.

Roosevelt, F. D. *Public papers and addresses.* Random House, New York, 1938. Cited in G. V. Rimlinger. *Welfare policy and industrialization in Europe, America, and Russia.* John Wiley & Sons, New York, 1971.

Sager, A. Estimating the costs of diverting patients from nursing homes to home care. Levinson Policy Inst., Brandeis Univ., Waltham, MA, 1977.

Salisbury, R. H. The analysis of public policy: A search for theories and roles. In A. Ranney (ed.), *Political science and public policy.* Markham, Chicago, 1968.

Samuelson, R. J. The withering freedom to govern. *Washington Post,* March 5, 1978, C1, C5.

Schulz, J. H. Income distribution and the aging. In R. H. Binstock & E. Shanas (Eds.), *Handbook of aging and the social sciences.* Van Nostrand Reinhold, New York, 1976.

Shanas, E. The health status of older persons: Comparisons of two national surveys. Paper presented to the 29th Annual Meeting of the Gerontological Soc., New York, 1976.

Skolnik, A. M. Private pension plans, 1950–1974. *Social Security Bulletin,* 1976, *39,* 3–17.

Steiner, G. Y. *Social insecurity.* Rand McNally, Chicago, 1966.

Steiner, G. Y. *The state of welfare.* The Brookings Inst., Washington, 1971.

Stevens, J. L. Testimony before the Subcommittee on Health and Long-term Care of the House Select Committee on Aging. *Recent Medicaid cutbacks: Shocking impact on the elderly.* USGPO, Washington, 1977.

Stockman, D. The social pork barrel. *Public Interest,* 1975, *39,* 3–30.

Surrey, S. S. *Pathways to tax reform—The concept of tax expenditures.* Harvard Univ. Press, Cambridge, MA, 1973.

U. S. Bureau of the Census. *Characteristics of the population below the poverty level.* Current Population Reports. Series P-60, No. 106. USGPO, Washington, 1977.

U. S. Bureau of the Census. *Demographic aspects of aging and the older population in the United States.* Current Population Reports. Special Studies. Series P-23, No. 59, USGPO, Washington, 1975.

U. S. Congressional Budget Office. *Long-term care for the elderly and disabled.* USGPO, Washington, 1977. (a)

U. S. Congressional Budget Office. *Poverty status of families under alternative definitions of income.* USGPO, Washington, 1977. (b)

U. S. National Ctr. for Health Statistics. *Health: United States, 1975.* DHEW, Washington, 1976.

U. S. Office of Management and Budget. *The budget of the United States Government: FY 1979.* USGPO, Washington, 1978. (a)

U. S. Office of Management and Budget. *Special analyses, budget of the United States Government, 1979.* USGPO, Washington, 1978. (b)

U. S. Office of the President. *Economic report of the President, 1976.* USGPO, Washington, 1976.

U. S. Social Security Admin. Current operating statistics. *Social Security Bulletin,* 1976, *39,* 36.

U. S. Social Security Admin. Current operating statistics. *Social Security Bulletin,* 1978, *41,* 54.

Watts, H., & Skidmore, F. An update of the poverty picture plus a new look at relative tax burdens. *Focus.* Inst. for Research on Poverty Newsletter, 1977, *2,* 5–7, 10.

Wershow, H. J. Reality orientation for gerontologists: Some thoughts about senility. *Gerontologist,* 1977, *17,* 297–302.

Worthington, N. L. National health expenditures, 1929–74. *Social Security Bulletin,* 1975, *38,* 3–20.

Article 16

THE LONG-RUN FINANCING PROBLEM: BASIC APPROACHES

Congressional Budget Office

. . . The Social Security program faces a long-run financing problem because of the expected growth in the number of beneficiaries relative to the size of the working population. This chapter considers the dimensions of that problem, provides some background information on the Social Security system, and outlines some options for improving trust fund balances over the long run.

MAGNITUDE OF THE LONG-RUN FINANCING PROBLEM

Over the next 75 years, the Social Security system is expected to have a deficit equal to about 13 percent of annual outlays, on average. Deficits will vary considerably over time, however, as Table 1 shows. Under current projections, trust fund balances will build up between 1990 and 2015, then decline fairly rapidly, and will be depleted sometime between 2025 and 2030.[1]

The estimates of tax rates, costs, and differences shown in Table 1 are all given as percentages of "taxable payroll," which is the total wage base subject to Social Security taxes—about $1.36 trillion in 1982.[2] Thus,

---

SOURCE: *Financing Social Security: Issues and Options for the Long Run*, Washington, DC: The Congress of the United States The Congressional Budget Office, December, 1982.

[1]Unless otherwise stated, all long-run projections given in this paper are based on the Alternative II-B economic and demographic assumptions of the 1982 Annual Report of the Board of Trustees, Federal Old Age and Survivors Insurance and Disability Trust Funds. The CBO does not develop long-run economic projections. The II-B assumptions are given in Appendix B, which also summarizes long-run actuarial cost and revenue estimation methods.

[2]The 1982 Trustees' Report defines taxable payroll as follows:

Taxable payroll is defined as that amount which, when multiplied by the combined employee-employer tax rate, yields the total amount of taxes paid by employees, employers, and the self-employed. In practice, the taxable payroll is calculated as a weighted average of the earnings on which employees, employers, and self-employed persons are taxed. The weighting takes into account the lower tax rates on self-employment income, on tips, and on multiple-employer "excess wages," as compared with the combined employee-employer rate.

TABLE 1   OASDI Tax Rates, Cost Rates, and Ratios of Balances to Outlays, Selected Years 1985–2060

Year	As a Percentage of Taxable Payroll[a]			Start-of-year Balances as a Percentage of Outlays
	Tax rate[b]	Cost rate[c]	Difference[d]	
1985	11.40	11.70	−0.30	−4
1990	12.40	11.64	0.76	−19
1995	12.40	11.42	0.98	15
2000	12.40	11.03	1.37	64
2005	12.40	10.95	1.45	128
2010	12.40	11.53	0.87	177
2015	12.40	12.82	−0.42	177
2020	12.40	14.44	−2.04	125
2025	12.40	15.97	−3.57	31
2030	12.40	16.83	−4.43	e
2035	12.40	17.02	−4.62	e
2040	12.40	16.80	−4.40	e
2045	12.40	16.66	−4.26	e
2050	12.40	16.72	−4.32	e
2055	12.40	16.81	−4.41	e
2060	12.40	16.81	−4.41	e
25-year Averages				
1982–2006	12.01	11.37	0.64	33
2007–2031	12.40	14.08	−1.68	e
2032–2056	12.40	16.81	−4.41	e
75-year Averages				
1982–2056	12.27	14.09	−1.82	e

a. Taxable payroll is the total of all wages on which Social Security taxes are paid, adjusted for differences in tax rates.

b. Combined employee-employer tax rate for the OASDI funds.

c. Cost rate is estimated outlays as a percentage of taxable payroll.

d. Difference between tax rates and cost rates.

e. Balances become negative during remainder of the projection period.

SOURCE: 1982 Annual Report of the Board of Trustees, Federal Old Age and Survivors Insurance and Disability Insurance Trust Funds; based on Alternative II-B assumptions.

the long-run average yearly deficit in OASDI of 1.82 percent of taxable payroll would be equivalent in 1982 to an annual deficit of about $25 billion.

Estimates of long-run Social Security costs and revenues are generally expressed as a percentage of taxable payroll rather than as dollar amounts because wages and prices are expected to grow at different rates over time, and it is therefore difficult to assess the meaning of estimates given in terms of future dollars. Taxable payroll provides a useful standard of comparison for long-run costs and revenues, since it is the basis on which revenues are calculated. Social Security revenues can be estimated simply by multiplying taxable payroll by the combined payroll tax rate, since payroll tax receipts account for almost all trust fund revenues.[3] If long-run costs (that is, benefit payments) are also expressed as a proportion of taxable payroll, they can be compared directly with tax rates, to get an estimate of the surplus or deficit in any given time period.

In considering these estimates, it may be helpful to remember that, in 1982, 1 percent of taxable payroll equals almost $14 billion. Thus, for example, a difference between Social Security costs and revenues of 4.43 percent of taxable payroll, as is projected in 2030, would equal about $60 billion if it occurred in 1982.

Several important factors must be considered in assessing the estimates of the magnitude of the long-run financing problems shown in Table 1. For example, although costs are projected to rise faster than revenues, they are not projected to rise as much relative to the gross national product (GNP). Over the next 20 years, total costs will actually decline relative to GNP, from about 5 percent now to less than 4.4 percent in 2005. They will then start to rise, reaching a peak of just over 6 percent of GNP in 2030 (see Table 2). Even if benefits are maintained at current law levels, therefore, the tax rates necessary to pay for them may not increase in proportion to the increase in the population who will be beneficiaries if the economy grows as projected over this period.

Because payroll tax revenues are not projected to increase as fast as GNP, however, the trust fund deficit will grow faster than outlays as a proportion of GNP, and will peak in 2035 at about 1.64 percent of GNP. In part, this growth in the deficit relative to GNP is attributable to the assumption that untaxed fringe benefits such as employer-provided pensions and health insurance will continue to grow as a proportion of employees' total compensation, so tax receipts will be based on a declining proportion of employees' total compensation. If the proportion of total compensation provided as fringe benefits grows more slowly than projected, however, the trust fund deficit will be smaller.

---

[3]In addition to payroll taxes, the OASDI trust funds also receive interest on their reserves, and a very small amount of income from general revenues that is used to pay for special benefits not funded through the payroll tax.

TABLE 2   OASDI Tax Revenues and Costs in Relation to Gross National Product, Selected Years 1985–2060

Year	As a Percentage of GNP		
	Tax Revenues	Costs	Difference[a]
1985	4.92	5.05	−0.13
1990	5.27	4.94	0.33
1995	5.17	4.76	0.41
2000	5.03	4.48	0.55
2005	4.95	4.36	0.59
2010	4.85	4.51	0.34
2015	4.76	4.92	−0.16
2020	4.66	5.44	−0.78
2025	4.58	5.90	−1.32
2030	4.49	6.10	−1.61
2035	4.41	6.05	−1.64
2040	4.33	5.86	−1.53
2045	4.24	5.70	−1.46
2050	4.17	5.62	−1.45
2055	4.09	5.54	−1.45
2060	4.01	5.44	−1.43

a. Negative numbers indicate a deficit.

SOURCE: Congressional Budget Office. Calculations based on Alternative II-B assumptions, 1982 OASDI Trustees' Report.

Both because the projected trust fund deficit is small, on average, relative to GNP, and because its size varies significantly over time, some analysts argue that action in the near future to resolve the long-run problem would be premature. As Table 1 shows, the problem is much larger after 2025 than before. Over the next 25 years, an average yearly surplus of 0.64 percent of payroll is projected for the OASDI trust funds under the Alternative II-B assumptions, and trust fund balances do not actually start to decline until about 2015. Moreover, any set of 75-year projections of economic behavior is subject to a wide range of error, so that the projected problems may never materialize.

On the other hand, projections of the long-run financial status of the trust funds are quite sensitive to the economic and demographic assumptions upon which they are based, and the risks associated with worse-than-expected economic and demographic conditions could be quite large. The 1982 Trustees' Report employs a range of economic and demographic assumptions to prepare estimates of long-run costs and revenues. Only under the most optimistic of these, known as Alternative I, is there no long-run deficit in the OASDI funds. Alternative I assumes, for example, that the rate of growth in real wages rises to 3 percent per year by 1987, and then levels off at 2.5 percent per year by 1992. This implies a faster rate of growth in wages than has been sustained for any period of time over the last 25 years. In contrast, under alternative III, the most pessimistic of the alternatives, the 75-year deficit in the OASDI trust funds is projected to average 6.47 percent of payroll per year—a percentage that would be equivalent to almost $90 billion in 1982. Also, under this alternative, an average yearly deficit of 0.72 percent of payroll in OASDI is projected even over the next 25 years. Alternative III assumes that prices continue to grow faster than wages until 1985, and that after 1985 real wages grow at a slowly increasing rate, leveling off at 1 percent per year in 1992 and later.[4]

Thus, while the financing problems of the trust funds may be much less than is now feared if the economy performs well, if the birth rate is high, and if mortality rates do not decline as sharply as expected, they could also be much worse if the opposite occurs. Given the high degree of uncertainty concerning the Social Security system's long-term financial well-being, it may be desirable to consider options to increase long-run balances in the near future, both to guarantee an adequate phase-in period and to restore public confidence in the system. Should the financial position of the trust funds turn out to be much better than anticipated, future benefits could be increased or taxes reduced.

The appropriate set of options for consideration depends to some extent on one's view of the long-run operation and purposes of the system. Before turning to a brief overview of possible types of options and some criteria for choosing among them, therefore, the next section provides some background information on the operation and development of the system.

THE SOCIAL SECURITY PROGRAM:
BACKGROUND INFORMATION

The Social Security system is a set of social insurance programs designed to protect workers and their families against income losses and medical costs associated with old age, disability, and death. Social Security cash benefits are paid to retired and disabled workers who have worked long enough to gain insured status, and to their spouses, children, and survivors. In addition, through the Hospital Insurance and Supplementary Medical Insurance programs, Medicare benefits are

---

[4]For more information on the details of these alternative sets of assumptions, see the 1982 Trustees' Report.

provided to those who are disabled or over the age of 65, and eligible for Social Security cash benefits.[5]

Social Security cash benefits are paid out of two trust funds—the OASI fund and the DI fund—which are both financed through a tax on wages. As discussed earlier, funding is on a pay-as-you-go basis— that is, current benefits are paid out of current tax receipts. Social Security payroll taxes are paid by both employers and employees, on earnings up to the maximum taxable wage, which increases every year to reflect general wage growth. Self-employed workers pay taxes at a rate between the employee rate and the combined employer- employee rate.[6]

Benefits are determined for eligible workers according to a formula based on a measure of lifetime earnings. Benefits for spouses, depen- dents, and survivors depend both on the insured worker's lifetime earnings and on the recipient's relationship to the insured worker. In addition, other factors such as the age of retirement, earnings after retirement, and benefits received by other family members can also affect benefits received.

Although Social Security benefits are based on lifetime earnings in covered employment, workers' benefits are not simply a fixed pro- portion of earnings. In addition to the adjustments for early retirement and for spouses, children, and so forth, mentioned above, the benefit computation formula itself has been designed to provide benefits that are a higher proportion of preretirement earnings for those with low lifetime earnings than for those with higher earnings. This reflects a perception that relatively high replacement rates—that is, benefits as a proportion of preretirement earnings—are necessary for those with relatively low earnings, in order to help provide them with adequate retirement incomes.[7]

Since the inception of the Social Security system, this concern for benefit adequacy has been balanced against a belief that benefits re- ceived should have some relationship to the contributions—that is, tax

---

[5]Disabled workers become eligible for Medicare only after a two-year waiting period.

[6]In 1982, the maximum taxable wage is $32,400, and the combined tax rate for the OASI and DI trust funds is 5.4 percent each for employers and employees. The rate for self-employed workers is 8.05 percent.

[7]Another reason for setting lower replacement rates for high earners is that such workers probably paid relatively high taxes during their working lives, so their bene- fits would be a higher proportion of their after-tax earnings, and their net, or after- tax, replacement rate would be closer to lower-wage earners' than their before-tax rate. In addition, low-wage earners probably benefit less from the tax-exempt status of Social Security.

payments—made by workers. Thus, additional taxable earnings result in benefit entitlements that are higher in absolute terms, but that are a declining proportion of average lifetime earnings. Up to the present, all retirees have had expected lifetime benefits exceeding their contributions; this will not be the case, however, under current projections for some future retirees with high lifetime earnings.

Both coverage and benefit levels have expanded substantially over the years, largely in response to concerns about the adequacy of retirement incomes. The percentage of persons 65 and over receiving Social Security benefits has risen from about 63 percent in 1959 to 91 percent in 1981, and average benefits in real terms have increased by over 60 percent during the same period. . . .[8] At the same time, the proportion of those over 65 in poverty has fallen from about 35 percent to about 15 percent.

Benefits have also increased relative to preretirement earnings, with the largest increases occurring during the early 1970s. The replacement rate for workers retiring at age 65 who always earned the average wage rose from about 35 percent in 1959 to a peak of about 54 percent in 1981, and is now about 49 percent.[9] Replacement rates are higher for those with lower lifetime earnings, and lower for those with higher lifetime earnings.

Much of the increase in benefits during the 1970s was due to a technical flaw in the indexing method contained in the 1972 Social Security amendments. This flaw caused benefits to rise faster than prices, and although it was corrected in the 1977 amendments, all those who were eligible for benefits in 1972 through 1979 now have higher benefit levels than they would have received in the absence of this flaw. Under the 1977 amendments, replacement rates will continue to fall until 1990, when they will stabilize at about 42 percent for an average wage earner retiring at 65.

As discussed earlier, funding is not projected to be available to pay for benefits at the levels scheduled under current law after about 2025. The next section briefly describes the basic approaches available for improving the long-run financial outlook for the trust funds, and discuss possible criteria for choosing among them.

---

[8]Calculation based on average retired-worker benefits.

[9]Because of differences in the treatment of workers born in different years that have resulted from the transitional benefit guarantees enacted in the 1977 Social Security amendments, a 62-year-old worker retiring in 1982 who had always earned the average wage would have a replacement rate (before adjusting for early retirement) of about 43 percent. . . .

POLICY OPTIONS: AN OVERVIEW

The financial status of the trust funds could be improved in two major ways over the long run: either benefits could be reduced relative to current law, or revenues could be increased. Each of these approaches could be implemented in a number of different ways, however. Nor are these approaches necessarily mutually exclusive—it would certainly be possible to design options that included both benefit reductions and tax increases.

Some important considerations apply to the assessment of either type of approach. These include the magnitude and timing of the impacts of each option, and its effects on different groups of workers and beneficiaries. Options that are similar or complementary in terms of the size and timing of their effects may have quite different impacts on those in different population groups. Some criteria with which options could be assessed include:

- Effects on the adequacy of beneficiaries' incomes, both now and in the future;

- Effects on rates of return on contributions—that is, total expected benefits relative to total contributions—for beneficiaries at different earnings levels and in different generations; and

- Focus of the effects—that is, the extent to which they have large impacts on a few persons or small impacts on many.

The first two of these criteria reflect the system's longstanding goals of maintaining benefit adequacy for low-income retirees, while providing a fair return on taxes paid by those with higher incomes. Most options involve some trade-offs between these goals. Under current law, workers with high earnings receive lower rates of return on their contributions than do those with low earnings.[10] If benefit reductions are focused on those with high earnings, this discrepancy will be increased. Reductions affecting beneficiaries with low lifetime earnings, however, may reduce benefit adequacy and increase poverty rates among the old.

The trade-off between benefit adequacy and the provision of a fair rate of return for all workers also occurs across generations of retirees.

---

[10]In assessing rate-of-return computations, it should be noted that most such computations are based on pretax income and do not include the advantages accruing to high-income beneficiaries from the tax-exempt status of Social Security benefits. In addition, allowance is rarely made for the insurance value of the benefit-indexing provisions.

Those who are not retired or who will retire in the near future will receive very high rates of return on their Social Security contributions, as compared with those in future generations. On the other hand, real wages, and therefore real benefits, are expected to grow over time, as are benefits from private pension plans, so future generations of retirees may have more resources available to them than do current retirees.

Finally, options could also be judged on the relative magnitude of their impacts for those they do affect. Those that affect a small number of people a great deal may cause greater hardships than those that have a relatively small impact on a large number of people.

The remainder of this paper examines specific options for improving trust fund balances, and assesses them against these broad criteria. These specific options include both benefit reductions and revenue increases. A brief overview of the advantages and drawbacks of each of these major approaches is given below.

Benefit Reductions

Major approaches to reducing benefits over the long run include changing the benefit computation formula and increasing the age of retirement.[11] The primary arguments in favor of such cuts are that real benefit levels and retirement incomes from other sources such as pensions are expected to grow over time, so future benefits could be reduced without reducing most retirees' standard of living, relative to the present. In other words, if retirees' incomes grow, benefit levels could be reduced without threatening their adequacy for most recipients.

On the other hand, sources of retirement income other than benefits are not evenly distributed across beneficiaries, and are not generally indexed, so benefit reductions could increase poverty among the elderly, especially if future periods of high inflation occur. If the cuts were concentrated on those with higher benefits, the threat to benefit adequacy would be reduced, but rates of return on contributions could fall to very low levels for some high earners. If incomes grow, cuts affecting primarily those retiring several decades from now would also pose less of a threat to benefit adequacy than cuts implemented now. Rates of return for future retirees will be low even under current law relative to those now received, however, and such options would reduce them further.

---

[11]. . . Although some do not regard increasing the age of retirement as a benefit cut, such an option would reduce lifetime benefits for all workers, and could be designed to have exactly the same effects on replacement rates at various ages as a formula change with comparable savings.

Finally, some options, such as changing the benefit computation formula, would affect all new retirees, while others, such as increasing the penalty for retiring early, would primarily affect certain smaller groups of retirees.

Revenue Increases

The financial outlook for the trust funds could also be improved by increasing revenues. This could be done either by increasing payroll taxes or by allocating revenue to the trust funds from some new source, such as income taxes on benefits. Most options to increase revenues would primarily affect workers, who in general have higher incomes than beneficiaries.[12] In addition, since at any time there are more workers than beneficiaries, a payroll tax increase of a given magnitude would affect workers' incomes less than a benefit cut with the same effect on the trust fund would affect beneficiaries' incomes.

On the other hand, a tax increase affecting workers would reduce workers' returns on contributions, and rates of return are already expected to fall over time as the system matures. If implemented in the near future, such a tax increase would further increase the burden on current workers relative to current retirees. In addition, increases on taxes affecting wages might also reduce work incentives, which could cause workers to work fewer hours and to retire earlier. If this occurred, additional revenues resulting from this approach could be significantly reduced.

Another type of option to increase trust fund revenues would be to transfer funds from general tax revenues, or to allow the trust funds to borrow from general funds. With given targets for the unified budget deficit, however, this option would require either reduced spending in other areas of the budget or increases in other taxes, as compared to other measures to improve trust fund balances.

Stabilization Measures

In addition to the problems associated with the projected long-run deficit, the trust funds could also face some temporary financing problems in future periods of poor economic performance. Even with benefit cuts or increases in revenues as compared with current law, Social Security reserves are likely to be low over the next 15 years, and may be low at other points in the future. Under these circumstances, as

---

[12]An exception would be taxing Social Security benefits. This would be comparable in its effects to a benefit cut focused on higher-income beneficiaries.

recent experience has shown, cyclical downturns in the economy can place severe strains on the funds. Thus, in addition to benefit reductions and tax increases aimed at improving average trust fund balances over the long run, this paper also presents several options that would stabilize trust fund balances by preventing large fluctuations in periods when the economy performed poorly.

There are two major approaches to this problem: either benefits could be linked more closely to wages, so that they would grow more slowly in periods of slow wage growth, or additional revenues could be provided to the trust funds in periods of high unemployment or rapid increases in prices relative to wages. In general, options of the first type would protect the trust funds, but could result in reductions in the purchasing power of benefits during economic downturns. Options of the second type would maintain benefit levels but would require additional taxes or spending reductions in other areas, if targets for the unified budget deficit are to be maintained.

Article 17

FAMILY MEDICAL EXPENSES IN A SINGLE YEAR

Congressional Budget Office

In any given year, a sizable number of families have medical expenses many times as great as those of the average family. The frequency and characteristics of these high-cost cases have important implications for health-care policy.

Importance for Policy

The importance of high-cost illness for policy stems in large part from the substantial portion of total medical expenses attributable to it. Because their medical expenses are atypically large, high-cost families contribute disproportionately to the total. Accordingly, high-cost illness is a major factor to consider in assessing both the problem of high national expenditures for medical care and the equity and efficiency with which health-care resources are allocated. For example, some would argue for directing additional resources into high-cost care for the seriously ill, while others would prefer to see a larger proportion of health-care resources devoted to lower-cost routine and preventive services. In either case, the costs currently associated with high-cost illness and the proportion of families affected by it are critical information.

The issue of high-cost illness arises frequently in the context of private or public efforts to insure individuals and families against the resulting financial burden. Among private employment-related insurance plans, reimbursement for large annual covered expenses is typically quite thorough and has been becoming more so over time.[1] Catastrophic health insurance plans have been enacted by a number of state governments, and a variety of proposals introduced in the Congress would either establish a federal catastrophic health insurance program or mandate that certain employers provide such insurance.

SOURCE: *Catastrophic Medical Expenses: Patterns in the Non-Elderly, Non-Poor Population,* Washington, DC: The Congress of the United States the Congressional Budget Office, December, 1982.
[1]See Congressional Budget Office, *Protection from Catastrophic Medical Expenses.*

Major Findings

The major findings of this chapter are the following:

• In the non-elderly, non-poor population, families exceeding the four catastrophic thresholds analyzed ($3,000, $5,000, $10,000, and $20,000) in any one year are relatively rare, but they account for a sizable proportion of total medical expenses. For example, about 5 percent of all families exceed $5,000 in expenses, but they account for about half of total expenses. (As explained, however, the proportion of families who exceed a catastrophic threshold at least once during a several-year period is far larger.)

• The expenses of these high-cost families tend to be concentrated in one family member, and this concentration becomes more pronounced when higher thresholds are used. In nearly three-fourths of families with expenses over $20,000, 95 percent or more of family medical expenses are attributable to one family member.

• The proportion of expenses attributable to inpatient charges is in general large among high-cost families and increases when higher thresholds are used.

Plan of the Chapter

This chapter begins with a detailed look at the national distribution of medical expenses. A subsequent section explores the role of individual family members in high-cost illness. . . .

THE NATIONAL DISTRIBUTION OF EXPENSES

The general shape of the distribution of medical expenses is that most families cluster at low levels of expense, with a long, thin "tail" of families stretching out to very high levels of expense. This is referred to as a "skewed" distribution: the low-expense end of the distribution is short and compact, while the high-expense end is long and thin. Figure 1 shows the skewed distribution of expenses graphically.[2]

---

[2]The distribution of medical expenses discussed in this chapter and displayed, for example, in Figure 1 and Table 1, are based on 1978 experience, projected forward such that the average expense is equal to the projected average expense in 1982. This method may slightly underestimate the proportion of families at very high levels of expense, because that proportion rose between 1974 and 1978 and might have continued growing between 1978 and 1982. The extent of the underestimation, however, is likely to be very small, and it would primarily affect only families with expenses above $20,000 per year. For example, the proportion of families exceeding $20,000 in

FIGURE 1   Distribution of Family Medical Expenses: Percent of Families with Annual Expenses in Given Intervals

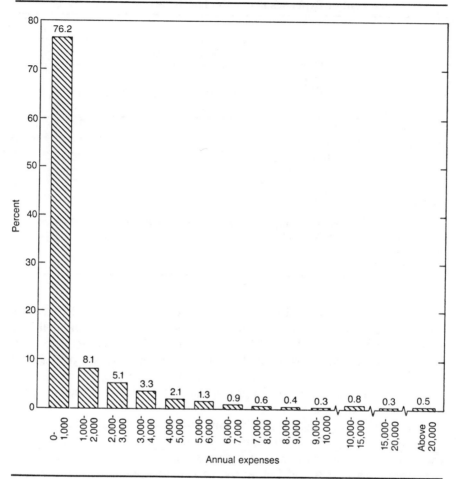

Another way to show the extreme "skewness" of medical expenses is to look at the percent of families exceeding certain annual levels of expense in any one year (see Table 1). Only 5 percent of all families exceed $5,000; 2 percent exceed $10,000, and 0.5 percent exceed $20,000.

The relatively few families with high expenses in a single year necessarily contribute disproportionately to total medical expenses (see

Table 1 is 0.5 percent. If underestimation is present, the correct figure most likely would be about six-tenths of one percent. Such a bias would not materially affect conclusions presented here.

TABLE 1   Percent of Families Exceeding Various Levels of Annual Expense, Percent of Total Medical Expenditures Attributable to Them, and Percent of Expenses above the Levels

Level of Expense	Percent of Families Exceeding Level	Expenses of Families Exceeding Levels, as Percent of Expenses of All Families	
		Total Expenses of Families Exceeding Level	Only Expenses Above Level[a]
1,130[b]	23	c	c
3,000	11	68	40
5,000	5	50	26
10,000	2	28	13
20,000	0.5	14	5
30,000	0.2	c	c

a. Includes all families exceeding the levels, but excludes the portion of their expenses that falls below the level.
b. Average annual expense.
c. Not estimated.

Table 1). This disproportion is more marked when higher thresholds are used, but even in the case of the lowest thresholds, it is striking. The 11 percent of families with expenses over $3,000 contribute fully two-thirds of all expenses, while the 5 percent with expenses over $5,000 account for half of all expenses. Families exceeding $20,000 in a single year comprise only about half a percent of all families, but they account for 14 percent of all expenses.

Another way of assessing the importance of high-cost illness is to consider only expenses in excess of a given threshold. That is, rather than considering all expenses of high-cost families—which include their expenses both above and below the threshold—one can tabulate only their expenses after they reach the threshold. Viewed this way, the disproportionate role of high-cost illness is necessarily smaller but is nonetheless still striking (see Table 1). For example, although 2 percent of all families exceed $10,000 per year, expenses in excess of $10,000 per year account for 13 percent of total medical expenditures. Similarly, even though families exceeding $20,000 comprise only 0.5 percent of all families, expenses in excess of $20,000 contribute 5 percent of all expenditures.

Inpatient expenses comprise a larger share of annual expenses in high-cost families than in the average family. Averaged across all families, about 75 percent of claims expenses were accounted for by inpatient charges. Among families exceeding a $3,000 threshold, this proportion was about 89 percent. Among families exceeding $20,000, inpatient charges accounted for 93 percent of total expenses. These proportions remained largely unchanged over the five years covered by the study.

THE ROLE OF INDIVIDUAL FAMILY MEMBERS IN HIGH-COST ILLNESS

To what extent are large family medical expenses attributable to a single family member? This question has important implications for plans to insure families against the expense of catastrophic illness, because eligibility for reimbursement could be based on either individuals' or families' expenses. This section examines the proportion of annual expenses attributable to a single family member and the number of high-cost individuals in high-cost families. . . .

The major findings of these analyses are the following:

- The bulk of the expenses incurred by high-cost families are attributable to one family member, and this pattern becomes more pronounced when higher thresholds are used.

- Most high-cost families include one, and only one, individual whose expenses taken alone exceed the threshold. This pattern is also more pronounced when higher thresholds are used.

The Proportion of Expenses Attributable to a Single Family Member

Family medical expenses are typically concentrated in an individual family member, and this concentration is more pronounced among families with high annual expenses. For example, in about three-fourths of all families filing claims,[3] one individual accounts for at least 75 percent of claimed expenses, and in more than half of all families filing claims, one individual accounts for 95 percent or more of the family's total (see Table 2). Among families exceeding $20,000 in expenses, the degree of concentration is substantially greater. In 92 percent of such families, one individual accounts for at least 75 percent of expenses, and in nearly three-fourths of such families, one individual accounts for at least 95 percent of expenses.[4]

---

[3]This excludes both families with no covered expenses and families that chose not to file claims because their expenses were small. The excluded families comprise about 34 percent of the sample.

[4]These percentages include single-person families, in which all expenses are necessarily attributable to one person. Deleting all single-person families, however, has little effect on the percentages in Table 4, particularly when high thresholds are used.

TABLE 2   Percent of Families in Which One Individual Accounts for More than Specified Percentages of Total Family Expenses, by Level of Expense

Percent of Expenses Attributable to One Family Member	All Families Filing Claims[a]	Families With Annual Expenses Exceeding			
		$3,000	$5,000	$10,000	$20,000
75 or more	75	77	77	82	92
80 or more	71	73	73	79	89
85 or more	67	68	68	74	85
90 or more	62	61	62	69	78
95 or more	56	51	53	62	71

a. Excludes the approximately 34 percent of families that had no expenses or chose not to file claims because their expenses were small.

The Number of High-Cost Individuals in High-Cost Families

Another way of looking at the role of individuals in high-cost illness is to calculate the number of high-cost individuals (that is, individuals exceeding catastrophic thresholds) within high-cost families. This can be done by separating the families that exceed a given threshold into categories: those in which no single family member alone exceeds the threshold, those in which only one family member exceeds the threshold, and those in which two or more family members exceed the threshold.

A sizable portion of high-cost families (from 15 to 21 percent, depending on the threshold), have no single family member whose expenses taken alone exceed the relevant threshold (see Table 3). These are the families that would be classified as high-cost cases under a family threshold, but not if the same dollar threshold was applied to the expenses of individuals.

The majority of high-cost families include only one family member whose expenses taken alone exceed the threshold. When the lower two thresholds are used, about three-fourths of high-cost families include only one high-cost individual. This proportion increases if higher thresholds are used, and with a $20,000 threshold, about 85 percent of high-cost families include only one high-cost individual.

Few high-cost families include two or more individuals who alone exceed the threshold, particularly when high thresholds are used. Using a $3,000 threshold, about 4 percent of all high-cost families include

TABLE 3   Percent of High-Expense Families with Zero, One, or Two or More Individuals Exceeding Individual Thresholds, by Threshold

| *Percent of Families* | *Threshold* | | | |
Exceeding Threshold With:	*$3,000*	*$5,000*	*$10,000*	*$20,000*
No Single Family Member Exceeding Threshold	17	21	18	15
One Family Member Exceeding Threshold	79	77	81	85
Two or More Family Members Exceeding Threshold	4	2	1	a

a. No reliable estimate available. This occurred in only one instance in the 1978 sample used here, corresponding (when weighted) to less than 0.02 percent of the families exceeding $20,000 in that year.

two or more high-cost individuals (see Table 3). This drops to 1 percent with a $10,000 threshold and to nearly zero with a $20,000 threshold.[5] In some cases, it is simply coincidence that two individuals in the same family exceed a threshold in the same year, but in other instances their illnesses are clearly related.[6]

---

[5]Only one family of the 126,590 for whom 1978 data were used included two or more individuals who exceeded $20,000 in that year.

It is possible that families with two or more high-cost individuals are somewhat underrepresented in these data. Extremely serious automobile accidents could lead to expenses over the threshold for each of several family members. Some portion of expenses stemming from such accidents would be reimbursed by automobile insurance policies rather than by Blue Cross. This should be a minor problem, however, because these data should include all related expenses if Blue Cross reimbursed even a small fraction of them. Only cases where the automobile policy paid the expenses in full should be omitted from these data.

[6]Maternity is one context in which two high-cost illnesses can be clearly related. A seriously ill newborn can generate large expenses in a short time, because charges for neonatal intensive care are typically high. Likewise, if delivery is complicated, the mother's expenses can mount rapidly. For example, in one case in the data used here, a newborn placed in intensive care accrued expenses of $10,400 in the first 11 days of life. The mother, who delivered by cesarean section, accrued expenses of $5,000 for delivery and related expenses. (Prenatal care and delivery are often billed together as a single charge at the time of delivery, and in this instance they clearly were.) Apart from that 11-day period, however, the family's total claims for the year amounted to less than $100.

Article 18

WORKFARE—INTRODUCTION

Congressional Budget Office

Work-related programs for recipients of public assistance—including job search assistance, training and education, and unpaid work experience (known as workfare)—have received considerable attention in recent years. Partly as a result of legislation enacted by the Congress in 1981 and 1982, many states have implemented programs to help welfare recipients attain the skills and work experience they need to become self-sufficient. The President, in his 1986 State of the Union Address, declared that the "success of welfare should be judged by how many of its recipients become independent of welfare" and called for the development of new approaches to achieve this objective. During the 99th Congress, several bills were introduced, and the topic is being addressed by various committees in the 100th Congress as well.

This report examines the issues surrounding the design, implementation, and evaluation of programs to provide work-related aid to recipients of public assistance, with an emphasis on federal programs for recipients of Aid to Families with Dependent Children (AFDC). As background, this chapter provides an overview of the AFDC program, the characteristics of AFDC recipients, and the history and goals of work-related programs for welfare recipients. Later chapters review current programs and evidence regarding their effectiveness, and examine a range of federal policy options.

BACKGROUND

Requirements and expectations regarding work by recipients of public assistance have changed substantially during the history of such programs. When AFDC—the major source of government cash assistance to low-income children and their families—was created a half-century ago, recipients were neither required nor expected to seek work outside the home. More recently, however, much attention has been focused on how to help recipients become self-sufficient through unsubsidized employment.

SOURCE: *Work-Related Programs for Welfare Recipients,* Washington, DC: The Congress of the United States The Congressional Budget Office, April 1987.

The AFDC Program in Brief

The program now known as Aid to Families with Dependent Children was established by Title IV of the Social Security Act of 1935. It authorized matching grants to states to help them provide financial assistance to needy children in families in which a parent had died, was absent from the home, or was incapacitated.[1]

Under current law, each state determines its own program eligibility criteria and benefit levels, subject to a number of federal requirements. In general, AFDC benefits are available to single-parent families with children under 18 years of age and with incomes and assets that are below specified amounts. States are permitted to extend eligibility until a child's nineteenth birthday if the child is a full-time student in a secondary or technical school. Since 1961, states also have been allowed to provide benefits to families in which both parents are present if certain conditions are met, one being that the principal earner is unemployed or works fewer than 100 yours a month. About half of the states have taken up this unemployed parent option (known today as AFDC-UP). AFDC-UP families account for less than one-tenth of all AFDC families and outlays.

Unless exempt, able-bodied recipients age 16 and over must register for work and training as a condition of eligibility. Every state operates a Work Incentive Program (WIN) that is used, in part, to enforce this requirement.[2] The most common reason for exempting adults is that they are caring for children under six years of age.[3] Children who are full-time students in secondary or vocational school are also exempt. If recipients fail to register for, or refuse without good cause to participate in, work-related activities to which they have been assigned by the welfare agency, they can lose some or all of their benefits.[4]

Each state establishes a standard of need and determines what percentage of this standard AFDC will provide for a family. Within

---

[1]The program was called Aid to Dependent Children (ADC) until 1962. Two-parent families in which one parent is incapacitated are treated as one-parent families in this report.

[2]States are permitted to operate alternative WIN Demonstration programs, as well as other work-related programs to which AFDC recipients and applicants may be assigned.

[3]States may request temporary waivers from the Secretary of Health and Human Services to enable them to require mothers of children under age six to fulfill work requirements.

[4]The principal earner in an AFDC-UP family must comply with this requirement or benefits for the entire family can be lost. If a single parent in other AFDC families fails to comply, the parent may lose his or her benefits, and payments on behalf of the children may be made to a third party instead of to the parent.

each jurisdiction, a family's monthly benefit level is determined primarily by family size and the amount and sources of other income. For example, in January 1987 the median state had a need standard of $428, and a maximum AFDC grant of $354, for a one-parent family of three.[5] In addition, receipt of AFDC benefits automatically establishes eligibility for Medicaid, the major federal/state program that provides health benefits for some low-income people.

Federal law requires states to disregard certain earned income in determining the amount of a family's benefits and prohibits states from paying AFDC benefits to a family whose total income exceeds 185 percent of its standard of need. Amounts ordinarily not counted as income during each of the first four months of a recipient's job include the first $105 of the individual's earnings, child care expenses of up to $160 a month per child, and one-third of the remaining earnings. After four months, the one-third "disregard" cannot be used. After 12 months, the initial disregard of $105 is lowered to $75. States are required to retain families on Medicaid for at least four months after they become ineligible for AFDC, if the reason for ineligibility is increased earnings.[6]

One result of these rules is that a recipient who takes a job would not have to earn very much before she (or he) would lose AFDC benefits entirely, particularly if she is in a state with low benefits. For example, for a mother in the median state with two children and no child care deductions, the breakeven point—that is, the amount of monthly earnings that would raise her countable income to the level at which she would no longer receive AFDC payments—is about $640 during the first four months, $460 during the next eight months, and $430 thereafter.[7] A person working full time in a job paying about $3.70 an hour would earn $640.

---

[5]In most jurisdictions, AFDC benefits, together with food stamps, provide families with incomes well below the poverty threshold. For example, the maximum AFDC benefit, combined with food stamps, in the median state for a family of three would equal about three-quarters of the 1986 poverty threshold for a family of this size. House Committee on Ways and Means, *Background Material and Data on Programs Within the Jurisdiction of the Committee on Ways and Means*, WMCP: 100–4, 100:1 (March 6, 1987), p. 407. The assumed amount of food stamps is based on the maximum food stamp allotment in most states of $214 for a family of three, after adjustments for receipt of AFDC benefits and for allowable deductions.

[6]States are required to continue Medicaid eligibility for nine months if loss of AFDC is the result of removing the one-third disregard. At their option, states may continue Medicaid coverage for these families for an additional six months. In addition, three-quarters of the states extend Medicaid coverage to "medically needy" families with dependent children. Under this option, families whose incomes—net of incurred medical expenses—are below a state's need standard are covered, even though they are not receiving AFDC.

[7]Child care expenses, up to the allowable limit of $160 per child, would raise the breakeven point on a dollar-for-dollar basis. The rules for disregarding certain earn-

AFDC benefits totaled an estimated $15.8 billion in fiscal year 1986, of which the federal government paid $8.5 billion. The federal share of the funding averaged about 54 percent for the nation as a whole and varied between a floor of 50 percent and about 78 percent, depending on each state's per capita income. The federal government also pays 50 percent of the costs of administering the program in every state, including the costs of certain work-related activities.[8] Combined federal and state administrative costs amounted to an estimated $2 billion in 1986.

Profile of AFDC Recipients

In an average month in 1986, 11 million people in 3.7 million families were estimated to be receiving AFDC benefits. The average monthly payment was $120 per person, or $352 per family. Two-thirds of the recipients were children; the rest were their mothers or other caretaker relatives. In most cases, the child's father was absent from the home.[9]

Large numbers of families move onto and off AFDC each year, even though the average monthly number of families receiving AFDC has not fluctuated very much during the past decade.[10] For some families, AFDC provides short-term assistance during a crisis; for others, it provides long-term aid. Much attention has been focused on identifying which recipients are most likely to be in the latter group.

Data from a sample of AFDC administrative records in 1985 provide a profile of mothers receiving AFDC and their families (see Table 1). The typical case consisted of a mother in her twenties, with one or two minor children (see the first column). About 60 percent of the mothers had at least one child under the age of six. Only 30 percent had to comply with WIN registration requirements; the remainder were exempted mainly because they were caring for young children (although some chose to register anyway).

Of the 3.3 million recipients in fiscal year 1985 represented in this sample, about 30 percent had been receiving AFDC for one year or less (see the second column), although some may also have received benefits in earlier periods. Another 30 percent had been receiving AFDC for

---

ings, and the changes that were made to them in 1967, 1981, and 1984, are described in "Costs and Effects of Expanding AFDC," Part III of House Committee on Ways and Means, *Children in Poverty*, WMCP: 99–8, 99:1 (May 22, 1985), pp. 414–417.

[8]Although the federal government reimburses states for half of most covered administrative costs, it provides 90 percent of certain costs for automated data processing.

[9]House Committee on Ways and Means, *Background Material* (1987), p. 429.

[10]Ibid. Between 1976 and 1980, the average monthly number of families on AFDC remained between 3.5 million and 3.6 million. It rose to 3.9 million families in 1981 and then decreased to 3.6 million in the following year. Since then, it has stayed between 3.6 million and 3.7 million families.

TABLE 1 Characteristics of Mothers Receiving AFDC in Fiscal Year 1985, by Time Since Case Was Opened (in percent)

Characteristic	Total	Months Since Case Was Opened		
		12 or Fewer	13 to 36	Over 36
Average Number of AFDC Mothers				
In thousands	3,310ª	990	980	1,340
As a percent of total	100	30	30	40
Current Age				
Under 20	6	13	7	1
20–21	9	12	13	4
22–30	45	45	47	44
Over 30	40	30	33	52
Age of Youngest Child				
Under 3	38	51	48	22
3–5	24	20	23	28
Over 5	38	29	29	50
Number of Children				
One	42	51	45	32
Two	31	29	31	34
Three	17	13	15	20
Four or more	10	7	9	14
Registration in Work Incentive Program				
Mandatory	30	24	25	38
Voluntary	3	3	3	3
Nonregistrant	67	73	72	59

a. Excludes 74,000 mothers for whom the number of months since case was opened is not available.

Note: These data may include a small number of adult women who receive AFDC and are the caretakers of the children, but are not their mothers.

SOURCE: Congressional Budget Office tabulations of information from the AFDC quality control case sample for 1985.

13 to 36 months, and the remaining 40 percent, for more than three years.

The "new" recipients were, not surprisingly, younger on average than the recipients already on the rolls, had fewer and younger children, and were less likely to be required to register with WIN (see the second column). For example, 25 percent of the new recipients were under age 22, compared with just 15 percent of all recipients.

The number of months since a case was opened, however, can seriously understate the extent to which mothers are dependent on AFDC for many years. These administrative statistics depict spells of receiving AFDC that are still in progress, not ones that have ended, so they cannot indicate total durations. Further, because previous and future spells are not included in the data, it is impossible to determine the extent to which these recipients were dependent up to the time of their current spell and the extent to which they may become dependent again in subsequent years. Thus, even though only about 40 percent of the recipients had been receiving AFDC for three years or more, the percentage who were or will be dependent for this length of time is much higher.

Data from the Panel Study of Income Dynamics (PSID), a nationwide survey that has tracked the experiences of members of about 5,000 households for over 15 years, provide important insights about long-term receipt of AFDC. An analysis of the PSID data for the years 1968 through 1982, conducted by David Ellwood, indicates that, of all mothers on AFDC for the first time, about half receive benefits for at least five years and about one-quarter do so for a total of nine years or more, though not necessarily in one continuous spell.[11] Precisely because the latter group receives payments for so many years, it accounts for the majority of the women receiving AFDC at any point in time and is the most costly group.

Further analysis by Ellwood suggests some of the characteristics of new recipients that are related to long-term receipt of AFDC, although the estimates are subject to a number of uncertainties.[12] In particular, he estimated that women who were young, who had young children, who were single when starting to receive benefits, or who had not worked recently before first going onto AFDC would be more likely to continue in the program for many years than other women

---

[11]David T. Ellwood, "Targeting 'Would-Be' Long-Term Recipients of AFDC" (Mathematica Policy Research, Inc., Princeton, N.J., January 1986).

[12]Several limitations of the data should be kept in mind. First, the data were collected over a 15-year period ending in 1982 and therefore mostly reflect the AFDC system as it was before major changes in the rules for disregarding certain earnings were made in 1981. Second, the number of AFDC recipients in the sample is small and may not be representative of the national AFDC population. Ellwood's results were based on analysis of only about 500 spells of receipt of AFDC during the 15-year period. AFDC mothers who did not head their own households—including young AFDC mothers living in their parents' home—and households that could not be found or refused to be interviewed were not included. Third, duration of the spells is measured by the number of years in which payments were received, even if only for part of a year. Therefore, estimates of movements on and off AFDC based on the PSID do not correspond to administrative data, which provide monthly information.

(see Figure 1). For example, women who had not worked during the two years before initially receiving AFDC were predicted to receive benefits, on average, for eight years, though not necessarily in a continuous spell. Women who had recent work experience, in contrast, were predicted to continue for six and a half years.

Work and Welfare

Perspectives on the proper relationship between work and welfare have changed substantially over time. Title IV of the Social Security Act of 1935 contained no mention of work. A premise of the original Aid to Dependent Children program was that the well-being of children raised in fatherless homes was closely linked to their mothers' not having to work outside the home. The Report of the Committee on Economic Security, submitted to President Roosevelt in 1935, spoke of

> . . .aid to release from the wage-earning role the person whose natural function is to give her children the physical and affectionate

FIGURE 1   Estimated Number of Years of AFDC Receipt, by Characteristics of Mother at Time of First Payment

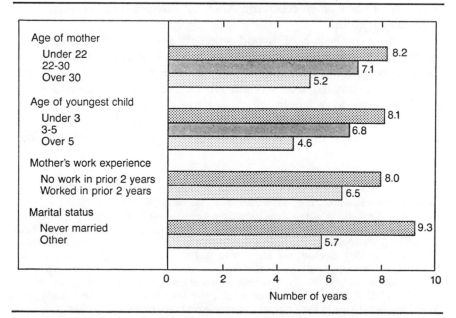

SOURCE: Congressional Budget Office using estimates from David T. Ellwood, "Targeting 'Would-be' Long-Term Recipients of AFDC" (Mathematica Policy Research, Inc., Princeton, N.J., January 1986) p. 42. Ellwood's estimates are based on analysis of the Panel Study of Income Dynamics, 1968–1982.

guardianship necessary not alone to keep them from falling into social misfortune, but more affirmatively to rear them into citizens capable of contributing to society.[13]

Three decades later, however, the Congress established the Work Incentive Program (Public Law 90-248) to foster

> . . .a sense of dignity, self-worth, and confidence which will flow from being recognized as a wage-earning member of society and . . . [in the belief that] the example of a working adult in these families will have beneficial effects on the children in such families.

What happened? Several factors may account for the change. One factor was the enactment of the unemployed parent option in 1961, which permitted states to offer benefits to two-parent families in which the principal wage earner was unemployed. The assumption that welfare mothers were needed at home apparently did not extend to the fathers. The inclusion of able-bodied men in the program contributed to an interest in helping recipients prepare for, and find, jobs.

Another factor was the tremendous growth in the number of families receiving AFDC during the 1960s and in the program's cost. Between 1960 and 1970, for example, the number of families receiving AFDC each month almost tripled—from 800,000 to 2.2 million. Total payments increased from about $1 billion to almost $5 billion during that decade (an almost fourfold increase after adjusting for inflation), reflecting increases both in the average value of benefits during this period and in the number of recipients.[14]

The third factor—and perhaps the most germane to the current debate on work and welfare—was the dramatic change in the role of women in American society since the program was originally developed. In 1935, the expectation was that mothers would stay home to rear their children. By the mid-1960s this was no longer the case, at least for mothers of school-age children. For example, as recently as 1948 only 26 percent of married women with children between the ages of 6 and 17, and 11 percent of married women with younger children, were in the paid labor force; by 1965, these rates of participation in the labor force had risen to 43 percent and 23 percent, respectively. During 1985, two-thirds of all mothers of children under age 18 worked for pay sometime during the year; almost half of these women worked

---

[13]Report reprinted in Project on the Federal Social Role, *50th Anniversary Edition, The Report of the Committee on Economic Security of 1935* (Washington, D.C.: National Conference on Social Welfare, 1985), p. 56.

[14]Calculated from Social Security Administration, *Social Security Bulletin, Annual Statistical Supplement, 1984–85*, p. 254, and *Economic Report of the President*, House Doc. No. 99–142, 99:2 (February 1986), p. 315.

year-round full-time.[15] (About 60 percent of mothers with children under age six worked sometime during that year, although only about one-third of these women worked year-round full-time.)

One consequence of the changing role of women is that some non-recipients who are in families in which mothers work outside the home consider it unfair for recipients not to work too, at least on a part-time basis. Another consequence is that paid employment is increasingly seen as a viable option for raising the living standards of recipients.

This changing view about the relationship between work and welfare is reflected in much of the welfare reform debate that has taken place since the 1960s. Should certain recipients be required to participate in work-related programs? How would such a requirement be enforced? What rewards or penalties should be provided to encourage recipients to choose work over welfare? How can a welfare system be designed that simultaneously provides adequate resources for people who cannot work and work incentives for those who can? These questions arose during the debates over the Family Assistance Plan of the Nixon Administration and the Better Jobs and Income Act proposed by the Carter Administration; they are still being discussed today.[16]

GOALS OF WORK-RELATED PROGRAMS FOR RECIPIENTS

The arguments in favor of work/welfare programs reflect several different goals, including:

- Raising the immediate or future living standards of recipients and their families;

---

[15]Congressional Budget Office tabulations of the March 1986 Current Population Survey indicate that about 22 million of the 33 million mothers of children under age 18 worked for pay sometime during 1985. About 15 million of these workers indicated that, when they work, they primarily worked on full-time schedules (that is, at least 35 hours per week). About 10 million reported that they worked at least 50 weeks during 1985 primarily on full-time schedules; this group (almost half of mothers who worked anytime during the year and 30 percent of all mothers) are classified as "year-round full-time workers."

[16]See *Work and Welfare*, prepared by Margaret Malone for the Subcommittee on Employment and Productivity of the Committee on Labor and Human Resources and the Subcommittee on Social Security and Income Maintenance of the Committee on Finance, U.S. Senate, S. Prt. 99–177, 99:2 (August 1986).

Issues concerning the relationships between welfare and work are not confined to the AFDC program. In the Food Stamp program, for example, certain recipients are required to search for work and accept suitable employment. The Food Security Act of 1985 requires all states to implement work-related programs for food stamp recipients in 1987. The Congressional Budget Office is preparing a report on the characteristics of work registrants in the Food Stamp program and on programs to help them become self-sufficient.

- Reducing welfare costs; and
- Requiring recipients to contribute to society in whatever ways they can.

The design of work-related programs for welfare recipients depends, in part, on which goals are emphasized. These goals may also overlap, in that success in achieving one could also help to achieve another. Increasing a recipient's long-term earnings potential, for example, could increase her (or his) future living standard, as well as reduce future welfare costs. Similarly, requiring recipients to participate in work-related activities could encourage more of them to search actively for paid employment, thereby raising their earnings.

Some participants in the work/welfare debate argue that one or more of these goals could be accomplished best by policies other than work-related programs—for example, that living standards could be raised by providing higher benefits or increasing the amount of child support provided by absent fathers, and that dependency could be reduced by tightening eligibility criteria or replacing cash assistance programs with guaranteed jobs. These approaches are beyond the scope of this paper, however, which focuses on options that explicitly involve work-related programs for recipients. Some of these other options— such as establishing nationwide minimum benefits for changing the extent to which benefits are reduced as earnings increase—have been discussed in earlier CBO reports.[17] The remainder of this section reviews these major goals and discusses some of their implications for the design and assessment of work/welfare programs.

Raising Living Standards

People who meet the eligibility criteria for AFDC usually have incomes that provide a low standard of living relative to that of the general population. One major goal of work-related programs for welfare recipients would be to raise the living standards of their families, primarily by increasing their immediate or future earnings. Programs designed with this goal in mind would be akin to many other programs intended to increase the earnings of their participants. For example, for many years the federal government has sponsored job training programs for economically disadvantaged people, including welfare recipients.

Whether increased earnings of recipients would result in higher living standards would depend, however, on the extent to which increased earnings would be offset by reductions in cash welfare and

---

[17]*Welfare Reform: Issues, Objectives, and Approaches* (July 1977); and *Reducing Poverty Among Children* (May 1985).

related benefits or by increases in work-related expenses. Moreover, the increased employment of program participants would not necessarily reflect higher total employment nationwide. One result of a work-related program could be that employers substituted the participants for other workers. On the other hand, even if total employment were not increased, it might be desirable to redistribute job opportunities to AFDC recipients as a means of preventing or ending long-term dependence on welfare.

Reducing Welfare Costs

Another major goal of work-related programs for welfare recipients is to reduce government costs for public assistance. Work/welfare options could achieve this goal by reducing the number of people on welfare or decreasing their monthly benefits.

The mechanisms for reducing government costs could be the same as those for meeting the goal of raising living standards, because one way of cutting welfare costs is to help recipients increase their earnings. Under such a program, however, a participant whose earnings increased might then become ineligible for welfare—a success in terms of this goal, even though the participant's standard of living declined because of lost AFDC and related benefits. The opposite also could occur; for example, the program might help someone who would have gone off welfare anyway attain a higher-paying job than she could have found without the program. In this case, there might be no savings to the government, even though the participant was able to attain a higher standard of living. Another way in which work-related programs might reduce welfare costs is by deterring people from applying for or continuing to receive benefits. In this case, costs would fall without necessarily being accompanied by higher earnings for recipients, whose standards of living would be lower.

Success in achieving this goal can be measured by whether a work-related program reduces outlays for welfare and other benefits such as Medicaid. Another, more demanding standard is whether the program reduces outlays by at least as much as it costs—that is, does the program pay for itself? If welfare costs were cut by less than the cost of the work-related program, then evaluations of the program would focus on whether the other benefits of the program were sufficient to warrant its net cost.

Requiring Recipients to Contribute to Society

A third major goal of work/welfare programs is to help assure that all members of society contribute to it in whatever ways they can. From this perspective, the recipient of welfare benefits has an obligation to do something in return for income support—for example, participate in designated activities such as job search assistance programs, training, or unpaid work. As articulated by the previously cited Committee on Economic Security in 1935, mothers receiving public assistance could best fulfill their obligation to society by raising their children to be useful citizens. Today, some proponents of modifying the AFDC program argue that recipients should be asked or required to do more.

Proponents of enforcing a work-related obligation on recipients offer various rationales for this view, but all conclude that more recipients should be required to participate in work-related programs in order to obtain benefits. Some advocates believe that certain recipients who could get jobs are choosing not to do so. Stricter enforcement of work requirements would, in effect, be a means of policing the welfare system. They argue that the current system provides little, if any, incentive for some recipients to seek paid employment or to acquire job skills, because the rate at which benefits are reduced to offset earnings is very high.[18] Obligating recipients to participate in some kind of activity, even if it does not produce something of value, would provide a means of discouraging individuals from becoming dependent on public assistance.

Others who want to require recipients to contribute to society believe that popular support for AFDC would be greater—and, hence, benefit levels might be raised—if the recipients were seen to be doing something in return. Likewise, "earning" their benefits would give recipients a greater sense of self-worth and would provide a better example for their children.

On the other hand, some advocates of work-related programs for welfare recipients believe it is neither necessary nor desirable to require participation. They argue that most recipients would rather be self-sufficient but lack good opportunities, and that work requirements are demeaning. Instead of requiring participation, they would prefer to develop programs that would be of sufficiently high quality that recipients would volunteer to participate.

COSTS OF WORK-RELATED PROGRAMS

Work-related programs for AFDC recipients cost money to operate, regardless of their goals. Last year, for example, about $200 million was spent on WIN. The enforcement of a work-related obligation involves administrative costs for registering and assessing individuals, keeping

---

[18]In addition to the loss of cash benefits, recipients might be discouraged from actively seeking work by the potential loss of other means-tested benefits such as Medicaid, Food Stamps, and subsidized housing.

track of their activities, and, if necessary, penalizing individuals who do not comply. Job search assistance, training and education, and workfare programs require expenditures for staff to develop and operate the programs. Costs for child care, transportation, and other supportive services for the participants may also be required, depending on the nature of the program and the needs of the participants.

A general issue, then, is whether the benefits of a program (or the expected benefits of a proposed program) are large enough to warrant the costs. This report examines both the extent to which past or current programs achieve the three goals described above and the costs to governments of implementing such activities. Conclusions about whether the benefits exceed the costs are not given, however, because they would depend on judgments about the value of achieving these goals and about competing uses for the funds expended.

Article 19

COMMUNITY MENTAL HEALTH CENTERS: A LOOK AHEAD

Allan Beigel, M.D.

Predicting the future of community health centers (CMHCs), even their status five years from now, is a difficult task. If there is any doubt about our capacity for predictive inaccuracy in this area, consider what might have been said in early 1977 when the Carter Administration came into office and the President's Commission on Mental Health was appointed. Only the staunchest pessimist would have dared to predict anything less than an optimistic future for community mental health centers. Thus, the predictions contained are based on the assumption that current pressures, which derive in part from political and economic considerations, will remain strong for the next several years.

Current Pressures

Between 1977 and 1981, federal appropriations for community mental health services ranged from $233.8 million to $313.7 million with an average of $282.2 million (1). Beginning in 1982, given the new budgetary restraint of the current administration, the amount appropriated for alcohol, drug abuse, and mental health (ADM) services could be as low as $428.2 million (the latest Reagan budget), or as high as $485 million (the House-approved figure).[1] Even though under the Omnibus Budget Reconciliation Act of 1981 states have the option of transferring funds between the three ADM categories, it is likely that relatively little shifting of funds will take place. It can be expected that approximately 47 per cent of the ADM appropriation will go for mental health care (1). It is also likely that the overall amount available for community mental health services will be at least 25 to 34 per cent less than originally appropriated for fiscal year 1981, even before any federal money is withheld by the states to cover administrative costs.

Some observers believe that since the act bars the use of block-grant funds for inpatient services the funds available for noninpatient

SOURCE: *Community Mental Health Centers: A Look Ahead*, Vol. 33, pp. 741–745, 1982. Copyright 1982, The American Psychiatric Association. Reprinted by permission.

[1]The actual amount approved for fiscal year 1982 was $432 million; the budget resolution passed for fiscal year 1983 froze the funding level at that amount.

services will decrease by less than 25 to 34 per cent. That probably will not happen. In fiscal year 1981 only an estimated 11 per cent of the federal funds available for CMHCs were used for inpatient services (1). Consequently that portion of federal money which cannot, because of the law, be used for inpatient care probably will be replaced by state-appropriated money transferred from current noninpatient uses, resulting in a simple budgetary transfer rather than any real change in the availability of funds for either kind of care.

The use of block grants to transfer federal funds for mental health services to the states is an equally important influence on future trends. While mental health funds have been "protected" for now by their inclusion in a separate ADM block grant rather than in the health services block grant originally proposed by the administration, it is unclear how long this situation will last if Congress accepts President Reagan's New Federalism proposals. First, it is possible that mental health eventually will be placed in a health services block grant but, even if that does not occur, it is probable that current controls on the use of federal money by the states will be relaxed further so that funds may be transferred more freely between the three ADM services or between ADM and other health or human service areas.

Recently an administration recommendation that the ADM block-grant funds be transferred administratively from the Alcohol, Drug Abuse, and Mental Health Administration to the Office of the Assistant Secretary for Health in the Department of Health and Human Services was rejected by a congressional committee.

Alternatively, the ADM block-grant legislation may not be renewed in three years, if the present legislation represents only an intermediate step in the eventual elimination of all federal support for ADM services.

At his press conference on October 2, 1981, President Reagan demonstrated the impact of his deregulation policy by holding up in one hand 318 pages of regulations for the categorical health programs that existed before January 20, 1981, and in the other hand the six pages to which they had been reduced after the implementation of the block grant.

Deregulation, coupled with the block-grant initiative, has freed from most federal regulations the 49 states and assorted possessions that to date have applied for the block grant funds. Therefore, even though grantees must continue to provide basic services (screening for state mental health facilities, emergency, outpatient, partial hospitalization, and consultation and education services), they have been freed from most other regulations that existed before October 1, 1981, and from most of the mandates of the Mental Health Systems Act of 1980, which, in essence, was repealed by Congress.

Considerable concern has been expressed over the failure of CMHCs to respond adequately to the needs of chronic mentally ill persons who have been discharged from institutional care, who are no longer able to obtain that care because of budgetary cutbacks, or who cannot be sent to state hospitals because of restrictive civil commitment laws (2–7). There is a growing perception that many of the chronic mentally ill who previously were treated in institutions are not better off in the community and that future mental health systems may need to develop a new type of institution that can provide 24-hour protective care in a humane setting (8,9).

As more articles reporting on the plight of the chronic mentally ill in our large urban areas are published in the popular press (10–13), pressure on community mental health centers will build, and the impact of deinstitutionalization will continue to influence future program trends.

Prediction of Future Trends

Based on the current pressures outlined above, it is possible to make some tentative predictions of how centers will change over the next several years.

Staffing Patterns.   In the face of continuing or increased demands for service, CMHC administrators will attempt to retain as many clinical staff as possible even as available dollars for services decline. They will minimize staff reductions by employing less highly trained and skilled individuals. In situations where services must be delivered or supervised by professionals to qualify for third-party dollars, administrators may favor employing less experienced, lower-salaried persons to minimize expenditures.

Catchment-Area Philosophy.   While the philosophy of serving a geographically specific catchment area will be retained, one can anticipate that this concept will be broadened in its implementation. Because of decreasing dollars and the absence of regulatory requirements, catchment areas probably will grow even larger; residents of the catchment area will continue to have access to services, but because of the large demands of the new expanded clientele, access to services may be more theoretical than actual.

Similarly, decentralization of services in the catchment area will be less possible even though the area will grow in size. Many satellite clinics started during the last several years will be closed (14). One justification for this policy will be the need to lower administrative overhead costs through increased centralization of services.

Consolidation and Merger.   In some catchment areas, the system of services was developed by multiple agencies working in a consortium or under the aegis of a single nonprofit corporation. Because of decreased dollars, the increased authority of the states under the block grant to contract for services, and the desire to save on administrative costs, fewer agencies will be involved in service delivery. Some will merge so that they can continue to be part of the action, reducing the range of options that consumers previously had when seeking services.

Competition with the Private Sector.   In 1977 federal categorical funding accounted for 19 per cent of the average CMHC's budget. In addition, 14.2 per cent of the budget was derived from Medicare and Medicaid (1). Since there already has been a 24 to 35 per cent decrease in the amount of federal categorical funds and since further cutbacks are likely in both categorical and reimbursement resources, it is reasonable to assume that CMHCs need to find alternative sources to replace these funds. Given the current economic climate, it is unlikely that state and local governments will replace these funds, and thus private insurance is a more probable resource for recouping some of these losses.

However, increased competition with the private sector for patients with adequate third-party psychiatric insurance will necessitate a shift in CMHC programs toward such services as short- and medium-term inpatient and outpatient care. Programs that would be de-emphasized because of the new emphasis on collecting psychiatric insurance include partial hospitalization programs, consultation and education services, and long-term inpatient and outpatient treatment. Since it is mostly chronic mentally ill patients who are high users of long-term services, one can anticipate a decreased emphasis on treating these populations within community mental health centers, and a corresponding increase in the number of less seriously mentally ill patients who need shorter periods of treatment.

Comprehensiveness.   Any shift away from the current system of CMHC services will result in a reduced emphasis on the principle of comprehensiveness. While centers may not disappear, the comprehensive CMHC so often mentioned in the past probably will, aided in part by the absence of any regulations requiring it.

The Role of the States.   As a result of the current changes the states, while receiving increased responsibility through the administration of federal funds, at the same time are being forced into competition with the programs they are being asked to administer. To increase their ability to manage the new funds, state authorities also may have to find new dollars, and those most easily available are the ones being passed on to them by the federal government. By using part of the federal money to expand administrative ability, state authorities could increase the antagonism of local CMHCs rather than foster a cooperative state-local partnership (15).

Increased Hospital Utilization. The reduction of services to patients with chronic mental illness will exacerbate already existing problems in caring for this population, and will lead, in turn, to increased community and professional pressure to rely more heavily on institutional settings. At the same time, decision-makers will respond to criticism by assuring the public and CMHCs that today's state hospitals are significantly improved compared with those that were so severely criticized in the late 1940s and early 1950s.

Some state hospital administrators probably will point out that without increased resources their institutions cannot expand their role in caring for the chronically mentally ill. It is possible that as long as hospitals are prevented from using federal block-grant funds for inpatient services, these extra funds will come from current state appropriations for CMHCs.

Consumer and Citizen Involvement. States and CMHCs will be under increased pressure from consumer and citizen advocacy groups. With federal funds turned over to the states and with the total amount of awards decreased, consumers and citizens will recognize that maintenance of their priorities will require more active involvement. Thus the potential for conflict between consumer and citizen groups, professionals, and program administrators may increase. In past years patient rights were a primary focus of these conflicts; now issues related to how the reduced funds should be spent will be at the center of the debate.

Professional Advocacy. Membership in professional and service delivery organizations was readily available to CMHCs and their staffs during the years federal funds were managed by the federal government. Now that these funds have been turned over to the states, where policies on the use of public dollars for memberships and out-of-state travel are more restrictive, national organizations like the National Council of Community Mental Health Centers that have relied on

CMHCs and their staffs for membership and advocacy will find themselves hard pressed to carry out their responsibilities. Similarly, attendance at national training conferences, an important vehicle for professional growth, will decline.

Alternate Strategies, Outcomes

Many of the projected trends described above could be harmful to the future of patient care and community-based mental health services. A number of alternative policies could be implemented to limit the negative impact of current influences.

One such strategy would be to serve fewer people. It is unwise for community mental health centers to adjust to the decrease in dollars while attempting to serve about the same number of clients. CMHC advocates should make it clear that as a result of reductions in appropriations fewer clients will be served. Strategies designed to maintain or increase the number of clients served despite reduced appropriations are ill conceived because they would undermine many of the basic principles upon which CMHCs were built.

Centers also should take the position that it is inappropriate to adjust to the new fiscal constraints by eliminating key elements of the service delivery system. The adoption of a philosophy that the service that cannot pay for itself should not exist will jeopardize severely the concept of comprehensiveness that distinguishes CMHCs from other mental health programs. This principle should be adhered to even though many service elements may need to exist in a smaller version than before, or may need to merge or consolidate with similar services in the community.

Maintenance of a comprehensive range of services does not necessarily mean that CMHCs need to continue to serve equally the seriously and chronically mentally ill and the worried well (16). It is important to recognize that one of the major byproducts of the CMHC movement during the past two decades has been the development of a whole range of alternative community services that can be invaluable to individuals whose emotional problems are not severe enough to require the extensive professional intervention a CMHC can offer (17). Therefore, while maintaining a system of peer review and accountability to ensure that services are used efficiently, CMHCs should give increased priority to the seriously and chronically mentally ill for whom no other services than institutionalization are available (18–20).

An attempt to cope with the current fiscal constraints by increasing competition with the private sector for the same pool of available insurance dollars and the same population of patients will be antithetical to the needs of the community. While CMHCs must have balanced budgets to survive, that survival should not be at the expense of the original objectives of the centers (21). Therefore, even though it could result in maintenance of the same budgetary level for CMHCs as that of the late 1970s, competition with the private sector would be unwise if the price is a reduction in the scope or range of services that are unavailable except through the center.

If the CMHC is to design its programs with increased attention to the seriously and chronically mentally ill patient, it will be necessary to ensure that competent and well-trained staff are available to treat this population (22). That goal will not be accomplished if one of the approaches to declining fiscal resources is to de-professionalize staff in order to maintain the same number of employees. Center administrators should point out that quantity can never replace quality and that, for the priorities of the 1980s, quality is essential. Centers should reduce the total number of personnel if necessary to ensure the availability of the highly skilled professionals needed to treat seriously and chronically ill patients.

While it is recognized that under the block-grant initiative states have assumed increased administrative responsibilities, it is hoped that states will refrain from using these limited dollars to underwrite any resulting increase in state administrative costs. Just as state authorities have asked centers to reduce their administrative overhead, states should reduce their own administrative overhead to a minimum and find other ways to meet the new costs than by tapping into available services dollars.

While that may not seem fair to state mental health authorities, it is important to remember that patients and CMHCs already are being penalized through a reduction in available service dollars as a result of federal budgetary cutbacks. To increase this penalty because of the state's need for funds to expand its monitoring capacity will not serve state or community programs well in the long run.

Effective and comprehensive community-based systems of care for chronic mentally ill patients are in short supply. However, an expanded use of institutionalization is not indicated, despite pressure from communities disenchanted with seeing the "crazies walking the street" (11) and from the problems presented by decreasing federal appropriations. While the easiest solution is to expand the use of institutions, this course would be regressive. Instead, alternative approaches such as the development of sheltered living programs are needed.

The progress made over the last 35 years toward community acceptance of mental illness should not be abandoned. If it is necessary to impose constraints on any aspect of the system to ensure that funds are available for effective community-based systems for the seriously and chronically mentally ill, then they should be imposed on care for those who are less seriously mentally ill and not at risk for hospitalization.

National organizations that have played a significant role in mental health advocacy at the federal level should redirect the influence of their constituencies toward state and local authorities. Just as the federal government has transferred resources to the states, these national organizations could do the same, perhaps by reducing national dues to accommodate increased dues for local and state entities. These organizations might also expand their information collection and dissemination role as they reduce their involvement in federal-level advocacy.

Conclusion

It is clear that as a result of reduced federal appropriations, block grants, deregulation, and the continuing impact of deinstitutionalization, significant re-directions in CMHC programming will take place over the next several years. It is entirely possible that the total impact of these influences will be negative, particularly if the changes are not thoughtfully planned. I hope it is clear from this brief analysis that the trends for the immediate future will depend largely on the choices made by program administrators, staff, consumers, and citizen advocates.

In most risk situations, opportunities for change are created. While the size of the community mental health center may decrease, both in terms of the number of patients served and the staff available, these are not the only criteria by which the future effectiveness of the center should be measured. Thoughtful program planning can lead to reordered priorities, increased quality of care, and program renewal as a result of cooperative relationships between communities and the state.

REFERENCES

1. Cravens, RB: Personal communication. Division of Mental Health Services Program, National Institute of Mental Health, Rockville, Md, 1981
2. Rieder, RO: Hospitals, patients, and politics. Schizophrenia Bulletin 11:9–15, 1974
3. Robbins, E, Robbins L: Charge to the community: some early effects of a state hospital's change of policy. American Journal of Psychiatry 131:641–645, 1974
4. Arnoff, FN: Social consequences of policy toward mental illness. Science 188:1277–1281, 1975
5. Kirk, SA, Thierren, ME: Community mental health myths and the fate of former hospitalized patients. Psychiatry 38: 209–217, 1975
6. Shapiro, R: Providing care for former institutional patients puts challenge on psychiatrists. Clinical Psychiatry News, April 1976, pp. 1, 28–30.

7. Talbott, JA (ed): Proposal for public policy on the chronic mental patient, in The Chronic Mental Patient: Problems, Solutions, and Recommendations for a Public Policy. Washington, DC, American Psychiatric Association, 1978
8. Bachrach, LL: Is the least restrictive environment always the best? sociological and semantic implications. Hospital & Community Psychiatry 31:97–103, 1980
9. Miller, RD: Beyond the old state hospital: new opportunities ahead. Hospital & Community Psychiatry 32:27–31, 1981
10. Civil liberty for what? (edtl) New York Times, April 8, 1974, p 34
11. Why are the insane walking the streets? Tucson Citizen, June 10, 1977, p 1
12. Sheehan, S: The patient: is there no place on earth for me: New Yorker, June 8, 1981, pp 50–96
13. McGuire, PA: Mental patients try their wings outside. Baltimore Sun, November 22, 1981, pp A1, A26–27
14. Weirich TW: Effects of decentralizing mental health services. Community Mental Health Journal (in press)
15. Final Report of the President's Commission on Mental Health. Washington, DC, US Government Printing Office, 1977
16. Borus, JF: Issues critical to the survival of community mental health. American Journal of Psychiatry 135:1029–1035, 1978
17. Glasscote, RM, Raybin, JB, Reifler, CB: The alternate services: Their role in mental health. Washington, DC, Joint Information Service, American Psychiatric Association, 1975
18. Bachrach, LL: Deinstitutionalization: An analytical review and sociological perspective. Rockville, Md, National Institute of Mental Health, 1976
19. James, JF: Principles in developing a community support system. Hospital & Community Psychiatry 29:34–35, 1978
20. Bachrach, LL: Planning mental health services for chronic patients. Hospital & Community Psychiatry 30:387–393, 1979
21. Kennedy, JF: Message from the President of the United States Relative to Mental Illness and Mental Retardation, Document 58, 86th Congress, February 5, 1963, p 12
22. Beigel, A, Sharfstein, S, Wolfe, C: Increased psychiatric presence in community mental health centers. Hospital & Community Psychiatry 30:763–767, 1979

Article 20

PULLING TOGETHER OR TEARING APART
Birds of a Feather Must Choose

Robert J. Wineburg

The human services system is changing. It is becoming more locally oriented, demanding greater community initiative in response to local needs. The local human services network faces new responsibilities and obstacles. Complicating this is the emergence of four dynamic challenges—largely precipitated by federal budget cuts—whose simultaneous interplay could fragment the system at a crucial period in its redevelopment. A unified service system is preferable, of course, to one that is not. Coordinated efforts to manage community problems clearly are mandatory at a time when resources are scarce.

Those seeking to develop a responsive human services network should be alert to possible barriers to their goal. Moreover, creativity will be essential in addressing the new and multiple tasks. Two strategies can serve as guideposts for developing innovations in light of these changing conditions. The strategies can be a springboard for countering the combined force and interaction of these four major challenges. One, increased responsibilities for planning, administering, and financing of programs must be balanced against decreased financial resources. Two, communities will face these new responsibilities with a growing number of social problems. Three, the resultant service demand will give rise to heightened lobbying by special interest groups. Four, expanded service responsibilities with less money and a rise in social problems leading to increased service demands will compel both legislators and providers to seek private sector money and technical help to manage problems at the community level. The challenges may be unique in each community, but they must be met in order to satisfy the urgent service needs of the eighties and beyond.

Increased Responsibilities

The successful transition from today's system to one that is administratively small, approachable, and accountable will be difficult. While

SOURCE: "Pulling Together or Tearing Apart, Birds of a Feather Must Choose," by Robert J. Wineburg, *Public Welfare* Vol. 42, No. 3 (1984), pp. 26–30.

the existing system has been labeled as top heavy, distant, and unresponsive, it had developed an internal consistency comprehensible to recipients as well as providers. Communities expected to handle certain problems through their publicly financed mental health, public health, and community and social services agencies. Were they unable to manage problems, they contracted with private agencies for support services. Such agencies—some independent and others under the United Way umbrella—had developed staffs and budgets partly because of the back-up and support roles they assumed in a community services network. Supplementing the public and private agencies were the service organizations, self-help groups, and churches.

Prior to the budget cuts, coordinated relationships between public and private agencies for the most part were contractual, founded on financial incentives. In Greensboro, North Carolina, for example, the mobile meals program was administered by a private agency and financed by a contract with the local department of social services. The decrease in social service block grant funds forced the cancelling of the contract, eliminating the program. Funds have been restored through private sources, but the coordinated relationship in this service area is no longer strong.

From January 1981 to July 1983, there was a 20 percent cut in federal funding for human resources programs. It was expected that private agencies would expand their roles to compensate for service reductions. Many private agencies, however, lost public funding as well. Numerous contracts with public agencies, large numbers of grants, and programs such as the Comprehensive Employment and Training Act were eliminated. The Urban Institute projected that by 1985 many private agencies, especially those emphasizing community services, would lose up to 65 percent of their federal support. In 1982, a Campaign for Human Development survey found that 80 percent of private voluntary agencies experienced funding cutbacks, 46 percent lost staff, and 23 percent lost more than half of their paid staff.

These reductions are drastically curtailing agency capacities. With less money for their own programs and for contractual support, agencies will be forced to reduce optional services, eliminate support service contracts, and economize across the board.[1] Private agencies, because of fewer contracts with public agencies and less federal money, will seek more revenue from the private sector. In short, they will spend more time meeting their own organizational needs at a time when their resources are in great demand.

The capacities of the community human services network have been hindered by federal budget reductions in two important ways. Public agencies, the major service providers in a community services system, must concentrate on providing mandated services. Their efforts will

center on efficient management of operations. This in itself is not drastic—but private agencies at the same time are seeking ways to survive.
Public agencies will look inward to cost-saving measures. Private agencies will venture outward to find money to stay afloat. Survival measures may take precedence over community problems. The initial cuts
have hampered the development of a new and more responsive local
system. Public agencies have been forced to manage caseloads with
less money, while private agencies have been dividing their efforts between raising money and delivering services.

To compound these problems, few state and local governments have
replaced lost federal aid with their own money.[2] In time, the community human services system may become less comprehensive and more
selective in the range of services offered and the type of clients served.[3]
More important, should this be a permanent change, it may lead to
greater fragmentation. While collective strategies are needed to solve
multiple community problems, increased responsibilities coupled with
reduced funds contribute to "coordination inertia." This is a state of
immobility in the community human services system resulting from
the independent pursuit of resources by different system participants.
In this instance, two major subsystems are being forced to operate sep-
arately at a time when progress hinges on their union. If coordination
inertia is not overcome, the evolving system will be no better at preventing and managing human problems than the one it is replacing—
and may very well be worse. While local initiatives must fill service
gaps engendered by the federal budget cuts, those very cuts may have
polarized local initiatives.

Growing Social Problems

Coincident with agency reduction of funds is a growth in social
problems. To a certain degree, public agencies have been forced to focus directly on problems facing clients, thus forsaking prevention and
education programs.[4] If the growth of social problems were to plateau,
community members might be able to redevelop responsive service
networks. That is unlikely to occur, however. Major concerns facing the
elderly are projected to grow sizeably over the next fifty years. Joanne
F. Selinske, in the Summer 1983 PUBLIC WELFARE, reports that child
protection services are reeling from cutbacks and notes that reports of
child abuse have risen 89 percent from 1976 to 1980. In the same issue,
Judith H. Cassetty and Ruth McRoy assert that poor families headed
by women will find it increasingly difficult to meet basic survival needs
such as food, housing, and medical care. Providers face these realities
and a host of others: drug and alcohol abuse; infant mortality rates;

and overcrowded jails. Communities will be required to confront these pressing problems and halt their growth.

The simultaneous rise in the volume of community problems and reduction in funds may force public and private cooperation. An undesirable outcome of that merger, however, may be hastily conceived plans resulting in ineffective services. Local human services networks are limited in their technical capacity to conduct comprehensive planning.[5] That limitation, when added to the potential for worker burnout brought about by growing responsibilities, decreasing funds, and increasing social problems, will cause the second dimension of coordination inertia—reunification of two weakened subsystems. This union of public and private agencies may be incapable of appropriate planning and effective delivery of service.

Special Interest Groups

Maintaining service levels will depend on the power of state and local special interest groups and on the fiscal capacities of states and localities, says Sara Rosenberry in the Winter 1983 *Journal of Urban Affairs*. Welfare theorists Frances Fox Piven and Richard A. Cloward agree and outline various strategies for involving service professionals, students, and clients in the electoral process. Local officials probably will feel increasing pressure from a host of emerging interest groups, each one calling for increased funds. The Bay Area Advocates for Human Services in California was formed after the Reagan cuts. One of its long-term goals is to "increase the ability to lobby more effectively at both county and state levels for funding for all human services," according to Stan Wisner in "Social Services Review (June 1983). In Greensboro, North Carolina, a local group called Community Alternatives to Budget Cuts joined with the Young Women's Christian Association, Junior League, and Parent Teacher Association to sponsor candidates' hearings focusing on human services issues. Efforts such as these are likely to proliferate as communities assume greater service responsibilities.

If needs are not met, there is little question that professional, neighborhood, and recipient groups will clamor for better management of services. But official response will depend on the fiscal capacity of localities to meet demands. Heightened lobbying efforts, especially at the local level, may result in further fragmentation. Possibly the issues espoused by the strongest lobbying effort, or issues that are politically "acceptable," will be considered at the expense of equally important needs. It is important to examine how the interaction of increased local lobbying efforts with increased service responsibilities, reduced funding levels, and growing service demands may further contribute to coordination inertia.

The community human services network faces continued reductions in federal money. Service providers should expect increased responsibilities and expanded demand. Pressure groups will lobby more intensively. The system, already constrained by its limited ability in comprehensive service planning, will become increasingly burdened by political pressures. Legislative solutions to social problems usually are incremental and often irrational; sometimes they inhibit comprehensive service planning. A sober examination of the problems by the community is necessary. Legislators, caught between reluctance to raise taxes and the need to be more accountable to the human services constituency, may be forced into drafting legislation that intensifies competition for dwindling local funds.

Rising antagonism spawned by competition for funds will thwart efforts to coordinate community-wide service planning. Furthermore, the public will hold local legislators accountable for larger expenditures for services. And it is quite likely that legislators will blame service providers for the system's inadequacies. Local political action will thrust providers into a detrimental political whirlwind. The volatile combination of broader responsibilities, increased service demands, and stepped-up pressure by interest groups may further retard coordinated network management. Stepped-up community action may spur the activities of different elements in the human services system, but there is no guarantee that the outcome will be beneficial to the system as a whole. Broadened, unplanned, uncoordinated incremental efforts to solve local problems will be the third dimension of coordination inertia that impedes the progress of the new system.

Private Sector Initiatives

While it is essential to devise strategies to minimize inertia, one more challenge must be examined and understood before action can be planned. Many authors have outlined ways that service gaps now are being filled or how they should be filled. Robert Agranoff reports in the *New England Journal of Human Services* (Spring 1983) that some foundations and businesses are funding creative, long-term, self-sustaining solutions to service problems at the community level. Jerry S. Turem and Catherine Born in *Social Work* (June 1983) cite the need for agencies to rekindle relationships with service groups, enlisting them to help fill some service gaps. Across the country, United Ways have initiated campaigns to assess local community needs, a major step in developing long-range service plans. These private-sector initiatives must be viewed cautiously—they may present a challenge to successful service coordination at the community level.

Efforts by businesses and foundations to stimulate self-sustaining community agency programs pose at least one troublesome issue. Frequently, solutions to service problems hinge upon the effective use of volunteers. Volunteers are finite resources. Fierce competition for their services may result in some agencies having too many and some too few. Also, agencies may overlook the need for coordinated recruiting, an essential element in comprehensive, community-wide problem solving. Self-sustaining efforts also may shift valuable resources to service sectors where staff have the best proposal-writing skills—but not the most need.

The use of service groups must be carefully planned and their capabilities matched to the needs of the community. Recent budget cuts at the North Carolina Services to the Blind and Visually Impaired resulted in the elimination of thirty highly skilled professionals. Asking the Lions Club to make up for the loss of these skilled people would be foolish; they cannot possibly deliver such services as mobility training. Successful service delivery at the community level will be determined in part by how well groups like the Lions are integrated into the delivery scheme. Agencies face many constraints in successfully and accurately analyzing community needs. The new complications facing the system must be taken into account prior to any needs analysis. Often volunteers carry out sophisticated assignments like comprehensive assessment of community needs. Even under the guidance of an expert planning director and staff, the analyses may be skewed.

Private sector initiatives are riddled with uncertainty, and they may contribute to the coordination inertia that threatens the community human services system. Facing the prospect of being pulled apart, forced back together in a weaker form, and then being fragmented again, it is not too difficult to imagine the community services network being whirled around willy-nilly. Private dollars and volunteers may gravitate to one part of the system, and service organizations could be drawn into areas without the skills to provide services or the resources to offer much financial support. This kind of aimless scrambling could be precipitated by less than professional attempts to assess community problems that are based on incomplete data and misinformation. The interaction of the private sector initiatives with the other challenges facing communities constitute the fourth dimension of coordination inertia. The mix of these challenges could spell chaos for the community services system.

Preparing for Change

It is possible for communities to emerge from the quicksand of coordination inertia. Needs must be defined accurately, planning groups must be designated, and agencies must be at the forefront of the effort. Coming to grips with community perception of the human services will be an important first step for both public and private groups.

Providers on each tier—public, private, and volunteer—must work toward changing the perceptions of the human services. Continuous efforts must be made to educate the community about the nature of problems and need for services. This will not be easy in the face of a rising conservative attack on liberal social welfare policies and programs. Community members must learn that the system is highly complex and effectual. Until citizens perceive the system as serving the needs of the young, the elderly, the sick, the homeless, the jobless, the battered, the abused, and countless others, innovations may fail to draw support.

Educating the community is no small task. Douglas Bicklen in *Community Organizing: Theory and Practice* mentions radio and TV talk shows, public service announcements, and letters to the editor as possible avenues of communication. Bradley Googins in *Social Work* (July–August 1983) stresses that one of the most important elements of gaining acceptance for a plan depends on the interpersonal qualities of the planner. But planners will have to be much more than personable to overcome the barriers faced by human services managers. As meeting human needs becomes more crucial to the well-being of a community, it will be essential that the public understand the role of the human services in this task. To establish the basis of understanding, planners first must educate important members of the community media—television, press, and radio. (See "On the Line," Summer 1983 PUBLIC WELFARE.)

Conferences with editors and members of the print media are important; they enhance the chances of reporters being assigned to cover particular projects. Media representatives should be given clear information about current and future projects. Names and telephone numbers of contact people should be included, as well as written biographical information of major project staff. In early 1983, the Greensboro Group held conferences with the city editor and the editorial page editor of the *Greensboro Daily News*. The subject was a five-week series of public discussions aimed at addressing Greensboro's response to the budget cuts. As a result of the conferences, the project was covered four of the five weeks. In addition, organizers published an 800-word guest editorial by one of the project's organizers in a Sunday edition, the most widely-read edition of the paper.

Published and aired stories often include facts that are incorrect or information that is incomplete. These situations can be alleviated by agency and project managers if they take the time to educate interested reporters about present and future projects and about ongoing programs and program changes. This can be done by providing reporters with copies of proposals, drafts of proposals, and fact sheets. Such efforts would provide reporters with solid background information on which they can build their stories. As reporters become better educated, so do communities.

In-depth position papers often are welcomed by editors and reporters because the papers provide important background information and save media representatives untold hours of legwork in unfamiliar territory. A group in Greensboro, Community Alternatives to the Budget (CAB), employed this strategy. CAB invited a reporter to a subcommittee meeting where he learned about community services issues and was given a copy of an in-depth position paper. Several months later an excellent article appeared in the *Greensboro Daily News* telling how health care cuts could be expensive for the community in the long run. The article stimulated serious discussions about how the community should respond to health concerns.

Communities must move toward a comprehensive understanding of the problems they face as well as the means they possess to solve these problems. Enlisting the aid of the media is a prime means of developing this understanding and should be considered a first step in overcoming coordination inertia. Such efforts could result in the development of new methods for teaching communities about their service problems and needs. Critical to such undertakings is the building of trust between agencies and the media.

A Central Forum

A new arm must be added to the community human services network, one that steers the community away from autonomous pursuits toward unified service. At one time, the United Way may have served this function, at another, universities or colleges. Now it is important for communities to find ways to meet the complicated challenges of the 1980s and beyond. The name of such a vehicle is not as important as its function: it might be called an institute, a center, or a consortium. Through it, human services participants—directors, providers, volunteers, recipients—who give the service network its character and life can explore ways to reshape the community system. Thirty communities across the country have established such education centers based on Harvard University's Principal's Center model.[6] Centers such as these for the human services could provide a forum to identify promising practices and encourage their visibility and exchange.

Instead of public money and private sector initiatives funding the solution of isolated problems in partial ways, funds in such cases are devoted to unification of the community services system. At a human services center, the participants could share experiences, explore new approaches to service design and delivery, and learn new service technologies. More important, a center of this kind would be devoted to the betterment of the whole system.

A community services center would facilitate technologically advanced needs assessments. Professional development workshops for agency staff would help them update skills in particular areas. The center also would allow directors or providers to debate complicated matters in an open setting. Conferences featuring experts from different service areas would be an ongoing aspect of such a center. The possibilities seemingly are endless, and the prospect of unifying a fragmented system is realistic and exciting.

Members of the Greensboro human services network completed the first phase of developing a human services institute in 1984. The pilot project convened sixty agency directors for a week-long program directed by two consultants specializing in human services development. The purpose of the meeting was to build the necessary trust that is the foundation of a unified services system. Financial support for those efforts came from the business community, the universities, service organizations, and the agencies themselves.

The second phase of development includes regional unification efforts. Thus, a second pilot project is being planned. Like the first, it will emphasize informal, creative exploration of mutual "regional" concerns. After both the local and regional networking efforts have been evaluated, the group will establish a permanent regional human services institute. It will be a mechanism that fosters creativity and strengthens bonds among human services colleagues, one that ultimately will improve the lives of those they serve.

Looking Ahead

Those who are responsible for the broad spectrum of services in the various community networks may find that they are creating as many problems for the human services system as they hope to solve. Agencies managing growing problems with less money will compete for the support of church, civic, and service groups. Interest groups may pressure local officials to create poorly planned service relationships between public agencies and voluntary groups. Private sector initiatives might be isolated, undermining their potential for success

Groups eager to see results may fail to acknowledge the need to shape community perceptions through public education.

In short, the system is fluid and dynamic. Uncoordinated moves will only create inertia forcing us back beyond past accomplishments. The test we face is to construct cooperative efforts that lead to systemic benefits. If each agency is forced—or permitted—to go it alone, more fragmentation is inevitable. Communities must tackle the challenges with an integrated program. There may have been a time when competitive service development enhanced service delivery. That time has passed.

NOTES

1. Paul Terrell and Stan Wisner, "Facing Up to Proposition 13: Human Services Impacts and Strategies," in *The Social Welfare Forum: Official Proceedings, 1981* (New York: Columbia University Press for the National Conference on Social Welfare, 1982): 160–174.
2. Richard Nathan, "State and Local Governments Under Federal Grants," *Political Science Quarterly* 1 (Spring 1983):54.
3. Henry A. Coleman and John P. Ross, "The New Federalism Strategy and State-Local Government Finances," *Journal of Urban Affairs* 1 (Winter 1983): 29–39.
4. Paul Terrell and Stan Wisner, "Facing Up to Proposition 13."
5. Mark I. Gelfand, *A Nation of Cities: The Federal Government and Urban America 1933–1965* (New York: Oxford University Press, 1975).
6. Roland S. Barth, "The Principal's Center at Harvard University," unpublished mission statement. The idea for an institute, center, or the like is based in part on the Principal's Center at Harvard University's Graduate School of Education.

PART IV

Practice, Politics, and the Social Welfare Agenda

The National Association of Social Workers' (NASW) Code of Ethics specifies that the practitioner is responsible to clients, colleagues, the community, the employing agency, and the profession at large and states that the social worker (Code of Ethics, 1980)

> should advocate changes in policy and legislation to improve the social conditions and to promote social justice . . . encourage informed participation by the public in shaping social policies and institutions.

In effect, the social worker has dual responsibilities. First, the worker provides quality services to a client, and, second, he or she has the ethical dictate to improve the form of public policy to facilitate society's responsiveness to *all* population groups.

Mary Richmond, one of the premiere social work leaders at the turn of the century, put it another way when she said that social workers help people out of the ditch and then try to get rid of the ditch.

Previous readings have sharpened our policy focus—at this point in our learning, we have an understanding of basic concepts, coupled with differing perspectives on the purpose of social welfare, knowledge of historical social welfare patterns, and awareness of issues impacting present-day social welfare. Now we are ready to look at how to get rid of the ditch, alluded to by Richmond, by improving the quality of public policy.

Social workers generally view themselves as helping agents; that is, providing a direct service in a noncumbersome, sensitive, and caring mode to clients. On the other hand, social workers often react with disdain to the political arena, the birthplace of public policy—stereotypes of negative manipulation and corrupt politicians run counter to social work beliefs. Yet, if we return to the premise that social work practice is governed by policy, then social workers too must become active players in the political milieu.

This section of articles directs our attention to the political world with some general points to consider: how to work in this somewhat foreign sphere and what goals to be looking toward. In a sense, these articles serve as a primer on politics; as we examine this section's readings, we need to remind ourselves of one basic question: What is my role in the politics of social welfare?

All too often social workers approach politicians with apprehension—how do I talk to them, they are important people who are on television, they have access to other leaders, they have power. Yes, all of these statements are true, but only to a point. For a moment, consider various functions individuals assume in society. For a society or a community to function, people take on different roles: doctors, dentists, mechanics, electricians, farmers, teachers, and so on. A person develops expertise in the hows and whys of a particular role to carry it out successfully. When we are in need of a specific service, we go to a specialist in that field, and sometime they too may require our knowhow. This is referred to as *reciprocity,* a fundamental component of social living.

A politician is skilled in making laws (as well as getting elected). Social workers are adroit in human behavior in the social environment, counseling, social problem analysis, and so on.[1] Politicians need our expertise and guidance in putting together effective legislation. Some politicians, on the other hand, abhor social workers because of our beliefs. Yet, we are experts with specialized knowledge and knowledge is power. Our approach to the political world should be based on viewing ourselves as significant partners rather than minor actors.

ARTICLE 21: "FACTORS INFLUENCING SENATE VOTING PATTERNS ON SOCIAL WORK RELATED LEGISLATION"

Are politicians supportive of social work concerns? Given the seemingly differently perceived worlds of politics and social work, we might think that there is little support for social welfare issues. Joyce Littell Smith and Gail Sullivan examine politicians' general reactions to the nature of social work and specify key points to consider for lobbying efforts.

---

[1]Social workers nationwide are running for office and being elected at all levels of government. For example, in the spring of 1988, social workers held the elected offices of mayor in San Francisco and New Orleans. Social workers were also elected members of both the United States Senate and the House of Representatives. The idea that politics is limited to lawyers is an outdated notion. Our expertise on the human condition, coupled with our communication skills, provides the electorate a viable choice for political office.

Their article, a result of a master's thesis in the late 1970s, provides a brief glimpse of the politician's view of social work and the welfare agenda. To work with others, whether they are politicians or psychiatrists, it is imperative that we are aware of commonly held perceptions and beliefs regarding our profession. Other professionals' ideas and perceptions of social work shape their responses and levels of acceptance to the issues social workers advocate.

Littell Smith and Sullivan examine two broad areas: First, are there specific variables which impact voting patterns for social work-related legislation and, second, what are the perceptions of politicians, in this case members of the U.S. Senate, to the profession of social work? By interviewing U.S. Senators and staff, the authors conclude that there is a positive image regarding the social work profession. Further, they identify specific variables which influence the degree of support, or lack thereof, for social work legislation.

This work is important for political involvement. Awareness of factors which influence, one way or another, a politician's perception of social work clarifies our direction, strengths, and weaknesses for lobbying. Further, understanding which variables strengthen a social work position helps map out a strategy for effective political participation. As you read the article, think of politicians in your hometown or others you may have come across in your experiences—how do they respond to social welfare issues? Can you nurture the variables identified by Littell Smith and Sullivan to positively impact the politician's stance with regard to social welfare?

ARTICLE 22: "LOBBYING AND SOCIAL WORK"

How do you lobby? Do you buy lunch for a politician? Do you work in his or her campaign? Do you make financial contributions? It won't hurt your cause if you do each of these, but lobbying is much more than direct or indirect campaign involvement. Lobbying is assertive, and at times aggressive, behavior to educate, persuade, and gain an individual's support for a certain issue. Lobbying involves skills familiar to the social worker—talking, active listening, teaching, advocating, referring, supporting, and negotiating. These practices are implemented in a different agency context with a different type of client.

Maryann Mahaffey examines the how-to of lobbying. Based on her experiences in politics and as a social worker, Mahaffey describes how social workers can become active partners in the political process. She examines a variety of lobbying strategies, barriers, and tasks for the social worker. The article cuts to the heart of politics and details specific techniques for effective lobbying.

Consider how you can incorporate Mahaffey's ideas into your practice repertoire. Are the ideas behind lobbying similar to ideas behind other social work practice techniques? How can you develop expertise in lobbying? Thinking back to the issues discussed in Part 3, where and how would you begin lobbying efforts?

ARTICLE 23: "INCOME SECURITY"

As seen in the preceding reading, lobbying is an art and a science—the *art* addresses the specific skills developed to be effective, the *science* includes the knowledge of the issue to be lobbied. Involvement in the political arena in the 1980s and 1990s mandates that our science or knowledge be grounded in programs and services of the same time periods. Part 2 of this anthology provided us with a historical perspective of social welfare, while Part 3 examined issues within social welfare, both significant parts to the science. Now we add a third piece to our ever-strengthening foundation—understanding the "Reagan Revolution," the 1980s federal strategy underpinning public social welfare programs. Understanding the how and results of the present and past establishes a solid foundation to advocate for different and new programs.

The so-called Reagan Revolution involved a redirection of federal allocation of resources, responsibility for programs, and, in essence, a philosophy of government different from other post–World War II presidential administrations. The Reagan plan included four dominant themes: (Major Themes, 1983)

a. Governments closest to the people—the state and local governments—are more responsive to the needs and desires of their citizens than is the federal government.

b. The most efficient means of allocating resources and meeting the needs of nearly all people is the free enterprise market. The federal government's role in the marketplace should be one of creating incentives for growth and opportunity.

c. A stronger and more modern defense capability is essential to deter attack and coercion, to protect the vital interests, and to lay the groundwork for negotiating mutual force reductions.

d. The federal government is the taxpayer's steward. It has the obligation to ensure that the resources surrendered to advance the public welfare are put to the most effective and proper uses.

In his 1983 budget message to the U.S. Congress, President Reagan noted that he wanted to limit tax burdens "necessary to finance essential government services," eliminate programs that do not belong in the federal realm, reduce federal regulations, and bring inflation under control (United States Budget, 1983, p. 4). The revolution aimed to minimize federal intervention in both the public and private sectors in order to revitalize economic growth.

James Storey provides an in-depth analysis of how the Reagan administration impacted income security programs. Discussion includes a descriptive, albeit brief, overview of related policy prior to 1981 and attention to changes in social insurance and public assistance programs in the early to mid-1980s.

As you consider this work, think back to earlier social welfare programs in the 1980s. What views have been implemented and muted? What role does welfare play in Reaganomics? How do Gilder's ideas in reading 4 play out in the revolution? What welfare programs are most susceptible to fiscal manipulation? What do you see for the future of the welfare state if the Reagan direction continues?

ARTICLE 24: "A SOCIAL AGENDA FOR THE EIGHTIES"

The preceding article examined social welfare from a "what it is" perspective; this manuscript allows us look at "what might have been."

In October 1979, President Jimmy Carter established the "President's Commission for a National Agenda for the Eighties." The commission was staffed by forty-five individuals representing a variety of interest groups—business, labor, arts, science, humanities. The members worked on nine panels which examined various facets of American life. Some areas studied included social justice, the economy, urban living, and the quality of American life. In December 1980, the commission's final reports were forwarded to the President.

This reading outlines social issues that the commission felt should be part of the national welfare agenda. In particular, information examining health issues, children and the aged, and education are detailed.

Consider what happened to this proposed agenda under the Reagan Revolution? Have certain ideas been set aside in favor of others? How valid do you feel the commission's social concerns are—were they made for political convenience (for reelection purposes) or for moral imperatives? What would the present-day welfare system be like had the commission's recommendations been followed?

ARTICLE 25: "NONWHITES AND THE DEMOGRAPHIC IMPERATIVE IN SOCIAL WELFARE SPENDING"

Welfare programs are structured by the amounts of available dollars for funding. Goals are one thing; fiscal appropriations, however, determine the extent of opportunity to reach a given goal. As we look toward the future welfare agenda, we must consider how social workers can positively impact the budget-setting process and resulting program development. The answer rests with having access to future trends. However, it is virtually impossible to have exact projections for the future; we can, and do, make educated estimates based on what we already know.

Martha Ozawa brings to our attention a key area for effective forecasting—the relationship between demographics and welfare spending. Ozawa takes an interesting position in this paper: She argues that demographics will be the primary influence in future welfare expenditures. Her introductory comments set the tone for the article:

> As the baby-boom generation starts to retire, we will face a large proportion of elderly and a shrinking proportion of children and working people. The issue of race . . . could become explosive as the demographic distribution of old and young emerges along white versus nonwhite lines.

Demographics are clear—the workforce is shrinking while the elder population increases. For future workers, this translates into increased taxes on salary to support public senior programs. Ozawa, however, raises the issue of race and the critical implications beyond the mere allocation of fiscal resources. She contends that, unless some immediate steps are taken to rectify the current programming for children, the future will face a funding battle based on race—social welfare for white elders or program funding for nonwhite children.

Ozawa's insight to the future highlights the extent to which two of the most vulnerable population groups, elders and children, may be set against each other. As we look at this insightful work, consider how such a situation may be averted: Why will children have to be played against seniors, and vice versa? How can we ensure that enough resources are available to both groups?

ARTICLE 26: "A WELFARE AGENDA FOR THE END OF THE CENTURY: RECASTING THE FUTURE ON FOUNDATIONS OF THE PAST"

This final article reflects on the future of social welfare. You should write this article, because you are the future. Your actions of today impact and form the reality of tomorrow.

In looking toward the future, loosen the bonds of the present and fantasize what you really would like for an ideal society. How do you want people, groups, and communities to be treated? What types of resources will be available? Who will be responsible to provide these various resources? What is the role of government and the private sector in the future welfare state?

Robert Morris's manuscript brings us to the beginning of the twenty-first century as he proposes a welfare agenda for the future. His subtitle, "Recasting the Future on Foundations of the Past," implies that the future is directly linked to the past; that is, we can't deny what has occurred, but we can shape our destiny if we want to be active participants in the process. When reading Morris's work, consider your ideas and what you want for the "welfare future": national health insurance, workfare, negative income tax, comprehensive educational programs. Do you envision welfare as a right or a privilege? Should programs be universal or selective with minimal or optimal services?

Your ideas on the future are important. As practitioners, you will be writing the policy of the future, administering programs of the future, and delivering services of the future. You will be major actors in the welfare of tomorrow, a role that will impact others throughout our society and far into the twenty-first century. Consider Morris's words closely, but more importantly, look to yourself and your vision.

BIBLIOGRAPHY

Executive Office of the President, *The United States Budget in Brief, Fiscal Year 1984*, Washington, D.C.: Office of Management and Budget, 1983.

———, *Major Themes and Additional Budget Details, Fiscal Year, 1983*, Washington, D.C.: Office of Management and Budget, nd.

National Association of Social Workers, *Code of Ethics*, Silver Spring, MD: National Association of Social Workers, 1980.

Article 21

FACTORS INFLUENCING SENATE VOTING PATTERNS ON SOCIAL WORK RELATED LEGISLATION

Joyce Littell Smith, MSW

Gail Marie Sullivan, MSW

Abstract

This study analyzes several influences on Senate voting patterns on key legislation selected by NASW. Party affiliation, region, ratio of NASW registered social workers to state population, liberal and conservative ideology, and judgment of social work were found to be significantly associated with voting patterns. Results of a questionnaire distributed to each Senator indicate a favorable perception of the field of social work.

The Carter Administration and the 95th and 96th Congresses have demonstrated a conservative trend. Social programs have been reduced in favor of increased military spending, apparently in heed of vocal conservative groups who criticize social program funding as a major cause of inflation (Dewar, 1980; "Social Program Cuts," 1980).[1] In view of the increasingly conservative approach evidenced in federal budget spending priorities and in light of the fact that major social service decisions are made in the political arena, it is important that social workers, in order to have an impact on policy formulation, continue developing greater understanding of political process. Knowledge of legislators' voting behavior is fundamental to understanding and influencing policy decision-making. The central question raised in this article is what factors influence voting behavior.

Political scientists have identified many pressures that influence legislative voting decisions. These pressures emanate from a large number of directions and may be summarized in terms of six types: (1) political parties; (2) members' constituencies; (3) interest groups; (4) members' personal values, preferences and beliefs; (5) the executive branch; and (6) colleagues within the Congress (Froman, 1963; Jackson, 1974; Kingdon, 1973; Turner, 1951). In addition to these pressures, there are always budgetary constraints which may conflict with the policy

SOURCE: *Journal of Sociology and Social Welfare*, Vol. 7, Nov. 1980, pp. 857–869.

interests of the Congressman. This study examines some major variables selected from the first four types of influences on Congressional decision-making.

The National Association of Social Workers (NASW) selected ten important pieces of legislation during the 95th Congress and tallied roll call votes of Senators, supporting or opposing the NASW position, in order to assess Senators' compatibility with its philosophy. Although a Senator's voting record is only one of the many components of his political stance, it remains the best single objective indicator of his position on a specific issue and of his general ideological persuasion (Barone, Ujifusa, Matthews, 1977; xv). The authors also examined the perception Senators have of the field of social work through a questionnaire given to each Senator. The questionnaire was designed to determine his attitude toward social work, his general knowledge of the profession, and his judgment as to its importance. Studies focusing on such areas have been used to ascertain the way social work is perceived by the general public (Condie, Hanson, Lang, Moss, Kane, 1978; Kadushin, 1958; Weinberger, 1976; White, 1955), and by other professions (Brennan and Khinduke, 1971; Ferris, 1968; Garrett, 1968; Olsen and Olsen, 1967; Robinson, 1967), but the authors' review of the literature uncovered no study of Senators' views of the profession. The number of times a Senator voted in line with NASW's position was compared with six empirical variables and with responses to the questionnaire to determine if there was a significant association between these variables and the voting patterns of the Senator.

Design

The general plan of the study was guided by the following research questions:

1. What are some of the major variables associated with voting patterns of Senators on significant pieces of legislation selected by NASW?

2. How do members of the United States Senate perceive the field of social work, and does this perception have an influence on their voting patterns?

The population under study was the 95th Congress of the United States Senate (100 members), serving in office as of January 1978. One recently appointed Senator was discounted (thereby reducing the population to 99) in that he replaced a deceased Senator who had cast the votes under study. In order to answer the first research question, the population was analyzed in terms of votes cast in line with NASW's position on ten legislative items and in terms of six empirical variables.

The second question was investigated by a questionnaire designed to ascertain each Senator's perception of the field of social work. The answers were analyzed in terms of votes cast in line with NASW's stand. The following six hypotheses were postulated and tested:

Hypothesis 1: Age is associated with voting patterns of Senators on key pieces of legislation selected by NASW.

Hypothesis 2: Party of affiliation (Democrat, Republican) is associated with voting patterns of Senators on key pieces of legislation selected by NASW.

Hypothesis 3: Region represented (Northeast, South, North Central, West) ("Statistical Abstracts", 1978), is associated with voting patterns of Senators on key pieces of legislation selected by NASW.

Hypothesis 4: Ratio of NASW registered social workers ("Annual Report of Membership", 1978) in each state to state population ("Current Population Reports", 1978) is associated with voting patterns of Senators on key pieces of legislation selected by NASW.

Hypothesis 5: Liberal (Americans for Democratic Action) (Barone et al., 1977)[2] ratings are associated with voting patterns of Senators on key pieces of legislation selected by NASW.

Hypothesis 6: Conservative (National Taxpayers Union) (Barone et al., 1977) ratings are associated with voting patterns of Senators on key pieces of legislation selected by NASW.

The dependent variable, voting patterns of members of the 95th Congress, was defined as Senate votes cast *in line with* NASW's position on ten bills and amendments dealing with the following subjects: revision of the Criminal Code (S. 1437), fiscal 1978 supplemental defense appropriations (H.R. 9375), federal funds for abortion (H.R. 9555), loan guarantees for New York City (H.R. 12426), labor law revisions (H.R. 8410), the CETA Program (S. 2570), District of Columbia voting representation (H.J. Res. 554), court-ordered busing (S. 1753), appropriations for HUD (H.R. 12936), and health planning (S. 2410) ("Senate Votes Compiled", 1979).

The questionnaire contained 15 items (summarized in results section). Two items designed to measure attitude focused on the status of the field of social work and licensing regulations for social workers. One item asked if there was a need for more social workers in the Senator's state. It was assumed that both attitude and knowledge of the Senator would be reflected in his awareness of whether the current number of social workers in each state is sufficient to meet the needs of the population. Knowledge of social work was also ascertained by asking about nine practice settings. It is well known that social workers are employed by public welfare agencies and protective services, but many people are unaware of the numerous diverse settings in which social workers practice ("Social Work Month", 1979). Over 300 professional social workers currently hold political office (Humphreys, 1979; 6), indicating that social workers are not only implementors of social policies but actual decision-makers as well. The Senator's judgment as to the extent of decision-making authority which should be properly invested in social workers was addressed by three items. To determine if the Senator's attitude toward, knowledge and judgment of social work had any significant influence in voting patterns, each item was analyzed as an independent variable.

A cover letter and questionnaire were hand-delivered to the office of each Senator. For those Senators failing to respond, a second letter and questionnaire were issued. The cover letter, delivered to the staff Legislative Assistant responsible for social welfare/work related issues, requested that the Senator personally fill out the questionnaire. However, since studies have found that staff members have a high degree of fundamental agreement with the attitudes and beliefs of their Congress member, as well as with the voting position taken by the Congress member (Kingdon, 1973; 192–197), it was requested that the Legislative Assistant fill out the questionnaire if the Senator was unable to do so.

Fifty-eight completed questionnaires were returned: 9 percent from Senators, 72 percent from Legislative Assistants, and 19 percent from other professional staff members. Seven questionnaires filled out by staff members were, in addition, reviewed by Senators. In order to see if there were differences between the 58 questionnaire respondents and 41 non-respondents in terms of the six empirical variables investigated in this study, Chi Square tests were run. No significant difference was found between Senators responding and those failing to respond to the questionnaire for each of the empirical variables, thus indicating that respondents were representative of the total Senate population in terms of the variables analyzed in this study.

Results

The distributions of the dependent and six empirical independent variables in the population are presented in Tables 1 and 2. Analysis of the six hypotheses found that age is the only variable of the six tested which was not significantly associated with voting patterns of Senators on the ten key pieces of legislation selected by NASW. Analysis of the six hypotheses is as follows:

1. *Age.* The mean age of the Senators is 55.5 years. A Pearson product-moment correlation $[r = -.07; p < .26]$ was obtained signifying that age is not significantly associated with how Senators voted on legislation selected by NASW.

TABLE 1   Distribution of Dependent Variable in Study Population: Voting Patterns of Senators Agreeing with NASW's Position

Number of votes cast in agreement with NASW's position on key bills	Number of times Senators voted in agreement with NASW's position
0	3
1	12
2	9
3	11
4	6
5	11
6	10
7	12
8	13
9	12
10	0
	Total 99
Mean = 5.03	

2. *Party Affiliation.* A pooled variance estimate for the means of voting patterns by party revealed a significant difference between Democrats ($\bar{x}$ = 6.05) and Republicans ($\bar{x}$ = 3.46), [$t(3.37)$ = 5.03; d.f. = 97; p < .001] signifying that Democrats voted more in line with NASW than Republicans.

3. *Region of the Country.* A one-way analysis of variance of region by voting patterns yielded a significant difference between Senators from the Northeast region ($\bar{x}$ = 7.28), North Central region ($\bar{x}$ = 6.04), West region ($\bar{x}$ = 4.31) and South region ($\bar{x}$ = 3.55) of the United States in terms of voting patterns [$F(3.98)$ = 10.994; d.f. = 3,95; p = < .001] signifying that Senators from the Northeast and North Central regions voted more in line with NASW than Senators from the West and South regions.

4. *Ratio of NASW Registered Social Workers to State Population.* The national mean ratio of NASW registered social workers to state population is one social worker to 3,831. A Pearson product-moment correlation [r = −.463; p < .001] was obtained showing a significant negative correlation of ratio of social workers per state capita with voting patterns, indicating that the smaller the difference between number of NASW registered social workers and state population (i.e., higher the ratio of social workers per capita), the more the Senator votes in line with NASW's stand and the larger the difference between the number of NASW registered social workers and state population (i.e., the lower the ratio of social

TABLE 2   Distribution of Independent Variables in Study Population

Variables		Frequency		
		Number		Percentage
Age				
35–50		33		33.3
51–59		35		35.4
60–80		31		31.3
	Total	99	Total	100.0
Party				
Democrats		60		60.6
Republicans		39		39.4
	Total	99	Total	100.0
Region				
Northeast		18		18.2
South		31		31.3
North Central		24		24.2
West		26		26.3
	Total	99	Total	100.0
Ratio of NASW Social Workers Per State Population				
1,000–2,599		22		22.2
2,600–3,399		24		24.2
3,400–4,999		28		28.3
5,000–8,999		25		25.3
	Total	99	Total	100.0
ADA Ratings				
0–26		28		33.7
31–75		28		33.7
79–100		27		32.6
	Total	83	Total	100.0
NTU Ratings				
0–30		27		32.6
31–46		28		33.7
47–83		28		33.7
	Total	83	Total	100.0

workers per capita), the less the Senator votes in line with NASW's stand.

5. *Liberal (Americans for Democratic Action) Ratings.* Eighty-three of the 99 Senators were rated by ADA on a scale from 0 to 100 ($\bar{x} = 51.34$). A Pearson product-moment correlation coefficient,

$[r = .80; p < .001]$ was obtained showing a significant positive correlation of liberal ideology with voting patterns (i.e., the more liberal the Senator is rated the more he voted in line with NASW's stand).

6. *Conservative (National Taxpayers Union) Ratings.* Eighty-three of the 99 Senators were rated by NTU on a scale of 0 to 100 ($\bar{x}$ = 40.92). A Pearson product-moment correlation coefficient $[r = -.67; p < .001]$ was obtained showing a significant negative correlation of conservative ideology with voting patterns (i.e., the more conservative the Senator is rated the less he voted in line with NASW's stand).

Through the use of a 4-way analysis of variance, the authors were able to test for the effects of each of the four independent variables on voting patterns as well as for interaction effects. Three of the independent variables were found to be significant: party ($F = 11.228, p < .01$), region ($F = 3.475, p < .05$), and liberal ratings ($F = 16.256, p < .001$). Ratio of NASW registered social workers to state population was not found to be significant. Of the two- and three-way interactions, only party by area was significantly related to voting patterns ($F = 3.13, p < .05$). In terms of hypotheses tested, the analysis of interaction effects indicated that no important combinations of the independent variables account for more than the independent variables taken singly.

Questionnaire results, shown in Table 3, indicate that generally the majority of Senators (79 percent) have a positive attitude toward social work, considering it a profession. Most Senators seem to have a broad knowledge of settings in which social workers practice. The majority indicated hospitals (95 percent), prisons (95 percent), community action programs (93 percent), schools (88 percent), police departments (81 percent), and armed forces (71 percent) as appropriate places for employment of social workers. Most Senators (62 percent) indicated that the Bureau of the Budget was not an appropriate place for social workers. Senators were split on seeing a mayor's office (59 percent) and private practice in psychotherapy (50 percent) as appropriate social work practice settings. The majority of Senators (90 percent) judged that having an identifiable clientele should not disqualify social workers from making policy decisions regarding social programs in Government. Senators were divided in their attitude toward state licensing for social workers: 47 percent of the Senators were in favor of state licensing and 35 percent were opposed. Most comment answers supported leaving licensing up to the states.

The great majority of Senators (78 percent) were of the opinion that trained social workers should play decision-making roles in the Office of Management and Budget determining the budgets for HEW/

TABLE 3   Distribution of Questionnaire Responses (N = 58)

Variables	Number of Respondents	Percentage
Attitude		
Social work is:		
profession	46	79
para-profession	9	15
other	3	6
	58	100
In favor of state licensing for social workers:		
yes	27	47
no	20	35
comments	11	18
	58	100
Attitude and Knowledge		
Need for more social workers in state:		
yes	25	43
no	7	12
don't know	26	45
	58	100
Knowledge		
Practice settings checked:		
Hospitals	55	95
Prisons	55	95
Community Action Programs	54	93
Schools	51	88
Police Department	47	81
Armed Forces	41	71
Mayor's Office	34	59
Private Practice in Psychotherapy	29	50
Bureau of the Budget	22	38
Judgment		
Identifiable clientele disqualifies social workers from making policy decisions regarding social programs in Government:		
yes	5	9
no	52	90
comments	1	1
	58	100

TABLE 3 *(concluded)*

Variables	Number of Respondents	Percentage
Trained social workers are qualified to play decision-making roles in government:		
yes	45	78
no	8	14
comments	5	8
	58	100
Level where social worker's decision-making authority should stop:		
direct service to clients	6	10
managing agency	1	2
authority at county level	3	5
authority at state level	3	5
authority at federal level	28	48
no answer	17	30
	58	100

HUD and other federal social programs. Senators were divided in their judgment as to where social workers' decision-making authority should stop: 48 percent believed this authority should stop at the federal level and 22 percent placed authority at the state and more local levels. Thirty percent of the Senators did not answer the question. As to their knowledge of the need for more social workers in their states, 43 percent indicated there was currently a need for more social workers while 12 percent said there was no need, and 45 percent did not know if there was a need.

In order to see if judgment, knowledge, and attitude of the Senator were associated with voting patterns, a test of analysis of variance was performed on each question. Two of the 15 items, both measuring judgment, were found to be significantly associated with voting patterns of Senators on the ten key bills. One of these items asked, "Should the fact that social workers have an identifiable clientele disqualify social workers from making policy decisions regarding social programs in the Government?" Ninety-nine percent of the respondents answered this question. A pooled variance estimate revealed a significant difference between those who responded *yes* ($\bar{x} = 5.13$) and those who responded *no* ($\bar{x} = 2.2$) in terms of voting patterns [$t(2.01) = 2.32$;

d.f. = 55; $p < .05$] indicating that Senators who responded *no* to the question, voted more in line with NASW's stand, than those responding *yes.*

The second item asked, "Where should social workers' decision-making authority stop: local to state level or federal level?" A pooled variance estimate for the 70 percent who answered this question revealed a significant difference between those who felt authority should stop at the local to state level ($\bar{x} = 5.0$) as opposed to the federal level ($\bar{x} = 2.8$), in terms of voting patterns [$t(2.70) = 12.45$; d.f. = 39, $p < .001$]. Senators who believe that decision-making authority should stop at the federal level voted more in line with NASW's stand than those who favored the more local to state level. The above analyses of questions indicate that Senators with a more favorable judgment of social work vote more in line with NASW's position. This suggests that a Senator's judgment of social work significantly influences his voting on social work related legislation.

Two additional items were found to be significantly associated with voting patterns slightly over the .05 probability level. One item which measured knowledge asked if schools were an appropriate setting in which social workers practiced. A pooled variance estimate on the 85 percent who responded revealed a significant difference between those who recognized schools as a social work practice setting ($\bar{x} = 5.2$) and those who did not ($\bar{x} = 3$), in terms of voting patterns [$t(1.67) = 1.99$; d.f. = 56; $p < .052$]. This indicates that Senators checking schools voted more in line with NASW's stand than those who did not.

The second item which measured both knowledge and attitude asked, "Is there currently a need for more social workers in your state?" There was a 100 percent response to this question. A one-way analysis of variance revealed a significant difference between those Senators answering *yes* ($\bar{x} = 5.96$), *no* ($\bar{x} = 4.14$), and *do not know* ($\bar{x} = 4.19$), in terms of voting patterns [$F(3.17) = 2.99$; d.f. = 2,55; $p < .058$]. It is interesting to note that those Senators who said there was a need for more social workers voted more in line with NASW's position than those who did not indicate a need and those who did not know.

Discussion

This study has demonstrated that party affiliation, region, ratio of NASW registered social workers to state population, liberal and conservative ideology, and judgment of social work, each has significantly influenced the way Senators voted on ten pieces of legislation selected by NASW. Age, knowledge and attitude toward social work were found to have no significance in terms of voting patterns. From these findings it can be concluded that Democratic Senators, with a liberal rating from

Northeast states with a high ratio of social workers per population, tended to vote in line with NASW's stand on social work related legislation. Republican senators, with a conservative rating from Southern states with a low ratio of social workers per population, tended to vote least in line with NASW's stand on social work related legislation. Although these results are somewhat predictable, NASW has not analyzed these specific factors, nor were the authors able to find any studies in which these factors were analyzed.

Results of the questionnaire indicate that the majority of Senators have a positive perception of the field of social work. Most of the respondents considered social work to be a profession and were aware that social workers function in a broad range of roles and practice settings. The majority also recognized that trained social workers are qualified to formulate and implement social policy. Recent articles suggest that the general perception of the field of social work is more favorable than in previous years (Alexander, 1979; Bartlett, 1970; Clearfield, 1973; Condie et al., 1978; Meyer and Siegel, 1977). The present study confirms this supposition in that Senators, as representatives of the public, likewise hold a favorable view of social work. The questionnaire results are encouraging for they suggest that social work is currently considered by Senators to be a valuable profession, whose practitioners are qualified to formulate and implement policy decisions. These findings should enhance the self-image of social work as well as encourage social workers to interpret and implement their unique understanding of people in policy decision-making activities.

Although the present study examines only some of the major factors which can be used to understand voting behavior of Senators on issues pertaining to social work, the findings suggest that some of the factors identified play a significant role in determining how Senators vote on social work related legislation. These factors may assist social work political practice by identifying Senators who are more likely than others to be receptive to arguments in favor of or against legislation upon which the social work community has taken a stand. The results suggest that social workers can influence political process in favor of social services by concentrating lobbying efforts where most effective, that is, on liberal Senators from northern states with a high ratio of social workers per population, who have a favorable judgment for the professional decision-making roles of social workers. This being an election year, it would be timely for social workers also to concentrate campaign efforts where they would have the most impact. The factors isolated in this study can be used to identify those candidates who are most likely to vote favorably in the future on social legislation.

On the other hand, some of the factors identified in this study do not play a significant role in determining how Senators vote on legislation pertaining to social work. A common assumption is that older Senators tend to vote more conservatively on social issues. However, this study found that age does not play a significant role in determining how Senators vote on social work related legislation. It appears that social workers have done a good job in educating Senators about the field of social work. Results show that the majority of Senators are knowledgeable about and have a positive attitude toward social work. However their knowledge and attitude do not significantly influence their voting behavior. Accordingly, these results suggest that in the future the education of Senators about the field of social work need not be a priority focus.

Complex factors influence legislative voting decisions. This study, by isolating a few of these factors, is an important first step toward more wide ranging and intensive investigations of a larger number of complex influences. Important factors requiring further study include: composition of the Senator's constituency; number, size and types of social work agencies in each state; the extent of political activism of NASW state chapters; and social issues of primarily state-wide interest.

FOOTNOTES

This article is a revision of a research project which the authors conducted toward their Master of Social Work degrees, May 1979, National Catholic School of Social Service, The Catholic University of America. The authors wish to thank James Rooney, Ph.D. for his assistance.

1. The anti-inflation strategy proposed by Administration and Congressional Budget Committees for fiscal 1981 requires wide-ranging cuts in social programs to accommodate increases in military outlays within the confines of a balanced budget. Proposed domestic spending cuts are spread over broad categories of services, affecting primarily spending for social services, employment and income assistance programs.
2. The Americans for Democratic Action rate Senate members on a broad spectrum of issues and the National Taxpayers Union rate members on every spending vote. These political interest groups represent the extremes of liberalism and conservativism, respectively.

REFERENCES

Alexander, Chauncey A.
  1979 "NASW Executive Director Reviews Practice of Professionalism in Social Work History." Better Times 60 (March 26): 6.
Barone, Michael, Grant Ujifusa, and Douglas Matthews
  1977 The Almanac of American Politics 1978. New York: E.P. Dutton.

Bartlett, Harriet M.
1970 The Common Base of Social Work Practice. Washington, D.C.: National Association of Social Workers, Inc.

Brennan, William C. and Shanti Khinduke
1971 "Role Expectations of Social Workers and Lawyers in the Juvenile Court." Crime and Delinquency 17 (April):191–201.

Bureau of the Census, U.S. Department of Commerce
1978a Current Population Reports, Population Estimates and Projections. Series P-25, 790. Washington, D.C.: U.S. Government Printing Office.
1978b Statistical Abstracts of the United States, 1978. Washington, D.C.: U.S. Government Printing Office.

Clearfield, Sidney M.
1973 A Study of Selected Aspects of the Professional Self-Image of Members of The National Association of Social Workers in Three Locales. Unpublished doctoral dissertation. Washington, D.C.: The National Catholic School of Social Service, The Catholic University of America.

Condie, C. David, Janet Hanson, Nancy Lang, Deanne Moss and Rosalie Kane
1978 "How the Public Views Social Work." Social Work 23 (January):47–53.

Dewar, Helen
1980 "Congress Clears Balanced Budget Stressing Defense." The Washington Post 191 (June 13): 1–2.

Ferris, Ellen Walsh
1968 Social Work Function as Perceived by Student and Resident Physicians and Social Work Experts. Unpublished doctoral dissertation. New York: School of Social Work, Columbia University.

Froman, Louis A.
1963 Congressmen and Their Constituencies. Chicago: Rand McNally and Co.

Garrett, Richard
1968 The Image of Social Work Perceived by The Professions of Education and Social Work. Unpublished MSW Thesis. Utah: Graduate School of Social Work, University of Utah.

Humphreys, Nancy
1979 "Where Social Workers Practice? Dr. Humphreys Has Answers." Better Times 60 (February 26):6.

Jackson, John E.
1974 Constituencies and Leaders in Congress: Their Effects on Senate Voting Behavior. Cambridge: Harvard University Press.

Kadushin, Alfred
1958 "Prestige of Social Work—Facts and Factors." Social Work 3 (April): 37–43.

Kingdon, John W.
1973 Congressmen's Voting Decisions. New York: Harper and Row.

Meyer, Henry J. and Sheldon Siegel
1977 "Profession of Social Work: Contemporary Characteristics." Pp. 1067–1081 in John B. Turner, et al. (eds.), Encyclopedia of Social Work. Seventeenth Edition. New York: National Association of Social Workers.

National Association of Social Workers
1979 Annual Report of Membership Statistics, December 1978. Washington, D.C.: National Association of Social Workers, Inc.

Olsen, Katherine M. and Marvin E. Olsen
1967 "Role Expectations and Perceptions for Social Workers in Medical Settings." Social Work 12 (July): 70–78.

Robinson, Sally
1967 "Is There a Difference?" Nursing Outlook 15 (November): 34–36.

"Senate Votes Compiled on Key Issues."
1978 The Advocate 7 (September).

"Social Work Month—Promoting a Profession."
1979 NASW News 24 (March): 1, 10.

"Social Program Cuts for Balanced Budget Okayed in Committee."
1980 NASW News 25 (May): 1, 18–19

Turner, Julius
1951 Party and Constituency: Pressures on Congress. Baltimore: Johns Hopkins Press.

Weinberger, Paul
1976 "Assessing Professional Status in Social Welfare." Personnel Information 10 (July):1, 44–47.

White, R. Clyde
1955 "Prestige of Social Work and the Social Worker." Social Work Journal 36 (January):21–23, 33.

Article 22

LOBBYING AND SOCIAL WORK

Maryann Mahaffey

The specific and immediate goals of the social work profession vary widely in the different fields of practice, but, in general, social workers consistently seek to expand and improve social and rehabilitative services for those who are powerless, discriminated against, shackled by circumstances, and deprived of opportunities to achieve their maximum individual potential. In recognition of societal and environmental effects on personal well-being, social workers also seek to change the environment. The extent to which the social work professional is able to achieve these objectives, particularly those related to environmental and social change, depends at least in part on social policy and, consequently, on the principal forces in the formulation of social policy—politics and government.

Despite the importance of government's legislative and administrative processes to the profession's objectives, the literature of social work (and other human service professions as well) is virtually devoid of materials delineating the discrete sequence of actions necessary to achieve political goals. The purpose of this article is to describe how social workers can advance their professional goals by undertaking political activities and, in particular, by lobbying to influence the legislative process.

Political Strategies

Politics has been variously termed the art or science of government, the art of balancing, the art of compromise, the art of the possible, the art of dissimulation, and the exercise of power. In a governmental system that involves widely disparate groups, interests, and forces in the checks and balances of multiple decision centers, those active in the political process are inevitably concerned with dialectics—with opposing forces that are dying or coming to life and with the new problems created by solving old ones. Politics and government therefore involve participants in such strategies and tactics as struggle, confrontation, negotiation, compromise, building coalitions, and utilizing power. It is useful to review how some of these strategies apply to the political process.

Struggle.   Through struggle and striving for reform, people learn to identify their self-interest and distinguish friends from enemies. They begin to understand what the real issues are and to avoid secondary concerns that deplete their energies and deflect them from major goals. They learn to work together and build power based on numbers that can counteract other kinds and levels of power, such as money or position. For example, those participating in various liberation struggles, such as women, blacks, Chicanos, American Indians, and other oppressed minorities, are learning that by working together they can exert power to reduce the exploitation of any group or individual. Struggle often requires confronting the opposition and demands a willingness to fight for rights as well as privileges.

Negotiation.   Lobbying, and other forms of political activity as well, can be compared to union negotiating. Both union negotiator and lobbyist have to come to terms with the boss—the owner, manager, decision maker, or legislator—in a small group meeting, and both must continually remember the fundamental interests of their constituents or employing organization. Negotiators or lobbyists who forget the power of their supporters and the thrust of their goals cannot be effective; they can even sell out their constituents. Nor can negotiators be effective unless they understand the interests and power of the opposition. They must know the realm of the possible and continuously probe to expand its limits. They must struggle for definition and clarity and for agreement or closure on specific terms.

Cooperation.   Perhaps the most telling political axiom is "Union gives strength." Little can be done alone, and the cooperation of others is essential to most political and lobbying activities. Colleagues must be enlisted to expedite certain measures, and coalitions and alliances must be formed deliberately to serve organizational ends.

Compromise.   Lobbyists must be prepared to fight for as much as they can get and often be willing to forfeit one objective to obtain another. Compromise should lead to long-term gains rather than losses. Negotiations to achieve the best that is possible at the moment may involve accepting unfavorable conditions for the sake of advancing the major objective. For example, a lobbyist might support a family assistance plan because it established the principle of federal responsibility for ensuring a minimum income for families. Securing this principle might require accepting family allowances that were grossly inadequate, but the lobbyist might draw the line on supporting the measure if it included forced work and a means test. Before negotiating a compromise, the lobbyist should resolve three key questions: What principles are basic? Where is the line drawn between establishing a principle and selling out? What is acceptable to the sponsoring group? In addition, the positions must be clear and argued out before the compromise is struck, for attempting to avoid resistance by settling before positions have been firmed is to ask for trouble later.

Step-by-Step Progress.   Once a principle is established by a legislative measure, there is always hope that the measure can be improved in the future. Amendments may relate, for instance, to expanding coverage, broadening services, or revising disadvantageous provisions. Small as well as big victories in the negotiating process process strengthen massive demonstrations and protest movements. It is difficult to sustain a massive effort without periodic concrete achievements. Small victories build people's faith both in their ability to create change and in their change agent. The challenge lies in helping people see that the immediate success is a step along the way to the larger victory and to recognize that step-by-step progress is a way of building power.

Use of Power.   The political process inevitably involves strategies for using power. These range from simple persuasion to bargaining and exchanging and to manipulation, dissimulation, and coercion. It is the wise lobbyist who uses power in such a way that friends are retained while objectives are achieved.

Sometimes those engaged in the political process become enthralled with the game, the means, and the power, developing an inflated pride in their own cleverness and skill with words and facts. It is a cardinal rule that lobbyists must never lose sight of their objectives. They must always remember that lobbying occurs within a system of political processes and is a methodology for creating change. Lobbying is not an end in itself.

Barriers to Interaction

Social workers have many illusions and misconceptions about the political process and politicians. These misapprehensions, coupled with the public stereotypes of social workers, form barriers to effective relationships between social workers and politicians. Such barriers must be broken down if social workers are to achieve credibility and influence as lobbyists.

Many social workers have a limited knowledge of government structures and even of the basic principles of civics and economics. Too few understand that a bill goes through a series of steps before it is voted on and that, in consequence, few bills can survive the legislative process in their original form. While a bill is in process, the sponsoring legislators prove they are on the job by proposing, supporting, or opposing—often in concert with colleagues—various deletions, revisions, and additions, taking whatever actions seem most appropriate to protect their own and their constituents' interests.

It is important for social workers to recognize that politicians serving as ombudsmen for constituents continually deal with the messes that powerful interests, bureaucracies, and politicians themselves create and that result in constituents' being cheated or harassed by complicated regulations and inefficient administrators. Politicians are thus under constant pressure to find immediate solutions to these and other difficult problems. Moreover, politicians know that all issues are strongly linked to feelings, including their colleagues' competitiveness for position.

All too often social workers look on the political process with disdain and aversion. Many consider politicians reactionary, venal old men who make deals and sell out their principles. These generalizations may sweep the social worker off course and deter actions dictated by social work training. The social worker's responsibility is to diagnose the politician's concerns and relationships, locate people who can be helpful allies or supporters, and search for areas of common interest and consequent influence.

Social workers also tend to become impatient with the prolonged time involved in creating change, and some lack the staying power to survive the compromises and twists and turns of the political process. They forget that the larger the system, the more complex and difficult it is to change. Many social workers consider that their rights of self-determination and individual decision making are eroded by the disciplined group effort necessary to remain in the political mainstream, keep track of the complex interplay of forces, and maintain effective coalitions.

Illusions

Much has been written about politicians' tendency to react to crises of the moment, but the notion that all politicians lack values and long-range goals is an illusion. One state senator in Michigan, for example, measures every bill and governmental action by its effect on the poor blacks who make up his constituency. He is a supporter of government as the employer of last resort. He thinks the government subsidizes the rich and penalizes the poor, and he wants to reverse that. Believing in accountability to those who elected him, he holds an annual legislative conference and monthly public sessions with constituents. He works assiduously to build support in his district.

Another state senator in Michigan has introduced legislation to establish subsidized adoption and increase the assets elderly citizens can have and still qualify for old age assistance. Nevertheless, he also introduced legislation to reduce the allotment under Aid to Families with Dependent Children called for by the state's governor. He is a businessman from a rural area, concerned with preserving free enterprise, limiting the central government's powers, and, if possible, reducing governmental expenditures.

Some social workers' naiveté about politicians and the political process leads them to believe that politicians are so powerful that they are unapproachable. They forget that politicians usually want to get reelected, move to higher office, or increase their power and influence. Politicians, therefore, are vulnerable to voter pressure, especially pressure from those in their own districts. Social workers forget, too, that politicians are not always consistent and that some politicians, by virtue of their work to maintain bases in their districts, have been able to take advanced positions and continue in office. The support of national health care by Congressman Ron Dellums of California is an example.

Social workers who view themselves as morally and ethically superior and who rely on individual moral suasion to influence politicians are not being realistic. Legislators know that however strongly they may believe in a moral principle, they cannot use morality to sway colleagues who may be trying, for example, to avoid raising taxes. Politicians have long memories about casualties at the polls and recall all too vividly those who were defeated because they sponsored tax increases at the wrong time, although for altruistic reasons.

Social workers are just one of the many lobbyist groups trying to influence politicians, and they are not generally in a favorable position at the outset. Politicians often believe that the social worker lacks political sophistication. They think social workers avoid conflict they cannot control and consequently lack the will to join in long-term struggles on controversial positions. Also, some politicians distrust intellectual professionals. Because of such negative attitudes, social worker–lobbyists do not always receive prompt and warm receptions. The need, therefore, is for the worker-lobbyist to maintain a delicate balance—to avoid oversensitivity, keep long-range goals in mind, and remain sensitive to the legislator's feelings while being alert to the issues at hand.

The social worker's position is also potentially advantageous. The social worker can be perceived not as a suppliant, but as the supplier of life-giving skills and coveted information. Politicians are perpetually concerned about getting feedback from varied sources to check their facts and impressions. They are constantly searching for reliable information about conditions and relationships in communities they represent. Social worker-lobbyists, who have training in social relationships and specific knowledge about people's needs and the services existing to meet needs, should be perennially helpful. It is necessary to be persistent, however, and to prove the value of the social worker's expertise.

Many politicians believe that change could be accelerated and people helped more if social workers showed less concern for self-protection and greater eagerness to help clean up politics, including a willingness to run for public office. Because the elected governing bodies of the nation are major sites for potential change, the stakes are high. They are especially high if social worker-lobbyists are ready to engage in the long, arduous, and time-consuming task of educating people to their self-interest and organizing them to influence the political process. It is essential that social workers be elected to public office and that others support them with time and money.

Lobbyists' Functions and Skills

The lobbyist is a person paid to represent an organization officially with government officeholders and agencies. Most lobbying focuses on legislation relating to special interests. It is pursued with legislative and administrative leaders and does not ordinarily receive public attention. In recent years, citizens' groups concerned with specific issues have been on the increase.

The responsibility of the social worker-lobbyist is to protect the employing organization's interests in legislatures and with administrative units. Endeavoring to present a personal image of tact, integrity, and discretion, social worker-lobbyists establish governmental contacts for the professional organization, ascertaining the limits of action and apprising the organization's leaders of findings so they can determine an appropriate course.

Effective lobbyists have varied skills and they can be depended on by both the employing organization and by legislators. They are friendly, outgoing, articulate, and persuasive. They can work independently, following the organization's general directives, and they must be flexible and willing to maintain irregular work hours if necessary. A good lobbyist has the maturity to argue vociferously on one issue, be a friendly partner on another, and ignore personal rebuffs by either friend or foe. Above all, the lobbyist knows when to talk and when to listen. The effective lobbyist also knows how to wait. It is unnecessary to buy lunches, but politicians remember who supports them at election time and who contributes money to their campaigns. Campaigns are expensive, and politicians hate fund raising.

The social worker-lobbyist should be skilled and experienced in the strategies and tactics of politics and have a sophisticated sense of timing and appropriateness. For example, if there is to be a demonstration, the lobbyist should be able to recommend astutely when and where it might be held, how many might participate, and what the target should be. If the time and place are wrong, if few or too many take part, or if the target is poorly chosen, the results may be psychologically damaging for participants and may weaken the cause itself.

Lobbyists must be familiar with parliamentary procedure, with the structure of the legislature and other governmental bodies, and with the concerns and circumstances of incumbent officeholders and legislators. They must develop the skills needed to glamorize a specific issue and keep it alive with legislators who are inundated with issues. Lobbyists must know how and when to seize the initiative and put the pressure on through telephone and letter campaigns and meetings with constituents. It is important to remember that most legislation is modified and defeated in committee and that many times it is easier to defeat a bill than to pass it.

Good lobbyists develop the ability to diagnose the motivation of individuals and groups; they know how to analyze forces operative in the field and probe for areas of compromise. It is also important for lobbyists to become aware of the stresses and strains between the houses of the legislature, among various levels and branches of government, and among parties, factions, and individual officeholders. Lobbyists learn about the power of those who chair a committee and those who are committee members, and they acquaint themselves with secretaries and aides, who are sometimes the key to reaching officeholders. Aides should be cultivated, for the politician is often too busy to go into detail on many issues and must rely on aides to analyze and summarize them and recommend actions and strategies. This is particularly true of administrators. Because a major portion of the politician's work is to respond to the complaints of constituents, it is important that the lobbyist gear discussions to the needs of each politician's constituents.

A lobbyist may discover that the person who chairs a powerful committee is unshakable on certain issues but willing to compromise on others. The head of another committee may lack leadership ability and be unable to twist arms, trade on bills, or get legislation through. If a legislator is tough and a good diagnostician, is willing to take political risks for the sake of crucial issues, has clearly defined political and legislative goals, and wields power through control over the agenda and skillful use of the gavel, he or she may be the key to achieving the organization's objectives.

Major Tasks

The major tasks of the social worker-lobbyist may therefore be summarized as follows:

• Offering the expertise of the social work profession to legislators, who find it impossible to study and understand all the numerous bills they must consider. The lobbyist volunteers to give support and information and, in turn, seeks support and data helpful to the employing organization. The lobbyist offers technical assistance at the appropriate moment on one bill, provides research results before a crisis is reached on another, and organizes and exerts constituent pressure on still another, maintaining bipartisan relationships on all bills. Sometimes the lobbyist organizes support for the politician, enabling the politician go to out on a limb.

• Keeping track of all pertinent legislation, regardless of whether it is sponsored or opposed by the employing organization. The lobbyist finds out who would best support certain legislation and works closely with that lawmaker, discovering who wants to amend the bill and checking on the positions of administrative departments, the chief executive's office, and others concerned. Amendments agreed to by the employing organization are offered to legislators.

• Paying special attention to committee votes. These votes are not publicized and are often difficult to ascertain, but they are vital in targeting organizational influence. The lobbyist also seeks to know what is happening in party caucuses because positions are hammered out and deals often made in these important meetings.

• Developing relationships with other lobbyists, sharing information with them, looking for common goals, and sounding out possibilities for coalitions.

• Developing liaisons between the employing organization and the legislative body. The lobbyist pins down votes and follows up on why legislators voted the way they did. This information is fed back to the client organization and its members. Lobbyists may also be helpful in contacting the press, setting up press conferences, and working with the organization's public relations director or committee.

• Assisting the employing organization in training and organizing its members to influence the political process. This includes working with the organization and planning and coordinating delegations, demonstrations, and members' appearances at committee hearings and at sessions when votes are taken.

Employing Organization

Political power develops when people are organized, united, and active. Social work organizations should organize their members and be able to mobilize them as necessary. Having a lobbyist may stimulate such action. In employing one, the organization clearly indicates the lobbyist's responsibilities and the person to whom he or she answers. The organization itself remains primarily responsible for organizing its members, educating them on issues, keeping them informed about events, and unearthing those, including board members of social agencies, who know and have influence with legislators. However, it may be part of the lobbyist's job to assist in all this work.

The organization is also responsible for keeping issues alive among its members, which involves the constant struggle of competing with countless other demands on members' time, attention, and finances. A piece of legislation can take five years or more to pass, and in the prolonged process, members can forget reasons for early compromises and priorities. When an organization is splintered at a crucial moment, it can lose the legislation because legislators will say, "If you're not together, we're not going to bother with the bill and your position on it." Alerting members to progress on major issues is vital. This can be done through newsletters or special bulletins, which should cover questions raised, arguments used, and key opposition or support gained or lost. Telephone trees and networks, such as the Educational Legislative Action Network of the National Association of Social Workers, are essential.

The social work organization should train its members in working with politicians so that they can take on the tasks needed to push legislation ahead. If members are organized, they can be mobilized when a critical point in the legislative process is reached. Appropriate actions might include the use of such tactics as carefully timed telephone campaigns with messages left with politicians' secretaries or aides; contacts in meetings; handwritten, one-paragraph letters; presence in numbers (sometimes with signs) at hearings; testimony at hearings;

visible presence when the vote on a bill is taken; and, after the voting, thank-you letters or acknowledgments regardless of the results.

In all this, it is important that the organization establish priorities and stick to them. A lobbyist can work well on only a limited number of bills. An organization's members can devote time and enthusiasm to a limited number of issues. The organization might be wise to concentrate on a few significant legislative measures that have some likelihood of passage, rather than scatter its efforts on a dozen or more minor measures or waste time on provisions that are perennially defeated. At the same time, it must always be ready to mobilize forces to defeat or change legislation that may not be on its priority list, but that suddenly develops strength in the legislative body.

Expert Knowledge

As noted earlier, elected officials often rely on social workers for expertise in specific fields. They look to social workers to provide supporting data for bills related to social work concerns, give requested advice, analyze bills, and draft legislative proposals or amendments. Those who are experienced in preparing such information for legislators know that a premium is placed on brevity, and they learn to prepare one-page summaries that begin with a one-sentence statement of the problem and that document needs, state pros and cons, and furnish precedents and costs. It is important to deal with just a few issues at a time, or, preferably, just one, and to be willing to talk to the legislator's aides, who often read the summaries aloud to the legislator. Above all, the materials provided must be honest.

At times, the outstanding expertise, authority, or influence of a specific social worker—perhaps the director of an agency or a board member—may be called for. For example, influential social workers may affect the committee assignment of bills, thus helping to save favored legislation.

Appearances at hearings by members of the social work organization should be coordinated through the lobbyist and the designated organizational chairman or chairwoman. In general, members should be prepared to testify before committees. The lobbyist should hold an orientation session with them, telling them what to expect, pointing out the elements of an impressive presentation, and warning of pitfalls. Role playing is helpful. Common faults that create hazards for the testifying social worker are issuing moral arguments without concrete accompanying proposals, making statements that are not backed by adequate research and documentation, and using confrontational tactics that can alienate the politician. Attacks may win an audience, but they turn off legislators. It is also important to be concise in presentations.

Unfortunately, some public hearings merely seek to document positions already determined. Realizing this, some legislators are not influenced by hearings. Nevertheless, hearings serve several useful purposes. They provide opportunities to (1) spotlight issues, (2) educate the public and arouse public opinion, (3) publicize the positions and proposed solutions of those testifying, (4) educate committee members, and (5) permit legislators to test public reactions to their positions. Although the publicity arising out of hearings may be useful to politicians, it is often essential to groups that are unable to draw media coverage unless a politician is willing to share the spotlight with them in a hearing.

Model for Legislative Action

Assuming a January session of a state legislature as the target date, the following is a model for a legislative action program by a social work organization. The model identifies only the tasks that need doing, without specifying whether they are to be made the responsibility of the lobbyist, the organization's board of directors, or other agents of the organization.

Previous Spring.   Discuss with key members of the organization the specific legislative propositions to be worked on in the following session, including areas of agreement with the proposed measure and items that can be compromised if need be.

Previous Summer.   Form an organizational steering committee and select a coordinator to work with the lobbyist in planning and carrying out the following activities:

• Collect evidence providing a rationale for the proposed legislation.

• Draft a petition for social workers and community residents. The petition should be addressed to legislators and signed according to legislative districts. (Social workers' refusal to sign may indicate opposition within the organization.)

• Arrange for the organization's members to form district delegations and name a chairman or chairwoman for each delegation. Each district delegation should then hold meetings with its lawmakers to explore support. If it is an election year, there should be meetings with all candidates to ascertain their position on issues. Two members of the organization who are constituents of the appropriate district should be assigned to get to know each legislator and to maintain a relationship before and during the session. These members should make appointments with the legislators they have been assigned and prepare for the meetings by outlining in writing the issues (no more than three) they wish to discuss. These visits should be short and the presentations succinct.

Previous Fall.   Form a small committee representing a cross section of the membership. These people should have the enthusiasm and the time to be part of periodic delegations to the government halls. Their work during the fall is exploratory; demands and pressure come later:

- Arrange for an official visit with the chief executive by the committee to ascertain the executive's viewpoint. After the meeting, the committee should leave a brief written account of the points it wants to make, including solutions and documentation.

- Meet with appropriate leaders of the organization to report findings and to select and order priorities.

- If it is not an election year, select legislators to sponsor new bills and meet with them. Tie each issue to their constituents' interests.

- If it is an election year, arrange delegation meetings in each legislative district to meet with primary winners and assess their support on issues of high priority. After the election, arrange for the committee to meet with the winners and obtain commitments.

- Obtain commitments from allies and from coalitions when possible.

- Discuss legislation with key administrators, ascertaining their level of support or opposition and the changes they may favor.

January Session.   Because all important contacts have already been made, the beginning of the legislative session is a time for consolidating positions with lawmakers, exerting preliminary pressure regarding major measures, and offering social work expertise on bills under consideration:

- Arrange for a committee delegation to visit the chief executive and his or her aides to obtain active support for targeted legislation. The delegation should present letters from the organization's members favoring the legislation. Similar visits might also be arranged with key lawmakers and their aides.

- Present each legislator with a list of bills the organization supports and opposes.

- Continue to collect and analyze background information about lawmakers. Records should be kept of all political contacts and actions.
- Report to the organization's members via newsletter.

Throughout the Session.   After the legislative bodies have chosen their officers, and their committee heads and members—about mid-January—the work goes forward and continues until the session:

- Make sure of promised support
- Work with legislators on the introduction of measures.
- Visit lawmakers to enlist allies and assess strength.
- Send newsletters regularly, perhaps weekly, to key members of the organization, including the chairmen and chairwomen of the district delegations.
- Send monthly letters reporting on the effects of the legislative efforts to the organization's total membership.
- Hold organizational steering committee meetings regularly to decide compromises, arrange members' visits to legislators, discuss coalitions, and so on. This feedback system is crucial to success in influencing the political process.
- Thank legislators, administrators, and all others who provided support.

Summary

Lawmakers are always influenced by a variety of people and organizations, and social workers should increasingly be among those who exert influence. However, if social workers are to serve effectively as lobbyists, they must have training in the political process and increase their political sophistication. The profession as a whole must grow in the ability to use conflict, develop power, be decisive, and take risks while at the same time pursuing the art of compromise. Lobbying demands that social workers use to the fullest their diagnostic and organizational skills. It may well prove easier to train a social worker to be a lobbyist than to train a lobbyist to understand and represent social work goals.

The social worker-lobbyist must marry social action with practice. To achieve change, the lobbyist must have the experience, skills, and knowledge to be authoritative in providing lawmakers with the information they need. The lobbyist can maintain a commitment to the philosophy and values of social work only by clearly defining objectives, relating means to ends, and establishing proximate and middle-range goals that are consonant with and directed toward long-range goals. Compromise can establish a principle to be developed in future legislation, but the lobbyist must be willing to continue the fight to expand the principle and be clear about where to draw the line so that a sell-out is avoided.

The knowledge and skills of social workers are appropriate to gaining and using political influence. The very principles social work has isolated as useful in clinical practice and policy development are integral to the political process; the problem-solving process as social workers use it in working with individuals, groups, and communities is crucial to lobbying. Both the politician and the lobbyist must be sensitive to individuals, understand group process and complex organizations, and know what to do to effect change.

Fortunately, social workers are becoming more active politically as elected officials, lobbyists, campaign workers, and members of commissions and of politicians' staffs. The stakes are high. Elected officials ultimately determine policy, including the implementation of programs. Among the issues they will determine during the next decade is whether social security and Medicare will continue as public programs or be absorbed by the private sector, forcing people to buy protection from private insurers.

Article 23

INCOME SECURITY

James R. Storey

Since 1935 the federal government has played a major role in assuring a degree of financial security for most Americans. This income security function has been realized through two quite distinct approaches. The broader of the two is aimed at the partial replacement of wages lost due to the retirement, death, disablement, or unemployment of a breadwinner. The primary federal activities included here are the major cash social insurance programs, Social Security and unemployment compensation, and various tax provisions and regulation of fringe benefits in the private sector. The second approach provides assistance or welfare that is means-tested or conditioned upon family income. Programs of this type provide both cash assistance, such as Aid to Families with Dependent Children (AFDC); Supplemental Security Income (SSI) for the aged, blind, or disabled; and in-kind assistance such as Food Stamps and housing subsidies.

This varied assortment of activities has developed over four decades in response to a great many social and economic concerns. However, the preponderance of public policies for income security has evolved in reaction to two major policy objectives. First, government has attempted to encourage the development of a fair and adequate retirement income system through a combination of public benefit entitlements, regulation of private pension plans, favorable tax treatment of income in old age, and tax incentives for retirement saving. Second, for persons of working age who experience economic deprivation—particularly those who are heads of families with children—public policy has struggled with two interrelated concerns: (1) how to design welfare programs that are equitable and meet a family's needs without unduly disrupting the family head's work incentives; and (2) how to structure federal and state roles in welfare programs so that the degree of cost sharing and program control is acceptable to both levels of government.

These major policy issues have come to be dominated in recent years by an overriding policy consideration—the need for greater budgetary control and restraint. Spending for income security purposes (which is defined exclusive of health insurance programs in this chapter) now exceeds all other components of the federal budget, and the annual growth in such spending generally accounts for over one-third of all nondefense program spending increases. Slowing this normal growth in income security outlays is difficult politically because it requires changes in legal entitlements that affect the current or future income of virtually everyone. Thus, the budgetary control objective collides with other policy goals. Its pursuit shapes significantly the possible directions for initiatives aimed at rationalizing retirement income systems or restructuring welfare programs.

An essential part of the Reagan administration's budgetary policy is to reduce the growth in income security outlays that would have occurred under the laws in effect in 1980. Sizable reductions were achieved in congressional actions on the 1982 budget, and the president has proposed further large cuts for 1983 and beyond. The reductions in programs directed to the low-income population have been substantial and generally involve lowering benefit amounts for recipients with earnings. Increased state control over welfare policies is also emphasized and is formally embodied in President Reagan's "New Federalism" initiative.

The budget cuts in social insurance programs to date have been proportionately much smaller and have had only a mildly restraining effect on long-run growth rates. However, movement toward a new policy on retirement income is evident. The Reagan administration is less inclined than its predecessors to use pension plan regulation as a means of changing policy. Instead, greater personal retirement saving is being encouraged through expanded tax subsidies for that purpose. Major changes in Social Security were proposed but rejected by Congress. The president has established a commission on social security reform in an effort to build a consensus for significant change in this area.

This chapter examines the Reagan Administration's policy initiatives in income security and their implications. It begins with a summary of major policy developments prior to 1981 and the most important issues confronting President Reagan when he took office. The next section discusses the specific changes that have already been implemented or proposed by the president. The third section assesses the immediate and likely longer-term consequences of these changes. The chapter concludes with speculation about future policy implications.

POLICY DEVELOPMENT PRIOR TO 1981

The Social Security Act of 1935 established the basic framework of income security programs that persists today: the federal Social Security system; the state unemployment insurance system; and federal grants to states for public assistance to certain categories of needy people. Spawned in reaction to the Great Depression, these programs were greatly expanded during the 1950s and 1960s with that period's economic growth and the burgeoning popularity of Social Security. The 1960s and early 1970s saw a proliferation of aid programs for the needy as the War on Poverty and Great Society initiatives focused public attention on those people not benefiting sufficiently from economic growth.

The increased costs of income security benefits were a growing concern by the mid-1970s as economic stagnation took hold. The need to constrain costs, coupled with other concerns, led to major attempts to improve and simplify the welfare system and to rationalize the provision of retirement income. Although many improvements resulted from these reform efforts, the 1970s ended with the central purposes of reformers still out of reach and heightened concern about mounting program costs. The problem of budgetary control, dissatisfaction with the welfare system, and unresolved concerns about Social Security and pensions were paramount on the agenda of the incoming Reagan administration.

Trends in Income Security Spending

Between 1935 and 1980, federal outlays for income security programs[1] grew from less than $1 billion to $217 billion, or 8 percent of the Gross National Product (GNP). Their current 37 percent share of the federal budget is the largest of any functional area. Programs that operate as federal grants to state governments account for a significant part of overall nonfederal spending as well—39 percent of all state spending on public welfare and 6 percent of total state expenditures for all purposes.

The pattern of growth in income security spending is shown for major programs in Table 1. Income security's share of the federal budget has tripled since 1935 and more than doubled since 1955. These benefits have quadrupled as a share of GNP since 1955, and their proportion of total personal income rose from 3 to 10 percent. The expansion and maturation of Social Security was the largest factor behind this growth. However, these relative measures of spending magnitude remained level from 1975 to 1980 as program expansions all but ceased and Social Security approached maturity. Still, large year-to-year dollar

TABLE 1 Federal Outlays for Income Security Programs, 1935–1980 (in $ billions)

Program	1935	1945	1955	1965	1970	1975	1980
Social insurance and related programs							
Social Security (OASDI)	—	0.2	4.3	16.6	29.7	63.6	117.1
Income security for veterans (excl. non-service-connected pensions)	0.5	0.8	2.3	2.2	3.8	5.1	8.1
Federal employee retirement and disability	0.1	0.2	0.8	2.8	5.6	13.3	26.8
Unemployment compensation	—	a	0.1	0.2	3.4	13.5	18.0
Other programs[b]	—	0.1	0.6	1.1	1.6	4.1	6.5
Subtotal	0.6	1.3	8.1	22.9	44.1	99.6	176.5
Low-income assistance programs							
Aid to Families with Dependent Children (AFDC)	—	a	0.4	1.0	2.1	5.1	7.3
Supplemental Security Income (SSI)	—	0.3[c]	1.0[c]	1.7[c]	1.9[c]	4.8	6.4
Veterans non-service-connected pensions	a	0.1	0.8	1.9	2.3	2.7	3.6
Earned income tax credit	—	—	—	—	—	—	1.3
Low-income energy assistance	—	—	—	—	—	—	1.6
Other cash assistance	—	a	—	a	0.1	0.2	0.7
Food Stamps	—	—	—	a	0.6	4.6	9.1
Other food programs[d]	0.2	a	0.3	0.7	1.0	2.0	4.9
Housing assistance	a	a	0.1	0.2	0.5	2.1	5.5
Subtotal	0.2	0.4	2.6	5.5	8.5	21.5	40.4
Total	0.8	1.7	10.7	28.4	52.6	121.1	216.9

TABLE 1 *(concluded)*

Program	1935	1945	1955	1965	1970	1975	1980
Addendum							
Total as a percentage of							
Gross National Product (GNP)	0.3	0.3	2	4	5	8	8
Total personal income	1	1	3	5	6	10	10
Federal budget outlays	12	2	16	24	27	37	37

a. Less than $50 million.

b. Includes railroad retirement system and benefits for disabled coal miners.

c. Figures prior to 1975 are for the old program of assistance to the aged, blind and disabled that SSI replaced.

d. Includes child nutrition programs and distribution of surplus commodities.

SOURCE: Data for 1935 through 1965 are from *Social Welfare Expenditures, 1929–1966,* Social Security Administration Research Report No. 25 (Washington, D.C.: GPO, March 1968); Data for 1970 through 1980 are from various *Budgets of the United States Government* (Washington, D.C.: GPO); Data in addendum are from various *Budgets of the United States Government* and *Economic Reports of the President* (Washington, D.C.: GPO).

increases in spending arise due to rising numbers of eligible beneficiaries, benefit increases for new beneficiaries due to increases in the wages upon which benefits are based, and cost-of-living benefit increases for current beneficiaries.

Although the number of need-related programs proliferated in the 1960s and 1970s and their spending in 1980 was more than seven times the 1965 level, the share of income security benefits devoted to this type of aid has actually been less since 1965 than before. About 25 percent of total benefits were spent on aid to the needy before 1965, but this proportion has since ranged between 15 and 20 percent.

The $96 billion increase in federal income security outlays from 1975 to 1980 consisted of a $77 billion growth in social insurance benefits ($54 billion from Social Security alone) and a $19 billion rise in need-related aid. Only a quarter of the latter increase resulted from growth in the traditional cash aid programs (AFDC, SSI, veterans pensions). Most of the growth in low-income aid resulted from increased Food Stamp participation and benefit levels that rose with food prices (24 percent), new commitments for subsidized housing (18 percent), and enactment of new forms of aid (15 percent).

Income security programs are also significant on the revenue side of the federal budget since Social Security and several others have their own dedicated revenue sources. The payroll taxes collected at the federal level now amount to 30 percent of all federal revenues.

Furthermore, the income tax code contains numerous exemptions, deduction, and credits that serve an income security purpose (Table 2). Most of these tax expenditures are associated with the exclusion of social insurance benefits from taxation and tax incentives for retirement saving. Retirement saving incentives are now the largest tax expenditures associated with income security.

This huge growth in government's income security role resulted from a complex of economic factors, demographic change, and significant shifts in public opinion regarding social policies. The remainder of this section provides an overview of major income security policy developments of the past several decades, first for the social insurance systems and then for low-income assistance.

Development of Social Insurance Policies

Enactment of the Social Security Act in 1935 heralded a major turning point in federal intervention to protect individuals against precipitous financial loss. Two major systems of social insurance were created. Unemployment insurance has changed little in terms of basic structure and purpose between 1935 and 1980. Social Security, on the other hand, expanded greatly and now has many features not included

TABLE 2   Selected Tax Expenditures for Income Security Purposes, 1970–1980 (in $ billions)

Tax Expenditure	CY 1970	FY 1975	FY 1980
Tax expenditures related to social insurance			
Exclusion of benefit payments			
Social Security (retirement)	3.0[a]	2.7	6.9
Social Security (disability)	0.1	0.3	0.7
Social Security (dependents, survivors)	a	0.4	1.0
Unemployment compensation	0.4	2.3	2.5
Workers compensation	0.2	0.5	1.2
Veterans compensation	0.6[b]	0.5	1.0
Net exclusion of pension contributions and earnings			
Employer plans	3.1	5.2	12.9
Other plans	0.2	0.4	2.1
Exclusion of insurance benefits	0.5	0.8	1.6
Additional exemptions and credits for blind and elderly	a	1.2	2.1
Tax expenditures related to low-income assistance			
Exclusion of benefit payments			
Public assistance	0.1	0.1	0.4
Veterans pensions	b	c	0.1
Earned income tax credit	—	—	0.4

a. For 1970, data for Social Security (dependents, survivors) and additional exemptions and credits for blind and elderly are included with Social Security (retirement).

b. For 1970, the veterans pension figure is included in the veterans compensation figure.

c. Less than $50 million.

SOURCE: Congressional Budget Office, *Tax Expenditures: Current Issues and Five-Year Budget Projections for Fiscal Years 1982–1986* (Washington, D.C.: GPO, Sept. 1981), table 1.

in the original law. The federal role in retirement income provision also underwent a major change with enactment of the Employee Retirement Income Security Act (ERISA) in 1974.

Unemployment Insurance.   The only major structural change in unemployment benefits prior to 1970 was a provision adopted in the 1960s to extend benefits to unemployed workers for an additional thirteen weeks whenever the unemployment rate exceeded a threshold level. The 1970s saw much more change as the economy reached its worst condition since the Great Depression. Coverage of state and local employees, farm workers, and domestic workers was expanded, and a temporary twenty-six-week extension of benefits was in force during the 1975 recession. A new program of trade adjustment assistance was established to aid unemployed workers in industries adversely affected by U.S. trade policy, and its coverage was liberalized substantially after the initial implementation.

Social Security. The expansion of Social Security occurred in a long series of amendments that began before anyone actually retired under the system and continued through 1972. The system was broadened by adding new categories of beneficiaries—survivors of covered workers, the dependents of retirees and survivors, disabled workers, and early retirees aged sixty-two to sixty-four. Coverage of the work force expanded to include virtually all privately employed workers and many government employees.

Benefit entitlements were also modified frequently. First, benefits directly proportional to wages were discarded in favor of a progressive formula that replaced a considerably larger share of earnings in retirement for lower-wage workers. Second, benefit amounts were increased over time by Congress as economic growth continually presented the system with an unplanned surplus of payroll tax revenues. Third, Congress continually liberalized the "retirement test"—the provision for reducing benefits according to a beneficiary's earnings—so that those who worked could realize larger total incomes.

The 1972 amendments, which included a 20 percent benefit increase, marked the end of the expansion of Social Security coverage and benefits. Ad hoc benefit increases gave way to automatic adjustments linked to the Consumer Price Index (CPI), an approach adopted (also in 1972) in part as a means of constraining costs. In 1977 Congress selectively trimmed future benefit costs and increased payroll taxes, and it was recognized that further benefit savings or revenues might be needed to meet long-run commitments. This abrupt turnaround from expansion to retrenchment was caused by a combination of circumstances. The trust fund reserves became dangerously low as inflation drove up benefits and a stagnant economy did not produce the expected payroll tax revenues. The long-run funding outlook also turned sour as fertility and mortality projections proved wrong. Despite the 1977 legislation, by 1981 the short-run funding outlook was once again problematic due to the state of the economy.

Regulation of Private Pensions. Even though Social Security benefits have risen dramatically, the system has always been regarded as a floor under retirement income that should be supplemented by pension benefits and personal savings. During the 1970s Congress also became concerned about the pension component of this retirement system and enacted the Employee Retirement Income Security Act (ERISA) to improve private pension coverage and funding and protect the pension rights of plan participants.

After a long period of growth in pension plans, coverage had stagnated far short of universality in the 1970s, with about one-half of private, nonfarm jobs covered by plans. Only about one-fourth of Social Security retirees were also receiving a private pension. Even many of these retirees had financial difficulties. They usually retired with adequate incomes, but the real value of the pension was often severely eroded over time since pensions are almost never fully adjusted for inflation. Finally, poor funding and management of some pension plans jeopardized the retirement security of millions of workers with private coverage.

ERISA dealt with some of these concerns by setting minimum standards for employee participation and vesting, funding, and rules of fiduciary conduct. The Pension Benefit Guaranty Corporation was established to protect the benefit rights of workers and pensioners when plans are terminated. These reforms have been beneficial to many workers, although the new requirements imposed by ERISA were probably a factor in the decline in the number of plans that occurred soon after enactment.

Efforts to extend ERISA to public pension plans have not succeeded, and a recommendation of President Carter's Pension Policy Commission to mandate minimum universal pension coverage found little support. Thus, the momentum for further improvement in retirement income through pension regulation had waned shortly before the Reagan administration took office.

Low-Income Assistance

The Social Security Act provided for federal matching grants for state assistance to needy persons who were aged or blind and to families with dependent children with a deceased, absent, or incapacitated parent. Prior to 1960 the only major change in this program was the addition in 1950 of a fourth category of recipients (the permanently and totally disabled) eligible for such federal matching. Subsequently, however, low-income assistance changed considerably as public policy focused on the problems of poverty in the 1960s and then sought in the 1970s to rationalize and improve the numerous, ill-coordinated programs that had developed.

The War on Poverty.   Prior to the 1960s there had been little systematic federal policy concerning poverty and its alleviation. Rather, the focus had been on society's insuring against the primary risks of income loss faced by working people and on ameliorating the plight of the "deserving poor"—that is, the categories of needy people that society did not expect to be self-sufficient. As the politics of the 1960s led to a new awareness of chronic regional economic problems, other structural labor market problems, and past civil rights violations, the prior notion of a "deserving poor" category began to break down. The idea that a wealthy nation should attempt to pull everyone up to at least a minimal living standard took root and grew. Efforts to improve direct aid for the needy resulted in higher federal matching for state welfare payments, enactment of the Medicaid program, and the extension at state option of AFDC to two-parent families where one parent was unemployed.

Steps also were taken both to require and to encourage AFDC families to move off the welfare rolls. These efforts were spurred not only by the antipoverty crusade but also by a growing opinion that many nonworking AFDC mothers should be in the labor force. This changing opinion was grounded in part in the fact that more women generally were working, but it also reflected a fear that AFDC was creating a "welfare class" of families with no breadwinners to serve as role models for their children. Legislation was enacted to increase job-related services, require mothers without preschool children to work, and provide AFDC recipients with a positive incentive to work. Whereas previously any earnings resulted in an equivalent reduction in benefits, a 1967 law disregarded the first $30 of monthly earnings and one-third of any excess over $30 plus work expenses.

New programmatic approaches were also developed to assist needy persons not covered by the public assistance categories and to supplement the benefits of those who were. The Food Stamp program was initiated in 1964 and was greatly expanded in the late 1960s. New forms of subsidized housing assistance for low-income families were established, not only for renters but also for home buyers. A longstanding policy of providing a federal subsidy for elementary and secondary school meals was augmented to provide a deeper subsidy for meals served to children from low-income families.

The Welfare Reform Era.   This surge in benefit expansion was followed by major attempts at systematic reform that spanned the Nixon, Ford, and Carter years. The impetus for welfare reform originated in 1969, when advocates of the poor who wanted to eradicate the remaining poverty gap formed an alliance with Nixon administration officials who sought to restructure welfare programs. The goals were to (1) establish a federal benefit floor more generous than that paid in the poorest states; (2) reduce the inequity between the "working poor" not eligible for welfare and the welfare eligibles; (3) step up efforts to move into jobs those able-bodied AFDC parents not caring for preschool children; (4) begin a resorting of roles between the federal and state governments, with the federal government running a streamlined national income maintenance system; and (5) head off the proliferation of new aid programs.

The reform efforts of Nixon, Carter, and various members of Congress never realized their central purpose of replacing AFDC with a federal income maintenance system. This failure stemmed largely from two difficulties. First, to provide both adequate benefit levels for the penniless and substantial incentives for recipients to work at an acceptable program cost proved to be impossible. The combination of a reasonable benefit level and only a partial reduction of benefits for earnings results in a large eligible population. Second, it was feared that a federal benefit floor high enough to replace AFDC in a large number of states would create political and economic problems in states where wages for unskilled labor were quite low.

The welfare reform effort did spawn a series of important initiatives, however. The state programs of aid to the aged, blind, and disabled were replaced with the federal Supplemental Security Income (SSI) program. Major improvements in Food Stamps fashioned the program into a "funny money" version of the national income floor President Nixon had sought as a replacement for AFDC. Enactment of a refundable earned income tax credit provided a wage subsidy to working poor heads of families with children.

Several other major program expansions occurred during the 1970s independent of the welfare reform effort. Commitments to subsidized housing rose substantially, child nutrition assistance took on new forms, and rising oil prices led to special aid to low-income households to help pay their fuel bills.

The overall incidence of poverty had declined significantly during the 1960s (from 22 to 13 percent of the population) with economic growth and expanded social insurance and low-income assistance. The leaner years of the 1970s saw little further poverty reduction (one percentage point); however, increased benefits resulted in further improvement for the neediest groups. The poverty rate among the aged fell from 24 to 15 percent, and for female-headed families from 37 to 33 percent.

Income Security Issues When Reagan Took Office

The Reagan administration took office with restraint of federal spending as one of its main objectives. Thus a key item on the agenda was to reduce the normal growth in income security outlays in ways that were in harmony with other income security policy goals. However, this budgetary objective had to be sought in the context of the policy developments just discussed. Welfare programs were widely regarded as inequitable among states and recipient groups, and the combinations of multiple benefits were thought to result in inadequate work incentives. A dozen years of attempts to gain more national control over the system, better coordinate the various programs, and improve their management had succeeded only partially.

The situation of Social Security seemed even more critical. Unforeseen economic and demographic trends had already halted the once common use of the program as a vehicle for improving the social welfare; now even its fiscal integrity was in doubt. Regulatory efforts to fashion pension benefits into a more predictable partnership with Social Security in providing a decent retirement income had left basic issues of coverage and benefit protection unresolved. Lost pension credits due to job mobility and the effects of inflation on benefit values were particularly troublesome. The third component of retirement income, personal savings, was not a major income source for most elderly, and the saving rate nationally for the years 1977 through 1980 was at its lowest level since the late 1940s.

POLICY CHANGES UNDER PRESIDENT REAGAN

The income security area would pose a series of difficult choices for any administration in the early 1980s but particularly for one committed to domestic budgetary restraint. If policy goes unchanged, income security outlays will continue to rise, driven by rising prices and wages, growth in eligible recipients, and, in recessionary periods, by rising unemployment. These outlay increases limit any flexibility to reorder budget priorities or alter the size of government. However, to change policy requires enactment of legislation that will affect the personal income of potentially millions of people who fall mostly into categories of great social concern. Policy changes also upset existing federal-state fiscal arrangements and the distribution of federal grants. Alterations in public retirement systems may have substantial repercussions for the private pension industry. Phasing in policy changes over long time periods—while mitigating such problems—totally eliminates short-term budgetary flexibility.

The Reagan administration has approached income security with three apparent major goals: (1) to reduce the short-term growth in spending that would otherwise occur by making a variety of changes in entitlements that can be implemented quickly; (2) to turn over greater responsibility for welfare assistance to the states; and (3) to promote greater reliance by individuals on their own resources through work and asset accumulation and lessen dependence on public benefits.

Budgetary Restraint Measures

Generally speaking, the actions the Reagan administration proposed in conjunction with the 1982 budget revisions and 1983 budget request reflect a short-run view that policy changes should result in immediate budgetary savings. The impacts of such changes have to be politically acceptable to Congress based on current effects on constituents. Therefore, cuts enacted in 1981 in social insurance and related programs were limited to the most questionable benefits. Many of the welfare cuts were designed to avoid reducing benefits of the poorest recipients; savings were also sought based on evidence of need for administrative improvements. For the most part, the administration's 1983 proposals follow the pattern established for 1982.

The major failures of Reagan's 1982 budget proposals in Congress resulted where short-term income losses would have hit politically favored groups. Elimination of the minimum floor on Social Security benefits was accepted only after Congress agreed to apply it solely to new beneficiaries. Major Social Security proposals that would have immediately reduced early retirement benefits for new beneficiaries were never seriously considered by Congress.

Viewed as a one-time budgetary action, the administration's attempt to reduce income security spending was amazingly successful. (However, as indicated in the next section, enacted measures may not be as significant in curbing long-term trends.) President Reagan proposed income security entitlement cuts rising to an estimated $17 billion by 1984. He obtained the enabling legislation to achieve about three-quarters of such savings. Many recent presidents had proposed savings in income security entitlements, but rarely was the necessary legislation enacted. In fact, such savings proposals were often regarded as one of several budget "gimmicks" to disguise the real outlay and deficit implications of overall budget requests.

The expected outlay savings in 1984 arising from 1981 actions ($12.8 billion) are about 4 percent of projected income security spending under previous policies, or about half the normal yearly increase in income security outlays. The extent of the cuts varies greatly among program areas (Table 3). Nearly 60 percent occurred in low-income assistance programs, although these account for only 18 percent of income security outlays. Within this category, the cuts fell most heavily on programs offering aid for specific consumption goods (food, housing, fuel) rather than general cash assistance. These in-kind programs

TABLE 3 Baseline Income Security Outlays and Enacted Savings Projected to 1984, by Program

Program	Baseline Outlays (In $ billions)	Percentage of Total	Estimated Outlay Savings (In $ billions)	Program Savings as Percentage of Baseline	Program Savings as Percentage of Total Savings
Social insurance and related programs					
Social Security (OASDI)	194.1	58.6	3.1	1.6	24.2
Income security for veterans (excl. non-service-connected pensions)	12.0	3.6	0.1	0.8	0.8
Federal employee retirement and disability	42.9	12.9	0.7	1.6	5.5
Unemployment compensation	18.4	5.6	1.2	6.5	9.4
Other programs[a]	5.8	1.8	0.2	3.4	1.6
Subtotal	273.2	82.4	5.3	1.9	41.4

TABLE 3 (concluded)

Program	Baseline Outlays (In $ billions)	Percentage of Total	Estimated Outlay Savings (In $ billions)	Program Savings as Percentage of Baseline	Program Savings as Percentage of Total Savings
Low-income assistance programs					
Aid to Families with Dependent Children (AFDC)	9.2	2.8	1.5	16.3	11.7
Supplemental Security Income (SSI)	8.4	2.5	0.1	1.2	0.8
Veterans non-service-connected pensions	4.2	1.3	0.0	0.0	0.0
Earned income tax credit	1.0	0.3	0.0	0.0	0.0
Low-income energy assistance	2.9	0.9	1.0	34.5	7.8
Other cash assistance	1.2	0.4	0.1	8.3	0.8
Food Stamps	12.9	3.9	2.4	18.6	18.8
Other food programs[b]	6.8	2.1	1.7	25.0	13.3
Housing assistance	11.6	3.5	0.7	6.0	5.5
Subtotal	58.2	17.6	7.5	12.9	58.6
Total	331.4	100.0	12.8	3.9	100.0

Note: Detail may not add to totals due to rounding.

a. Includes railroad retirement system and benefits for disabled coal miners.

b. Includes school lunch and other child nutrition programs.

SOURCE: Unpublished projections, Congressional Budget Office, July 28, 1981 and August 6, 1981.

384

sustained nearly half the income security cuts, though they comprise only a tenth of all income security spending. AFDC and unemployment compensation were also reduced in size by amounts greater than a pro rata reduction would have yielded.

The president's 1983 budget proposals again sought substantial savings in income security benefits—$9 billion in 1984, rising to $11 billion in 1986. Almost 80 percent of the 1984 savings would fall on the low-income aid programs. Most of the remainder would come from limits on federal retiree benefit adjustments.

Cuts in Low-Income Assistance Programs

The savings already enacted in low-income assistance programs fall into three categories. First, benefit amounts were reduced for welfare recipients with earnings by lowering AFDC and Food Stamp income eligibility limits and partially or totally eliminating certain allowable deductions from countable income. These actions were by far the most profound from a policy viewpoint, as they reversed past efforts to increase recipients' financial incentives to work. Such changes reduced outlays to $2.0 billion. These enacted provisions and further changes proposed in the president's 1983 budget are listed in Table 4.

Substantial savings were also realized through reductions in funding levels of several programs administered at the state or local level. Low-income energy assistance and the Puerto Rico Food Stamp program were both converted to block grants and reduced by a total of $1.3 billion. Another major saving ($1.7 billion) was achieved by reducing the federal subsidy for school meals. The administration's 1983 budget proposed further block grants for food programs, various savings in AFDC, and an eventual turnover of AFDC and Food Stamps to state control. . . .

The third category of savings is related to administrative efficiency. Congress changed the procedure for income accounting in the AFDC, SSI, and Food Stamp programs so that income is now measured retrospectively. Prospective income accounting, while more sensitive to recipient needs, results in greater overpayments. These changes saved $0.8 billion.

The administration's welfare cuts were designed to avoid reducing the benefits of recipients with the least income. However, a 1983 budget proposal would deny new SSI recipients the existing $20 monthly income disregard. Since most SSI eligibles have income from Social Security or elsewhere, dropping this disregard would be tantamount to lowering the federal income floor for the needy aged, blind, and disabled by $240 a year.

TABLE 4   Policy Changes and Proposals to Reduce Benefits for Welfare Recipients with Earnings

Program	Changes Enacted in 1981	1981 Administration Proposals Not Enacted	1982 Administration Proposals
AFDC	Limitations on child care and work expense deductions from countable income		
	Cap on gross income allowed for eligibility		
	Limitation on "$30 + ⅓" monthly earnings disregard to first 4 months as recipient		
	Option for states to run "workfare" programs[a]	Require states to have "workfare" programs[a]	Require states to have "workfare" programs[a]
	Eligibility for unemployed-parent families restricted to those where primary earner is the person unemployed		Limit unemployed-parent eligibles to those participating in "workfare" program
			Delete benefit for parent who deliberately quits job, reduces hours, or refuses job
Food Stamps	Cap on gross income allowed for eligibility		
	Limit indexing of income deductions and repeal newly enacted deductions		
	Reduce earnings disregard from 20 percent to 18 percent of wages		Eliminate earnings disregard
			Increase benefit reduction rate to 35 percent of countable income

a. "Workfare" refers to the Community Work Experience program in which certain categories of welfare recipients are required to work without pay for a number of hours sufficient to offset the cost of the welfare benefit.

Cuts in Social Insurance and Related Benefits

With one exception, enacted reductions in social insurance benefits were not large relative to pre-Reagan spending. That exception is unemployment compensation, where 1982 budget savings of $1.2 billion (6.5 percent of baseline outlays) were achieved, mainly from a narrowing of benefits for long-term unemployment. A more restrictive trigger was adopted for the thirteen-week extension of unemployment benefits that occurs when unemployment is high, and eligibility for trade adjustment assistance (TAA) was drastically curtailed. (A 1983 budget proposal would eliminate TAA.) These changes are consistent with Reagan administration objectives to limit government interference in the market economy and to induce able-bodied people to depend less on public benefits.

Social Security savings of $2.5 billion in the 1982 budget were obtained from a variety of provisions, none of which affected the basic entitlements of retired workers. The Social Security minimum benefit was dropped for beneficiaries coming on the rolls after December 31, 1981. Social Security dependents' and survivors' benefits to college students are being phased out. A cap was placed on total public disability benefits equal to 80 percent of final wages. Implementation of a planned liberalization in the Social Security retirement test was delayed. Death benefits under Social Security (and also veterans programs) were eliminated for certain cases.

The changes made in Social Security did not deal with the system's funding problems, although the major benefit reductions rejected by Congress would have done so. Social Security still could become insolvent as early as 1983 unless Congress acts to increase the system's revenues or reduce its costs. Because of its political sensitivity, the administration has chosen to defer major initiatives on these questions until 1983 while awaiting recommendations from a new National Commission on Social Security Reform due to report by the end of 1982. It also has abstained from any new initiatives to address the principal long-run issues—the Social Security trust fund deficit anticipated in the next century, and the need to rationalize public and private retirement programs into a more sensible and equitable overall system.

Changes in Tax Expenditures

While benefit savings were being achieved through the budget review process, tax expenditures for the purpose of encouraging retirement saving increased dramatically (Table 5). This increase was due in part to provisions of the 1981 Economic Recovery Tax Act but also to the growth in earnings of pension fund assets. On the other hand, the

TABLE 5   Estimated Income Security Tax Expenditures for Fiscal Years 1981 and 1983 and Percentage Change, for Selected Tax Expenditures

Tax Expenditure	Estimated Revenue Loss (In $ billions)		Percentage Change in Revenue Loss
	FY 1981	FY 1983	
Tax expenditures related to social insurance			
Exclusion of benefit payments			
Social Security and railroad retirement	11.8	13.8	+16.7
Unemployment compensation	2.0	2.7	+36.5
Veterans compensation and pensions	1.4	1.5	+8.9
Net exclusion of pension contributions and earnings			
Employer plans	23.4	27.5	+17.6
Keogh plans, IRAs, other	2.2	3.8	+73.3
Additional exemptions and credits for blind and elderly	2.4	2.5	+5.2
Tax expenditures related to low-income assistance			
Exclusion of public assistance benefits	0.4	0.4	−4.4
Earned income tax credit	0.6	0.5	−18.9

SOURCE: Office of Management and Budget, *Budget of the United States Government, Fiscal Year 1983* (Washington, D.C.: GPO, February 1982), Special Analysis G. Tax Expenditures.

income tax rate reductions had the effect of slowing growth in pre-existing tax expenditures associated with the exclusion of income security benefits from taxable income. The major tax expenditure for low-income families—the earned income tax credit—actually declined in value because eligibility limits and maximum amounts were not adjusted for inflation.

Because of the broadening of individual retirement account (IRA) eligibility to include all wage earners and their nonworking spouses and an increased contribution limit for both IRAs and Keogh plans, the tax expenditures for these exclusions are expected to rise by 73 percent over the two-year period. By 1983 they are expected to amount to more than a tenth of all pension-related tax expenditures.

Tax expenditures associated with exclusion of public benefits are generally rising more slowly than the benefits themselves. In fact, the revenue loss due to excluding public assistance will actually fall by 4 percent because of both tax rate reductions and cuts in benefits for those on welfare who work. The revenue loss from the earned income credit will decline by nearly a fifth over the two years.

CONSEQUENCES OF THE POLICY CHANGES

The changes made in 1981 have already had an impact on program recipients. Immediate effects on available benefits can be determined. However, the longer-term consequences of these policy changes cannot yet be fully measured since they depend on responses by individuals, state and local governments, and private organizations. This section first presents an analysis of the immediate effects of selected benefit changes for the group most affected—welfare recipients who also have wage income. It then discusses several longer-term implications regarding the national commitment to a "social safety net," the efficiency of policies aimed at the working poor, the likely future course for the retirement income system, and the impact of budget cuts on future growth in program spending.

Short-Term Effects of Welfare Savings

The magnitude of the Reagan welfare cuts has been widely discussed by the media in budgetary terms, and the impacts on typical families have been shown. However, information has not been available on how important the cutbacks are as reductions in total family income, how the relative impact varies among different kinds of families, and the numbers of people so affected. A study by the Congressional Budget Office (CBO)[2] . . . analyzed the distribution of benefit cuts by income class, but it did not distinguish the relative impacts within the lowest income bracket ($10,000 and below) or among family types. This section reports on a more detailed analysis of a national sample of families conducted by the author using a computer model that simulates the AFDC and Food Stamp program changes and measures their consequences for individual family incomes.[3]

Three comparisons between old law and new law benefits were made based on (1) actual 1979 income data, (2) income projected to 1984 using CBO's low economic growth scenario, and (3) 1984 projections using CBO's high economic growth scenario.[4]

The average changes in income that would have occurred had the 1981 welfare cuts been in effect in 1979 are shown in Table 6 for various recipient groups. The income of families receiving AFDC but no other welfare benefit would have been reduced by an average of 2 percent ($194) a year. AFDC families also receiving Food Stamps would have

TABLE 6 Changes in Mean 1979 Income, Program Eligibility, and Poverty Status Due to Welfare Benefit Reductions, for Selected Recipient Groups

Eligibility Group	Mean Pretax Posttransfer Annual Family Income 1979[a] ($)	Change in 1979 Mean Income		Change in Number of Eligible Families		Change in Number of Families in Poverty	
		($)	(%)	(Number)	(%)	(Number)	(%)
Eligible for							
Any transfer payment	13,764	−24	−0.2	−135,029	−0.4	+137,156	+1.5
AFDC only	9,898	−194	−2.0	−31,446	−1.3	+74,477	+6.2
AFDC and Food Stamps	7,989	−231	−2.9	−47,164	−4.5	+15,271	+4.0
SSI and Food Stamps[b]	5,582	−11	−0.2	−1,566	−0.2	+2,111	+0.9
AFDC, SSI and Food Stamps	10,576	−97	−0.9	−1,685	−1.3	c	c

a. Income data include the value of Food Stamps as well as cash income. The data on income and changes in income use the family as the unit of analysis. Since welfare-eligible units will differ somewhat from the family definition because of program rules, the income data generally are higher than the incomes for the welfare-eligible units.

b. There is no change in income for SSI-only cases that could be measured in the TRIM model. The only programmatic change was the switch from prospective to retrospective income accounting.

c. Sample size is too small.

Source: Urban Institute simulations of policy changes using the TRIM model and the March 1980 Current Population Survey.

lost $231 in benefits. (Actual total losses to AFDC families are greater than shown here since some families lost Medicaid eligibility, some now pay more than before for school lunches, and some who live in public housing now pay higher rents.) SSI recipients who received Food Stamps would have experienced a small average loss of $11 in benefits.

Within these recipient groups, as expected, the losses are greatest for recipients with earnings. For example, AFDC-Food Stamp families with working female heads would have lost an average of 6 to 7 percent of annual income. For two-parent families with a male earner, the reductions would have been smaller (less than 2 percent) because welfare benefits are a smaller part of their total family income.

The administration's 1983 budget proposals would deepen these losses. The proposed cuts again would affect primarily benefits for recipients with earnings. However, unlike the enacted cuts, the proposed savings would affect substantially most Food Stamp recipients, all new SSI beneficiaries, and AFDC family units that share a household with other individuals.

The number of families losing eligibility for various combinations of benefits or falling below the poverty level because of the enacted cuts is substantial. Nearly 5 percent of the AFDC-Food Stamp cases lose their combined eligibility, most becoming AFDC-only cases. Even so, the number of AFDC-only families declines because of lost eligibility. The welfare cuts move an estimated 137,156 families below the poverty level, a 1.5 percent increase in the number of poor families. Most of this increase occurs in the AFDC-only population, whose poverty rate increases by 6 percent.

Projections of the enacted welfare changes to 1984 indicate that the effects will be smaller relative to gross family incomes than in 1979. That is, in both the low- and high-growth scenarios, mean family incomes are estimated to rise faster than will the benefit reduction amounts caused by the policy changes. For example, the $231 average reduction found in 1979 for AFDC-Food Stamp families would rise to $247 in 1984 (low growth path), but this latter amount would be a smaller part of gross income (2.3 percent in 1984 compared to 2.9 percent in 1979).

Long-Term Welfare Policy Issues

The administration argues that the long-term implications of its policies are favorable for those persons now on welfare. The objective of strong economic growth, if realized, will benefit everyone through greater job opportunities and faster wage growth. Officials anticipate that steps taken to reduce welfare eligibility and implement state "workfare" projects will promote greater work effort by low-income family heads. This section deals with the implications of benefit changes in a welfare policy context.

The welfare changes enacted thus far, while important, are relatively modest in scope and do not depict accurately the profound policy redirection set in motion by the administration. Two basic tenets of welfare policy have been called into question. What responsibility does the federal government bear to assure that a "safety net" is in place for those who find themselves in need of financial help? How should welfare assistance be provided to those who can work but have wages insufficient to meet family needs?

The "Safety Net" and the Federal Role in Income Support. When the Reagan administration announced its Program for Economic Recovery in February 1981, it established "preservation of the social safety net" as the first among nine criteria used in revising the Carter administration's fiscal 1982 budget. Although the rhetoric about the safety net was subjected to a wide range of interpretations, the February document did identify a set of "social safety net programs":[5] "social insurance benefits for the elderly; basic unemployment benefits; cash benefits for dependent families, elderly and disabled; and social obligation to veterans." These descriptive labels were not formal program titles; instead, they were general characterizations of the parts of programs that the administration did not seek to change.

The adjectives in the above quotation took on more definition in light of subsequent administration proposals. Exempted from proposed 1982 budget cutbacks were Social Security age sixty-five retirement benefits; unemployment benefits for the first thirteen weeks of unemployment; cash welfare aid to eligibles with no other source of income; and the major veterans programs. Thus, the "safety net" did not in fact include early retirees, disabled workers or retirees' dependents under Social Security; workers unemployed longer than thirteen weeks; the typical welfare recipient (who has income other than welfare); and recipients of noncash aid regardless of their income. "Safety net" proved to be a term that categorized people neither by their degree of current financial need nor by their vulnerability to future economic insecurity. Rather, it appears to have been used primarily to delineate and protect the benefits of those for whom cutbacks would likely have aroused the strongest reaction in Congress. The proposed savings for the 1983 budget mostly abide by the safety net concept that evolved in the 1982 budget, though greater savings are being sought than before in veterans benefits.

The confusion over what a safety net should include highlights the fact that a national income floor has never actually been adopted. The closest approximation is provided by the Food Stamp program, which supplements cash income with food coupons scaled to income according to a nationally uniform schedule for all people who meet the needs test. Ironically, this program has been treated most harshly under President Reagan.

The administration's New Federalism proposal would transfer to state control a number of federal programs, including AFDC and Food Stamps. In its most extreme form this would constitute a complete turning away from any federal responsibility for an income floor for all but the aged and disabled. While state-run welfare systems could be required to meet minimum federal standards, strong standards might be rejected or circumvented and would make little sense in any case under the New Federalism concept.

Thus far, the states have not been willing to accept this federalism proposal. A majority seem to favor the idea that there is a need for federal responsibility for an income floor. Their argument is based on the nationwide impact of economic change and the fact that states with serious economic problems usually experience simultaneously a rising welfare burden and declining tax revenues. Given the president's twin emphases of welfare cost reductions and transfer of authority to state government, the most basic questions about the safety net have gone unasked. Is the current protection afforded the neediest Americans adequate, and is this income floor fair in its variation among states, localities, and population groups?

Reversal of Past Policy on the Working Poor.   However the battle of state versus federal roles is resolved, the direction of policies regarding the working poor has already been reversed from that of the 1960s and 1970s. Through actions taken at the president's request in 1981, Congress moved away from the notion that low-income people are to be encouraged to work through positive financial incentives. To illustrate how the changes in AFDC and Food Stamps alter disposable incomes and financial work incentives, it is helpful to focus on a single parent with two children (the most common AFDC family).[6] Disposable income for such a family whose head has earnings typical of AFDC eligibles has declined in 1982 in every state compared to prior law. In some states the degree of decline is substantial—for example, from $731 to $534 a month in Connecticut, a 27 percent drop. In low-payment states, the decline tended to be less in degree but perhaps more severe in terms of the hardship that may result—for example, from $449 to $371 (67 percent of the poverty level) in Louisiana. The 1981 changes result in a nonworking AFDC parent and two children being better off than the example family with a working parent in twelve states.

These policy changes also altered dramatically the marginal gain to AFDC recipients from working an extra hour or seeking a higher wage. For example, in California a recipient formerly could keep about 30 cents of an extra dollar of wages over a wide earnings range ($100 to $450 a month). Now that same recipient would realize almost no gain over the $100 to $350 range and would lose income at the margin by earning more than $350.

Prior to 1981 presidential welfare initiatives had placed strong emphasis on lowering effective tax rates (taxes plus benefit offsets) applied to wages of low-income family heads and on eliminating precipitous loss of large benefits due to minor increases in earnings. Supporting arguments emphasized both work incentives and equity (i.e., that families of low-income workers should end up with greater total income than is available to comparable families without working members.) In deciding to reverse this policy, the Reagan administration had several arguments in its favor. First, if federal welfare spending had to be cut, the most humane way may be to reduce benefits for the least poor recipients (i.e., the working poor). Such action necessarily reduces financial work incentives for those still eligible for assistance. Second, there has been great public resentment surrounding the extension of welfare eligibility to persons with five-figure earnings levels, even though such cases are a small proportion of the caseload. This circumstance is necessitated by a program design that combines payment amounts based on both need standards related to family size and benefit reduction rates well below 100 percent.

A third administration argument—that the marginal tax rate is not an important determinant of work effort for lower-income people—is one that will be long debated. This incentives question was studied extensively in the 1960s and 1970s using both AFDC program experience and specially designed field experiments.[7] The analytic evidence is imprecise, but a general conclusion of the experiments is that the variation in work response to different benefit levels and reduction rates was modest. The studies are based on circumstances not exactly the same as those facing today's AFDC families. For instance, implicit tax rates on earnings greater than 100 percent and a possible loss of Medicaid eligibility were not analyzed. Still, existing evidence does generally support the administration view in two respects. Eliminating the "$30 plus one-third" disregard will probably lower program costs, and the work effort of those affected will not be greatly reduced. One well-regarded study of AFDC data concluded that "liberalized work incentives may encourage current recipients to increase labor supply, but these increases will be more than offset by work reductions of former nonrecipients who are now attracted onto the program."[8] Also, some sociological research suggests that economic incentives are not the only important consideration in a person's decision to work, since work itself has been found to have an intrinsic value independent of income.[9]

Whatever the effects of marginal tax rates, there is a way in which the nominal work incentive for a welfare eligible can indisputably be increased without lowering the payment level or the benefit offset rate.

This approach is to increase the personal cost to eligibles of applying for and continuing to receive benefits. Several administration AFDC proposals have this effect. The prime example is the proposed mandatory "workfare" program to require certain AFDC family heads to "work off" their benefits. (Congress thus far has left this program a state option.) It is thought that such measures serve to deter would-be recipients from applying for benefits, perhaps more than offsetting any caseload increase that might result from the reduced financial work incentives. Administration officials have argued that those so deterred are not really in need of assistance by definition, for a person in dire need would not hesitate to apply.

Critics of the administration's policy on work incentives have countered with several arguments. First, they argue that welfare applicants should be served, not hassled, by the bureaucracy and thus should not be subject to provisions aimed at deterring applications. Second, there is an equity argument in favor of having substantial financial work incentives for welfare recipients; that is, persons with incomes low enough to qualify for welfare should still be able to reap financial gain from working just as any other worker would expect. Third, the idea that low-income people will not respond to positive work incentives, whether or not an accurate notion, runs counter to the supply side theory that greatly increased economic activity will flow from lowered tax rates. This contradiction in policy may add to the perception held by many that the administration has treated poor people relatively harshly.

The fourth argument against this administration policy direction is one of feasibility. To make workfare programs perform well in providing relevant work experience to all eligibles may involve program costs much larger than the benefits will justify. While programs designed to move welfare recipients into jobs have a long history, none has been applied to all eligibles statewide, and until recently states could not restrict remuneration of job program participants to cover only their welfare benefits. The demonstrations of workfare for AFDC recipients that occurred in several states prior to the Reagan administration generally have been judged ineffective.[10] Similar tests for persons receiving Food Stamps or local general assistance have been successful in some instances. However, this success is probably because the clientele involved (single individuals and male family heads) were different than those of the AFDC program.

One major problem in previous AFDC workfare projects has been resistance by local administrators. The new round of workfare tests will benefit from the strong support and encouragement of the administration, and that fact may mitigate problems of implementation. However, acceptance of the community work experience program advocated by the administration will ultimately hinge on actual state experience. The problems they will encounter are predictable: potentially large administrative costs with unknown and perhaps immeasurable results; problems in enforcing work force discipline; resentment of those who desire public service jobs but are not eligible for them; a reduction in the incentive of public agencies to improve productivity; and taxpayer irritation with the provision of public services by a poorly trained and perhaps unmotivated welfare work force.

These problems will have to be weighed against several redeeming factors: the provision of job experience to unskilled people who may benefit from even the most limited work opportunities; a positive feeling among local taxpayers that they are getting a tangible service in return for the taxes paid to otherwise idle neighbors; and the availability of workers for local projects for which no other funds are available.

Long-Term Implications for Retirement Policy

Although public retirement benefits have largely escaped budget cuts, the immediate and long-term funding problems of Social Security suggest a continued focus by policy makers on retirement issues. Administration initiatives are discussed below with respect to two key questions: Will society come to rely more on personal savings in retirement: Will a major restructuring of Social Security be attempted?

The Potential for Privatization of Retirement Income.   Public benefits have become increasingly important as a source of income in old age. For example, in 1978 Social Security benefits accounted for 38 percent of all cash income for persons age sixty-five and over, up from 3 percent in 1950 and 30 percent in 1962. They amount to at least half of the income of more than half of the elderly and comprise 90 percent or more of the income of nearly a quarter of the elderly.[11] Wages and asset income accounted for 23 and 19 percent, respectively, of the income of the elderly in 1978. These two sources totaled 79 percent in 1950 and 46 percent in 1962. Pension plans accounted for 14 percent in 1978, up from 9 percent in 1962.

Despite this large and growing role of public benefits, we may soon be at a turning point that eventually will result in a greater proportion of income in old age flowing from wages and assets. The likelihood of this occurrence stems largely from the financial limitations of the Social Security system. The Social Security funding problem may result in reductions in scheduled future benefit levels. Further, the administration, several key members of Congress, and two recent government commissions have urged changes in Social Security designed to delay retirement age and increase the labor force activity of older people.

Another factor that may encourage greater reliance on work and savings is that, during a period of rapid economic change, employees cannot count on improvements in the value of their future pension benefits relative to wages. Many people retiring today will do better than earlier cohorts because of past pension gains. But a young or middle-aged worker today must plan under the assumption that spells of unemployment are more likely and, for many, a change in career, firm, or industry is a real possibility. Since the majority of workers cannot take their pension credits with them when they change jobs, they lose those credits or see them reduced in value by inflation before reaching retirement age. This lack of portability of credits when workers change jobs cannot be corrected without major federal intervention. Such action would fly in the face of the current trend toward deregulation of private businesses.

While most older workers may be able to retire for some years to come with more adequate incomes than their predecessors, many younger workers may be forced to consider the possibility of, at best, stagnation in the availability and adequacy of retirement income and, at worst, a substantial reduction in Social Security benefits. Thus, it is logical that these employees may work longer and save more to improve their financial prospects in old age. Two new measures—one enacted, one proposed—will act to support such behavior.

The measure enacted in 1981 provides an added incentive for personal retirement saving by changing the tax law to permit all wage earners a tax-deferred $2,000 annual contribution to an individual retirement account (IRA). If large numbers of people take advantage of this provision and keep the funds intact until retirement age, there could be a major increase in the asset income available in old age. Should IRAs prove popular, Congress may increase allowable contribution levels over time. Such a step might strengthen a trend toward privatization by encouraging less federal regulation of pension plans or a reduced role for Social Security.

There are three principal stumbling blocks to a greater reliance on IRAs in their present form. First, the higher a person's tax rate, the higher the incentive to save through an IRA. The incentive is weakest for low-income workers who are the least likely to have pension coverage. Thus, for many workers IRAs may not serve well as an alternative to an employer pension plan. A second problem is that any voluntary saving program will inevitably result in a substantial number of people who fail to take advantage of it. This can create a social problem if Social Security is cut back. Third, the flexibility of personal control

over IRA funds increases the risk of poor management of one's retirement assets. Again, a major social problem could result.

A 1982 proposal by President Reagan to prohibit mandatory retirement rules would serve to delay the time of retirement for some older
workers. Currently, employers can compel workers to retire at age sev-
enty. Elimination of such rules would have two effects. First, an estimated 5 percent of older workers would continue working beyond the
ages at which they now retire.[12] Second, employers would be pressured
to provide pension credits for work past the "normal retirement age"
(usually age sixty-five). A good many pension plans provide little or
no credit for delayed retirement, thereby inducing employees to retire
earlier than they might otherwise.

The Need for Long-Term Social Security Reforms.   A potential
insolvency of the Social Security trust funds in 1983 due mainly to poor
economic conditions will force Congress to address the system's financing. But a long-term funding issue also requires attention since
actuarial projections indicate that the system's financing cannot cover
fully the expected benefit costs when the post-World War II "baby boom"
generation retires in the next century. Legislated payroll taxes are at
historically high levels, and there seems to be little interest in Congress in raising them further. Thus, if the projections prove to be correct, either the system will have to be pared back and provide fewer
benefits, or it will have to tap new revenue sources and leave fewer
funds for other public purposes or for private investment.

Adjustments in revenue sources and tax rates can be made with
little lead time, though other budgetary factors and tax considerations
may limit what can be done in any one year. Measures to reduce costs,
on the other hand, have to be phased in over a long period to avoid
undesirable effects on people who are too near retirement age to alter
their behavior. There is no scarcity of ideas for achieving long-range
savings since this topic has been addressed by several governmental
studies and legislative proposals. However, the Reagan administration,
despite its emphasis on reducing the size of government, failed to
capitalize on a potential opportunity in 1981 to enact long-term cost-
saving Social Security reforms. Proposals were offered in May 1981
that would have greatly reduced long-term spending, but they were
poorly conceived and politically infeasible. Any political momentum
for such initiatives that may have existed in 1981 has declined sharply
only a year later.

Administration failure to mount an effective reform effort can be
attributed to the top priority assigned to short-term budget cuts and
the attention that execution of the budget plan required. Short-term
Social Security benefit cuts through structural changes are hard to

achieve, as the administration has now learned. The May proposals were guided too much by the logic Budget Director David Stockman applied to such issues in William Greider's *Atlantic Monthly* article. "I'm just not going to spend a lot of political capital solving some other guy's problem in 2010."[13]

Of course, it is the year 2010 or thereabouts when the sharp rise expected in the aged population will occur and the beginning of a substantial funding shortfall is projected. This shortfall may not materialize, in fact, since many long-range assumptions are involved in such estimates. Furthermore, even if it does, Congress may well choose to devote more resources to benefits for the elderly as the society grows older. However, if curbing the system's cost is to remain an option to meet the projected long-run constraints, then action in the near term is advisable. This would allow a long phase-in time for any benefit reduction measures and facilitate long-range individual career and financial planning. Whether the bipartisan National Commission on Social Security Reform will propose long-term reforms—and how effective its report will be in persuading Congress—remains to be seen.

Implications of Budget Cuts for Future Budgetary Growth

When the Reagan administration revised the Carter 1982 budget, it sought income security savings amounting to 10 percent of outlays in 1984 and a one-third reduction in outlay growth from 1982 to 1986. The actual result was a 4 percent outlay savings and a lowering of the growth rate by one-fifth. Although congressional inaction is partly responsible for the lesser figures, the main reason is the much poorer economic performance than the administration expected.

It was noted earlier that the 1982 budget reductions were proportionally far greater for low-income assistance (13 percent) than for social insurance and related programs (2 percent). A similarly large differential is found when these reductions are viewed in terms of the restraint this introduced on long-term budgetary growth. The income security budget data presented . . . indicate that without the Reagan cuts the annual growth rate in outlays from 1982 to 1986 would have been 7.4 percent. Taking the cuts into account, the expected annual growth rate is 6.0 percent. For low-income assistance, the spending growth rate was slashed by more than half, from 5.9 to 2.7 percent. However, the growth rate for social insurance spending was reduced by only one percentage point, from 7.6 to 6.5 percent.

Although the potential for curbing growth in low-income assistance is significant, the actual experience could prove to be less dramatic. Because changes in AFDC and Food Stamps raised the rate at which benefits decline with earnings, benefits will rise more rapidly as earnings fall. Thus, the present recession may result in greater welfare costs than have been predicted. Another factor that may undermine the assumed reduction in welfare spending growth is the unknown work response of recipients to the higher offset rates. If, as some observers predict, large numbers of people quit work because they are now better off on welfare, spending will be higher than expected.

Social insurance spending growth will still be determined largely by factors the president's budget reduction measures did not seriously confront: cost-of-living increases, the normal growth in entitled individuals, and real benefit increases due to the rising wage base upon which benefits are computed. Some small cuts were made that address each of these factors, but spending growth will still depend heavily on such uncontrollable factors as economic performance and the numbers and longevity of Social Security retirees.

In one case, unemployment compensation, the administration did succeed in reducing the sensitivity of spending to economic performance. In July 1981 the Congressional Budget Office estimated that a one-percentage-point increase in the unemployment rate would add $5.9 billion to unemployment benefit outlays. In February 1982, after enactment of the cutback in the thirteen-week extended benefit program, CBO estimated an outlay increase of only $4 billion for a one-point rise in unemployment. Thus, the present recession is raising these outlays by about $2 billion less per point of unemployment than would have occurred without the cuts. Of course, this change attenuates one original purpose of the program, which is to support consumer demand automatically in an economic downturn.

CONCLUSIONS

The Reagan administration's first year brought a change in direction for certain income security policies and substantial budget reductions. These reductions affected low-income assistance proportionately much more than social insurance programs. Benefit cuts were greatest for those low-income people who work. The effectiveness of the cutbacks as a restraint on long-term spending growth was minimal since the annual growth rate for the large social insurance systems was reduced by only one percentage point. The administration sought substantial income security savings in its 1983 budget request, with the cuts again falling most heavily on the low-income assistance programs. Any major initiative to change Social Security has been deferred until the commission established by President Reagan reports its recommendations in late 1982.

The administration has launched a redirection of welfare policy on two fronts. A devolution of responsibility for income support to the states is being sought, and steps have already been taken to change welfare recipients' work incentives and work requirements. The first of these initiatives is most evident in the New Federalism proposal to turn over to the states complete responsibility for the AFDC and Food Stamp programs. Lengthy negotiations with the states over this proposal are likely. State officials are concerned about the financial impacts of economic change on their populations and budgets and the potential for adverse effects from welfare policies in neighboring states. Thus, any politically viable plan probably will have to impose some national standards on program rules and provide a federal guarantee against costs exceeding a ceiling.

Two new developments regarding welfare recipients and work experience will receive close scrutiny. The benefit cuts for recipients with earnings, enacted in 1981, have become a primary focus of those concerned about welfare policy. If evidence on the subsequent behavior of recipients indicates that they are less likely to work, then the recent curtailment of financial work incentives will become a major issue. The second development is the state experimentation with "workfare" projects. Whether or not "workfare" becomes a significant factor in welfare policy, as the administration advocates, should hinge on a critical assessment of the initial demonstration efforts now getting underway.

Less attention has been given to the reductions in income security benefits that affect a middle-class clientele, mainly because the effects are being felt more slowly. However these cuts—the Social Security minimum and college student benefit phase-outs, the administrative review of disability claims, the limitations on unemployment benefits, the drastic reduction in trade adjustment assistance, the cuts in federal subsidies for school meals—need to be analyzed to capture their overall impacts on beneficiaries' well-being and to inform future debate on proposals for further reductions in social insurance and related benefits.

The reaction of wage earners to the liberalized IRA rules will be crucial in determining future retirement policy developments. If participation is at a high level across a broad spectrum of the eligible population, then policy makers may want to consider measures to promote greater reliance on private retirement saving relative to public benefits. A key question will be the extent to which IRA contributions represent net additional saving that would not have occurred without the provisions of the 1981 tax law.

A major debate over Social Security reform will likely begin in 1983 after the commission reports. It appears that a consensus for any action either to reduce the system's costs or increase its revenues will require strong presidential leadership. How President Reagan decides to respond on this issue will be a key factor in income security policy for the remainder of his term in office.

The president's position on Social Security will also be a major determinant of the extent to which his budget policy will limit growth in federal spending. If the most conservative president since before the New Deal chooses to leave the future growth of these entitlements largely untouched, the continued strength of public support for Social Security will be affirmed. The long-term implication of such an eventuality is that either the federal government will become larger relative to the total economy, or its role in other areas ultimately will have to be reduced.

NOTES

1. The federal programs discussed in this chapter include several that are not in the income security function in the federal budget. The additional programs are military retirement, veterans income security programs, Coast Guard retirement, and Public Health service officers' retirement. Budget data for housing assistance are included in this chapter, but issues are discussed in the context of housing policy in chapter 13.
2. Congressional Budget Office, *Effects of Tax and Benefit Reductions Enacted in 1981 for Households in Different Income Categories* (Washington, D.C.: CBO, February 1982).
3. The immediate effects of other income security cuts (e.g., in unemployment benefits, Social Security, and child nutrition) could not be analyzed at this level of detail in the time available for the study due to the limitations of the simulation model used.
4. The methodology used in the simulation and the economic assumptions are discussed in chapter 16.
5. *America's New Beginning: A Program for Economic Recovery* (Washington, D.C.: GPO, 1981), table 6, p. 14.
6. Information for this example is drawn from Tom Joe, "Profiles of Families in Poverty: Effects of the 1983 Budget Proposals on the Poor" (Washington, D.C.: Center for the Study of Social Policy, February 1982).
7. For a review of the experimental studies, see Robert A. Moffit, "The Effect of a Negative Income Tax on Work Effort: A Summary of the Experimental Results," chapter 11 in Paul M. Somers, ed., *Welfare Reform in America: Perspectives and Prospects* (Boston: Kluwer-Nijhoff Publishing, 1982). Studies of AFDC are reviewed in Sheldon Danziger, Robert Haveman, and Robert Plotnick, "How Income Transfer Programs Affect Work, Savings, and the Income Distribution: A Critical Review," *Journal of Economic Literature*, vol. 19 (September 1981), pp. 975–1028.
8. Frank Levy, "The Labor Supply of Female Household Heads, or AFDC Work Incentives Don't Work Too Well," *Journal of Human Resources*, vol. 14, no. 1 (winter 1979), p. 76.

9. For example, see Leonard Goodwin, *Do the Poor Want to Work?* (Washington, D.C.: The Brookings Institution, 1972).

10. Prior experience is summarized in Demetra Smith Nightingale, "Workfare and Work Requirement Alternatives for AFDC Recipients: New Priority on an Old Issue" (Paper presented at the 1982 Annual Forum of the National Conference on Social Welfare, Boston, Mass., April 26, 1982).

11. U.S. Department of Health and Human Services, Social Security Administration, *Income of the Population 55 and Over, 1978* (Washington, D.C.: GPO, 1981), p. 49.

12. James R. Storey, "The National Age Discrimination in Employment Act Studies: Results and National Policy" (Paper presented at the 34th Annual Meeting of the Gerontological Society of America, Toronto, Ontario, November 10, 1981).

13. William Greider, "The Education of David Stockman," *Atlantic Monthly,* December 1981, p. 43.

Article 24

A SOCIAL AGENDA FOR THE EIGHTIES

President's Commission for a National Agenda for the Eighties

The theme of hard choices applies to the social justice and urban policy areas just as it does to the other segments of public policy. In an expanding economy, making a choice becomes easier since it then becomes possible to devote greater resources to equalizing opportunities among Americans in gaining access to education, jobs, and health care. Adverse economic circumstances, however, must never become an excuse for abandoning our pursuit of social justice. Many social and urban programs form a defense against hardships caused by unemployment and recession; others contribute to long-run economic growth by reducing economic discrimination in the labor market and by increasing the nation's stock of human capital.

The country no longer needs to debate the legitimacy of federal government participation in the provision of human services. The successes of earlier programs in easing the suffering of the sick and poor have settled this matter. During the New Deal, the federal government began to maintain people's income through social insurance programs, such as unemployment compensation and Old Age and Survivors' Insurance. Thirty years later, the Great Society expanded upon the New Deal tradition with the passage of civil rights legislation to protect the rights of minority citizens, of Medicare and Medicaid to insure the elderly and the poor against the financial catastrophe of serious illness, and of programs to provide compensatory education for the nation's poor.

The programs on this Commission's social agenda do not back away from the tradition of the New Deal and the Great Society. Instead, the new agenda builds upon the old. It suggests ways in which the federal government's performance in health, welfare, education, and civil rights can be improved and strengthened by examining the interactions among programs and by determining whether programs achieve their basic purposes.

Acceptance of the reform tradition, then, does not exempt each of the human service areas from a list of hard questions that includes:

SOURCE: *A National Agenda for the Eighties,* Washington, DC: The President's Commission for the Eighties, 1981.

What are we intending to do? Can the government best do it? Which level of government? What is the best means of administering the program in order to obtain the desired results?

Nor does the desire to use and improve upon older programs exempt this Commission's proposals from coming to grips with a very fundamental dilemma: the Commission recommends new and expanded human service programs at the same time that the nation is already confronted with the problem of meeting the "uncontrollable" costs of some existing programs. Many of these programs, such as food stamps, began as experiments; others, such as Social Security, were created with a tight fit between program benefits and the money collected to pay those benefits. Over the years, these programs have expanded their coverage and increased their benefit levels. In some cases this expansion occurred because of a conscious public decision to provide support for individuals in need; in other cases the expansion was almost inadvertent, the result of legislative desires to make old programs achieve new purposes. The end product of these expansions, however, has been to create a new class of programs that provide services which individuals perceive almost as an inherent right; such services have come to be called entitlements. They differ from other services that are supplied by the market on the basis of an individual's willingness or ability to pay.

As the analysis by the Quality of Life Panel makes clear, there is no question that meeting the costs of these entitlements poses a serious problem; nearly half of the federal budget is taken up with programs over which neither Congress nor the President can exert much control. The costs of these programs are often not related to the resources available to pay for them. Participation rates go up or down without consideration of the total costs of the program; instead, these rates depend upon things like the demographic structure of the population. If anything, the countercyclical nature of many entitlement programs causes participation rates to rise when federal revenues fall. Benefit levels in many of these programs also move automatically with the price level, and in some cases rise faster than do federal revenues. All of these factors combine to increase the costs of entitlement programs and to give society less and less flexibility to alter the mix of public goods.

The nation now needs to gain control over its existing programs and to set priorities for the creation of new ones. The reports of the Panels on Social Justice and on Metropolitan-Nonmetropolitan Policies suggest goals for which we should strive in the Eighties—a guaranteed minimum income, a coherent urban policy, an effective educational system, universal health insurance, and the advancement of civil rights. All of these goals cannot be reached at once, for they must be balanced against other important goals, such as controlling inflation or reducing the nation's dependence on foreign oil. In the cases where legislation is required to create new programs, Congress may not be able to pass such legislation immediately; even before such programs are created, the country will have to assess the merits of the older programs and determine if they contribute toward meeting modern social goals.

When the nation does address these important matters, some confusions that have pervaded the discussion of human services will have to be clarified. Considerations related to the proper implementation of services often get mixed up with questions related to the generosity of benefit levels. In fact, these questions exist independently of one another; there are better and worse ways of spending any given level of money. Implementing programs differs from simply mandating the achievement of goals and starting the flow of funds; concern for the proper design and administration of programs makes an important difference in meeting goals. Government programs and market forces need not operate at cross-purposes; government is capable of using private markets to help achieve public goals.

Because of these confusions and because of the incremental nature of the policymaking process, the country often does not pursue its human service goals in either an efficient or a caring manner. Legislators, executive branch agencies, and private interest groups together perpetuate a narrow view of problems that often helps to create fragmented programs. Piled one on top of another, these programs too often conflict with one another and produce unintended results. At the same time, overlaps between programs and gaps among programs occur.

This chapter offers ways of remedying these problems and includes specific recommendations in urban policy, civil rights, health, welfare, education, and the country's approach toward dependency. In essence, the hard choices in this area lead the Commission to recommend that the aims of past reform eras be combined with new knowledge about implementing social programs and with a concern for the costs that entitlement programs generate. Such a combination will produce a constructive synthesis that can serve as a basis for meeting the country's social goals.

Civil Rights

In none of the human service areas does the federal government have a clearer and more compelling responsibility than in civil rights.

During this decade the nation must reaffirm its commitment to eliminate the past effects of discrimination. The task will be more difficult than in previous decades because of the state of the economy and the persistence of racism among segments of the population. These difficulties only underscore the need for strong national leadership that is capable of creating a national climate in which civil rights issues are addressed with seriousness and intensity. Only when the victims of racial, ethnic, and sexual discrimination are made whole can this country realize its egalitarian ideal.

In this decade, the major civil rights laws of the Sixties and Seventies must be vigorously enforced; efforts to repeal or dilute such legislation or to frustrate compliance must be repelled. Weak civil rights laws—such as those dealing with fair housing—need to be strengthened, and the Voting Rights Act of 1965, which is due to expire in this decade, should be extended so that blacks and other minorities can retain this needed protection.

In recent years, the civil rights movement has broadened both in the range of its concerns and in the number of groups who benefit from its gains. Black Americans have led the way in this regard; the example of the struggle to attain civil rights for black Americans has inspired similar efforts by other disadvantaged and minority groups. All of these groups are involved in a wide-ranging effort to make the United States a country in which race, ethnicity, age, and physical handicap do not form barriers that block advancement or limit participation in American life.

What is clear, as this Commission puts forward its social agenda, is that many of the nation's problems—those of its educational system, its provision of health care, its attempts to maintain the income of the poor, its efforts to ensure quality housing for all, and its steps to lessen alienation from the electoral and democratic process—have a more adverse impact on minorities and families headed by women than on other Americans. For that reason, it becomes necessary to offer a civil rights program addressed specifically to ending the barriers of racial, sexual, and age-related prejudice and ultimately to stopping the disparities in employment, housing, and voting rights that separate minority citizens from the rest of the population.

The current civil rights agenda deals with both abstract rights and tangible results; the achievement of one does not necessarily imply the attainment of the other. For example, the long Constitutional struggle for black equality may have ended, but we have yet to achieve true equality. No area demonstrates this truth more dramatically than employment. Sixteen years after Title VII of the Civil Rights Act of 1964 made discriminatory employment practices illegal, the black unemployment rate remains double the white rate.

The nation's public policy needs to demonstrate a sensitivity to this employment gap and to produce responses that work toward eliminating it. One such response is to encourage affirmative action plans. In the *Weber* and *Bakke* cases, the Supreme Court recently established the Constitutional validity of race-conscious, voluntary affirmative action plans. The support of the executive branch is now required so that employers will implement such plans and monitor their results.

More direct federal action is needed in the area of employment training. The private sector should receive financial subsidies to hire and train those with traditionally high unemployment levels. If the private sector proves incapable of solving this problem, however, government must be ready to expand its training and employment efforts through such vehicles as the Comprehensive Employment and Training Act and the Youth Employment and Initiatives plan.

Voting rights also occupy a place on a civil rights agenda for the Eighties. Spurred by the passage of a voting rights act in 1965 and by a new interest in the potential of the political process, voter participation among minorities has increased dramatically over the past 15 years. To increase this participation, the 1965 act needs to be improved and its life extended beyond its present termination date in 1982. In addition, minorities require the benefit of an easier voter registration process—one unencumbered by bureaucratic red tape and racial discrimination. One practical measure that accomplishes this end is postcard registration. Short of this measure, the country may wish to experiment with a system in which young people register to vote through their schools, thereby facilitating and encouraging participation in the electoral process.

In addition to these positive steps, care needs to be taken to discourage measures that reduce minority representation in government. Redistricting Congressional, state, or local voting districts so as to reduce the political influence of minorities should be guarded against and challenged in court.

As for the vital area of fair housing, the federal government still needs to implement the provisions of the Fair Housing Act of 1968 and the Housing and Community Development Acts of 1974, 1977, and 1980 more efficiently. This area is one in which Congress has boldly declared that discrimination in the sale or rental of housing is against the law. The executive branch, however, consumed an entire decade before issuing regulations to enforce the laws.

The law itself is limited and should be strengthened. Under its terms, the Department of Housing and Urban Development (HUD) has only the power to conciliate when investigation of a complaint shows probable discrimination; it has no authority to take action against private discriminators. The Commission urges the passage and aggressive implementation of legislation that would provide an administrative enforcement mechanism.

Other priorities in the area of fair housing include the need to develop protections against the displacement of low-income families as the result of neighborhood revitalization and economic development activities. Standards must also be established for selecting sites for subsidized housing, and a procedure should be developed that allows tenants eligible for subsidized housing a wider range of options.

Closing the gap in the employment levels of whites and blacks, protecting and encouraging the right of black citizens to vote, and eliminating discrimination in the housing market are all important items on a black agenda for the Eighties. But these matters do not exhaust the list of black concerns. The resurgence of the Ku Klux Klan and the continuation of violence directed against minorities pose a growing threat to the security of blacks and members of other minority groups and heighten racial tensions. Enactment of special legislation to control racial violence and to provide stricter enforcement of existing civil rights laws deserves serious consideration.

The Commission has also considered issues that relate to the rights of women in this nation. Today more than half of the nation's adult females are in the labor force. Despite this momentous change, the nation continues to act upon outdated assumptions that confine women to certain jobs, that often place women in positions subservient to men, or that pay less than comparable jobs held chiefly by men. The assumptions violate the norms of equity and social justice.

To remedy the situation, the Equal Employment Opportunity Commission (EEOC) should monitor employment practices and make sure that the nation's jobs are as accessible to women as they are to men. Women should not be forced to accept what has been traditionally regarded as women's work—nursing, teaching, and secretarial duties. Instead, they should be free to choose from the entire spectrum of jobs and to advance within a job or profession with the same ease as men.

Something more fundamental may also be required: equal pay for work of comparable value. Because of segmentation in the labor market, the wage levels in some traditional women's jobs are below those in jobs traditionally held by men. In time, the forces of supply and demand in a labor market unimpeded by prejudice should correct this problem, as women find employment in traditionally male occupations and exercise their talents fully. Such is simply not the case at present, however, which leads the Social Justice Panel to suggest that wage structures in different occupations be examined in this decade, with an eye to adjusting them so that women and racial minorities receive equal pay for work of comparable value.

On the job, women should enjoy working conditions free from sexual harassment; the definition and prosecution of sexual harassment on the job stand out as important matters with which the EEOC and private employers need to concern themselves in the Eighties.

The job of the EEOC and other government agencies will be made much easier if the legal status of women becomes clarified. Women no longer require special protection; they deserve equality instead. To guarantee the equal rights of women under the law, the Commission urges that the nation complete the matter of enacting the Equal Rights Amendment (ERA).

Passage of ERA will not lessen the need to preserve the civil rights of poor women. The Commission notes that the Hyde Amendment to the Labor/Health and Human Services appropriations bill (which prohibits the use of Medicaid funds to perform abortions unless necessary to save the life of the mother) and the 1980 Supreme Court decision that upholds the constitutionality of the Hyde Amendment and prohibits federal reimbursements for abortion under the Medicaid program, unfairly discriminate against the women that are served by that program.

Poor women—and poor men—who are also alienated by the barrier of language face difficult circumstances in this country. In March 1978, for example, the median income of a non-Hispanic family in this country was $16,300; an Hispanic family, by way of contrast, made do with an income of $11,400, significantly less than the non-Hispanic figure. Although non-English-speaking Americans have much in common with other minorities, they also must confront their own special problems.

Among the matters that concern these groups is public policy toward immigration. The Immigration and Naturalization Service (INS) has the power to police the U.S. border with Mexico and to return undocumented aliens to Mexico and other foreign countries. Local law enforcement agencies, however, frequently stop Americans of Hispanic heritage on roadways and incarcerate them. The civil rights of American citizens and aliens are often abused by this process.

The difficult matter of determining the extent of local, state, and federal responsibility toward undocumented aliens also requires resolution during this decade. In a recent case, a federal District Court in Texas held that the children of undocumented aliens need not pay tuition to attend American public schools. Despite this decision, the rights of undocumented aliens with regard to all of the social services—education, welfare, and health—remain unclear.

At the very least, people who lack the ability to speak English must not have their rights abridged for that reason alone. Agencies that enforce civil rights laws and dispense social services must, for example, make their work accessible to Spanish-speaking citizens. States with a high concentration of Spanish-speaking residents should consider using public monies to establish English language instruction centers.

Hispanics, it should be emphasized, have problems that are more similar than dissimilar from those of the rest of the minority population. The matters of crucial concern to Hispanics are of equal concern to blacks, native Americans, and all other minority groups. These matters go to the heart of the government's performance in the coming decade: civil rights must not be put in the back of this country's public consciousness. The stark fact is that reducing disparities among groups in housing, employment, and the other life essentials constitutes as important a mission as any this country has in the coming decade.

This Commission, then, joins many of its predecessors in urging that this decade be the one that closes the gap between the rhetoric of American promise and the reality of American performance.

From an Urban Policy to a Social Policy: New Perspectives on Urban America

Over the past several decades, demographic and economic forces have transformed urban America dramatically. Understanding the scale, direction, and pace of these forces is essential before making coherent policy recommendations. Also, prior to recommending what government should or should not do, there is a need to consider carefully what government is and is not capable of accomplishing in such a complex policy area.

In general, we recommend that the nation respond to urban change by promoting strategies of adjustment, rather than attempt to reverse the changes experienced by communities across the land. In large measure, these changes—including the transformation of local economies, the lower density settlement patterns, and the growth in locations beyond metropolitan areas—are often beneficial to the nation as a whole, even though they may have undesirable short-term effects on specific communities. The pace, if not the direction, of larger scale trends can occasionally be influenced by wise public policy; adjusting to the direction of change, as well as moderating its pace, then, should be our primary objectives.

From a long-range perspective, we urge the federal government to assign priority to the development of a blend of social and economic policies that encourages the health and vitality of the nation as a whole and all of its citizens regardless of where in the nation they might live. The urban consequences of essentially nonurban policies will continue to outweigh those of narrow and explicitly urban policies. The general implication is that, in the long run, the fates and fortunes of specific places be allowed to fluctuate. Throughout the process of economic change, people—more so than places—should be insulated from the multiple hardships that accompany the transformation of the nation—in its communities, its economy, and the larger society.

Earlier we urged the government to adopt economic policies that promote steady economic growth, encourage investment, create jobs, and inhibit inflation. We must retain the capability to create wealth even as we continue to develop more equitable means of distributing it. Here we urge the government to adopt social policies that have as their collective aim ensuring that those who can work are able to and those who cannot work are able to lead a life of dignity while their welfare is provided through alternative means. The government should aim principally to remove barriers between people and economic opportunity. We believe that a people-to-jobs strategy based on vigorous government programs of assisted migration and skill acquisition should receive the emphasis that has been reserved in recent years for job-to-people strategies dependent upon local economic development. Efforts must be redoubled to train the unskilled, to retrain the displaced, and to assist those who wish to relocate to areas where employment opportunities abound.

In the interim—until such a major policy reorientation can be accomplished—the federal government can take important steps toward easing the plight of beleaguered urban areas, without foreclosing its long-range policy. There is a recognized need for reorganizing and coordinating its major community and economic development programs. A number of grant-in-aid programs should be consolidated and their resources more carefully targeted to localities most in need. Grants to localities should be accompanied by sufficient transfer of authority so that local officials have the flexibility to address diverse local needs with external funds. Responsibilities should not be mandated to localities without the assurance of the availability of the resources needed to execute them. In general, federal urban policy efforts should be evaluated by their collective capacity to ease the burdens on Governors, mayors, and others of local and state governance.

The Transformation of Cities.   Contrary to conventional wisdom, cities are not permanent; their strength is related to their ability to reflect change rather than to fend it off. Their imposing physical features—the vast interwoven networks of factories, homes, commercial establishments, and the transportation routes linking them—belie cities' underlying susceptibility to historical trends. Standing at the intersection of virtually all the important shaping forces of an era—demographic, economic, political, cultural—cities articulate, and continuously re-articulate, our changing national circumstances. Although they are the settings for all manner of abiding cultural institutions, cities serve us better as mirrors than as museums. They must be permitted to reflect changing technological capabilities and social circumstances, rather than be constrained by an attempt to preserve under glass any particular historical combination of them. To attempt to restrict or reverse the processes of change—for whatever noble intentions—is to deny the benefits that the future may hold for us as a nation.

Whatever else they are, cities are economic entities; first and foremost they are the settings where great wealth is produced and distributed. A city's physical arrangements and material life are largely determined by the technological state of the art that existed as the city grew and by its role in a local and regional economy for which it serves as a linchpin. Much evidence exists to suggest that the economy of the United States, like that of many of the older industrial societies, has for years now been undergoing a critical transition from being geographically concentrated, centralized, and manufacturing-based to being increasingly deconcentrated, decentralized, and service-based. In the process, many cities of the old industrial heartland—for example, in the states of New York, Pennsylvania, Ohio, Michigan, and Illinois—are losing their status as thriving industrial capitals, a position they have held through the first half of the century.

These cities are not dying. Rather, they are transforming, and in the future they will likely perform a narrower range of vital and specialized tasks for the larger urban society. Central location and compactness will continue to be essential to many urban enterprises and attractive to many urban dwellers. These older cities are gradually evolving; their physical appearance and economic function are becoming increasingly reflective of the newer social roles that history is assigning them. This transformation of older cities from centers of manufacturing and production to centers of services and consumption will require that their "health" be defined at new, and often lower, levels of population and employment.

The central city in the future will likely experience great increases in the number of white-collar office jobs in managerial, professional, financial, and "knowledge" occupations. Also nurtured will be the allied services that these workers, their families, and employing institutions will require during and after the working day. The proportion of manufacturing jobs will decline, and the blue-collar labor force will be much reduced from previous levels as a result of the loss of manufacturing and allied jobs from central cities.

Cities can no longer be expected to perform alone the traditional role of providing employment for the unskilled, unemployed, poor, and dependent urban underclass.

The general decline in rural migration to cities may well remove from a municipality's shoulders the traditional burden of acculturating newcomers to urban life and assimilating them into urban society. (The rising tide of foreign immigrants—particularly from the Caribbean—may in fact restore some of these functions to a few cities.) The older industrial cities will continue to be national and regional centers performing important commercial, service, financial, governmental, and cultural functions. But they will share many of those tasks with smaller communities far removed from central locations. They will become scaled-down residential centers for households defined by a narrower range of age, composition, and income differences.

Geographically, population shifts and economic trends within cities will create an urban landscape characterized by lower density industrial and residential settlements oriented around multiple smaller and more specialized centers of concentration (e.g., large suburban shopping malls, office and industrial parks). The historical dominance of core central cities will be diminished as certain production, residential, commercial, and cultural functions disperse to places beyond them. In demographic terms, continuing suburbanization within metropolitan areas will be accompanied by both a broader dispersion of people to the periphery of metropolitan areas and a reconcentration of population in the countryside. For the foreseeable future, the rate of growth in nonurban areas will continue to exceed that in metropolitan areas, and the South and West will grow at rates exceeding those in the North and East.

An often-noted "urban renaissance" within cities—while enriching and laudable—seems not to be taking place on anything like the scale suggested in popular commentary. On the contrary, we have no evidence of a return *en masse* of the upper middle class to the cities nor any accompanying large-scale residential and civic rejuvenation. To be sure, certain inner-city neighborhoods are unmistakably enjoying forms of real estate upgrading and restoration, but statistically such changes amount only to a thin patina across the urban landscape. Thus, between 1968 and 1979, only one-half of one percent of the nearly 20 million housing units in cities has been affected by revitalization or restoration efforts. Moreover, in excess of 70 percent of the people residing in revitalized central city units were already central city dwellers, not returning suburban immigrants. What the statistical indices do reveal, however, is the ongoing, relentless deterioration of living conditions and income levels, relative to suburban locations, as old central cities progress toward economic transformation.

Change, however, while inevitable, is often as unwelcome in public matters as it is in our private lives. It is seldom more unwelcome than when it threatens arrangements to whose preservation we may be deeply committed. Often, in revering the cities where we are born, live, or work, we unconsciously cling to a certain image of what that city *is*—an image inextricably tied to a specific timeframe—and we forget that cities, like all living things, change. Change invariably entails a mix of advantages and disadvantages; yet the disadvantages are usually perceived to be clear and unmistakable, while the current advantages may be less easily recognized and long-range advantages may be imperceptible. The special challenge for policymakers confronting change, therefore, is to weather the disillusionments and deprivations occasioned by major change and to try to discern the underlying trends, and, if possible, to adjust to them.

This, of course, is an ideal scenario. In fact, few of us are so philosophical and visionary in the face of profound change. Government, however—as an important locus of authority, planning, and guidance in a society—has a greater responsibility than its citizens to understand change and to facilitate those changes that it can or should not try to prevent. Admittedly, that is not always an easy task in a system such as ours where government is continuously responsible to the people, many of whom are suffering from the accompaniments of change.

Indeed, we do not need scholarly treatises to remind us of the lamentable byproducts of urban deconcentration for the older industrial cities: the erosion of the tax base, hence of fiscal solvency; the increased ghettoization of the poor and minorities; the enduring high rates of unemployment and chronic economic depression in poverty neighborhoods; the deterioration of municipal services and their delivery systems; the "excessive" use of resources per capita; the fear of crime—all of which are associated with the dispersion of urban America into lower density social and economic arrangements.

The burden for people left in central cities is heavy. For many—the young and old, racial or ethnic minorities, and women—access to the traditional avenues to success has been blocked by discrimination and the dispersal of economic opportunity to places outside central cities. Whereas the city's process of upgrading had enabled earlier generations of migrants and their offspring to use the city as a launching pad, a growing proportion of urban residents are now left behind, consigned to become a nearly permanent urban underclass.

The relative decline of the older urban centers in the North-Central and Northeast regions has been accompanied by a corresponding growth of newer cities in the Sunbelt regions of the South and Southwest. These changes are the predictable results of economic change, but they are no less traumatic. Understandably, pressures have built up rapidly for special programs of compensatory aid, in some instances bailouts to avoid bankruptcy. We cannot confront these problems with disinterest and detachment, yet we cannot avoid the fact that growth and decline are integral parts of the same dynamic process in urban life. When the federal government steps in to try to alter these dynamics, it generates a flood of demands that may sap the initiative of urban governments because of the expectation of continuing support. There must be a better way.

Federal Urban Policy in the Eighties.   In instances of deep-seated and inexorable historical transformation, there is a fundamental problem in attempting to halt the shrinkage of a metropolitan area or to revitalize obsolete industries that in the past have been expected to adapt themselves to changing circumstances. In our view, the moral and material resources of government would be better expended in planning for the future and helping people to adjust to new imperatives in ways that derive from an understanding and acceptance of change.

Because the negative consequences of change visit people first and foremost, we should try to help people bear their often painful burdens, and, as quickly as possible, facilitate transition to new locations and jobs. This is not, we recognize, the customary or popular view. Traditionally, the government has focused much of its resources on localities, in part because of the growing political demands of jurisdictions undergoing traumatic change and in part because it is politically safer to aid places (and their political leadership) than people directly. Thus, we have allocated billions of public dollars in recent years to develop selected localities in the hope that the endeavor will help people, albeit indirectly. Much evidence seems to indicate, however, that such strategies achieve very little in upgrading those localities, let alone in helping the unemployed, underemployed, and dependent whose fortunes are not directly tied to the functioning of local economies. Localities have proved to be very difficult to shore up or "revitalize," despite all our place-oriented redevelopment programs. Federal assistance to local government has often been ineffective in eliminating the multiple distresses of "pockets of poverty" within "pockets of plenty."

It is time, then, despite all the difficulties entailed, to alter the pattern of place-oriented, spatially sensitive, national urban policies, and to ask, instead, what more people-oriented, spatially neutral, national social and economic policies might accomplish, if not in the immediate future, then certainly in the long run. In return, federal programs must be employed to assist the transformation of local communities to achieve health and vitality at lower population levels, and with a transformed economic base, and to ameliorate the undesirable impacts of these transitions.

Thus, as the major long-term goal of federal urban policy, the Commission urges government to place greater emphasis on retraining and relocation assistance efforts designed to link people with economic opportunity, wherever that opportunity might be. Specific measures to emphasize would include job creation, skill acquisition and assisted relocation programs targeted to the employable, cash assistance plans for those who cannot work and for the "working poor," and, finally, subsidies to private employers to ensure that jobs created by government are only temporary and supplemental bridges to eventual employment in the private sector. The principal purpose of such programs would be to increase people's mobility by helping them acquire the necessary skills to ensure their continuing relevance to a changing economy. In short, much greater attention should be given to developing strategies that allow people to adjust to shifts in the location of economic opportunity. Assisting people to follow jobs, rather than concentrating solely on attempting to steer jobs to where people are, is a major goal in any adjustment strategy. Without the prospect of acquiring necessary retraining to participate in the rapidly changing economy, large segments of the urban lower classes face nearly permanent exclusion from an increasingly specialized economy that has less and less use for unskilled labor.

In the final analysis, however, the best national urban policy is the restoration of steady growth in the economy. Ultimately, people acquiring new skills and moving to new job opportunities constitute the best antipoverty program we can devise. For that reason, public sector activity should endeavor to encourage private sector vitality, taking care to try to alleviate its undesirable consequences without hampering that vitality.

We have tried to set forth a difficult but, in our opinion, necessary long-range reorientation of federal urban policy. The task cannot, of course, be accomplished overnight without traumatic consequences for a score of our struggling largest and oldest cities. There is much that can be done in the interim, however. Prior to any effort at substantial reform, policymakers should take a hard look at the current assignment of responsibilities among federal, state, and local governments. An important basis for the clarification of the present confused division of labor in the federal system is the recognition that the federal government, with its access to the widest possible tax base, is an efficient and reliable collector of revenues. This strength should not be surrendered in any "decongestion" of the federal system. The federal government should also retain overall responsibility for the formation of broad national goals and of programs to implement them. In certain special instances, the federal government should assume the financial and administrative responsibility for programs of national significance. Thus, for example, as we have stated earlier, Washington would certainly assume leadership in areas of national health care financing and reform of the welfare system.

At the same time, the federal government has often shown itself to be an inefficient and inflexible administrator of the myriad grant-in-aid programs dispensed to state and local governments. There are now over 500 such grant-in-aid programs, totaling some $88 billion. Some 88 percent of these programs are administered via relatively narrow categorical grants. The Advisory Commission on Intergovernmental Relations, and state and local officials—Governors, state legislators, mayors, city council members, and county executives—convincingly argue that the time has come to unclutter this system. While retaining responsibility for broad national purposes—particularly concerning the civil rights of all citizens—the federal government should begin to turn over to state and local governments more responsibility for implementing many of these grant-in-aid programs, as well as consolidating a number of the narrow categorical problems in the areas that it continues to control.

The federal government should explore the possibility of better coordinating the largest urban and rural development programs, including those currently administered by the Department of Housing and Urban Development, the Economic Development Administration, the Community Services Administration, the Farmers Home Administration, and the Small Business Administration. Policy tools including CDBGs (Community Development Block Grants), CETA (Comprehensive Employment and Training Act), UDAGs (Urban Development Action Grants), EDA (Economic Development Administration) grants, and possibly EPA (Environmental Protection Agency) water and sewer grants might be usefully employed by a single authority. This would permit a more concentrated and administratively efficient interim response to place-oriented urban problems.

Finally, the federal government—both Congress and executive branch agencies—should begin to exercise more restraint when mandating responsibilities to local governments without providing the resources necessary to carry them out. In addition, during the coming years, the federal government, in close cooperation with state and local officials, should explore means of improving the fiscal underpinnings of state and local governments. Especially important is an examination of the mesh of the national and subnational systems of taxation, with the goal of revising them to reflect more faithfully the programmatic division of responsibilities among the federal, state, and local governments. Ultimately, clarity is the assignment of responsibilities, recognition of the special competencies of different levels of government, and appreciation of the importance of coordinating public with private sector activities can do much to lessen the dislocation accompanying changes that will surely continue to unfold.

A Welfare Agenda for the Eighties

Welfare represents another human service area in which we have not paid enough attention to the design and implementation of individual programs and to the manner in which these programs interact with one another. As a result, this jerry-built system satisfies almost no one.

More than 45 years after the New Deal and 15 years after the Great Society, the fact remains that poverty persists in America. The Census Bureau estimates that the income of 25 million people (11.8 percent of the population) fell below the official poverty line in 1976.* Women, blacks, and Southerners accounted for a disproportionate share of the total.

In welfare policy, as in urban policy, we are the victims of history. In fact, the only rationale for the existing system is historical. Each program represents a small piece of history: it stands for a politically acceptable approach to a particular problem at the time of the program's creation. As a direct result, today's system is an uncoordinated collection of all that has come before.

Analyzing the American welfare system requires the skills of an archeologist, the ability to sift patiently through layer upon layer of government programs. Sorting out the layers, one finds at least five distinct types of welfare programs. They vary by the era of their creation, and by whether they offer the poor money, advice, or a particular commodity. These types of programs include aid to the poor, which are programs that offer money and advice, such as the Aid to Families with Dependent Children (AFDC) program; social insurance programs, like Social Security, that provide money as a right; government aid to purchase essential commodities, as in food stamps; government provision of minimum standards, such as minimum wages; and government provision of opportunity, such as vocational rehabilitation.

Despite pleas for simplification, each type of program continues to play a role in the American welfare system. As a result, this system amounts to a catalogue of historical approaches to social welfare. The trouble is that this catalogue features the very oldest as well as the very newest in ideas.

Because of the additive nature of the welfare system, an individual who seeks aid from the system encounters a bewildering array of overlapping programs. One might consider the case of a recently widowed mother with children, one of whom is disabled. Under present conditions, this mother must apply to at least seven different programs to

*This official poverty definition fails to take in-kind transfers such as Medicaid and food stamps into account. It may therefore overstate the poverty level.

receive the aid to which she is entitled. In a typical jurisdiction, she needs to travel to at least 4 different offices and fill out at least 5 different forms, answering 300 separate questions. The programs may treat the information obtained from these forms differently. On one program, for example, the value of a car may differ from the value of the same car in another program. Because each welfare program follows its own traditions, it may take 1,400 pieces of information just to determine accurately the level of the woman's income. This illustration underscores the findings of a 1974 subcommittee of the Joint Economic Committee. "Instead of forming a coordinated network," the subcommittee wrote, "our . . . income maintenance programs are an assortment of fragmented efforts that distribute income to various persons for various purposes, sometimes on conflicting terms with unforeseen results."

Any effort to change the welfare system in the Eighties must take into account the institutional landscape and its layer upon layer of programs. An effective agenda must deal with the problems created by the persistence of programs long after the rationale for their existence has disappeared.

The development of the AFDC program serves as a case in point. Originally, the program aided needy widows upon the death of their wage-earning husbands. The idea was to keep mothers out of the labor force so that they could stay home with their children. Over the years, however, AFDC has grown to become the nation's largest public assistance program. Despite its new importance, it continues to provide aid only to single-parent families and to serve as an incentive for women not to join the labor force. Although society's ideas about the goals of welfare programs have changed, AFDC has remained substantially the same—a throwback to an earlier era that nonetheless cost a great deal of money and impeded efforts to reform the welfare system more comprehensively.

The present welfare system contains other problems as well. Many of them concern the three central goals of a modern welfare system— equity, adequacy, and efficiency. Ideally, the nation's welfare system should treat similar people in a similar manner—the notion of equity. (The notion of equity may also be extended to allow for differences in the cost of living from one region of the country to another.) It should provide benefits that give all households an income above the poverty level—the goal of adequacy—and it should contain incentives to substitute work for welfare wherever possible—the target of efficiency. The present system meets none of these criteria.

In order to remedy these problems, we need to look at the system of welfare programs rather than at the individual programs themselves. In recent years, a number of reform proposals have taken this broad view. Many of them rely upon the concept of a negative income tax, an idea that will continue to be on the public agenda for the Eighties. The idea follows from the observation that welfare programs penalize work. If a person who earns a dollar loses a dollar in benefits, he has little incentive to work, because in effect he pays a 100-percent "tax" on his earnings. To remedy the problem, he must be allowed to keep a certain percentage of his earnings.

The virtue of the negative income tax is that it provides a means by which all families receive the guarantee of a minimum cash benefit and, at the same time, pay less than a 100-percent tax on their earnings. The negative income tax, therefore, enables welfare programs to reach the working poor without taking away the incentive of those poor people to work.

Although the negative income tax presented many problems, Congress made a serious attempt to enact it into law during the Seventies. By the end of that decade, acceptance of its general principles, if not the exact political details of how it could be implemented, was common among welfare reformers. There was widespread agreement that coverage needed to be expanded, benefits made more equitable, and work incentives improved. Passage of the Supplemental Security Income program, with its income guarantee for the elderly and the permanently disabled, marked another step toward creation of a negative income tax for all Americans.

The Commission has also considered other welfare reform proposals, including plans to guarantee the welfare population jobs and efforts to provide the states with block grants for welfare purposes. The job proposals contain the beneficial features of moving toward universal coverage of the poor and reorienting manpower programs toward providing actual jobs to people. On the other hand, no one knows if the nation has the ability to create jobs for the welfare recipients that are expected to work, to separate the welfare population that is expected to work from the welfare population that is not able to work, and to manage such a complicated program. The block grant idea suffers from the fact that it would perpetuate current problems: states withlow benefits would continue to pay benefits well below the povertyline.

After reviewing these various reform proposals, the Commission recommends that Congress legislate a minimum security income for all Americans. The income guarantee should be related to the poverty level—within a possible range, as determined by Congress, of from two-thirds to three-quarters of that amount—and the tax on earnings should be relatively low—perhaps 50 percent. The new program would replace the current AFDC, food stamp, and general assistance programs. It would provide the sort of permanent, effective reform that would obviate the need for new crash programs, such as the recently proposed "energy stamps."*

The minimum security income would not serve as a substitute or replacement for all existing or proposed welfare programs. Because we recognize the importance of the gains made in the past decade, the Supplemental Security Income program would remain in place for the elderly and the disabled—groups that require a higher guarantee because they are not expected to work.

Once in existence, the new system will aid millions of the working poor neglected by current programs and raise the level of welfare benefits in many states to adequate levels. But it will also cost the federal government more than it now spends on welfare. The Commission has obtained estimates that place the additional federal cost of the program (using a guarantee of three-quarters of the poverty line) at from $15 to $20 billion. By ensuring that our welfare system functions coherently, however, and because the new national minimum income will replace a number of expensive and overlapping programs, the enactment of the program may lead to substantial administrative savings. In addition, it will relieve state and local governments of much of their welfare burden and enable them to perform the sorts of functions they perform best: providing social services rather than income transfers. And under the new program, a meaningful reform of Social Security could occur, since that program would be free of much of its welfare burden.†

If the goal of ending poverty appears to be too distant to reach in the decade ahead, we should at least take the first step and reform our welfare system. For this area is one in which we are not spending the available money wisely; the nation's performance in the field of welfare can be improved.

The Nation's Health System

During this century, a veritable revolution has occurred in medical science, much of it emanating from this country. In many respects, medical care in the United States is second to none in the world, with

---

*Since Congress will not be able to act immediately on welfare reform and since rising fuel prices place a burden upon the poor, some thought does need to be given to ways of helping the poor meet energy costs.

†The financing of Social Security, although a very important topic, is one of those matters on which the Commission feels it lacks technical competence. Accordingly, it leaves this subject to other bodies with more direct mandates to provide actuarial analyses of the Social Security program, notably the President's Commission on Pension Policy.

advances accumulating at a startling rate. Yet we face a disquieting scene in which some of us have access to the finest health care in the world, while many others must make do with care that is inadequate. Medical science is not to blame for these inadequacies, but the system we have developed for delivering needed care to our citizens is woefully inadequate. It is fitting, therefore, that the Commission address health care, not from the perspective of the state of medical science, but from that of the health care system.

Social justice in America embraces the right of all citizens to secure adequate health care. We can no longer consider this a privilege but must develop a national health policy that will protect everyone against the financial burden of ill health. Curiously, there has been extensive agreement for the past 30 years on the need for such a policy—indeed, rarely has a public issue generated more popular and political enthusiasm—yet thus far no encompassing legislative action has been produced.

Instead, as in the case of welfare, the nation has advanced by historical increment. Since 1938, if not earlier, Congress has kept pace with public interest by scheduling hearings and producing, over the years, several historical layers of health programs and policies. The passage of the Social Security Amendments in 1965 marked a strong beginning toward a comprehensive federal health policy. The amendments created Medicaid for the poor and Medicare for the elderly. As a result of these programs, the government's role has become so large that in 1980, 40 percent of all health expenditures in this country were underwritten by federal and state governments—a figure that does not include expenditures through tax subsidies—in the form of deductions from income or exclusions of medical costs and insurance premiums paid by employers.

As significant as Medicaid and Medicare have been, however, they have serious shortcomings. Perhaps the most basic is a lack of comprehensiveness. In much the same fashion as the nation's welfare programs, its health policies fail to extend benefits to everyone in need of them. Far too many people—an estimated 12.6 percent of the population—are not covered by any health insurance at all. Many others are inadequately covered.

Although the Commission believes that financing health care is of the highest priority, all of the following issues and concerns should be addressed in any truly comprehensive national health policy:

- Assuring access of the economically disadvantaged to high-quality health care services;
- Protecting all Americans from the threat of financial catastrophe caused by major illness;

- Encouraging efficient production of health care services so that high-quality care is produced at minimum cost, whether this cost is borne by the public or the private sector;
- Assuring the elderly that they will be able to live with the dignity, mobility, and independence that their health status permits;
- Removing disparities in health status and risk of disease among groups of Americans by applying our advanced state of medical technology to illnesses that are preventable, regardless of the patient's social or economic circumstances.

To achieve these goals, the Commission proposes a three-part national health policy—universal comprehensive national health insurance, an enlarged program of disease prevention and health promotion, and a program for providing a greater range of health and social services for the elderly.

Its first and most extensive provision—a national health insurance program—would extend coverage to all Americans, regardless of income, and would significantly alter the way we finance health care in this country. The health care system in the United States has grown in a way that reflects the way we pay for this care. All insurers, both public and private, have generally adhered to the principle that all "medically authorized" services for a patient would be paid for, regardless of cost or actual necessity. As a result of this perverse incentive system, we now face a situation in which we have more hospital beds than we need and more physicians, more specialists, and more expensive equipment that we can efficiently use. Attempts have been made to regulate physicians and hospitals to improve efficiency and to contain costs, but these attempts are deeply flawed, with half-hearted regulation put on top of a dynamic industry. There are no doubt more successful, less expensive alternatives to our present "worst of two worlds" health policy.

The Commission has considered a number of financing proposals to remedy these defects. One approach would mandate expanded coverage for catastrophic medical expenses for all Americans. While addressing one defect in the system, more basic problems in the way services are produced and delivered would remain. Another approach would create a single, government-administered financing program, thereby enlarging the scope of government control over the health industry in a fundamental way. This program would apply cost-containment requirements to all providers of care. These might include negotiated fees and charges for other services, utilization review, and prospective budgeting to encourage efficiency in hospitals. A third approach to reform of the system would stimulate competition among a diverse mix of insurers and would largely replace regulation by economic incentives for both consumers and producers.

The government-administered health insurance program has important and attractive features, not the least of which is its generally successful implementation by our neighbor, Canada. Under this type of insurance program, reimbursement for services would be made by a government insurance fund to providers agreeing to comply with the fund's regulations. These regulations would probably require cost-containment programs that have already been implemented in a limited and often voluntary way, such as prospective reimbursement, health planning, utilization review, and negotiated uniform fee schedules. In addition, a ceiling on total health expenditures would also be set so that growth of these expenditures could be controlled. This degree of control over the health care delivery sector would fundamentally alter the income distribution of physicians, the number and nature of hospitals, and the type of services produced. Because the degree of mandated restructuring inherent in this sort of insurance program is so great, implementation and achievement of provider compliance would be very difficult to attain.

The Commission feels, on balance, that an expansion of the role of competition, consumer choice, and market incentives rather than government control is more likely to create the much needed stimulus toward greater efficiency, cost consciousness, and responsiveness to consumer preferences so visibly lacking in our present arrangements for providing medical care.

This competitive program would provide all individuals with a flat premium subsidy which would be applicable to a number of insurance and delivery options. It would enable people to select a health insurance plan best suited to their preferences and needs, with respect to the type of health system desired, amenities, extent of coverage, and the total cost of the care.

Every available plan would provide a minimum level of coverage for basic health care services. Additional services would be covered by additional, more expensive insurance options, paid for by the individual. All health insurance plans would cover "catastrophic" medical costs attendant to major and/or long-term illness. This minimum insurance program would cover the poor and the unemployed at no cost, but it could also be applied toward other health insurance plans as well. This program would especially benefit the poor, who now face a restricted medical system because of the way Medicaid is structured in most states. Thus, all Americans would be covered by a basic comprehensive health insurance plan, but would retain the right to select any other health insurance plan if this basic plan did not perform satisfactorily.

With the appropriate information, a consumer could compare the different plans and choose the one that best met his needs. Presumably, some insurers would offer "closed panel" plans, which would reimburse consumers only when they used a health care provider who had promised the insurer to deliver services at a negotiated price. This system is in marked contrast to the typical health insurance plan today, whereby nearly all private and public insurance plans reimburse patients for reasonable medical care provided by essentially any doctor and hospital. The closed panel plans would encourage health care providers to make their prices competitive. Moreover, since closed panel plans often cost less than comparable plans that contain no restrictions on a consumer's choice of providers, other insurance companies would have an incentive to find ways to contain insurance premium costs. Thus, encouraging a diversity of insurance plans would create a more competitive market for health care and would ultimately lead to lower overall medical costs.

Consumers would decide themselves whether they preferred a constrained or an unconstrained system—one with full first-dollar coverage for all services, or one that requires some sharing of medical costs which would encourage needed care, while discouraging frivolous use. Every consumer would decide what type of health system was personally most desirable and would be responsible for the costs (or cost savings) that the choice brings.

Serious problems of program design and implementation must be overcome, of course, in any attempt to reform the present system. This report notes, however, that there are a number of policy areas, health care being only one, in which concern is expressed that attempts to regulate the behavior of individuals to achieve efficiency are likely to be more expensive—and less successful—than approaches that encourage freedom of choice within an appropriate system of incentives.

The second element of the proposed health policy concerns the application of existing medical technology to those medical problems that are preventable by appropriately structuring and financing health promotion services. In order to take needed steps forward in preventing disease, programs for maternal and child screening, for immunization, and for nutrition services need to be enlarged. Equally important, the Commission suggests that an increased effort be directed toward extending preventive services and health education, especially among high-risk groups of the population, so that the burden of chronic illness can be reduced and the wide disparities that currently exist across groups for illnesses such as stroke, heart disease, tuberculosis, and some types of cancer could be lessened or eliminated. Further efforts must be made to identify the sources of occupational illnesses and to remove them insofar as practicable. Outright prevention may be unattainable for these conditions, but the high vulnerability to risk among certain population groups relative to the rest of the population can certainly be lowered.

A third element in the nation's health policy is the provision of noninstitutional forms of care for the elderly so that they will be able to live at home for as long as they choose and their health permits. There is concern that nursing home admissions too often reflect a lack of appropriate social support services for the frail elderly who would rather remain in their home and social setting. (See the next section of this chapter.)

These health policy recommendations entail significant costs—costs which in a period of fiscal stringency constitute a serious barrier to enactment. The Commission notes, however, that each of the new health insurance, disease prevention, and long-term care programs will generate important savings in both private and public expenditures, as current patterns of health care production and consumption are made more efficient. Although estimates put the annual costs of a national health insurance program such as the Commission recommends at approximately $14 billion, the program will reduce out-of-pocket spending by those formerly without insurance. In addition, savings from increased incentives to produce health care efficiently and consume it prudently are estimated to be $2.5 billion.

An expansion of disease prevention programs, such as would be provided by the recently proposed health incentive grants program, would cost slightly under $1 billion per year, according to the Congressional Budget Office. These programs, however, will generate significant savings by lowering the costs of illness, disability, and premature death.

A program for expanded use of home-based and day-care services for the elderly will reduce our present expenditures on institutional care, which constitute an enormous burden on both the Medicaid and Medicare programs. By using nursing homes for only those patients who are too frail and dependent to live at home with support services, we will need fewer of these facilities. Community-based care is a far less expensive alternative for those not needing the intensive care of a nursing home. The Congressional Budget Office has estimated that the liberalization of Medicare and Medicaid coverage for noninstitutional care would have increased direct federal costs by just over $1.5 billion in 1980.

Adoption of a health policy with these three components—comprehensive insurance, disease prevention, and care for the elderly—will not only improve the health of Americans, but will reduce the outstanding inequities that are inconsistent with the broader goals of social justice for America in the Eighties.

Dependency: Children and the Elderly

Consideration of urban policy, welfare, and health has left some important gaps in our discussion of human services. The most significant of these concerns the role of public policy toward children and the elderly.

We are increasingly becoming a society of the very young and the very old. Although the number and percentage of children in the population will decline in the Nineties, the immediate decade before us may witness a "baby boomlet." One estimate has the number of preschool children increasing by 36 percent to 23,400,000. Because of declining mortality rates, the number of elderly will also increase in the next decade. The Eighties, then, will be a threshold to an era when one-fifth of America's population will be elderly, and another one-fifth infants. More to the point, people over 65 will constitute roughly half of the dependent population by the year 2000.

In the past, the family has assumed primary responsibility for caring for all dependents, young and old. But over the past two decades, the American family has undergone a dramatic transformation. The most significant change affecting children and the elderly has been the increasing disappearance of their traditional caretakers. Women have entered the labor force in large numbers, reducing the time they can spend with children and old people. With the rapidly growing number of single-parent households, women are becoming increasingly the sole, or main, source of support for families. In short, although women will likely continue to perform the care function, their growing presence in the labor force requires a variety of new arrangements and programs to help carry the traditional burden of caring for children and old people.

One pressing need is for a wider range of adequate, affordable child care options. While many children now receive care through a variety of formal and informal arrangements, convenient and affordable alternatives do not exist for many families. The Census Bureau estimates that more than 2 million children between the ages of 7 and 13 are "latchkey" children who are left to take care of themselves after school. At least 20,000 preschoolers are left alone while their parents work. Clearly, alternatives to the present situation are needed.

Not all families require child care; this Commission feels strongly that such decisions must be left to the discretion of individual families. The responsibility of government, industry, and nonprofit organizations lies in facilitating the availability of affordable child care options for those families who choose to use them.

Options for public and private sector initiatives include more widespread provision of child care subsidies as part of employee benefit packages, expansion of tax credit systems for child care services, and creation of more options for working parents such as job sharing, flextime, and parental leave with pay.

A second item on the dependency agenda would be the improved availability of a broader range of support services permitting the elderly to remain at home. This item has already been discussed with regard to reforming the Medicare program to allow more health care to take place in community, rather than in institutional settings such as nursing homes. Other useful initiatives in this regard include encouraging the present trend toward delayed retirement, creating a broad spectrum of volunteer and paid job opportunities for the elderly— opportunities that permit intergenerational contact—expanding existing transportation systems for the elderly, instituting more out-of-home day programs for the elderly whose families work during the day, and providing incentives for the construction of multigenerational housing, especially rental units.

In sum, no new major or overarching policies are needed to care for dependents, just an increased social awareness and expansion of existing programs. The combined private and public costs of implementing the recommendations made for dependent care will be in the $2- to $4-billion range. The numbers of the young and the old will grow, and families—a rapidly increasing number of which contain working women—will be obligated to seek newer and more flexible means of maintaining care. In this search, private and public institutions must act as vital, sympathetic, and helpful allies.

Education

The Commission believes that public schools are failing in significant ways to provide the quality of education desired by the American public. A successful education system would assure that every student receives the basic skills and social experience required to become a functional and productive citizen in a democratic society. Barriers to the education of the nation's students—barriers of poverty, inequality, ignorance, and mediocrity—must be removed. A continued commitment to equal access to learning opportunities is of critical importance, and it should be accomplished in a way that enhances the quality of public schools. Thus, equality, competence, and excellence are the essential items on the national education agenda. To achieve these goals, public schools must receive the support of the community at large, but at the same time, taxpayers, through local school boards, have a right to hold school personnel accountable for the students' achievements in the required academic, vocational, and life skills.

The public schools are being asked to perform their traditional role more effectively and efficiently while developing, as rapidly as possible, realistic responses to an additional set of educational needs—needs that will have considerable impact upon American society. Thus, in the 1980s, the school system will be called upon to satisfy a widening public insistence on equity in educational opportunities; to offer greater diversity and choice; to set higher standards; to respond to demands for accountability, sometimes expressed through cumbersome and prescriptive regulations; and to meet society's requirements for educated, skilled workers in new fields. Rapidly expanding technologies, especially in the processing and transmittal of information, will need to be accommodated, along with a gradual shift in the schools' focus from a school-based learning environment to one that involves more interaction with other learning resources. Educators will have to develop programs that will foster the professional growth of the individuals who work in educational institutions and that make schools more responsive to changing community priorities. The achievement of these concerns while improving on the traditional role is the central problem facing public education. At present, funds and trained staff are not sufficient to meet this need.

Continued failure by the schools to perform their traditional role adequately, together with a failure to respond to the emerging needs of the 1980s, may have disastrous consequences for this nation. Such a prospect is particularly inopportune as public schools are being reminded of the importance of their contribution to the current national priorities of defense, technology, and productivity. Some observers claim that the public's expectations for the schools are unrealistic and do not sufficiently acknowledge the extent to which society's problems beset the schools themselves. On the other hand, many observers believe that societal explanations are a poor excuse for the decline in school quality and productivity. Public schools, they say, simply are failing to meet the needs of students.

Although there is no public consensus about the specific inadequacies of the public school system or the reasons for them, it is clear that many people are dissatisfied with one or more aspects of public school education. Included among the dissatisfactions is the performance of the school system in providing:

- A minimum level of basic skill proficiency;
- Desegregated schools and quality integrated education;

- The training necessary for an increasingly complex and changing job market;
- Proficiency in the skills required to attend higher education institutions;
- Adequate accountability for the achievement, or lack of achievement, of students;
- Funding and design of compensatory programs for the handicapped and disadvantaged;
- Adequate understanding of topics such as conservation, world interdependence, and sex-role stereotyping.

Numerous other dissatisfactions exist. Each tends to generate the formation of special interest groups which often work at cross-purposes with each other as they advocate differing notions of what the schools should do and how.

This Commission has not attempted to provide specific solutions to these problems. Moreover, the Report does not contain a full education agenda with definitive answers. Instead, the challenge is defined, and some suggestions are offered for improving public education in a few areas.

The Commission believes that the current crisis of confidence in public schooling—more widespread, persistent, and intense than at any previous point in our history—is precisely the time to reaffirm the legacy and potential of public education. A renewed commitment to excellence in public education for children of all abilities is fundamental to the American ideal of a just society. Temporary confusion of purpose and disappointment with lowered test scores are not sufficient cause to permit the permanent weakening of this mainstay of a pluralistic democracy. Although the school system is falling far short of success, there are many examples of improvement which indicate that quality can be achieved.

Demographic and Social Context.* One reason for some of the public schools' difficulties is the absence of planning for future demographic and social changes. Many school systems learned during the 1970s that it costs them much more to react to changes than to anticipate them. For the 1980s, certain demographic and social trends will bear heavily on the education system. Continuing a decade of decline,

---

*Although the Commission believes that the topic of higher education is important, it did not have the resources to examine the issue thoroughly. For this topic, the Commission defers to the recent study conducted by the Carnegie Council on Higher Education, entitled *Three Thousand Futures: The Next Twenty Years in Higher Education.*

the number of elementary school-age children is expected to drop another 4 percent in the early 1980s and then begin to increase. By 1990, there should be approximately as many children between the ages of 5 and 13 as there were in 1960. Racial minority representation in this cohort will be 17.7 percent in 1990, compared to an expected racial minority representation of 14.8 percent in the total population.

The number of young people of high school age is expected to decline about 19 percent during the 1980s. Racial minority representation in the 14- to 17-year-old cohort will probably increase to 19.4 percent in 1990. The representation of Hispanics in both the younger and older age groups is expected to grow more rapidly than either the black or majority populations. For both age groups, the pattern of enrollment decline and recovery will vary greatly from locality to locality, principally because of differential migration.

Equal Education Opportunity and Compensatory Education. The Commission is of the opinion that more, not less, concerted action is needed on the part of the federal government, the courts, and the states to implement the spirit and letter of the *Brown* decision. Active federal support should be provided for methods of achieving desegregation, such as redistricting, pairing of schools, and court-approved transportation plans. Other solutions to the problem of segregated schools will require comprehensive, coordinated government programs in housing, transportation, commerce, education, and criminal justice. Added support is also needed for special programs such as bilingual education, pre-elementary education, and education of the disadvantaged and the handicapped. This is important to central city districts where the problems of schools are most acute and where low-income blacks, Hispanics, and native Americans are disproportionately affected. Evidence indicates that compensatory education programs have helped, but more can and should be done.

Federal education policy must remain committed to its central mission of promoting equality of opportunity and providing compensatory educational services, while at the same time being careful not to hinder the efficient and equitable management of schools by state and local governments. Controversy surrounds the question of the remaining objectives of federal education policy. The amount of federal involvement in maintaining or improving the public schools will continue to be a difficult issue in the 1980s.

Improving the Educational System. In the 1980s, students must be offered competent instruction—particularly in reading, writing, mathematics, and processes of logical thought—and the chance to develop their individual talents to the fullest. A renewed commitment to proficiency in basic skills is requisite. However, to function successfully in society, students also must be taught how to apply these skills to practical tasks and decisions they will face daily.

The Commission must also caution against overemphasizing basic skills. Abuse occurs when "back to basics" is used as an excuse to block other curriculum and programmatic development, to eliminate "frills" (such as art, music, foreign language, books, and personal instruction) in order to reduce school budgets, or as a means of constraining the pursuit of excellence. Public schools must also maximize the talents of promising and high-achieving students; otherwise there is the prospect that schools will fail to produce the skilled people that society needs and that more families may choose private education.

As one of many possible incentives for students and staff, schools might establish a student evaluation and promotion system that is based upon mastery of subject matter, not on time in class or years in school. Students would progress at their own rate upon learning what the school has set out to teach. Tests in elementary and secondary schools should be used as a means of diagnosing students' abilities and disabilities, as a basis for supplying additional resources and individualized attention as early and as often as needed, and as one of a number of factors in grade promotion and graduation decisions. The controversy surrounding I.Q. tests, minimum competency tests, truth-in-testing laws, and other aspects of testing suggests that thorough consideration should be given to the design of new tests, to the calibration of existing tests, and to the training of the teachers who will use them.

Teacher training programs should be critically reviewed, and more emphasis should be placed on in-service training. Teachers' salaries must be kept at competitive levels to attract talented, well-trained entrants to the profession—and more importantly to keep good teachers already in the schools. At the same time, new procedures should be established for accountability in order to relieve the school system of those teachers who are indifferent, ineffective, and unwilling (or unable) to improve. School administrators must expect more from their teachers, and teachers must expect more from their students. Teachers must also begin to take more personal responsibility for students' successes and failures.

A new spirit of collaboration is needed—within the schools; among administrators, teachers, parents, and students; and between the schools and the surrounding community. Organizations and individuals should be encouraged to offer their resources to the public schools. The involvement of the private sector in the improvement of public schools should be expanded.

The Needs of Youth.   The structure and operation of public schools have changed very little in response to the altered needs of their students. Schools have often avoided the necessity of matching parts of the school curriculum with the current and future needs of society. Possibly the most significant condition affecting youth is the lack of responsible social, economic, and political roles within their families, institutions, and communities. Citizenship skills such as participation and negotiation are rarely learned in experiential ways. Many parents and teachers feel that a balance of "real world" experiences and classroom theory is essential to prepare teenagers for adult work, citizenship, and family responsibilities. Students' determination to study can increase as they develop a more sophisticated understanding of the correlation between education, employment, community status, and choices of lifestyles. To prepare youth better for the world of work, reforms in junior and senior high schools should include an emphasis on basic skill remediation, vocational exploration, and learning in community settings outside the school.

The Census Bureau projects that 48 percent of all children born in 1980 will live "a considerable time" with only one parent before they reach the age of 18. A recent national study has concluded that children living with only one parent encounter significantly more academic and disciplinary problems than their peers. Important questions have yet to be answered. Should these children be treated differently? Is there a greater need in the 1980s for family and sex education courses? What should be the organizational, pedagogical, or curricula response, if any, to the pervasive changes in "family" characteristics? Can the schools afford to assume even greater caretaking roles?

Financing Elementary and Secondary Education.   The critical need facing school finance in the 1980s is the resolution of the conflicts among rising educational costs, higher public expectations, and mounting voter resistance to higher taxes: The decline in school enrollments, which might have been expected to help free funds for increased per pupil expenditures, has not had that result in many communities. School costs, sensitive to inflationary pressures, have risen 187 percent over the past 10 years. State support, and some federal allocations, are based on average daily attendance figures and tend to decline, at least in constant dollars, when enrollment falls. Moreover, it takes time for school systems to realize any savings resulting from a decline—that is, to lose enough students in the right places to cut a teaching slot, to drop a program, to close and sell a building, or to be able to reallocate resources.

The dominant trend has been to close or consolidate underused school buildings. Few school districts have used enrollment decline to reduce class size, despite abundant evidence supporting the positive effect of small classes on learning. In addition, while managing present contraction, school administrators must assess each decision in terms of its consequences for increased enrollment in the future.

Adequate school financing alone is not the answer to improved education, but helping poorer school districts provide better educational services is an essential element in the improvement of education and the advancement of social justice. Consequently, the Commission suggests that the states which have not acted should seek reform of their school finance systems in order to make local taxable wealth substantially irrelevant in determining the quality of a student's education; that equitable financing of elementary and secondary education, particularly in urban areas, be regarded by federal and state governments as an integral part of the larger problem of intergovernmental finance for which solutions must be found; and that states, in providing financial assistance to local school districts, recognize the greater costs that some localities incur because of larger concentrations of disadvantaged families and the higher costs of virtually all services in such areas.

The voucher system and tuition tax credits are two of a number of proposals under discussion to develop alternative school financing methods. Advocates believe that these proposals would encourage greater consumer accountability and choice, and promote a competitive incentive to improve school quality. Those opposed to the use of public funds in support of private education fear that such efforts would impair and contravene the nation's historic commitment to universally available, free education and equality of opportunity. The education agenda for the 1980s should include an examination of the consequences of the policy choices for and against vouchers, tax credits, and other means of channeling public funds to the private sector of education. The options require extended study by a competent and objective body of public policy experts outside partisan politics, although in the long run only our elected representatives can decide to institute such measures.

A movement to consolidate and simplify the array of categorical educational aid programs will continue to attract support in the 1980s. A majority of school administrators believes that federal education funds are often accompanied by excessive and conflicting regulations governing their use. The federal government should explore the possibility of moving to less restrictive means of supplying aid and offering more discretion to administrators at the local level, while still vigorously enforcing larger national equity goals.

The Prospect.   The factionalism that engulfed public education during the 1970s was not conducive to learning or excellence in the public schools, nor was it healthy for the scientific, technological, and economic growth that is stimulated by a thriving educational system. In this context, specific financial, structural, and programmatic recommendations constitute only part of the challenge of improvement. The real task lies in finding the will and the creativity to carry out the recommendations—especially in a setting almost devoid of the use of compromise. First, a positive image of schools and youth as resources, not as problems, should be revived. Second, public education should respond to societal needs by clearly separating that which it can accomplish alone, that which it cannot accomplish at all, and that which it can accomplish only by acknowledging and using the resources of nonschool organizations. Third, the administration of public schools should be the responsibility of people who can be leaders as well as managers.

The task of restoring confidence and quality in public schools requires leaders who have the skills to mediate among factions in a way that produces a constructive consensus. At the same time, the future of public education will require leaders who not only can improve school quality, but can also market school quality to an increasingly competitive and distrustful public. Leadership of this caliber will help keep in the public mind the truth that effective education of all children is a public good, and that society ultimately pays for ignorance and social injustice, just as it pays for disease and crime. In the 1980s, education's leaders, teachers, parents, and students, in concert with the larger community, must work together to realize the full promise of public education.

Article 25

NONWHITES AND THE DEMOGRAPHIC IMPERATIVE IN SOCIAL WELFARE SPENDING

Martha N. Ozawa

If the reelection of President Reagan symbolized anything significant, it is the recapturing of our national identity and the regaining of a vision of this country's future. Why was such reassurance necessary? In the 1960s, the United States launched a noble social movement to eradicate poverty. But before winning the War on Poverty, the United States got bogged down in the Vietnam War, an unpopular war that could not create victors. The Watergate scandal then demoralized millions of young people. And the oil shortage of 1973 to 1974 left a lasting economic effect. With all these forces impinging on the nation, Americans lost ground in international economic competition as well as credibility in international politics.

In his 1980 presidential campaign, Ronald Reagan helped the nation articulate a future agenda so that our confused and weakened nation could once again find the way toward national progress. He told us that the road to progress could be found if we focused on increasing defense expenditures, deregulating industry, lightening the tax burden of business and of high-income individuals, and minimizing government expenditures for transfer programs, especially means-tested welfare programs. Whether these policies have been responsible for the recent economic recovery is not clear, but President Reagan managed to bring about a vigorous recovery with no apparent inflation. Thanks to the economic recovery, the real income of the average American increased. Furthermore, the nation was at peace throughout the first Reagan Administration. As a result, a majority of American voters felt good about themselves, their economic condition, and their standing in the world, and they had confidence in their government. Thus in 1984, Ronald Reagan was again elected president of the United States.

SOURCE: Copyright 1986, National Association of Social Workers, Inc. Reprinted with permission from *Social Work*, Vol. 31, No. 6 (November-December, 1986) pp. 441–446. An earlier version of this article was presented at the symposium on "Social Work Policy and Practice in the 80s and 90s: Impact on Oppressed Minorities," Hunter College School of Social Work, New York, NY, December 7, 1984, and at the Ninth NASW Professional Symposium, "The People Yes," Chicago, Illinois, November 8, 1985.

In the process of recapturing national identity, however, the War on Poverty, which had been started in the 1960s, was put on the back burner. Although the incidence of poverty—especially among children—has been steadily on the rise since 1970, a majority of politicians of both parties as well as a majority of informed citizens seem unconcerned about this rise and the fact that the poor are getting poorer and the rich are getting richer.[1] Instead, these groups have found a new strategy: Increase the national income pie rather than distribute the pie more equally as it exists. Should we, as social workers, go along with the political tide and acquiesce to further cuts in federal spending for social welfare programs for low-income families, which certainly will hurt nonwhite families disproportionately?

It is this author's belief that, the current ideological tide notwithstanding, the demographic imperative will dictate future social welfare spending. The demographic imperative—that is, the mandatory force of population changes—is so strong and significant today that future demographic shifts will override other forces in determining the allocations and levels of social welfare expenditures. As the baby-boom generation starts to retire, we will face a large proportion of the elderly and a shrinking proportion of children and working people. The issue of race in the allocation of resources could become explosive as the demographic distribution of old and young emerges along white versus nonwhite lines. That is, in coming decades, the country will have a disproportionately large number of "white" elderly and a disproportionately large number of "nonwhite" children.[2] How can we make sure that enough resources are available to support the elderly—especially the very elderly who are over 75 years of age—without creating a political battle in the allocation of resources to children? How can we avert a situation in which transfer payments for the elderly—be they social security, Medicare and Medicaid, or other in-kind benefits—will be made at the expense of transfers for children? Unless we develop new strategies for constructive resource allocation to support the old and nurture the young, we may face an ugly political battle with strong racial overtones: a battle about social welfare expenditures for white elderly versus social welfare expenditures for nonwhite children.

DEMOGRAPHIC IMPERATIVE

As this nation marches into the twenty-first century, it will go through profound changes in demographic composition. As in many other industrialized societies, the population will continue to age. The median age, which was 30.6 years in 1982, is expected to reach 36.3 in 2000 and 41.6 in 2050. The proportion of persons age 65 or over will increase from the current 11.6 percent to 13.0 percent in 2000 and to 21.8 percent in 2050.[3] Among the elderly, the 75-plus group is increasing most rapidly. By the middle of the next century, this group's proportion will be larger than the current proportion of the elderly age 65 and over.[4]

With the elderly population rapidly increasing in the next century, the governmental burden for financing various types of social welfare programs is expected to grow. Despite 1983 Amendments to the Social Security Act devised to curtail future growth in benefits, the social security tax rate will go up. Governmental outlays for other programs— Medicare, nursing home care, housing, and related social services— are expected to grow as well. Taken together, in 1983 the federal government spent 27 percent of its total outlays for the nation's elderly. The percentage was only 21 percent in 1971.[5] Projections indicate that it will rise to 35 percent by the year 2000 and 65 percent by 2020.[6]

The increasing expenditures for the elderly will have to be met by a working population that is shrinking in relation to the aged population. Currently, there are 19 elderly persons per 100 working-age individuals. But by the time the baby-boom generation retires in the early years of the next century, there will be 38 elderly persons per 100 working-age individuals. True, the proportion of children will continue to decline. But because the rate of increase of the elderly is accelerating faster than the rate of decrease of children is declining, the dependent ratio (the ratio of children and elderly to working-age individuals) will start climbing again in 2010.[7] All factors considered, social welfare expenditures for the elderly are bound to grow.

Perhaps there is a danger in lumping all persons age 65 and over as a dependent population. The health condition of the elderly continues to improve. More jobs may become available to the elderly as fewer children grow up and enter the work force. Increasing service jobs may open up job opportunities for the elderly. And, if given the option, more elderly persons may choose to work rather than retire.

Yet past experiences tell us otherwise. Labor force participation among the elderly has been steadily declining. As a result, the number of elderly who could have received social security benefits but did not because of excess earnings has steadily declined. In 1970, 13 percent of elderly workers age 62 through 71 earned enough to forgo all social security benefits. In 1983, the comparable figure was only 3.0 percent.[8] However, a provision under the 1983 Amendments to the Social Security Act that levies taxes on up to one-half of social security benefits for high-income individuals and couples may influence the work behavior of the elderly. Some may work more to make up for the reduction in benefits; others may work less because more income through work would result in a further cut in benefits. Only an empirical study can measure the exact effect of this provision. Furthermore, unlike the federal government, which, through recent legislation, is attempting to encourage the postponement of retirement, corporate America and many nonprofit employers have not yet moved toward establishing such a policy.[9] In the meantime, the proportion of the elderly continues to increase. It is safe to say, therefore, that a smaller number of workers will be available to support each social security beneficiary in the future. This is exactly what the actuary of the Social Security Administration predicts: When the baby-boom generation retires, there will be only two workers, instead of the current three, to support each beneficiary.[10]

How is this pertinent to nonwhites? Whether this nation can fulfill its commitment to strong support of the elderly depends to a major extent on how quickly the nonwhite segment becomes more productive. This is because the nonwhite population is a growing segment of the total population and because nonwhites will have a disproportionately large number of children.

As Table 1 indicates, the percentage of nonwhites as a whole is increasing in relation to whites. Nonwhites constituted 14.5 percent of the total population in 1982; the percentage will reach 20.7 by 2030 and 23.0 by 2050.[11] Within this context, nonwhites will have a disproportionately large number of children. For any given year up to 2050, nonwhite children will be overrepresented proportionally among all children. In contrast, the nonwhite elderly will be underrepresented among all elderly persons, although the relative growth rate of the nonwhite elderly is faster than that of nonwhite children. Thus, one can say that, within the whole population, nonwhites will have a disproportionately large number of children, whereas whites will have a disproportionately large number of elderly. This condition will persist for the foreseeable future.

These data imply that the degree to which the baby-boom generation will be economically secure in old age will depend largely on how productive current nonwhite children are when they reach adulthood. As they become adults, will they have developed earning power? In social security, this question will be crucial in determining future benefit levels. That is, future benefit levels will be mathematically determined by the average earnings of workers, the tax rate, and the ratio of workers to beneficiaries.[12] Because the ratio of workers to beneficiaries will decrease, average earnings will need to go up to provide future retirees with social security benefits that are as adequate as those received by current retirees. Otherwise, the tax rate will skyrocket. To boost average earnings, nonwhite earnings must increase.

If opportunities for nonwhite children remain as limited as they are today, it is certain that the earning power of nonwhite adults will not be rising as it should. A variety of indicators show that, today,

TABLE 1   Distribution of U.S. Population by Race, 1984–2050 (percentage)

| Year | U.S. Population | | Total |
	White	Nonwhite	
All Persons			
1984	85.5	14.5	100.0
1990	84.4	15.6	100.0
2000	83.1	16.9	100.0
2010	81.7	18.3	100.0
2020	80.5	19.5	100.0
2030	79.3	20.7	100.0
2040	78.1	21.9	100.0
2050	77.0	23.0	100.0
Children[a]			
1984	81.6	18.4	100.0
1990	80.7	19.3	100.0
2000	79.4	20.6	100.0
2010	77.8	22.2	100.0
2020	76.8	23.2	100.0
2030	76.0	24.0	100.0
2040	75.2	24.8	100.0
2050	74.8	25.2	100.0
Elderly[b]			
1984	90.5	9.5	100.0
1990	90.2	9.8	100.0
2000	89.1	10.9	100.0
2010	87.7	12.3	100.0
2020	86.2	13.8	100.0
2030	84.5	15.5	100.0
2040	82.8	17.2	100.0
2050	80.9	19.1	100.0

[a]Children refers to persons age 17 or under.
[b]Elderly refers to persons 65 years of age and over.

SOURCE: U.S. Bureau of the Census, "Projections of the Population of the United States, by Age, Sex, and Race: 1983 to 2080." *Current Population Reports.* Series P-25 (Washington, D.C.: U.S. Government Printing Office, 1984), Table 6, pp. 41–94.

nonwhite children indeed have less chance than white children to develop to their fullest potential.

Blacks and Other Nonwhites

Because blacks continue to be the dominant group among nonwhites (82.0 percent in 1984), and projected to be 75.3 percent in 2030 and 73.4 percent in 2050), the plight of nonwhite children can be estimated, with a margin of error, on the basis of data pertaining to blacks.[13]

First, chances are greater for nonwhite babies to be born prematurely. For instance, in 1982, among blacks, 12.4 percent of infants weighed less than 2,500 grams (5 pounds 8 ounces) compared with 5.6 percent among whites.[14] Studies have shown that low-weight infants have a greater risk of developing major handicaps such as low IQ, hearing loss, and spastic disorders.[15] Low-weight births, in turn, are closely related to infant mortality. Again taking blacks as an example, their infant mortality rate is almost twice as high as that of whites. All these deplorable conditions are caused, to a great extent, by insufficient prenatal care for blacks.[16]

Second, the rate of illegitimate births is higher among nonwhites than among whites. Again, data indicating the black versus the white differential are available. In 1982, 566 per 1,000 black infants were born out of wedlock compared with 120 per 1,000 white infants. Most mothers of such infants eventually marry, but many of these marriages end in divorce. These mothers may have wanted the children before birth but later regard them as a burden. As a result, many children born out of wedlock become victims of abuse and neglect.[17]

Third, the rate of female-headed families is higher among nonwhites than among whites. Again, the black-white differential is startling. In 1982, as many as 41 percent of all black families were headed by females, compared with 13 percent of all white families.[18] Like other women, many of the nonwhite and the white female heads-of-households work outside of the home. The rate of labor force participation is higher for separated or divorced women with children under 6 years of age than for married women with such children.[19] Under the best of circumstances, it is hard for any female head-of-household to provide an environment conducive to the healthy development of children. It is especially hard for nonwhite female heads to do so.

After an early childhood of struggle, nonwhite children generally receive an education of lower quality than do white children. To a large extent, quality of education depends on per-pupil expenditures, which in turn are dictated by a funding mechanism that depends heavily on property taxes. As long as residential patterns do not change, funding differentials will persist. There is a sizable gap in test scores of nonwhite and white children.[20]

Whether they graduate from high school or drop out, nonwhite children have fewer opportunities to find jobs. The unemployment rate among black teenagers is approaching 50 percent—more than twice the rate for white teenagers. Black teenagers who find employment are likely to end up with less desirable jobs than white teenagers. They may also have to fight discrimination in the labor market. Anticipating a bleak future, many black female teenagers may consider that giving birth to an infant and establishing an independent household are a viable alternative to trying to break into the labor force. (Research shows that Aid to Families with Dependent Children [AFDC] facilitates establishing independent households, although it does not cause illegitimate births.[21]) Then the cycle of childhood misery and deprivation starts all over again. Of course, nonwhite children include other minority groups as well as blacks. Indeed, it is widely known that most Chinese-American and Japanese-American children do well in school and, as a result, find high-paying jobs. But because birth rates of these two groups are even lower than that of whites, they continue to be a small segment of the nonwhite population.[22]

The loss of opportunities for developing human capital during childhood is one of the decisive factors that contribute to nonwhites' inability to extract resources from society. This inability is clearly reflected in the differences in the average amount and the sources of income received by white and nonwhite persons aged 15 and over in the United States.

As seen in Table 2, per capita money income of nonwhite persons is significantly lower than that of white persons. Nonwhites' annual per capita income ($8,088) in 1982 was only 67 percent of whites' per

TABLE 2   Shares of Per Capita Income of Persons 15 Years Old and Over in 1982, by Race

	White		Nonwhite	
Source of Income	Amount	Percentage	Amount	Percentage
Earnings	$9,560	78.9	$6,637	82.0
Income from assets	920	7.6	167	2.1
Transfer payments				
Social security	800	6.6	490	6.1
Public assistance and Supplemental Security Income	73	0.6	303	3.7
Pension and annuities	435	3.6	178	2.2
Other[a]	331	2.7	313	3.9
Total	$12,119	100.0	$8,088	100.0

[a]Includes veterans' payments, unemployment insurance benefits, workers' compensation, alimony payments, and other contributions.

SOURCE: Estimated from U.S. Bureau of the Census. "Money Income of Households, Families, and Persons in the United States: 1982," *Current Population Reports*, Series P-60. No. 142 (Washington, D.C.: U.S. Government Printing Office, 1984). Table 49, pp. 166-169.

capita income ($12,119). In that year, per capita earnings of nonwhites ($6,637) were only 69 percent of the earnings of whites ($9,560).[23]

Furthermore, nonwhites and whites derive their income in different magnitudes from different sources. This is revealed by an analysis of the composition of their income. On the average, earnings are a more important source of income for nonwhites than for whites. So are public assistance and Supplemental Security Income (SSI) payments. At the same time, nonwhites do not derive as much of their income from assets as whites do. Pensions and annuities do not constitute as large a portion of per capita income for nonwhites as for whites.

Hispanics

Although this article focuses on the nation's nonwhite population and thus includes only 44 percent of Hispanics in the overall data analysis, policymakers should pay attention to all Hispanics as well as to nonwhites when they put forth strategies for developing the productive work force so as to be able to finance social welfare programs adequately for the elderly. Hispanics will constitute an increasing proportion of the total population,[24] but the prospect of their economic productivity seems destined to lag behind that of the total population.

Hispanics frequently have a value system and lifestyle quite different from those of blacks and other nonwhite groups. However, their economic and demographic characteristics are similar to those of nonwhites. Like most nonwhite groups, Hispanics have a higher birth rate and lower life expectancy in comparison to those of whites. As a result, the demographic composition of Hispanics is far different from that of the white population, with a larger proportion of children among the former than among the latter. For that matter, the age profile of Hispanics is even more skewed than that of nonwhites as a whole. In 1982, as many as 38.4 percent of Hispanics were children, whereas only 4.0 percent were elderly. Compare these figures with those of nonwhites as a whole: In 1982, 33.4 percent were children, and 7.6 percent were elderly.[25]

In 1982, the median household income of Hispanics was $15,178 compared with $21,117 for whites and $11,968 for blacks. The poverty rate of Hispanic families in the same year was 27.2 percent compared with 9.6 percent for white and 33.0 percent for black families. The rate of female headship among Hispanic families was 22.7 percent compared with 13.0 percent for white and 41.0 percent for black families.[26] On the educational front, Hispanics do worse than blacks. In 1982, 41.7 percent of Hispanics aged 25–34 had not finished high school, compared with 20.8 percent for blacks and 12.8 percent for whites.[27]

Problems Ahead

There is a clear indication of problems in decades ahead. Projections indicate that federal outlays to support the elderly will continue to accelerate as years go by. Along the way, nonwhite workers will become a larger segment of the working population. The development of the earning capability of nonwhites will become crucial in determining whether and to what extent this action can ensure a satisfying quality of life for the elderly. This means that whether the baby-boom generation will have sufficient income security in old age will depend heavily on how fast and to what extent this nation can develop human capital among today's nonwhite children.

LIMITATIONS IN THE WELFARE APPROACH

Although there is great need to develop human capital among nonwhite children, the public appears less and less supportive of governmental expenditures for social welfare purposes. This, in part, has been proved by the reelection of President Reagan, who preaches cutbacks in the federal budget for social welfare programs. To recapture public support for social welfare spending, we need to instill a new vision and a new rationale for the legitimacy of governmental involvement in social welfare programs. To do this, we need to evaluate the welfare approach to helping low-income families and see its flaws and limitations.

It seems to me that the seeds of current welfare problems were planted in the early 1960s when policymakers defined poverty in this nation and set poverty levels in dollar amounts. Since that time, poor people have been defined as persons who did not have sufficient money—in other words those whose income was below the poverty threshold. The policymakers believed that poverty could be eliminated by applying the negative income tax concept—that is, by making federal subsidy payments to those families having less than poverty-level income. Eradicating poverty simply meant filling the gap between the official poverty line and the actual income level of poor people.

To preserve work incentives, the gap was not to be filled dollar for dollar with public income transfers. It was necessary to fill the gap in such a way that earnings through work brought additional net income. These ideas were straightforward and easy for all to understand. The negative income tax as a plan for transferring income captured the imagination of many academics and government officials. The government later incorporated basically the same ideas in various social welfare programs, such as the Food Stamp program and other income-tested noncategorical transfer programs.

In developing new programs, there were two central policy objectives: (1) the improvement of work incentives and (2) the implementation of horizontal equity—which meant adopting a noncategorical approach to the provision of social welfare. To improve work incentives, the benefit withdrawal rate (or the implicit tax rate) had to be lower than that in traditional welfare programs like AFDC. To put it another way, as recipients increased their earnings, benefits were to be reduced more gradually than under traditional welfare program. Implementing horizontal equity (as is done in the Food Stamp program) meant that benefits would be made available to all households regardless of sex and marital status of household heads or the presence of children, as long as households met an income-testing measure also. The result of applying these policy objectives was twofold: First, it enlarged the pool of eligible households, some of whom had income above the poverty line. Second, many male-headed families among the working poor became eligible. Thus, many near-poor households applied for and received benefits. In 1981, for example, 33 percent of the households receiving food stamps were not poor, 47 percent of the households receiving public housing assistance were not poor, and 46 percent of the households receiving Medicaid benefits were not poor. However, it is important to note that many poor households did not receive benefits: In 1981, 59 percent of poor households did not receive food stamps, 87 percent did not receive public housing, and 61 percent did not receive Medicaid.[28]

The pursuit of the policy objectives of improving work incentives and implementing horizontal equity in welfare programs produced a serious side effect: More and more public funds were required to fill the poverty gap. In terms of cash income, the poverty gap in 1967 was $22.6 billion before transfers. After the government had spent $17.5 billion for cash transfer programs, a $10 billion poverty gap remained. In 1982, the pretransfer poverty gap was $114.9 billion. After the government had spent $118.1 billion, a $45.3 billion poverty gap remained. The rate at which the poverty gap has been reduced because of cash transfers has been declining since 1974.[29] Unless the poor can earn more through work, the poverty gap will persist, in spite of increasing cash transfers.

What about the issue of work incentives? Do people work less when they receive benefits from welfare programs developed along negative income tax lines? The New Jersey Income-Maintenance Experiment found that men did not change their work behavior even after they started receiving transfer payments, but women—especially white women—did.[30] Looking at the effect of all income transfer programs taken together, Danziger, Haveman, and Plotnick argued that the decline in the labor force participation rate due to these programs has been negligible—perhaps a few percentage points.[31]

Despite empirical findings showing that income-tested transfer programs do not diminish work incentives, the public's support for such programs seems to have declined. Why? First, many families receive welfare benefits not just from one program but from multiple programs. Governmental data show that in 1981, two or more noncash welfare benefits were received by 6.2 million households, many of whom received cash assistance in addition.[32] When the same household receives benefits from multiple sources, the benefit withdrawal rates of these programs interact with each other; the result is a much higher cumulative implicit tax rate than the rate of each program, creating the effect of a stronger disincentive to work. The idea of a negative income tax originally appeared simple, straightforward, and conducive to preserving work incentives. But when the principle is incorporated in numerous programs benefiting the same clientele, the original strengths associated with the negative income tax are dissipated quickly. Observing this phenomenon in negative income taxation, Lampman, an authority on poverty and income distribution, warns that there is a limit to eradicating poverty through income-tested transfer programs.[33]

Another reason for the public's apprehension about income-tested transfer programs might be that as a result of expanding these programs, many working families became recipients of benefits. The public might think that the inclusion of the working poor is bad for preserving work incentives. Why? It was originally thought that decreasing the rate for the withdrawal of benefits was effective for increasing work incentives of those who were already on welfare and who had been subjected to an implicit tax rate as high as 100 percent. But the public might suspect that the inclusion of the working poor resulted in increasing the work disincentives of other groups. Inclusion of the working poor meant that, for the first time, they would be subjected to an implicit tax rate. Whether the implicit tax rate was lower than it had been was immaterial for them. Getting on welfare brought about their subjection to both the implicit tax rates involved in welfare programs and the positive tax rate involved in income tax: An extra dollar of earnings brought a decreasing amount of net additional income through work. Even if the public does not understand the complex relationship between work and welfare, many might think it undesirable to have a large segment of the population depending on welfare for daily living—especially if that segment includes working households. Perhaps this might have been one of the major concerns of the Reagan Administration when it drastically changed AFDC and other welfare programs and made working-poor households ineligible for benefits. However, these changes brought back greater disincentives to work among those who stayed on welfare.[34]

Probably, a more serious flaw in the welfare approach of transferring income to low-income families is that governmental intervention occurs after individuals or families have lost their capacity to be independent. The approach has at least two negative consequences. First, since governmental intervention takes place in relation to the economic behavior of adults (parents in most cases), transferring income interferes with the incentive structure of the labor market. This is clearly seen in the case of the working poor who receive transfer payments. Even for the nonworking poor on welfare, the receipt of transfer payments may influence the decision about future work. Second, because transfer payments are related inversely to the earnings level of the household head, governmental interest is concentrated on the economic behavior of household heads. The human capital development of children growing up in welfare families becomes unimportant as an objective of governmental intervention.

Beyond the specific problems in the welfare approach of transferring income to low-income families, there is a broader question of how the general public looks at the national objective of eradicating poverty through welfare programs. Many taxpayers may accept the eradication of poverty through welfare programs as a worthy cause: To some, it may signify public benevolence; to others, it may symbolize social justice; to still others, it simply may mean charity. For each taxpayer supporting governmental spending for low-income families, however, there may be another taxpayer opposing it. At any rate, even among those who support governmental spending, motives are likely to be short of "national interest." Taxpayers probably do not regard such government spending as a positive investment for the United States. Instead they may consider it something that is desirable but that can be cut out when the chips are down. It seems to me that taxpayers' strong sustaining support for governmental spending becomes a reality only when they realize that at least a portion of the ultimate benefits from such spending accrue to them. They must see it as a positive investment.

PUBLIC INVESTMENT IN CHILDREN

The foregoing discussion indicates that the welfare approach is inappropriate and even counterproductive for ensuring the optimal development of our country's low-income children, among whom nonwhite children are overrepresented. It is clear that the nation needs a new approach—a new vision, impetus, social policy, and set of programs—if it is to succeed in developing new generations of children who eventually will be called on to support the growing number of elderly. And remember that nonwhite children will be a growing segment of the population of children. If this nation is to be financially ready to support the baby-boom retirees adequately in the next century, it needs to launch a program immediately for developing human capital among today's children and those yet to be born.

The new approach—let us call it "the public investment approach"—should be almost an antithesis of the welfare approach. Under the public investment approach, public spending would be justified, not because certain segments of society need a public handout but because taxpayers regard it as wise to invest in the nation's children. They would have come to see that such an investment would not only be in the interest of the children and the nation but in their individual interest as well. Unlike welfare programs, which generally target benefits to low-income families, public investment programs would target benefits to *all* children regardless of family income level. When spending is targeted to children, this ensures benefit provision independent of parents' employment status or level of earnings. As a result, governmental resources—financial, personnel, and material—would be mobilized toward achieving the goal of the program: *the physical, mental, and intellectual development of children.* The government would no longer need to waste its resources in monitoring, regulating, and controlling the behavior of the children's parents.

Under the public investment approach, a package of public programs would be developed, all of which would be directly related to achieving the stated goal. Programs would deal with the provision of prenatal and postnatal medical care, cash payments, medical care in childhood, and high-quality education.

Prenatal and Postnatal Care.   Under this program, all expectant mothers would receive free prenatal and postnatal care. The government might contract with private physicians to provide needed services, or it might hire physicians for this purpose. To facilitate the participation of all mothers, maternity cash benefits might be provided beginning six months before and ending six months after the birth of a child.

Cash Payments.   All children would receive flat-amount cash payments. The payments might take the form of either refundable tax credits or children's allowances. (As discussed elsewhere, there are advantages and disadvantages to either approach.[35]) The level of payments might be set at the poverty line—that is, the amount necessary to support a dependent who is living in a poverty-line household.

Free Access to Basic Medical Care. A health clinic might be established as an integral part of the public school system. For example, each school district might establish a health clinic that would provide basic medical care for all infants, preschool children, and school children. Or, the government might develop a heavily subsidized health insurance program for children, financing of which could be fashioned after the Supplemental Medical Insurance for the elderly and disabled (Part B of Medicare). (More than three-quarters of the total expenditures for this program are currently subsidized by the federal government, although, initially, enrollees and the federal government shared the cost equally through general revenues.[36])

High-Quality Education. As mentioned earlier, per-pupil spending for education depends heavily on property taxes as a fiscal source. Thus, the first order of educational reform might be to change the way public schools are financed. That is, the amount of public money spent for a particular school district should be made independent of the value of properties in the district. One way to do this would be to make each state government totally responsible for financing all schools within the state. The federal government might provide funds for equalizing interstate differentials in funding resources. Of course, increased funding alone would not guarantee improvement in the quality of education: however, it would at least help attract more qualified teachers to low-income school districts where disproportionate numbers of nonwhite children are located.

If policymakers decided to adopt these new programs, current welfare and related programs, including AFDC, could be either eliminated or scaled down drastically. The portion of SSI that deals with disabled children could be eliminated. Medicaid could concentrate on the aged and disabled poor. The government might altogether revamp the Food Stamp program and public housing assistance. Dependent benefits for children under social security could be eliminated. Personal exemptions for children could be curtailed.

What would be the net cost of the investment approach? It is hard to tell. It would depend on the scope of the new programs and on the extent to which current programs were eliminated or curtailed.

Beyond these arithmetical calculations, taxpayers would consider the programs for public investment in children worth the public spending. They could clearly see the direct payoff from the investment. They could see the linkage between child development and the assurance of old age income security. Of course, some may not support the programs for public investment in children in anticipation of a direct return to them 20 or 30 years later, but even they would have an attitude more positive to these programs than to the current welfare programs. In welfare programs, all they are concerned with is the program cost. In programs for public investment in children, their primary concern is the results beneficial to society as well as to themselves: the program cost is a secondary concern.

INTERDEPENDENCE

Future social welfare spending will be dictated by the demographic imperative. The government increasingly will be called on to channel public monies to the growing proportion of the nation's elderly. The demographic imperative is so powerful that the ideology of a political tide will not make much difference in the level of the government's commitment to supporting the elderly—especially the 75 and over group. Whether the government can meet the growing needs of the elderly depends largely on the productivity of the nation's present and future children when they reach adulthood.

Because nonwhite children constitute an ever-growing segment of the relatively shrinking population of children, the optimal development of each nonwhite child will be crucial for creating future generations of productive workers. Because of demographic changes, the interests of nonwhite children and the interests of the elderly—especially the white elderly—will be interlocked. Informed white adults will have a vested interest in supporting public spending for nonwhite children so that their own old age will be secure. Taxpayers who understand the demographic imperative will accept the future vision for public spending: public investment in children to ensure adequate provision for the elderly. At last the inevitability of mutual interdependence between the young and the old and, more pointedly, between nonwhite children and white elderly can be seen—interdependence that means either the survival or the decline of a satisfying quality of life for all.

NOTES AND REFERENCES

1. U.S. House of Representatives, Select Committee on Children, Youth, and Families. *Children, Youth, and Families: 1983,* 98th Cong., 2nd sess. (Washington, D.C.: U.S. Government Printing Office, 1984). Table 12, p. 136.
2. In this article, "nonwhite children" denotes black, American Indian, Asian-American, and nonwhite Hispanic children.
3. U.S. Bureau of the Census, "Projections of the Population of the United States, by Age, Sex, and Race: 1983 to 2080." *Current Population Reports,* Series P-25, No. 952 (Washington, D.C.: U.S. Government Printing Office, 1984). Tables C and F, pp. 6 and 8.
4. U.S. Senate Special Committee on Aging in conjunction with the American Association of Retired Persons, *Aging America: Trends and Projections*

(Washington, D.C.: American Association of Retired Persons, 1984), Chart 7, p. 3.

5. U.S. Bureau of the Census, *Statistical Abstract of the United States: 1984* (104th ed.: Washington, D.C.: U.S. Government Printing Office, 1983), Tables 604 and 616, pp. 367 and 376.

6. A. Pifer, "Final Thoughts," *Annual Report 1982* (New York: Carnegie Corporation of New York, 1982), p. 7.

7. U.S. Bureau of the Census, "Projections of the Population of the United States, by Age, Sex, and Race: 1983 to 2080," Table D, p. 6.

8. See U.S. Department of Health, Education & Welfare, Social Security Administration, *Social Security Administration, Social Security Bulletin: Annual Statistical Supplement, 1970* (Washington, D.C.: Social Security Administration, 1970), Tables 67 and 104, pp. 73 and 109: and U.S. Department of Health and Human Services, Social Security Administration, *Administration, Social Security Bulletin: Annual Statistical Supplement, 1983* (Washington, D.C.: Social Security Administration, 1983), Tables 59 and 117, pp. 119 and 193.

9. For example, under the 1983 Amendments to the Social Security Act, the earnings test will be further liberalized beginning in 1990, and the delayed retirement credit will increase beginning in 1990 from the current 3 percent per year to an eventual 8 percent for those attaining the normal retirement age in 2009. See J. A. Svahn and M. Ross, "Social Security Amendments of 1983: Legislative History and Summary of Provisions," *Social Security Bulletin*, 46 (July 1983), pp. 3–48.

10. *1982 Annual Report of the Board of Trustees of the Federal Old-Age and Survivors Insurance and Disability Insurance Trust Funds* (Washington, D.C.: Social Security Administration, 1982). Table 8. (Mimeographed.)

11. U.S. Bureau of the Census, "Projections of the Population of the United States by Age, Sex, and Race: 1983 to 2080." Table 6, pp. 41–94.

12. The mathematics of social security benefits can be expressed as follows: $t \times Nw \times W = Nb \times B$: therefore, $B = t(Nw/Nb) \times W$, in which total tax receipts = total benefits; tax receipts = the payroll tax rate (t) times the number of workers (Nw) times average covered earnings (W); total benefits = the number of beneficiaries (Nb) times the average benefits (B). See S. J. Schieber, *Social Security: Perspectives on Preserving the System* (Washington, D.C.: Employee Benefit Research Institute, 1982), p. 136.

13. U.S. Bureau of the Census, "Projections of the Population of the United States, by Age, Sex, and Race: 1983 to 2080," Table 6, pp. 39–106.

14. *Monthly Vital Statistics Report*, 33, No. 6, Supplement (September 1984), Table 6, p. 29.

15. S. P. Kumar et al., "Follow-Up Studies of Very Low Birth Weight Infants (1,250 grams or less) Born and Treated within a Perinatal Center," *Pediatrics*, 66 (September 1980), pp. 438–444: and R. S. Cohen et al., "Favorable Results of Neonatal Intensive Care for Very Low-Birth-Weight Infants," *Pediatrics*, 60 (May 1982), pp. 621–625.

16. U.S. House of Representatives, Select Committee on Children, Youth, and Families, *Children, Youth, and Families, 1983: A Year-End Report*, 98th

Cong. 2nd sess. (Washington, D.C.: U.S. Government Printing Office, 1984), Tables 1 and 2, pp. 131–132.

17. V. R. Fuchs, *How We Live* (Cambridge, Mass.: Harvard University Press, 1983), pp. 28–29.

18. U.S. Bureau of the Census, *Statistical Abstract of the United States: 1984*, Table 56, p. 46.

19. U.S. House of Representatives, Select Committee on Children, Youth, and Families, *Children, Youth, and Families, 1983*, Table G, p. 100.

20. Fuchs, *How We Live*, p. 69.

21. M. J. Bane, "Household Composition and Poverty," paper presented at the Conference on Poverty and Policy: Retrospect and Prospects, sponsored by the Institute for Research on Poverty (University of Wisconsin, Madison), and the U.S. Department of Health and Human Services, Williamsburg, Va., December 6–8, 1984 (photocopied); see also Bane and D. T. Ellwood, "Single Mothers and Their Living Arrangements," working paper supported by Contract No. HHS-100-82-0038. U.S. Department of Health and Human Services, undated (photocopied).

22. In 1970, the average number of children ever born to Chinese-American women age 35–44 was 2.83 and 2.15 for Japanese-American women. This compares with 2.85 for white women (excluding Hispanics). Fuchs, *How We Live*, p. 63; see also U.S. Bureau of the Census, "Detailed Population Characteristics," *Census of Population, 1980*, United States Summary, PC80-1–D1–A (Washington, D.C.: U.S. Government Printing Office, 1984), Table 270, pp. 103–105.

23. U.S. Bureau of the Census, "Money Income of Households, Families, and Persons in the United States: 1982," *Current Population Reports*, Series P-60, No. 142 (Washington, D.C.: U.S. Government Printing Office, 1984), Table 49, pp. 166–169.

24. In 1970, the average number of children ever born to Hispanic women age 35–44 was 3.65. This compared with 3.49 for blacks, 2.85 for whites (excluding Hispanics), 2.83 for Chinese-Americans, and 2.15 for Japanese-Americans. Fuchs, *How We Live*, p. 63: See also U.S. Bureau of the Census, "Detailed Population Characteristics," Table 270, pp. 103–105.

25. U.S. Bureau of the Census, "Persons of Spanish Origin in the United States: March 1982." *Current Population Reports*, Series P-20, No. 396 (Washington, D.C.: U.S. Government Printing Office, 1985), Table 1, p. 7; and U.S. Bureau of the Census, "Projections of the Population of the United States, by Age, Sex, and Race: 1983 to 2080," Table 6, pp. 39–106.

26. U.S. Bureau of the Census, *Statistical Abstract of the United States: 1984*, Table 782, p. 474.

27. Ibid., Table 226, p. 146.

28. U.S. Bureau of the Census, *Statistical Abstract of the United States: 1984*, Tables 610 and 611, pp. 372–373.

29. S. Danziger, "Alternative Measures of the Recent Rise in Poverty," IRP Discussion Paper No. 740–83 (Madison: University of Wisconsin, Institute for Research on Poverty), p. 10. Note that cash transfers include social insurance benefits as well as public assistance payments.

30. D. Kershaw and J. Fair, *The New Jersey Income-Maintenance Experiment,* Vol. 1, *Operations, Surveys, and Administration* (New York: Academic Press, 1976).
31. S. Danziger, R. Haveman, and R. Plotnick, "How Income Transfer Programs Affect Work, Savings, and the Income Distribution: A Critical Review," *Journal of Economic Literature,* 19 (1981), pp. 975–1028.
32. U.S. Bureau of the Census, *Statistical Abstract of the United States: 1984,* Table 610, p. 372.
33. R. J. Lampman, "Scaling Welfare Benefits to Income: An Idea That is Being Overworked," *Policy Analysis,* 1 (Winter 1975), pp. 1–10.
34. See P. L. 97–035. *Omnibus Budget Reconciliation Act of 1981,* Title XXIII, "Public Assistance Programs," 97th Cong., 1st sess. (Washington, D.C.: U.S. Government Printing Office, 1981).
35. For detailed discussion, see M. N. Ozawa, "Income Security: The Case of Nonwhite Children," *Social Work,* 28 (September-October 1983), pp. 347–353.
36. R. J. Meyers, *Social Security* (2nd ed.: Homewood, Ill.: Richard D. Irwin, 1981), Table 8.3, p. 478.

Article 26

A WELFARE AGENDA FOR THE
END OF THE CENTURY
Recasting the Future on Foundations of the Past

Robert Morris

The central tenets or premises of the welfare state, on which many national social programs are based, lie midway between those of an unrestrained free market of capitalism and a planned society controlled by government in all important respects. These principles or premises are the foundation for collective efforts in America to humanize the social and economic relationships among all members of the society without subjecting all to collective decision making. Put another way, they are efforts to balance personal freedom and collective obligation.

The pattern of this "middle way" changes as economic, cultural and social trends shift. For the U.S., the twentieth century brought a rapid succession of trend shifts which make it difficult to identify the solid foundations on which public support for social welfare programs can be maintained. The economic condition of most citizens improved in absolute and relative terms; social programs slowly became more extensive, universal and costly; and after a period when welfare helped redistribute national income, these effects were reversed.

In such times, it is easy to call for a new articulation of public or governmental responsibility for social needs; or to restate old principles for a welfare state in the hope that, by reiteration, those principles will reassert their power as an intellectual guide for social development. But, a successful effort is much more demanding. Much of the unease in arguments about welfare derives from the tendency for advocates to press for action toward the extremes of much more or much less government responsibility without having agreed upon a central foundation of public opinion about public obligation. In other words, there has not been articulated a value base about government social obligation which enjoys such wide support that all parties must use it as the starting point for future evolution of the welfare state idea (Freeman, 1983).

The challenge of the immediate future is to establish the core foundations and the basic programs for social responsibility on a more firm basis. This requires that advocates differentiate between what is essential as a foundation for governmental obligation, and what is desirable but not essential. The criteria for essentiality are not easily fixed and it is this to which believers in government responsibility must address their efforts—they need to agree among themselves on this essential base. Without such consensus, advocates are likely to dissipate their efforts by arguing among themselves more than they argue with the opponents of welfare.

There is common belief held by nonprofessional advocates of a political agenda that vigorous presentation of any set of ideas can lead a people and thus determine the choices of any governing system. Without demeaning the power of ideas, it is worth considering that ideas flourish best when there is an environment ready to receive them. The great men or great ideas interpretation of history is balanced by the equally persuasive interpretation that leaders lead because they sense and express the inchoate wishes and beliefs of faceless citizens. If this interpretation has validity, it may also explain the support which sustained the 1975—1984 efforts to radically revise American social welfare policy. Action to reverse the fifty-year growth in national governmental responsibility for social difficulties may be rooted in public beliefs rather than being an aberrant political episode.

The proposed agenda for social welfare seeks to combine these two interpretations, but it relies mainly on a conviction that, in the short run, that agenda is most likely to succeed which is rooted in the contemporary beliefs and perceptions of a majority of citizens.

The Function of Values, Traditions and Ethics

Some ambiguous but nonetheless potent forces join the recognizable realities of new social and economic pressures to shape the essential core for public responsibility. Given the traditions of the past, it is difficult to long ignore an ethical or value dimension which has to be incorporated in economic and political decisions. The tendency to self-realization and selfishness . . . is a strong, but not exclusive, motivating force of the times. But, to reduce the destructive effects of self-centeredness requires some reaffirmation of ethical or moral obligations which individuals have to each other and to the social institutions which they create to express those obligations. The period of the 1980s is one in which those institutions are more denigrated than they have been for several generations.

However, it is not possible to assert with much confidence that any one or single ethical expression is the correct or preferred one. An ethical guide may precede the welfare program but an ethical base has to be restated. For the immediate future, it is important to seek some agreement about whether the inherited traditions of caring for some dependent others are to be expanded at all, and, if so, how far. For example, can the future build a deep conviction that the able-bodied adults without work opportunity are *entitled* to as secure social protection as the traditionally dependent classes? Or, do we want to assert that all people are entitled to care and help regardless of what they do, or fail to do, to "deserve" it? Or, must they deserve charity? Or, do we want to embrace an ethical doctrine of equality in condition for all people regardless of their contribution to the collective society? All of these views have been advanced historically, and today. But, a practical agenda for the future calls for some coalescing of opinion around one or the other.

Fairness of Reciprocity

In practical terms, a claim for ethical justice needs to be attached to practical economic and political steps for its realization. The traditions of helping others which still persist carry with them ideas about helplessness (e.g., children, aged and sick)—about which reciprocity and fairness were self-evident in small societies. Widows once considered helpless have been replaced by unwed mothers considered able to work. A modern view which uses a term like *fairness* is hard to operationalize in mass society where helper and helped seldom know each other, but fairness is still associated with beliefs about reciprocity, as it was historically. The future form of welfare can be enlarged, over the present, if it is rooted in these twin convictions: that people in organized societies not only need each other and depend on each other, but each needs to contribute to the general well-being within his or her capability. Both terms—*fairness* and *reciprocity*—are ambiguous, but advocates will need to settle the ambiguity for practical purposes by agreeing with each other about some definition. Reciprocity can mean work as hard as you can, or it can mean doing the best of which you are capable, or it can mean behaving in collectively sanctioned and approved ways. At one time, behaving well meant being grateful for charity; today, it may mean doing something useful to some others but not necessarily work at wages, or it can mean deserved reward for effort or behavior.

These slippery ideas are introduced because they seem inextricably tied to the more practical actions which have to be taken to reestablish and define the future direction for social programs in the U.S. There will be practical conflicts over economic distribution and there will be struggles for power and dominance among various group interests—conflicts which will engage most of our organized efforts. Success for those who believe in social obligation may well depend on their ability to also articulate ideas about fairness and reciprocity which build on the tradition of the past, which go beyond them, but not so far beyond that the support of average citizens is lost. The question to be agonized over is how to formulate positions on which most advocates can agree.

Dependency as Practical Ethics

A practical issue, debate over which can enlarge our ethical views about responsibility, is that of dependency. The view which citizens take about independence and dependence through life may replace the recent concern over poverty, or a change in their views about dependence may be a necessary prelude to a renewed attack on poverty. Small children are necessarily dependent on adults although the American culture of independent striving and personal achievement seems to be pushing independence of children into earlier and earlier years. But, as children enter adult life, the emphasis is almost entirely upon independent self-sufficiency and achievement. Then, to be dependent on others, except in some abstract economic transaction sense, is not only frowned upon but is considered demeaning. Social programs of the welfare state address unavoidable dependencies which arise in raising children, feeble old age, and illness. It is no accident that programs for the elderly occupy a central place in welfare: the state of growing old has long been accepted as a part of life processes, not because of personal inadequacy. If life begins with dependence on parents, old age can mean some growing dependence on family or on society, acceptable because inevitable. But, American culture has always taken an ambiguous stance regarding other dependency; little place has been left in daily affairs for most other dependents. Pity is left for them, but not full citizenship or full regard. Dependency is not viewed as a natural part of living, but as some aberration to be cured or shelved. Dependency is usually something to be "treated" as a disease, with optimistic faith in modern technology or science to achieve success. A youth-oriented, activist society tries to make some room for the inevitably dependent, but the effort is not wholehearted and results in more contradictions.

Dependency has another dimension: the authority of professionals and bureaucracy over individuals. Professional care, on which all depend at some time, gives control over decisions affecting life to professionals. Those who are economically and physically dependent on others lack the freedom to change caregivers, so they are even more dependent than most on decisions made by a bureaucracy, as well as by professionals. Medical care is the best example, but most services for the dependent are governed by decisions made by caretakers over the lives of those to be cared for, another example of the way in which dependency becomes demeaning in an activist society. How dependent should service users be on professionals? How much decision making can providers allow their clients?

Such moral dimensions of the problem involve open awareness of the inevitable hazards of birth, growing up and growing old. But, this awareness is not much debated at any level which will locate a respectable place for the dependent in the life of the society. Instead, the activist and competitive pressures of the times rely on the competition of interests and the pragmatic adoption of short-term solutions to long-standing social problems. The results have been generous in fiscal terms, but less generous in human relationship terms. Reduced to its most elementary level, the competitive character of American economic and social life produces change and material gain, but also leaves in limbo those who lose in the competition. Little attention is given to the central characteristic of a wholly, unrelieved, competitive society—for each winner there must be a loser. This reality is masked by doctrines of economic growth which point to increased productivity and wealth which *should* take care of losers. But, in the short run—and life itself is brief—the adjustment does not take place quickly enough for individual human beings. The national commitment to individual freedom, competitiveness and growth is not congenial to discussion about collective obligations to dependents; and government action continues to satisfy the needs of the independent better than those of dependents.

The recasting of a viable platform for governmental and collective responsibility for welfare will depend on how the electorate chooses to define the relationships between the dependent and the independent—a relationship which gives a respectable place for dependency, or for some cases of dependency at least, or a place of ignominy. Recent use of the phrase "the truly needy" begins the discussion, but the phrase itself is full of condescension, as if the condition of being needy is some residual aberration of some human beings rather than a condition for which place has to be given.

If we are to approach such matters intelligently, we need a constant reminder that most, but not all, of the dilemmas of dependency are of our own making. The number of young single mothers is a product of our open, freer culture with its constantly rising level of individual expectations. The same rise in expectations, a basic part of our culture, helps us understand why some low paying, insecure, despised service jobs are hard to fill with native labor and are filled by new immigrants whom our beliefs about freedom encourage to come. Some of minority youth employment is traceable to persisting racial prejudices. And the new class of able-bodied retired is a product of our new science. Altogether they present us with unprecedented problems which we seek to resolve within our historic values of freedom, concern for others and openness.

ELEMENTS FOR AN AGENDA

The challenges already noted suggest an agenda for the last fifth of the twentieth century which might establish basic government responsibility more firmly in terms acceptable to the citizens of the nation. It consists of four parts:

1. Agreeing to agree among advocates of any governmental responsibility;
2. selecting a basic core of government responsibility: Work and Income, plus a national health system;
3. redesigning social programs before expansion; and
4. creating an institutional capability for analysis, research and development (or diffusion).

A forward looking strategy involves a choice between at least two alternatives. We, that is, social or citizen activists, can limit our efforts to the very poorest and join a minority element in public thinking, in effect joining some party of the further left, hoping to change public attitudes, or awaiting some major economic catastrophe which will convert this minority into a majority. The alternative is to develop a program for the deprived which is consonant with the current attitudes of a large majority of citizens. The first of these suggests a very long-range outlook without much influence on current policy developments during the next decade. The second has the potential to influence current policy choices. The second works within the framework of cultural institutions and seeks to modify them. The first awaits a major transformation of social and political institutions. The following analysis is based on the second alternative.

Agenda 1: Agreeing to Agree

A new consensus among advocates may seem obvious, but it is also the most difficult to realize. The unresolved questions embedded in the current retreat from government welfare make it doubtful if any simple, direct, or quick resolution will be found without an extensive discussion and debate among advocates themselves, even more important than the debate between antagonists and supporters. Some welfare proposals have dealt with special categories of dependencies, the advocates for which are competing with others for some share of a welfare resource pie (the retarded versus the mentally ill, or children versus aged). The next period needs a consolidation of forces around a limited platform. It is not a time to advance many platforms, each claiming the loyalty of a small population, but no single one sufficiently broad in appeal or deep enough in its potential for future evolution to command widespread support. The period is one for exploration of new forms and new ideological centers for broad coalition around a core program. It may be frustrating but necessary to begin with some restatement of basic principles before the practical details of a political program are put into motion, but to begin with the details, lacking a wide enough base in principle or concept guarantees continuation of the present uncertainty.

A new consensus will be strongest if built on a few criteria. For one, the goals should reflect the beliefs of a majority of ordinary citizen-voters as much as they capture the wishes of active advocates. If they go beyond present acceptability, the added goals need to be sufficiently close to the beliefs of most citizens to be capable of acceptance. A basic and incremental program will inevitably have to start with the inherited views about public obligation and add on the new requirements of twentieth century society where they are most congruent with old beliefs.

A base from which to approach consensus might be found in the present Social Security system. It may require adjustments over time, but its basic integrity, a few basic principles, should be preserved at all costs. These include the non-means testing basis for benefits, the use of payroll, pay as you go, taxes, and coverage of the entire population for whatever benefits are authorized. An unstated corollary of such premises is that the benefit structure be contained by whatever level can be actuarially justified within the level of premiums or payroll taxes as authorized by a political process. Such premises have a firm foundation in public thought. If they are abandoned in search of a more generous or more redistributive system, then it is widely accepted that an anchor for public support is lost. This is not to suggest that other more redistributive programs are not necessary, only that they should grow out of and not in place of the present system of social security.

Securing a primary consensus will be exceptionally difficult, calling for statesmanship as well as leadership. The present fragmented character of organization among supporters of public responsibility for social well-being will be especially troublesome. Most of those who work in and for social welfare and who have even rudimentary organizations to work with are devoted to an array of specialized social services each with a narrow constituency. It is asking much that they turn away from their present primary interest in securing federal funding for rehabilitation, mental illness, etc., as the foundation for their specialized efforts and redirect their energies to the other more general issues such as work and income to which they have given lip service but not wholehearted effort.

This is a hard decision for the involved organizations to take for it violates a long-standing tradition of floating coalitions in which numerous supporting organizations nominally join forces behind one issue but in reality continue their major efforts along individual sectional lines at the same time. As a result, least effort goes toward a major objective, although the nominal listing of many organizations gives a spurious impression of major effort. The crucial dilemma is how to assure that the scant resources which such organizations have can be concentrated for a time upon a few issues—when their diverse memberships may not consider the selected priority issues to be theirs.

Much political coalition activity involves organizations which maintain their separate agendas and activities and allocate a minor fraction of their resources to the coalition effort. What is proposed here is a reversal of that procedure in order to increase the chances for success on one or two significant fronts at a time.

The effort to create a new consensus might succeed if it can capture the enthusiasm and energy of the numerous specialized groupings which now coexist. That enthusiasm can be generated if it becomes clear to all that the consensus embodies the best of past tradition and the demands of the twentieth century. What is at stake is the evolution in welfare thinking from a basically charitable foundation of the past to a universal right foundation for the future. The charitable foundation was one of concern for the clearly helpless and dependent. The universal right future is based on confidence that most disadvantaged people (not all) can manage their affairs reasonably well if they have reasonable means with which to live. The universal right future is not based on any belief that each and every human need gives its victim an absolute right to have the need taken care of by specialized care and service efforts financed and defined by government. But, a *few* universal rights are the basis for future evolution in welfare.

The next section outlines the case for work and income as the base for a universal rights based government obligation, but for Agenda 1, the task is for advocates to agree upon *any* course of action most likely to generate widest support for the most widely reaching programs.

In making a choice about strategy, advocates will need to weight most seriously the equation between ends and means, or aims and resources. It is at this level of strategy assessment that advocates need to be most hardheaded, and least emotional or self-deceiving about their strengths.

A number of myths about welfare strategy will need to be re-evaluated in the course of any serious new consensus and coalition building:

1. That the voting public is responsive to an open-ended and indefinitely expanding role for national government in welfare. A close analysis of opinion polls (. . .) indicates how risky it would be to assume that because respondents to opinion polls seem to support many specialized activities that this translates into comparable support for indefinite growth in public responsibility. Public support is not a zero sum game, but neither is it infinitely expandable. There are limits to both economic growth and to public willingness to tax itself. Judgment is necessary about the best foundation for available public support. The assertion by advocates that *some* need exists does not inevitably translate into governmental support.

2. That there are available sufficient tax funds for all wants, if only funds were redirected, say from military to welfare purposes. Of course, redirection of tax funds would ease the welfare difficulties of the 1980s, but it is not only untrue that public dollars are part of a zero sum budget but neither are they fully fungible. Medical or military dollars are not automatically transferable to welfare. In simpler terms, the amount of tax dollars which an electorate will make available for welfare can be changed, either up or down, but the voter decision about how much to be taxed for welfare will be determined by the collective beliefs about welfare which voters hold, not by their readiness to give up one public good for another, when each is highly valued by a large part of the electorate. . . ., the beliefs about welfare are, as of today, less open-ended than advocates have believed to be the case. For such reasons, advocates, in reaching consensus will need to weigh what is empirically known about voter support, rather than making assumptions about support based on the wishes or wants of the advocates.

3. That past coalition building strategies for welfare will suffice in the future. In the past, the means and resources of advocacy groups have generally been not only modest, but minuscule when related to the large ends which have been sought. Modest resources have not been linked or leveraged to either larger financial or manpower resources, or to large citizen membership organizations. The final outcome of coalition agreement and consensus building will be most satisfying when it is based on a realistic matching of aims or purposes with resources mobilized for their realization. As will be argued next, the income and work focus

seems to offer better opportunity to achieve large aims with linkage to larger resources and support than any of the other alternatives.

Agenda 2—Choosing a Core—Work or Income Plus National Health

The first task for a consensus-seeking coalition is to find agreement on what constitutes a minimum but significant core for national social responsibility. There will be many candidates. It is here suggested that the core consist of national responsibility for work and income plus a national health system ahead of anything else.

In choosing what core program to support, questions of principle and metapolicy need to be settled. Once that task is completed, a few key technical issues become paramount, which are worth noting here. A key technical issue, once policy is adopted, is whether to design programs based on earnings or on insurance principles. Each has advantages and drawbacks and, since no ideal solution is evident, awkward technical decisions will have to be made. The choices are quite different from those proposed by the Reagan administration between 1980 and 1984, which argued for direct public investment in economic development rather than welfare as a path to economic strength via human development. Insurance- and earnings-related programs result in differences in provision among population groups; neither is egalitarian unless one uses the phrase "social" insurance to mean programs which are based on resource redistribution and not on actuarial principles of economic insurance measures. They also differ in the effect on employment practices and in the degree of consumer choice. While such matters lie outside the scope of this work they will continue to be the object of serious technical and political debate while new national policies are being reshaped.

Work at fair wages or some universal income security program for all citizens have been an accepted foundation for thinking about social welfare for a long time. Only upon some such foundation has it been possible to advance other social programs like health care, home help for the severely disabled, child day care and so on, all of which are premised on a belief in the autonomy of society's most vulnerable as well as for the able-bodied. Unfortunately, America's system for income maintenance is poorly understood, complex to administer, and insecurely rooted in public acceptance (with the possible exception of retirement provision). This uncertainty is compounded by the emergence of a body of adult able-bodied workers for whom work is not steadily available as a result of the major structural changes in the economy which continue to take place and which produce discontinuities between labor force demand and supply. These persist for long transitional periods of time, making the promise of work and economic growth in the distant future unsatisfactory.

Both work and income have received attention by government in recent decades but satisfactory results have not yet been achieved. Work, the preferred end for most citizens, eludes many, and income provision is uncertain. The extent of government responsibility for both is still contested, and advocates have not agreed on which approach, among many proposed, offers the best prospect for effective policy. Until agreement is reached on work and income obligation of government, the entire concept of government obligation for the vulnerable wavers between the charitable and the punitive. The needy are stigmatized as either helpless and incompetent, or as needing the prod of hunger to look after themselves. The search for better policy has also been obscured by the rhetoric of debate which makes it seem as if supporters of welfare want equal income shares for all, whereas the argument is really about reducing or increasing, not abolishing, the gap between incomes of those who have and those who do not.

The practical reasons for the salience of this issue are not limited to any abstract conviction about the saving virtues of work as a religious imperative. In the American tradition, the independence which comes from having earned one's means of livelihood is most valued. Whether sensible or not, this does represent what the electorate uses first as its criterion of full membership in society. It is the touchstone of reciprocity and fairness. This view was not only historically determined, when men and women over the millennia had no alternative to labor. People are also most free, most autonomous, when they are not dependent on someone else for choices and decisions which govern the lives of each. And, that independence comes first when each individual earns the means to acquire necessities or luxuries to choose what and where and how to use them. When the means are provided gratuitously by others, even at the distance which modern welfare places between giver and beneficiary, the recipient is never wholly free or self-confident. It is also arguable that such a "dependent" individual also has his or her own self-respect and self-confidence diminished and eroded. The issue is not only one for the individual. The foundations of a democratic society rest upon assumptions that citizens are autonomous actors in society. Unfortunately, the conditions for autonomy in modern society are not automatically self-realizing.

Others may argue that autonomy and self-respect are not dependent on earning or on work, and that such ideas are old fashioned, but it is hard to deny the force of reciprocity. A recipient of income from another is likely to feel more equal if some return is given to the giver, if not in work then in some other form of service or gift, or contribution to the social well-being. Work and earning can have different forms, but their basic relationship remains. Such concepts of reciprocity were first articulated in ancient Greece where poets, artists and dramatists were seen as valued contributors to society; although they were not considered to be "at work," they "earned" their respect. For such reasons, relief, or guaranteed welfare, is not a substitute for income earned by some socially valued activity and the resulting sense of achievement. This view is supported by the eagerness with which relief recipients seek work when opportunities are realistically available. It is also supported by the reactions of relief recipients about the degradation they feel as relief recipients.

In a narrower sense, many of the nonfinancial social problems which the public wants attended to and which social agencies seek to alleviate can only be adequately dealt with if socially, mentally or physically troubled persons have economic security and opportunity to lead independent lives. Treating physical or mental disability or emotional stress when the individual is suffering from unrelieved economic insecurity or deprivation is usually a losing effort (Bremner, 1956).

The evidence about a close association among socially useful activity, economic status and social psychological illness is not definitive, but is widespread and suggestive that valued work has therapeutic value in itself. During World War II, hundreds of thousands of adults who were previously out of work were suddenly in demand as youth were drafted into military service. Not only did the volume of dependency decline, but the salience of many sociopsychological problems began to recede or were redefined. Other studies reveal that the rate of mental hospital admissions and demand for mental health services rises during economic depressions and recedes during booming economic periods (Bremner, 1956). This is not to argue that social problems are only economic in origin, but to note that some part of many sociopsychological difficulties are either diminished in intensity, or are shaped by lack of opportunity to fit into the dominant culture of the times which values work as a vital part of group citizenship.

The salience of work is also seen in the success of efforts to develop work opportunities for the retarded, the physically and mentally disabled, and the elderly, an outcome desired by the disabled themselves.

This foundation of work as a basis for social policy is weakened by blind spots in public thinking. One is how to value motherhood and family. The blind spot is most evident in the reactions to single parents with small children who are economically dependent on others. The public seems to simultaneously want them to be out working so they will not have to depend on welfare payments, and also to be at home to "earn" respect as nurturing parents. If work is assured for all, should single parents of small children have to "earn" their support by work outside the home, or can their "work" within the home be considered of such social importance that it satisfies the desire for reciprocity necessary to justify support by others? In many ways these parents could be viewed the same as other able-bodied adults unable to find work, if a reasonable income program supplements a work program.

Another blind spot is the attitude about human nature and the willingness to work. It is assumed by some that the poor will work only if forced by hunger. The evidence is overwhelmingly in the other direction when every announcement of work brings out a flood of applicants. But, the best test for this view would be a wider availability of work at reasonable income.

Some critics of social intervention argue that social benefits only keep the poor from working (Murray, 1984), and that withdrawing benefits will be a sharp incentive for the dependent able-bodied to find work, or to work harder. A contrary view is supported by substantial economic analysis. Lampman (1984, pp. 141–144) found that at best there may be an aggregate reduction in hours worked by those in the labor pool of about 6 percent. A large part of the reduction is offset by investment in health and education which increases productivity in the long run as well as improves the quality of life for all. The reduction is also offset by a widespread natural human tendency to reduce working hours slightly as income rises in order to enjoy a higher standard of life.

Approaches to Work and to Income Assurance: Dilemmas of Past Programs

If the salience of work-derived income is accepted, the question remains of what to do and how to proceed? The last decades have witnessed numerous governmental efforts, so what should or can be done differently? Or, do we only need more of what we have tried? Advocates are not yet agreed about the answer.

Public Service Employment.   Numerous federal and state initiatives have been undertaken since the pioneer works programs of the 1930s. These programs employed a total of 15,582,000 workers between 1932 and 1942, mainly on public investment projects such as construction of highways, public buildings, water and sewer facilities and recreational facilities. In 1941, they accounted for 36 percent of the non-self-employed workforce, and cost about half of the defense expenditure for 1942 (Kesselman, 1978).

In 1971, an Emergency Employment Act was passed to: improve work chances for groups such as Vietnam veterans and older workers; to reduce barriers to work in private and civil service workplaces; to seek transfer of one-half of these workers to regular and permanent public or private sector jobs. About 185,000 workers were hired at the program peak, or about one in twenty-five of the unemployed. Fifty-four percent of the people hired secured more permanent work and 26 percent were not employed after the end of the project.

Other efforts were generated under Title X of the Public Works and Economic Development Act. A 1974 Job Opportunities program was authorized under this Title which employed over 100,000 persons at an average cost of $13,881 per person per year (Evans, 1984).

The major approaches now available are: government stimulation of employment in the private sector; subsidy of special work efforts by private employers; public service employment; training and relocation; and work for welfare recipients only (Joint Economic Committee, 1974).

Experience with such programs has highlighted the limitations of each approach as much as it has revealed the controversies among various interest groups.

Job Subsidy and Job Creation Programs.   Such programs are costly ($10,000 to $25,000 for each job); and less than half of the jobs represent new job creation. Although used in England, Japan and West Germany, as well as in the U.S., they may displace other employees whose wage is not partly subsidized; they can lead to reducing wage levels; the turnover of workers is high and, therefore, inefficient, increasing the costs of producing goods; they may become inflationary if pursued on a large scale; and, become very costly if made large enough to perceptibly reduce unemployment levels (Garfinkle, 1978; Department of Labor, 1979; CBO, 1982).

In Japan and Western Europe, between 60 and 85 percent of subsidized jobs involve displacement, not additional jobs. In the U.S. such displacement has ranged between 15 and 65 percent (Haveman, 1982). Attempts to target programs to those who have no work or cannot find work on their own have not been especially successful to date and have been administratively costly.

The sum of past experiences is large, but does not satisfactorily answer the objections of poor targeting, cost, effectiveness. For example, the 1982 Public Service Employment program reduced total unemployment by only 0.2 percent. There are great difficulties in deciding how to target public employment programs. Shall they be only for workers displaced from dying industries: Or, for those who had worked in such industries ten years or more? Or, for youthful new job seekers? Not every displaced worker will be long out of a job; many quickly find work themselves. Is it really useful to subsidize public jobs when some proportion of workers soon find jobs in the private sector? How to discriminate between these and others who fail to find new work? (Borus, 1980).

There are also substantial budgetary costs involved. One estimate (Ball, 1981) estimates that one billion dollars in public works construction would support 24,000 jobs, one-half directly in construction and the rest in related work. But, in 1984, several million people were out of work. To offset this, the Department of Labor has estimated that as many as three million jobs, one-half for low-skill workers, can be created by a public service employment program.

Training and retraining is a popular approach, and one premised on the assumption that, once trained, jobs are there for the filling by trainees. If we omit vocational training for youth as part of basic education, and consider retraining for youth not in school and for adults displaced from former jobs, then both government and industry have tried various approaches. A few large corporations undergoing technological transformation have undertaken to retrain at least part of the labor force for new tasks. Others have offered to move workers and their families to new plants in new parts of the country. Such efforts do not characterize most industries, and are limited to those few which are large in scale, strongly organized by a trade union, use scarce skilled workers, or are financially secure enough to absorb the costs.

Publicly supported retraining programs are a basic part of the Department of Labor's mandate. The results of these programs are mixed. They do retrain workers and some do find new jobs. However, some studies have noted that many more workers who would be eligible for such training seem to find work on their own, often more rapidly and at better pay than those who opt to take time out for retraining (Borus, 1980). As with public service employment, the question of targeting such programs is serious, for the answer determines whether public funds are used to retrain workers unnecessarily, or whether they are used only for a minority of workers who cannot make the transition between jobs on their own. A variation on conventional retraining methods is suggested by "individual training accounts." These could be set up in any industry and paid into by both employer and employee. In case of unemployment the fund can be drawn on by the employee to learn new skills and to pay for relocation to a new area. It is limited in that it would reach only workers in larger, better organized industries and would work only if alternative work were available in a reasonable time (Hormats, 1984). If unused, the account reverts to the employees' retirement account.

Basic Vocational Training Programs.   These programs are a part of the Department of Labor and Department of Education mandate to attend to the needs of the economy. Major training programs include:

Vocational Education, Manpower Development and Training legislation. They have had some impact, but have not dealt with the lack of work opportunity which still exists. They have usually been narrow in focus, concerned with work in a locality, short term in nature, dealing with the lowest work levels, assuming a strong labor demand. They often fail to meet the requirements for continuous technical learning in a scientifically changing economy; for a national framework where work opportunity moves fluidly around the country.

Youth programs for either work or training have been tried intermittently since the Civilian Conservation Corp (CCC) and the National Youth Administration (NYA) of the 1930s. These were not much in evidence between World War II and the 1970s, but later numerous programs were tried: Youth Conservation Corps, Neighborhood Youth Corps, Youth Employment and Demonstration Projects. While all of them had a training component, analysis of results suggest that lack of job opportunity was as much or more a criterion than training itself (Sherraden, 1980; Ginzberg, 1979).

Recent analyses indicate that in a period when the economy is improving, as in the early 1980s, a well-designed training and job placement program may be more effective than public employment programs. In part this is explained by the fact that the next decade is expected to be one with a relatively smaller cohort of youth entering the labor market, thus creating a situation with less "overcrowding" of the workplace. Poor and minority teenagers can be expected to benefit if aided by better education, better focused training, and job placement activities (Rivlin, 1984; Gueron, 1984).

Much the same conclusion can be drawn for young mothers who wish to work provided their children are cared for; and for the able-bodied elderly who wish to remain economically active. For the latter, new forms for economic and social activity can be considered and are being tested in small-scale demonstrations: cooperatives, mutual aid, reduced work and pay schemes as workers near retirement, reducing work time but stretching work life in the later years, and many others (Cahn, 1984; Morris, 1985).

Welfare Work

A number of efforts have been made to prepare welfare recipients for early work. Given that most recipients, other than those receiving Aid for Dependent Children, are disabled or aged, such programs have concentrated on single parent families where the parent is a woman with small children and no mate or spouse to share income production. Various approaches have been tried, such as work incentives and Work-Fare (required work for welfare). Some have been punitive, requiring relief recipients to work hours necessary to make up for their relief payments. Some variations have been declared unconstitutional although voluntary work for relief programs have been upheld. More sophisticated efforts have combined several elements: an able-bodied relief recipient must apply for work, he or she is evaluated and either must, or is encouraged to, enter into some work training program. Training can be a combination of on-the-job experience and education. Such programs seek to locate jobs or to facilitate job location by relief recipients. They have not been notably successful so far (Sanger, 1984; Department of Labor, 1978). However, those which are based on voluntary participation with training work best in giving gratifying experience to many people which may in time lead to work (Ford Foundation letter, 1984). Most of the jobs thus provided have been low skill at low wage, and incentives have been inadequate, compounded by poor administration.

There remain critical ethical questions about pressure to force young mothers to work when there are small children at home, especially when day care services are not readily available. There are also serious obstacles in that work may be temporary, during which relief security is lost, and regained with so much delay and difficulty that the real income position of recipients is worse than before. Also, even steady work at low wages often leads to a loss of such benefits as food stamps, medical care, and housing supplements, so that the net position is worsened. To offset this, many young people find the job experience one which truly makes them more confident in going out to find work, when there is work to be had (Sanger, 1984; Ford, 1984).

On balance, one must conclude that the national government and private industry have tried to tackle the problems of unemployment, during periods of high and low employment. The efforts have not been adequate for the task in a shifting economy but they provide an experience base out of which more effective programs might be shaped if the obligation to act by government is secured. Advocates will want to concentrate rather than disperse their efforts to find a preferred solution to the work option (Bluestone, 1984).

The Income Alternative

Even if work for all is assured, some groups will still lack income. Their needs have been met in one way or another through all of recorded history, and the present is no exception. In fact, present programs have enlarged the definitions of need beyond the traditional sick and aged to include some of the able-bodied. The core agenda for the future calls for ways to restructure and redesign income programs for these groups.

Income security involves attention to five overlapping and not clearly separable groups: the able-bodied unemployed in the workforce, those never in the workforce, those with severe handicap or illness which removes them at least temporarily from the workforce, the retired with low benefits due to low lifetime earnings, and the retired with other sources of income. These groups are differentiated by different legal statuses regarding their entitlements. Some have paid into contributory insurance funds (the regularly employed temporarily out of work, the retired); others have earned benefits without cash contributions to a fund (veterans); others have never had an opportunity to acquire legal entitlement through contribution or service (the severely handicapped, and those who never worked because of lack of opportunity or will or ability). Each group is treated differently in present arrangements, producing an impenetrable maze of rules and regulations and eligibilities. The intent of the complex varieties is to treat each group according to a different conception of entitlement or desert, but the criteria for deservedness are ambiguous and often unfair.

The nation has dealt with the problem through several categorical programs: AFDC, SSI, Workmen's Compensation, Veterans' Benefits, Food Stamps. Each of these is intended to meet the needs of different populations and each involves complex administrative and monitoring procedures, large staffs, hard to rationalize eligibility procedures and widely differing standards. They have proven costly in administration and unsatisfactory as to results. If we except veterans and the work injury program, the two main elements of income support lie in AFDC for the able-bodied and SSI for those presumed to be permanently out of the labor force. The first is full of inequity in treatment among the different states and heavily stigmatizing. The latter is somewhat more generous and treats all alike anywhere in the country.

In recent years, advocates have pressed for enlarging public responsibility in new areas and for increasing expenditures in each category in order to reduce the gaps which separate the poor from the better-off—a major redistribution of national income. This objective has been obscured by some of the argument which leads opponents to suspect that advocates seek an equalization of incomes, not just a reduction in the gap. A standard is still lacking about the basic income entitlement which is so related to earned income that wide acceptance is possible. The level to which the well-to-do think the poor are entitled as a matter of right remains to be identified.

The most vexing design problem involves the provision of basic income for the able-bodied, usually through AFDC or local General Relief, unable to find work even after the work programs are introduced. It has eluded resolution for many reasons: how to give security without major income redistribution between working and nonworking populations; how to void the "poverty (or welfare) trap" in the transition between income provision and earned income; and, what support level is consensually acceptable. If the level of guaranteed income support for the unemployed is high, then very large numbers of fully employed workers become eligible for supplementation of earnings and since their numbers exceed those of the unemployed, costs escalate so high that irresistible opposition is activated. And, if benefits are cut off when very low wages are earned (say at a bare subsistence rather than at an economy level), then the poor are worse-off when working, thus, other opposition arises so that no consensus has been reached. The last major effort at welfare reform was attempted by the Nixon administration, when a version of a negative income tax was proposed. It failed in part because supporters of the idea were divided over the level of income to be assured.

A major obstacle to solving this problem lies in deeply rooted views about reciprocity, the balance between rights and obligations. On one hand there are clearly identified groups without income through no fault of their own. On the other hand there are less well-defined groups which resist work that is low in pay, status or security. The attitude about the latter is often used to resist any income support programs, without recognizing that our culture is pervaded by education and belief that individuals are entitled to the best that life has to offer. Certain job categories do not fit into this national model. So we are left with the ideal, but also some belief that individuals in need do not fit into the model because they will not try. The disparity between an idealized middle class American lifestyle and economic reality of the poor is thus blurred by arguments over who has earned the right—a modern version of the old Greek view about reciprocity. The evidence is seen in the resistance of native Americans to performing such tasks as stoop farm labor, crop picking, staffing restaurants, serving as attendants in nursing homes and hospitals. Many of these jobs involve dirty and taxing labor, they are poorly and erratically paid, and are not well regarded by most citizens. They do not at all fit into the vision of life which the national ideal holds out for all citizens who work.

There are other contributing obstacles—the racial minority makeup of part of the poor population to mention one—but the major trouble lies in the variety of poor people whose needs must be addressed but whose conditions vary so much that no single simple administrative approach seems to work. There is also the fear, held by some, that a too generous income guarantee will lead many able-bodied people to leave the workforce to live in presumed comfort without work. The rather ambiguous evidence of major negative income-tax experiments conducted in the last decade do indicate that there is a slight decrease in employment rates, but most of this was accounted for by wives or single mothers who had left part-time, low paid work when family income was secured (Pechman, 1975; C. Brown, 1980; Kershaw, 1976).

While the concern about labor force erosion due to relief is real, it is also paradoxical in a period when all evidence suggests a surplus of labor, not a shortage. Such labor shortages as exist are mainly in skilled work for which the unemployed are generally ill equipped.

Since there has been no "perfect" income solution yet devised, the agenda needs to open debate on second-best alternatives which can rally sufficient popular support to pass a legislature. In other words, aiming for the best need not drive out an effort to achieve the less ideal good. Such debate has to deal with persistent contradictions in the wishes of advocates. In the past, one of the ideal solutions envisaged an individual focused relief system to meet the multiple and diverse needs of all people in all possible conditions. This required large staffing, extensive bureaucratic monitoring, control, and complex management procedures. This has been rejected since 1960 as both costly and intrusive.

American ambiguity, even schizophrenia, about helping the able-bodied poor is nowhere more evident than in the maze of procedures and routines imposed by legislation and by regulation designed to control expenditure and reduce fraud. The controls are subject to annual revision because of the continuous tug-of-war between those who seek to reduce programs and those who seek to improve them. A recent well-documented case study of the consequences of this situation found that relief entitlement and eligibility for poor, part-time working mothers had to be recalculated fourteen times in thirty two months. Each change involved a minimum of two hours of form filling and checking for each case plus an unspecified amount of central computer and administrative or supervisory time. This came to about half of each staff member's total work time. In addition the recipients sustained income loss when they had to report periodically in person (no time off for that) and risked losing their jobs because of their absence (Joe, 1985). With 3.8 million AFDC recipients (of whom about 500,000 work) these administering complexities become obstacles in themselves. No acceptable resolution of this dilemma has yet been found and any to be devised will require compromises by both protagonists and antagonists.

One alternative is to fix a national minimum floor of income which all persons should be assured of receiving if in or out of work, or unable to work, i.e., a negative income tax. Low income workers would receive supplements if earnings are below the minimum. Individuals out of work could be free to supplement their guaranteed income with private part-time earnings without suffering a dollar-for-dollar loss of public income, at least until total income climbs above the economy budget level. When welfare advocates considered past efforts—the Nixon welfare reform and a negative income tax—they could not accept a rather low national floor for entitlement to start with, in exchange for a secure national system which would replace abolition of poverty or income equalization as a national objective. Opponents of welfare could not give up or trade off their opposition to supporting able-bodied adults and especially single women with small children. It is worth searching for some compromise in which conservative opponents and liberal supporters each give up something to achieve a more secure foundation for income assurance.

Another less comprehensive alternative would be to concentrate on the needs of children. A uniform children's allowance or a family allowance has long been advocated whereby a standard sum is paid *all* families with minor children, the fact of having children being sufficient justification for the program. One rationale for such allowances is that it corrects inequities which result from wage policies based on the worker not on family needs. This could replace AFDC but be awarded to all families: those with higher earnings would have this payment subject to income tax retrieval so that those paying tax would not benefit unfairly. A less palatable approach would be to pay the allowance only to poor and working poor families (with children) alike, a variation of present AFDC (Handel, 1982).

Since all of this has been proposed before, it is here suggested that the agenda requires a new strategic and tactical approach which will reassess what level of generosity can be made acceptable to enough people to ensure passage—a revised welfare reform package. A variation of the negative income tax approach has been proposed by the Institute for Fiscal Studies in England, which proposes a system of benefit credits which entitled individuals would receive in proportion to their other income: 100 if no income, proportionally less as other income rises or falls (Dilnot, 1984). The issue is whether universal certainty of income is worth the price of a lower level income floor to trigger government action. Such trade-offs are the core of compromise to get action in a consensual society.

If we broaden reform efforts to erase the invidious distinction between the so-called able-bodied and other traditionally "helpless" groups, then the contradictions to be addressed multiply. But, the possible results in a universal income program might be worth the difficulties.

A national income program for all—able-bodied and physically or mentally incapacitated and socially disadvantaged alike—makes a kind of appeal for simplicity. But, it does skirt the fact that such diverse groups do have different needs. Aside from that, the various interest groups, the legal history and the advantages of current protection are embodied in large federal program such as Supplementary Security Income, AFDC, Unemployment Insurance, Veterans Benefits and Food

Stamps. Can they, or should they, all be treated alike? And, if yes, at whose level of support, e.g., veterans are treated much better, in relative terms, than others. The range of unresolved issues is still formidable. Supporters of each category will have to reconcile their own differences in order to mobilize sufficient influence to overcome the opposition of those who have always been unsympathetic to social programs. Most of the conceivable remedies have already been proposed, without wide agreement, and new ones are lacking. Issues in need of resolution are:

1. Equal treatment and adequacy in benefits. Should the condition of the worse-off among citizens be slightly improved, or should their conditions be brought up to the average level of all others in society? Or, somewhere in between? And, should poor people in similar circumstances be treated alike? In other words, is the objective to be fair, by some measure not yet agreed upon, or shall it be equality? Equality in treatment of all citizens by government as to an income floor is both desirable and achievable, at least for those in comparable circumstances. But, does this extend to equality of income for those who work full time, and at what level? Or, to all who work and all who do not or cannot work? And, at what level? There has been little call for absolute equality but there has been great ambiguity in the effort to reduce income disparities.

The following suggests the disparities which have evolved in the ad hoc, specialized approach of the past, disparities which are hard to fully justify in logic or in humanity:

TABLE 1   Average Monthly Benefit Payments in Some Federal Maintenance Programs in 1981

Families under Aid to Families and Children	$282.00	(range $89.00 to $416.00 per month)
Supplementary Security Income for Aged	146.00	
Supplementary Security Income for Disabled	229.00	
Unemployment Benefits ($107 per week)	560.00	
Miner Families, Black Lung Disease:		
Miner with family	442.00	
Widow and family	315.00	
Social Security, Retired	386.00	
Social Security, Disabled	413.00	
Social Security, Widows	349.00	

SOURCE: *Statistical Abstract of the U.S., 1984,* Washington, D.C., Department of Commerce.

Only the inherited prejudices about work, earning, race or marital status justifies the basic income differentials between aged, disabled, unemployed males and unmarried mothers. Such inequalities could be remedied by a common base income standard for all federally funded income programs. But agreement about a level which is widely acceptable is not in sight. A compromise between equal treatment and high benefit levels seems necessary.

2. Equity in treatment. Equity is not the same as adequacy or equality for it requires some measure of just desert or fairness for all, in like circumstances, the helper and the helped (. . .). For welfare, a classic example is the differential in treatment accorded AFDC family recipients in the various states where monthly income can be as low as $89 a month (plus Food Stamps) in Mississippi, or as high as $416 in California although the subsistence needs of recipients do not differ (Statistical Abstract, 1984). Reorganization to alter this situation can take the form of a federally standardized and regulated program, much like that of Supplementary Security Income for the aged and disabled. It should be relatively easy to rally supporters to the claim that all dependent adults (and their minor children) are entitled to a minimum income and that this level should be the same everywhere. However, supporters still need to resolve several serious differences among themselves before a unified demand for reform is raised.

3. Income redistribution versus ameliorating distress is an issue which separates more radical from more moderate advocates. Each relief program involves some redistribution, but the key issue is whether an income program is intended to radically alter the income distribution pattern which results from the working of the basic economic system. Although there is a natural desire to find simple and comprehensive solutions, it is more realistic and promising to separate the two. The main function for social welfare is to press for an acceptable, decent and humane base for existence for all citizens.

This objective so stated obscures two difficulties which need to be overcome. The present stage of American public belief will not accept a welfare income base which exceeds the income which a full-time employed low income worker can earn. The issue is to find agreement about the size of the gap between the two. The welfare base cannot yet compete with the level fixed by the workplace. In like fashion, welfare is not yet acceptable as a way to raise the level of low income workers whose earned income is below the poverty level which public opinion has thus far set. This supplementation does occur in some extreme cases where welfare is sometimes used to supplement labor market income: full-time unskilled workers with large families and the seasonally employed. But, welfare is an unlikely instrument to remedy more widespread flaws in the workplace through labor rate subsidy. If the workplace pattern is unjust, economic workplace remedies seem more suitable, e.g., labor organization, minimum wage laws. Although welfare can contribute its testimony about the consequences of workplace inequity, such as poverty with full-time low wage work, it is not equipped to devise relevant economic remedies, except for the few extreme cases noted.

What welfare can do is concentrate on the most acceptable and human program for those who are in and out of the labor market. At this level can the advocates come to some agreement about a minimum common standard of income for all citizens who lack the means to support themselves which is linked to but still can be below the level of full-time earned income?

One approach could evolve along the following lines:

1. a standard flat but low assured income base for all dependent adults, able-bodied or not;
2. a separate children's allowance for each child;
3. an aid attendance allowance for the extra personal care required by the physically and mentally disabled and provided by another adult and determined necessary by medical screening.

This has a certain logical consistency, but it also involves technical, administrative and political difficulty as does any attempt to rationalize the existing categorical system of many programs.

After considering all the difficulties which impede a meaningful redesign of income programs, a final alternative remains—to accept the categorical approach of today with all its administrative costs, complexities and inequities. It can be argued, not unreasonably, that competition among special interest groups is the best way in which Americans can raise the total level of public concern for the disadvantaged, even if at the price of high cost and inequity. If this is to be the conclusion, then it would be wise to avoid muddying the advocacy waters by also trying to wipe out differences among categories or to rationalize relationships among them in the hope of saving money through coordination.

Other Core Programs: National Health?

Once the provision of work, or income security lacking work, has been solidly established, the question arises—should other services become the natural obligation of the national government which governs so much of economic behavior? If one accepts the argument for limited federal obligation in the current phase of American maturity, the one additional subject for a national obligation may be health although other human needs, such as housing or child care might compete with it. The major gap in the American system of social obligation is a reasonable arrangement to meet the hazards of illness and disease, hazards to which all are subject; the costs of which are very high for the sick; and the solution for which relies on a powerful set of professions and economic interests whose participation in a solution is essential. These groups include physicians, nurses, and the drug industry. In extreme cases, inattention to serious health risks reduces individuals to poverty and dependency.

The present halfway measures taken by government—Medicare and Medicaid—have proven to be costly and unsatisfying. They introduce financial support into an otherwise unreconstructed health delivery system where choice about what is to be delivered and the pricing of that delivery is left to multiple private forces which are not competitive. That system is built around the most costly forms of medical care—hospitals—and is built around illness rather than health development. It depends on decisions made by physicians who are governed by professional plus economic motives. Despite these flaws, there is wide public acceptance of medical care as a necessity, of the drive for new technology, and of some form of insurance protection. It is only lately that the flaws in the current system have become so visible as to force public attention toward a change: extraordinary increases in the rate of expenditure; the explosion in medical technology; the neglect of health services in the community as compared to the institution; and the impenetrable complexity of present financing and insurance procedures (Starr, 1982).

Several social difficulties could be minimized if a more rationalized health system were to evolve, with better distribution of health care and more equitable financing. The threat of impoverishment and insecurity for the working and middle classes would be reduced if such a health care system could be devised at a controlled cost. The difficulties encountered by many social protection programs—for the aged, the young physically handicapped, the drug and alcohol addicted and the delinquent would be reduced if all citizens had comparable access to whatever medicine has to contribute.

A further strong argument for a universal national approach to this subject is financial. The central place which medical and health care holds in American policy and thinking has encouraged a rapid growth in public expenditures for health, a much more rapid and proportionate increase than in any other human sector service. Such costs now total about 10 percent of the gross national product and are still growing more rapidly than any other sector of the economy. This not only makes it more and more difficult to secure funds for other human needs, but it also places health and medical services in a strategic position when it comes to defining the approach to all other needs.

As the health dollar squeezes the rest of welfare financing more and more, social programs are drawn into close relationships with that medical system—care of aged, treatment of children's health, drug and alcohol addiction, mental illness, child abuse and occupational disability. Basic economic institutions, such as hospitals, nursing homes, the drug industry, and the health institutions and insurance companies, already have a major stake in the welfare sector.

Such considerations call for some resolution of the provision of health care, an issue which has been battled over politically at least since 1929. Public or professional action to establish public responsibility is more promising in the health field for it touches on the income and lives of all citizens, not only a deprived few; it is also an area of public interest sanctioned by the respect accorded the healing professions. There is a 60-year history of effort to draw upon. For the next few years, it should be possible for those interested in federal social responsibility to adopt a joint strategy which focuses on this issue, assigning subordinate effort to the many other less established welfare interests.

Agreement about a comprehensive national approach to health service delivery can be sought along with agreements about work and income, but compromises are necessary by advocates on a few central issues: the balance between hospital and in-community or at-home medical care; the balance of effort between cure and prevention, or between high technology support and community health; the use of insurance or general revenue financing; the extent of physician or public control in allocation decision making; limitation on medical system freedom to charge without control (i.e., fee for service, individual practice versus group or managed health care in some combination); and, some control over the speed of technological change in medical care.

If the case is accepted for health provision as a core choice for national responsibility on some universal basis, the realizing of the case also requires some painful choices among equally desirable ends which advocates need to settle. An idealized amalgam of the main desires of advocates would look like this: the scheme should make health services available to all, at a moderate cost, with free consumer choice of providers and with incentives for scientific advance and growth in the health system, and both freedom and remuneration for its professionals and staffs—without excessive gain by either personnel or institutions. Such an ideal has serious built-in contradictions. It is not too difficult to construct a plan which is universal and which sustains free choice and the provider system; but, such a system is likely to be very costly and the providers gain disproportionately fast in comparison with the rest of the population. If cost is contained, free choice is probably going to be impaired, and medical provider freedom will also be circumscribed. So, the task is to find the best compromise among these desirable ends: freedom, low cost, universality and scientific progress.

One of the aims of any widely acceptable compromise will be limitation on health system income and control over the direction and pace of growth. This can result from a system of insurance in which benefits are determined by what consumers or insurers are willing or able to pay, with inequities in access and coverage. Or, it can result from capping the total invested by government and consumers combined, leaving the system to adjust its services as it can. Access to care, and control over growth and direction will be controversial. The compromise may have to be in who makes the decisions or in how decision making is shared.

In the current national environment, hopes for a national health system patterned after the English Health Service is unrealistic, but the tempo for moving more of medical care into some form of group, prepaid practice has accelerated. Health maintenance organizations and medical care contracted between insurance companies and preferred medical care providers (to secure a discount in payments) are far advanced, as in the growth of proprietary and investor-owned-for-profit medical agencies. A universal network of health maintenance organizations may be the way of the future, but those interested in a better health care system will still need to look closely to see if the promises of such organizations will be realized, lacking a national pattern of government or of consumer standards and financing. As HMOs grow in number, they may begin to behave as private physicians and hospitals do today, in which case the problems will remain: high cost, uneven coverage, inequity in access. Mass HMOs will still be forced to make or to save money, and trim services accordingly unless some external framework for service and cost is set. Such groups can be directed by physician interests acted out collectively rather than in private offices. Such collective decisions can be in self- or in public interest.

The National Association for Public Health Policy has advanced a broad agenda consisting of these elements:

1. investment in prevention programs where changes in lifestyle can reduce illness;
2. federal financing of comprehensive health care for the entire population in place of the present programs for the poor and aged;
3. Physician payments *only* through group prepaid practices (HMOs), community health centers or independent medical practice associations; prospective payment to both public and private hospitals in lieu of cost reimbursement;

4. federal grants for capital construction;
5. differential financial incentives for health care in rural or under served regions;
6. regional planning for education;
7. administration through health departments;
8. federal-state joint development of health care uniform standards. (National Association for Public Health Policy, 1984)

This platform assumes that there will be an increase in federal health care expenditure.

One approach to enormously complicated relationships would be to develop the means for making the core of the health system (e.g., medical professions, institutions, drug companies) responsible and accountable for a wider range of outcomes than the narrow acute care formulae now provide for. For example, to lead the health system to link directly community health and care, primary care, long-term care (with social supports as needed), prevention, and acute hospital and medical care; and do all this within whatever funds are provided whether through insurance, government or private payments. This would tilt medical care away from the bias to use its resources for acute, crisis, in-hospital care (Sheps, 1983).

Modest steps in such a direction were being taken in 1984. The pressures to contain hospital costs is forcing some medical care out of hospitals back into the community. Some of the response takes place under proprietary auspices; in others, some hospitals have begun to broaden their responsibility to encompass out-patient, at-home, nursing home, home nursing, and long-term social support care services, as well as in-hospital treatment. In a more experimental mode, the idea of a social HMO is being tested in four sites through backing of the federal government and several foundations. In this experiment (thus far limited to the elderly), patients enroll for more comprehensive benefits than are normally provided, combining hospital, nursing home, home care, and social support services, as well as preventive health and ambulatory medical care. Financing is on a capitation basis, with a fixed sum paid in advance and based on the scope of benefits contracted for in an insurance, not a welfare, model (Morris, 1976; Callahan, 1981). In a more traditional mode, several communities, among them the city of Boston, Blue Cross/Blue Shield of Massachusetts, and the State of Massachusetts are experimenting with enrollment of the poor in managed health programs operating out of neighborhood health centers.

Because of the efforts to contain medical costs, the field of health care has entered a period of much turmoil and change which can either produce a new system or create enough chaos that government will have to take leadership in creating a new approach in the next decade. The opportunity is certainly present for a coalescing of interests by compromise behind a new pattern for national responsibility which can differ from those proposed in the past.

Agenda 3: Redesigning Social Programs before Expansion

In practical political terms, some secondary activities will have to be carried on while primary interests are being coalesced and a new platform is being worked on. Many social services, other than those already discussed, could regain credibility and security if their services were redesigned. While less crucial to the future than income reform, the redesign of other social service programs could further public confidence in welfare as a basic institution. Social welfare personnel have devoted much more attention to these many less universal services, but usually on a case, not system or structural level.

A lower priority has been assigned by the author to these "other" services, but not because they are unworthy of attention. These other welfare activities address the needs of beneficiaries who are more or less helpless. A decent and humane society finds ways to help the helpless. What is at issue is how best should the American society approach *this* human need, and is national government the only or major guarantor of action? In a period when the relations between national government and all other parties to the social order—state and local government, voluntary organization, philanthropy and industry—are being reviewed, the responsibility for the miscellany of personal social services is an especially promising area for re-examination. A solidly rooted national program of income assurance provides the foundation for organizing other welfare, and that solid foundation has yet to be constructed in an effective and acceptable structure. The residual service programs also command wide popular sympathy which can be drawn upon to reconstruct the division of responsibility between government and voluntary or private action. The outcome may be a new form of social contract among the parties, including families of the stricken, or it may be more agreement about the growth of national responsibility. The outcome will be hastened if advocates give attention now to some of the troubling aspects of service organization outlined in the next section.

Those other social programs represent a small part of federal expenditure: child welfare, mental illness, developmental disability, rehabilitation, substance abuse (drugs and alcohol), family life, etc. But, they do involve a disproportionate amount of effort by professional personnel and affect the lives of many citizens. The following identifies some of the areas in which reorganization or basic improvement would be useful, but about which a sufficiently broad agreement has not yet been reached to assure major change. Public acceptance of such social programs will be more readily achieved if the technical difficulties are resolved before there is any major effort to further increase federal commitments for very specialized activities, which are not universal in their reach.

Centralization or Decentralization: Coordination and Integration of Services.   Where there exist many specialized services, coordination among them becomes important as human social needs are not easily segmented. Independent service agencies resist those coordinating proposals which infringe on their freedom of action, but coordination which does not alter relationships among agencies is also meaningless. Efforts to break out of this dilemma encounter differences among social welfare advocates which are as great as the differences between them and the opponents of any government responsibility. To cite one national example, the argument for smoothing out state differences in treatment of AFDC families usually requires a uniform national income standard, which carries with it an extension of federal power. However, to reduce the federal role through decentralizing opens up the door to even greater diversity among the states in the way similar classes of people are treated. Decentralization and equity seem to oppose each other, and both are valued by advocates. It would be salutary if advocates could agree more than they do now about the advantages and disadvantages of a federally controlled program—or of centralization at any level—and then accept the price of that control. Or, alternatively, to assess the advantages and disadvantages of decentralization with its greater reliance on the states as "laboratories for experimentation." This approach brings program decisions closer to where people live, but it assures more diversity in treatment. And, it demands much more intensive supporter mobilization state by state which may strain the resources of most advocacy groups.

Decentralization of large service agencies may also need attention. Present service agencies depend for the most part on centralized control of both financing and services—whether either or both can be decentralized remains untested. Some experiences in industry seem to succeed but marketplace forces have provided an external framework for choices that are made. The major welfare markets lack such a disciplining control and clients seldom have control over their own assets in buying services. Service providers are also unfamiliar with work patterns in which their daily decisions might be affected by marketplace influences, so that bureaucratic procedures have evolved to mediate the exchange relationship between providers and consumers. Some efforts in public welfare have shown small but promising gains in this direction but the evidence is not yet available on which to base any major decentralization design (Orlans, 1982).

At the level of local organization, there is also a continuous search for better methods for coordinating the work of diverse local service programs. Unfortunately, local coordination is as elusive as decentralization. Social agencies persist, serving different populations with widely differing needs, which leads to specialization in care and fragmentation of eligibility standards for entitlement.

Marginal improvements can be sought by agency agreements over two approaches. One is the simplification of application procedures for services and standardized assessment procedures, so that applicants can know the rules of each program from which they seek help, and so that agencies can more readily accept referrals from each other. This calls for a better articulated client movement among many agencies plus a common application form so that frustrating visits and reapplications can be reduced for people in trouble. In effect, the aim should be to structure services so that each agency welcomes applicants from others rather than trying to discourage them by procedural obstacles.

The second approach is to increase the use of the case manager principle, developed recently in health agencies for long-term patients. Case managers specialize in helping applicants through the maze of agencies and procedures on the premise that if the maze cannot be simplified, professional guides through it can be provided. Case managers need not control the applicants so much as act as specialists to size up what combination of agencies might possibly help an applicant with his or her presenting problem and then help the applicant negotiate the maze. This approach has worked but is administratively costly. In reality, every service agency tends to hire its own case managers. But, they often act as gatekeepers to control access to their own agency. There are few examples where a communitywide case manager system has authority to affect admission to independent agencies; instead, each agency maintains its barriers.

Administrative Reorganization: Who Is in Control.   Many dissatisfactions result from the complexity of welfare procedures. The public has difficulty in understanding these procedures, and operating confusions result. In theory, good administration should be able to settle such matters, but most social welfare programs, and especially those which depend on federal or state subsidy, are burdened by two elements of control: professional and administrative. At one level, professional welfare workers (as is true for medicine and nursing) believe they can manage their work best if unencumbered with too much red tape. On the other hand, it is widely believed that some management and fiscal control is necessary in any organization which handles public or private funds to control professional expenditure or to guard against fraud. In the past 20 years, most social programs have seen top level control shift from welfare trained personnel to accountants and fiscal or business management trained administrators with little prior knowledge of the welfare service they administer. The result has been to tilt agencies from service (with efficiency) to efficiency (and less priority to service).

However, a new, more professional cadre may be in the making— a new blend of social worker and administrator. The future will be more secure if the components of this new staff are defined; and if they can be concerted in a career-stable manpower cadre which can count on a career ladder to run a welfare service enterprise (as a service) efficiently—rather than to run a business in which service is secondary.

Bureaucracy and Simplified Procedures.   Organization in welfare is compounded by the reliance on detailed, procedural rules and regulations and on a heavy flow of justifying paper reporting which, in turn, is subject to constant post-auditing. In income maintenance agencies, where this trend is most pronounced, the regulations which staff must observe may fill hundreds of pages of manuals, the contents of which are constantly being changed. This trend has spread to nonfinancial services where agencies depend on several third party incomes. Despite the growth of computers and of management information systems, there has also been a reduction in the ratio of staff to total load so that the service systems are still cluttered with confusion and uncertainty and unhappiness among all parties.

Part of the explanation for this accumulation of procedural detail may be found in the distrust which surrounds so much of welfare. Some voters are convinced that no one associated with welfare can be both honest and efficient; officials at different levels of government share some of these views; and the persistent suspicion about people who must depend on others for help leads to the creation of numerous checks and counterchecks to remove the taint of fraud or deceit.

Computers and management information systems have been hailed as the remedy. But, these systems depend upon difficult to achieve accuracy of explicit and detailed information fed into the process. The capacity to retrieve the vast amounts of such information requires an added level of manpower to analyze and report findings in staff usable form which introduces a new source of potential error. To date, the new technology has permitted centralized staff to acquire valuable insight into a system's working, but has not yet proven capable of reducing the complexity of system operations for front line use by those who directly deliver help.

Another major obstacle to bureaucratic simplification lies in the rapid staff turnover and low state of career esteem to which much of major social welfare has fallen. The major public welfare agencies, the largest employers, are usually considered way stations for young people while they seek their major career lines. The result is a rapid turnover in front line staff, leaving relatively few who are satisfied to remain and give some continuity to programs. To make any important operation work with unskilled staff in constant turnover requires extensive supervision at many levels, and the accumulation of complex procedural manuals which break down the functions into their simplest units. But, middle and top management also turn over rapidly in state agencies. The situation makes for the most extensive bureaucracy, which relies on breaking procedures down into repetitive, small decision units more suitable for processing things than for people (Morris, 1976).

Extensive professional supervision is sometimes offered as a solution to the poor fit between routine operations, management, and human behavior. Supervision has its own complex of difficulties but above all, a great increase in supervising personnel is seen as an unacceptably high level of administrative cost and as proof of inefficient management.

Reorganization and simplification of structure should be possible, though difficult. Reduction of bureaucratic procedures may be less difficult. Sustained attention to such issues at the level of service delivery can improve confidence while larger issues of the scope of national responsibility are being sorted out.

The Challenge of Welfare for Profit.   If we think of redesigning a social service system rather than changing a specific service like child protection, then the field needs to deal with the emergence of proprietary social welfare and fashion the relationships between it and more conventional nonprofit and public activity. It is only possible here to outline the issues that will be involved in redesigning a system which contains the full range of providers. In the areas of day care for children, child welfare, nursing homes, home health care, home social support services, medical care (hospitals), mental health, personal counseling, to name a few, service providers now include: profit-making corporations, nonprofit voluntary agencies with a community base, nonprofit agencies without a community structure, governmental agencies, and services provided by industrial or commercial employers for their employees. The proprietary agencies are better named as investor owned (they have stockholders who expect an ultimate return for their investment) and some of these providers are financed by stock issues on a national basis listed on a national stock exchange.

The ensuing competition has several potential consequences. The profit agencies may serve those who can afford to pay leaving the poor for the nonprofit sector. This would involve a major change in financing the nonprofit sector since many of these agencies depend on fees from clients which might be lost. On the other hand, the financial resources for capital investment of the profit sector are enhanced by their superior management capacity to make economic management decisions without major regard for community group pressures. The nonprofit sector could conceivably be forced to behave more and more like the proprietaries in order to survive economically. Still another consequence is that in the new competition, all types of agencies will compete against each other for governmental reimbursement wherever a government benefit is involved. Since government has begun a trend to purchase services for which it is responsible from nongovernmental agencies—that is to contract out its public obligation to private providers—the division of services will come under new kinds of scrutiny: will the governmental criterion be the cheapest service or the best, and how will the best or the cheapest be measured. The least costly service may be the most efficient but it may also be the shoddiest and the assertion that the nonprofit sector is always the best is not sustained by present evidence.

The current competition is forcing the kind of restructuring of services which occurred, on a smaller scale, at the turn of the century when children's agencies and agencies for the aged began to specialize and break up into institutional and noninstitutional services—both under voluntary nonprofit auspices. Although much smaller in scale than the present competition among more diverse providers, the conflict persisted for some decades before a reasonable accommodation was found.

Agenda 4: A Research and Development Capacity

The sketchy review of some of the trouble some contradictions which plague many efforts to advance or to solidify social welfare programs provides the basis for the final agenda item. Advocate effort in the next few years could profitably be directed to these contradictions in a systematic fashion in an attempt to discover ways of resolving them. Trial and error experimentation is useful but not sufficient. More systematic analysis and testing is called for. In many ways, this large area of national activity—social welfare—still functions at an eighteenth century apprentice level, with hardly any significant application of modern research and development technology. Except for minimal professional education for frontline service delivery, there is no powerful intellectual infrastructure to carry out the self-criticism, analyses and testing which the contradictions call for. There are valuable national and regional organizations and a few government or university research centers, but most of them are poorly financed and overcommitted to the daily problems of maintaining a large and complex welfare system under daily emergency conditions. Support has not yet emerged for a network of research and development centers (R and D) similar to those which have made such useful contributions to the evolution of modernsociety in the physical sciences, medicine, military capability and business.

During the next few years, some portion of welfare effort will need to be devoted to developing comparable analytic centers and to confronting the kinds of dilemmas noted above. Such centers can grow around or out of major national welfare service associations, out of major universities or out of professional associations. To succeed, such associations may have to decide how much of their meager resources they are willing to set aside for long-term purposes, rather than devoting so much to the promotion of current short-term objectives without ever confronting the internal contradictions which continue to make the ends of social welfare so uncertain.

The kind of R and D capability which is necessary has three major components: a policy oriented research and data analysis staff; collection, updating and maintenance of a data base focused on the R and D objectives, which can synthesize data collected by government, research data of other centers accessed on a sharing basis, and original data gathered directly by the welfare R and D centers; and, a network of links between several research analysis-type centers and consumers of findings. The last of these is perhaps most important. The standard pattern of the past has been to communicate research results via publication or within one community. This is valuable for research and academic personnel, and may slowly filter into use by developers of policy or of programs. But the process of use and idea diffusion is slow, unpredictable and wasteful. What modern R and D technology has shown in so many fields is the potential in more actively connecting information with organization use structures or networks which are interested in putting into practice and into use the implications of evidence. Business develops its market this way; science has extended its influence this way; and conservative political movements opposed to government welfare have also extended their influence in policy making by similar developmental means.

Social welfare has several handicaps as it attempts to adopt these methods of research and of linked development. Its base constituency is fragmented and not motivated by a common impulse which governs business or political ideology. Welfare is still sometimes conceived of as a layman's spare time activity or as the realm of minor functionaries carrying out distasteful tasks of social rescue through welfare. Instead, as we have seen, welfare has become an important factor in modern economic, political and social development. What is called for is readiness to act in technical and strategic ways commensurate with these roles.

Dreams of the Future

The limited platform suggested previously is not the outer boundary of welfare conceptions, but it represents the essential foundation building which must be completed if social programs are to be secure, or if America is to become something other than a grudging and reluctant welfare state. Broader concepts of social justice, other actions by government to create a more equitable and cohesive society can be dreamed of and planned for, but they are unlikely to be realized unless the foundation is securely in place. But, the welfare agenda outcome will also be shaped, in time, by the beliefs which citizens have about the kind of society they have anticipate in the coming decades. Three main models of the future have emerged:

1. *A world of boundless abundance* provided by the existing economic and social order. This model applies equally to capitalist and socialist societies. It envisages a world in which maximizing economic growth is possible, without destroying basic resources, that work for all will result naturally, that basic political and economic structures do not need to be altered, and that minor dependencies which persist can be taken care of by modest diversions from personal and public incomes through family, charity or public provision for the helpless.

2. *A world of leisure and creativity* without dependence on any forced labor. New productivity forces, in this model, will cut the link between work and income; work will take on a new form, without compulsion. The Athenian world would become general in which 10 percent of the population which then have leisure to pursue intellectual and artistic interests will now become 100 percent, but without the Athenian 90 percent of the population who had to work with their hands and were either slaves or poor craftsmen.

3. *A third or middle road accepts the constancy of change* in economic and social relationships, *but accepts a continuing tension* between differing interests without removing the tensions or by removing some of the interests. The tension persists within a sta-

ble consensus seeking order which does not lapse into anomie and lethargy, nor into class conflict and polarization. (Cornes, 1984)

The main agenda issues could be addressed in each of these models of the future, but the way the issues are answered for political and policy action purposes will differ. The first and second scenarios call for little welfare action, for they presuppose that economic growth will abolish both poverty and dependency. That is only slightly oversimplified for even in such a future some people will be sick or unable to work. But, for the most part, such life hazards are assumed manageable by savings or insurance with which any need can be met. They call for the creation of wholly new patterns of living and of self-realization. While the hazards of illness and injury are still present, these views place much more confidence in the promise of scientific advance to deal with most of such conditions. Welfare needs or wants are seen as at best a minor residual flaw in an otherwise benign world of self-realization.

For those who are concerned with the realities of human existence in today's world, those who look for answers in such futurism can only seem to be dreamers and escapists, but the attractiveness of escape from trouble is undeniable.

The proposed agenda is set in the context of the third, or middle, course which most closely approximates the world we now live in and the world as it is likely to be for some generations to come. This approach is realistic—visions of cataclysmic changes which will remake society in the span of one lifetime are not supported by any historical evidence. Great upheavals which destroy the foundations of a society in one generation recreate a new order after the passage of decades or generations. In the interim, changes in the attitudes and behaviors of people change quite slowly. The time frame for this agenda is only the next two decades. It calls advocates to the practical and the basic work necessary to enrich a tradition of caring for others and to modernize and reshape social support programs of government in their lifetime in the U.S.

BIBLIOGRAPHY

Ball, Robert, "Employment Created By Construction Expenditure," *Monthly Labor Review,* 104, Dec. 1981, p. 39.

Bluestone, Barry, B. Harrison, and L. Gorbach, *How to Create Jobs,* Washington, DC: Center for National Policy, 1984.

Borus, Michael, "Assessing the Impact of Training Programs," In Eli Ginzberg, *Employing the Unemployed,* New York: Basic Books, 1980.

Bremner, R. H., *From the Depths,* New York: New York University Press, 1956, Chapters 4 and 5.

Brown, Charles, *Taxation and the Incentive to Work,* New York: Oxford University Press, 1980.

Cahn, Edgar, "Surplus People." Unpublished manuscript. Coral Gables, FL, University of Florida Law School, 1984.

Callahan, James, and Stanley Wallack, *Reforming the Long-Term Care System,* Lexington, MA: Lexington Books, 1981, pp. 185–218.

Congressional Budget Office (CBO), *Dislocated Workers,* Washington, DC: U.S. Government Printing Office, July 1982, p. 38.

Cornes, Paul, "The Future of Work for People with Disabilities," *Interchange,* New York: World Rehabilitation Fund, June 1984, No. 9.

Dilnot, A. W. Kay, J. A., & Morris, C. N., *The Reform of Social Security,* London: Clarendon Press, 1984.

Evans, Robert, "A Job Program." Unpublished manuscript. Waltham, MA: Brandeis University, March 29, 1984.

Ford Foundation Letter, April 1, 1984. Citing Experiences of the Manpower Demonstration Research Corporation.

Freeman, Gary, and Paul Adams. "Ideology and Analysis in American Social Security Making," *Journal of Social Policy,* January, 1983, Vol. 12, Part 1, pp. 75–95.

Garfinkle, Irving, and John Palmer, ed. "Issues, Evidence, and Implications," in *Creating Jobs.* Washington, DC: Brookings Institution, 1978, p. 1.

Ginzberg, Eli, *Good Jobs, Bad Jobs, No Jobs.* Cambridge, MA: Harvard University Press, 1979.

Gueron, Judith, *Lessons from a Job Guarantee: The Youth Incentive Entitlement Pilot Projects.* New York: Manpower Demonstration Research Corporation, June 1984.

Handle, Gerald, *Social Welfare in Western Society.* New York: Random House, 1982.

Haveman, and John Palmer, eds. *Jobs for Disadvantaged Workers.* Washington, DC: Brookings Institution, 1982.

Hormats, Robert, "A Western Strategy for Jobs and Growth." *Transatlantic Perspective,* German Marshall Fund of the U.S., September, 1984, No. 12, p. 11.

Joe, Tom, and Lorna Potter. "The Welfare System: A Briar Patch for Anna Burns." *Public Welfare,* Vol. 43, No. 1, Winter 1985 p. 4.

Joint Economic Committee of the Congress, *Studies in Public Welfare.* Paper 19 in Public Employment and Wage Subsidies. Washington, D.C.: U.S. Government Printing Office, December 30, 1974.

Kershaw, David, *The New Jersey Income Maintenance Experiment*. Vols. 1–3, Vol. 1, Labor Supply, New York: Academic Press, 1976.

Kessel, am. Jonathon R., "Work Relief Programs in the Great Depression" in *Creating Jobs*, Palmer, J. OP. CIT.

Labor, Department of. R & D Monograph No. 67, ±979, p. 171. *Assessing Large Scale Job Creations and Perspectives on Public Job Creations*. R & D Monograph No. 52, 1977. Washington, D.C.: U.S. Government Printing Office.

———, & Department of Health, Education, and Welfare. WIN: 1968–1978: A *Report at Ten Years, Ninth Annual Report to the Congress*, Washington, D.C.: U.S. Government Printing Office, 1978.

Lampman, Robert. *Social Welfare Spending: Accounting for Changes 1950–1978*. New York: Academic Press, 1984.

Morris, Robert, "Alternative Forms of Care for the Disabled." In *Developmental Disabilities: Psychological and Social Implications*. New York: Alan Liss, 1976.

———, "Diffusion of Innovation." Mimeo unpublished report of a study to the National Science Foundation, Washington, D.C., at Waltham, Brandeis University, Levinson Policy Institute, 1976.

———, "The Elderly as Surplus People: Is There a Role for Higher Education?" *The Gerontologist*, Washington, D.C.: The Gerontological Society of American, forthcoming, Fall, 1985.

Murray, Charles, *Losing Ground: American Social Policy*, 1950–1980, New York: Basic Books, 1984.

National Association for Public Health Policy. "A National Health Program for the United States." South Burlington, VT, 1984.

Orlans, Harold, ed. *Human Services Coordination*. New York: Pica Press, 1982.

Pechman, Joseph, and M.P. Timpane. *Work Incentives and Income Guarantees: The New Jersey Negative Income Tax Experiment*. Washington, D.C.: Brookings Institution, 1975.

Rivlin, Alice, "Helping the Poor" in *Economic Choices 1984*, Rivlin, ed. Washington, D.C.: Brookings Institution, 1984.

Sanger, Mary Bryna, "Generating Employment for AFDC Mothers." In *Social Service Review*, March 1984, Vol. 38, No. 1, pp. 28–47.

Sheps, Cecil, and Irving Lewis, *The Sick Citadel*. Cambridge, MA: Oelgeschlager, Gunn and Hain, 1983.

Sherraden, Michael. "Youth Employment & Education: Federal Programs from the New Deal through the 1970's." In *Children & Youth Services Review*, 1980, Vol. 2, pp. 17–39; Also: *National Service*. New York: Pergamon Press, 1982.

Starr, Paul. *The Social Transformation of American Medicine*. New York: Basic Books, 1982.

494   Part IV   Practice, Politics, and the Social Welfare Agenda

Statistical Abstract of the United States; Bureau of the Census, Washington, D.C.: U.S. Government Printing Office, 1984. These disparities also reflect differences in state economic resources, but not accurately. In the 20 years since 1960, southern states once poor, like Louisiana and Texas, have become well off and northern states, once wealthy, have suffered economic losses.

About the Author

Ira C. Colby is an associate professor of social work and director of the Criminal Justice Program at the University of Texas at Arlington. Previously, he directed the undergraduate social work program at Ferrum College, Ferrum, VA. He served as president of the Rural Social Work Caucus, chairperson of the National Rural Task Force of the National Association of Social Workers, and vice president of Virginia Chapter of the NASW. In 1988, he received the Galloday Teaching Award from the University of Texas at Arlington, and in 1984 he was chosen "Social Worker of the Year" by the Tarrant County Chapter (TX) of NASW.

Dr. Colby has authored over a dozen articles on a number of social work topics ranging from child sexual abuse to rural social work. He also serves as a manuscript reviewer for a number of national social work journals.

He received his master degree in social work from Virginia Commonwealth University and doctorate in social work from the University of Pennsylvania. Presently he is certified as an Advanced Clinical Practitioner by the Texas Department of Human Services.

A NOTE ON THE TYPE

The text of this book was set 10/12 Palatino using a film version of the face designed by Hermann Zapf that was first released in 1950 by Germany's Stempel Foundry. The face is named after Giovanni Battista Palatino, a famous penman of the sixteenth century. In its calligraphic quality, Palatino is reminiscent of the Italian Renaissance type designs, yet with its wide, open letters and unique proportions it still retains a modern feel. Palatino is considered one of the most important faces from one of Europe's most influential type designers.

Composed by Weimer Typesetting Co., Inc.

Printed and bound by R. R. Donnelley & Sons Company

DATE DUE

Demco, Inc. 38-293